INTERVENTION, CIVIL WAR, AND COMMUNISM IN RUSSIA

IN RUSSIA

April–December, 1918

THE WALTER HINES PAGE SCHOOL OF INTERNATIONAL RELATIONS
THE JOHNS HOPKINS UNIVERSITY

INTERVENTION, CIVIL WAR, AND COMMUNISM IN RUSSIA

APRIL—DECEMBER 1918

DOCUMENTS AND MATERIALS

By

JAMES BUNYAN

OCTAGON BOOKS

A DIVISION OF FARRAR, STRAUS AND GIROUX

New York   1976

Reprinted 1976
by special arrangement with The Johns Hopkins Press

OCTAGON BOOKS
A DIVISION OF FARRAR, STRAUS & GIROUX, INC.
19 Union Square West
New York, N.Y. 10003

Library of Congress Cataloging in Publication Data

Bunyan, James, 1898-   comp.
    Intervention, civil war, and communism in Russia, April-December, 1918.

    At head of title: The Walter Hines Page School of International Relations, the Johns Hopkins University.
    Reprint of the ed. published by the Johns Hopkins Press, Baltimore.

    Bibliography: p.
    1. Russia—History—Revolution, 1917-1921—Sources.   2. Russia—History—Allied intervention, 1918-1920—Sources.   3. Communism—Russia.   I. Johns Hopkins University. Walter Hines Page School of International Relations.   II. Title.

DK265.B94   1976   947.084'1   75-42073
ISBN 0-374-91097-9

Manufactured by Braun-Brumfield, Inc.
Ann Arbor, Michigan
Printed in the United States of America

TO THE MEMORY OF

FRANK ALFRED GOLDER

FOREWORD

It is the purpose of this work to make available in English translation a selected body of Russian materials which portray the history of both the domestic affairs and the international relations of Russia during the crucial period of April to December 1918. The volume follows chronologically *The Bolshevik Revolution 1917-1918* (published in 1934 under the auspices of the Hoover War Library, Stanford University), in which a similar method was used to depict the Bolshevik seizure of power in Russia and the history of the Soviet régime from its inception to April 1918. December 1918 has been taken as the terminus of the present work because about that time developments ensuing from the end of the World War placed Russia in an international position materially different from that occupied during the previous eight months.

Though of brief duration, the period covered in the following chapters is of great significance as one of the most critical in the recent history of Russia. The political and social struggle which attended the establishment of the Soviet Government did not come to an end with the spread and consolidation of Bolshevik power during the winter months of 1917-1918. The following spring witnessed far-reaching changes which intensified the conflict marking the Russian revolutionary drama. One of the new factors was the intervention of the Great Powers in Russian affairs after Russia's formal withdrawal from the World War. A second development, given impetus by foreign intervention, was the intensification of civil war, which during the months under consideration spread rapidly through most of Russia. Finally, in this period the Bolsheviks greatly widened the scope of their economic and social experimentation, thereby effecting a transformation in the ways of collective living as radical as any in the previous history of human society. It was inevitable that this sudden break with the past should deepen the crisis in Russia's body politic.

The chapters of the book are grouped around these three major factors. Chapters I-III deal with the intervention of the two rival coalitions of the Great Powers and with the attitude and policy of the Bolsheviks toward that intervention; chapters IV-VI relate to the spread of civil war in Central Russia and the borderlands; chapters VII-XI are concerned with the institutions and effects of the communist order. The materials included were selected from official records, party resolutions, collected works of Bolshevik leaders, memoirs and diaries of participants, the daily press, and reports of foreigners who lived in Russia through those stirring days. The length of most of the materials has frequently prevented translating them in their entirety. However, care has been taken to reproduce their essential parts, and it is trusted that their meaning has not been altered as a result of the omissions. The materials are arranged to constitute as clear a narrative as possible and, whenever necessary, have been supplemented by exposition designed to assist the reader in following the main connections of events.

I wish to acknowledge my gratitude to the many who have aided me in the preparation of the book. I am particularly thankful to Dr. Albert K. Weinberg, of the Walter Hines Page School of International Relations, who has read and re-read every page of the manuscript and the proofs and has acted as constant critic. To Professor DeWitt C. Poole, Director of the School of Public and International Affairs, Princeton University, I am indebted for his reading of the manuscript and for many valuable suggestions based on his experience as American Consul General at Moscow in 1918. I desire to thank the Committee of the Page School of International Relations—Professors Gilbert Chinard, James Hart, W. Stull Holt, Johannes Mattern, and William O. Weyforth—for their encouragement and help. I also wish to thank Professor Kent R. Greenfield and the members of his Seminar in History at the Johns Hopkins University for illuminating criticism of a portion of the manuscript. Dr. Leon Sachs was kind enough to give advice upon a number of questions involving legal terminology, and Dr. N. B. Fagin and Dr. W. T. Feldman to help in reading the proofs. For the drafting of the map in this book I am deeply indebted to the helpfulness of Captain Parker M. Reeve. Miss Maria Wade has had the burden of typing the manuscript and I wish to express my great appreciation of her assistance. Finally, I take pleasure in acknowledging the courteous help given me by the staffs of the Hoover War Library, Stanford University, and of the Slavic Division of the Library of Congress, especially by Miss Nina Almond, Mr. D. Krassovsky, Mr. P. McLean, Mr. N. Rodionoff, Dr. V. Gzovski, and Mr. G. Novossiltzeff.

In dedicating this volume to the late Professor Frank Alfred Golder, I desire to pay a tribute to his service in conceiving the project of a documentary study of recent Russian history and in making notable contributions to it in his *Documents of Russian History 1914-1917* and in many materials used in *The Bolshevik Revolution 1917-1918*.

JAMES BUNYAN

The Walter Hines Page School
of International Relations
October, 1936

CONTENTS

xi

B. Distribution. Disruption of private trade. Function of consumers' cooperatives. Foreign trade policy. Wages in kind. Abolition of private trade. Exclusion of kulaks from cooperatives. Plan for distribution of goods.

C. Finance. Taxing the bourgeoisie. The state budget. Extraordinary revolutionary tax on the bourgeoisie. Taxes in kind. Krestinsky on the extraordinary tax. Issue of bank notes. Krestinsky on paper money. Moneyless economy.

CHAPTER I

AUSTRO-GERMAN INTERVENTION

During the winter of 1918 Bolshevik power spread at a rapid pace throughout Russia, particularly in the South and Southeast, where Soviet armies, aided by local sympathizers, gained control over the Ukraine, the Don and Kuban regions, and the Crimea, and established there Soviet forms of government.[1] However, this extension of Bolshevik ascendency was definitely checked when, toward the end of February 1918, the troops of the Central Powers entered the Ukraine at the invitation of the deposed Ukrainian authorities. On March 3 the Bolsheviks formally accepted at Brest-Litovsk the German peace terms, which forced the Soviet Government to recognize the independence of the Ukraine, Finland, Esthonia, and Livonia, and to withdraw its troops from these regions, which were shortly afterwards occupied by the Central Powers. In Southern Russia the Austro-German forces advanced far beyond the Ukrainian borders. They helped the Don Cossacks to drive the Soviet armies from the Don region, occupied the Crimea, and sent an expeditionary force to the Caucasus. These developments placed under the control of the Central Powers some of the most productive agricultural and metallurgical areas of Russia and enabled them to draw from these regions food and raw materials, which they so badly needed for the continuation of the war. The Bolsheviks were powerless to resist Austro-German occupation of Southern Russia; nor were the Entente Powers in any

---

[1] Materials relating to the early Bolshevik victories in the South are given in James Bunyan and H. H. Fisher, *The Bolshevik Revolution 1917-1918, Documents and Materials*, pp. 404-51. This work will hereafter be cited as *The Bolshevik Revolution*.

1

degree successful in their efforts to dislodge the Germans
and Austrians through intervention in Russia. The Central Powers remained in control of Southern Russia until
the end of the World War, when they withdrew their forces
in accordance with the terms of the Armistice.

A. OCCUPATION OF THE UKRAINE

The occupation of the Ukraine by the Central Powers
was a sequel to the separate peace treaty which they concluded with the Ukrainian Government at Brest-Litovsk
on February 9, 1918. The feature of that treaty which was
most important to Germany and Austria was the promise
of the Ukrainians to deliver bread to these Powers. But at
the moment of concluding peace with the Central Powers the
Ukrainian Government was in flight before invading forces
of Soviet Russia. The Germans immediately sent an army
to drive the Bolsheviks out of the Ukraine—a task which
they accomplished with great rapidity. Kiev was occupied
on March 1, 1918; the same day saw the reestablishment of
the Ukrainian Government which the Bolsheviks had expelled from the capital. In a week all the principal cities of
the Ukraine were in the hands of the Germans and Austrians. But the Ukrainian Government, consisting of
moderate socialists, was not destined to enjoy power for a
great length of time. Its land and labor policies,[2] hardly
distinguishable from those of the Bolsheviks, did not seem
to the Germans compatible with their desire for order and
supplies. The Ukrainian peasants were occupied very little
with production but chiefly with the division of the landlords' estates and intra-village warfare incident to that
division.

[2] These were proclaimed in the Third Universal of the Rada, quoted in
ibid., pp. 435-37. Rada is the name of the Ukrainian National Council.

To insure an at least partial collection of the coming harvest, General von Eichhorn, commander in chief of the German army of occupation, on April 6, 1918, issued a decree announcing to the peasants that the next harvest would belong to the cultivator of the land, whether he were peasant or landlord. This decree was published without the knowledge of the Ukrainian authorities and first came to their attention two weeks after it had been issued and circulated in the villages. Alarmed at this interference by the German Command in the domestic life of the country, the Rada protested to the authorities in Berlin, but the order was never revoked.[3]

Soon the German Military Command took more drastic action, and by the middle of April it decided to do away with the Ukrainian Government altogether. An ally was found in Pavlo Skoropadsky, a former Russian general of Ukrainian descent, who on April 24 reached an understanding with the Germans whereby the Ukrainian Government was to be overthrown and Skoropadsky was to become dictator of the country.

The military side of the coup d'état, which by design coincided with the sessions of a congress of landowners and well-to-do peasants known as the "Khleboroby,"[4] was carried out entirely by the Germans. In the afternoon of April 28, 1918, a detachment of German soldiers entered the building of the Pedagogical Museum, where the Rada was in session. The commanding officer announced that the members of the Rada and the government were under arrest, and the coup d'état was accomplished in a few minutes. The next day, General Skoropadsky and members of the landowners' congress assembled at the Sofiisky Square and

---

[3] S. Sumsky, "Odinnadtsat perevorotov," in *Letopis Revoliutsii*, I, 237-42.
[4] Literally "bread-producers."

Skoropadsky was proclaimed hetman (chief executive) of the Ukraine.[5] The Skoropadsky régime lasted until the departure of the German troops in December 1918.

CONDITIONS IN THE UKRAINE IN MARCH 1918

[Report to the German Eastern Command] [6]

When the German forces entered the Ukraine they found absolute chaos. . . . There was no central government . . . and the country was divided into a number of areas not larger than a uezd—often not larger than one city or even a single village . . . ; these areas were ruled by different political parties or by dictators, atamans, and all sorts of adventurers. Not infrequently one came across neighboring villages surrounded by trenches and fighting each other for the land of the former landlords. . . .

It is not true that the Bolsheviks are supported only by the Russian soldiers who remained in the Ukraine. . . . They have a large following in the country. All the industrial workers are with them, as is also a considerable part of the demobilized soldiers. The attitude of the peasants, however, is very difficult to ascertain. The villages that have once been visited by Bolshevik gangs . . . are, as a rule, anti-Bolshevik. In other places Bolshevik propaganda seems to be successful among the peasants.

The peasants are concerned chiefly with the dividing up of the land; they will follow the Rada if it allows them to take the estates of the landlords . . . as proclaimed in the Third and Fourth Universals.[7] . . . Otherwise they will go with the Bolsheviks. Although

---

[5] A. Goldenweiser, "Iz Kievskikh vospominanii (1917-1921 gg.)," in *Arkhiv Russkoi Revoliutsii,* VI, 209-16; N. Mogiliansky, "Tragediia Ukrainy," *ibid.,* XI, 84-90; D. Doroshenko, *Istoriia Ukraini,* II, 2-35. The *Arkhiv Russkoi Revoliutsii* will hereafter be cited as *A. R. R.*

[6] "Doklad . . . o polozhenii del na Ukraine . . .," in *A. R. R.,* I, 288-92. The author of this report is the German writer Collin Ross, who served from 1914 to the end of the war with the military division of the Ministry of Foreign Affairs (*Militärische Stelle des Auswärtigen Amtes*). Upon the occupation of the Ukraine he was sent to Kiev to investigate conditions and report to the German Eastern Command (*Ober-Ost*).

[7] The Third Universal, proclaiming the Ukrainian People's Republic, was published on November 20, 1918; the Fourth Universal, declaring the Ukraine an independent republic and defining the rights of the different classes of citizens, appeared on January 22, 1918. Both are quoted in *The Bolshevik Revolution,* pp. 435-37, 444-48.

the Bolsheviks lost out in many places because of their system of terror, their slogan "Take everything, all is yours" is too attractive and tempting to the masses.

The Ukrainian separatist movement, on which the Rada is relying, has no true roots in the country and is supported only by a small group of political dreamers. The people as a whole show complete indifference to national self-determination. Politically they do not form a compact group but are divided into a number of socialist parties. To be sure, with the arrival of the Germans the Rada is gradually gaining power, but that power is based chiefly on German bayonets and is likely to remain so for some time. . . .

With the backing of the Germans the Rada is developing considerable initiative, but it must overcome enormous difficulties because of . . . the irreconcilable differences among the various classes of the population. Civil war is not likely to cease for a long time. . . .

The Ukrainian army consists of hired soldiers, mostly former officers and soldiers out of work. . . . Its organization is thoroughly democratic, with no distinction of rank except for one commanding officer to a detachment. The soldiers receive 333 rubles a month, with food, quarters, and clothing. Their families are also supported. . . . The army numbers two thousand. . . . The Commander in Chief is Minister of War Zhukovsky, the Chief of Staff . . . is Ozhetsky, both former officers of the Russian General Staff. . . .

The Ukraine . . . is abundantly supplied with everything. . . . But it will be very difficult to obtain supplies from the peasants . . ., who refuse to sell their grain for paper money. Because of the unlimited issue of money there is so much of it here that it has lost all value to the peasant, who is not certain that he will be able to purchase his necessities with it. . . . The peasant is willing, however, to exchange his grain for goods. . . .

The Rada is of the opinion that the peasants have unlawfully acquired from government storehouses grain kept to supply the front, and now wishes to requisition that grain with the aid of German troops. . . . This procedure, if carried on for any length of time, is certain to create an intense hatred of the Germans. It would be a better policy to try to obtain grain in exchange for goods. . . .

GENERAL EICHHORN'S ORDER TO THE UKRAINIAN PEASANTS [8]

[April 6, 1918]

1. The harvest will belong to those who have cultivated the land. They will receive cash payments for it at fixed rates.

2. A peasant who acquires more land than he can cultivate thereby does harm to the Ukrainian state and people and is liable to punishment.

3. If the peasants of a certain area are not in a position to sow all the land, the landlord of the area will be required to attend to the sowing . . . , in which case the peasants must not interfere with the landlord's activities. The land committees must supply the landlord with the seeds, horses, and machinery required for sowing and harvesting. . . .

AGREEMENT BETWEEN SKOROPADSKY AND GENERAL GROENER [9]

[April 24, 1918]

1. The Brest-Litovsk Treaty will be recognized.

2. The Central Rada will be dissolved. . . . New elections may be held only upon restoration of order in the country and with the permission of the German Command. . . .

4. All offenses against German troops come within the jurisdiction of the German Court Martial.

5. . . . All land committees will be dissolved. . . .

6. Pending the promulgation of Ukrainian laws on compulsory military service, the laws in force shall be those of the Central Powers.

7. Free trade is to be legalized. . . .

8. Private property in land is to be reestablished. The peasants are to pay for the land which they received during the partition. In the interests of agriculture large landed estates are to be preserved.

9. The Central Powers are to be compensated for their military aid to the Ukraine. The extent and method of compensation are to be determined later.

[8] Doroshenko, *op. cit.,* II, 18.

[9] *Ibid.,* pp. 31-52. General Groener was chief of staff of the German army of occupation.

THE RADA PROTESTS AGAINST GERMAN INTERFERENCE
[Rada Session, April 25-26, 1918] [10]

During the session of the Small Rada which took place in Kiev on April 25 there was an interpellation concerning the order of Field Marshal Eichhorn. . . . The interpellation was made by the Ukrainian Socialist-Revolutionists. After reading the order Yanko declared that it was a violation of the fundamental rights of the Ukrainian people, . . . an interference in their internal affairs and rights. . . . The speaker concluded: "Now that the order is published, what steps has the Government taken to prevent its enforcement and stop interference in the Ukraine's internal affairs?"

. . . The next day Kovalevsky, Minister of Agriculture, replied to the interpellation. He substantiated the statement that the order had been published. "I too received a German copy [of the order]. . . . After reading it I could not help realizing that it came as a result of the agitating in connection with the land question. Recently numerous delegations have come here to demand the annulment of the land law and the replacement of the socialist government by a business administration. The Field Marshal's order coincided with . . . these attacks upon socialism. The order is a direct interference in our domestic affairs. It shows a lack of confidence in me as Minister of Agriculture. . . . I have therefore tendered my resignation."

Liubinsky, Minister of Foreign Affairs, spoke next. "This order," he said, "is the result of propaganda [against us]. The Germans definitely promised not to interfere in our domestic affairs . . . , [but] they find it too difficult to understand our internal situation. . . ."

[At the conclusion of the debates there was adopted a resolution which protested against German policies in the Ukraine and repudiated Eichhorn's order.]

KIEV DECLARED UNDER MARTIAL LAW
[Field Marshal Eichhorn's Order, April 26, 1918] [11]

Irresponsible individuals and groups are attempting to terrorize the population. In violation of law and justice they are making

[10] *Svoboda Rossii*, No. 16, April 30, 1918, p. 2.
[11] *Svoboda Rossii*, No. 19, May 4, 1918, p. 2.

arrests with the object of frightening those who, in the interests of the country and of the newly born state, are ready to work hand in hand with Germany. I shall tolerate no such lawlessness in the places where German troops are stationed. I therefore order that special measures be taken to safeguard the city of Kiev and that all those committing lawless acts be turned over to the court.

I hereby order: (1) All infringements of public order—criminal offenses as well as offenses directed against German and allied troops, including all individuals attached [to those troops]—fall under the exclusive jurisdiction of a special German court martial. (2) Infringements of public order, particularly street gatherings, are forbidden. (3) It is likewise forbidden to disturb order or public safety by propaganda expressed in speech, the press, or any other medium. Newspapers committing these offenses will be suppressed immediately. (4) The regular Ukrainian courts shall continue their functions except as provided in Section I. (5) These regulations become law immediately upon publication. . . . (6) The staff of the 37th Army Corps will enforce this order.

FIELD MARSHAL VON EICHHORN
Commander in Chief of German Troops in the Ukraine

REASONS FOR MARTIAL LAW

[German Diplomatic Mission to the Kaiser] [12]

There has recently been evidenced an intense agitation against German influence in the Ukraine. The efforts of the Germans to introduce order have not met with the support of the [Ukrainian] Government. There are indications that even members of the Government have been taking part in this agitation. Quite recently the director of the Bank for Foreign Trade, Dobryi, was arrested. He had been working in close contact with the Germans and the members of the Economic Commission. Field Marshal Eichhorn, with the approval of the Imperial Envoy, von Mumm, has taken special measures to protect Kiev. [These measures] relate chiefly to the establishing of courts and the imposing of severe punishment for the disruption of order. Investigation by the

[12] *Ibid.*

German court of the circumstances under which Dobryi was arrested led to the imprisonment of the Ukrainian Minister of War, the Chief of the Ministry of the Interior, the Chief of the City Militia, and the Chief of the Ministry of Foreign Affairs.

THE LAST DAYS OF THE UKRAINIAN RADA
[Session of April 27, 1918] [13]

. . . The session of the Rada, which opened very late and was attended by a great number of outsiders, quickly settled the question of additional elections to the Ukrainian Constituent Assembly, the meeting of which was fixed by the Rada for May 12. Minister of War Zhukovsky replied to an interpellation by Yanko, a member of the Rada, concerning the disarming of Ukrainian troops.[14] The explanations amounted to this:

The War Ministry intended to disarm two divisions recruited from prisoners of war of Ukrainian nationality, in view of the fact that these divisions had proved incapable of performing military service. Last night delegates of the First and Fourth regiments came to me and said that they were surrounded by German troops and were being disarmed. To prevent bloodshed I sent officers to quiet the soldiers and dispatched a vigorous protest to the Chief of the German Staff. The German Command replied that it had no intention of insulting Ukrainian troops but was merely endeavoring to make sure that arms and ammunition were surrendered in full.

The explanations of the Minister of War . . . were followed by a speech of the President of the Council of Ministers, Golubovich. He touched upon the latest order of Field Marshal Eichhorn and said:

"Already the first order of General Eichhorn, relating to the compulsory sowing of land, has aroused the protest of the Rada. Now we are confronted with a new act of the German Command about which the Rada Government was not consulted. Furthermore, the Government learned about the order only when it was posted in the streets yesterday, April 26. The German Command

[13] *Svoboda Rossii,* No. 20, May 9, 1918, p. 5.
[14] A division of Ukrainian soldiers was disarmed by the Germans during the night of April 26-27.

accuses us of weakness and makes reference to the existence of secret organizations. But the real crux of the matter is that the German Command has fallen under the influence of groups hostile to the Rada and cannot adequately grasp the situation.

"When we invited German troops to come to the Ukraine we intended to safeguard the national and social conquests of the revolution, which, as we firmly believed, were seriously threatened by Bolshevism. In our negotiations it was always emphasized that the Germans would come to us as friends of the Ukraine and would under no circumstances interfere in our domestic affairs. I could cite as evidence the telegrams which I exchanged with Berlin after Kiev was occupied by German troops. Even now the German Government and people do not approve of the policies of the German Command, as is evident from the Reichstag debates of April 24-25 on Eichhorn's orders. [The policy of the German Command] is especially fraught with dangers to our common interests now that we have just signed a commercial treaty and sent three million puds of grain to Germany.

"What can we do now? We must call the attention of the German Government to what is going on and insist that the men who do not fit in with the situation be removed. . . ."

On the motion of Yanko the Rada postponed further debate until the next day.

[Session of April 28] [15]

. . . The debates were opened by Porsh, . . . chairman of the commission which had concluded a commercial treaty with Germany. Contrary to expectations, he began to criticize the policies of the Government. General Eichhorn's orders [he said] merely revealed the weaknesses of the Government, which has no real support in the country and no "constructive program." Nevertheless, Eichhorn's orders are fraught with grave consequences, especially now that the commercial treaty has been successfully concluded. . . . We should protest most energetically in order that Berlin and Vienna may understand the actual situation.

Martov spoke for the Government party of Ukrainian Socialist-

[15] *Svoboda Rossii,* No. 20, May 9, 1918, p. 5.

Revolutionists. He testified that the peasant population had absolute confidence in the Rada. He felt, however, that a grave danger was threatening the Ukraine. "It is better for the Rada to perish than to compromise with the German Command. Even if the Ukraine should have to share the fate of Belgium, we must see to it that we do not become like the obedient and helpless *Sfatul Tserii*." [16]

Zarubin, a Russian Socialist-Revolutionist, spoke amid violent protests from the benches of the Government majority. [He said:] "What we predicted has come to pass and it is but a logical result of the policies which the Rada has been following. General Eichhorn's order introduces the death penalty and does away with all civil liberties. There is only one way of salvation left to us: to appeal to the Ukrainian democracy and the democracies of the world. The Government does not want to do this because it is afraid of democracy and is even suppressing it." Zarubin enumerated the non-democratic acts of the Rada. . . . He was interrupted with shouts of "Go to the Bolsheviks and Eichhorn!" . . .

Vinnichenko, the former leader of the Rada, mounted the platform: "The reason for our tragedy is not by any means the fact that the Germans are here. They saved us from the Bolsheviks. The reason for our tragedy is the fact that, though economically the Ukraine and Germany are friendly, yet socially they are hostile. Furthermore, the non-Ukrainian democracy still continues to dream of a united and undivided Russia. The Germans wish to obtain the support of the circles which formerly favored the Allies. Our own forces are weak and our principal hope is the socialist movement in the West."

Rafes, representative of the Bund,[17] began to speak. During his speech Grushevsky, the President, received information that the building of the Rada was surrounded by German troops. At 3:45 [P. M.] the door leading to the presidium quarters was opened, and a German lieutenant gave a loud command in Russian, "Attention! Hands up! Hands up!"

More and more soldiers entered the premises of the Rada. They

---

[16] The reference here is to the Bessarabian National Assembly, which voted on April 9 for union with Roumania. See *The Bolshevik Revolution*, pp. 462-64.

[17] Jewish Social Democratic party.

approached the members of the Rada, pointing revolvers at their heads. Members of the Rada and the public stood up and raised their hands. The President, Professor Grushevsky, attempted to protest against the introduction of soldiers into the session of the Rada. "Who are you?" shouted the German lieutenant. When told that this was Professor Grushevsky, he said: "We do not want you." He then called out the names of Ministers Zhukovsky, Tkachenko, Kovalevsky, and the Chief of the Political Section of the Ministry of the Interior, Gaevsky. Only the last was present. He, together with Liubinsky, Minister of Foreign Affairs, was placed under arrest and taken into an automobile.

"Surrender your arms," ordered the lieutenant. "If arms are found on anyone during the search he will be severely punished." "He will be shot," added another lieutenant in German. Members of the Rada, accompanied by soldiers, came one after another to the presidium table and gave up their revolvers. The German soldiers removed the cartridges. Members of the Rada were led into a separate room, where they were questioned. Professor Grushevsky was placed under house arrest. . . . After some time the members of the Rada . . . were set free. The German soldiers left the building. The Rada was free again but the evening session was not held.

[Session of April 29] [18]

On the morning of April 29 large crowds assembled near the building of the Rada; there were no German soldiers in evidence. All kinds of rumors were in circulation: that the Rada Government no longer existed; that the Congress of Khleborobs and the Sech Cossacks were on their way to break up the Rada. Nevertheless, a closed session took place in the building of the Rada. It was decided to send to the German representative in Kiev, Baron Mumm, a delegation of three: Porsh, Golubovich, [and] Korchinsky. The delegation was to ask Baron Mumm [to tell] on whose initiative the recent events had taken place—that of the military officers or that of the German Government. The delegation was also to point out that if the German Government adopted a conciliatory attitude the Rada was ready to meet Germany's de-

[18] *Svoboda Rossii,* No. 20, May 9, 1918, p. 5.

mands to a greater extent than previously. In case of necessity the government could resign; also, the land law could be changed to meet the requirements of the times.

About three o'clock the official session [of the Rada] began. Professor Grushevsky made the following announcement: "Late last night the German Military Attaché . . . called on me. I protested vigorously against all the infringements of the rights of the Rada which the German troops had taken the liberty of perpetrating. The Attaché replied that the arrests had been occasioned by the Dobryi affair; as for the rest, he promised to make a careful investigation. This morning the Chief of Staff called and stated that the German Supreme Command did not approve of the methods which the subordinate officers had used during the arrest of Rada members. The Supreme Command thought that the bringing of soldiers into the premises of the Rada had been a mistake."

With this, the session of the Rada came to a close. At four o'clock the building of the Rada and the adjacent streets were surrounded by Sech Cossacks armed with machine guns. At the same time the Khleborob Congress, together with Hetman Skoropadsky, set out for the Sofiisky Square.

THE CONGRESS OF LANDOWNERS
[Session of April 28, 1918] [19]

On April 28 the solemn opening of the Congress of Khleborobs took place, attended by several hundred delegates of peasants and landowners chiefly from Poltava, Ekaterinoslav, and Kiev gubernias. The voting for the Executive Committee of the Congress apparently caused no conflict, but when the results of the election were announced a minority of the assembled delegates broke away and formed their own "Democratic Congress of Khleborobs." Voronovich was elected chairman of the principal congress.

The first [speech of] greeting disclosed the state of mind of the assembly. Speaking for the union of landed proprietors, Dusson said:

"We greet you as the first freely elected congress, expressing

[19] *Ibid.*

the true attitude of the khleborobs. In all previous congresses delegates were not elected but appointed by party organizations, [with the result] that the peasants and the khleborobs never had a voice. . . . The principal wealth of our Ukraine is bread. If the khleborob proves able to stand up for himself and his land . . . our country will be saved and prosperous."

Reichert, a representative of the Cooperative Land Bank of Kherson, declared amid shouts of applause that the socialists who had ruined the country could have no place in the government. Healthy social and cultural forces should be called upon to undertake the task of national reconstruction.

[Session of April 29] [20]

The session opened with a report on the land question by Professor Kistiakovsky. After stressing the fact that during recent years the land had passed into the hands of the peasants, the speaker said: "Is it possible to call that government a people's government which abolished land ownership at a time when the land and the toil on the land were becoming more and more diffused among the people?" At the insistent demand of the audience the speaker specified the government he meant—the Ukrainian Rada. A tumult was raised in the hall and for several minutes there were heard the shouts: "Down with it, to hell with it!" The statement of the speaker that the land committees should be abolished was received with loud applause. By way of characterizing the policies of the Rada, Professor Kistiakovsky said that whereas in the domain of commerce the Ukrainian Rada recognized private property, in agriculture the land was being taken away from the khleborobs. Once more there were heard the cries: "It is our land; we did not steal it and we will not give it up!" The speaker's concluding statement, that the khleborobs would succeed in abolishing the land law, was received with an outburst of enthusiasm. . . . The whole congress shouted: "Down with the Rada!" The speaker could not resume his speech for a long time. [He ended as follows:] "You citizens must tell the ministers: 'The land law must be abolished at once. We do not wish to be

[20] Ibid.

the charges of the committees. They have ruled over us long enough. We shall now take care of ourselves. What has been plundered under the guise of law must be restored, and what has been set on fire must be paid for.'" (*Shouts of applause.*)

[Several other speakers also criticized the Rada and the Ukrainian Constituent Assembly which was scheduled to meet in May. There were passed resolutions favoring abolition of the Rada's land law, reestablishment of private property in land, and turning the government over to "competent" authorities. Then the question of forming a new government was brought up for consideration.]

One of the speakers raised the question of forming a new government. It was clear that this suggestion met with general approval. A representative of Ekaterinoslav Gubernia . . . proposed to send a delegation to the German Command. Kovalenko asked what form the new government was to assume. . . . For the first time the word "hetman" was heard. It was repeated time after time, reverberating in every corner of the circus.[21]

It was three o'clock when the General of the Guards, Pavlo Skoropadsky, surrounded by an officers' escort, appeared in one of the loges. The circus trembled with applause. General Skoropadsky was invited to take a seat at the presiding table and the chairman said: "The next speaker is the illustrious Hetman Skoropadsky."

Skoropadsky made . . . a brief speech in Ukrainian. He said that he was not assuming power for his own benefit. He accepted authority from the Congress in order to put an end to anarchy. "I pray God that He may help me to save the Ukraine from the blood and ruin which she is now facing." The Hetman was carried shoulder-high. The circus roared with enthusiastic shouts.

A religious ceremony was set for 4:00 P. M. in the Sofiisky Square. Here assembled the presidium of the Khleborob Congress, representatives of the landed aristocracy, generals, fashionable ladies, etc. At 3:30 Hetman Skoropadsky arrived, accompanied by a guard. The Hetman entered the Sofiisky Cathedral and after prayer came out to the Square, where Bishop Nikodim prayed for the long life of Hetman Pavlo.

[21] The Congress was held in the Kiev Circus.

PROCLAMATION OF HETMAN SKOROPADSKY [22]
[April 30, 1918]

Citizens of the Ukraine! You all remember the time when the blood of our best citizens was being shed profusely and the newly formed sovereign state of the Ukraine was on the brink of ruin.

We owe our salvation to the mighty support of the Central Empires, which continue . . . to fight with us for the integrity and peace of the Ukraine.

Everyone hoped that with the support of the Germans order would soon be established in our country and the economic life of the Ukraine at last resume its normal course.

These hopes, however, have not been realized. The former government of the Ukraine proved incompetent. Disorder and anarchy reign throughout the country and economic disorganization and unemployment are steadily on the increase, with the result that the once prosperous Ukraine is now threatened by the approaching phantom of starvation.

All the working classes of the people have become profoundly alarmed by this situation . . . and have come forward with a categorical demand for the immediate creation of a government which will prove itself able to guarantee to the people peace, order, and the opportunity to engage in productive labor.

As a faithful son of the Ukraine, I choose to respond to the call and to assume provisionally the responsibility of power.

I hereby declare myself the Hetman of the Ukraine!

I shall appoint a cabinet of ministers to govern the country on the basis of the provisional constitution of the Ukrainian Empire, which is published with this declaration.

Both the Central and the Small Radas are dissolved and with them all land committees. The former ministers and their assistants are dismissed. All other employees of state institutions are to remain at their posts and continue their duties.

A law dealing with elections to the Ukrainian Seim will soon be announced. Until then I shall firmly uphold law and order. I shall require absolute obedience to all government regulations and

[22] *Pravda,* No. 88, May 9, 1918, p. 3; Doroshenko, *op. cit.,* II, 48-49, gives the text in Ukrainian.

maintain the authority of the government by measures as extreme as necessity demands.

The right of private property, which is the basis of civilization and culture, is hereby fully restored. All ordinances of the previous Ukrainian Government and of the Russian Provisional Government, in so far as they infringed upon the right of private property, are declared null and void. Complete freedom to buy and sell land is also reestablished.

Measures will be taken toward the alienation of lands of large landowners at their actual cost and toward their distribution among needy peasants.

The rights of the working class will likewise be safeguarded and special attention will be paid to railway employees, who continued their important work under most difficult circumstances.

In the domain of economics and finance, complete freedom of trade is reestablished and opportunity is given to private enterprise and initiative.

I am fully aware of the burdens which await me and I pray to the Almighty that He may give me sufficient strength to fulfill adequately my duties to my Ukrainian fatherland. . . . What impels me to assume this burden is not personal ambition but the welfare of the people. I therefore call upon every Ukrainian citizen to help me and my assistants in our difficult and important task.[23]

PAVLO SKOROPADSKY
All-Ukrainian Hetman

---

[23] A provisional statute for the Ukrainian state which was made public on the same date gave the Hetman full dictatorial power. He was to appoint the prime minister and the cabinet of ministers, to be without restriction in international affairs, and to command the army and navy. (*Novaia Zhizn*, No. 84, May 8, 1918, p. 3.) Skoropadsky's first cabinet was composed of the following members: F. A. Lizogub, Prime Minister and Minister of the Interior; D. I. Doroshenko, Minister of Foreign Affairs; N. P. Vasilenko, Minister of Education; A. K. Rzhepetsky, Minister of Finance; M. Chubinksy, Minister of Justice; Yu. Vagner, Minister of Labor; C. Gutnik, Minister of Trade and Industry; General Rogoza, Minister of War; Yu. Sokolovsky, Minister of Agriculture; V. Zenkovsky, Minister of Cults. (Goldenweiser, in *A. R. R.*, VI, 217.)

PROTEST AGAINST THE HETMAN'S GOVERNMENT
[Resolution of the All-Ukrainian Peasant Congress] [24]

The Second All-Ukrainian Peasant Congress . . . declares its protest against German interference in the internal political life of the Ukraine . . . and proclaims to all Ukrainian citizens the following:

1. The peasantry does not recognize the Hetman elected by the landlords.

2. . . . The land must by no means revert to the landlords as is implied in the Hetman's declaration.

3. The peasantry appeals to the German people not to go against the Ukrainian people and not to allow bloodshed between these two peoples.

4. The Congress recognizes the Constituent Assembly, which is soon to meet, as the highest central Ukrainian authority. . . .

6. The Peasant Congress appeals to all workers and democratic organizations to come to the defense of the revolution . . . and to unite with the peasantry in the fight against counter-revolution.

THE KADETS AND THE SKOROPADSKY RÉGIME
[From the Proceedings of the Congress of the Party of People's Freedom, May 11, 1918] [25]

. . . Mr. Grigorovich-Barsky put to a vote the following question: Does the Congress approve the participation of party members in the present government? By a majority of seventy to thirteen, with six not voting, the Congress replied to this question in the affirmative. It then accepted the following resolution:

"Having heard the report of the Kiev Regional Committee on the organization of the government, the Congress of the Ukrainian Party of People's Freedom, while remaining loyal to the ideals and the program of the party . . . , considers it imperative for the party to share in governmental activity and finds it possible to allow individual members of the party to enter the newly formed ministry. . . ."

[24] P. Khristiuk, *Zamitki i materiali do istorii Ukraniskoi revoliutsii*, III, 15. The Congress was in session from May 8 to May 10, 1918.

[25] *Svoboda Rossii*, No. 30, May 21, 1918, p. 2.

The Congress also accepted the following resolutions concerning the land and labor problems:

THE LAND PROBLEM

"An adequate solution of the land problem in the Ukraine, which is predominantly an agricultural country, is the most pressing task of the day. Refusal to undertake agrarian reforms, and a return to past forms of the ownership and utilization of land, even if such a return were made possible by the use of external force, would inevitably lead to economic and cultural stagnation. . . . The satisfaction of the agrarian needs of the toiling peasant population and the removal of existing abnormalities in the use of land will prove the best means of counteracting the demagogic slogans of land socialization, which have brought ruin to agriculture and anarchy to the country. However, unrestricted freedom to sell land without state regulation is bound to lead to chaotic liquidation of land ownership, to speculative buying, and to transfer of the land to foreigners. . . . In view of the fact that land reform cannot be realized through the efforts of a single party, the Congress considers it necessary to support any group which advocates the following: (a) consolidation of small private property; (b) opposition to transferring Ukrainian land to foreigners; (c) limitation of land ownership, and purchase by the state of lands above the established standards; (d) assistance to small owners in increasing their holdings. . . ."

THE LABOR PROBLEM

"Workers should be given extensive freedom to organize unions for the purpose of defending their rights and needs; but these unions may not exercise general administrative functions. The eight-hour working day shall be continued in industry, provided that this does not lead to a decrease in the normal productivity of labor, which during the revolutionary period has sharply declined."

GERMAN ECONOMIC POLICY IN THE UKRAINE [26]

The fall of the Ukrainian Rada was doubtless accelerated by the Rada's inability to fulfill the obligations of providing food which

[26] *Ibid.*, No. 26, May 16, 1918, p. 2.

were imposed on the Ukraine by the commercial treaty with Germany. According to that treaty, Germany was to receive seven million puds of bread from the Ukraine by May 1.[27] Hardly three million puds were shipped by that date. Bread supplies which had accumulated at railway junctions fell very easily into the hands of the German troops, but no further progress could be made. . . . Not long before the overthrow of the Rada one German representative described the situation as follows: "We readily believe the declarations of the Ukrainian Government that the Ukraine has plenty of bread, but up to now we have not seen it."

It seems that it was this necessity of obtaining Ukrainian bread as soon as possible which primarily determined German policy. At the same time, the representatives of the German Government, both military and civil, acted with great caution. . . . In their negotiations with the Ukrainian Government the Germans constantly emphasized that they preferred a peaceful settlement of the problem. The reason for this attitude is that the military force at the disposal of the Central Powers—so far seven hundred echelons (about four hundred thousand soldiers) have arrived—is far from sufficient to undertake a military requisition of bread. Furthermore, Germany and Austria-Hungary count on Ukrainian bread not only for this year but for the next agricultural year as well. That is why the representatives of the German Government in the Ukraine are so attentive to every complaint of landowners and peasants. When they became convinced that the agrarian reforms . . . met with strong opposition from a considerable part of the peasantry, the German envoy, Baron Mumm, twice made energetic representations to the Ukrainian Government on the necessity of a radical change in land policy. The Socialist-Revolutionist representatives in the government, especially Golubovich and Kovalevsky, were actively opposed to [Mumm's] plans. Apparently Baron Mumm soon came to the conclusion that Germany was "backing the wrong horse."

By this time negotiations with Skoropadsky and the Union of

---

[27] The economic agreement between Germany and the Ukraine called for the following shipments of grain: April, nine million puds; May, fifteen; June, twenty; and July, nineteen million puds. (R. Lutz, *Fall of the German Empire, 1914-1917*, I, 828.)

Landed Proprietors had reached a definite stage, and the coup
d'état took place.

Just now it is difficult to foresee its immediate consequences.
Will Skoropadsky's government justify the German hopes of receiving Ukrainian bread? In any event, the German Command is
displaying exceptional energy in facilitating the [Government's]
task. . . . All Ukrainian . . . railways and the Dnieper steamship lines are in the hands of the Germans. German railway agents
have taken stock of all railway properties. . . . Officially this is
being justified on the ground that German troops are waging war
on Ukrainian territory and that therefore all ways of communication must be under German administration. . . .

In the domain of financial policy, the former government had
outlined a series of measures such as selling alcohol supplies and
introducing vodka and sugar monopolies. These measures, however, were not carried out, and Ukrainian finances were based on
paper money printed in Germany. Till very recently the German
Government hesitated to give the money to the Rada. The money
was given to Skoropadsky's government, and the newly printed
karbovantsy [28] immediately became known as *skoropadki*.[29] Close
commercial relations between the South and the North of Russia
form no part of German economic policy, and in their negotiations with the Rada the representatives of the German Government were decidedly opposed to the making of a commercial treaty
between the Ukraine and Velikorossiia.[30]

Austro-German occupation of the Ukraine inaugurated
a period of violent peasant insurrections, which played an
important part in bringing about the downfall of Skoropadsky's government. The requisitioning of grain and other
foodstuffs from the peasants, together with the restoration to their former owners of the land and other property
seized by the peasants during the early stages of the revolution, led to frequent sanguinary conflicts between the forces

---

[28] The Ukrainian word for rubles.

[29] Designation of Skoropadsky's paper money as *skoropadki* involves a pun; in
Russian and Ukrainian the word means "rapidly falling."

[30] Great Russia.

of occupation and the Hetman police on the one hand, and the peasant partisan bands on the other. Evidence of these conflicts is found in the daily press and in personal reminiscences. These accounts show that while in some instances, as in the case of the peasant leader Makhno, the partisan bands caused considerable trouble to the German and Austrian forces of occupation, in most cases the uprisings were easily crushed.

PEASANT UPRISINGS IN THE UKRAINE
[Newspaper Reports]

In the Ukraine there is a strong movement against the German and the Gaidamak [31] forces. Partisan bands of peasants have been formed at a number of places in Kiev and Chernigov gubernias. The bands assume the name of "Forest Brothers." The German . . . troops handle the insurgents very brutally. A number of villages have been destroyed. . . . The peasants of Kursk Gubernia are forming peasant armies to fight the Germans. . . . Local soldiers are in command of these armies.[32]

Peasant uprisings are taking place all over the Ukraine. The peasants refuse to give back the agricultural implements which they have taken from the landlords. The Germans are using artillery against the peasants. In the fighting near Kremenchug the peasants were armed with heavy artillery and machine guns.[33]

General Skoropadsky called a special conference of representatives of German authorities and the Ukrainian War Ministry to consider the question of liquidating peasant disturbances, which have spread almost throughout the Ukraine. . . .

General Skoropadsky made a long speech . . . , saying that . . . [eight] gubernias were affected by the peasant rebellion. The disturbances have reached their highest point in Podol, Kharkov, and Ekaterinoslav gubernias, where the local authorities appointed by the Skoropadsky Government are being arrested and slaughtered by the peasants. . . . In many places workers are joining the peas-

---

[31] Troops of the Ukrainian Government.
[32] *Svoboda Rossii*, No. 19, May 4, 1918, p. 3.
[33] *Novaia Zhizn*, No. 108, June 5, 1918, p. 2.

ants, and according to the latest information Krivorozhsky Uezd is in the hands of the insurgents. Troops have been sent to put down the insurgents, but the latter are offering serious resistance. . . . In Podol Gubernia punitive detachments succeeded at first in localizing the peasant movement, but serious disturbances have arisen again. Peasants are burning landlords' estates and killing our representatives. As a partial measure . . . General Skoropadsky suggested declaration of martial law in all territories of the Ukraine, immediate formation of special Cossack detachments for the liquidation of the movement, [and] establishment of contact with the German Supreme Command in the Ukraine. . . .

General Eichhorn, who was present at the conference, declared that he would take every measure to liquidate the disorders. . . .[34]

Peasant insurrections in the Ukraine are beginning to assume an organized form. The first band of revolting peasants appeared in the village of Boguslav (Kiev Gubernia). . . . On June 13 . . . groups of armed . . . peasants entered the village. The chief of the group ordered that the militia be disarmed and the population searched. For some reason only Jewish homes were searched, and the searches were accompanied by plunder. The partisan band did not stay in the village very long. The chief of the local militia managed to inform the Germans . . . , and on June 15 . . . the peasants fled.

With the departure of the Germans the partisan bands reappeared. They were now in greater number, better organized . . . , and armed with machine guns. The chief of the bands . . . issued an order requiring the inhabitants to surrender arms. . . . A levy of one hundred thousand rubles was then imposed on the village. However, the peasant bands did not succeed in maintaining their rule over Boguslav for a long time. Soon a German detachment arrived and forced the peasants to retreat.[35]

Peasant disturbances in Kiev Gubernia are increasing considerably. The punitive detachments which General Eichhorn sent to Uman . . . and Belaia Tserkov . . . did not have any success. General Eichhorn therefore issued orders to send German reserves stationed at Kiev to those regions. . . .

The peasants of Uman Uezd succeeded in deposing the uezd

[34] *Ibid.*, No. 110, June 7, 1918, p. 3.   [35] *Ibid.*, No. 128, July 3, 1918, p. 3.

starostas and in establishing special committees of their own. According to the latest information, large detachments of German troops are engaged in wholesale slaughter of peasants. . . . The German Command declared Belaia Tserkov and its environs under martial law.

Peasant insurrections occurred in Verkhnedneprorsky Uezd (Ekaterinoslav Gubernia) and in Yuzimsky Uezd (Kharkov Gubernia). . . . The peasants kill German colonists for giving help to the Germans. . . .[36]

A UKRAINIAN PEASANT HERO

[From the Memoirs of Gerasimenko] [37]

Makhno's activities in the South of Russia began in March 1918. . . . He formed a small band . . . and engaged in daring robberies, roving from one place to another. . . . As his band gradually increased in number through the influx of [people] dissatisfied with the Hetman régime . . . , Makhno was able to make raids on landlords' estates, small towns, and railroad stations. The raids were usually accompanied by brutal murders in which Makhno's followers settled their personal grievances against those who in one way or another had offended them.

The freedom which Makhno felt is well illustrated by a story told by the manager of one of the large estates in Taurida Gubernia. . . . Makhno arrived at the estate . . . to settle personal accounts with a certain employee . . . , who fortunately was absent at the time.

"We can wait until he arrives," said Makhno smilingly. "We are not in a hurry."

For three days Makhno ruled the estate. His followers abandoned themselves to debauchery and departed only when they were given a large sum of money. Upon his departure Makhno promised to come again.

During June the anarchist group . . . "Nabat" . . . and other anarchists . . . from various cities of Southern Russia . . .

[36] *Ibid.*, No. 129, July 4, 1918, p. 3.

[37] K. V. Gerasimenko, " Makhno," in *Istorik i Sovremennik*, III, 151-54. Gerasimenko was associated for a time with the Makhno movement, and his memoirs, from which this excerpt is taken, tell the story of Makhno's activities up to the end of 1920, when Makhno was finally defeated by the Bolsheviks.

joined Makhno. From this time on Makhno's activities proceeded in a different direction. He now dreamt of establishing . . . a peasants' republic . . . based on anarchist principles. . . .

Circumstances greatly favored Makhno. The Crimea and the Ukraine were occupied by foreign troops, which were hated by the peasants. The Hetman authorities . . . were engaged in introducing "order" in the villages. . . . The landlords who came back to their estates were treating the peasants brutally in reprisal for the damage which their estates had suffered. The peasants were becoming more and more enraged and were looking for aid from various atamans. . . .

Makhno's band was daily increasing in numbers and adopted a regular military organization. It had its infantry, cavalry, machine guns, and even artillery. . . . Makhno's daring . . . and successful raids . . . on small German detachments and the Hetman's police authorities made him a peasant hero.

"Let's join Makhno," became the cry of the peasant masses.

Spurred on by success, Makhno entered upon open hostilities against the German and Austrians. The Austrians were terrorized by Makhno's followers to such an extent that they were afraid to appear farther than Ekaterinoslav and recalled their detachments from the villages and small towns. The Germans took a different stand in the matter. Irritated by Makhno's daring raids, the German Commander in Chief at Kiev ordered the concentration of a large force to exterminate Makhno's army.

Makhno was forced to retreat under pressure from the German army and found himself surrounded in the region of Alexandrovsk. . . . [He managed, however, to escape with a small group of his followers.] The Germans issued a special announcement stating that "Makhno, the bandit, has been wiped out," but five days later Makhno slaughtered a detachment of Austrians . . . and forced a few captured officers, including the commander of the detachment, to play cards with him. The game continued for two days, after which the officers were shot. . . .

It is difficult to give an estimate of the casualties which the Germans and Austrians suffered as a result of encounters with Makhno.

According to official data of the Hetman authorities, during the months of April and June Makhno made 118 raids, each leading to bloodshed. . . .

To the peasant masses Makhno became a legendary figure . . . , acquiring the reputation of a man fighting for peasant freedom and peasant justice. . . .

SKOROPADSKY'S RÉGIME

[From an Account by Goldenweiser] [38]

The revolution brought about by the Hetman . . . met [at the outset] with no opposition anywhere in the Ukraine. The new power needed only to organize itself and show its character. . . .

At first the formation of a ministry presented some difficulties. The Ukrainian parties, particularly the Socialist-Federalists, with whom negotiations were conducted, refused to take part in the government. The conservative parties were willing to enter the cabinet, but at the beginning there was reluctance to give a reactionary color to the cabinet. The Constitutional Democrats were invited to take part in the government, and a split took place in their ranks on this question. The majority, however, was in favor of entering the cabinet. . . . The cabinet was finally formed under the presidency of F. A. Lizogub. . . . The first cabinet of the Hetman was far from being reactionary; quite the contrary. Alongside a few moderate conservatives there were members with definitely progressive tendencies. But . . . the policy of the Hetman Government was of no consequence at all. Over and above this government there was a force on which everything depended.

In his memoirs General Ludendorff writes: "In Hetman Skoropadsky we found a man with whom it was very easy to get along." [39] Naturally the Germans tried to take full advantage of this possibility and directed the Hetman's policy toward their own gain. The real head of the Ukrainian state was not the . . . Hetman, nor the Prime Minister, but the chief of staff of Eichhorn's army group, General Groener. . . .

The Hetman revolution was accomplished under the banner of the restoration of landed property and freedom of trade. On these

[38] Goldenweiser, "Iz Kievskikh vospominanii," in *A. R. R.*, VI, 217-30.
[39] *Meine Kriegserinnerungen*, p. 502.

points the government had the full approval of the Germans. . . .
At first, commercial interests were under protection; later, as the
government moved to the right, the landed gentry became the re-
cipients of special favors. . . .

The period of the Hetman's rule was marked by a substantial
economic revival. . . . In the first place, industrial and commercial circles, being close to those in power, were able to create favorable conditions for themselves; in the second place, the enormous German and Austrian markets for every kind of goods
created a very favorable economic situation for our region. We
were then passing through an era . . . of speculative fever. The
paralyzed bourgeoisie of the North [Central Russia] streamed to
Kiev. Stock companies grew like mushrooms and did an enormous business. . . .

The German court martial [40] imposed very severe sentences. . . .
The situation of the accused, most of whom did not know German, was tragic; while the arbitrariness of the "Gerichtsherr"
. . . gave the court proceedings only a very slight resemblance to
a well-regulated administration of justice. But if one compares
these courts with some of the other forms of political persecution
practiced at the time, it will have to be acknowledged that the
courts were the lesser evil. . . .

Those who suffered most from persecutions were the peasants.
Special commissions were formed to ascertain the damages suffered by landowners during the revolutionary period. The peasants were forced to pay the damages . . . , the entire village being
made responsible for the payments of individual members. The
peasants offered resistance but were crushed with great severity.

Among the city-dwellers the Jews in particular were persecuted.
. . . All the excesses of the revolution were ascribed to them. . . .

The Germans were firmly in control of the Ukraine, the Crimea,
and the Azov region. The character of their relation to the Moscow Sovnarkom was uncertain.[41] It was clear, however, that the

---

[40] *Ibid.,* p. 223.

[41] In his memoirs Ludendorff expresses regret for the dual policy which
German statesmen pursued toward the Bolsheviks. The Germans, he says, should
have delivered a rapid blow at Petrograd and Moscow and set up a new government there, even at the cost of changing the Brest Treaty. [This note of
Goldenweiser is based on Ludendorff's *Kriegserinnerungen,* p. 529.]

Germans were determined to prevent the spread of Bolshevism in the fertile Russian South; and as long as the German army occupied the Ukraine, Bolshevism had no chance there. As for the [Moscow] Bolsheviks, they pretended at that time to recognize the independence of the Ukrainian state. Ukrainian consulates were established at Petrograd and Moscow . . . and conducted a thriving business in the issuance of more or less legal affidavits of Ukrainian origin and citizenship, thus giving an opportunity to thousands of people to leave Soviet Russia.

In the middle of the summer a Soviet peace delegation headed by Rakovsky arrived at Kiev. . . . The negotiations were conducted in Bolshevik style, i. e., publicly and with stenographic records of proceedings. For the sake of greater expedition the conversations were carried on through interpreters, though each side understood perfectly what the other was saying. In actuality, the proceedings consisted largely in the utterance of disparaging remarks and led to no results. The Bolsheviks used the occasion for propaganda . . . , but it is difficult to see why the Ukrainians and the Germans who stood behind them needed these negotiations. . . .

In July Field Marshal Eichhorn . . . was assassinated on his way home from staff headquarters.[42] . . . Germany was not then in a position to reply to the assassination in the same way in which she retaliated against the Chinese Boxers in 1900 when her ambassador, Keller, was assassinated. . . .

The sudden defeat of the German army [in the West] . . . radically changed the direction of the Hetman Government. . . . In November [October] the Socialist-Federalists entered the cabinet and a policy of Ukrainization was adopted. . . . Then came the German Revolution and the Ukrainian Government was

[42] Eichhorn was assassinated on July 30 by a youth named Boris Donskoi, a Russian Socialist-Revolutionist of the Left. Earlier in the month (on July 6) Count Mirbach, German Ambassador to Moscow, was assassinated by another Socialist-Revolutionist of the Left. (See below, p. 213.) After killing Field Marshal Eichhorn, Donskoi made no attempt to escape. He was seized by German authorities, and when questioned in jail made the following statement: "The Central Committee of the Socialist-Revolutionists of the Left condemned Eichhorn to death because he . . . strangled the Ukrainian Revolution . . . and took the land away from the peasants." (*Letopis Revoliutsii*, I, 226.) Donskoi was hanged by the Germans on August 10, 1918, in a public square in Kiev.

again reorganized. . . . A former tsarist minister . . . became prime minister . . . and contacts were established with the Volunteer Army. . . . This government lasted only a month. The peasant uprisings led by Petliura brought the Hetman régime to an end [on December 14, 1918].

As their military power began to decline, the Central Powers withdrew the support which they had given to Skoropadsky, the Hetman of the Ukraine. Desirous of making up for this loss of aid by securing help from Russian elements, the Hetman changed his internal policies with the view of making them more acceptable to these elements. He removed from his government the members who stood for Ukrainian independence and proclaimed the Ukraine an integral part of Russia.[43] His new cabinet, headed by Gerbel, former tsarist minister, consisted mostly of Russian monarchists. These steps only aggravated the political situation and accelerated the Hetman's downfall; for the Ukrainian conservative nationalists who previously supported the Hetman now turned against him. The leadership of the anti-Skoropadsky movement, however, was assumed by the more radical Ukrainian nationalists, members of the Rada government overthrown by the Germans toward the end of April. Taking advantage of the widespread discontent among the peasants, Petliura, Vinnichenko, and others proclaimed at Balaia Tserkov, near Kiev, a Ukrainian People's Republic and a Directory as its government. Thousands of peasants began to flock to the banner of the Directory and in a short time there was formed a large peasant army. It captured Kiev on December 14 and thereby brought the Hetman régime to an end.

[43] The proclamation is quoted in *Severnaia Kommuna,* No. 155, November 16, 1918, p. 3.

PROCLAMATION OF THE UKRAINIAN DIRECTORY
[December 25, 1918] [44]

The heroic efforts of the armed Ukrainian people have swept the monarchical-landlord government of the Hetman from the land of the Ukraine. The Ukraine is now freed from punitive expeditions, . . . gendarmes, and other institutions of the ruling classes. National-personal autonomy [45] is reestablished in order to guarantee each nation free development. The dumas and zemstvos which represented the propertied classes and were appointed by the Hetman government are abolished. In their place democratic governments, elected by popular vote, are reestablished.

Pending the final solution of the land problem, the Directory of the Ukrainian People's Republic has resolved that all small-scale agricultural holdings are . . . to remain the property of their former owners. All other lands become the property of peasants who have little or no land, and revert first to those who enlisted in the republican army which fought the Hetman.

Supreme jurisdiction over land belongs to the Directory. . . . This resolution applies also to monastery, church, and state lands. People's land councils are established to introduce the agrarian reforms. . . .

By its resolution of December 9 the Directory has annulled all laws and ordinances of the Hetman government relating to labor. The eight-hour work-day is reestablished; collective agreements are reintroduced; the right of association and strike is upheld; and factory-shop committees are reinstated.

The laws and ordinances of the Hetman government, which were directed against the interests of the toiling people . . . , are hereby annulled by the Directory. . . .

[44] *Revoliutsiia na Ukraine po memuaram belykh* (S. A. Alexeev, ed.), pp. 293-96.

[45] "National-personal autonomy" was a popular slogan of the time. It stood for the organization of national minorities into autonomous unions with complete self-government in such matters as education, culture, mutal aid, emigration. The idea underlying the movement was that nationality is determined not by geographical or political factors but by the complex of beliefs and customs common to a society. This conception was elaborated by the Austrian socialist Karl Renner in *Das Selbstbestimmungsrecht der Nationen in besonderer Anwendung auf Oesterreich.*

Having been authorized by the toiling classes of the Ukraine to assume sovereign power, . . . the Directory, by the above measures, has completed the first stage in the social and national liberation of the Ukrainian people. The next stage of our revolution will consist in creating new, just, and healthy . . . social reforms. . . .

The so-called "ruling" classes, the landed and industrial bourgeoisie, have demonstrated during seven months of unlimited rule their complete incapacity to govern the country. . . . The plundering policy of the propertied classes surrendered a considerable part of the national wealth to foreign imperialist hands. . . . Industry was completely ruined . . . and speculation reached unprecedented dimensions. . . .

The Directory declares that the non-toiling and exploiting . . . classes, responsible for the ruin of the national economy . . . , can have no voice in the administration of the country. The right to rule belongs to the toilers of the independent Ukrainian People's Republic. . . .

1. The peasants, who were among the first to . . . raise arms against the *pans*,[46] . . . should elect delegates to a congress of Ukrainian toilers. These delegates will represent the will of the armed peasantry as well as of those who contribute by peaceful work to the upbuilding of the new order of life.

2. The city workers should elect . . . delegates to a congress of Ukrainian toilers.

One part of the workers of non-Ukrainian nationality joined the fight of the Ukrainian people against the Hetman with little enthusiasm, while another was entirely neutral. The Directory believes that in the struggle for the liberation of all toilers the non-Ukrainian workers will forget their national prejudices and cheerfully join the rest of the people.

3. The toiling intelligentsia . . . , viz., workers in the field of education, cooperative workers, office employees, etc., should also elect representatives to the congress of the toiling people.

The time and place of meeting of the congress, as well as the electoral rules, will be announced later. The congress will have all

[46] Nobility.

sovereign rights and will decide all questions affecting the social, economic, and political life of the Republic. . . .

The Directory . . . will introduce workers' control in factories, shops, and other industrial enterprises . . . ; it will organize the national economy in accordance with the requirements of the present transition period, when the old, capitalist order is in ruins and a new order free from exploitation . . . is emerging. . . .

The toiling intelligentsia is called upon to join the productive classes and apply its energies and knowledge to the building of a new and just life. . . .

V. Vinnichenko
President of the Directory

Petliura, Shvetz, Andrievsky, Makarenko
Members of the Directory

The rule of the Directory lasted only a few months. By the end of November 1918 the Bolsheviks had already formed a "worker-peasant" government for the Ukraine, and soon they sent an army from Soviet Russia to bring that government into power. After two months of fighting against the forces of the Directory, the Bolsheviks occupied Kiev on February 5, 1919, and established once more a Ukrainian Soviet Government.

B. The Don

The early attempts of the Don Cossack leaders and the Volunteer Army to keep the Bolsheviks out of the Don and to organize opposition to the Soviet Government resulted in failure. General Kaledin committed suicide, the Volunteer Army fled to the Kuban, the newly elected Ataman Nazarov was killed by the Bolsheviks, and a Soviet form of government was established in the Don at the end of February 1918.[47] The Soviet régime, however, could not take root

[47] See *The Bolshevik Revolution*, pp. 420-28.

here. Directed against ancient Cossack customs and privileges, it soon aroused the open hostility of the Cossack settlements. Here and there and in increasing numbers, Cossacks rose and drove out the Soviet officials, and on April 13 a detachment of Cossacks made a raid on Novocherkassk, the Don capital, which they captured and held for a few days.[48] The strength and spirit of the Cossacks increased and a revived Cossack army began to press against the capital. At the same time—late in April—German forces in the Ukraine were moving eastward, blocking the Bolshevik lines of communication with the Don. On May 6 the Cossacks, aided by Colonel Drozdovsky's detachment of volunteers, which reached the scene after a march of sixty-one days from the Roumanian front, captured Novocherkassk. Two days later Cossack troops entered Rostov, where the Germans had already arrived from the west.

On May 11, delegates from adjacent Cossack villages met at Novocherkassk under the name of the Krug to Save the Don. The Krug elected General Krasnov [49] as provisional ataman enjoying absolute power until a new meeting of the Grand Krug in August. Krasnov immediately adopted a friendly attitude toward the Germans, hoping that with their aid he could keep the Soviet forces out of the Don region and form a new Don-Caucasian Republic, independent of Russia and close to Germany.

REESTABLISHMENT OF THE DON COSSACK GOVERNMENT

[Announcement of the Don Government, May 9, 1918] [50]

When the Bolsheviks usurped governmental power in the Don region and proceeded to rule the country on the principle of the

---

[48] I. Borisenko, *Sovetskie respubliki na severnom kavkaze v 1918 godu*, I, 93.

[49] During the November uprising in Petrograd Krasnov was in charge of Kerensky's military expedition against the Bolsheviks.

[50] S. A. Piontkovsky, *Grazhdanskaia voina v Rossii 1918-1921gg.*, pp. 405-07. This work will hereafter be cited as *G. V. R.*

dictatorship of the proletariat . . . , they completely uprooted the old forms of Cossack self-government. The result was that when the toiling Cossacks, realizing the fraud and treason of Bolshevik rule, raised the banner of insurrection and overthrew the Soviet Government at Novocherkassk, our region found itself without a central government capable of assuming the great responsibility of liberating our native land and of establishing all necessary state institutions. Such a government has now been formed (on April 28). . . .

The first and most essential aim of this Provisional Government is to free the Don from the destructive rule of the Soviet Government and the Red Guards. . . .

The [next] task of the Provisional Government is to call as soon as possible the "Krug to Save the Don." The Krug [51] will consist of representatives of army detachments—regiments, platoons, and batteries—which helped to free the Don; there will be no discrimination between Cossack and non-Cossack. Also, each stanitsa [52] will send one representative to the Krug. . . . The present Provisional Government will turn over its power to the Krug . . . , which will have the right to appoint a second provisional government. . . .

. . . Meanwhile the Provisional Government takes upon itself the task . . . of reestablishing the normal functioning of all regional institutions which were suppressed during Bolshevik rule. . . . It will endeavor to safeguard the independence of the Don . . . but will engage in no undertaking that goes beyond the borders of the Don.

The Provisional Government, taking upon itself the heavy burden of power for the sake of the common good, calls upon all . . . to unite their efforts and crush the Soviet Government together with its Red Guards, who keep the toiling masses in constant fear for the possessions acquired by the sweat of their brows.

THE PROVISIONAL GOVERNMENT OF THE DON

The Krug to Save the Don was in session from May 11 to May 18. Although it did not represent the entire Don, a large part of which was still under Bolshevik control, the

[51] A Cossack assembly.   [52] A Cossack settlement.

Krug adopted important political measures. It elected General Krasnov to the post of ataman and at Krasnov's demand accepted a constitution which closely resembled the fundamental laws of Imperial Russia. In doing this it abolished all the institutions of the revolution, including the laws of the Provisional Government, and virtually restored the old order in the Don region.[53]

Meanwhile the Moscow Bolsheviks continued to look upon the Don as a part of the Soviet Republic and on May 31 issued a statute for the organization of the Cossack regions. However, on June 5 the newly elected ataman proclaimed the Don an independent democratic republic.

GENERAL KRASNOV ELECTED ATAMAN OF THE DON

[Krasnov's Proclamation, May 17, 1918] [54]

By the will of the Krug to Save the Don I was elected Ataman of the Don to exercise supreme authority in every field. . . . Our former enemies, the Germans and Austrians, have entered the territory of the Voisko to help us in the struggle against the Red Army bands and to restore law and order in the Don. Not all of our land is yet freed from robbers and the dark forces which mislead the simple minds of our Cossacks. . . .

Cossacks and citizens! I call upon you to preserve order and tranquillity. No matter how much the Cossack heart may suffer at the sight of German troops, I demand that you refrain from molesting them. . . . Knowing the strict discipline of the German army, I am confident that we shall succeed in preserving amicable relations with the Germans until . . . we organize an army of our own, capable of maintaining order without the aid of foreigners. We must remember that we were defeated not by German soldiers but by our own ignorance and the grave illness which overpowered our Voisko . . . and the whole of Russia. . . . Let every one attend to his business. . . . You are now masters of your own land

[53] The constitution adopted by the Krug is quoted in *A. R. R.*, V, 194-97.
[54] *Donskaia Letopis*, III, 320-21.

. . . and may be sure that no one will hinder you from enjoying the fruits of your own labor.

As for myself, I would have you know that I place above all else the honor, glory, and prosperity of the Grand Voisko of the Don. I give you my oath, Cossacks and citizens . . . , that I shall serve the interests of the Voisko with honesty and fidelity. . . .

THE SOVNARKOM APPEALS TO THE DON AND KUBAN COSSACKS [55]

[May 30, 1918]

Toiling Cossacks of the Don and the Kuban!

A great danger is menacing you. The enemies of the toiling Cossacks have raised their heads. The former landlords . . . threaten to seize power in the Don and the Kuban and to deliver this prosperous and fertile region to foreign plunderers. Former General Krasnov, who in the November [1917] days marched with Kerensky against Petrograd, is now . . . negotiating with Skoropadsky, the oppressor of the Ukrainian workers and peasants, and with the representatives of the German Empire.

Do you know all this, Cossacks of the Don? No, you do not know it, because the traitors act behind the backs of the toiling people. They declare in your name that you wish to separate from Russia and to become, like the Ukrainians, the slaves of the pomeshchiks [landlords] and capitalists. To get back . . . the land and the rank of general, traitors of the Krasnov type are ready to betray your native Don region to foreign landlords and capitalists. . . .

The Soviet of People's Commissars hereby declares that the Don region is an integral part of the Russian Socialist Federated Soviet Republic. The pomeshchiks and generals have no right to speak for the toiling Cossacks and to bargain with your land, your bread, and your blood. Rise, toiling Cossacks, as one man, and declare that you remain as before in fraternal union with the workers and peasants of Russia!

The Soviet of People's Commissars declares the former General Krasnov and his helpers and allies to be enemies of the people and

[55] *Vestnik Narodnago Komisariata Vnutrennikh Del,* Nos. 15-16, 1918, pp. 11-12.

places them outside the law. There is no place for them in the free land of the toiling Cossacks! Death to the traitors and betrayers!

Expressing the will of the workers, peasants, and Cossacks of the whole of Russia, the Soviet of People's Commissars orders you to take up arms at once in defense of your land against traitors and plunderers. The Soviets of Cossacks' Deputies are charged with the duty of forming a powerful and reliable army ready to fight for your land and freedom. Every toiling Cossack is in duty bound to join the army at the first call of his soviet. We shall supply you with necessary ammunition and arms and reinforce you with fraternal armies.

A great danger is threatening you, Cossacks of the Don and the Kuban! You must demonstrate by deeds that you do not wish to become slaves. . . .

Rise, Cossacks of the Don! Rise, Cossacks of the Kuban! Death to the enemies of the people! Death to the traitors! Hail the toiling Cossacks! Long live the fraternal union of workers, peasants, and Cossacks! Long live the Russian Socialist Federated Soviet Republic!

V. Ulianov (Lenin)

President of the Sovnarkom

Trotsky, Chicherin, Stalin

People's Commissars

ORGANIZATION OF COSSACK VOISKOS

[Decree of the Sovnarkom, May 31, 1918] [56]

1. Every Cossack region and voisko shall be considered a separate administrative unit. . . .

2. The toiling Cossacks have the right to organize Soviet institutions of government provided they share that right equally with the toiling peasants and workers inhabiting Cossack lands. . . .

3. To coordinate the work and facilitate the solution of questions of regional and state importance, the voisko soviets . . . are to send their representatives to the regional soviet unions and the

[56] *Ibid.*, No. 17, 1918, pp. 10-11. Voisko is a Cossack community.

All-Russian Central Executive Committee of Soviets. In the latter the toiling Cossacks are to have the following representation: Don Region, four seats; Kuban Region, four seats; Orenburg Voisko, one seat; Terek Voisko, one seat; Ussury Voisko, one seat; Uralsk Voisko, one seat; Astrakhan Voisko, one seat; Siberian Voisko, one seat; Transbaikal Voisko, one seat; Amur Voisko, one seat; Semirechie Voisko, one seat; Yenisei Voisko, one seat; Irkutsk Voisko, one seat.

4. Representatives of the toiling Cossacks are to form a special section of the [All-Russian] Central Executive Committee and are to send delegates to every people's commissariat to help in solving questions relating to Cossack lands and voiskos. . . .

6. The immediate task [of Cossack soviets] is to strengthen the Soviet form of government and fight counter-revolution. . . .

7. The land formerly owned by Cossack voiskos is to remain, in accordance with the Fundamental Law of Land Socialization, in the use of the toilers domiciled in the Cossack territories and engaged in agriculture. . . . Pending the final solution of the land problem all voisko reserve lands, as well as those formerly owned by [army] officers, church, etc., revert to the voisko land committees . . . for distribution among those in need of land; . . . care, however, must be taken that the area under cultivation is not diminished. . . .

9. The Voisko Soviets of Cossacks' . . . Deputies are to undertake at once the formation of Cossack sections of the Red Army . . . in conformity with the decree of the Soviet of People's Commissars on the organization of the Red Army. . . .

V. ULIANOV (LENIN)
President of the Soviet of People's Commissars

THE DECLARATION OF INDEPENDENCE OF THE DON
REPUBLIC

[Communication to Foreign Powers, June 5, 1918] [57]

The Grand Voisko of the Don began its existence as an independent state in 1570. It became an integral part of Russia in

[57] Translation from the French text of the declaration. A copy is in the Hoover War Library, Stanford University, Cheriachukin Papers, File 1, No. 5.

1645 and since then has remained faithful to the Russian Empire. It continued so after the revolution, endeavoring in cooperation with the Provisional Government to bring the country to the Constituent Assembly, where the future form of government . . . was to be finally settled.

The . . . Voisko Krug and its elected ataman, Kaledin, refused to acknowledge the Soviet of People's Commissars as the legitimate government of Russia. They broke away from Soviet Russia, which became a toy in the hands of degenerate adventurers—the Bolsheviks; they declared the Don an independent democratic republic and entered upon a bitter fight against the Soviet Government. . . . Thanks to the courage and energy of the Don Cossacks, the Don Voisko is now free once more. On May 17 I was elected . . . Ataman of the Don and vested with extraordinary powers. . . .

In communicating the above to you, I have the honor, Sir, to ask you to advise your government of the following:

1. Pending the formation of a united Russia, the Don Voisko is an independent democratic republic. . . .

6. The Don Voisko proposes that the Powers recognize its right to exist as an independent state until Russia is united. . . .

MAJOR GENERAL KRASNOV
Ataman of the Don

MAJOR GENERAL BOGAEVSKY
President of the Council of Ministers

The original purpose of the German advance into the Don region was to insure fuel for the Ukrainian railways by occupying the coal fields of the Donetz Basin. But when the Germans saw that General Krasnov was friendly to them they conceived the project of controlling the Southeast politically as well as economically.

On June 11 a messenger from General von Eichhorn arrived at Novocherkassk to make known the Kaiser's views on the Russian situation. According to the message delivered, the future was not to see a single Russian state. Instead, there were to be formed out of what was formerly the Russian Empire four independent states—the Ukraine, the Union of the Southeast, Central Russia, and Siberia. Krasnov's task was to organize the Union of the Southeast, expel the pro-Ally Volunteer Army from the Don, and support the Central Powers in case of the reestablishment by the Allies of an Eastern front. A similar exposition of German desires with regard to Russia was presented in a memorandum which the Chargé d'Affaires of the Don Embassy at Kiev, in close touch with German circles there, sent to General Krasnov on June 21. Seeking to win the support of the Germans, General Krasnov dispatched a letter to the Kaiser which assured him of the neutrality of the Don and announced the formation of a Dono-Caucasian Union friendly to Germany.[58]

A PROPOSED DON FOREIGN POLICY

[Memorandum of General Svechin, Chargé d'Affaires of the Don Embassy at Kiev, to the Hetman of the Don, June 21, 1918] [59]

GERMAN ASPIRATIONS

. . . There seems to be a unanimous opinion in Germany that for the near future, at least, Russia must remain divided into several independent parts.

The Germans know perfectly well that the war in the West is far from being at an end, that our former allies will make great efforts, and that the European struggle will require much time and energy on their own part. . . . The Germans also realize that they cannot succeed in the near future in gaining the sincere good will of the Russians; and this means that Russia, if united, would constitute a new menace to Germany. . . . Kaiser Wilhelm would like to see Russia divided into four or five parts: Central Russia,

---

[58] *Donskaia Letopis,* III, 92-94; " Germanskaia interventsia i Donskoe pravitelstvo v 1918g.," in *Krasnyi Arkhiv,* LXVII (1934), 97, 120.
[59] *Ibid.,* pp. 120-22.

the Ukraine, the Union of the Southeast, Transcaucasia, and Siberia. It can be seen from this that the desire of every Russian patriot to see Russia united in the near future . . . is bound to encounter the most energetic opposition from the Central Powers. . . .

THE POSITION OF THE DON AND THE RUSSIAN SOUTHEAST

The position of the Southeastern regions of Russia and particularly of the Don is that of being between the hammer and the anvil. The Germans, if they so desire, can give one part of our territory to the Ukraine and leave the other to be plundered by the Red Guards. The consequences of Red Guard domination are too well known; nor is becoming a part of the Ukraine an attractive prospect. The Ukrainian Central Rada deposed by the Germans had invited German troops to its aid in order to have a semi-socialist government; [but] the conditions to which the Rada had to subscribe were such as to make the present Ukrainian rulers shudder. . . .

OUR ADVANTAGES

However, we have one enormous advantage possessed by neither Moscow nor Kiev and we should use it in full measure.

The point is that we and the Cossacks of the Southeast constitute an enigma for the Germans. As one representative of the German Command puts it, we are a "Sphinx" to them. On the one hand, they would like to help us and in this way secure our good will as well as certain material advantages; on the other hand, however, they are afraid to see us grow strong lest we do them injury. At the same time, it is not to their advantage to quarrel with us or to arouse us against them. As it is, the Germans find it rather difficult to control the Ukrainian peasant movement. The Ukrainian Government cannot fulfill the terms of the agreement with the Germans on the supply of food, and the Austro-German troops must use force in collecting grain from the villages. They encounter considerable opposition . . . and instead of three army corps . . . the Germans were compelled to send six corps for the occupation of the Ukraine, and they will need more in reinforcements. Naturally, under such circumstances the Germans have no desire to arouse the hostility of the Cossacks and thus to find themselves under the necessity of sending one or two more army corps and of weakening the Western front, which, according to Field Marshal Eichhorn, "is sitting on their necks." . . .

The things for us to do are:

1. To refrain from expressing any hope of seeing Russia united.

2. To maintain correct relations with the uninvited guests now in our territory. . . .

3. To have no relations with our former allies, who thus far have given us nothing and in many ways have betrayed us. They can give us no aid and the Germans will see to it that their influence does not extend beyond the Urals.

4. To proclaim our readiness to defend our territory against any hostile invasion.

5. To make a commercial agreement with Germany on the basis of the most-favored-nation principle.

In return we shall receive:

1. All necessary arms, supplies, and military equipment.

2. The settlement of our boundaries with Kiev and Moscow in accordance with our aspirations.

3. A stable organization of the Union of the Southeast. . . .

To bring about this Union it is necessary:

1. That the Ataman of the Don Voisko assume . . . the title of Ataman of the Union of the Southeast.

2. That the Don . . . and Kuban Governments draw up at once a constitution of the Union.

3. That an appropriate declaration be issued.

THE ATAMAN OF THE DON APPEALS FOR GERMAN
PROTECTION

[Krasnov's Letter to the Kaiser, July 11, 1918] [60]

Your Imperial and Royal Highness!

The bearers of this letter . . . , Major General Duke of Lichtenberg and . . . Major General Cheriachukin, are authorized by

[60] A copy of the original is in the Hoover War Library, Stanford University, Cheriachukin Papers, File I, No. 11.

me, the Ataman of the Don, to greet Your Imperial Highness, the Illustrious Monarch of Great Germany, and to deliver the following message:

Two months of fighting, in which the glorious Don Cossacks were engaged for the freedom of their country and fought with a courage equalled only by that displayed in recent years in the war against the English by a people of Germanic stock, the Boers, have resulted in our complete victory. . . . The land of the Grand Voisko of the Don is now nine-tenths liberated from licentious Bolshevik bands. Order has been reestablished . . . with the aid of the troops of Your Imperial Highness. . . .

The new state, however, . . . cannot exist in isolation. It has entered, therefore, a close alliance with the heads of the Astrakhan and Kuban voiskos, . . . Prince Tundutov and Colonel Filimonov. The object of the alliance is to organize . . . on federal principles an independent state, consisting of the Grand Don Voisko, the Astrakhan Voisko (with the Kalmuks of Stavropol Gubernia), the Kuban Voisko, . . . the Terek Voisko, and the peoples of the Northern Caucasus. These Powers have already given their consent and have decided . . . to be neutral in the present international conflict.

I authorize [the bearers of this letter] . . . to petition for the following:

That Your Imperial Highness recognize the independence of the Grand Voisko of the Don . . . and the federation of states to be known as the Dono-Caucasian Union. That Your Imperial Highness recognize the boundaries of the Grand Voisko of the Don to be the geographical and ethnographical limits of the past, and help settle our quarrel with the Ukraine over the Taganrog region in our favor. . . .

That Your Imperial Highness assist the Don in acquiring the cities of Tsaritsyn and Kamyshin, both of Saratov Gubernia, and the city of Voronezh . . . , because they are strategically important for the Don. . . .

That Your Imperial Highness exert pressure on the Soviet authorities in Moscow to remove their . . . Red Guard from the territories of the Don and the other states entering the Dono-Caucasian Union. . . .

That Your Imperial Highness assist our young state with cannon, rifles, ammunition, and supplies, and, if you consider this advantageous, set up in the Don territory factories for the manufacture of cannon, firearms, shells, and bullets. . . . In exchange for the favors of Your Imperial Highness, the Grand Voisko of the Don will observe strict neutrality in the World War . . . and will grant to Germany the exclusive right to export foodstuffs and raw materials . . . in exchange for agricultural machinery [and other manufactured products]. In addition Germany will be given special privileges in investing capital in Don industries and in developing new enterprises. . . .

A close alliance with us is certain to bring mutual benefits . . . , and a friendship cemented in bloodshed on common battlefields by the warlike Germans and the Cossacks is bound to evolve into a tremendous force in the struggle against our common enemies. . . .

Respectfully yours,

PETER KRASNOV

ATTEMPT TO ESTABLISH A DONO-CAUCASIAN FEDERATION

[A Constitution Proposed by Krasnov] [61]

When our country lay prostrate under the heavy blows of fate . . . , the peoples of the Southeast, animated by the desire to defend their independence . . . and common interests, proclaimed themselves in October 1917 a Union of the Southeast, in the hope that by united effort they would be able to resist the advance of the dark forces which were trampling in the dust all human and divine laws.

The struggle against the Bolsheviks which shortly commenced gave a temporary advantage to them; but now God has blessed our arms and our region has once more come to life.

However, in view of the fact that new armies are being organized for an invasion of our steppes and mountains, the Atamans of the Don, Kuban, Astrakhan, and Terek voiskos, and the Chief of the Mountaineers of the North Caucasus, assuming the pre-

[61] A. I. Denikin, *Ocherki russkoi smuty,* III, 246-47.

rogatives of supreme state authority, have resolved to proclaim the Dono-Caucasian Union a sovereign state.

Announcing this resolution, we beg you, Sir, to transmit to your government the following:

1. The Dono-Caucasian Union consists of the following independently governed states: the Grand Voisko of the Don, the Kuban Voisko, the Astrakhan Voisko, the Mountaineers of the Northern Caucasus and of Daghestan. They have decided to unite in one state on the principle of federation.

2. Each state belonging to the Dono-Caucasian Union will be governed in its internal affairs by local laws and on the principle of complete autonomy.

3. The laws of the Dono-Caucasian Union are divided into general laws, i. e., those for the whole union, and local laws, which each state makes for its own use.

4. The Dono-Caucasian Union has its own flag, emblem, and national anthem.

5. At the head of the Dono-Caucasian Union is a Supreme Council consisting of the Atamans (or their assistants) of the Don, Kuban, Terek, Astrakhan, and the Chief of the Mountaineers of the Northern Caucasus and of Daghestan. The Supreme Council elects a president, who acts as chief executive of the Supreme Council.

6. A Seim of representatives of the peoples of all states entering into the Dono-Caucasian Union will meet with the Supreme Council not less than once a year.

7. The function of the Seim is to formulate general state laws for ratification by the Supreme Council.

8. The Dono-Caucasian Union will have one army and one navy. The commander in chief of all armed forces of the Union will be appointed by the Supreme Council.

9. The following ministers . . . will be appointed by the Supreme Council: Foreign Affairs, War and Navy, Finance, Commerce, Transport, Post and Telegraph, State Comptroller, and the Chief Clerk.

10. The provisional capital of the Dono-Caucasian Union will be Novocherkassk.

11. The Dono-Caucasian Union wil¹ have common money, . . . postage and revenue stamps, and tariffs. . . .

12. The Dono-Caucasian Union . . . declares its neutrality [in the World War]. . . . It will fight only against Bolshevik troops invading the territories of the Union.

13. The Dono-Caucasian Union intends to maintain peaceful relations in the future with all states and will resist invasion of its territories by any foreign troops. . . .

14. The Dono-Caucasian Union hereby declares its intention of entering into commercial relations with any state recognizing its sovereignty.

15. The frontiers of the Dono-Caucasian Union are indicated on a special map. . . . For strategic reasons the Union must incorporate the southern part of Voronezh Gubernia, including Liski and Voronezh, part of Saratov Gubernia with Kamyshin and Tsaritsyn, and the district of Sarepta.

16. The Dono-Caucasian Union entertains the hopes that its emergence into life will be welcomed by the Powers interested in its existence and that an exchange of diplomatic representatives between those Powers and the Union will soon take place.

The statement of General Krasnov to the Kaiser that the governments of the Southeast consented to the formation of the Dono-Caucasian federation was not in accord with the facts. On the very day that Krasnov made the claim (July 11), representatives of the peoples which were alleged to be entering the federation held a conference at Novocherkassk and, with the exception of Prince Tundutov, Ataman of the Kalmucks, refused to sign the draft of the constitution submitted to them by Krasnov.[62] Opposition to Krasnov's plan came also from General Denikin, who thus added a new disruptive element to the already strained relations between the two anti-Bolshevik leaders.

Denikin, who assumed command of the Volunteer Army after its defeat in the Kuban in April 1918, had managed to retreat to the Don region by early May.[63] He hoped to

[62] K. Kaliugin, "Donskoi ataman P. N. Krasnov i ego vremia," in *Donskaia Letopis,* III, 96-97; Denikin, *op. cit.,* III, 247.
[63] See *The Bolshevik Revolution,* pp. 427-28.

join forces with the Cossacks and soon entered into negotiations with representatives of the Don Government.[64] But no agreement could be reached. Krasnov refused to place himself under Denikin, and Denikin disliked Krasnov's pro-German attitude. Under the circumstances the leaders of the Volunteer Army decided to merge their fortunes with those of the Kuban Cossacks and to undertake a second campaign into the Kuban, which was still under Bolshevik control.

This campaign began at the end of June, and after two months of bitter fighting the Volunteer Army succeeded on August 16 in taking the Kuban capital, Ekaterinodar.[65] A few days later Novorossiisk, a Black Sea port, was captured. Thus the Volunteer Army cleared a large part of the Northern Caucasus of the Bolsheviks, and secured a base where it could undertake preparations for a drive against the Bolsheviks of Central Russia.

On August 26 Denikin promulgated a statement which defined the aim of the Volunteer Army as the restoration of a united sovereign Russia. Two days later he issued a statute for the civil administration of the territories under the Army's occupation.

AIM OF THE VOLUNTEER ARMY

[General Denikin's Speech, August 26, 1918] [66]

. . . The Volunteer Army has undertaken the task of restoring a united sovereign Russia. Hence, murmurs from centrifugal elements and from disappointed local ambitions.

[64] The first meeting took place on May 11 at Novocherkassk and was followed by a conference between Denikin and Krasnov at Manych on May 28. *Donskaia Letopis,* III, 52; *A. R. R.,* V, 200-02.

[65] Accounts of the Second Kuban Campaign are given in W. H. Chamberlin, *The Russian Revolution,* II, 135-40; A. Zaitsov, *1918god. Ocherki po istorii russkoi grazhdanskoi voiny,* pp. 191-228.

[66] Denikin, *op. cit.,* III, 262.

The Volunteer Army cannot, even temporarily, bind itself to foreigners and enchain the free course of the Russian ship of state. Hence, murmurs and threats from without.

The Volunteer Army, proceeding on its thorny path, wishes to rest on the support of all nationally-minded groups of the population. It cannot be the tool of any political party or social organization. In that case it would cease to be the Russian National Army. Hence dissatisfaction, impatience, and political strife within the Army. But the Army, if it is to live up to its traditions, cannot take upon itself the suppression of the ideas of others. It says directly and openly: be Right or Left, but love our harassed fatherland and help us save it.

Similarly the Volunteer Army, fighting with all its might against the corrupters of the people's soul and the spoilers of the people's wealth, is beyond the ambitions of social strife and class struggle. . . . This is not the time to settle social problems, and no section of the Russian Empire has the right to build Russian life according to its biased ideas.

The leaders of the Volunteer Army . . . do not intend to attempt legislative reorganization [of the country]. Their sole aim is to maintain a minimum of conditions requisite for decent living . . . until an all-Russian legislative body, representing the reason and conscience of the Russian people, shall direct Russian life into new channels—toward light and truth.

CIVIL ADMINISTRATION OF THE VOLUNTEER ARMY
[August 28, 1918] [67]

Until the scattered fragments of the Russian state are reunited and a legal all-Russian government is formed, the administration of the regions occupied by the Volunteer Army is to be conducted on the basis of the following provisional statute:

PROVISIONAL STATUTE FOR THE ADMINISTRATION OF THE REGIONS OCCUPIED BY THE VOLUNTEER ARMY

Part I

1. Supreme authority in the regions occupied by the Volunteer Army is vested in . . . the Commander of the Volunteer Army.

[67] *Ibid.*, p. 267.

2. In the regions occupied by the Volunteer Army the laws which were valid in the territories of the Russian state prior to October 25 [November 7] shall remain in force, with such amendments as follow from the present statute as well as from the laws to be enacted on the basis of this statute.

3. All citizens of the Russian state, irrespective of nationality, social status, and religion, have equal civil rights. The special rights and privileges enjoyed by the Cossacks shall be held inviolable.

4. The established church in these regions is the Russian Orthodox Church, headed by the Most Holy Patriarch of Moscow and All Russia. Other recognized churches and religious societies have full liberty and are under the protection of law.

5. The national language is Russian. The use of local languages and dialects in state and social institutions will be permitted within the limits indicated by law.

6. The Russian tri-colored (white-blue-red) flag will be the national flag.

Part II

7. In the regions occupied by the Volunteer Army, Russian citizens enjoy inviolability of person, residence, and private correspondence. No one is to suffer restriction or loss of freedom except through due process of law. Search and arrest can be carried out only in cases provided for by law and in a manner defined by law.

8. Freedom of the press is recognized. The procedure of inspecting the press and of [establishing] responsibility for crimes and misdemeanors committed through the press are to be defined by law.

9. Russian citizens may assemble peaceably and without arms, and likewise organize societies and unions for purposes not contrary to law. The manner of using these rights of civil liberty is to be defined by law.

10. Property is inviolable. Compulsory expropriation of immovable property, when necessary in the interests of the state and of society, will be carried out in accordance with law and with fair compensation. . . .

[Part III concerns the rights of the commander in chief; Part

3

IV sets up a special council for civil administration; Part V deals with the judiciary; and Part VI provides for the autonomy of the Kuban region.]

C. THE CAUCASUS

The Commissariat of Transcaucasia, though not formally declaring independence, began to function independently immediately after the dissolution of the Russian Constituent Assembly on January 19, 1918. The delegates to that body, together with other elected representatives of Georgia, Armenia, and Azerbaijan, formed a representative assembly called the Seim, which appointed a cabinet to govern the region. But in the domain of foreign affairs Transcaucasia's fate still depended in large measure on the rest of Russia; for the negotiations at Brest-Litovsk between the Bolsheviks and the Central Powers and Turkey involved Transcaucasia as well as the territories under Soviet control. When, on March 2, the Sovnarkom accepted the revised German terms, which ceded three Caucasian provinces to Turkey, the Transcaucasian Government resolved to adopt an independent foreign policy. It first repudiated the Brest-Litovsk Treaty and attempted direct negotiations with Turkey; when these negotiations failed it declared war against "Turkish imperialism." The war ended in a quick and decisive defeat for Transcaucasia. The fact that peace had to be negotiated made it necessary to proclaim Transcaucasia an independent republic—a step taken on April 22.

The Transcaucasian Republic lasted only a little over a month. After the resumption of peace negotiations with Turkey, which opened at Batum on May 11, 1918, disagreements developed among the three nationalities composing the federation over the peace terms which Turkey was trying to impose on the new state. Thereupon the federation was dissolved and each component nation entered upon independent existence.[68]

Continually pressed by the Turks, who with their Moslem Tartar allies held nearly all of Russian Armenia and Azerbaijan, the Georgians turned for aid to Germany. Interested in forestalling their Turkish allies in seizing control of petroleum and other natural resources in the region, the Germans encouraged the Georgians.[69] On May 26 the Georgians declared their independence. By an agreement of May 28 with the Georgians Germany received control of the Transcaucasian Railroad and the use of Georgian ships for the duration of the war. On June 11 the Georgian Republic received de facto recognition in the Reichstag, and a diplomatic mission headed by Colonel von Kress came to Tiflis with a few battalions of German soldiers.

DISSOLUTION OF THE TRANSCAUCASIAN REPUBLIC

[Resolution of the Seim, May 26, 1918] [70]

In view of the fact that radical disagreements on the question of peace have appeared between the peoples composing the independent Transcaucasian Republic, the functioning of an authoritative body capable of speaking for the whole of Transcaucasia becomes impossible and the Seim is obliged to acknowledge that the Transcaucasian Republic is dissolved.

DECLARATION OF THE INDEPENDENCE OF GEORGIA [71]

[May 26, 1918]

For many centuries Georgia existed as a free and independent state.

At the end of the eighteenth century, surrounded on all sides

[68] *Dokumenty i materialy po vneshnei politike Zakavkazia i Gruzii*, pp. 222-23; see also *The Bolshevik Revolution*, pp. 456-57.

[69] Ludendorff, *op. cit.*, p. 530.

[70] *Documenty i materialy po vneshnei politike Zakavkazia i Gruzii*, p. 330.

[71] Piontkovsky, *G. V. R.*, pp. 678-79.

by enemies, Georgia voluntarily joined Russia on condition that Russia defend her from external enemies.

During the years of the great Russian Revolution, an order was established in Russia which made for the destruction of the military front and the abandonment of Transcaucasia by the Russian army.

Left to her own resources, Georgia, together with all Transcaucasia, took the management of her destinies into her own hands and created appropriate organs for that purpose; however, the pressure of outside forces brought about the disruption of the union which had held together the peoples of Transcaucasia, and caused the downfall of the new political entity.

The present situation of the Georgian people imperatively dictates the necessity of creating an independent political organization as a safeguard against hostile powers and a solid foundation for free development.

Accordingly, the National Council of Georgia, elected by the National Assembly of Georgia on November 22, 1917, now publicly proclaims:

1. Henceforth the people of Georgia are a sovereign people and Georgia is a legally independent state.

2. Georgia is politically . . . a democratic republic.

3. In the event of any international conflict Georgia will remain neutral.

4. The Georgian Democratic Republic endeavors to establish friendly relations with all members of the society of nations, particularly with neighboring peoples and states.

5. The Georgian Democratic Republic guarantees civil and political rights to all citizens within its boundaries without regard to nationality, creed, social position, or sex.

6. The Georgian Democratic Republic offers wide opportunities for free development to all peoples living within its territory.

7. Pending the convocation of the Constituent Assembly, the government of Georgia is headed by the National Council, augmented by representatives of national minorities, and by a Provisional Government, responsible to the National Council.[72]

[72] The personnel of the Georgian Provisional Government was as follows: Noi Ramishvili, President and Minister of the Interior; Akakii Chkhenkeli, Minister

AGREEMENT BETWEEN GEORGIA AND GERMANY [73]
[Concluded at Poti, May 28, 1918]

1. Georgia acknowledges the Brest-Litovsk Treaty of March 3, 1918, as a basis for its dealings with Germany.

2. Until the end of the war Georgia will allow Germany to use Georgian railroads for the transport of troops and war materials of the Quadruple Alliance. . . . [74]

3. All railroad stations and the port of Poti will be controlled by Germany. . . .

[An additional commercial agreement was drawn up to provide for the organization of a German-Georgian mining concern with monopoly rights to all minerals.]

The action of Georgia forced the Armenians and the Tartars to make similar declarations, and on May 28 the independence of the republics of Armenia and Azerbaijan was proclaimed. Neither nation, however, controlled the most important cities of the areas which they claimed. Armenia found itself squeezed within a territory of some eleven thousand square versts of barren land with fourteen versts of railroad and about six hundred thousand refugees. Her borders were threatened on every side by hostile armies: the Turks on the west, the Kurds on the south, the Tartars of Azerbaijan on the east, and the Georgians on the north. Since Armenia had neither oil nor other mineral deposits, Germany showed less interest in her fortunes than in those of Georgia.

Azerbaijan laid claim to what was formerly Elizavetpol, Baku, and Transkataliia gubernias. But the city of Baku,

of Foreign Affairs; Grigorii Georgadze, Minister of War; Georgii Zhuruli, Minister of Finance, Trade, and Industry; Georgii Laskhishvili, Minister of People's Education; Noi Khomeriki, Minister of Agriculture and Labor; S. Meskhishvili, Minister of Justice; Ivan Lordkipanidze, Minister of Ways and Communications.

[73] Z. Avalov, *Nezavisimost Gruzii v mezhdunarodnoi politike 1918-21gg.*, pp. 65-66.

[74] To the Mesopotamian front against the British.

with its mixed population, did not recognize the authority
of the Azerbaijan Government, which nevertheless was
determined to make that city the capital of its future state.
Turkey, which aspired toward the possession of Baku,
promised to help Azerbaijan to occupy that city, which
since the end of March 1918 had been ruled by a Soviet
composed of Russian Bolsheviks and Armenians. A Turko-
Azerbaijan army under the command of Mursal-Pasha
made a rapid advance toward Baku, and by the middle of
June the city was surrounded. The Armenians, fearing for
the fate of their nationals in the event of a Tartar victory in
Baku, sent to the British general Dunsterville, who was
stationed at Enzeli, Persia, a delegation asking for help in
the defense of Baku against the Turks. Dunsterville first
sent Bicherakhov, a Russian colonel, with a force of eighteen hundred Cossacks who were in the British service.
Bicherakhov held back the Turks for about a week and then
left the front.

On July 31 the Armenians and the Caspian sailors, dissatisfied with Bolshevik policies in Baku, set up a new government under the name of the Dictatorship of Tsentro-
kaspiia, consisting of Socialist-Revolutionists, Mensheviks,
and members of the Armenian party "Dashnaktsiutun."
Twenty-six Bolshevik commissars attempted to flee to
Astrakhan by way of the Caspian Sea but were arrested
at Krasnovodsk and shot on September 20 while being conveyed to Askhabad.[75]

About the middle of August, Dunsterville himself arrived
at Baku with a small force of British soldiers. The attempts
of the British general to strengthen the defense of the city
were unsuccessful, and Baku fell to the Turks on Septem-

[75] According to Bolshevik accounts the execution of the Baku commissars took
place at the demand of the English consul at Askhabad, T. Johns. (Piontkovsky,
G. V. R., pp. 668-69.)

ber 14, 1918. The capture of the city was accompanied by a massacre in which, according to Armenian sources, over thirty thousand Armenians were killed. The Azerbaijan Government, under Khan-Khoisky, was then established at Baku.[76]

D. THE CRIMEA

During the latter half of April German troops began to move into the Crimean Peninsula. In anticipation of that move the Collegium of the Navy Commissariat ordered on March 27 that preparations be made for the transfer of the Black Sea fleet from Sevastopol to Novorossiisk.[77] But in view of the difficulties of making Novorossiisk suitable as a naval base the transfer of the fleet was delayed.

On April 22 Chicherin protested against Germany's invasion of the Crimea on the ground that it was Russian territory, but the German advance continued and the Black Sea fortress Sevastopol was occupied on April 30. Three days earlier all first-line battleships left Sevastopol for Novorossiisk. Thereupon the Germans presented the Soviet Government an ultimatum demanding the return of the battleships.[78] The Sovnarkom sent orders to Novorossiisk for the fleet to return to Sevastopol, but the sailors of a number of warships refused to obey the orders and decided to sink their vessels—a gesture which was carried out on June 18, 1918.[79]

[76] B. Baikov, "Vospominaniia o revoliutsii v Zakavkazi," in *A. R. R.*, IX, 119-33; Major General Dunsterville, *The Adventures of the Dunster-force*; V. I. Lenin, *Sochineniia*, XXIII, 557-58.

[77] "Dokumenty po istorii chernomorskago flota v marte-iiune 1918g.," in *A. R. R.*, XIV, 160-61.

[78] *Ibid.*, p. 187. Article 5 of the Brest-Litovsk Treaty provided that "Russia will either bring her warships into Russian ports and keep them there until general peace is concluded, or will disarm them at once." (United States Department of State, *Papers Relating to the Foreign Relations of the United States, 1918, Russia*, I, 443. This publication will hereafter be cited as *U. S. Foreign Relations, 1918, Russia*.)

[79] V. Lukin, "Chernoe more v rukakh Germanii," in *Grazhdanskaia voina*

In the meantime General Koch, commander of the German troops in the Crimea, summoned the Tartar National Assembly (Kurultai) which had been broken up by the Bolsheviks at the end of January 1918, and authorized a Tartar nationalist leader, Dzhafer Seit-Ametov, to form a Crimean government. Representatives of Russian political groups were also invited to participate in the government on condition that they recognize the sovereignty of the Tartar parliament. The Russians declined the invitation on the ground that the Tartars were a minority (one-third) of the region. They also objected to Seit-Ametov's candidacy for the post of prime minister in view of his Turkophile tendencies. In the end the government was formed without the Russian political parties and under the premiership of General Sulkevich, with Seit-Ametov as Minister of Foreign Affairs.[80]

SOVIET PROTEST AGAINST GERMAN OCCUPATION OF THE CRIMEA

[Chicherin to the German Secretary of Foreign Affairs, April 21, 1918] [81]

We are in receipt of dispatches indicating that German-Ukrainian forces have crossed Perekop and are proceeding in the direction of Simferopol. Even the ex parte declaration of the Ukrainian Government, as reported by you, makes no claim that the Crimea is a part of the Ukrainian People's Republic.

The invasion of the Crimea is a flagrant violation of the Brest Treaty in that it is tantamount to invasion of the territory of the Soviet Republic. The invasion threatens our Black Sea front and may lead to clashes occasioned by the necessity of defending our fleet. The People's Commissariat of Foreign Affairs entertains the hope that further penetration will be stopped. . . .

Boevye deistviia na mariakh, rechnykh i ozernykh sistemakh, III, 13-26. This source also reveals that the Sovnarkom, at the same time that it issued the official order for the fleet to return to Sevastopol, sent a messenger to urge the sailors not to return but to sink their ships in the Black Sea.

[80] V. Obolensky, "Krym v 1917-1920 gg.," in Na chuzhoi storone, V, 29-34; Pasmanik, Revoliutsionnye gody v Krymu, pp. 96-103.

[81] Izvestiia (Omsk), No. 82, April 25, 1918, p. 3.

GERMANY AUTHORIZES THE ESTABLISHMENT OF A TARTAR GOVERNMENT

[General Koch to Dzhafer Seit-Ametov, May 1918] [82]

German troops have entered Crimean territory with the aim of reestablishing order . . . and of helping the Crimean people freely to decide their future. The Tartars were the first to present to the German Command a project of forming a regional government. . . . I charge you with forming a cabinet. The German Command will give every possible support to that cabinet in its efforts to reestablish order and tranquillity.

GERMAN POLICY IN THE CRIMEA

[From an account by N. N. Bogdanov] [83]

It is evident that the Germans were planning to occupy the Crimea much more thoroughly and for a much longer period than the Ukraine. This can be seen from the fact that the Germans were buying up real estate and making plans for the construction of railways and seaports. They were undoubtedly counting on using the local Tartar government in the same way as the small Moslem governments of Northern Africa were used. . . . Under German influence Tartars were developing the desire to form an independent Crimean state. . . . On July 21, 1918, the Moslem National Council of Crimea sent to the German Government a memorandum describing the historical development of the Crimean Tartars . . . and proposing reorganization of the Crimea into an independent and neutral khanate, free from the domination and political influence of Russia. . . .

RELATIONS OF THE CRIMEA WITH THE UKRAINE

[From an account by N. N. Bogdanov] [84]

In its endeavor to create a "Great Ukraine," Skoropadsky's government tried . . . to include in its borders the Crimean Peninsula with the port of Sevastopol. . . . The Crimean Government refused the demands of the Ukraine; thereupon the latter

---

[82] *Svoboda Rossii,* No. 48, June 16, 1918, p. 3.
[83] From an unpublished manuscript in the Hoover War Library, Crimean Government Documents, File 19, p. 5. Bogdanov was a member of the Crimean Government. [84] *Ibid.,* pp. 6-7.

declared a customs war, closing its borders to the export and import of goods. Commercial and industrial circles became alarmed. We had difficulty in obtaining continental products . . . and could not ship our fruit into the Ukraine. . . . I was sent to Kiev to negotiate. . . . F. A. Lizogub proposed as conditions for agreement: recognition of the Ukrainian state; a common customs border; cession of the port of Sevastopol to the Ukraine; retention of our own institutions; and use of the Russian language in internal administration, local economy, and education. We were told that until the agreement was concluded not one pud of goods would be allowed to pass the border. . . . The negotiations would probably have come to a successful conclusion, as we [Crimeans] were ready to compromise . . . , but the general situation underwent a radical change. News reached Kiev of German failures on the French front. . . . We then broke off negotiations. . . . In a few days the Ukrainians stopped the customs war on their own initiative.

With the defeat of the Central Empires the entire situation in the Crimea became transformed. On November 16 General Koch notified the Tartar nationalists that he would no longer support their government. Thereupon zemstvo representatives and members of the Constitutional Democratic party formed a new government, which established contacts with General Denikin and the Allies.

DENIKIN TO THE CRIMEAN PEOPLE

[Proclamation of November 20, 1918] [85]

In view of the fact that detachments of the Volunteer Army are moving toward the Crimea, I order that the population be widely informed: First, that the Volunteer Army is coming to the Crimea exclusively for the purpose of upholding order and not of interfering in internal affairs; second, that the Volunteer Army has no reactionary aims, its purpose being the reestablishment of a united and undivided Russia. Without anticipating the future form of government, the Volunteer Army concedes . . . the

[85] A copy of the original is in the Hoover War Library, Crimean Government Documents, File 18.

widest possible autonomy to the component parts of the Russian state. . . . It repudiates with great indignation any attempt to incite one nationality or class against another. I call upon all who love Russia . . . to unite for the sake of the country's welfare.

GENERAL DENIKIN
Commander in Chief

PLEA TO SEND ALLIED TROOPS TO RUSSIA

[Radio Communication from the Crimean Minister of Foreign Affairs to Nabokov, Russian Ambassador to Great Britain, December 14, 1918] [86]

I consider it my duty to call your attention to the Ukrainian situation. The complete collapse of the Hetman's power and the absence of any other authority are throwing the country into a state of anarchy. In this way we are losing the territorial base from which to start a movement on Moscow. The Bolsheviks are already seizing town after town, and the entire shore line of the Black Sea may soon find itself in their hands. The movements of Petliura and of the Bolsheviks are directly menacing the Crimea. It is necessary to bring the seriousness of the situation to the special attention of the Allies and to urge them to send a large force to the Ukraine immediately. It is possible to occupy the Ukraine now; later it will be necessary to conquer that territory. There are plenty of healthy elements in the Ukraine on which it is possible to rely. One only has to know how to find them. It is important that statesmen capable of understanding the situation come with the Allied troops. . . .

Even before the Crimean Government sent its plea for Allied aid, a small Allied force had already arrived in Southern Russia. This force, which consisted of French and British troops dispatched after the Armistice, landed at Odessa on November 26. From this time on the Allies played an important part in the long civil war in Southern Russia, especially through the support which they lent the Volunteer Army of General Denikin.

[86] The original is in *ibid.*, File 9. A similar communication was sent to Maklakov in Paris on December 17, 1918.

CHAPTER II

ALLIED INTERVENTION AND THE CZECHOSLOVAKS

While the Central Powers were seizing vast territories in Southern Russia, the Bolsheviks faced the threat of even more extensive encroachment in the form of intervention by the Entente. The Allies had begun to consider intervention upon Russia's withdrawal from the World War, which, enabling Germany to increase considerably its military forces in France, seemed to the Allied military authorities to necessitate the reestablishment in Russia of a front that would again deflect German troops from the West. An additional incentive to Allied intervention arose when the Central Powers occupied Southern Russia, thereby gaining a great aggrandizement of their economic resources for continuing the war. But for about seven months, despite these incentives, the Allies undertook no measures of intervention outside of such local actions as the dispatch of a small British force to Murmansk in March and the landing of some Japanese and British troops at Vladivostok early in April. The Allies were deterred from extensive intervention by the opposition of President Wilson to Japanese single-handed action in Siberia, by the reluctance of one group among the Allies to intervene without Bolshevik consent, and by the failure of the Bolsheviks to give that consent.

However, the entire issue of Allied policy toward Russia was brought to a head in June 1918 by a development in Siberia in connection with the Czechoslovaks, former Austrian subjects fighting with the encouragement of the Allies in behalf of the independence of their people. Journeying through Russia in order to reach France and participate in the war against Germany, the Czechoslovaks eventually came into conflict with the Bolsheviks and succeeded in gaining control of vast territories in the Volga region and Siberia. Thereupon the Allies decided to use the Czechoslovak Corps for the purpose of reestablishing the Russian front against the Germans. At the same time the Allied Powers resolved to intervene in Russia with an expeditionary force of their own, and early in August they landed troops at Archangel and Vladivostok.

A. EARLY PLANS OF INTERVENTION

After the Bolshevik Revolution the policy of the Powers at war with Germany had as its objective the keeping of Russia in the war. This objective, however, was sought by two divergent paths. While certain Allied diplomats encouraged anti-Bolshevik groups to overthrow the Soviets and reestablish the Eastern front, other representatives of the Allies, and some American officials as well, conferred with Bolshevik leaders and suggested that should Russia continue the war against Germany it would again receive Allied aid. Uncertain of the outcome of the Brest-Litovsk negotiations, Trotsky welcomed their suggestion and endeavored to secure a definite promise that the Allies and the United States would help the Bolsheviks in case they broke with the Central Powers. That promise was given by Sadoul, Robins, and Lockhart; and during the February advance of the Central Powers in Russia the Bolshevik Central Committee resolved to accept Allied help in resisting the Germans.[1]

[1] See *The Bolshevik Revolution*, pp. 515 ff. Sadoul was the personal representative of Albert Thomas, French Assistant Minister of War; Robins was the

These discussions of collaboration with the Soviets continued even after the signing and ratification of the Brest Treaty. Sadoul, Lockhart, and Robins—and even Ambassador Francis for a time—proceeded on the theory that they could still secure Bolshevik cooperation in the war against Germany. Trotsky, alarmed at both the Austro-German advance into Southern Russia and the possibility of an Allied intervention directed against the Bolsheviks, encouraged the consideration of such cooperation. He welcomed the landing at Murmansk early in March of a small British force which was sent to oppose the Germans and Finns who were threatening the Murmansk Railway; [2] moreover, he suggested to Sadoul and Lockhart the possibility of using the Czechoslovak Legion, then stationed in the Ukraine, for the same purpose.[3] Trotsky's chief aim, however, was to secure the assistance of Allied military experts in the organization of the Red Army. On March 19 Robins telegraphed to Francis, who had established residence in Vologda, as follows: "Conference with Trotsky yesterday was most satisfactory. He asks for five American army officers to act as inspectors of the organization . . . of the Soviet army. . . . Trotsky asks further for railroad operators, men, and equipment." [4] A few days later (on March 26), Sadoul wrote to Thomas: "The collaboration of the Allied missions with the Bolsheviks, directed toward the building of a new, disciplined army . . . , is under way. The French Mission must, naturally, play the principal rôle in that reorganization. Several officers will be attached directly to Trotsky, forming a kind of

chief of the American Red Cross Mission to Russia and acted as Ambassador Francis' unofficial observer; Lockhart served as the special representative of Great Britain in Russia.

[2] David Francis, *Russia from the American Embassy*, pp. 264-65.

[3] J. Papoušek, *Chekhoslovaki i Sovety*, p. 13.

[4] *Russian-American Relations, March 1917-March 1920. Documents and Papers* (C. K. Cumming and W. W. Pettit, eds.), p. 104.

military cabinet and supervising the different activities of the Commissariat of War." [5] The new Soviet army, according to the advocates of collaboration, was to be reinforced by Allied troops landing at Archangel, Murmansk, and Vladivostok, and the Eastern front was to be reestablished in Russia. "I insist," wrote Sadoul to Thomas on March 30, "that we can obtain the consent of the Soviet Government to intervention under certain conditions. It is necessary that (1) the intervention be not purely Japanese . . . ; (2) that the Allies give a pledge that the intervention would be of a purely military character and would not lead to any interference in Russian domestic affairs . . . ; (3) that a precise statement be made as to what price, territorial and economic, the Bolsheviks would have to offer to the Japanese realists." [6]

Meanwhile the Allies were by no means agreed as to the best way of handling the Russian situation. France and Japan advocated intervention against the Bolsheviks; Great Britain favored intervention against the Germans but hoped that the Bolsheviks would be prevailed upon to invite it; and the United States was decidedly opposed to any intervention in the Russian Far East.

As early as December 1917 Clemenceau urged upon Colonel House the desirability of asking the Japanese to send an expeditionary force to Siberia.[7] On January 8, 1918, the French Ambassador addressed a communication to the Secretary of State informing him that the French Government was considering the dispatch of an expeditionary force to Harbin and thence to Irkutsk for the purpose of supporting those groups in Siberia "that have remained true to the

[5] J. Sadoul, *Notes sur la révolution bolshevique, Octobre 1917-Janvier 1919,* p. 272.
[6] *Ibid.*, pp. 284-85.
[7] Charles Seymour, *The Intimate Papers of Colonel House,* III, 387.

cause of the Entente." The force was to consist of French occupation troups in China and detachments of Chinese soldiers. The note concluded with a proposal that the United States Government cooperate in the expedition. Similar proposals were made by the French Government to Great Britain and Japan.[8]

On January 16 the American Secretary of State replied that the United States was not prepared to support the proposed expedition in view of the fact that the state of affairs in Siberia did not justify intervention and that such intervention "would be likely to offend those Russians who are now in sympathy with the United States and its cobelligerents."[9] The British reply to the French proposal was "evasive and not at all encouraging," while the Japanese Government answered that it was prepared to meet the situation single-handed and without the cooperation of other governments.[10]

The desire of the Japanese Government for a free hand in case of intervention in Siberia was acceded to by the French Government[11] and was recommended by Great Britain in a note to the American State Department on January 28, 1918. The British communication urged that Japan be asked to act as the mandatory of the Allies in the occupation of the Trans-Siberian Railway.[12] In a memorandum of the Department of State to the British Embassy on February 8 this recommendation was rejected. The memorandum argued that the necessity of intervention had not yet arisen and that "should intervention unfortunately become necessary in the future . . . any military expedition to Siberia or the occupation of the whole or of a part of the Trans-Siberian Railway should be undertaken by international

[8] *U. S. Foreign Relations, 1918, Russia*, II, 21.
[9] *Ibid.*, p. 29. [10] *Ibid.*, p. 32. [11] *Ibid.*, p. 45.
[12] *Ibid.*, pp. 35-36; and Seymour, *op. cit.*, pp. 390-91.

cooperation and not by any one power acting as the mandatory of the others." [13]

France and Great Britain, however, continued to insist that intervention was necessary [14] and finally prevailed upon President Wilson to withdraw his objections to Japan's acting in Siberia as the mandatory of the Allies. Toward the end of February the President drafted a note in which he stated that while "the Government of the United States has not thought it wise to join the Governments of the Entente in asking the Japanese Government to act in Siberia," it now "has no objection to that request being made." [15] On March 1 Wilson's note was shown to the French Ambassador and the Chargé d'Affaires of the British Embassy, who took a copy of the note and dispatched it to London.

When the note was received in London the British Government instructed its ambassador in Japan to tell the Japanese Government that Great Britain approved the proposal of Japan that it be appointed the mandatory of the Allies in Siberia. This message was communicated to the Japanese Government on March 11.[16] On March 4, however, President Wilson had again changed his mind, reverting to his original opposition to intervention. On March 5 the State Department dispatched to Japan and the Allied Governments the following note:

THE UNITED STATES OPPOSES INTERVENTION IN RUSSIA

[Note to the Japanese and Allied Governments, March 5, 1918] [17]

The Government of the United States has been giving the most careful and anxious consideration to the conditions now prevail-

[13] *U. S. Foreign Relations, 1918, Russia,* II, 42.
[14] See *ibid.,* pp. 49-52, 58-60.
[15] Seymour, *op. cit.,* p. 419.
[16] *U. S. Foreign Relations, 1918, Russia,* II, 68, 78.
[17] *Ibid.,* pp. 67-68.

ing in Siberia and their possible remedy. It realizes the extreme
danger of anarchy to which the Siberian provinces are exposed
and the imminent risk also of German invasion and domination.
It shares with the Governments of the Entente the view that, if
invasion is deemed wise, the Government of Japan is in the best
situation to undertake it and could accomplish it most efficiently.
It has, moreover, the utmost confidence in the Japanese Government and would be entirely willing, so far as its own feelings to-
wards that Government are concerned, to entrust the enterprise to
it. But it is bound in frankness to say that the wisdom of intervention seems to it most questionable. If it were undertaken the Government of the United States assumes that the most explicit assurances would be given that it was undertaken by Japan as an ally
of Russia, in Russia's interest, and with the sole view of holding
it safe against Germany and at the absolute disposal of the final
peace conference. Otherwise the Central Powers could and would
make it appear that Japan was doing in the East exactly what
Germany is doing in the West and so seek to counter the condem-
nation which all the world must pronounce against Germany's
invasion of Russia, which she attempts to justify on the pretext
of restoring order. And it is the judgment of the Government of
the United States, uttered with the utmost respect, that, even with
such assurances given, they could in the same way be discredited
by those whose interest it was to discredit them; that a hot resentment would be general in Russia itself, and that the whole action
might play into the hands of the enemies of Russia, and particularly of the enemies of the Russian revolution, for which the Government of the United States entertains the greatest sympathy, in
spite of all the unhappiness and misfortunes which have for the
time being sprung out of it. The Government of the United States
begs once more to express to the Government of Japan its warmest friendship and confidence and once more begs it to accept its
expressions of judgment as uttered only in the frankness of
friendship.

The American note opposing intervention did not dis-
courage the French Government in its efforts to win the
acquiescence of President Wilson in the Allied plan of a

Japanese occupation of Siberia. On March 12 the French Ambassador to the United States wrote a note to the Secretary of State in which he predicted that refusal of the Allies to allow Japan to intervene in the Russian Far East would have serious consequences. The note declared that "Japan must and will interfere in Asia in defense of her present position and of her future," and that "if she does so without our assent she will do it against us and there is some likelihood of her later arriving at an understanding with Germany." [18]

However, the Japanese reply of March 19 to the note of the American Government was in large part conciliatory. It called attention to the fact that the proposal of intervention had originated not with Japan but with the Allies, and it gave assurances that Japan would "refrain from taking any action on which due understanding has not been reached between the United States and the other great powers of the Entente." On the other hand, the note concluded by declaring that "should the hostile activities in Siberia develop to such a degree as to jeopardize the national security or vital interests of Japan she may be compelled to resort to prompt and efficient measures of self-defense." [19]

The warning which Japan thus gave was very shortly to be carried out. The occasion for Japan's resort to "measures of self-defense" was the killing of two Japanese at Vladivostok on April 4. On the following day the Japanese fleet landed an armed force which took over the patrolling of the city. Later in the same day the British disembarked fifty marines to guard their consulate.

The Bolsheviks interpreted the landing of the Japanese and the British as the beginning of an intervention directed against the Soviets. On April 5 the Sovnarkom issued a

[18] *Ibid.*, p. 75.   [19] *Ibid.*, p. 81.

proclamation protesting against the landing and calling upon the "toiling masses" to resist "the imperialist attack from the east."

SOVIET DENUNCIATION OF THE JAPANESE LANDING AT VLADIVOSTOK

[Proclamation of the Sovnarkom, April 5, 1918] [20]

Japan has invaded Russia, having landed troops at Vladivostok; England is apparently following in the footsteps of Japan. A statement has been received from the Soviet authorities in Vladivostok and Irkutsk to the effect that Admiral Kato, commander of the Japanese fleet, has landed troops at Vladivostok and issued a proclamation to the local inhabitants informing them of the fact that Japan was taking upon itself the preservation of order. As a pretext for the landing they use the murder of two Japanese in Vladivostok by unidentified persons.

Regarding this murder—its causes and the culprits—the Soviet Government has at present no information whatsoever. But it knows, as does the whole world, that the Japanese imperialists have for months been preparing for a landing at Vladivostok. The official Japanese press wrote that Japan was called upon to reestablish order in Siberia as far as Irkutsk and even to the Urals. The Japanese authorities were looking for a suitable pretext for their plunderous raid into Russian territory. The Tokio General Staff indulges in the invention of monstrous statements concerning conditions in Siberia, the German prisoners of war, etc. The Japanese Ambassador at Rome stated a few weeks ago that the German war prisoners were armed and ready to seize the Siberian Railroad. This statement has made the rounds of the world press. The military authorities of the Soviet Republic sent British and American officers along the Siberian line and gave them every opportunity to convince themselves of the falsity of the official Japanese statement. When this excuse was removed the Japanese imperialists were forced to look for other excuses; and the murder of two Japanese was very opportune. The murder took place on the 4th of April, and on the 5th the Japanese Ad-

[20] *Rannee Utro*, No. 57, April 6, 1918, p. 1.

miral, without awaiting any investigation, made a landing. The course of events leaves no doubt whatsoever that all this was pre-arranged and that the murder of the two Japanese was only a pre-text for the imperialist attack from the east which had been con-templated for some time. The imperialists of Japan wish to strangle the Soviet Revolution, to cut off Russia from the Pacific Ocean, to seize the rich territories of Siberia, and to enslave the Siberian workers and peasants.

Japan is acting as the deadly enemy of the Soviet Republic. What are the plans of the other governments of the Entente—of the United States of America, England, France, and Italy?

Up to the present moment, their policy in regard to the preda-tory intentions of Japan has evidently been one of vacillation. The American Government, it seems, was against the Japanese inva-sion; but the situation cannot remain indefinite any longer. Eng-land apparently . . . intends to go hand in hand with Japan in working for Russia's ruin.

The above question must be put to the British Government most explicitly. The same question must be asked of the diplomatic representatives of the United States and the other countries of the Entente. The answer given, and, even more, the steps taken by the Allied countries, will inevitably have a profound influence on the future international policy of the Soviet Government.

Though taking proper diplomatic steps, the Soviet Government is at the same time issuing an order to the Soviets in Siberia to offer resistance to any forcible invasion of Russian territory.

WORKERS and PEASANTS! HONEST CITIZENS! A new horri-ble trial is coming from the East. Within the country dark forces are raising their heads. The bourgeoisie of Siberia is stretching out its hand to foreign invaders. The city Duma of Vladivostok, consisting of Mensheviks and Socialist-Revolutionists of the Right, has passed a resolution welcoming the armed Japanese in-vasion aiming to wrest from the workers and peasants political power, the land, and control of industry; the Russian bourgeoisie and its hirelings—the Mensheviks and Socialist-Revolutionists—are acting in concert with the Japanese plunderers.

Resistance to Japanese invasion and merciless struggle against Japanese agents and helpers within the country are matters of life and death for the Soviet Republic, for the toiling masses of all Russia.

The landing of the Japanese and the British at Vladivostok had not been anticipated by the advocates of Allied-Soviet cooperation. On April 7 Sadoul wrote to Thomas: "The unexpected Anglo-Japanese landing will not facilitate the efforts which I, in collaboration with Lockhart and Robins, am making to secure the consent of the Soviets to an Interallied intervention in Siberia and European Russia." [21] Francis disclaimed any knowledge of the reason for Japan's act and on April 7 instructed Robins to assure the Bolsheviks that the Allies did not sanction the Japanese landing.[22] On the same day Balfour telegraphed Lockhart to explain to Trotsky that the landing was made solely for the protection of foreign residents at Vladivostok and that he regretted that an attack on Japanese residents should have taken place at a time when "the Allied governments are desirous to do everything they can to afford support and assistance to Trotsky." [23] However, the statement given out in Russia by the French Ambassador was less reassuring. While declaring that the armed intervention was designed merely to protect the security of foreigners and could be localized in Vladivostok if Japan were given due satisfaction, he went on to say that the continuation of the German advance might compel the Allies to intervene in Siberia in order to stop German aggression in Russia.

Noulens' statement appeared in the Russian press on April 23, the day of the arrival at Moscow of Count von Mirbach, the newly appointed German Ambassador to Russia. Count Mirbach protested against the statement of the

[21] Sadoul, op. cit., p. 294.
[22] U. S. Foreign Relations, 1918, Russia, II, 107.
[23] Ibid., p. 109.

French Ambassador and the Soviet Government demanded Noulens' recall. However, Noulens was not recalled.

THE FRENCH AMBASSADOR ON INTERVENTION IN RUSSIA

[Press Interview with Noulens, April 23, 1918] [24]

The landing of Japanese troops at Vladivostok came as a result of long-standing troubles and disturbances in that city. Sooner or later there was bound to occur an incident calling for armed interference to provide for the security of foreigners. . . . The Japanese question, in so far as it is purely Japanese, can be localized in Vladivostok, provided that the Tokio Government is given the satisfaction which it has the right to demand.

However, the Allies cannot remain indifferent to the advance of the Austro-Germans in the North and the South—an advance which goes far beyond the limits which it was possible to anticipate after the Brest Treaty. The Germanic states are, in fact, aiming to establish exclusive control over the economic life of all Russia. Furthermore, they are endeavoring through their prisoners of war to organize colonization centers in Siberia. The Allies may be compelled to intervene in order to meet this menace, which is directed against them and, to a much greater extent, against the Russian people. Should the Allies at any time be forced to resort to military operations, they will act solely in the capacity of friends. They will fight against German aggression in Eastern Europe without interfering in Russian internal affairs, with no ulterior motive of conquest, but solely for the protection of common interests and in full accord with Russian opinion. I have no data of any kind relative to the intentions of the governments in this question; but, no matter what happens, I feel confident in saying that should armed intervention take place in Siberia, it would have an Interallied and distinctly friendly character.

---

[24] *Svoboda Rossii*, No. 10, April 23, 1918, p. 2.

THE SOVIET GOVERNMENT DEMANDS THE RECALL OF THE FRENCH AMBASSADOR

[Chicherin's Note to the French Government, April 27, 1918] [25]

On April 23 there appeared in the Moscow newspapers the following declaration of the French Ambassador, Noulens. . . . [The text of the press interview follows.]

Upon our inquiry as to the authenticity of M. Noulens' declaration we received confirmation through M. Le Bonn, the French Consul at Moscow.

In the critical period through which Russia is now passing M. Noulens' declaration can hardly contribute to amicable relations between the French and Russian peoples. A representative of the French Government who helps to impair the relations between France and Russia cannot be tolerated within the Russian Republic.

The Government of the Russian Socialist Federated Soviet Republic expresses its confidence that M. Noulens will immediately be recalled by the Government of the French Republic.

CHICHERIN
People's Commissar of Foreign Affairs

Meanwhile the advocates of Allied-Bolshevik cooperation continued negotiations with Trotsky. Lockhart reported to the British Foreign Office that Trotsky would welcome the sending of an Interallied force to Russia provided definite guarantees were given.[26] Thereupon the British Secretary of State for Foreign Affairs proposed to the American Government that in place of having Japan act as the mandatory of the Allies an Interallied expedition be sent to Russia.

[25] Ibid., No. 15, April 28, 1918, p. 3.
[26] R. H. Bruce Lockhart, British Agent, p. 271.

GREAT BRITAIN PROPOSES THE SENDING OF AN INTERALLIED FORCE TO RUSSIA

[Extract from Balfour's Note, April 25, 1918] [27]

The British War Cabinet have now further considered the general military problem before the Allies, and have reached the conclusion that it is essential to treat Europe and Asia . . . as a single front. The transfer of German divisions from east to west is still continuing and, under present conditions, can be further continued, and it is imperative to stop this movement if it can possibly be done.

Germany can now draw food and raw materials from Asia, and in these conditions, even if our defensive is successful, there is little chance that we could make a successful offensive. . . . It thus becomes of the greatest urgency to reestablish an Allied front in Russia. . . .

The British Government considers that it is necessary for the Allies to unite in order to bring about a Russian national revival, and in order to adopt a policy of freeing Russia from foreign control by means of Allied intervention. The Allies must, of course, avoid taking sides in Russian politics, and, if the Bolshevist government will cooperate in resisting Germany, it seems necessary to act with them as the *de facto* Russian Government. Trotsky, at least, has for some time shown signs of recognizing that cooperation with the Allies is the only hope of freeing Russia from the Germans. . . . He has now definitely asked for a statement of the help which the Allies could give, and of the guarantee which they would furnish, and says that he considers an agreement desirable if the conditions are satisfactory. The British Government are of opinion that the Allies should avail themselves of this opportunity to offer Allied intervention against Germany, accompanied by a suitable declaration of disinterestedness and by proper guarantees as to the evacuation of Russian territory. If such an offer was accepted the whole position might be transformed, and if it was refused, the position of the Bolshevist government would at least be defined. . . .

The British War Cabinet are anxious to learn whether the

[27] *U. S. Foreign Relations, 1918, Russia*, II, 135-37.

President would be disposed to agree to the following course of action:

1. Great Britain and the United States to make a simultaneous proposal to the Bolshevist government for intervention by the Allies on the lines indicated, an undertaking to be given for the withdrawal of all Allied forces at the conclusion of hostilities.

2. An American force . . . to be sent to the Far East.

If this general policy is acceptable, the question of approaching the Japanese Government remains. Japan would under this scheme intervene in Siberia as part of a joint intervention by the Allies . . . and it would probably be necessary for her to use her troops, in conjunction with Russian and Allied forces, in European Russia as well as in Asia. . . .

Before consulting the other Allied powers the British Government think the most important step is to ascertain whether the President concurs in these proposals, for without his concurrence the British Government would not care to proceed further with them.

While the British Government was seeking to obtain President Wilson's consent to the new plan of an Interallied expedition to Russia, the French Government endeavored to hasten the transport to France of the Czechoslovak Legion, then on its way to the Western front via Siberia. Acting on instructions from the French Ministry of War, General Lavergne, French military representative in Russia, submitted to Trotsky a proposal to divert a part of the Legion to Murmansk and Archangel as more expeditious points of departure than Vladivostok.[28] Trotsky agreed to the French proposal and the Soviet Government issued orders early in May to turn the Czech trains west of Omsk toward Archangel. The Czechoslovaks, who knew nothing of the negotiations of General Lavergne but suspected an un-

[28] J. Noulens, *Mon ambassade en russie sovietique*, II, 86.

friendly move by the Bolsheviks and the Germans, refused to obey the orders to change their itinerary. This refusal led to a conflict between the Bolsheviks and the Czechoslovaks which was ultimately to decide the entire question of Allied intervention in Russia.

B. THE CLASH OF THE CZECHOSLOVAKS WITH THE BOLSHEVIKS

At the outbreak of the World War a group of Czech and Slovak residents of Russia, hoping to liberate Czechoslovakia from Austria-Hungary, organized a detachment which fought in the Russian army against the Central Powers. In 1916 Czechoslovak leaders in Paris conceived the idea of expanding that detachment into an army by recruiting the Czech and Slovak prisoners taken from the Austrians. The Russian Imperial Government was not very receptive to the plan. However, when the Provisional Government came into power it granted its permission to the Czechoslovak leaders to form an army in Russia, and by the end of 1917 the Czechoslovak Legion numbered about forty-five thousand soldiers and occupied a separate section of the Southwestern front, in the Ukraine.

Unlike the rest of the Russian army, which after the seizure of power by the Bolsheviks began rapidly to disintegrate, the Czechoslovak Corps retained its military organization. When the Bolsheviks opened armistice negotiations with the Central Powers the Czechoslovaks withdrew to the rear and took up quarters in the vicinity of Kiev.

On December 16, 1917, by agreement between the French Government and the Czechoslovak National Council in Paris, the Czechoslovak Legion was placed under the French Supreme Command [29] with the understanding that it would be transported to France to fight on the Western front. Shortly afterwards the Czech leaders asked permission of the Soviet Government to pass through Soviet territory on their journey to France. They undertook to remain neutral in the civil war which was then going on in the South of Russia and accordingly did not respond to the efforts of the Ukrainian Central Rada and of General Alexeev, organizer and head of the Volunteer Army, to secure the aid of the Legion in fighting the Bolsheviks.[30]

On February 16 the commander of the Bolshevik troops in the Ukraine informed Professor Masaryk, President of the Czechoslovak National Council, that the Soviet Government would permit the Czechoslovaks to cross Soviet territory on their way to France.[31] A few days later the Germans began to invade the Ukraine, driving before them the demoralized Bolshevik troops. Ukrainian Bolsheviks then appealed to the Czechoslovaks for aid in resisting the Germans.[32] However, the Czechoslovaks, considering the German forces to be superior to their own both in number and in organization, ignored this appeal and began to withdraw from the Ukraine. At Bakhmach, an important railway junction, the Germans blocked the way of the retreating Czechoslovaks. A four-day engagement followed in which the Czechoslovaks lost about six hundred men but succeeded in getting their trains through and in entering Soviet territory.

At this very time (early in March) Trotsky was engaged in conversations with unofficial representatives of Powers

[29] The agreement is given in Margarete Klante, *Von der Volga zum Amur. Die tschechische Legion und der russische Bürgerkrieg,* p. 318.

[30] See *The Bolshevik Revolution,* pp. 425-27.

[31] T. G. Masaryk, *The Making of a State,* p. 196.

[32] E. Bosh, *God borby. Borba za vlast sovetov na Ukraine s Aprelia 1917 do nemetskoi okkupatsii,* pp. 188-90.

at war with Germany—Sadoul, Lockhart, and Robins—on the possibility of using the Czechoslovaks in the Archangel and Murmansk regions as the nucleus of a proposed Allied force which was to cooperate with the Bolsheviks in fighting the Germans and Finns. Trotsky approved the plan, and Lockhart reported to London on the new project of Allied-Bolshevik cooperation. On April 1 the British War Office sent the French Government a memorandum informing it of Trotsky's request that the Czechoslovaks remain in Russia and form a nucleus for the reorganization of the Russian army with the assistance of Allied military experts. The memorandum recommended that in view of the difficulties of transporting the Czechs to Europe "they should be employed in Russia or Siberia." Beneš, who was then in Paris, opposed the plan, and the French Government likewise objected.[33]

Lenin was also opposed to keeping the Czechs on Soviet territory, and as early as March 15 the Sovnarkom at his insistence resolved to allow the Czechoslovaks to leave Russia via Siberia, the port of Archangel being still ice-bound.[34] But before this resolution was announced several troop trains of the Czechoslovaks had reached Omsk or points farther east. They had suffered from numerous obstacles placed in their way by the Siberian Bolsheviks, who knew nothing of the Sovnarkom's resolution and feared that the Legion would be used by the anti-Bolsheviks to overthrow the Soviets. On March 21 the Omsk Soviet ordered that the Czechoslovak trains be stopped and suggested to Moscow that the Legion be turned back and sent via Archangel. But five days later there arrived from Stalin a telegram which, announcing the resolution of the Sovnarkom, removed for

[33] E. Beneš, *Souvenirs de guerre et de révolution, 1914-1919*, II, 185.
[34] Papoušek, *op. cit.*, pp. 13, 30.

the time being all obstacles to the journey of the Czecho-slovaks.

EARLY HISTORY OF THE CZECHOSLOVAK ARMY IN RUSSIA

[From the Report of Captain Hurban to Masaryk, President of the Czechoslovak National Council, Summer of 1918] [35]

. . . Our army in Russia was organized from Czech and Slovak prisoners of war under almost insurmountable difficulties. We were cooperating with the Russian army, and since 1917, during the first revolutionary offensive under Kerensky, it was only our army that really attacked and advanced.[36]

When the Bolshevik-Soviet Government signed the peace treaty at the beginning of March, our army of about 50,000 men was in the Ukraine, near Kiev. The former Ukrainian Government, to escape the Bolsheviks threw themselves into the arms of the Germans. . . . The position of our army was almost desperate. We were in a state which had concluded peace, into which, however, the Germans were advancing and occupying large territories without resistance; the Red Guards of the Soviets did not represent any real military power. . . . [They] seized the locomotives and were fleeing east in panic.

Under these circumstances Emperor Charles sent us a special envoy with the promise that if we disarm we will be "amnestied" and our land will receive "autonomy." We answered that we will not negotiate with the Austrian Emperor.

As we could not hold a front, we began a retreat to the east. Already then in agreement with the Allies (our army had been proclaimed a part of the Czechoslovak army on the Western front, and thus allied with the French army), it was decided to transport our army over Siberia and America to France. We began the difficult retreat from Kiev. The Germans in an overwhelming force were to prevent our escape. About a hundred miles behind us they seized the important railroad junction at Bachmac [Bakh-

---

[35] An English translation of the report, followed in the above text, is in the Hoover War Library, Stanford University.

[36] The July offensive is described in F. A. Golder, *Documents of Russian History, 1914-1917*, pp. 425-34.

mach], which we were obliged to pass in our trains on our retreat to the east.

When we arrived at Bachmac the Germans were already waiting for us. There began a battle lasting four days, in which the Germans were badly defeated and which enabled us to get our trains through. . . .

Our relations with the Bolsheviks were still good. We refrained from meddling with Russian internal affairs, and we did not react to the appeals of the different anti-Bolshevik circles. Therefore, when we found ourselves on the soil of Soviet Russia, we tried to come to an agreement with the Bolshevik government with respect to our departure. . . . We made it clear to the Bolsheviks that if we were not absolutely loyal it would suffice to order one of our regiments (our army was then, in March, near Moscow) to take Moscow, and in half a day there would be no Bolshevik government; for then we were all armed, having taken from the front everything we could carry, so as to prevent it from falling into the hands of the Germans (each of our regiments had 200 to 300 machine guns) and nobody in Russia, to say nothing of Moscow, could have at all contemplated an attempt at opposition. Moscow, moreover, would have received us with open arms. . . .

To prove indisputably our loyalty we turned over everything, all our arms, with the exception of a few rifles which we kept for our, so to say, personal safety (10 rifles for each 100 men) to the Bolsheviks. The equipment we turned over to the Bolsheviks, including arms, horses, automobiles, aeroplanes, etc., was worth more than 1,000,000,000 rubles, and it was logically our possession, for we took it away from the Germans, to whom it was abandoned by the fleeing Bolsheviks. This transfer of the equipment was, of course, preceded by an agreement made between us and the Moscow government, by which we were guaranteed unmolested passage through Siberia. . . .

Already then there were signs that the Germans were beginning to be uneasy about our movement. Today we have documentary evidence of the fact that in March the Germans considered our progress as a naïve adventure which would soon end in failure. When they saw, however, the "impossibility," as they called it, was becoming a reality, they began to do their best to frustrate our efforts, and organized an army of agents against us. . . . The Bolsheviks, though not exceptionally friendly to us, refrained so far from all direct action against us. Their only desire in this respect, to which they devoted much money, was to persuade our volunteers to join their Red Guards. After getting our support and the support of the Letts, Lenin and Trotsky felt they would be safe. This agitation was carried on vigorously and not by very honest methods. We did practically nothing to oppose it, but we knew our men. Our people are too well educated politically and in every other way to be carried away by the methods of Lenin and Trotsky. . . .

Under such circumstances we began our pilgrimage east. . . .

THE SOVIET COMMANDER IN CHIEF AUTHORIZES THE CZECHOSLOVAKS TO LEAVE THE UKRAINE

[Antonov's Announcement, March 16, 1918] [37]

Our comrades of the Czechoslovak Corps, who have fought faithfully and valiantly in the region of Zhitomir . . . , Grebenko, and Bakhmach, are now leaving the Ukraine and are returning a part of their arms. The revolutionary troops will never forget the fraternal help which the Czechoslovak Corps has rendered the working people of the Ukraine in their struggle against the imperialist looters. The revolutionary troops accept as a token of friendship the arms which the Czechoslovaks are leaving.

ANTONOV

THE OMSK SOVIET ORDERS THE STOPPING OF THE CZECHOSLOVAK LEGION

[From the Minutes of the Session of Tsentrosibir, March 22, 1918] [38]

. . . Comrade Stremberg received news that armed Czechoslovak soldiers were moving through Siberia on the way to Vladivostok. Fearing that the Czechoslovaks might be used by counter-revolutionists and imperialists against the Soviet Government, the Presidium . . . ordered them to stop their movements and com-

[37] V. A. Antonov-Ovseenko, *Zapiski o grazhdanskoi voine*, II, 47.
[38] V. Maksakov i A. Turunov, *Khronika grazhdanskoi voiny v Sibiri 1917-1918*, p. 146. Tsentrosibir was the name of the Soviet Government of Siberia.

municated the order by direct wire to the Soviet of People's Commissars. Comrade Stalin . . . replied that no armed forces except Soviet troops could be tolerated in the territories of the Soviet Republic and ordered the Czechoslovaks to disarm. The Presidium suggested to the Sovnarkom that the Czechoslovaks be sent out by way of Archangel. . . .

[Omsk to the Kazan Soviet] [39]

Sixty trains of Czechoslovaks armed to the teeth are proceeding from Kursk to Eastern Siberia. To let them through is treason to the Soviet. Tsentrosibir . . . considers it urgent that their movement be halted, that the echelons be disarmed and sent out by way of Archangel. . . . You are hereby ordered to stop these trains at any cost. . . . Mobilize all available forces and do your duty. Issue necessary orders to all railway lines. . . .

KRUTIKOV
Commissar of War

THE SOVIET GOVERNMENT GRANTS THE CZECHOSLOVAKS PASSAGE TO VLADIVOSTOK

[Stalin, Commissar of Nationalities, to the Czechoslovak National Council, March 26, 1918] [40]

The Soviet of People's Commissars considers the proposal of the Czechoslovak Army Corps to be just and fully acceptable; on the inflexible conditions, however, that the Corps immediately start for Vladivostok and that the counter-revolutionary commanders be immediately removed.

The Czechoslovaks shall proceed not as fighting units but as a group of free citizens, taking with them a certain quantity of arms [41] for self-defense against the attacks of counter-revolutionists.

[39] K. Zmrhal, *Armada ducha druhe mile*, p. 22.
[40] Jaroslav Kratochvil, *Česta Revoluče*, p. 42.
[41] The agreement between the Sovnarkom and the Czechoslovak National Council of March 27 permitted the retention of 168 rifles and one machine gun for each train. The rest of the arms was to be surrendered at Penza. This arrangement is often referred to as the Penza Agreement. (V. Vladimirova, *God sluzhby "sotsialistov" kapitalistam*, p. 222.)

4

The Soviet of People's Commissars orders the Penza Soviet
. . . to remove all the old commissars and appoint new ones who
can be depended upon to accompany and protect the Czechoslovaks
as an organized unit on their way to Vladivostok and to keep the
Soviet of People's Commissars informed of all events connected
with their movements. . . . The Soviet of People's Commissars
wishes to be of assistance to the Czechoslovaks while they are on
Russian territory, provided they are honest and sincerely loyal.

By order of the Soviet of People's Commissars

STALIN

The Japanese landing at Vladivostok on April 5 brought
a new complication into the relations of the Czechoslovak
Legion and the Soviet Government. Lenin, interpreting the
descent as the beginning of Allied intervention, on April 7
wired the Vladivostok Soviet that he "considered the situation very serious" and warned it "not to entertain any
illusion as the Japanese are almost certain to start an
advance." [42] Accordingly, orders were issued to stop the
Czechoslovak trains.[43] But on April 10 the Vladivostok
Soviet replied to Lenin that "the situation is not hopeless
as there appear to be great disagreements among the Allies.
. . . The whole question of occupation is an open one." [44]
On April 12 the Sovnarkom issued another order, allowing
the Czechoslovaks to proceed to Vladivostok. This was published by the daily newspaper of the Czechoslovak Legion
on April 15, 1918, but on the preceding day the commanders
of the First Division of the Czechoslovak Corps, meeting
in secret conference at Kirsanov, had passed a resolution to
resist by force any attempt to obstruct the progress of the
Legion.

[42] Maksakov i Turunov, op. cit., p. 160.
[43] L. Trotsky, Kak vooruzhalas revoliutsiia. Na voennoi rabote, I, 212.
[44] Maksakov i Turunov, loc. cit.

THE CZECHOSLOVAKS THREATEN RESISTANCE TO THE SOVIETS

[The Kirsanov Resolution, April 14, 1918] [45]

The extremely slow movement of the units of the Czechoslovak Army Corps, the violation of the agreement made by the Soviet authorities with the O. C. S. N. R.[46] to move five echelons daily, as well as rumors reaching the division that some echelons of the Fifth and Eighth regiments, after surrendering a part of their arms in conformity with this agreement, were forced to surrender the rest—all this causes apprehension among the volunteers and their commanding officers that the transportation of the Army Corps will be stopped completely and that the example set by the Soviets in disarming the echelons of the Fifth and Eighth regiments will be repeated with all the other units of the Army Corps.

Considering the fact that the Soviet authorities who have taken obligations upon themselves are powerless to force local soviets to fulfill them, the meeting has decided to notify the commanders of the Army Corps and the O. C. S. N. R. of the following:

1. The interruption of transport and the lack of certainty that it will be resumed have a demoralizing effect upon the units. . . .

2. The breaking up of the Army Corps will end the struggle which the Czechoslovak volunteers are waging against Austro-German imperialism in behalf of the freedom of the Czechoslovak democracy.

3. Delay in the transportation of the Army Corps will inevitably have the result that its aid to the Allies will either come too late or will not be as effective as it could be. . . .

4. The stopping of the Army Corps and the unsystematic character of the transportation interfere with the proper provisioning of the Army Corps, on the one hand, and exhaust the food supply of the local population, on the other.

5. Our experience in Great-Russian territory during six weeks has brought us to the conclusion that it is impossible to count upon reaching an agreement with the Soviet Government. . . . So far the Bolsheviks have met many obligations, because they

[45] Kratochvil, *op. cit.*, pp. 59-61.
[46] Russian branch of the Czechoslovak National Council.

feared the strength of the Army Corps. As soon as we surrender our arms their attitude toward us will change and we shall have no means of bringing pressure. In view of this fact the First Czechoslovak Hussite Artillery Division, as represented by its commanding officers, considers it absolutely necessary:

1. To stop immediately all further surrender of arms and to see to it that the arms and ammunition which have been surrendered at Penza are recovered.

2. To obtain additional supplies of ammunition.

3. To secure secretly complete control of locomotives and fuel in all railway centers where the Army Corps is located.

4. Upon the completion of these . . . preparations, to propose to the Soviet authorities most resolutely, in the name of the whole Army Corps, that all echelons be immediately dispatched, and to declare that: (a) Due to the violation of the former agreement and the attempts to disarm the Czechoslovaks by force, the Army Corps will under no condition surrender its arms before reaching Vladivostok. (b) If within twenty-four hours after an appropriate telegram is sent the request is not complied with, we shall take it for granted that hidden elements within the Soviet Government are acting against the Czechoslovak army in accordance with instructions of the German Command. . . . (c) We affirm again that our only aim in going to Vladivostok is to embark upon our voyage to France and to render the earliest possible help to the Allies, who are especially in need of aid now that the Soviet Government has concluded a separate peace. (d) The Czechoslovak army declares that on leaving Russian territory it retains its old brotherly feelings for the Russian democracy and that under no circumstances will it take part in political strife. In the event, however, that irresponsible elements engage in operations against Czechoslovak units . . . they will be met with due resistance. (e) We propose to the Soviet authorities that we leave behind hostages as a pledge that the Czechoslovak units will remain strictly neutral in crossing Great Russian and Siberian territory and that they will not be used by the Allies for purposes of occupation in Russia and Siberia. (f) In return, the Czechoslovak Army Corps will be given hostages by the Soviet Government as a pledge that it will refrain from any form of attack upon

the Czechoslovaks and that the Soviet Government will take no measures to impede our passage.

5. To make public this proclamation, in order that the local inhabitants may be informed of the purpose of the Czechoslovaks in their journey.

6. This declaration of the Army Corps is to be considered as final and irrevocable. Failure to receive a reply at the time stated will be considered a signal for immediate resumption of the journey.

MAJOR GENERAL KOLOMENSKIJ
Commander of the First Czechoslovak Hussite Artillery

The day after the Kirsanov Resolution was adopted, news came that the anti-Bolshevik Cossack leader Semenov, who was advancing along the Harbin Railway, had reached a point one hundred miles east of Karymsk, an important railway junction where the Trans-Siberian Railroad divides into two lines. Once more the Bolsheviks became alarmed, fearing that Eastern Siberia would be cut off from the rest of Russia. On April 17 martial law was declared in Siberia,[47] and four days later Chicherin telegraphed that all Czechoslovak trains should be stopped. On April 30 Chicherin modified this order. He issued instructions that the Czechoslovak troop trains east of Omsk should proceed to Vladivostok but that those west of Omsk should be turned back toward Archangel and Murmansk. The Czechoslovak leaders were puzzled by this change in itinerary and were even more surprised when on May 8 they received a telegram from Dr. Starka, the Czech representative at Vologda, stating that the new order had been issued by the Sovnarkom after reaching an agreement on the matter with Allied representatives.[48]

[47] Maksakov i Turunov, op. cit., pp. 164-65.
[48] Papoušek, op. cit., p. 28. The agreement was reported by General Lavergne to the French Ministry of War on May 5. It is quoted in Beneš, op. cit., II, 258-59.

On May 9 Maxa and Markovič, both of the Czechoslovak National Council, left Omsk for Moscow to clear up matters. They arrived at Moscow on May 13 and discussed the question with General Lavergne, of the French Military Mission, who confirmed the report that the change in route was in accordance with the wishes of the Allies. Trotsky promised every assistance in the new plan of transporting the First Division by way of Archangel,[49] and the members of the Czechoslovak National Council decided to return to Omsk to order the carrying out of the new arrangements. But the situation suddenly altered when, on May 18, news reached Moscow of a Czechoslovak mutiny at Cheliabinsk. The trouble had started on May 14, when a Czech soldier was wounded by a piece of iron thrown from a train carrying Hungarian prisoners. A fight promptly ensued between the Czechs and Hungarians and a Hungarian soldier was killed. During the investigation of the affair by Bolshevik authorities, a number of Czechs called as witnesses were imprisoned by the Soviet. A delegation sent by the Czechs to demand their release was also placed under arrest. This occurrence enraged the Czechoslovaks. On the 17th they released the prisoners by force, disarmed the Red Guards, and took possession of the arsenal. The Cheliabinsk affair was soon peacefully settled by the local disputants, but Moscow decided on a more drastic policy toward the Czechoslovaks. On May 20 Trotsky's assistant, Aralov, telegraphed to the soviets along the Penza-Omsk railroad to detrain the Czechoslovaks; they were to be organized into labor artels or drafted into the Red Army. The next day Maxa and Čermak were arrested and forced to sign an order to the Czechoslovaks to surrender their arms. Four days later Trotsky dispatched his famous telegram ordering "every

[49] Zmrhal, op. cit., p. 28.

armed Czechoslovak to be shot on the spot." Meanwhile the Czechoslovak army delegates, holding a congress at Cheliabinsk, decided (on May 22) to disregard the orders from Moscow and elected a new committee to take charge of all operations connected with the continuation of the journey to Vladivostok. The breach between the Sovnarkom and the Czechoslovaks was thus complete. In a few days open hostilities began. When the Soviet authorities in Penza attempted on May 26 to carry out Trotsky's order, they met with determined resistance from the Czechoslovaks. An engagement followed and Penza was taken by the Czechs on May 28. However, the Czechs did not stop there but continued their way east through Syzran and on June 8 occupied Samara. Here their movement came to a temporary halt, and their activities became closely linked with those of the anti-Bolshevik elements of Samara, organized under the leadership of the Committee of Members of the Constituent Assembly. This committee proclaimed itself the government of the region and prevailed upon the Czechs to remain at Samara until the new government could organize an army of its own to resist the Bolsheviks.

Similar developments took place in Siberia. Cheliabinsk fell on May 26, Omsk was captured on June 7, and a local anti-Bolshevik government, known as the Siberian Provisional Government, came into existence at Omsk.

THE SOVNARKOM ORDERS THE CZECHOSLOVAK EASTWARD MOVEMENT STOPPED

[Chicherin's Telegram to Siberian Soviets, April 21, 1918] [50]

Fearing that Japan will advance into Siberia, Germany is categorically demanding that German war prisoners held in Eastern Siberia be removed at once to either Western Siberia or European Russia. Please take all necessary measures. The Czechoslovak detachments must not go farther east.

CHICHERIN

[50] *Volia Rossii,* VIII-IX (1928), 307.

FRENCH PROPOSAL TO TRANSPORT THE CZECHOSLOVAKS VIA ARCHANGEL

[Clemenceau to Pichon, April 26, 1918] [51]

. . . I believe that all units of the Czech Corps should be transported by the swiftest means to the Western front, where the presence of these excellent troops is very important; for this reason I have taken appropriate steps with the British Government to obtain transportation for a part of these troops by way of Archangel. . . .

THE SOVNARKOM ORDERS THE DISBANDING OF THE CZECHOSLOVAK CORPS

[Aralov's Telegram to Siberian Soviets, May 20, 1918] [52]

By order of the Chairman of the Commissariat of War, Comrade Trotsky, you are to detrain the Czechoslovaks and organize them into labor artels or draft them into the Soviet Red Army. Do everything in your power to assist the Czechoslovak Communists. . . . [53]

CZECHOSLOVAKS ORDERED BY THEIR DELEGATES AT MOSCOW TO SURRENDER ARMS [54]

[May 21, 1918]

In view of the unfortunate misunderstandings between the Czechoslovak trains and the local Soviet organs, and in order to prevent such misunderstandings, the O. C. S. N. R. orders all com-

---

[51] Beneš, *op. cit.*, II, 192-93.

[52] Papoušek, *op. cit.*, p. 52.

[53] In a statement of May 31, 1918, Trotsky gave the following interpretation of Aralov's telegram: "Through Comrade Aralov I made the Czechoslovaks the following proposal: In case the continuation of their journey should be rendered impossible by failure of the English and French to provide the necessary ships, they [the Czechoslovaks] would be given an opportunity to remain in Russia and choose an occupation most suited to their training and desires, i. e., to enter the Red Army or take up a trade. But this proposal, dictated by the best of intentions . . . , was used by counter-revolutionary elements . . . to poison the minds of the Czechoslovaks and make them believe that the Soviet Government was scheming to hand them over to the Germans." (*Kak vooruzhalas revoliutsiia*, I, 213.)

[54] Kratochvil, *op. cit.*, pp. 79-80.

manders of the Czechoslovak trains to deliver unconditionally all their arms to the local Soviet representatives. The protection of the trains devolves completely upon the Soviet organs of the Russian Federated Republic. Anyone not complying with this order will be considered a traitor and declared outside the law.

MAXA

ČERMAK

CZECH DECISION NOT TO SURRENDER ARMS

[Resolution of May 22, 1918] [55]

The Congress of the Czechoslovak Revolutionary Army, assembled at Cheliabinsk, declares in the presence of War Commissar Sadlutsky its feeling of sympathy with the Russian revolutionary people in their difficult struggle for the consolidation of the revolution. However, the Congress is convinced that the Soviet Government is powerless to guarantee our troops free and safe passage to Vladivostok and therefore has unanimously decided not to surrender its arms until it receives assurance that the Corps will be allowed to depart and will be protected against counter-revolutionary trains.

ORDER TO DRAFT THE CZECHOSLOVAKS INTO SOVIET SERVICE

[Aralov's Telegram to Siberian Soviets, May 23, 1918] [56]

Supplementing the previously given instruction, I order you to proceed immediately with . . . the disarming and disbanding of all echelons and units of the Czechoslovak Army Corps. . . . From the present Army Corps you are to form Red Army units and labor detachments. If you need the help of Czechoslovak commissars, you are to turn to the Czechoslovak Social-Democrat consulates at Penza, Samara, Petropavlovsk, and Omsk. Report to the People's Commissar of War at Moscow on the steps taken and the results achieved.

[55] *Ibid.,* p. 80.   [56] *Ibid.,* p. 81.

THE CZECHOSLOVAK ARMY CONGRESS REPUDIATES THE NATIONAL COUNCIL
[Resolution of May 23, 1918] [57]

The Congress of the Czechoslovak Army Corps hereby suspends the authority of the O. C. S. N. R. in all matters pertaining to the transportation of the army on its way to Vladivostok and transfers that authority to the Provisional Executive Committee. . . . Orders issued by the O. C. S. N. R. are invalid.

DECISION TO RETAIN ARMS COMMUNICATED TO THE SOVNARKOM
[Telegram, May 23, 1918] [58]

The Congress of Representatives of the Czechoslovak Corps at Cheliabinsk has resolved to delegate exclusive charge of the transportation of Czechoslovak troops to the Provisional Executive Committee chosen by the Congress. Orders issued by representatives of any other Czechoslovak organization are invalid. With reference to the order to surrender arms, issued by the representative of the Czechoslovak National Council, Maxa, and War Commissar Aralov, the Congress has unanimously decided not to surrender arms before reaching Vladivostok, considering them a guarantee of safe travel. The assurances of safe transportation from the authorities of the Federal Soviet Republic cannot satisfy us. . . . The Congress protests against the repeated attempts to disarm and stop Czechoslovak echelons. . . . Although taking certain precautionary measures, the Czechoslovak Executive Committee entertains the hope that the Soviet Government will place no obstacles in the way of the departing Czechoslovak revolutionary troops. . . .

Our hope for a peaceful settlement of this involved situation is the greater since every conflict would only prejudice the position of the local Soviet organs in Siberia.

BOHDAN PAVLU
Chairman of the Czechoslovak Executive Committee

[57] Ibid.
[58] Za Svobodu. Obrazkova kronika československeho revolučniho hnuti na Rusi, 1914-1920, III, 195.

ORDERS TO DISARM THE CZECHOSLOVAKS

[Trotsky's Telegram, May 25, 1918] [59]

To all Sovdeps along the Penza-Omsk Railway Line:

All Soviets are hereby ordered to disarm the Czechoslovaks immediately. Every armed Czechoslovak found on the railway is to be shot on the spot; every troop train in which even one armed man is found shall be unloaded, and its soldiers shall be interned in a war prisoners' camp. Local war commissars must proceed at once to carry out this order; every delay will be considered treason and will bring the offender severe punishment. At the same time, reliable forces entrusted with teaching the rebels a lesson are being sent to the rear of the Czechoslovaks. Honest Czechoslovaks who surrender their arms and submit to the Soviet Government will be treated as brothers and given every assistance. Inform all railway workers that not a single car of armed Czechoslovaks is to be allowed to move eastward. Those who submit to violence and assist the Czechoslovaks in their movement east will be severely punished.

This order is to be read to all Czechoslovak units and to all railway workers in places where Czechoslovaks are found. War commissars will report on its execution.

L. TROTSKY
People's Commissar of War

[Order of Tsentrosibir to All Siberian Soviets, May 26, 1918] [60]

Make preparations to disarm the Czechoslovak echelons which are on the way. If your forces are not adequate to disarm them, do everything possible to stop the echelons: side-track them, take their locomotives, in urgent cases tear up the railway tracks. . . .

PROKOPIEV
Member of the Military-Revolutionary Staff

[59] Maksakov i Turunov, *op. cit.*, p. 168.
[60] *Za Svobodu*, III, 249.

[The Penza Soviet to Trotsky, May 26, 1918] [61]

Upon the receipt of Aralov's telegram . . . we held a conference which was attended by Czechoslovak Communists. . . . We
arrived at the conclusion that we could not carry out the order in
its full sense as you demand. . . .

MINIKIN
Chairman of the [Penza] Gubernia Soviet

[Trotsky's Reply, May 26, 1918] [62]

Comrades! Military orders . . . should not be discussed but
obeyed. Any representative of the War Commissariat who is so
cowardly as to evade disarming the Czechoslovaks will be brought
by me before the Military Tribunal. It is your duty to act immediately and energetically.

L. TROTSKY

An important factor in determining the attitude of both
the Czechoslovaks and the Allies toward the Bolsheviks was
the presence in Siberia of a large number of German and
Hungarian war prisoners. It has been estimated that during the World War Russia took close to two million prisoners, about two-thirds of whom were subjects of Austria-
Hungary. The larger part of these prisoners (about 54 per
cent) were kept in European Russia—in regions immediately adjoining the Western borders, in the Don, and in the
Caucasus; the rest were held in the Volga region and in
Siberia.[63]

While German and Austrian commissions for the exchange of prisoners were engaged in repatriating their
nationals, the Bolsheviks were active in propaganda among
war prisoners and in the formation of international legions
of the Red Army for the defense of the Soviet régime

[61] Zmrhal, op. cit., p. 46.
[62] Ibid., p. 47.
[63] Rossiia v mirovoi voine 1914-1918g. v tsifrakh, p. 41.

and the expected world revolution. After his arrival at Moscow, Mirbach, the German Ambassador, protested on several occasions against Bolshevik activities among war prisoners, and Trotsky issued orders to keep the prisoners isolated in the camps.[64] But local authorities paid no attention to these orders and continued to recruit war prisoners for Soviet armies.

Reports of the arming of German and Austrian war prisoners soon began to circulate in Allied countries, where the fear was expressed that this activity was going on with the approval of the Central Powers and for the purpose of giving them control over Siberian resources. When Lockhart and Robins approached Trotsky on this subject he denied that prisoners were being armed and proposed that the Allies send their own representatives to Siberia to investigate the situation. W. B. Webster, member of the American Red Cross Commission, and W. L. Hicks, of the British Mission at Moscow, were sent to Siberia on March 19. They reported to Robins and Lockhart in April that they could count only 931 prisoners under arms and that the Central Siberian Soviet gave them a written guarantee that not more than 1,500 war prisoners would be armed.[65]

From the material given below it appears that the Central Siberian Soviet did not live up to the promise given to the American and British investigators and that many thousands of Austrian and German war prisoners served in the Red Army. Large numbers of them were used by the Soviet authorities in their attempts to disarm the Czecho-

[64] See *U. S. Foreign Relations, 1918, Russia*, II, 131.
[65] The Webster-Hicks reports are given in *Russian-American Relations*, pp. 165-86. See also F. L. Schuman's *American Policy toward Russia since 1917*, pp. 87-88, which declares that "all evidence points to the validity" of the Webster-Hicks report; and Louis Fischer's *The Soviets in World Affairs*, I, 103-05, which subscribes to the same view. Additional reports on the arming of war prisoners are given in *U. S. Foreign Relations, 1918, Russia*, II.

slovaks—a fact which only strengthened the conviction of the Legion that the interferences with its journey to Vladivostok had been inspired by the Central Powers. Whatever be the truth as to the number of Austrian and German war prisoners armed by the Soviets, there is no doubt that the belief in their menace to the Czechs contributed very largely to President Wilson's ultimate approval of intervention in Russia.

WAR PRISONERS IN SIBERIA

[Newspaper Report, April 13, 1918] [66]

According to information received at the neutral missions in Petrograd, a very strained atmosphere has come to prevail in the concentration camps of war prisoners in Siberia, in connection with the enlistment of some of the war prisoners in the Red Army. . . .

At Krasnoiarsk, Irkutsk, and other cities war prisoners who have joined the ranks of the Red Army are fighting those of their comrades who will not follow their example but remain neutral. Two officers who refused to enlist in the Red Army were deported to Chita, despite the protest of the Danish Consul. . . .

. . . The neutral diplomats intend to take up the question of the status of war prisoners and their evacuation from Siberian concentration camps with the Commissariat of Foreign Affairs.

[Statement of the Danish Minister April 18, 1918] [67]

. . . War prisoners who refuse to identify themselves with the Bolsheviks are subjected to disagreeable treatment, and we are forced to come to their defense since from the beginning of the war the Danish Embassy has undertaken to represent the interests of war prisoners. . . . The report that war prisoners in Siberia are being supplied with arms is not subject to doubt. The number of men thus armed is very considerable and the Siberian authorities compel them to go into action. . . .

[66] *Strana*, No. 14, April 13, 1918, p. 2.
[67] *Novaia Zhizn*, No. 71, April 19, 1918, p. 3.

[Propaganda Among War Prisoners] [68]

. . . Revolutionary propaganda among war prisoners is assuming a wide extent. In addition to sending agitators among prisoners, [Communists] have started a number of publications—revolutionary leaflets and pamphlets in all languages. These publications are being distributed in all war prisoners' camps, in hundreds of thousands of copies. . . . At Moscow there has been formed a committee the duty of which is to organize international legions of the Red Army. This committee has recently published, in English, French, German, Italian, and Russian, the following proclamation:

"Comrades Internationalists! Russia has been caught in a vise but her voice, thundering above the din of the World War, calls humanity to truth and justice for the poor and oppressed. Russia has many enemies, external and internal, mighty and perfidious. Russia does not need words and empty expressions of sympathy. She needs work, discipline, organization, and fearless fighters. Have you faith in the Revolution, in the International, in the Soviet Government? If you have, join at once the International Legion of the Red Army. . . ."

WAR PRISONERS AND THE RUSSIAN CIVIL WAR

. . . The long awaited Siberian congress of war prisoners . . . opened at Irkutsk on April 15, 1918. Sixty delegates came from [various] war prisoners' camps and the armed units composed of Internationalists. At that time most of the so-called International Battalion of the Red Army at Irkutsk and a number of Red Army detachments at Chita, Krasnoiarsk, Tomsk, and Barnaul consisted of former war prisoners, as did various units on guard duty, such as the Angora Battalion at Irkutsk. About the same time the First Omsk International Detachment, numbering eight hundred men, mostly Magyars . . . , was organized and sent to the Semenov front. . . .

Semenov's offensive in Transbaikalia served as a signal for the consolidation of all the revolutionary forces of Siberia. . . . New detachments of Internationalists came into existence. At Chita an

[68] *Znamia Truda,* April 19, 1918, p. 3.

insurrection was suppressed, chiefly with the aid of a Hungarian unit. . . . From Kansk, Achinsk, Krasnoiarsk, Barnaul, from all the war prisoners' camps, new forces came to join the Red Army. . . . When the Czechoslovaks were being disarmed at the Irkutsk station, it was chiefly the decisive action of one of our Internationalist machine-gun detachments . . . which saved the day. . . .[69]

. . . According to the estimates of the Central Committee of War Prisoners, the war prisoners in the ranks of the Red Army before the German Revolution totalled fifty thousand. All of these were recommended by revolutionary organizations of war prisoners and fought on all the internal fronts in Russia. . . .[70]

The proletarian element of the war prisoners, chiefly Germans and Hungarians, organized so-called International Battalions which rendered great service to the Bolsheviks in establishing Soviet rule in Siberia and in fighting counter-revolutionists. These battalions helped to suppress the counter-revolutionary uprisings at Omsk, Tomsk, and Irkutsk, fought successfully against Semenov's bands, and . . . defended Soviet territory against the Czechoslovaks. . . .[71]

CLASHES BETWEEN CZECHS AND AUSTRO-GERMAN PRISONERS OF WAR

[American Consul General at Irkutsk to the Secretary of State, June 2, 1918][72]

On the afternoon of May 26 a train arrived in Irkutsk carrying Czechoslovaks to Vladivostok. I may add here that according to a statement of the Central Siberian government here in Irkutsk instructions have been received from the Bolshevik government in Moscow to disarm all the Czechoslovak trains.

An attempt was made to carry out this program and it resulted in a clash in which according to the official Czech report, 8 were killed, 7 died of wounds, 36 wounded, and 5 wounded who were

[69] D. Frid, in *Proletarskaia Revoliutsiia*, No. 5, 1928, pp. 159-60.

[70] I. Ulianov, "Oktiabrskaia revoliutsiia i voennoplennye," in *Proletarskaia Revoliutsiia*, No. 7, 1929, p. 109.

[71] V. Vegman, "Voennoplennye imperialisticheskoi voiny," in *Sibirskaia sovetskaia entsiklopediia*, I, 519.

[72] U. S. Dept. of State, Confidential Report on Matters Relating to Russia, No. 16, August 16, 1918, pp. 35-36.

subject afterwards to surgical amputations. There were about 600 Czechs engaged. The official report of the Red Guard losses has not been made public but I am certain that they were even heavier than those of the Czechs. However, it would appear that the Czechs finally gave up their arms voluntarily and further bloodshed was avoided, and this particular train shortly proceeded on its way.

About 10 o'clock that night two further Czech trains arrived at a station called Innokentevskaya seven versts west of Irkutsk and directly opposite an Austro-German prison camp. . . . From the best information obtainable and supported by the personal investigations of the French Consul General and myself on the spot it would appear that these two trains were attacked about midnight by armed Austrian and German prisoners. There were about 1,000 Czechs engaged and they evidently made short work of the Austrians and Germans who made the attack. While the conflict was on, the Soviet sent two Commissars of Foreign Affairs to me urging my intervention in order to stop further bloodshed. I immediately called upon the French Consul General and we proceeded at daybreak under a flag of truce to the scene of action. The Czechs had captured 22 Austrians, 4 Germans, and 9 Russians who were members of the Red Guard. There were also a large number of Austrians and Germans wounded who had been removed to the camp. I at once called upon the Russian commandant of the prison camp in order to get all the facts from both sides. An Austrian officer was permitted to accompany me back to the Czech trains in order to establish the nationality of the prisoners. In addition to the prisoners above mentioned 5 had been killed and already buried before my arrival. These I had disinterred in order to establish their nationality. The Austrian officer identified these as being four Austrians and one German. I desire to state in this connection that the dead and all the prisoners, with the exception of two or three, were all in the uniforms of their respective nationalities. This seems to establish beyond doubt the question that a large number of the prisoners in Irkutsk are armed. From the best authority obtainable I have it that there are now 600 prisoners armed in this city and they compose a large part of the Red Guard. I have seen a few Austrian prisoners on the streets in Austrian uniforms bearing arms.

Under the good offices of the French Consul General and myself we succeeded in disarming these two trains of Czechs, also a third train which had arrived in the meantime at another station a few versts farther west. . . .

ACTIVITIES OF CZECHOSLOVAK COMMUNISTS

[Report of the Commissariat of Nationalities] [73]

Even before the counter-revolutionary insurrection of the Czechoslovaks . . . , the Czech Communists were engaged in propaganda . . . in favor of forming a Czechoslovak Red Army. . . .

In Penza a [Czechoslovak] Secretariat was organized to carry on propaganda among Czechs and Slovaks, and a Czechoslovak revolutionary regiment was formed from the men who came over to our side. One part of that regiment is now fighting on the X front; the other part, which remained at Penza during the Czechoslovak insurrection, participated in the defense of the city and suffered heavy losses. . . . The Penza Secretariat published in Czech various broadsides and . . . a propaganda paper. . . .

A similar secretariat functioned in Samara, where proclamations were issued and a Czechoslovak detachment of the Red Army was formed. . . .

When the Czechoslovaks mutinied . . . every effort was being made to liquidate the mutiny. On May 20 agitators were sent to Irkutsk, Samara, and Penza with Trotsky's order to disarm all echelons without exception. . . . At the same time, the Congress of Czechoslovak Communists (May 25-27) protested unanimously against the adventure of the Czech bourgeoisie and called upon Czech workers to desert their leaders and join the Russian Revolution. . . .

Throughout the period of military operations the Czechoslovak Section of the Commissariat of Nationalities sent agitators and revolutionary literature to the front.

The final break between the Bolsheviks and the Czechoslovaks occurred on June 11 when, by order of the Sovnarkom, the Russian Branch of the Czechoslovak National

[73] *Zhizn Natsionalnostei,* No. 1, November 9, 1918, p. 1.

Council was dissolved and its properties were transferred to the Czech Communists attached to the Commissariat of Nationalities. The order stated that the motive of the Sovnarkom's act was to help "the Czech soldiers brought up in the spirit of bourgeois nationalism . . . to reeducate themselves and become class-conscious." However, by the time the order was issued the Czechoslovak army had elected a new executive committee, which assumed control of the movements of the Czech troops in Siberia. In a memorandum dated June 5 and addressed to the French Mission, the Czechoslovak Executive Committee gave the following reasons for the break of the Czechs with the Soviets:

WHY THE CZECHOSLOVAKS TOOK TO ARMS

[The Czechoslovak Executive Committee to the French Mission, June 5, 1918] [74]

1. The Czechoslovak action along the Penza-Irkutsk railway line was prompted by the threats of the Soviet Government to break up our units, intern them as war prisoners, and shoot all armed Czechoslovaks. We had reliable information that . . . our military organization was to be completely disbanded and that its units were to be forced into service in the Red Army. This compelled us to prepare for armed defense.

2. The spark that set us into action . . . was the treacherous attack upon our echelon at Marianovka, near Omsk, on May 25. We retaliated by occupying all important stations along the line Cheliabinsk-Omsk-Irkutsk . . . on May 27 and 28.

3. Our tactics were directed at first toward insuring a safe and unimpeded passage to France for ourselves. We did not want to interfere in Russian internal affairs and allowed the soviets to remain in their places. Soon, however, we became convinced that the Cheliabinsk Soviet . . . had organized an armed strike movement against us. Thereupon we decided to remove the Soviet authorities from their positions, especially after we received new reports . . . that the Soviet Government was mobilizing all its forces against us.

[74] *Za Svobodu,* III, 293.

4. Under these circumstances we decided to give up our policy of political neutrality and to summon to our help all the best elements of the local population.

DISSOLUTION OF THE CZECHOSLOVAK NATIONAL COUNCIL
[Decree of the Sovnarkom, June 11, 1918] [75]

In connection with the insurrection of the Czechoslovak regiments against the Soviet Government the Sovnarkom has decreed:

The Czechoslovak National Council (Russian Branch) and all organizations and committees associated with it are dissolved.

The property, capital, archives, etc. of the above-mentioned organizations are turned over to the Czechoslovak Section attached to the People's Commissariat of Nationalities.

V. ULIANOV (LENIN)
President of the Sovnarkom

L. TROTSKY
People's Commissar of War

CHICHERIN
People's Commissar of Foreign Affairs

MOTIVATION [76]

The Czechoslovak National Council . . . opposed the Soviets . . . and supported the Ukrainian Central Rada at Kiev against Soviet Russia. Its organ [a Czech daily paper], . . . took a position hostile to the Soviets in their endeavors to build . . . a socialist republic. . . . With the consent of Professor Maxa, Czech regiments were sent to Kiev in October to suppress the uprising of the proletariat. . . . During the retreat of the Czech Corps from the Ukraine its leaders, especially Maxa, prevented an agreement with the Soviet Government of the Ukraine [to fight the Germans].[77] . . . At that time a military party was

[75] *Izvestiia*, No. 119, June 12, 1918, p. 3.   [76] *Ibid.*

[77] In a message dated June 25, 1918, addressed to the People's Commissar of Foreign Affairs, Masaryk repudiated the charge that the Czechoslovaks had been disloyal. The message is quoted in *U. S. Foreign Relations, 1918, Russia*, II, 225.

formed among the leaders of the Czechoslovaks, who thought that since they were the only organized force in Russia they could do as they pleased. The most recent events indicate that the plans of the military party . . . are being carried out. . . .

The Czech soldiers, brought up in the spirit of bourgeois nationalism and kept in ignorance . . . of the actual policy of the Soviet Government, now became a tool in the hands of irresponsible intriguers and adventurers who hate the very word "socialism." Wishing to free the Czech soldiers from that bondage and to give them a chance to reeducate themselves and become class-conscious, we find it necessary to abolish the organization. . . .

C. The Decision of the Allies to Intervene

The clash of the Czechs with the Soviets led the Allies to view the question of intervention in an entirely new light. They considered that the Legion's seizure of strategic points on the Trans-Siberian Railway and the presence of a Czech contingent of five thousand soldiers in the Volga region presented an opportunity to rebuild the Eastern front. It only remained to prevail upon President Wilson to sanction the enterprise.

Even before the news of the Czech action reached Central Russia the advocates of Allied-Bolshevik cooperation against Germany were forced to abandon their plan. This plan, as has been seen, was based on the expectation that Trotsky would invite the Allies to land an army in the Far East. But the invitation was not forthcoming. On May 28 the Allied ambassadors, holding a conference at Vologda which was also attended by the British special representative, Lockhart, and French military attachés, decided to urge intervention regardless of Bolshevik consent.[78]

On June 1 General Lavergne, French Military Attaché, sent to the French Ministry of War a memorandum describ-

---

[78] *Ibid.*, p. 179; Lockhart, *op. cit.*, pp. 280-81.

ing the new situation which had arisen in consequence of the break of the Czechoslovaks with the Soviets. He reported that a new committee had been appointed to direct the Czechoslovaks in their voyage and that Trotsky was irreconcilable on the question of disarming the Czechoslovaks; from these facts he drew the conclusion that the presence of Czech forces at strategic points along the Trans-Siberian Railway could well be utilized for purposes of intervention.[79] Three days later, Allied representatives at Moscow delivered a formal protest against the attempts to disarm the Czechoslovak Legion.

Chicherin justified the disarming in a note of June 12 addressed to the Allied diplomatic representatives at Moscow, and Trotsky issued a warning against Allied interference in Russian affairs.

CHICHERIN TO THE ALLIED DIPLOMATIC REPRESENTATIVES

[Note of June 12, 1918] [80]

On June 4 representatives of . . . England, France, Italy, and . . . the United States presented a statement concerning the Czechoslovaks in which they declared that the disarming of the Czechoslovaks would be considered by their governments as an unfriendly act . . . , since the Czechoslovak troops are Allied troops and are under the protection and care of the Entente Powers.

The People's Commissariat of Foreign Affairs has the honor . . . to make the following explanation:

The disarming of the Czechoslovaks cannot be considered an act unfriendly to the Entente Powers. It is necessitated primarily by the fact that Russia is a neutral power and cannot tolerate the presence in her territories of armed forces not belonging to the army of the Soviet Republic. But the immediate cause of the tak-

---

[79] Beneš, op. cit., II, 250-51.

[80] Yu. Kliuchnikov i A. Sabanin, Mezhdunarodnaia politika noveishego vremeni v dogovorakh, notakh i deklaratsiiakh, II, 144-46.

ing of decisive and strong measures to disarm the Czechoslovaks is to be found in their activities. . . . They began a rebellion in Cheliabinsk on May 26, . . . seized the city and ammunition, and arrested . . . the local authorities. . . . The subsequent spread of the rebellion led to the occupation by the Czechoslovaks of Penza, Samara, Novonikolaevsk, Omsk, and other cities. . . . Everywhere the Czechoslovaks acted in cooperation with White Guards and counter-revolutionary Russian officers, . . . restoring the institutions which had been abolished by the Soviet Republic of Workers and Peasants. . . .

The Soviet Government has taken the most energetic steps to suppress . . . and disarm the Czechoslovaks. . . . The People's Commissar of Foreign Affairs is confident that the Entente Powers . . . will approve of these measures of the Soviet Government . . . and will condemn the Czechoslovaks . . . for their counter-revolutionary armed rebellion [sic], which constitutes a most flagrant interference in the internal affairs of Russia.

CHICHERIN

People's Commissar of Foreign Affairs

TROTSKY DENOUNCES ALLIED INTERVENTION

[Excerpt from Trotsky's Speech of June 22, 1918] [81]

. . . We cannot regard the intervention of the Allied imperialists in any other light than as a hostile attempt on the freedom and independence of Soviet Russia. If they make a landing we shall defend ourselves with all our strength. . . . Between the Germans and the encroachments of armies of the "friendly" Allies we see no difference. . . . The "Allies" could make no serious attack without the help of the Japanese army. Only fools can imagine that the Japanese would enter this fight for no other purpose than to help the Allies free Russia from the Germans. If Japan interferes in Russian affairs it will be solely for the purpose of enslaving Russia. . . . As between Japanese and German occupation . . . , the former is more dangerous for . . . Russia since there is much less reason to expect an early internal change in Japan than in Germany. . . . Those who twist this statement

---

[81] Trotsky, *Kak vooruzhalas revoliutsiia,* I, 199-200.

into an argument that we plan an alliance with the Germans against the "Allies" are either naturally stupid or are being paid to be stupid. . . .

In the meantime, the Supreme War Council, meeting at Versailles on June 1, reaffirmed its previous resolutions [82] to transport the Czechoslovaks to France [83] and addressed to the Japanèse Government a request to furnish the necessary ships.[84] It also resolved upon a formal proposal to the Japanese Government that it send an army to Siberia on the conditions that it respect the territorial integrity of Russia, take no sides in Russian internal politics, and advance as far west as possible for the purpose of encountering the Germans.[85] The Council also decided to send reinforcements to Murmansk, which had been held by the British since March, and, if possible, to occupy Archangel.[86]

The expedition to the North of Russia encountered no opposition from President Wilson. The American cruiser "Olympia" arrived at Murmansk toward the end of May, and on June 3 Admiral Sims announced that a force of six hundred American soldiers had been sent to Murmansk.[87] The President agreed to send an additional force to Archangel [88] but still temporized on the question of intervention in Siberia, for which Japan was expected to provide the major armed force.

According to Beneš, the first definite proposal to utilize the Czechoslovaks for intervention in Russia was in the instructions of the French Ministry of War to General Lavergne on June 20. The instructions urged that the Czechoslovaks hold their positions along the Trans-Siberian

[82] The one at Aberville on May 2, 1918, and the other at London on May 28. The two resolutions are quoted in Beneš, op. cit., II, 194, 219-20.
[83] Ibid., p. 249.
[84] U. S. Foreign Relations, 1918, Russia, II, 199-200.
[85] Ibid., p. 202.   [87] Ibid., p. 489.
[86] Ibid., p. 485.   [88] Ibid., pp. 484-85.

Railway and refuse to surrender their arms, thus making intervention possible if it should be decided upon.[89] It was probably on the basis of these instructions, which were received in Russia on June 27, that Major A. Guinet, a French officer attached to the Czechoslovak Corps, announced on June 29 that the Allies had decided to intervene in Russia. The actual decision, however, was not made until July 2, 1918, when the Supreme War Council met at Versailles. For this meeting there was prepared a lengthy memorandum setting forth the reasons why the Council considered the sending of an Allied expedition to Russia "an urgent and imperative necessity." The memorandum argued in part as follows: ". . . Allied intervention is essential to win the war. . . . [The Germans] know as well as we know that there is but the smallest chance of an Allied victory on the western front in 1919 unless Germany is compelled to transfer a considerable amount of her strength back again from west to east. It will therefore be a primary object of her policy to prevent the re-creation of an eastern Allied front. During the forthcoming autumn and winter she will endeavor to do this either by establishing in Russia a government favorable to herself or destroying all possibility of organized resistance to her domination. If the Allies are to win the war in 1919 it should be a primary object of their policy to foster and assist the national movement in Russia in order to reform an Eastern front. . . ."[90] The memorandum concluded with an appeal to President Wilson to approve the policy of the Supreme War Council.

[89] Beneš, *op. cit.*, II, 252.
[90] *U. S. Foreign Relations, 1918, Russia*, II, 243-44.

A FRENCH PLEDGE TO SUPPORT THE CZECHS

[Major A. Guinet's Message to the Czechoslovaks, June 29, 1918] [91]

I hereby inform the Provisional Executive Committee of the Czechoslovak Army that I have received from the French Ambassador a ciphered telegram informing me of the intervention of the Allies in Russia. In transmitting this information, I wish to add that I have been authorized to express the thanks of the Allies to the Czechoslovak troops for their action in Russia. The behavior of the Czechoslovaks, arising out of a clear understanding of the situation, is to the greater honor of the whole Czechoslovak Army. . . .

Only a short time ago members of the French Mission were making efforts to maintain relations with the Russian Soviet Government. But this government no longer deserves such consideration in the eyes of the Allies and the civilized world. We are no longer in contact with the Bolsheviks. . . .

From now on you will see us straining every effort to support . . . the Czechoslovak Army. It is to you that we owe the reestablishment of the Russian front . . . against the real enemy of Russia and of the Allies. . . . The French Mission, always a faithful ally of Russia, is fighting at her side in the first trench of this new front.[92]

THE SUPREME WAR COUNCIL DECIDES ON INTERVENTION IN RUSSIA

[Resolution of July 2, 1918] [93]

. . . The Supreme War Council, having carefully considered the military situation and the prospects of the Allies in all the theaters of war, have come to conclusion—

I. That immediate Allied armed assistance to Russia is imperatively necessary for the following reasons:

(a) To assist the Russian nation to throw off their German

[91] *Izvestiia*, No. 140, July 13, 1918, p. 4.

[92] Chicherin protested against this message. In reply, Noulens stated on July 18 that Guinet had not been authorized to make the announcement. (Zaitsov, *1918god. Ocherki po istorii russkoi grazhdanskoi voiny*, p. 172.)

[93] *U. S. Foreign Relations, 1918, Russia*, II, pp. 245-46.

oppressors and to prevent the unlimited military and economic domination of Russia by Germany in her own interests.

(b) For the decisive military reason given by General Foch in his telegram to President Wilson; i. e., that the Germans have already called back from Russia a number of divisions and sent them to the western front. Allied intervention will be the first step in stimulating the national uprising in Russia against German domination which will have an immediate effect in renewing German anxiety in regard to the east and compelling her to refrain from removing further troops westward and perhaps to move troops back to the east.

(c) To shorten the war by the reconstitution of the Russian front.

(d) To prevent the isolation of Russia from western Europe. They are advised that if action is not taken in Siberia the existing Allied forces in Northern Russia may have to be withdrawn and Russia will be completely cut off from the Allies.

(e) To deny to Germany the supplies of western Siberia and the important military stores at Vladivostok and to render these available for the Russian population.

(f) To bring assistance to the Czecho-Slovak forces which have made great sacrifices to the cause for which we are fighting.

II. That the intervention should be Allied in character, should be accompanied by pledges to the Russian people as agreed to at the last Versailles conference, and should include the following:

1. An Allied force to operate in Siberia. Circumstances render imperative that the force shall be considerable in number, military in character and Allied in composition, and that above all things it should operate immediately; delay would be fatal. It is recognized that owing to geographical and shipping conditions Japanese troops will comprise the larger portion of the force but its Allied character must be maintained and it must include American and Allied units. The force should be under a single command appointed by the power that provides the largest number of troops.

2. Such developments of the Allied forces in Murmansk and Archangel as the military advisers of the Allies may recommend.

3. Relief expeditions under American direction and control to supply the wants and alleviate the sufferings of the Russian people.

The primary object of Allied action being to cooperate with the Russian nation in re-creating the eastern front as a first step toward freeing Russia, the closest coordination must exist between the above forces and the Russian people.

III. Therefore, in view of—

1. The unanimous opinion of General Foch and the Allied military advisers of the Supreme War Council that immediate dispatch of a considerable Allied force to Siberia is essential for the victory of the Allied armies;

2. The fact that no adequate expedition can be sent without Japanese cooperation and that Japan will not undertake effective action without the encouragement and support of the United States Government; and

3. The shortness of the time available before the winter for initiating active operations in Siberia and the rapid German penetration into Russia:

the Supreme War Council appeal to President Wilson to approve the policy here recommended and thus to enable it to be carried into effect before it is too late.

The resolution of the Supreme War Council formed the subject of a special conference at the White House on July 6. This conference accepted the resolution in principle but limited the scope of intervention very considerably. Specifically, the White House conference concluded that the establishment of an Eastern front was a physical impossibility and did not deserve further consideration; that the situation of the Czechoslovaks required Allied assistance; and that, provided the Japanese Government was willing to cooperate, the United States was ready to furnish arms to the Czechoslovaks and to send to Vladivostok a military force of seven thousand Americans and an equal number of Japanese to guard the lines of communication of the Czechoslovaks.[94] On July 17 these conclusions were communicated by the

[94] *Ibid.*, pp. 262-63.

Secretary of State to the Allied ambassadors at Washington in the form of an *aide-mémoire*.

Meanwhile the Allies were proceeding with their own plans for intervention. On July 7 Ček, commander of the western part of the Czechoslovak Corps, issued an order stating that by agreement with the Allies the Czechoslovaks were to remain in Russia and form the vanguard of an Eastern front against Germany. More detailed instructions for the establishment of the Eastern front were sent by the French Ministry of War on August 7 to General Janin, French commander of the Czechoslovak troops.

CZECHOSLOVAKS TO REMAIN IN RUSSIA
[Ček's Order, July 7, 1918] [95]

Notify all brothers that in conformity with the decision of the Congress of the Army Corps and our National Council, and with the concurrence of the Allies, our Corps has been made a vanguard of the Allied forces. The instructions issued by the Staff of the Army Corps aim at the establishment of an anti-German front in Russia in conjunction with the whole Russian nation and our allies. . . .

AMERICAN PLAN FOR INTERVENTION IN RUSSIA
[Extract from the Communication of the Secretary of State to the Allied Ambassadors, July 17, 1918] [96]

. . . It is the clear and fixed judgment of the Government of the United States, arrived at after repeated and very searching reconsiderations of the whole situation in Russia, that military intervention there would add to the present sad confusion in Russia rather than cure it, injure her rather than help her, and that it would be of no advantage in the prosecution of our main design, to win the war against Germany. It can not, therefore, take part in such intervention or sanction it in principle. . . . Military ac-

[95] F. V. Steidler, *Československi hnuti na Rusi*, p. 69.
[96] *U. S. Foreign Relations, 1918, Russia*, II, 288-89.

tion is admissible in Russia, as the Government of the United States sees the circumstances, only to help the Czecho-Slovaks consolidate their forces and get into successful cooperation with their Slavic kinsmen and to steady any efforts at self-government or self-defense in which the Russians themselves may be willing to accept assistance. Whether from Vladivostok or from Murmansk and Archangel, the only legitimate object for which American or Allied troops can be employed, it submits, is to guard military stores which may subsequently be needed by Russian forces and to render such aid as may be acceptable to the Russians in the organization of their own self-defense. For helping the Czecho-Slovaks there is immediate necessity and sufficient justification. . . . It yields, also, to the judgment of the Supreme Command in the matter of establishing a small force at Murmansk, to guard the military stores at Kola, and to make it safe for Russian forces to come together in organized bodies in the north. But it owes it to frank counsel to say that it can go no further than these modest and experimental plans. It is not in a position, and has no expectation of being in a position, to take part in organized intervention in adequate force from either Vladivostok or Murmansk and Archangel. It feels that it ought to add, also, that it will feel at liberty to use the few troops it can spare only for the purposes here stated and shall feel obliged to withdraw those forces, in order to add them to the forces at the western front, if the plans in whose execution it is now intended that they should cooperate should develop into others inconsistent with the policy to which the Government of the United States feels constrained to restrict itself.

At the same time the Government of the United States wishes to say with the utmost cordiality and good will that none of the conclusions here stated is meant to wear the least color of criticism of what the other governments associated against Germany may think it wise to undertake. It wishes in no way to embarrass their choices of policy. All that is intended here is a perfectly frank and definite statement of the policy which the United States feels obliged to adopt for herself and in the use of her own military forces. The Government of the United States does not wish it to be understood that in so restricting its own activities it is seeking, even by implication, to set limits to the action or to define the policies of its associates. . . .

ALLIED PLAN FOR ARMED INTERVENTION

[Instructions of the French Ministry of War to General Janin, August 7, 1918] [97]

The aim of the Czechoslovak forces acting in cooperation with the Allied intervention forces is to effect direct contact between Siberia . . . , the Allied bases in the Arctic Ocean, and the groups in Southern Russia which are sympathetic to us.

The specific goal pursued is the restoration of continuity on the whole Trans-Siberian Railway and the establishment of as many strategic points as possible between the White and the Black seas in order to stem Germany's eastward expansion. . . .

The first goal is the occupation of the territory around Irkutsk in order to facilitate contact between the Czech contingents in Vladivostok and the echelons stranded west of Baikal.

The advance . . . should then be continued toward the Urals and the interior of Russia.

It is important, however, that the Czech echelons from Central and Western Siberia be immediately induced to cooperate toward the establishment of contact with the Vladivostok group and the bases in the Arctic Ocean . . . by way of Ekaterinburg, Viatka, Dvina, and later through Samara and Vologda.

It is very important that these contacts be assured before winter sets in.

Toward the end of July the United States Government reached an agreement with the Japanese Government on the terms of the Siberian expedition, and early in August the two governments made public statements defining their aims in sending troops to Russia.[98]

---

[97] Maurice Janin, *Moje účast na československém boji za svobodu*, p. 102.

[98] The Japanese statement was published on August 2 and is given in *U. S. Foreign Relations*, 1918, *Russia*, II, 324-25; the American statement, identical with the communication of July 17 quoted on pp. 109-10, above, was published on August 3.

CHAPTER III

THE BOLSHEVIKS FACE INTERVENTION

Early Soviet foreign policies were largely determined by the faith of the Bolsheviks in the imminence of an international proletarian revolution caused by the politico-economic disturbances of the World War and the revolutionary example of Russia. In numerous appeals to the "toiling and exploited masses," the Bolsheviks urged that the "imperialist" war be turned into a civil war with a view to the overthrow of capitalist governments and the establishment of socialism. However, the governments of the warring nations not only survived these revolutionary appeals but were sufficiently strong to menace Soviet Russia with two-fold intervention, proceeding from both the Central Powers and the Allies.

Intervention largely dispelled the hopes of the Bolsheviks for the early triumph of the world revolution and at the same time introduced a change in their conception of the rôle of Soviet Russia in that revolution. Instead of acting as the shock force in an immediate movement for the overthrow of capitalism, Russia was for the present to conserve carefully its own existence in order to lend powerful aid to the world proletarian revolt when it finally matured. It followed that intervention was to be actively opposed when it menaced the existence of the Soviet régime but not when it entailed merely the loss of portions of Russian territory which, as it was believed, would eventually be regained when the world revolution broke out. Accordingly, the Bolsheviks reacted to the intervention of the Central Powers and to that of the Allies in very different ways.

They did not resist the first by arms because for the time being it did not jeopardize the existence of the Soviet régime in Central Russia. On the other hand, the Bolsheviks took steps to oppose Allied intervention because they considered that this represented an attack upon the very life of the lone socialist republic.

While during the spring and summer the Bolsheviks were entirely on the defensive, in the fall of 1918 certain international developments brought about a reversion to the more aggressive attitude which had originally marked Soviet foreign policy. These developments were the setback suffered by the Central Powers on the Western front and the political unrest which simultaneously arose in those countries. The Bolsheviks believed that these events had, in the words of Lenin, "quickened the pace of the proletarian world revolution," in the sense that they were the preliminaries to an uprising of the German and Austrian proletariat, to be shortly followed by revolts in other countries. On this assumption the Bolsheviks proceeded to make preparations for assisting the working class of Germany and Austria, and at the same time intensified their opposition to the Allied forces of intervention.

A. The Bolsheviks and the Central Powers

Having recognized the independence of the Ukrainian Republic in the Treaty of Brest-Litovsk, the Bolsheviks could raise no formal objection to the Austro-German occupation of the territories belonging to that republic. However, the German advance did not stop at the demarcation line fixed by the Treaty of Brest-Litovsk but extended southward to the Don region and the Crimea and northward into Central Russia. On April 21 Chicherin, in a note addressed to the German Secretary for Foreign Affairs,

5

protested against Germany's invasion of the Crimea.[1] A few days later the Commissar of Foreign Affairs dispatched to the German Government a note which, though it denounced Germany's violation of the Brest-Litovsk Treaty, concluded by inquiring what new terms would have to be accepted by Russia to secure stable relations with Germany.

PROTEST AGAINST GERMANY'S VIOLATION OF THE BREST TREATY

[Chicherin to the German Government, April 27, 1918] [2]

The Russian Soviet Government has taken every measure to observe strictly the terms of the treaty in order to safeguard for our people its essential purpose—a state of peace. In reality, however, peace does not exist. In the region of the South there is taking place a further penetration by German troops. . . . They are moving on Orel, Kursk, and Voronezh—territories which beyond question are Russian. They have also penetrated the Taurida Peninsula. At the same time, in the north of Finland, White Guard troops, acting in conjunction with [German] landing forces and under the direct leadership of German officers, are seizing Russian war materials.

In conformity with the Brest-Litovsk Treaty . . . the Soviet Government officially declared its readiness to open peace negotiations with the Central Ukrainian Rada. But no reply was received from that government, controlled by Germany. . . . Instead, as was stated above, a further advance of German-Ukrainian forces into Russia is in progress.

In view of these circumstances, the Soviet Government was compelled to mobilize troops necessary to protect the freedom and independence of the Russian Republic within the limits stipulated by the Brest-Litovsk Treaty.

It is perfectly obvious that such a state of affairs cannot last very long. Considering it necessary to bring about a perfect understanding for the purpose of securing peace, the Soviet Government reaffirms its readiness to observe the terms of the Brest-

---

[1] See p. 56, above.
[2] *Svoboda Rossii,* No. 15, April 28, 1918, p. 2.

Litovsk Treaty in the future. At the very moment when Mirbach, the German Ambassador, is presenting his credentials to the Russian Government, the Soviet Government expresses its confidence that he will take every step to insure that the Government of the German Empire declares precisely whether or not it considers the terms of the Brest-Litovsk Treaty as being in force. If it does, what steps does it intend to take in order to terminate the above-mentioned military operations, which are obviously menacing the state of peace between Russia and Germany?

If [on the other hand] the German Government thinks that it can no longer observe the terms of the peace treaty which was ratified by both states, it becomes absolutely necessary that the German Government state clearly the new demands for the sake of which it directs the Ukrainian, Finnish, and German forces against the Russian Soviet Republic. . . .

The protests of the Commissar of Foreign Affairs neither stopped military operations on the Ukrainian front nor brought about a clarification of the relations between Germany and Soviet Russia. During the early part of May influential military circles in Germany favored an aggressive policy toward the Bolsheviks, and certain generals even advocated the capture of Moscow and the overthrow of the Soviet régime.[3]

On May 8 the German Government presented a demand that Russia cede to Finland Fort Ino, important for the defense of Petrograd. The Germans also required that the Russians force the British out of Murmansk, which the latter had occupied early in March. It was in connection with these demands that the Central Executive Committee, the Moscow Soviet, and representatives of trade unions and factory-shop committees assembled on May 14 to hear Lenin discuss Russia's foreign relations.

[3] Max Hoffman, *Der Krieg der versäumten Gelegenheiten,* pp. 223-24; Ludendorff, *op. cit.,* pp. 505, 529.

SOVIET RUSSIA'S FOREIGN RELATIONS

[Lenin's Speech at the Plenary Session of the Central Executive Committee, the Moscow Soviet of Workers' Deputies, and the Representatives of Trade Unions and Factory-Shop Committees, May 14, 1918] [4]

Comrades! Allow me to acquaint you with the present state of affairs in our foreign politics. The situation, Comrades, has changed considerably during the past few days in view of the fact that general conditions have become more critical and that, as a consequence, the bourgeois press and its hireling, the bourgeois-socialist press, are deliberately spreading alarm and doing dark and dirty work to restore the Kornilov régime.

Comrades, I shall call your attention first of all to the facts which determine the essentials of the international position of the Soviet Republic, in order to proceed to the external juridical forms which determine that position. With this as a foundation I shall attempt to outline the new difficulty, or more exactly, the turning-point, which is now before us and is at the heart of the crisis in the political situation.

Comrades, you know from the experience of the two Russian revolutions . . . that the deepest roots of the internal and external policies of our state are determined by economic interests, the economic position of the dominant classes of our state. These postulates, which are at the foundation of the whole Marxist conception of life, . . . must not be lost from sight even for a minute; otherwise we may lose ourselves in the obscurities and the maze of diplomatic cunning, a maze which is often created artificially and made more intricate by individuals, classes, parties, and groups, which are either disposed or forced to fish in muddy waters. . . .

In its essentials the situation can be reduced to this—that the Russian Socialist Soviet Republic is . . . an oasis [sic] in the midst of a raging ocean of imperialist plundering. . . . The imperialist war has divided the imperialist Powers into hostile groups . . . —a proof that under certain conditions a union between the imperialists of all countries is impossible. We witness a situation where the raging waves of imperialist reaction are bat-

[4] *Protokoly zasedanii Vserossiiskogo Tsentralnogo Ispolnitelnogo Komiteta 4-go sozyva,* pp. 263-70.

tering the little island of the Socialist Soviet Republic, ready, as it were, to submerge it, but destined in the end to break on each other.

The war has disclosed two fundamental contradictions which for the present determine the international position of the Socialist Soviet Republic. The first . . . is the struggle between Germany and England. . . . The fierceness of the conflict makes . . . the union of the greatest imperialist Powers against the Soviet Republic almost impossible. . . .

The second contradiction . . . is the rivalry between Japan and America. The economic development of these countries . . . has accumulated an enormous mass of explosive material which makes inevitable a desperate fight between them for supremacy in the Pacific. . . . This opposition, concealed for the time being by the Japanese-American alliance directed against Germany, keeps a check on the aggressiveness of Japanese imperialism against Russia. . . . It is possible, of course—and this is something which must not be forgotten—that the groupings of imperialist Powers, no matter how solid they appear, can be disrupted in a few days if the interests of sanctified private property, of the sanctified rights of concessions, etc., so demand. . . . For the present, however, the situation described above is sufficient to explain why our socialist island is capable of preserving itself in the midst of the raging storm. . . .

The situation, however, may change in a few days. . . . The American bourgeoisie, now at odds with Japan, may tomorrow come to an understanding with it because the Japanese bourgeoisie might [otherwise] come to an agreement with Germany. They have [in common] basic interests in partitioning the earth, [in safeguarding] the interests of the landowners, of capital, and in defending what they consider their national dignity and their national interests. . . . That is why the situation in the Far East is so unstable.

The realities of German political life are [as follows]: The majority of the imperialist classes, parties, and groups favor the carrying out of the Brest Peace and, of course, would be glad to make that peace more favorable to themselves and acquire a few more annexations at the expense of Russia. They are forced to this point of view by political and military considerations, as viewed from the standpoint of German national interests. . . . They prefer peace in the East so as to have a free hand in the West. . . . On the other hand, there is the military party, . . . which says: "Force must be used at once, irrespective of consequences.". . . We must be prepared to face a change in conformity with the interests of the extreme military party.

This makes clear how unstable the international situation is . . . , what circumspection, tact, and self-possession are required from the Soviet Government in defining clearly its aim. . . .

I know that there are learned men, men believing themselves very clever, even calling themselves "socialists," who maintain that we should have postponed assuming power until the revolution had broken out in other countries. They do not realize that by talking as they do they renounce revolution and join the bourgeoisie. To wait until the toiling classes bring about the revolution on an international scale is to condemn oneself to a state of inactivity and mere waiting. This is nonsense. The difficulties of revolution are well known. Having started as a spectacular success in one country, revolution may have to go through periods of trial because the final victory is possible only on a world scale and through the united efforts of the workers in all countries. Our task is to exercise tact and caution; we must maneuver and retreat until reinforcements come to our aid. A change to these tactics is inevitable, no matter how they are ridiculed by those who call themselves "revolutionists" but understand nothing about revolution.

I have now finished with the general situation and shall go on to the facts which during the past few days aroused so much alarm and panic and gave the counter-revolutionists an opportunity to resume their work of undermining the Soviet Government.

The Brest-Litovsk Treaty and the general laws and conventions which define the position of neutral countries among belligerent nations constitute the legal framework of all the international relations in which the Soviet Socialist Republic is involved. The conclusion of peace with Finland, the Ukraine, and Turkey was directly implied in the Brest-Litovsk Treaty. Yet with each of these countries . . . we continue to be at war, [a war which is] inspired by their ruling classes. Under the circumstances, the only way out was the temporary breathing-spell which we secured by signing the Brest Peace, a breathing-spell about which much nonsense has been spoken . . . but which for the duration of two months brought very definite results. It enabled the majority of Russian soldiers to return to their homes . . . , to take advantage of the conquests of the revolution, to take over the land, to look around, and to gather new strength for the sacrifices that are ahead of them.

Of course, this temporary breathing-spell appears to be approaching an end now that the situation in Finland, the Ukraine, and Turkey has become critical . . . , and the question of war and peace has merely been postponed. . . . But once more you can see that the final solution [of this question] depends on the outcome of the vacillations of the two hostile groups of imperialist countries—the American [Japanese] conflict in the Far East and the Anglo-German in Western Europe.

The extreme military party of Germany thought that they would move large numbers of troops and obtain bread [in the Ukraine]. But it turned out that they had to overthrow the government. They could do this very easily because the Ukrainian Mensheviks agreed to it. But then they found that the coup d'état led to new gigantic difficulties because it proved necessary to conquer every step in order to get bread and raw materials, without which Germany cannot exist. . . . It is this situation in the Ukraine which inspired the hopes of the Russian counter-revolution.

. . . Russia, unable to reconstruct its army, has suffered and is suffering new losses, . . . new indemnities . . . , open and concealed. The partial armistices between the Russian and German troops [on the Ukrainian front] give little indication as to the general outcome. The question hangs in the air. The same is true in Georgia, where we witness a protracted counter-revolutionary struggle on the part of the government of the Caucasian Mensheviks . . . , who call themselves Social-Democrats. . . . Should the politicians of the Caucasian Seim receive help from German troops . . . the Russian Soviet Republic will face new difficulties, new wars, new dangers. . . .

This is the situation, Comrades, which has come into existence . . . , a situation which gives us new and plain confirmation of the correctness of the line of policy which the Russian Communist Party (Bolshevik), led by its majority, has followed and firmly insisted upon during the past months. We have accumulated an abundance of revolutionary experience and have learned from that experience that it is possible to adopt aggressive tactics when objective conditions allow. . . . However, [for the present] we are forced to a policy of waiting, to a slow gathering of strength. . . . Whoever does not close his eyes, whoever is not blind, knows that we are merely repeating what we have said before and what we have always insisted upon. We are not forgetting the weakness of the Russian working class. It is not our will but historical circumstances—the inheritance of the tsarist régime, the flabbiness of the Russian bourgeoisie—which are largely responsible for the fact that we found ourselves the vanguard of the international proletariat. . . . But we must remain at our post until the arrival of our ally, the international proletariat, for this ally is sure to arrive . . . even though moving much slower than we expected and wished. When we find that because of objective conditions the proletariat is moving too slowly, we shall continue to adhere to a waiting policy, a policy of taking advantage of the conflicts and oppositions between the imperialists, of accumulating strength and holding fast to the Soviet oasis . . . toward which, even now, the eyes of the workers and toilers of all countries are turned. That is why we say that if the extreme war party is able at any moment to overcome one of the imperialist coalitions and to form a new, unexpected imperialist coalition against us, we shall not be able to help it. If they move against us we shall defend ourselves. We shall do all we can, all that our diplomacy is capable of doing, to postpone that moment and to make the brief and unstable breathing-spell which we received in March last longer . . . , until the millions of workers and peasants . . . are ready for the last and decisive struggle.

Since November 7, 1917, we have become defensists. We have won the right to defend the fatherland. We do not defend secret treaties . . . nor [the privilege of being] a great Power. Of Russia there remains nothing but Velikorossiia.[5] . . . We say that the interests of socialism, the interests of world socialism, are

[5] Great Russia.

above national interests, above the interests of the state. We are for the defense of the socialist fatherland . . . , which requires the waging of a merciless war . . . against the bourgeoisie in our own country. This we have already begun and we know that we shall be victorious. What we have is only a small island surrounded by an imperialist world of war, but we have demonstrated what the working class is capable of doing. . . . Because we stand for the defense of the fatherland we say that we need a strong army . . . , but to have a strong army it is necessary that the dictatorship of the proletariat make itself felt not only at the center . . . but all over Russia. . . .

The question of peace with Finland centers on Fort Ino and Murmansk. Fort Ino, which is the bulwark of Petrograd, was among the territorial stipulations when we concluded a treaty with the Finnish workers' government. This government, while claiming all [Finnish] territories, made an exception of Fort Ino on the ground that it was a point of defense of the common interests of the Finnish Socialist Republic and the Russian Socialist Soviet Republic. . . . As was to be expected, the reactionary and counter-revolutionary bourgeoisie of Finland advanced a claim to the fortification. The issue was raised many times and continues to be critical. A source of even greater friction arose in connection with the question of Murmansk. The English and French made claims there because they spent tens of millions [of rubles] to build a port in order to protect their rear in their imperialist war against Germany. They respected neutrality to such an extent that they were ready to use everything which lay unguarded. . . . The English landed a force at Murmansk and we had no way of preventing the landing by force. The result was that we were presented [by the Germans] with a demand which almost has the character of an ultimatum [to the effect] that if we cannot defend our neutrality [the Germans] will fight on our territory. But the worker-peasant army has already been formed . . . and if we are attacked we shall fight the enemy as one man. . . .

Lenin's theses concerning foreign policy were bitterly attacked by the opposition groups in the Central Executive Committee. The Left Socialist-Revolutionists urged the abrogation of the Brest-Litovsk Treaty and the termination of the "breathing spell"; the Right Socialist-Revolutionists advocated the resumption of war on the side of the Allies; the Mensheviks likewise stressed the necessity of fighting against German imperialism but maintained that the achievement of Russia's salvation from foreign perils demanded as prerequisites the reestablishment of the Constituent Assembly and the substitution of a democratic republic for the Communist dictatorship.

ATTACKS ON LENIN'S FOREIGN POLICIES

[From the Proceedings of the Plenary Session of the Central Executive
Committee and the Moscow Soviet, May 14, 1918] [6]

Kogan-Bernstein [Socialist-Revolutionist of the Right] : . . . The speaker from the Sovnarkom has told us some of the old tales . . . about the breathing-spell, the clash of international imperialisms, . . . [and] how it was being used in the interests of the Soviet Republic, which has become a small island. . . . I agree that this island has become very, very small because of the policies inaugurated after the November Revolution, . . . but it is ridiculous to talk about a breathing-spell when German armies are advancing on every front. . . . We are helpless even before the reactionary bourgeoisie of little Finland. How can we utilize the clash of two imperialisms? . . . It would be better to accept the aid of the Allies, of Anglo-Franco-Japanese imperialism. . . . German imperialism, which is penetrating into Russia, . . . forces us to join the Allies . . . and to take the road that thanks to your November counter-revolution was abandoned. . . .

Karelin [7] [Socialist-Revolutionist of the Left] : If some future investigator . . . should attempt to draw a picture of present-day political conditions on the basis of Comrade Lenin's report, he might arrive at the conclusion . . . that the Soviet island fared rather well in the midst of the imperialist storm. We contempo-

[6] *Protokoly zasedanii Vserossiiskogo Tsentralnogo Ispolnitelnogo Komiteta 4-go sozyva*, pp. 277-78.
[7] *Ibid.*, pp. 281-82.

raries, who are able to judge the situation from viewpoints other than Lenin's report, are forced to different conclusions. . . . A sober analysis of the political situation forces the Left S. R.'s to the opinion that the revolution is in a critical condition and that we shall not be saved by the breathing-spell. . . .

It is important to realize that the cause of the present tragic condition of the revolution is a policy arising from fear and cowardice. It is this policy that inevitably leads us to two conclusions in our international orientation. . . . The first conclusion, . . . which one often finds in the newspapers, posits the inevitability of the German orientation. In view of our weakness and the fact that at present we cannot fight we are urged to remain temporarily within the orbit of German influence. The second conclusion, that of Kogan-Bernstein . . . , is [acceptance of] the Anglo-Franco-American influence. . . . The essence of our [Left S. R.'s] policy is that we repudiate any influence. We believe that the revolution is sufficiently strong to have its own orientation. . . . At this critical moment all the forces of the Soviet Republic should be mobilized for struggle. There are only two ways open to us. One is the revolutionary way; the other is the way of shameful retreat, of shameful concession and maneuvering, the way of death. The fight is inevitable . . . and it will be a fight to the finish.

PARTY RESOLUTIONS ON FOREIGN POLICY

[Resolution of the Bolsheviks] [8]

Having heard the report of the President of the Soviet of People's Commissars, the joint session of the Central Executive Committee and the Moscow Soviet fully approves the policy of the Soviet Government. . . .

[Resolution of the Mensheviks] [9]

The feudal imperialist caste of Germany has fully uncovered its plans and has openly joined the Russian counter-revolutionary landlords and capitalists in an effort to destroy the conquests of

---

[8] *Ibid.*, p. 290. The conference adopted this resolution.
[9] *Ibid.*, pp. 290-91.

the democracy. The reactionary coup d'état in the Ukraine is only the beginning of a general campaign of counter-revolutionary forces . . . to establish the dictatorship of the propertied classes with the aid of German bayonets. . . . The reestablishment of Russia's unity and independence, which is inherently connected with the triumph of the principles of political freedom and democracy, will be made possible only by means of a revolutionary-democratic struggle against all external and internal elements of reaction and primarily against German imperialism. It is this German imperialism which at present is leading all counter-revolutionary forces. . . .

The government as now organized . . . is absolutely incapable of handling the difficult task of defending the very foundation of the democratic revolution against . . . reaction and . . . German imperialism. . . . It is therefore necessary to call at once the Constituent Assembly dispersed on January 18. . . . Only the Constituent Assembly is capable of uniting the whole proletariat and the entire democracy in the struggle against Russian and German reaction. . . . It is also necessary . . . (1) to reestablish . . . local self-government . . . ; (2) to restore political and civil liberties; (3) to reject the new German demands . . . ; (4) to arm the whole people.

[Resolution of the Socialist-Revolutionists of the Right] [10]

1. Six months of Bolshevik rule have brought Russia to complete ruin. . . .

2. . . . German armies are penetrating into the interior of Russia and are taking advantage of the civil war, which the Bolsheviks began, to annex from Russia a number of territories. . . .

3. . . . German imperialism has now thrown off the mask of the Brest Peace and is openly at the head of the movement for social and political reaction. It has selected the Ukraine and Finland as its bases and is scheming to turn Velikorossiia into a German colony.

4. Under these difficult conditions the Bolshevik Government . . . has taken a number of provocative steps in relation to Rus-

[10] *Ibid.*, pp. 291-92.

sia's former allies while bowing servilely to the innumerable ultimata of the German conquerors.

5. The interests of the Allied democracies imperatively require
that Russia remain strong, independent, and capable of resisting
German designs in the East. . . .

6. In view of the foregoing . . . the joint session of the All-
Russian Central Executive Committee and of the Moscow Soviet
resolves: (a) To declare void the separate Brest Peace which Germany has been continually violating and to call upon all forces of
the country to resist the German aggressors. (b) To reestablish
the relations with the Allies . . . which the Bolshevik Government has broken off so unconcernedly. . . . (c) To take immediately all necessary steps toward the reestablishment of an all-
national democratic government as represented by the Constituent
Assembly. . . .

The tension caused by Germany's demands in the early
part of May was shortly eased when the Bolsheviks ceded
to Finland the western part of the Murmansk region. To
be sure, the presence of Allied troops in the North of Russia
remained for some time a sore spot in Soviet-German relations. But during the summer months Germany was en-
grossed in the Western front and preferred to leave its
relations with Soviet Russia unchanged. A résumé of these
relations is given in the following reports by Chicherin.

SOVIET-GERMAN RELATIONS

[From Chicherin's Report to the Fifth Congress of Soviets, July 5, 1918] [11]

During the period following the conclusion of the Brest Treaty,
Russia's foreign policy developed along lines different from those
followed during the first few months after the November Revolution. The essential characteristic of our foreign policy at the
end of 1917 and the beginning of 1918 was a revolutionary offensive aiming at the expected world revolution, for which the
Russian November Revolution was intended to be a signal. Ignor-

[11] *Izvestiia*, No. 138, July 5, 1918, p. 6.

ing the governments, it appealed to the revolutionary proletariat of all countries . . . in the hope of arousing it to an international revolutionary struggle against imperialism and capitalism.

When the failure of the proletariat of other countries to lend its immediate support brought about the defeat of revolutionary Russia by the armies of German and Austrian imperialism and led to the occupation of Finland, the Ukraine, the Baltic Provinces, Poland, Lithuania, and White Russia by the armed forces of Germany and Austria-Hungary, the foreign policies of Soviet Russia had to assume a radically new form. During the last four months we were compelled to adopt a waiting policy, to avoid the dangers which menaced us from all sides, and to gain as much time as possible in order to allow the growing proletarian movement in other countries to mature and to enable the new political and social relationships established by the Soviet Government to take firmer root among the masses of the Russian people. . . .

This policy of delay was made possible not only by the diversity of interests of the two coalitions but also by the conflict . . . within the ranks of each imperialist group. The struggle on the Western front engaged the forces of the two coalitions to such an extent that neither dared to strike a final blow at Russia. Within each imperialist group there are those who think of future . . . economic relations with Russia. . . . In place of plunder they would like a policy of bargaining for concessions and economic privileges. . . . [Again], the hope of drawing Russia into the war, now that she is regaining her military strength, plays a part in the calculations of both coalitions. . . .

The period immediately following the signing of the Brest Treaty is characterized by the fact that the German offensive on the whole Eastern front did not stop at the line of demarcation fixed by the treaty. Finland and the Ukraine were cleared of Soviet troops, although the peoples in these regions continued a desperate struggle. During this time the Entente Powers withdrew entirely their military support but remained in control . . . of the points at which the evacuation of their armed forces was to take place. The first turning-point in the direction of peaceful relations between Russian and the Central Empires was the arrival of the German representative, Count von Mirbach, at Moscow on April 23, 1918, and of the Russian representative, Comrade

Joffee, at Berlin on April 20, 1918. The Japanese landing at Vladivostok on April 5 must be considered as an unfavorable fact in relation to the former allies. However, assurances soon followed . . . that this was not an attempt to interfere in Russia's internal affairs. . . . [On the whole] the representatives of the Entente Powers adhered to a more careful policy toward Russia; the definitely friendly attitude of the United States of North America must be emphasized in particular.

. . . After having occupied the whole of Finland and the Ukraine, German-Austrian armies began to invade Soviet territory and encountered Soviet troops with the result that there were continuous skirmishes along the whole frontier. At that time Petrograd was directly menaced and White Guards were entering the Murmansk region. . . . At the same time the German army in the Ukraine continued its advance into Kursk and Voronezh gubernias, the Donetz Basin, and the Don. In the South the Germans occupied the Crimea . . . and made a landing at Poti in the Caucasus, and Turkish troops began to move into the interior of the Caucasus in the direction of Baku. This critical period was brought to a conclusion on the Finnish frontier by an agreement between the Russian and the German Governments concerning a basis for negotiations between Russia and Finland. The beginning of peace negotiations between Russia and the Hetman Government resulted in the gradual cessation of military activities on the Ukrainian front. . . .

[From Chicherin's Report to the Seventh Congress of Soviets, November 6, 1919] [12]

. . . On June 12 there was concluded with the Ukraine a treaty providing for an armistice, reciprocal repatriation, and trade relations. The whole of May was an extremely unsettled time because of the gradual movements to the north and northeast, partly by German troops and partly by irregular bands supported by the Germans. But the main blows of the Germans at this time were aimed at the southeast, at Bataisk and further points in the direction of the grain-producing Kuban, while the Turkish troops, dis-

[12] *Ibid.*, No. 249, November 6, 1919, p. 2.

regarding the treaties, were advancing in the Caucasus and supporting there the fictitious counter-revolutionary governments.

Considerable progress toward the stabilization of relations with Germany resulted from the exchange of notes between Moscow and Berlin which took place about the end of May and the beginning of June, with regard to both the question of the return of our warships from Novorossiisk to Sevastopol and that of a definite settlement of the boundary line. . . .

The excessive economic claims of the German representative in Moscow and the attempts of the Russian bourgeoisie, hiding behind him, to win back from the Soviet Government their expropriated wealth, demanded the speediest conclusion of the economic agreements provided for by the Brest Treaty. . . .

After the assassination of Mirbach [13] by the Socialist-Revolutionists of the Left on July 6 it so happened that German imperialism had its hands too full to try to take advantage of the splendid pretext for crushing Soviet Russia. But the German Government could argue the lack of safety for its embassy at Moscow; this in fact it did, and on July 14 it demanded permission to send to Moscow a battalion of German troops. It was the most critical moment of our relations with German imperialism. . . . Confronted with our resolute refusal, the German Government immediately gave in. An exchange of notes in the second half of July resulted in the following agreement: the auxiliary staff of the German Embassy and of the various German commissions was increased to three hundred persons, and additional forces were to come to Moscow in groups of thirty, without arms and without German uniforms.[14] . . . On July 28 the new German ambassador, Helfferich, one of the most prominent leaders in Berlin economic circles, arrived at Moscow. His appointment showed clearly the desire of Germany to strengthen its economic relations with Soviet

---

[13] *Ibid.*, No. 250, November 7, 1919, p. 3. The events which precipitated the assassination of Mirbach are treated in a subsequent chapter.

[14] In his report to the Central Executive Committee of September 2, 1918, Chicherin stated that during the latter part of July three hundred German soldiers were brought to Moscow to guard the German embassy. D. C. Poole, American Consul General at Moscow, asserted that he approached Chicherin at the time to ascertain the truth of the reports that there were German troops in Moscow, and that he "was given the most solemn assurances that [the reports] were quite unfounded." (*U. S. Foreign Relations, 1918, Russia,* I, 581.)

Russia. . . . On August 7 he left Moscow . . . and the German Embassy departed . . . to Pskov, in the occupied territory. . . .

Despite the weakening of German military power in the East, the pressure upon us was still sufficiently great to demand energetic activity on our part to overcome it. During this period an attempt was made to settle our relations with Finland. . . .

Germany demanded in a note dated May 8 that we surrender [Fort] Ino to Finland. . . . In the negotiations which followed we agreed under pressure from Germany to cede to Finland the western part of the Murmansk region, in exchange for which we were to retain Fort Ino, and Finland was to turn over to us the Raivola district in Vyborg Gubernia. . . . On August 3 a Russo-Finnish conference opened at Berlin. The Finnish representatives at the conference revealed the most unbridled appetites, desiring to annex the whole Kola peninsula and Karelia as far as the White Sea. It became clear that the negotiations were hopeless, and they were suspended. . . .

In August . . . the labors of the "Political Commission" and the "Economic Commission" were concluded by the three supplementary treaties of August 27. These fixed the amounts of our payments on various obligations to Germany, . . . assumed because of the losses inflicted on German nationals by our acts of nationalization up to July 1, at one and a half billion marks in gold and bank notes, payable in five instalments, one billion marks in commodities, and a loan of two and a half billion marks in Germany.[15] Simultaneously with our payment of these amounts Germany was to evacuate White Russia. . . . Germany obligated itself to evacuate a part of the Donetz Basin and Rostov. . . . The treaty acknowledged as a fact the recognition by Germany of Georgia's independence. Baku was recognized as belonging to us, and we bound ourselves to deliver a part of the naphtha [of Baku] to Germany. We were to receive a part of the coal from the Donetz.

---

[15] Of the total of six billion marks which the Bolsheviks undertook to pay to Germany, two and a half billions were to be met "by handing over securities of a loan at 6 per cent . . . with a sinking fund of one-half per cent, which will be taken up in Germany by the Prussian Government." As security for the loan there were to be assigned as pledges "specific national resources, in particular the rental dues for certain economic concessions to be granted to Germans." (Financial clause of the Supplementary Treaty of August 27, 1918, Article 3, Section 3. Quoted in *ibid.*, p. 605.)

We declared that in view of the de facto situation we recognized the end of Russia's sovereignty in Esthonia. We were assured an outlet to the sea through Reval, Riga, and Windau.

During this period strange relations were formed with Turkey. Germany pretended to be powerless to control Turkey. From the information in our possession we cannot tell to what degree certain elements in the German Government supported Turkey's campaign against Baku, but the fact remains that the capture of Baku by the Turks violated Germany's treaty with us. . . .

During the gradual advance of Nuri Pasha's army toward Baku, the German Government replied to all the protests of Comrade Joffe by presenting him telegrams from the German General Kress, from Tiflis, and from the Turkish Government which denied the very fact of a Turkish campaign. . . . After the capture of Baku by the Turks on September 16 we demanded its immediate evacuation. . . . To this demand . . . the Turkish Government did not agree, and on September 20 we notified Turkey that we considered the Brest Treaty abrogated by her and no longer in effect between Turkey and Russia.

We fulfilled correctly [16] our obligations toward Germany under the agreements of August 27, and the first payments in gold were made by us at the required time.[17] . . . [However] every day showed an ever sharper baiting of the Bolsheviks in the German press. The German Government began to shower us with complaints against our alleged violation of the second paragraph of the Brest Treaty, which prohibited each government from carrying on propaganda against the institutions of the other. . . . At this time there took place the first concerted diplomatic step of both imperialistic coalitions against the proletarian revolution. When on September 3 all the local foreign representatives at Petrograd visited Comrade Zinoviev to protest against the "Red Terror"—a protest which was officially confirmed in the note of

[16] *Izvestiia*, No. 251, November 9, 1919, p. 2.

[17] Apropos of this payment General Hoffman made the following entry in his diary: "September 11. . . . Yesterday the first instalment of the Russian indemnity—gold and paper—reached Orsha . . . and was taken over by the Reichsbank. The Bolsheviks are clever and know how to touch us. Now that they have begun to pay, the Foreign Office and the Reichstag are, of course, strongly for supporting the Bolsheviks, without regard to what the future may bring." (*War Diaries and Other Papers*, I, 236.)

September 5 of the Swiss representative, Odier—the German Consul General, Breiter, participated with other representatives in this demonstrative protest. But the days of German imperialism were drawing to a close. . . . On October 3 the All-Russian Central Executive Committee, in reply to a letter from Comrade Lenin, made the epoch-making declaration which stirred the whole world. In view of the expected attack of Anglo-French imperialism on the German working class after its liberation, [the All-Russian Central Executive Committee] promised its assistance [to the German workers]. . . . The policy of mutual aid of the revolutionary workers' states against attack on them by foreign imperialism has thus been given official international expression. . . . The rising revolutionary wave in Germany gradually forced the technical diplomatic work into the background. On November 5, three days before the German Revolution . . . , and after the vaudeville incident with our trunk, which quite opportunely broke at the Berlin railway station and disclosed leaflets that we had never put there, our Embassy, including the different commissions, was expelled from Germany . . . , and all German representatives . . . were recalled from Russia.

B. THE BOLSHEVIKS AND THE ALLIES

While in the early summer of 1918 the relations between the Soviet Government and the Central Powers were improving, Soviet-Allied relations were at that time growing steadily worse. Already the conflict with the Czechoslovaks in May had embittered the Bolsheviks against the Allies. But the Bolsheviks showed no open hostility until June, when the British undertook an extensive occupation of the North of Russia.

Early in March 1918, when German troops began to appear on Finnish territory and to threaten the Murmansk region, the British landed a small force at the port of Murmansk. The British force was shortly joined by French and American marines and a detachment of Serbian and Czechoslovak soldiers. While not objecting to the presence of Allied troops in the North, the Moscow Bolsheviks demanded, through a special emissary, Natsarenus, formal recognition of the Soviet Government by the Allied Powers. At the same time Trotsky discussed with Allied military representatives at Moscow a project of transferring the Czechoslovaks from the Ukraine to Murmansk as part of a general plan of Allied-Soviet military cooperation against Germany.[18] But Allied recognition was not forthcoming, and the Germans protested against the presence of Allied troops on Russian territory. Thus, when the clash with the Czechoslovaks occurred the Bolsheviks decided to contest the stay of the Allied forces at Murmansk.

On June 7 Lenin sent orders to the Murmansk Soviet to oppose the Allied occupation of the Murmansk region. But the Murmansk Soviet was not in complete sympathy with Bolshevik foreign policies; and when the issue was raised of obeying the Moscow Sovnarkom or of entering into a separate understanding with the Allies, the majority favored the latter course.[19] Toward the end of June an additional British force landed at Murmansk. While Chicherin protested against the British descent,[20] the Murmansk Soviet not only offered no opposition to it but on June 30 adopted a resolution approving cooperation with the Allies.

THE MURMANSK SOVIET APPROVES COOPERATION WITH THE ALLIED FORCES
[Resolution of June 30, 1918] [21]

1. The demands of Lenin and Trotsky . . . that the Allies be expelled from here and that we enter a protest against their presence are not to be obeyed.

---

[18] See pp. 76-77, above.

[19] M. Levidov, *K istorii soiuznoi interventsii v Rossii*, pp. 98-115; M. Kedrov, *Bez bolshevistskogo rukovodstva*, pp. 104-22; I. Mintz, *Angliiskaia interventsiia i severnaia kontrrevoliutsiia*, pp. 42-44.

[20] *Russian-American Relations*, p. 227.   [21] Kedrov, *op. cit.*, p. 125.

2. The Allies must remain here to help local Russian authorities—the District Soviet—in defending the region against Germano-Finns. . . .

3. The Murmansk District Soviet is the supreme authority of the region. . . . The Allies must not interfere in our internal affairs.

4. In order to give a precise and definite character to the relations between the District Soviet and the Allies, the Presidium . . . is authorized to begin negotiations with the Allies at once for the purpose of arriving at a specific . . . agreement . . . defining the rights and obligations of the District Soviet and the Allies.

The resolution of the Murmansk Soviet was telegraphed to the Sovnarkom, and Chicherin, in a last effort to win over the recalcitrant Soviet, had the following conversation with Yurev, its chairman.

ATTEMPT TO WIN OVER THE MURMANSK SOVIET

[Direct-Wire Conversation between Chicherin and Yurev, Chairman of the Murmansk Soviet, Midnight, July 1, 1918] [22]

[Chicherin:] Comrade Lenin refuses to talk with you. Those who hold the point of view set forth in your telegram, which we have just received, will be denounced as traitors to the revolution and Soviet Russia. In the struggle against both imperialist coalitions the Soviet army will do its duty to the very end. . . . We shall fight with all our power against any imperialist invasion, whether German or Anglo-French. Soviet Russia can expect no . . . aid from world capitalism and our class enemies. . . . We did not call the English to our territory . . . and considered their stay at Murmansk as temporary. . . . We reject the aid of the Germano-Finns and likewise the aid of the Anglo-French. . . .

Yurev: Comrade, has not life taught you to view things soberly? You constantly utter beautiful phrases but not once have you told how to go about realizing them. Russia has been reduced to a mere shadow as a result of these phrases. . . . The Germans

[22] *Ibid.*, pp. 130-32.

are strangling us and you go on hoping that they will become magnanimous. If you know a way out of our condition please tell it to us and the toiling people will follow you. I do not believe that the Soviet Government is to be blamed for everything. It is all the fault of certain individuals who undertook a job for which they were not fitted and are leading the people to ruin.

Chicherin: Look at the Ukrainian toilers rising against the imperialist plunderers. The Czechoslovak outrages should have taught you the lesson that Anglo-French imperialism, in the same way as German imperialism, will bring ruin to the revolution and slavery to the toilers. . . . Revolutionary troops are already on their way to Murmansk to defend Soviet territory against any invasion. . . . We know that Anglo-French imperialism wishes to extend its hand from Murmansk, Archangel, and Vladivostok to the Czechoslovaks, the White Guards, and Russian reactionaries. . . . Your duty is to protest against the invasion [of Murmansk], to make no agreements with the imperialist plunderers, . . . and to defend Soviet Russia.

Yurev: . . . Can you supply the region with the food which we are now lacking and send us a force sufficient to carry out your instructions . . . ? If not, there is no need of lecturing us. . . . We ourselves know that the Germans and the Allies are imperialists, but of two evils we have chosen the lesser. . . .

When Chicherin's effort failed, the Sovnarkom outlawed the chairman of the Murmansk Soviet and protested against the British landing. But the Murmansk Soviet continued negotiations with the Allied commanders and on July 6 signed an agreement which opened the Murmansk region to Allied penetration.[23]

THE CHAIRMAN OF THE MURMANSK SOVIET DECLARED AN ENEMY OF THE PEOPLE

[Announcement of the Sovnarkom, July 1, 1918] [24]

The chairman of the Murmansk Soviet, who went over to the Anglo-French imperialists and is taking part in hostilities against

---

[23] The agreement is given in *U. S. Foreign Relations, 1918, Russia,* II, 493-95.
[24] *Rannee Utro,* No. 121, July 2, 1918, p. 1.

the Soviet Republic, is hereby declared an enemy of the people and is placed outside the law.

LENIN

President of the Soviet of People's Commissars

TROTSKY

People's Commissar of War and the Navy

MEASURES TO OPPOSE THE MURMANSK LANDING

[Trotsky's Order, July 1, 1918] [25]

Notwithstanding the protest of the Commissar of Foreign Affairs, a foreign landing has been made at Murmansk. I have been ordered by the Soviet of People's Commissars to take the necessary measures to protect the White Sea coast from the foreign imperialists. In the fulfillment of this duty I declare:

1. Any aid, direct or indirect, given to the foreign force which is making its way into the Soviet Republic will be regarded as treason to the state, punishable by martial law.

2. The movement of war prisoners (armed or unarmed, companies or individuals) toward Murmansk or Archangel is unconditionally forbidden. Violation of this order is punishable by martial law.

3. No one, Russian or foreigner, can go to the White Sea coast without the permission of the nearest district war commissar.

. . .

THE SOVNARKOM PROTESTS AGAINST BRITISH INTERVENTION

[Chicherin to Lockhart, July 12, 1918] [26]

Despite repeated assurances by the Government of Great Britain that the landing of British troops in Murmansk is not an act of hostility to the Russian Soviet Republic, the Government of Great Britain has not only failed to comply with our elementary demand for the removal of troops from Soviet territory but has moved its detachments, together with French and Serbian auxiliary forces, south to the interior. Soviet officials are being arrested and some-

[25] *Ibid.*   [26] *Izvestiia*, No. 146, July 13, 1918, p. 4.

times even shot; railway guards are being disarmed, while the railroads and telegraph are brought under British control. After occupying Kem and Soroki, the British troops moved farther east and took Sumsky-Possad, which is on the way to Onega. Such acts of the British troops can only be considered an invasion of the Russian Soviet Republic. No other motive can explain the movement of the British troops eastward.

The People's Commissariat of Foreign Affairs expresses its most solemn protest against this unjustified aggression upon Soviet Russia. We have stated and are stating once more that Soviet troops will do everything possible to protect Russian territory and will meet foreign invasion with the most determined resistance. We call your attention especially to the indignation of the broad masses of Russia which is caused by the unprovoked British invasion, and to the effects which this feeling will have upon the people in the future.

CHICHERIN

People's Commissar of Foreign Affairs

While the British forces were extending their area of occupation along the Murmansk railway, Allied representatives in Russia encouraged anti-Bolshevik organizations to overthrow the Soviet Government.[27] One of these organizations started uprisings in a number of cities near Moscow.[28] Suspecting that the Allied representatives were instigating these uprisings, the Bolsheviks decided to transfer the Entente Diplomatic Corps from Vologda to Moscow.

On July 10 Ambassador Francis received an urgent message from Chicherin inviting the Allied ambassadors to move to Moscow. The alleged reason for the invitation was the fear of the Soviet Government that it might not be in a position to give the ambassadors adequate protection in Vologda.[29] After consultation with his colleagues, Francis

[27] Lockhart, op. cit., pp. 288-89.
[28] An account of these is given in Chapter IV below.
[29] U. S. Foreign Relations, 1918, Russia, I, 618; David Francis, Russia from the American Embassy, pp. 245-46.

replied that the ambassadors did not consider themselves to be in danger and had decided not to comply with Chicherin's request.

The next day Karl Radek, an official of the Commissariat of Foreign Affairs, arrived at Vologda to arrange for the removal of the Diplomatic Corps to Moscow. Having been informed by Francis that the Allied representatives had resolved not to accept Chicherin's invitation, he placed military guards around the embassies on July 13 and reported to Chicherin that he proposed to apply to the ambassadors "a moral siege of gentle reprisals such as isolating them from their entourage, limiting their supplies, stopping all persons desiring [to see] them, etc." [30]

The "moral siege" continued for several days but the ambassadors stood firm in their resolution not to go to Moscow.

On July 17 a messenger arrived from General Poole, the commander of the British forces at Murmansk, stating that the British intended to occupy Archangel early in August, and, since the presence of the Allied ambassadors at Vologda might complicate General Poole's plans, he advised that the ambassadors leave for Archangel as soon as possible. When on July 23 a second "urgent" message arrived from Chicherin pressing the Diplomatic Corps to come to Moscow, the ambassadors decided to leave for Archangel.[31] After some delay in securing a locomotive the Diplomatic Corps left Vologda on July 25. A few days later (August 2) the British landed a force at Archangel.

The departure of the Allied ambassadors from Vologda was interpreted by the Bolsheviks as a prelude to intervention if not a beginning of open hostilities on the part of

[30] *U. S. Foreign Relations, 1918, Russia,* I, 622.
[31] Francis, *op. cit.,* pp. 251-53; *U. S. Foreign Relations, 1918, Russia,* I, 636-40.

the Entente. On July 29, in the course of a speech before the joint session of the Central Executive Committee, the Moscow Soviet, and representatives of trade unions and factory-shop committees, Lenin declared that Soviet Russia was now in a state of war with "Anglo-French imperialism." He accused the Allies of having made an agreement with the Russian bourgeoisie to destroy the Soviet Government and urged the workers to strain every effort in the fight against counter-revolution.[32] On the motion of the Bolsheviks the assembly passed a resolution declaring the socialist fatherland in danger.

THE SOCIALIST FATHERLAND DECLARED IN DANGER

[Resolution of the Central Executive Committee, July 29, 1918] [33]

The joint session of the All-Russian Central Executive Committee of Soviets, the Moscow Soviet of Deputies, the Trade Unions, and the Factory-Shop Committees, having heard the reports of the representatives of the central Soviet Government, resolves:

1. To declare the socialist fatherland in danger.

2. To subordinate the work of all soviet and other workers' organizations to the basic tasks of the present moment: the repulsion of the attack of the Czechoslovaks and . . . the collection of grain.

4. To increase surveillance over the bourgeoisie, which is everywhere siding with counter-revolutionists. The Soviet Government must safeguard its rear by watching the bourgeoisie and subjecting it to mass terror.

5. With this in view the joint session considers it imperative to transfer responsible workers from soviet and trade-union organizations to military and food institutions. . . .

7. Mass campaign for bread, mass military training, mass arming of workers, the straining of all efforts in the fight against the

[32] Lenin, *Sochineniia*, XXIII, 163.
[33] *Piatyi sozyv Vserossiiskogo Tsentralnogo Ispolnitelnogo Komiteta Sovetov Rabochikh, Krestianskikh, Kazachikh i Krasnoarmeiskikh Deputatov*, pp. 8-9.

counter-revolutionary bourgeoisie with the slogan "Victory or death"—these are our common principles!

On July 30, Allied diplomatic representatives called on Chicherin and inquired whether Lenin's statement in the Central Executive Committee was to be construed as a formal declaration of war entailing a rupture of diplomatic relations and a departure of the Allied representatives from Russia. Chicherin replied that Lenin's statement need not be so construed, that thus far only a state of emergency had been declared, and that the Soviet Government desired the diplomatic representatives to remain in Russia.[34] But the antagonism of the Bolsheviks to the Allied diplomats and governments was fully expressed in an appeal addressed on August 1 to the "toiling masses" of France, England, America, Italy, and Japan.

TO THE TOILING MASSES OF FRANCE, ENGLAND, AMERICA, ITALY, AND JAPAN

[Appeal of the Sovnarkom, August 1, 1918] [35]

Workers!

Like a vicious dog loosed from its chain, the whole capitalist press of your countries howls for the "intervention" of your governments in Russian affairs and shrieks with hoarse voice: "Now or never!" But even at this moment, when these hirelings of your exploiters have thrown off their masks and shout openly of a campaign against the workers and peasants of Russia, even at this moment they lie without conscience and trick you without shame. For at the very moment when they threaten "intervention" in Russian affairs they are already carrying on military operations against the workers and peasants of Russia. The Anglo-French bandits are already shooting Soviet workers on the Murmansk Railway, which they have seized. In the Urals they are breaking

---

[34] *U. S. Foreign Relations, 1918, Russia,* I, 648-49.

[35] Kliuchnikov i Sabanin, *Mezhdunarodnaia politika noveishego vremeni,* II, 158-61.

up workers' soviets and having their representatives shot by Czechoslovak detachments, which are supported with the money of
the French people and are led by French officers. By order of
your governments they are cutting off the Russian people from
bread in order to force the workers and peasants to put their necks
once more in the noose of the Paris and London stock exchanges.
This open attack of Anglo-French capital on the workers of Russia is merely the culmination of an eight-month underground fight
against Soviet Russia. On the first day after the November Revolution . . . , when the Russian workers and peasants declared
that they would no longer shed either their own or other peoples'
blood in the interests of capital . . . , when they appealed to you
to follow their example and to have done with the international
slaughter, to have done with exploitation, at that very moment
your exploiters pledged themselves to make an end of this country,
the working class of which had dared for the first time in the history of humanity to throw off the yoke of capitalism and the noose
of war. Your governments supported the Ukrainian Rada against
the workers and peasants of Russia, the Rada which sold itself to
German imperialism and summoned German bayonets to its aid
against Ukrainian peasants and workers; they supported the Roumanian oligarchy, that same oligarchy which, by attacks on our
Southwestern front, helped to destroy Russia's defensive power.
Their agents bought for ready cash that same General Krasnov
who now, hand in hand with German soldiery, is trying to cut off
Russia from the coal of the Donetz and from the bread of the
Kuban in order to make her the defenseless victim of German and
Russian capital. They gave both money and moral support to the
Socialist-Revolutionists of the Right, the party which betrayed the
revolution and rose in arms against the authority of the workers
and peasants.

But when they saw that all their efforts had proved unsuccessful, when it became apparent that hired bandits were an insufficient force, they decided to sacrifice your blood as well and are
now undertaking an open attack on Russia. . . . You who are
shedding your blood in the interests of capital on the Marne and
the Aisne, in the Balkans, Syria, and Mesopotamia, you are also
to die in the snows of Northern Finland and in the Ural Mountains. In the interests of capital you are to be the executioners of

the Russian workers' revolution. To cover up this crusade against
the Russian workers' revolution your capitalists tell you that this
crusade is undertaken not against the Russian Revolution but . . .
against German imperialism, to which we are supposed to have
sold ourselves. The falsity and hypocrisy of this statement will be
clear to each one of you if you will only consider the following
facts:

1. We were forced to sign the Brest Peace, which dismem-
bered Russia, only because your governments, fully aware of the
fact that Russia was not in a condition to fight any longer, would
not agree to international peace negotiations, in which their
strength would have saved Russia and given you an honorable
peace. It is not Russia, which for three and a half years has been
bleeding to death, that has sold your cause; it is your own governments, which have thrown Russia under the heel of German
imperialism.

2. When we were forced to conclude the Brest Peace . . . and
the agents of your governments kept trying to drag us into the
war again, arguing that Germany would not allow us to remain at
peace with her, our press replied to them: "If Germany violates
the peace . . . , if she raises her hand against the Russian Revolution, we shall defend ourselves; if the Allies wish to help us in
our sacred work of defense, let them help us to restore our railways, to organize our economy." . . . But the Allies did not
respond to these advances. They thought only of how to squeeze
from us the interest on the old loans which French capital had
lent to tsarism in order to drag it into the war—loans which the
Russian people paid back long ago with a sea of blood and mountains of corpses.

3. The Allies have not only failed to give us help in reestablishing our power of defense but . . . have tried in all ways to
destroy that power by increasing our internal disorder and cutting
us off from our last reserves of bread.

4. The Allies warned us that the Germans would seize the Siberian and Murmansk railways. . . . In the end, however, these
lines were seized not by the Germans . . . but by our noble allies.
. . .

All that the press of your capitalists . . . says in defense of the barbarous attack on Russia is sheer hypocrisy. . . . They have other objectives in undertaking the campaign against Russia. . . . Their first aim is to seize as much Russian territory as possible in order to insure . . . the payment of interest on loans of French and English capital. Their second aim is to crush the workers' revolution lest it inspire you . . . to throw off the yoke of capitalism. Their third aim is to create a new Eastern front in order to divert Germans from the Western front to Russian territory.

The agents of your capitalists tell you that in this way they will lessen the pressure of the German hordes on you and hasten the moment of victory over German imperialism. They lie. They could not defeat Germany when a large Russian army was in the field, giving the Allies numerical superiority; they are less in a position to conquer on the field of battle now when the Russian army is just being created. German imperialism can be defeated only when the imperialism of all countries is defeated by the united attack of the world proletariat, . . . and the international civil war of the exploited against their exploiters will put an end to every kind of injustice, social as well as national. . . .

We have endured too long the mockery of Soviet Russia by the representatives of Allied imperialism. We have allowed those who licked the boots of tsarism to remain in Russia, although they did not recognize the government of the workers. We have not resorted to repressive measures against them, although the hand of their military missions was in every counter-revolutionary plot directed against us. Even now, when French officers are leading the Czechoslovaks and the Murmansk outrages have begun, even now we do not protest . . . against the presence of your diplomats in the territory of Soviet Russia, which they have not recognized. We have demanded only their removal from Vologda to Moscow, in order that we might protect them from attacks by people whom their crimes have profoundly stirred. . . . Even now, after the departure of the Allied envoys, not a single hair shall fall from the heads of those of your peaceful compatriots living among us who obey the laws of the Worker-Peasant Republic. . . .

We are convinced that every measure taken against those who are hatching plots on Russian soil against the Russian Revolution will meet with your sincere sympathy because these plots are directed against us. Forced to fight against Allied capitalism, which wishes to add new chains to those laid on us by German imperialism, we address ourselves to you with the appeal:

Long live the solidarity of the workers of the world!

Long live the solidarity of the proletariat of France, England, America, Italy, and Russia!

Down with the bandits of international imperialism! Long live the International Revolution!

Long live peace among nations!

On August 2 the expected intervention came. The British landed a force at Archangel, and for several days Moscow was the prey of rumor and alarm.[36] It was believed that the Allies had landed in strong force and would soon capture Moscow. According to Lockhart, the Bolsheviks "lost their heads and, in despair, began to pack their archives."[37] A number of years later, Chicherin told Louis Fischer that during those critical days the Bolsheviks approached the German Ambassador, Helfferich, with a proposal that the Germans send an army into Russia to oppose the Allied advance from Archangel. But Helfferich was not encouraging and left Moscow on August 6.[38]

The attitude of the Bolsheviks toward the Allies now became one of active hostility. On August 5 the Cheka rounded up as many British and French nationals as it could lay hands on (about two hundred) and put them in jail. On the same day the consular buildings of France and Great Britain were raided and a number of officials placed under arrest.[39] In a few days, however, it became known that the British troops at Archangel were only a small force transferred from Murmansk and therefore insufficient for

[36] The events at Archangel in connection with this landing are considered in Chapter VI, pp. 304-14.

[37] Lockhart, *op. cit.*, p. 306.

[38] Fischer, *The Soviets in World Affairs*, I, 128.

[39] *U. S. Foreign Relations, 1918, Russia*, I, 651-52.

large-scale operations against the Bolsheviks. While this fact relieved the Soviets of menace from the north, it did not remove the danger from other quarters. During August the Bolsheviks were seriously threatened from the east, where their Socialist-Revolutionist opponents, aided by the Czechoslovaks, gained control of a considerable territory in the middle Volga region, captured Kazan on August 7, and thus acquired a position favorable to an attack on Nizhny-Novgorod and Moscow.[40] At the same time the Allied and Associated Powers openly declared their intention of intervening in Russia and began to land their troops at the Russian port of Vladivostok.

Although not accompanied by a formal declaration of war, this landing ánd the ensuing hostilities endangered the Allied diplomatic and military representatives, who still remained in Central Russia. Negotiations for their departure began early in August and lasted throughout that month; but before permitting their departure the Bolsheviks formally charged a number of Allied representatives with conspiring to overthrow the Soviet Government.

On August 30 Uritsky, the head of the Petrograd Committee to Fight Counter-Revolution, known as the Cheka, was killed, and an attempt was made on the life of Lenin.[41] On the next day the British embassy at Petrograd was raided by the Cheka, and a British naval officer and one Cheka agent were killed during the raid. On September 1 Lockhart, the unofficial British representative in Soviet Russia, was arrested in Moscow and brought to the Cheka headquarters. There Lockhart was questioned about the attempt on Lenin's life, but he refused to answer any questions. After a few hours Lockhart was released, but he was rearrested several days later and imprisoned for almost a

[40] See Chapter VI, pp. 287-92, below.   [41] See Chapter V, pp. 236-38, below.

month. The alleged reasons for Lockhart's arrest, as well as for the raid on the British embassy, are given in Soviet official statements quoted below.

ACCUSATIONS AGAINST ALLIED DIPLOMATIC REPRESENTATIVES

[Announcement of the Sovnarkom, September 2, 1918] [42]

Today, September 2, there has been brought to an end a conspiracy which was planned by Anglo-French diplomats, at the head of which were the chief of the British Mission, Lockhart, the French consul, Grenard, the French general, Lavergne, and others. The purpose of the conspiracy was, by bribing Soviet troops, to seize the Soviet of People's Commissars and proclaim a military dictatorship in Moscow.

The entire organization, which was built up in strict secrecy and used bribery and forged documents, has now been exposed.

Among other things we found instructions to publish, in case the coup d'état succeeded, forged secret correspondence alleged to have passed between the Russian and German Governments; forged treaties were also to be produced for the purpose of creating sentiment in favor of resuming war with Germany.

The conspirators were acting under cover of diplomatic immunity and with certificates issued with the personal signature of the chief of the British Mission in Moscow, Mr. Lockhart. Several copies of these certificates are at present in the hands of the Cheka.

It has been established that in the past week and a half there passed through the hands of one of Lockhart's agents alone, the British Lieutenant Reilly, 1,200,000 rubles for bribery.

The conspiracy was disclosed thanks to the reliability of the Soviet army officers whom the conspirators offered bribes.

At the secret headquarters of the conspirators an Englishman was arrested. When brought to the Cheka he said that he was the British diplomatic representative, Lockhart. After the identity

[42] *Izvestiia*, No. 189, September 3, 1918, p. 3.

6

of the arrested Lockhart had been established he was immediately released.[43]

The investigation is being carried on energetically.

THE RAID ON THE BRITISH EMBASSY AT PETROGRAD
[Bolshevik Statement, September 5, 1918] [44]

Unprecedented and monstrous crimes are being perpetrated in our land. The English and French bourgeoisie, which prides itself on pacific democratic aspirations, has undertaken the task of restoring monarchy in Russia. The agents of French and English capital, including the official representatives of the English and French Governments, have entered into close contact with tsarist generals . . . , the Cadet party—those enemies of the people—, and the traitorous Socialist-Revolutionists and Mensheviks. . . . The Anglo-French capitalists, through hired assassins, have plotted a number of terroristic acts against the representatives of the workers' government. . . . The money bags of the English and French are being used to bribe various scoundrels. The English and French are the real murderers of Volodarsky and Uritsky and the organizers of the attempts on the lives of Lenin and Zinoviev.

According to very reliable information received by us, official

---

[43] Lockhart gives a different account of the circumstances of his arrest. He states that a group of Cheka agents broke into his apartment about 3:30 A. M. on September 1 and ordered him to come with them to the Cheka headquarters. (Lockhart, *op. cit.,* pp. 314-15.) Lockhart ridicules the charges which the Bolsheviks made against him, characterizing them as "Arabian Nights tales." He writes that on August 15 he was visited by two Lettish officers, one bearing a letter of introduction from Captain Cromie of the British Embassy at Petrograd, the other presenting himself as a colonel of the Lettish troops which had been supporting the Bolsheviks. The latter declared that the Letts were not willing to fight for the Bolsheviks indefinitely, that their present ambition was to return to their own country, and that since the fate of their country now depended upon the Allies, they would not be willing to fight the Allied forces at Archangel if ordered to do so by the Bolsheviks. He requested that Lockhart arrange matters with General Poole, commander of the Allied troops at Archangel, so that the Letts would not be shot down but would be permitted to surrender. Lockhart asserts that he made no commitment to the two Letts but merely gave them a letter requesting that they be permitted to pass through the British lines to consult with General Poole. (*Ibid.,* pp. 311-13.)

[44] *Izvestiia,* No. 191, September 5, 1918, p. 3. The Russian text of the statement carries the title: "An Appeal to the Civilized World."

representatives of England intend to blow up railroad bridges . . .
and cut us off completely from the bread supply coming from
Perm and Viatka. They plan to cause explosions in our factories
and shops, to wreck trains, and have already perpetrated a number
of terroristic deeds. In short, they are doing everything possible
to support the Czechoslovaks, to return the land to the Russian
landlords, to enslave the workers . . . , [and] to force us into a
new war against the Germans, their competitors.

The English murderers look upon Russia as their colony. They
wish to deal with our country in the same way in which the high-
waymen of European imperialism dealt with China during the
'nineties. The vile stranglers of freedom are ready to commit
any crime. They have murdered Comrade Uritsky because he
brought together the threads of an English conspiracy in Petrograd. But the English agents have not succeeded in destroying
the traces of their vile plot. On August 31, at 6:00 P. M., our
Commission to Fight Counter-Revolution succeeded in trapping
one of the principal groups of the English conspirators. At a
secret meeting in the consular building we arrested five Russian
counter-revolutionists, including Prince Shakhovskoi, Jr., and
about twenty-five English agents. We found a considerable quantity of arms and seized an enormous correspondence, soon to be
published, which fully incriminates the English plotters.

When the Cheka representatives entered the consular building,
the English conspirators, headed by [Captain] Cromie, began to
shoot, killing our Comrade Yanson and seriously wounding
Comrades Sheikman and Vortnovsky. . . .

The whole world knows that we did not wish . . . a war against
England and France. Nor do we wish a war now. We want
only . . . peace and socialism. We want the Russian working class
and peasantry to be allowed to organize their life in the way
desired by the people. We would never have infringed upon the
freedom of any Englishman or Frenchman. We would never have
resorted to a search of the embassy building. But we cannot
remain silent when the embassy is converted into quarters of
conspiracy for plotters and murderers, when officials living in our
territory weave about our country a net of bloody intrigue and
monstrous crime. We know that the mercenary press of England
and France will not tell the truth about what happened in Petro-

grad. The English and French peoples will be deceived. But truth will always assert itself. The whole civilized world is bound to learn of the dark crimes with which the agents of Anglo-French imperialism have covered themselves.

G. ZINOVIEV
Chairman of the Soviet of Commissars
of the Northern Region

DZERZHINSKY
Chairman of the All-Russian Cheka

B. POZERN
Commissar of War

A. LUNARCHARSKY
People's Commissar of Education

In reprisal for the arrest of Lockhart the British Government arrested Litvinov, who at the time was the unofficial Soviet representative in England. Balfour also protested, in a note to Chicherin on September 6, against the attack on the British embassy at Petrograd and threatened that "His Majesty's Government will hold the members of the Soviet Government individually responsible and will make every endeavor to secure that they shall be treated as outlaws by the governments of all civilized nations and that no place of refuge shall be left to them." [45]

In a reply to Balfour's note Chicherin justified the arrest of Lockhart. He reiterated the charge that the Allied representatives had been engaged in conspiracy and emphasized the fact that among those whom the Soviet Government had arrested there was not a single workman. However, he agreed to release "the representatives of the British and French bourgeoisie" as soon as Russian representatives in England were given an opportunity to leave that country. [46]

[45] Balfour's note is quoted in *U. S. Foreign Relations, 1918, Russia*, I, 665-66.
[46] *Izvestiia*, No. 193, September 7, 1918, p. 3.

Negotiations for the exchange of prisoners continued for some time, and an agreement was finally reached in accordance with which Lockhart and other Allied representatives were allowed to leave Russia early in October and Litvinov with a group of Bolsheviks left England at the same time.

C. Preparations for World Revolution

During the early fall of 1918 the internal and external affairs of the Soviet Government improved considerably. The Red Army made steady progress in its campaign against the Czechoslovaks and the People's Army in the Volga region,[47] and the failure of the German offensive in France held out the prospect of revolution in Germany and other countries. At Lenin's suggestion the Central Executive Committee adopted on October 4 a resolution placing all Soviet "forces and resources" at the disposal of the German proletariat in establishing itself in power, and on October 30 the Sovnarkom imposed on the Russian bourgeoisie a tax of ten billion rubles for the defense of the Russian and international revolutions. A few days after the collapse of the Imperial régime in Germany the Central Executive Committee denounced the Brest-Litovsk Treaty and invited Germany and Austria-Hungary to join "an alliance of the toiling masses . . . fighting for a socialist order."

LENIN URGES PREPARATIONS FOR WORLD REVOLUTION

[Letter to the Central Executive Committee, October 3, 1918] [48]

. . . The result of the crisis in Germany . . . will surely be the capture of the government by the German proletariat. The Russian proletariat is watching the course of events with close

[47] See Chapter VI below.
[48] Lenin, *op. cit.*, XXIII, 215-17.

attention and great enthusiasm. Even the blindest workers of other nations now see that the Bolsheviks were justified in building their tactics on the support of the workers' world revolution. . . . Even the most ignorant now understand the low treason to socialism committed by the Mensheviks and Socialist-Revolutionists in forming a coalition with the plundering Anglo-French bourgeoisie on the pretext of overthrowing the Brest Treaty. . . .

The Russian proletariat must realize that it will soon be necessary to make great sacrifices in the cause of internationalism. The time is approaching when circumstances will demand that we help the German people . . . against Anglo-French imperialism. Let us begin to prepare at once. Let us show that the Russian worker can work much more energetically, make greater sacrifices, and die more bravely when fighting for the cause of the international proletarian revolution. . . .

First of all let us . . . increase the supplies of bread. Let us put aside in each grain elevator a certain quantity of grain for the German workers in case they should need it in their struggle to free themselves from the imperialist monsters and beasts. Let every party organization, every trade union, every factory, machine-shop, etc., establish contact and strengthen the ties with . . . the peasants . . . , educate them and help them to conquer the kulaks and to collect all grain surpluses. Let us in the same way increase our efforts to organize the Red Army . . . of workers and peasants, ready to make every sacrifice for the cause of socialism. This army is growing stronger and more experienced in battles against the Czechoslovaks and White Guards. . . .

It was our intention to have an army of a million men by spring, but now we need an army of three millions. We can and will have it. The history of the world during the last few days has quickened the pace of the proletarian world revolution. The most rapid changes are now possible. It may be that German and Anglo-French imperialism will join forces against the Soviet Government.

We too must hasten our preparation and increase our efforts tenfold!

Let this be the slogan of the first anniversary of the great October Revolution of the proletariat!

Let this be the pledge of the ultimate victory of the world-proletarian revolution!

THE CENTRAL EXECUTIVE COMMITTEE PLEDGES SUPPORT
OF THE GERMAN PROLETARIAT

[Resolution of October 4, 1918] [49]

The Central Executive Committee considers it necessary to inform the working class of all countries of its position in regard to the events which are now taking place.

. . . The imperialist classes of the Central Empires are experiencing a catastrophic downfall. . . . The Anglo-French, American, and Japanese imperialist plunderers seem supreme. . . . After their new successes the Entente robbers are even more dangerous and staunch enemies of the Soviet Republic. . . . Just as during the Brest-Litovsk peace negotiations, so now the Soviet Government builds its policies on the anticipation of social revolution in both imperialist camps.

Firm conviction of the truth of these anticipations made it possible for us to accept the horrible conditions of the Brest-Litovsk Agreement. . . . Associating the future of the Ukraine, Poland, Lithuania, the Baltic provinces, and Finland with the future of the proletarian revolution, we rejected every idea of a *rapprochement* with Entente imperialism for the purpose of altering the Brest-Litovsk Treaty. The chains with which Anglo-American and Japanese-American plunderers bind nations are in no way better than Austro-German chains.

Military dictatorship in Germany is as incapable of changing the course of events as is the coalition between bourgeois speculators and their flunkeys from the camp of [socialist] compromisers. It is inevitable that the German working class should assume power; thus the struggle between Anglo-American and Austro-German plunderers may almost any day become a struggle of imperialism against proletarian Germany.

The All-Russian Central Executive Committee declares to the whole world that Soviet Russia will offer all its forces and resources to aid the German revolutionary government. The All-Russian Central Executive Committee has no doubt that the French, English, American, and Japanese proletariat will be in the same camp as Soviet Russia and revolutionary Germany.

[49] *Piaty sozyv Vserossiiskogo Tsentralnogo Ispolnitelnogo Komiteta Sovetov Rabochikh, Krestianskikh, Kazachikh i Krasnoarmeiskikh Deputatov,* pp. 251-53.

In anticipation of the rapidly approaching revolution, the All-Russian Central Executive Committee considers it the duty of Russian workers and peasants to redouble their fight against the Entente bandits who have invaded our country and to be ready to give food supplies and active military aid to the working class of Germany and Austria-Hungary.

The All-Russian Central Executive Committee hereby orders the Revolutionary War Council to adopt at once an extensive program of Red Army organization to meet the new international situation.

The All-Russian Central Executive Committee orders the People's Commissar of Food to create at once a supply of food for the toiling masses of Germany and Austria-Hungary to aid them in their fight against internal and external oppressors.

All Soviet institutions, both central and local, trade unions, factory-shop committees, committees of the poor, and cooperatives are under obligation to take the most active part in the formation of a powerful Red Army and the mobilization of food products as resources for the social revolution.

YA. SVERDLOV

Chairman of the Central Executive Committee

TAX FOR THE DEFENSE OF REVOLUTION

[Decree of the Sovnarkom, October 30, 1918] [50]

The international situation which has developed in connection with the late happenings in the theater of the imperialist World War and has given rise to a united front of the international proletarian army compels us to exert every effort in the defense of the Russian and international revolutions. The Russian Socialist Federated Soviet Republic has therefore resolved to create a powerful Red Army.

Stupendous resources will be required to organize, equip, and maintain such an army—resources which ordinary state revenues are incapable of providing. In the course of the imperialist war the city bourgeoisie and the village kulaks managed to accumulate

---

[50] *Sobranie Uzakonenii i Rasporiazhenii Rabochego i Krestianskogo Pravitelstva,* No. 80, 1918, p. 996. This publication will hereafter be cited as *S. U. R.*

and still continue to accumulate enormous amounts of money, chiefly by means of predatory speculation in the necessities of life, especially in grain. This money must now be immediately and completely taken away from the parasitic and counter-revolutionary elements of the population and used to meet the urgent needs of revolutionary organization and struggle.

The All-Russian Central Executive Committee has therefore resolved to levy on the propertied classes in cities and villages a lump-sum tax of ten billion rubles. . . .

DENUNCIATION OF THE BREST-LITOVSK TREATY

[Resolutions of the Central Executive Committee, November 13, 1918] [51]

To all peoples of Russia and the inhabitants of the occupied territories:

The All-Russian Central Executive Committee of Soviets hereby solemnly declares that the conditions of the peace with Germany signed at Brest-Litovsk on March 3, 1918, are null and void. The Brest-Litovsk Treaty (as well as the supplementary agreement signed at Berlin on August 27 and ratified by the Central Executive Committee on September 6, 1918) is revoked in its entirety and all its parts. All clauses of the Brest-Litovsk Treaty relating to contributions and the transfer of territories and regions are hereby abrogated.

The last act of the Wilhelm government, which forced this outrageous peace upon the Russian Socialist Federated Soviet Republic in order to weaken it . . . and have a chance to exploit freely its borderlands, was the expulsion of the Soviet Embassy from Berlin for engaging in activities directed toward the overthrow of the bourgeois-imperialist régime in Germany. The first act of the insurgent workers and soldiers of Germany after overthrowing the imperial régime was to request the return of the Embassy of the Soviet Republic. In this way the Brest-Litovsk Treaty of violence and plunder lies crushed under the simultaneous blows dealt by the German and Russian revolutionary proletariat.

The toiling masses of Russia, Lithuania, Esthonia, Poland,

[51] *S. U. R.*, No. 95, 1918, pp. 1207-08.

Latvia, the Ukraine, Finland, the Crimea, and the Caucasus, freed by the German Revolution from the yoke of an oppressive treaty dictated by the German militarists, are now called upon to decide their own fate. The imperialist peace must be replaced by a socialist peace concluded by the free toiling masses of Russia, Germany, and Austria-Hungary. The R. S. F. S. R. invites the fraternal peoples of Germany and Austria-Hungary, as represented by their soviets of workers' and soldiers' deputies, to start immediately negotiations for the annulment of the Brest Treaty. Peace among nations can be built only upon such principles as are conducive to fraternal relations between the toilers of all countries and peoples. The principles of that peace were proclaimed by the November Revolution and defended by the Russian delegation at Brest-Litovsk. All occupied regions of Russia must be evacuated and the right of self-determination fully recognized as belonging to the toiling nations of every people [sic]. All damages must be paid by those who are really guilty of the war—the bourgeois classes.

The revolutionary soldiers of Germany and Austria, now organizing their soviets of deputies in the occupied regions, should cooperate . . . in bringing about these aims after they have established relations with the local soviets of workers and peasants. By a fraternal union with the peasants and workers of Russia they will heal the wounds which German and Austrian generals, in the interests of the counter-revolution, inflicted upon the population of the occupied territory.

Such an international compact between Russia, Germany, and Austria-Hungary would be more than a peace treaty. It would be an alliance of the toiling masses of all nations, fighting for a socialist order built upon the ruins of militarism and economic slavery. The toiling masses of Russia, represented by the Soviet Government, invite the peoples of Germany and Austria-Hungary to enter such an alliance. They entertain the hope that this mighty alliance of the free peoples of Russia, Poland, Finland, the Ukraine, Latvia, the Baltic States, the Crimea, the Caucasus, Germany, and Austria-Hungary will be joined by all other nations which have not yet succeeded in throwing off the yoke of imperialism. Until that time the alliance will resist every attempt to force the capitalist bondage of a foreign bourgeoisie upon other peoples. The peoples of Russia, freed by the German Revolution from German imperialism, will hardly tolerate subjection by Anglo-American or Japanese imperialism.

The Government of the Soviet Republic has invited all countries still waging war against it to make peace agreements. It hopes that the toiling masses of those countries will force their governments to make peace with the workers, peasants, and soldiers of Russia. Meanwhile the Soviet Government will resist every attempt to restore the power of capital, whether foreign or native, and will summon to its aid all the revolutionary forces in Central and Eastern Europe.

Welcoming the peoples of the regions freed from German imperialism, the R. S. F. S. R. invites the toilers of those regions to form a brotherly alliance with the workers and peasants of Russia and promises them every assistance in their struggle to establish a socialist government of workers and peasants.

The oppressive peace of Brest-Litovsk has now been overthrown. Long live a real peace and a world-alliance of workers of all countries and peoples!

YA. SVERDLOV
Chairman of the Central Executive Committee

Upon the establishment of a republican régime in Germany the Bolsheviks made several attempts to resume diplomatic relations with the new government. They were especially desirous of sending representatives to the expected congress of delegates of German workers and soldiers. The German Government refused to resume diplomatic relations and prevented the Russian delegates, headed by Radek, Joffe, and Bukharin, from crossing the border into Germany. The Germans stated the reasons for their act in a radiogram of December 3 which charged the former Soviet Embassy to Germany with bad faith. Joffe, so the radiogram stated, not only engaged in Bolshevik propaganda but also purchased arms and ammunition for German revolutionists, spending for this purpose 105,000 marks.[52] The next day Joffe sent the following reply:

JOFFE TO THE GERMAN GOVERNMENT

[Radiogram of December 4, 1918] [53]

With reference to the radiogram of December 3 . . . , which accuses the former Embassy of the Soviet Government in Berlin not only of spreading Bolshevik propaganda but also of purchasing arms, I wish to state that the said propaganda was carried on with the help of the Independent Social-Democratic party. As regards the purchase of arms . . . , the amount mentioned in the radiogram is not correct. Minister Barth received not 105,000 marks but several hundred thousand marks for the purpose of acquiring arms. I desire to make known the real facts in the case and consider it as to my credit that by means of my above-mentioned activities, which were in full accord with the Independent [Socialists] . . . , I contributed to the full extent of my power to the triumph of the German Revolution.

JOFFE

[52] The radiogram is quoted in *Izvestiia*, No. 267, December 6, 1918, p. 3.
[53] *Ibid.*

CHAPTER IV

ANTI-BOLSHEVIK MOVEMENTS IN CENTRAL RUSSIA

Foreign intervention was not the only threat to their power which the Bolsheviks encountered during the spring and summer of 1918. While foreign armies were dislodging the Bolsheviks from control in Southern Russia, the Murmansk region, and Siberia, there was an intensification of opposition to Bolshevik rule in Central Russia, the relatively small part of Russia which the Communists still dominated. To be sure, the termination of hostilities with the Central Powers in December 1917 for a time left the Bolsheviks free to suppress the internal opposition which had assailed their rule from the beginning. However, the developments which followed the conclusion of the Brest-Litovsk Peace gave new impetus and direction to the anti-Bolshevik movements by introducing the factor of intervention. Foreign occupation of vast Russian territories, providing bases for the organization of native anti-Bolshevik forces, gave numerous opponents of the Soviet régime in Central Russia renewed hope for a speedy overthrow of Bolshevik rule through the combined assault of Russian and foreign armies. At the same time the passive attitude of the Soviet Government toward German intervention brought into the anti-Bolshevik camp many of the early supporters of Bolshevism.

The opposition forces in Central Russia comprised groups of the most diverse character—peasants and workers resentful of economic privation and government interference in economic life, inveterately hostile monarchists and conservatives, moderate socialists dissatisfied with Bolshevik dictatorial methods, and Left Socialist-Revolutionists denunciatory of the Bolsheviks for the Brest Treaty. Heterogeneous, too, were their activities, ranging from mere protests or strikes against specific governmental policies to the organization of conspiracies and open insurrections against the government. The very lack of cohesion among the opposition groups prevented them from achieving any considerable success either in changing the direction of Bolshevik policy or in organizing effective armed opposition. Strikes were suppressed and the numerous outbreaks of armed revolt were liquidated by the Red Army and the Cheka.

A. Discontent Among Workers and Peasants

During the spring and early summer of 1918 the Bolsheviks lost much of their popularity among city workers and peasants. The acute food shortage, the widespread unemployment, and the increasingly radical and dictatorial policies adopted by the Bolsheviks caused considerable disillusionment among large sections of the industrial proletariat. At the same time the extension of civil war to the villages, which received official sanction in May, intensified the opposition of the well-to-do and middle-class peasants to the Soviet régime.[1]

DISORDERS AT PAVLOVSKY POSAD [2]

[Pavlovsky Posad.] On May 12 . . . a group of peasants . . . and workers . . . stormed the Soviet. The building of the Soviet was set on fire while its members were inside. Six of the defenders of the Soviet and ten of its assailants were killed. Many were wounded. Red Army troops were called from Bogorsdsk, Orek-

---

[1] An account of the relations between the Bolsheviks and the peasants is given below in Chapter VIII.

[2] *Svoboda Rossii,* No. 24, May 14, 1918, p. 3.

hov-Zuev . . . , and Moscow. The mob disarmed the war prisoners and a part of the Red Army soldiers.

On May 13 the city was declared under martial law. From early morning on all passers-by were searched. . . . Numerous arrests were made. . . . Early in the morning [May 13] large crowds of peasants were seen coming into town with sacks and baskets in their hands. Rumors had reached the villages that " yesterday the Soviet was stormed and today the bourgeoisie would be stormed and bread distributed." When the peasants found out that Red Army detachments had arrived in the city they fled home. . . .

WORKERS CRITICIZE THE GOVERNMENT

[Resolution of Workers of the Bogatyr Factory, May 16, 1918] [3]

. . . We workers of the Bogatyr factory . . . , having considered at a general meeting the conditions of the working class, have resolved: to call the attention of the People's Commissars, who claim that they were elected by us and that they defend our interests, to the fact that we protest most energetically against their acts in relation to us as workers. We protest against the shooting of workers who ask for bread—an occurrence at Kolpino, Kolomna, and other Russian cities. We protest against the civil war which the commissars have started all over Russia. We protest against the food policy which in place of bread has given us an enormous army of bureaucrats living on our sweat. . . . We protest against the policy of the commissars which has delivered us to the enemies of the revolution—the Germans.

We categorically demand the transfer of the management of the food supply to the cooperative societies . . . , the calling of a new Constituent Assembly . . . , freedom of speech and press . . . , a cessation of the shooting of citizens and workers . . . , the immediate reestablishment of all abolished organs of local self-government. . . .

[3] *Novaia Zhizn,* No. 93, May 18, 1918, p. 3.

REVOLT IN THE RED ARMY AT SARATOV

[May 16-19]

[Saratov.] [4] A group of Red Army soldiers, numbering according to official figures about six hundred and according to unofficial estimates about three thousand, revolted against the Soviet authorities, demanding the reelection of the Soviet and free trade in flour and other food products. The Executive Committee rejected the demands, and the insurgents undertook a systematic siege of the building in which the Executive Committee held its sessions. The building was under fire . . . throughout the night of May 16, and the third story was completely demolished. The Executive Committee held continuous session and considered the question of surrender. The Bolshevik leaders, however, insisted on continuing the fight, as the telegraph office was left unoccupied by the soldiers and the Bolsheviks thus had an opportunity to communicate with other cities. To gain time they [the Bolsheviks] started negotiations for an agreement without making definite proposals. May 17, the second day of the revolt, passed without military action. The insurgents issued to the people an appeal stating that they had decided to put an end to Bolshevik violence and inviting the population to join . . . [the revolt].

. . . In the morning of May 18 machine guns and artillery got to work. The Red Guards who were defending the Soviet seized the Astoria Hotel and fortified it. A machine-gun engagement took place . . . during which several passers-by were killed. The Peasant Bank, where the Executive Committee was located, was also under fire. At first the insurgents had the advantage, but about 4 : 00 P. M. . . . Bolshevik reinforcements began to arrive from other cities. . . . An armored car, which soon made its appearance, decided the outcome of the insurrection. . . . The Red Army staff was captured; several hundred men were arrested . . . ; and many were shot.

In the morning of the 19th martial law was declared. . . . An order was given out which demanded that under penalty of death all arms be surrendered in three days. The Executive Committee also issued an appeal to the people explaining what had taken

[4] *Svoboda Rossii,* No. 33, May 24, 1918, p. 3.

place and putting the blame for the whole affair on the Socialist-Revolutionists of the Right and the Mensheviks. . . .

Saratov, May 22.[5] The city is full of rumors that the insurrectionists are being executed. Numerous arrests have taken place. [The authorities] are searching for Socialist-Revolutionists and Mensheviks. A number of Socialist-Revolutionists have been condemned to death. . . . The city is panic-stricken and is being abandoned by many. . . .

DISSATISFACTION AMONG INDUSTRIAL WORKERS [6]

Kostroma. Of late a sharp change has been in evidence among the working masses. Recent elections to the City Soviet gave a majority to the Mensheviks. The Council of National Economy is wholly in Menshevik hands. The same [party] dominates the factory-shop committees, being second only to the non-partisans.

The non-partisan elements now constitute a considerable force. They look at [economic] issues from a purely business standpoint, while in politics they are nationalistic.

This change of attitude occurred under the influence of the food crisis. The largest factory in the city of Kostroma, which employs eight thousand workers, excluding [office] employees, is going to close next week because of shortage of money, fuel, and raw material. The demand for free trade in grain is finding more and more supporters among the workers. . . .

CALL FOR A WORKERS' STRIKE AGAINST THE GOVERNMENT [7]
[May 23, 1918]

A plenary session of the special conference of factory and shop delegates took place today. The session attracted a large number of people. On the order of the day was the question of organizing a political strike as a protest against the acts and general policy of the Soviet Government.

The speaker . . . pointed out that the method which the workers had thus far been following, viz., passing resolutions against the mistaken policies of the Soviet Government and protesting against the practice of Red Terror, had proved a failure. More decisive

[5] *Ibid.*, No. 35, May 26, 1918, p. 4.   [7] *Ibid.*, p. 2.
[6] *Ibid.*, No. 33, May 24, 1918, p. 4.

measures, therefore, are necessary to force the Soviet Government to be attentive to the wishes of the people in general and the working class in particular. A general political strike of the workers would serve this purpose. The strike should be under democratic slogans, including a demand for a modified food policy, a protest against violence, an insistence upon the reestablishment of democratic organs of local self-government, abolition of the army of mercenaries, abandonment of the persecution of the press, etc. . . . A resolution on the necessity of immediately organizing a general workers' strike was unanimously adopted. . . .

THE RAILWAY WORKERS OPPOSE THE GOVERNMENT

[From an Account of the Proceedings of the Congress of Railway Workers, May 23, 1918] [8]

The second plenary session of the Congress of Railway Workers took place today. Mr. Kobozev, Special Commissar, delivered a . . . speech before the meeting.

The speaker thought that the essential condition for the improvement of transportation was the establishment of normal relations between the engineers and the workers. . . . The Soviet Government, Kobozev declared, had resolved to fight vigorously against those anarcho-syndicalist tendencies of railway employees and workers which had assumed abnormal forms. Stable administrative organs must be established. The employees and workers must understand that the railway organizations are not self-sufficient, that the slogan,"The railways are for the railwaymen," is a slogan which we do not want. All important questions will be solved by the central authorities. . . . The speaker thought that Vikzhedor [9] was a state within a state. It was because of Vikzhedor that the ideas of trade-union syndicalism had gained strength.

Kobozev was sharply attacked by the Vikzhedor representative, whose speech evoked a storm of applause. The representative maintained that the attempt to combine centralized administration with mass initiative was absurd. Kobozev retorted that he intended to do away with mass initiative in the form in which it

---

[8] *Ibid.,* p. 3.

[9] Vikzhedor is the abbreviation of *Vserossiikii Ispolnitelnyi Komitet Zheleznodorozhnikov*—All-Russian Executive Committee of Railway Workers.

was then expressing itself. The statement of the commissar caused great commotion. . . . In the debates which followed, the speakers declared that they could not follow Kobozev, that the wishes of Vikzhedor should be taken into consideration.

CLASH BETWEEN WORKERS AND RED ARMY SOLDIERS [10]

On June 16 a number of soldiers of the Red Army, led by Kapustiansky, a member of the Extraordinary Commission [to Fight Counter-Revolution], came to the factory village of Yuzha . . . and attempted to arrest five workers' delegates for attending the workers' conference at Sormovo. The factory workers prevented the arrest of their delegates and the Red Army soldiers were forced to leave.

On June 30 Kapustiansky appeared again with a detachment of thirty men and arrested [the delegates] during the night. . . . When on the next day the workers learned about the arrests, they quit work in the factory, went to the Sovdep, and demanded the release of those arrested. Kapustiansky began to threaten with his revolver, and one of the Red Army soldiers fired and wounded a worker. The workers then fell upon Kapustiansky, beat him until he was half-dead, disarmed the soldiers, and made them leave the village. A new Red Army detachment which arrived at the scene was also disarmed.

THE INSURRECTION AT TAMBOV

[An Account in Pravda, June 22, 1918] [11]

According to information received by the Extraordinary Commission to Fight Counter-Revolution, the unsuccessful attempt to overthrow Soviet rule in the city of Tambov was started and carried on under the direction of Socialist-Revolutionists of the Right. The lackeys of the bourgeoisie, crying at every crossroad about the submission of the Soviets to the Germans, everywhere and continually interfered with the creation of a powerful revolutionary Red Army. As soon as mobilization was called for, the counter-revolutionists started a widespread agitation against the

[10] *Svobodnaia Zhizn*, No. 4, July 5, 1918, p. 3.
[11] Piontkovsky, *G. V. R.*, p. 185.

Soviet. . . . Having assured themselves of the support of the petty-bourgeois and kulak elements, the betrayers of the working class risked making an attack on the Soviet. Kulaks were summoned from nearby villages to the aid of organized army officers. Almost the entire Soviet, together with prominent members of the Communist party, were unexpectedly arrested.

When the counter-revolutionists felt sure that their cause had won, they went completely mad: they shot the Commissar of Finance and two other Communists; the army officers donned glittering shoulder-straps and put on spurs.

At the head of the government stood the so-called " Military Committee," which included army officers and several kulaks.

This committee issued the following proclamation:

"The reign of the usurpers and robbers, who tore Russia asunder and betrayed her to the Germans, has come to an end. A new government, honest but strong, has been organized.

"Since the fight against the Bolsheviks demands that our forces be united, full power is vested in the Military Committee of Officers and Soldiers.

"All opposition to and agitation against the Military Committee will be punished with the death penalty. The supervision of supplies and economic conditions is entrusted to the authorities of the city of Tambov.

"Long live the insurgent Russian people!"

REVOLT OF RIAZAN WORKERS [12]

In the large factory village of Ozery . . . there recently took place an uprising of the workers against the Soviet. The events, according to official sources, were as follows:

Dissatisfied with the local Soviet authorities, a large crowd of workers, numbering about eight thousand, surrounded the building of the Soviet, in which at the time were three members of the Executive Committee, . . . eight Red Army soldiers, and six militia officers. The members of the Soviet pleaded with the workers not to resort to violence, but in vain. . . . Thereupon those besieged began to fire on the crowd, which fell back somewhat. . . . A number of workers secured rifles and bombs from some

[12] *Nashe Slovo*, No. 59, July 2, 1918, p. 4.

source, climbed on the roof of the house next to the Soviet, and began to fire on the building of the Soviet. One of the bombs thrown into the Soviet premises exploded and destroyed the floor, a number of bookcases, and papers. . . .

Seeing that the Soviet refused to surrender . . . , the assailants decided to set the building of the Soviet afire. . . . Soon the news spread that a train with Red Army soldiers from Kolomna was nearing Ozery. Some of the workers rushed to the railroad to destroy the railway tracks, but the soldiers' train was already at the station. The soldiers rescued the Soviet. . . . Among the beseiged there were two killed and four wounded; the casualties of the assailants are unknown. . . .

RAILWAY STRIKES

[Appeal of the Sovnarkom, June 22, 1918] [18]

The Soviet of People's Commissars, having discussed at the session of June 22 the events which took place on the Alexandrovsk Railroad, and having taken into consideration the data supplied by Vikzhedor [All-Russian Executive Committee of Railwaymen] and Vsoprofzhel [All-Russian Trade-Union Council of Railwaymen], resolved to make the following appeal to the . . . railwaymen:

There is now noticeable among the employees and workers of Russian railroads a deep discontent, which in certain places turns into unorganized action. Here and there conflicts arise which take on an extremely bad character. Local strikes are occurring and even strike committees are being organized.

Certain agents of the central and local authorities are known to have taken measures which are in manifest violation of their duties and discredit the Soviet Government. The orders which they have issued are contrary to the interests of the working class and the revolution. Such occurrences as shooting of railwaymen, threats of violence, illegal executions, dismissal apart from and contrary to the decisions of road committees and trade unions, etc., call forth the just indignation of the railwaymen. [At the same time] counter-revolutionists are utilizing this in-

[18] *Vestnik putei soobshcheniia*, No. 5, 1918, p. 1.

dignation . . . to bring the capitalists and landlords back into power.

The Soviet of People's Commissars hereby declares that it will show no mercy to those agents of the Soviet Government who by thoughtless and criminal acts intensify the dissatisfaction of the toiling masses, which has been growing because of famine and exhaustion.

Comrades Railwaymen! The discontent on the railways is in danger of assuming such character and dimensions as to spread to every existing railway organization. Remember that upon your perseverance . . . depends the regular shipment of food to the starving cities and villages, that the stoppage of transport at this critical moment for the Russian Revolution will fall as a disgrace on the railway proletariat, which played such a distinguished part in the revolutionary movement of Russia. Comrades, beware of provocation! The Soviet of People's Commissars takes upon itself the obligation of uprooting all those elements which, acting in the name of the Soviet Government, but in evident violation of official instructions and ordinances, perpetrate violence against employees and workers of Russian railways.

V. ULIANOV (LENIN)
President of the Sovnarkom

NEVSKY
Acting People's Commissar of
Ways and Communications

[Meetings of Railway Workers, July 1, 1918] [14]

A number of meetings took place yesterday on the Moscow Railroads. In the shops of the Alexandrovsk Road the meeting was attended by a large number of workers and proved very stormy.

Znamensky, a member of the Soviet of Workers' Deputies, tried to persuade the workers not to strike, because a strike would threaten the interests of the working class. It might be permissible [he said] to fight against the Bolsheviks, but not against the Soviets, which are the instruments by which the proletariat fights

[14] *Zaria Rossii*, No. 56, July 2, 1918, p. 1.

against the capitalist régime. The speaker maintained that the Bolsheviks were not at all interested in continuing in power. They would rather go to the front and fight the Germans or the Czechoslovaks. . . .

A worker stood up and asked in a loud voice: "Why is it that a government which calls itself the Workers' and Peasants' Government is shooting down workers and peasants?"

These words called forth a storm of applause.

The Menshevik and Right Socialist-Revolutionist speakers laid stress on the horrors of the political terror which reigns throughout the country. They drew comparisons between the Communists and monarchists of the type of Markov the Second.[15]

[From the Proceedings of the Joint Session of the Conference of Factory-Shop Committees, Moscow Soviet, and Representatives of Railway Committees, July 1, 1918][16]

Lozovsky, an Internationalist and chairman of the All-Russian Union of Railwaymen, spoke on the railway strike. In his opinion the cause of the railway strike is, in addition to difficulties with food supply, the acts of violence which local and central officials perpetrate against the railway workers. On June 21 a delegation of the Council of the All-Russian Union of Railwaymen was sent to Lenin to report on those acts of violence and to ask that the excesses be brought to an end. Lenin agreed to issue a special appeal to all railwaymen, and the Council assumed the moral obligation of stopping the use of violence against railway workers. . . . The strike, Lozovsky pointed out, was due on the one hand to the provocation of government agents, and on the other to . . . famine. The two must be fought with most decisive measures; otherwise an upheaval is possible. The Conference should take upon itself the task of defending the interests of the railway workers. A mere appeal against the strike will have no effect. . . .

Sverdlov spoke after Lozovsky. He stated that the Soviet Government was passing through a critical period and called upon the workers to unite and oppose the enemies on the Right. He declared that all acts of violence on the railroads would be sup-

[15] A notorious reactionary active during the last years of the old régime.
[16] *Zaria Rossii*, No. 56, July 2, 1918, p. 3.

pressed most resolutely. With those "elements who move from city to city with the purpose of provocation" Sverdlov promised to be merciless. . . .

When the debates came to an end, Sverdlov announced a resolution stating that by the decree of June 28 all large-scale enterprises, factories, and shops had passed to the control of the Republic. From now on the workers and their trade unions must assume the responsibility of preserving and consolidating these gains. . . .[17]

PEASANT RIOTS AND DISTURBANCES

[Extracts from Official Reports of the Petrograd Telegraph Agency]

Perm, July 1. . . . Enraged by the enforcement of the bread monopoly, the peasants of Shlykovsky Volost killed a member of the Gubernia Executive Committee, four Red Army soldiers, and a grain accountant.

Rzhev, July 1, 1918.ˈ The peasants of Staritsky Uezd killed the commissar of Tver Gubernia, Gusev, who arrived at the uezd with an expeditionary detachment. The soldiers of the detachment were disarmed. . . .

Tver, July 2. The kulaks of Selishchensky Volost . . . attempted to break up the committee of the poor, which was requisitioning food surpluses. The Extraordinary Commission to Fight Counter-Revolution arrested two leaders of the attack on the committee of the poor. . . .

Tver, July 2. In the village Spas a riot took place . . . during which a mob killed three Red Army soldiers. . . .[18]

Rzhev, July 3. The peasants of Chamerovsky Volost . . . offered energetic resistance to Red Army soldiers who came to requisition bread. The entire volost organized itself into detachments armed with rifles and hand grenades. . . . "Under pressure of superior forces" the Red Army soldiers retreated. . . . The next day the Red Army soldiers came back in greater numbers . . . , but the peasants entrenched themselves near the village Savina and put the Red Army soldiers to flight.[19]

[17] The resolution is quoted below, pp. 401-02.
[18] *Nashe Slovo*, No. 60, July 4, 1918, p. 4.
[19] *Ibid.*, No. 63, July 6, 1918, p. 4.

Tver, July 4. . . . In Maslovsky Volost there took place armed clashes between peasants and Red Army soldiers who came to requisition bread. Five peasants were wounded. The soldiers succeeded in disarming the peasants.[20]

DEMAND FOR THE INDEPENDENCE OF TRADE UNIONS

[Minority Resolution Presented at the Fourth Conference of Factory-Shop Committees and Trade Unions, July 2, 1918] [21]

1. The Russian Revolution is not a socialist but a bourgeois revolution.

2. The agrarian question is being solved instinctively and in the spirit of the institution of [private] property.

3. From this it follows that the emergence of a bourgeois political order (counter-revolutionary) is inevitable.

4. The working class faces, therefore, the necessity of safeguarding its political and economic independence. It follows that if they are to preserve full independence of the organs of the state and of the Commissariat of Labor the trade unions must insist on the following: (1) Complete non-interference in their internal affairs, and the ability to discharge unobstructedly their tasks as organs of the class struggle; (2) the arbitration of all disputes between capital and labor; (3) the carrying out of social reforms; (4) the formation, in connection with the Commissariat of Labor, of a special council consisting of representatives of workers and employers for the preliminary consideration of all legislative projects of the Commissariat of Labor.

The Mensheviks and Right Socialist-Revolutionists, aiming to create an organization which would express and direct the opposition of the workers to the Bolsheviks, in the middle of July summoned workers' delegates from all Central Russia to a conference at Moscow. About forty delegates came to the conference, which opened on July 21. After the body had been in session for two days the Extraordinary Commission to Fight Counter-Revolution arrested its entire

[20] *Svobodnaia Zhizn,* No. 4, July 5, 1918, p. 3.
[21] *Professionalnyi Vestnik,* No. 1, 1919, pp. 4-5.

membership. However, the conference succeeded in passing a resolution which condemned the policies of the Soviet Government.

RESOLUTION OF THE CONFERENCE OF WORKERS' DELEGATES [22]

[July 21, 1918]

The Workers' Conference believes:

1. That only by putting an end to the internal war and reestablishing the political rights of the workers and of the whole people can proper conditions be created for the restoration of industry and the lessening of unemployment.

2. That the economic plan which the Bolsheviks force upon the country aggravates the economic breakdown and increases unemployment and famine. . . .

3. That experiments with the socialization and nationalization of factories and mills must be stopped.

4. That there must be created conditions favorable for attracting Russian and foreign capital on the basis of free competition.

5. That measures must be taken for the reestablishment of credit and the denationalization of banks.

6. [That] state control of production and a planned distribution of raw materials among all factories and mills [must be established].

7. [That] regulation and distribution of articles of prime necessity [must be introduced].

FIGHTING THE KULAKS

A kulak insurrection took place in Saratov Gubernia. . . . The White Guards took advantage of the dissatisfaction in connection with mobilization and broke up the village soviets and the committees of the poor.

A special investigating commission and an armed detachment were dispatched to put down the kulaks of twelve villages. The detachment disarmed the villages, reinstated the soviets . . . ,

[22] *Izvestiia*, No. 158, July 27, 1918, pp. 3-6.

and exacted payments from the kulaks. . . . It took eight days to suppress the kulak insurrection. . . . We shot thirty-six persons. . . . A detachment of German Internationalists helped in the operation. This detachment was given orders to search out those guilty of bringing about the insurrection. . . . [23]

Vetluga, September 10. On August 28 the city was captured by a detachment of White Guards . . . and local kulaks. [Four] members of the uezd executive committee were brutally murdered. At present the city is in the hands of Soviet troops. Nineteen participants in the revolt were shot.[24]

Kulak insurrections took place in the villages of Matrenka, Driazgi, and Talinsk-Chemlyk. In several villages the insurgents succeeded in breaking up the soviets and the committees of the poor. . . . Upon the arrival of a detachment of the Uezd Cheka the leaders of the insurrections were shot and the soviets reestablished.[25]

INSURRECTIONS IN CENTRAL RUSSIA

[Announcement of the Moscow District Military Committee, November 22, 1918] [26]

During the early part of this month, in Riazan, Kaluga, and . . . Tula gubernias, counter-revolutionary elements and local kulaks revolted against the Soviet Government.

The rebels, organized in bands, overthrew local Soviet authorities . . . , broke up committees of the poor, and destroyed railway and telegraph lines. To reestablish order I dispatched a mixed detachment [of the Red Army] under the general command of Comrade Kraaze. . . .

Thanks to the energy . . . and loyalty . . . of the Red Army, order was reestablished in a week and the guilty received the deserved punishment. . . .

MURALOV

District Military Commissar

[23] *Ezhenedelnik chrezvychainykh komissii po borbe s kontr-revoliutsiei i spekuliatsiei*, No. 1, 1918, pp. 23-24.

[24] *Izvestiia*, No. 196, September 11, 1918, p. 5.

[25] *Pravda*, No. 265, 1918, p. 3.

[26] *Severnaia Kommuna*, No. 164, November 27, 1918, p. 2.

B. Anti-Soviet Organizations in Central Russia

The spring of 1918 witnessed in Central Russia a rapid growth of anti-Bolshevik groups willing to avail themselves of foreign aid in overthrowing the Bolsheviks. The most important of these groups were the Moscow Center of the Right, the Union for the Defense of the Fatherland and Freedom, the Union for the Regeneration of Russia, and the Socialist-Revolutionists of the Right. The Moscow Center of the Right, to which most of the conservatives belonged, looked to Germany for assistance and hoped to gain this aid through economic or other concessions. However, most of the anti-Bolshevik groups turned to the Allies, whom they were willing to join in the war against Germany. The hopes of these anti-Bolsheviks were fostered by the Allied representatives who advocated intervention against the Bolsheviks, particularly by the French Ambassador, Noulens.

POLITICAL LIFE IN MOSCOW

[Extract from a Letter . . . dated Moscow, April 24, 1918] [27]

I am here rather close to Prince E. Troubetskoi, Struve, Kishkin, Astrov (the former mayor), Gourko, Krivoshein, Manuilov, and . . . Speransky.

At the left, I meet Alexinsky and with the S. R., Avxentiev, Gotz, Zenzinov . . . at the farther left, Dan, and at the extreme left I happen to chat about Japan and other things with Chicherin, occasionally with Mrs. Kollontai. . . .

I kept for the last in the list my most precious gem: a few days ago I entered into relations with Savinkov, with whom I am on

[27] A copy of the original is in the Hoover War Library, Stanford University. The letter was written by a foreign resident at Moscow who was rather close to the Allied Missions. The spelling of proper names has been corrected to conform to the system of transliteration followed in this volume; otherwise the document, which is an English translation from the French, has been followed literally.

the best of terms; on this very day I have had a very quiet cup of tea with that man upon whose head a price has been set. . . .

Count Mirbach, the new master, fell upon us today. As was written yesterday we have a Prince Lvov period, a Kerensky period, a Lenin period. We are about to have a Mirbach term.

In the midst of the infinite passivity of the Russian people, in the midst of the infinite "aloofness" of the Allies, Mirbach comes to us in the aureole of pliant, but ruthless will, authority, order, order mainly, which envelopes Germany in the eyes of people who all yearn to shake off the nightmare by which they are harrassed.

It is no secret that the pro-German sentiment, or rather German orientation as it is put in good Russian, has made considerable headway. That pro-Germanism heretofore confined to the former officials of the Court and Imperial bureaucrats first seized the private individual fearing for his life and money box, then invaded the political sets of the Right, and is breaking into the K. D.s [Constitutional Democrats]. It is the trend of thought of the industrial groups, . . . the groups of the Rights, which may be our friends at heart, but believe that the two vital necessities of Russia are the monarchical principle and union with the Ukraine whose secession is artificial, and they hope to bring these about through an understanding with Germany. That is the ground on which we must fight with a hope that Germany will be blinded by her successes and Rohrbach theories to the point of being unable to parry the blow. But to achieve our purpose we must assume a well-defined position.

Some, many of the K. D's and especially those of the Left, have stood with the Allies throughout. Our most outspoken allies are among the laborites and particularly among the S. R's of the Right. These have learned and forgotten a good deal during the reign of the Bolsheviki. They are seriously thinking of many amendments to their program. They seem to be decidedly prone to Kadetism. Unfortunately, the K. D's and S. R's are Russian, Russian to the core, in their ideas when it comes to programs and phrases. A coalition of parties can hardly be hoped for, but a coalition of men may be worked out.

Yet the strength of the S. R's must not be overestimated. The Russian Revolution, their old standing dream, seems to have died with their offspring, the Constituent Assembly. Bolshevism had instilled in the peasant the one-sided idea of unrestrained license to lay hands on anything he covets. But after so taking hold, the peasant will be seized with the uncontrollable desire to keep hold of his booty. We may very well see, in the near future, the Russian muzhik turn into a regular bourgeois. And the S. R's who had built their doctrine on the idea that socialism was the evolved shape of the Russian peasant's ideal no doubt already see the spectre of the French small land holder looming up.

As for the extreme left: in their present condition, having lost all power outside of Moscow, the Bolsheviki can but carry out under protest Germany's ultimatums. . . .

Germany comes here as an unopposed master. No need of a military occupation of Petrograd or Moscow is felt at present. She will use her marks and ultimatums to whip them all into line; she will prop with her authority a government that is daily losing the respect of the masses and its self-confidence, but will cling to power as long as it can, then after draining, sucking, and assimilating all that is worth taking in Russia, she will think of strengthening her situation by throwing out the Bolsheviki and setting up a Monarchy eager to enter into perpetual alliance with her; she will draw up another treaty which being then accepted by all, will sanction the Brest-Litovsk Treaty under cover of immaterial concessions; she may go to the extreme of a nominal or very loose union of Russia and the Ukraine, and will be looked upon by grateful Russia as the restorer of public order, the deliverer of the bourgeois from the Bolshevik pest, and the rebuilder of union.

That may not be the true aim of the Germans, but at any rate, it is ascribed to them and has the advantage of placing them in a clear-cut position. As against this we, the "former allies," make a picture which, as a Russian student conversant with his classics, may compare to that drawn by Krylov in his famous fable. Japan, an enigma; France, intensely for Japanese intervention . . . , the [French] mission for "Sovietist orientation"; England wavering; Italy with but one thought, that of keeping Bolshevism out; Belgium in a trance; and lastly the Americans who would be "business men" and democrats at one and the same time and cast a sportsman's eye upon the Bolsheviki. There you are!

It seems that the "intervention" party will win. It is without doubt the only one from which we may yet expect some advantage. But we must lose no time in bringing into play all the forces concerned, down to the frailest.

Of all the organizations now in existence, and the Lord knows how many and how loose they are, that which seems to me most likely to make good is that led by the man I mentioned, Boris (Savinkov), as we discreetly call him here. He is by far the man who impressed me most, is endowed with self-possession, clear-mindedness, and energy. He does not seem to bother with questions of programs or scruples, a rather exceptional case here, whether this be said to his credit or not. And as he cannot but thwart our enemy's plans, we may trust him to the utmost. The difficulty lies in bringing the several organizations together, the partisan ideas predominating among them. But all those that are pro-Ally have ties with General Alexeev, who maintains close relations with Savinkov.

THE MOSCOW CENTER OF THE RIGHT

[From the Memoirs of V. Gurko, Member of the Organization] [28]

At the time of the Bolshevik coup d'état, there existed in Moscow an organization calling itself the League of Active Citizens. It was formed in August [1917], just before the Moscow State Conference. . . . With the inauguration of the Bolshevik era . . . certain members of the League, viz., Krivoshein, Struve, and Professor Novgorodtsev, realizing that the organization was not likely to accomplish anything substantial, decided to form an inner group whose purpose would be the establishment of contacts with military circles and the creation with their aid of a force sufficient to overthrow the Bolsheviks. The group was known first as the "Deviatka" because of the number [nine] of members composing it (three representatives of the League of Active Citizens, three of the Cadet party, and three of commercial and industrial circles). Later it came to be known as the Center of the Right. . . . The group was in possession of some resources, supplied principally by industrialists.

[28] V. I. Gurko, "Iz Petrograda cherez Moskvu, Parizh i London v Odessu," in *A. R. R.*, XV, 8-15.

In February 1918 the Center of the Right was in touch with a number of secret military organizations. . . . Moscow was flooded with former officers . . . , but there was no military leader with sufficient prestige to consolidate the scattered forces. . . . General Brusilov was at one time willing to head the movement on condition that we guarantee him at least six thousand men. . . . Strange as it may seem, it proved impossible to muster that number. This [failure] was due in part to the lack of money . . . but chiefly to the circumstance that, together with those attempting to form a military force for the overthrow of the Bolsheviks in Moscow, there were others who were trying to transfer the officers from Moscow to the Don to enter the Volunteer Army, and to the Urals to form a new Eastern front. Another factor was the ill-famed controversy of "orientation," in which one side leaned toward Germany, the other toward the Allies. . . . In vain I attempted to show that the Center of the Right had no preference other than the Russian, that in its choice between the Entente and Germany the Center of the Right was guided exclusively by the interests of the Russian state. I cited in this connection the well-known statement of Palmerston, that England had permanent interests but no permanent allies. A feeling of hostility toward a nation with which we had been at war for three years was understandable, but feelings alone, I argued, are not a safe guide in politics. Nor was it a question of loyalty to the Allies, since they were ready to support the Bolsheviks, Russia's oppressors, if they would only continue the war against Germany. . . .

It was this very question of which side should be favored that caused the final breach between the Center of the Right and the Union for the Regeneration of Russia. The specific occasion [of the breach] was the proposed landing of the Japanese in the Far East with the object of forming an anti-German front on the Urals which was to include the Czechoslovaks . . . and the Volunteer Army. The plan originated in Paris and was communicated . . . through Grenard, the French consul at Moscow, to Prince E. Trubetskoi. . . . It was a fantastic idea. . . . The Union for the Regeneration of Russia accepted it. . . . General Tsikhovich, representing the Center of the Right, made an estimate of the time needed for the concentration of a sufficient force in the Urals and found that there would be required a period of from six to eight months. It was also clear that Japan would not help us merely because of our beautiful eyes. . . . Moreover, there was the danger that the Germans would support the Bolsheviks in case an Eastern front was formed. The Center of the Right was firmly convinced that the Bolsheviks were Russia's principal evil . . . , and that they could be overthrown if the Germans assisted or remained neutral. . . .

While negotiations were taking place with the French about the formation of a front in the Urals, certain representatives of the German Government in Petrograd began to negotiate with a number of leaders of the Right. . . . The Moscow Center of the Right was brought into the negotiations, and for the first time there presented itself the question of using the Germans for the overthrow of the Bolsheviks. . . . When the Germans discovered that they could deal only with the circles of the Right, that the more radical political parties ignored them, the idea of restoring order in Russia was, naturally, abandoned by them. . . .

Among those favoring an understanding with Germany was the leader of the Constitutional Democrats, P. Miliukov. During the spring of 1918 Miliukov was in hiding in the Don region, but with the arrival of the Germans he moved to Kiev, where he carried on negotiations with the German authorities in the Ukraine. In these negotiations Miliukov endeavored to reach an understanding with reference to the modification of the Brest Treaty and the reestablishment of the monarchy in Russia.

MILIUKOV ADVOCATES AN AGREEMENT WITH THE GERMANS

[Memorandum to the Moscow Center of the Right] [29]

A communication of Prince Gr. Nik. [Troubetskoi] convinces me that our views as to the best way of leading Russia out of her present situation coincide in every particular. I too consider it our primary and most urgent duty to form a stable government and unite the various parts of Russia. This we must do as soon as

---

[29] Denikin, *Ocherki russkoi smuty,* III, 82-83.

7

possible . . . and with the aid of the Germans, who can help us establish in Moscow . . . a central government capable of uniting the rest of Russia. It is important, however, to obtain Germany's consent to the revision of the Brest-Litovsk Treaty *now* and not at the termination of the war.

With this in mind, I entered . . . at the suggestion of the Germans into unofficial negotiations with a representative of the *Oberkommando*. I had a talk . . . with Herr Mumm, in the course of which I discovered that there were two points of view in Germany regarding the Russian question. One, entertained by the diplomats and supported by the Reichstag, advocates the division of Russia by forming *Randstaaten,* and a *rapprochement* with England. The other point of view, held in dominant military circles and now finding favor among liberals and socialists, would make Russia a strong ally for a future fight against England and is ready . . . to revise the Brest-Litovsk Treaty.

The first policy was the official one, but with the resignation of Kühlmann it is losing support. The second is likely to become official. That it is gaining ground is evident from the appearance of a third point of view, one of compromise, which favors a partial revision of the treaty and a limited unification of Russia; this last is the most dangerous for us.

The Germans . . . will doubtless try to come to an agreement with those Russian groups that are willing to make the greatest concessions. . . . It is necessary, therefore, to unite all our forces on one definite program as a basis for future negotiations.

I suggest . . . the following principles:

1. The government which is to emerge must be an all-national government . . . , monarchical in character. . . . An effort should be made to determine the candidate for the throne at once. . . . I would suggest the Grand Duke Mikhail Alexandrovich, whose whereabouts must be known to his relatives in Moscow. . . .

2. All conversations with Germany should assume the integrity of the former Russian Empire, except for Finland (with strategic guarantees from the latter) and Poland (within the limits of the former Kingdom of Poland . . .). In my unofficial conversations Kurland offered considerable difficulty. . . . I can see no way of surrendering Libau. The Crimea and Transcaucasia were

not touched upon, and I suspect that Germany covets these provinces as a base for a future struggle with England. It is obvious, however, that we cannot sacrifice them. The Ukraine constitutes another difficulty. Germany wishes to give her rights similar to those of Bavaria. . . . But I insisted on the sovereignty of the central government, territorial unity, and unity of citizenship. . . .

3. Under the above-mentioned conditions Germany would have to look for compensations . . . of an economic character. It is important, therefore, that our industrialists consider the economic features of the treaty and state the limits of our concessions. . . .

5. We shall have to declare our neutrality, which must of necessity be friendly to Germany. . . . The new national government should prove able to give . . . the people a real peace—something which the Bolsheviks have failed to do. This will sanction its power in the eyes of the people.

The favorable attitude which the Center of the Right adopted toward the Germans soon caused a split within the ranks of that organization. The left wing, composed largely of Cadets, formed a separate organization, pro-Ally in sympathies, which became known as the National Center.[30] This organization shortly became affiliated with a group founded by Boris Savinkov under the name of "The Union for the Defense of the Fatherland and Freedom."

Savinkov, one-time Minister of War in the Provisional Government of Kerensky, helped to organize the Krasnov expedition against Petrograd immediately after the Bolshevik coup d'état.[31] When the expedition had failed, he went to the Don and entered the Administrative Council formed in connection with the Volunteer Army of Generals Alexeev

[30] At their party caucus in the middle of May 1918 the Cadets adopted the following resolution: "The Central Committee hereby reaffirms its previous attitude toward the Allies and expresses its opposition to every attempt, direct or indirect, to resort to the aid of the Germans in reestablishing the government. The Committee will refrain from giving any aid to the Germans. . _ ." (*Zaria Rossii*, No. 19, May 19, 1918, p. 3.)

[31] See *The Bolshevik Revolution,* pp. 173-74.

and Kornilov. Early in 1918 General Kornilov, wishing to get rid of Savinkov, sent him on a mission to Soviet Russia to recruit opposition forces and dispatch them to the Volunteer Army. Savinkov founded an organization of his own in Moscow . . . and his subsequent activities were independent of the Volunteer movement in the South.

THE UNION FOR THE DEFENSE OF THE FATHERLAND AND FREEDOM

[From Savinkov's Reminiscences] [32]

Early in March 1918 . . . I discovered in Moscow a secret organization which included about eight hundred army officers. . . . The organization was led by a number of citizens prominent in public life and aimed at the preparation of an armed insurrection [against the Bolsheviks] in the capital. . . . The Moscow organization avowedly broke away from democracy and contemplated a constitutional monarchy for Russia. Furthermore, a number of its leaders, blinded by the temporary success of the Germans in France, betrayed the Allies and advocated an understanding with Count Mirbach, the German ambassador at Moscow.[33] To the credit of Russian officers, it is necessary to say that these attempts to come to an agreement with the enemy produced a split in the organization, and only sixty out of the eight hundred were ready to go the German way.

. . . I decided to form a new secret society . . . , accepting the program of the "Civic Administration of the Don." [34] . . . With the aid of Colonel Perkhurov . . . I organized all available officers and cadets . . . and laid the foundation of what later came to be known as the "Union for the Defense of the Fatherland and Freedom." . . . In April the Czechoslovaks for the first time gave us financial aid, which enabled us to extend our activities. We formed army units. . . . We had our agents in the German embassy, the Sovnarkom, the Cheka, the Bolshevik Staff, and similar institutions. . . . We planned . . . to assassinate Lenin

[32] B. Savinkov, *Borba s bolshevikami*, pp. 24-28.
[33] The reference here is to the Moscow Center of the Right.
[34] See Kornilov's political program in *The Bolshevik Revolution*, pp. 424-25.

and Trotsky and made preparations for an armed insurrection. . . .

When the Union . . . became a sizeable organized force, there arose for consideration the question of political affiliation. . . . The Center of the Left,[35] which was formed in the spring of 1918, proposed that I become a member of that organization. After consulting my staff I refused. The Center of the Left . . . consisted mostly of Socialist-Revolutionists and Left Cadets. . . . I then accepted an invitation . . . for the National Center . . . to place my forces at its disposal . . . and start an armed uprising. That uprising could not take place in Moscow, since the Germans threatened to occupy the capital if the Bolsheviks were overthrown; it took place in Rybinsk, Yaroslav, and Murom. . . .

Our aim [36] was to cut off Moscow from Archangel, where the Allies proposed to land a force. According to that plan, the Allies, having landed at Archangel, could very easily take Vologda and menace Moscow if Yaroslav were in our hands. In addition to Rybinsk and Yaroslav we intended to capture Murom . . . , where the Bolshevik Stavka [37] was located, and, if possible, Vladimir to the east of Moscow and Kaluga to the south. . . . Moscow would then have found itself surrounded by insurgent cities . . . , seriously menacing the Bolsheviks.

The plan was only partly successful. . . . In Kaluga and Vladimir there were no insurrections. In Rybinsk it failed. However, Murom was taken . . . and Yaroslav . . . was held for seventeen days, a period more than would have been necessary for the Allies to arrive from Archangel. But the Allies did not come.[38]

---

[35] This was the original name of the Union for the Regeneration of Russia, described in the next document.

[36] Savinkov, *op. cit.*, p. 32.

[37] Army Headquarters.

[38] The Yaroslav insurrection took place on July 6, while the Allies did not land at Archangel until August 2. In his testimony given in August 1924, when he had been arrested by the G. P. U. and brought before the Revolutionary Tribunal, Savinkov spoke of the preparations for the Yaroslav uprising as follows: "Through Grenard, Noulens sent me a telegram from Vologda in which he definitely stated that the landing would take place between the 3rd and the 10th of July . . . and insisted that we begin the insurrection on the 5th of July. . . . Thus the French were closely connected with the affair but deceived us." (*Delo Borisa Savinkova*, p. 39.) F. Grenard, on the other hand, insists that Savinkov decided upon the revolt on his own initiative and "in violation of his promise not to undertake anything without the cooperation of other Russian parties." (*La révolution russe*, p. 322.)

It was not only conservative groups which worked for an overthrow of Bolshevik rule. In the anti-Soviet camp also were liberals and socialists who believed that economic reform should come about, not through dictatorship, but through gradual and democratic means. The most important of the opposition organizations holding this point of view were the Union for the Regeneration of Russia, composed of liberals and moderate socialists; the Socialist-Revolutionists of the Right, socialists believing in revolution but not in a class dictatorship; and in large part the Mensheviks, socialists who stressed the evolutionary aspect of Marx's teaching. Some of the Socialist-Revolutionists of the Right and of the Mensheviks joined the Union for the Regeneration of Russia, an organization which aimed to bring about the combined action of all the democratic groups opposed to the Soviet Government. Both the Union and the Socialist-Revolutionists negotiated with certain Allied representatives with a view of bringing about Allied intervention against the Bolsheviks.

THE UNION FOR THE REGENERATION OF RUSSIA

[From Accounts by Argunov and Miakotin, Members of the Union]

At the beginning of the year 1918,[39] . . . when the Bolsheviks had captured both capitals . . . and were celebrating one victory after another, . . . all anti-Bolshevik forces began to feel the need of uniting . . . [against the common enemy].

During the spring of 1918, almost all central committees of the different political parties moved to Moscow and began negotiations for common action. The negotiations, however, had no positive result . . . as it was difficult to overcome party differences. . . . The idea had to be abandoned . . . , but those most anxious to bring about cooperation . . . formed an organization which came to be known as the "Union for the Regeneration of

[39] A. Argunov, *Mezhdu dvumia bolshevizmami*, pp. 3-7.

Russia"; . . . this organization they entered in the capacity not of party members but of private individuals. . . .

The Union was composed of . . . Constitutional Democrats (almost every leading member of the left wing of that party), Socialist-Populists, Social-Democrats (Edinstvo group), Socialist-Revolutionists of the Right, non-partisans (from military and commercial-industrial circles), and members of the cooperative movement. . . . The platform of the Union, . . . viewed in its essentials, is reducible to the following points: (1) To fight the Bolsheviks and the Germans—a purpose which necessitated not only the formation of a Russian army but also the cooperation of Allied troops; (2) to reestablish the political and economic organization of the country on democratic principles and to call a new . . . Constituent Assembly. . . .

 Much attention was given . . . to the character . . . of the [proposed] all-Russian government. While agreeing that it had to be a strong government capable of swift . . . and independent action . . . , the Union was unhesitant in rejecting the idea of an individual dictatorship (military or civil) and instead determined upon a directory with five or . . . three members, belonging, if possible, to different parties and agreeing on a program. The . . . directory was to form a ministry . . . with the character of a business cabinet. . . .

At first the Union devoted itself . . . to the consolidation of all anti-Bolshevik forces. A military center was formed . . . which assumed the leadership of the different . . . military organizations (mostly of officers) . . . in Moscow, recruiting them for the proposed army and sending some of them to the provinces to take charge of local forces. According to the plans of the Union, the sporadic armed clashes with the Bolsheviks, which at this time were occurring . . . here and there and being easily crushed by the Bolsheviks with the aid of the Germans, were to give way at the most opportune moment to concentrated action on a large scale in a number of large cities simultaneously. The arrival of the Allies in more or less sufficient numbers was considered to be such a moment. . . .

From its very inception the Union maintained regular relations and frequent contacts with the representatives of the Allied missions at Moscow, Petrograd, and Vologda, mainly through the

French ambassador, Noulens. The Allied representatives were fully informed as to the aims of the Union and its membership and quite frequently expressed their readiness to help in every way. . . . In June 1918 M. Noulens sent the different political organizations of Moscow, including the Union for the Regeneration of Russia, a semi-official note stating the views of the Allies on the Russian problem. The note almost repeated the entire political program of the Union and confirmed . . . the readiness of the Allies to send an army . . . to fight the Germans and the Bolsheviks. . . . As a private opinion . . . the note suggested a series of measures for the internal reorganization of Russia. Rejecting the possibility of an agreement with the Bolsheviks, the Allies urged . . . the formation of an all-Russian coalition government in the form of a directory of three acting dictatorially until the Constituent Assembly should meet. . . .

. . . During one of the meetings [40] the representatives of the Entente Powers asked us what the attitude of the Russian people would be in case the Allies landed troops on Russian territory to fight the Germans. The representatives of the Union for the Regeneration of Russia replied that, though they were entitled to speak only for those groups which had entered the Union . . . , they were nevertheless of the opinion that the Russian people would welcome an Allied landing provided the Allied Governments gave a solemn pledge (1) . . . that at the peace conference Russian territory and sovereignty would not be impaired in consequence of that landing; (2) that no new burdens, . . . other than those involved in the fact of fighting, would be imposed upon Russia; and (3) that after landing on Russia's soil the Allies would not interfere in her internal affairs and would act in cooperation with the all-Russian government eventually emerging from the anti-Bolshevik movement. . . .

The representatives of the Entente Powers found these conditions fully acceptable, and an agreement with the Allies was thus considered feasible.

. . . The most important question for the Union . . . was that of forming an Eastern front against Germany and the Bolsheviks, whom the Germans were supporting. The nucleus of such

---

[40] V. Miakotin, "Iz nedalekago proshlago," in *Na chuzhoi storone*, II (1923), 189-93.

a front was to be composed of the officers' organizations, of which
Moscow had a great number. . . . Accordingly, the Union established connections with various anti-Bolshevik military organizations . . . and worked out a general plan of action. According to
this plan, at a previously fixed time all available forces were to be
transferred to the neighborhood of the region where the Allies
proposed to land their troops, an insurrection was to be started, a
new government proclaimed, and a new army mobilized to act in
conjunction with the Allies.

During the summer of 1918, however, an event occurred which
considerably changed the original plan. The clash between the
Bolsheviks and the Czechoslovaks . . . stimulated a strong anti-
Bolshevik movement which in a short time expelled the Bolsheviks
from Siberia and the Ural and Volga regions. Local governments
appeared in these sections, notably in Samara, where a committee
of members of the Constituent Assembly, composed of Socialist-
Revolutionists, took power into its hands. The result was that,
in addition to the Volunteer Army operating against the Bolsheviks in the South, there now appeared in the Northeast a new
force threatening the entire Volga line. . . . Since the Allied missions assured us that we could expect in a short time the landing
of a considerable Allied force in the North, it seemed to us that
the Eastern front had become a reality, a front stretching from
the White Sea to the Black Sea and directed against the Germans
and the Bolsheviks. Under the circumstances it was found . . .
unnecessary to retain the military organizations at the center, and
. . . the Union for the Regeneration of Russia transferred them
to the South and the East. . . .

THE SOCIALIST-REVOLUTIONISTS INVITE ALLIED INTERVENTION

[Resolution of the Eighth Conference of the Socialist-Revolutionists
of the Right, May 26, 1918] [41]

I. INTERNAL POLICY

The Eighth Party Conference of the Socialist-Revolutionists,
having considered the question of the immediate tasks of the
party, resolves:

[41] Piontkovsky, *G. V. R.*, pp. 154-56.

1. Bolshevik rule during the last six months has resulted in the political disintegration of the country, the complete ruin of its finances, and the total disorganization of economic life, with the result that Russia has ceased to function as a national and political entity. These destructive processes are accompanied by the growth of reactionary tendencies among the propertied classes, which are seeking an understanding with Germany . . . in order to bring about a restoration of the monarchy. . . . With the political restoration there is bound to come an economic and social restoration, bringing, as in the case of the Ukraine, the reestablishment of private property in land and the return of estates to the former landowners . . . , with compensation for damages suffered during the revolutionary period.

2. The principal aim of the Russian democracy is to reestablish the country's independence and its national and political unity on a basis that will guarantee an adequate solution of all political and social problems raised by the March [1917] Revolution.

3. The main obstacle to the achievement of the above aims is the Bolshevik Government. Therefore it is necessary first of all to put an end to that government. . . .

4. . . . . The Constituent Assembly, with the aid of local governmental organs, will then undertake the solution of . . . political, social, and economic questions.

II. RELATIONS WITH THE ALLIES

In view of the extreme complexity of Russia's international position, the Eighth Party Conference feels obliged to state that every additional day of Bolshevik rule is threatening revolutionary Russia with new calamities.

The Allies have two paths open to them. With the consent of the legitimate Russian government they can dispatch a military force sufficient . . . to resist German penetration by reestablishing a Russian army and front; or they can look upon Russia as a country . . . which has surrendered its political sovereignty to Germany, in which case the Allies may consider it necessary to occupy certain Russian territories in order to prevent Germany from utilizing those territories for military purposes. The first alternative, which is the more acceptable for Russia in her present military situation . . . , has been offered repeatedly by the Allies to the Bolsheviks, with no other aim than to defend Russia against German aggression. But the Bolsheviks invariably refuse, because they place party interests above those of the country.

Considering the fact that as a result of Bolshevik policies Russia is in danger of losing her independence and of being partitioned into spheres of influence . . . , the Eighth Party Conference holds that the only way of averting the danger is to overthrow the Bolshevik dictatorship and to establish a government based on universal suffrage and willing to accept Allied assistance in the war against Germany . . . , on condition that Russia's territorial integrity and political sovereignty will not be violated . . . and that the appearance of the Allies in Russian territory will be for strategic reasons only. . . .

The Eighth Conference of the Socialist-Revolutionists authorizes the Central Committee to take whatever measures may be necessary to secure for Russia the course of action [on the part of the Allies] which will prove of greatest benefit to it.

THE MENSHEVIKS AND THE CIVIL WAR

[From an Account of the Proceedings of the All-Russian Conference of Mensheviks, May 22, 1918] [42]

The all-Russian conference of representatives of Menshevik organizations opened yesterday. . . . Three reports dealing with the tasks of the present moment were heard. F. Dan [spoke] on war and peace; Lieber, on the same theme; and L. Martov, on the political disruption of Russia.

F. Dan declared that in order to insure the safety of the revolution it was necessary to do away with the situation created by the Brest Treaty and to reestablish the independence and unity of Russia. This task [he thought] could not be realized while anarchy was crushing the country, while industry and finance were being destroyed by pseudo-socialistic experiments, and while the reconstruction of the army was aimed not so much at liberation from the German yoke as at maintenance of the Bolshevik party in power. The speaker thought that the only way out was to con-

[42] *Svoboda Rossii,* No. 32, May 23, 1918, p. 4. The conference was held in Moscow from May 21 to May 27.

solidate and organize all the revolutionary forces of the country. Every attempt to attract foreign bayonets was bound to lead to a greater enslavement of Russia by world imperialism. It was necessary, therefore, to fight against the so-called "German orientation" . . . and the attitude of bourgeois circles. At the same time the party [Menshevik] must repudiate most decisively the "Anglo-French orientation," which finds adherents in certain circles of the democracy counting on foreign aid for the overthrow of the Bolshevik Government.

L. Martov observed that the political disruption of Russia was the artificial result of the victory of imperialist reaction in the World War. He said that until the struggle between the two coalitions came to an end this disruption could not be considered as final [in the sense of] determining the historical future of the peoples [of Russia]. Thus the fundamental task of the Russian Revolution was to fight against the artificial disruption of the country and to reestablish its unity. . . .

Lieber held that it was necessary for the proletariat to take the most active part in the elemental movement for the liberation and unification of Russia. At the same time [it was important] to resist counter-revolution. The speaker was very much opposed to the German orientation but he thought that a certain understanding with the anti-German coalition was permissible. . . .

The evening session was devoted to discussion of the reports. . . . In the statements of the speakers there were clearly asserted two tendencies—the one favoring "no orientation," and the other defending the "Anglo-French orientation."

A CRITICISM OF MENSHEVIK POLICY

[Maisky's Letter to the Menshevik Central Committee] [43]

When the Bolsheviks seized the government and took a course headed straight for social revolution, the Social-Democratic party

[43] I. Maisky, *Demokraticheskaia kontr-revoliutsiia*, pp. 8-11. Maisky-Liakhovetsky, a prominent member of the Menshevik group of the Russian Social-Democratic party, was expelled from the Central Committee of the Mensheviks for joining the Committee of Members of the Constituent Assembly in Samara. He entered the cabinet of the Samara Government but later joined the Bolsheviks.

[Menshevik] was confronted with the question of future policy. Three positions, obviously, were open to the party: It could support the Bolsheviks, fight them, or remain neutral. After some hesitation, our party rejected the first and third possibilities and decided to fight against the "Communist dictatorship" which was leading the country to civil war, economic ruin, and the destruction of freedom. In opposition to the "Communist dictatorship," the Social-Democrats advocated the principles of democracy, most clearly embodied in the All-Russian Constituent Assembly.

Did our party carry out the officially adopted line of policy consistently? My answer is that it did not. Through all last winter [1917-1918] the party was in a state of irresolution, which reached its climax during the spring of 1918. The general situation in May and June was, briefly, as follows: In the vigor of life, Bolshevism was energetically pursuing its destructive policy in the political and economic spheres. Far from coming to any agreement with other socialist parties, the Bolsheviks engaged more and more in openly persecuting them. All legal possibilities of struggle . . . were disappearing, one after another. At first civil liberties were destroyed, then terror was introduced, and finally there began to rage a civil war in which the Bolsheviks were only too anxious to receive aid from German imperialism.

Under the circumstances, the struggle against Bolshevism was bound to assume very strenuous forms. It was time to act and not to talk. Strikes, insurrections, plots of army officers, rebellions of workers and peasants were everywhere in evidence. The Czechoslovaks commenced military operations at the end of May, and soon a committee of members of the Constituent Assembly was formed in Samara. The political atmosphere was rising to a climax of excitement; and it was the duty of our party to give its adherents a clear and definite answer to the question of what to do, whether to take part in the anti-Bolshevik movement or refrain from such participation. . . . Has the Central Committee fulfilled its duty? No!

I recall the endless meetings of the Central Committee, during May and June, devoted to a "permanent" discussion of "current problems," and I cannot but feel a resentment against that continuous orgy of equivocal phrases and ambiguous resolutions. To tell the members of the party, "Side with the Bolsheviks," was something which the majority of the Central Committee found impossible, because the rule of the Bolsheviks was leading the country to ruin. On the other hand, they did not have the courage to say, "Rise against the Bolsheviks, support the Czechoslovaks, seek the aid of the Allies," because they were apprehensive of the reactionary elements in the anti-Bolshevik camp and feared that the activities of the party might be utilized in the interest of a restoration. . . . The result was that in spite of the official party policy of fighting the Communist dictatorship the Central Committee actually adopted a policy of "neutrality." . . .

Though the anti-Soviet organizations acted in strict secrecy, traces of their activities soon leaked out and the Extraordinary Commission to Fight Counter-Revolution, known as the Cheka, succeeded in arresting several members of Savinkov's group. Moscow was proclaimed under martial law and a number of conspirators were shot. Somewhat later the Socialist-Revolutionists and the Mensheviks were expelled from the Central Executive Committee and other Soviet institutions.

MARTIAL LAW IN MOSCOW
[Decree of the Sovnarkom, May 29, 1918] [44]

Because of the discovery of a close connection between the Moscow counter-revolutionary plotters, headed by the Socialist-Revolutionists of the Right, and the uprising . . . at Saratov, the rebellion of the Don Cossack General Krasnov, and the insurrection of the White Guards in Siberia; and in view of the licentious agitation of the counter-revolutionists, who take advantage of the difficulties in connection with the food supply by trying to restore the power of the capitalists and landlords, the Sovnarkom resolves:

TO DECLARE MARTIAL LAW IN MOSCOW.

N. I. Muralov is charged with the duty of taking all emergency measures to maintain revolutionary order.

V. Ulianov (Lenin)
President of the Sovnarkom

[44] *Izvestiia*, No. 108, May 30, 1918, p. 1.

EXPULSION OF RIGHT SOCIALIST PARTIES FROM THE SOVIETS

[Decree of the Central Executive Committee, June 14, 1918] [45]

Taking into consideration that:

(1) The Soviet Government is living through its most difficult period, having to withstand at the same time the attacks of international imperialism . . . and those of its allies within the Russian Republic, who spare no means, from the most shameless calumny to conspiracy and armed uprisings, in the struggle against the Workers' and Peasants' Government.

(2) The presence in Soviet organizations of representatives of parties which are obviously endeavoring to discredit and overthrow the Soviet Government is absolutely intolerable.

(3) From previously published documents, as well as from those cited at the present meeting, it is clear that representatives of the Socialist-Revolutionists (of the Right and Center) and the Russian Social-Democratic Labor Party (Menshevik) . . . are guilty of organizing armed attacks against the workers and peasants, in association with notorious counter-revolutionists — on the Don with Kaledin and Kornilov, in the Urals with Dutov, in Siberia with Semenov, Horvath and Kolchak, and recently with the Czechoslovaks. . . .

The All-Russian Central Executive Committee of Soviets resolves:

To exclude from its membership the representatives of the Socialist-Revolutionists (of the Right and Center) and the Russian Social-Democratic Labor Party (Menshevik), and to urge all Soviets of Workers', Soldiers', Peasants' and Cossacks' Deputies to remove representatives of these parties from their ranks.

YA. SVERDLOV
Chairman of the Central Executive Committee

[Resolution of the Kazan Soviet] [46]

In accordance with the resolution of the Soviet of Deputies, all representatives of Right socialist parties—Right S. R.'s, Center

[45] *S. U. R.*, No. 44, 1918, p. 538.
[46] *Rannee Utro*, No. 121, July 2, 1918, p. 3.

S. R.'s, Mensheviks, the Bund, and the United Jewish Party—
were excluded from membership in the Soviet. In this way eleven
members lost their seats.

Continually harassed by the Cheka and finding little
popular support in the capital, some of the anti-Soviet
groups transferred their activities to the provinces, thereby
carrying out a previously adopted plan of organizing insurrections outside Moscow and of forcing the surrender of
the Bolsheviks by attacks from without. Members of the
Union for the Regeneration of Russia and Socialist-Revolutionists of the Right went to the Volga region, Siberia, and
Northern Russia and helped to organize the Eastern front.[47]
On the other hand, Savinkov's group remained in Central
Russia and started insurrections in a number of cities near
the Soviet capital. The most serious of the insurrections
were those at Yaroslav and Murom.

On July 6 a group of army officers, led by Colonel
Perkhurov, captured Yaroslav by a surprise attack. They
disarmed the militia, seized a number of Soviet buildings,
and shot several Bolshevik commissars. During the first
days the anti-Bolshevik forces were aided by local workers
and peasants from neighboring villages. But despite the
early successes of the insurgents Soviet troops remained in
control of a part of the city and continued to fight against
the Whites for over two weeks. Toward the end of this
period Bolshevik reinforcements arrived from Moscow and
other cities. Yaroslav was subjected to a heavy artillery
bombardment which caused great damage to the city and
forced the surrender of the insurgents.

The Murom revolt was suppressed more quickly than
that of Yaroslav. On July 8 Savinkov's men captured
Murom, together with the headquarters of the Bolshevik

[47] See Chapter VI.

Supreme War Council, which were located in that city. Only two days later, however, the rebels were forced to abandon Murom.

THE YAROSLAV REVOLT

[Proclamation of the Insurrectionists, July 6, 1918] [48]

Citizens! Bolshevik rule in Yaroslav Gubernia has been overthrown. Those who seized power a few months ago by means of deceit and kept that power with unheard-of violence . . . , those who brought upon our people famine and unemployment, who instigated brother against brother and ruined the national treasury, are now in prison awaiting punishment. Those who have overthrown this authority aim at the establishment of popular representative government. The foundations of political organization must be laid by a legally elected . . . popular assembly which will establish political and civil liberties and will pass a law turning over all land to the toiling peasantry as private property.

First of all, legal order must be reestablished. Any violation of life or property . . . will be mercilessly punished. . . . All restrictions of trade will be removed and private capital will be permitted to participate in supplying the population with goods. . . . The new authority will demand unconditional obedience to its orders and will mercilessly persecute all who interfere with the activity of institutions and enterprises.

Events similar to those in Yaroslav have also taken place in other cities along the Volga. We are acting in cooperation with the Northern and Samara Governments and are under the command of General Alexeev. The Northern army is under the command of Boris Savinkov, an old revolutionist. Moscow is now surrounded, in a closed circle. Few more efforts are needed and the Bolsheviks who seized the Kremlin . . . will be wiped off the face of the earth. Let everyone able to carry arms join the Volunteer Army. Three hundred years ago our warriors, animated by great patriotic enthusiasm, succeeded in healing the wounds of

[48] S. Broide, *Yaroslavskii miatezh*, pp. 123-25.

their suffering fatherland; we too shall succeed in saving our country and our people from shame, slavery, and famine.

COLONEL PERKHUROV
Commander of the Northern Volunteer
Army of the Yaroslav Region

SUPPRESSION OF THE YAROSLAV REVOLT

[Trotsky's Announcement, July 23, 1918] [49]

During the past week Yaroslav was the center of a carefully organized insurrection. Agents of Anglo-French imperialism, White Guards of monarchist and Socialist-Revolutionist tendencies, bourgeois adventurers, monks, university students, and criminals joined in a cruel revolt against the workers and peasants. Due to treason large artillery supplies passed into the hands of the insurgents.

The participation of many army officers in the revolt gave the insurrectionists a superiority in military-technical knowledge. In spite of this, Soviet troops recaptured the city, suppressed the revolt, [and] disarmed and imprisoned hundreds of rebels. The heavy hand of the Revolution has fallen on the heads of the criminal enemies of the people.[50]

The banner of the Soviet Republic again waves over Yaroslav.

L. TROTSKY
People's Commissar of War and the Navy

APPEAL OF THE INSURRECTIONISTS AT MUROM

[Proclamation of the Whites, July 8, 1918] [51]

To the Workers and Peasants:

Citizens! The events of the last few days compel all those who love their country and the Russian people, all true defenders of freedom, to take up arms against the Soviet Government and de-

[49] *Pravda,* No. 152, July 23, 1918, p. 3.
[50] After the city was retaken the Bolsheviks shot about four hundred persons. See the next chapter, p. 228; also Chamberlin, *op. cit.,* II, 59.
[51] *Krasnaia Kniga V. Ch. K.* (Makintsian, ed.), I, 75-77. This work will hereafter be cited as *Krasnaia Kniga.*

feat the usurpers who are disguising their nefarious acts by using the name of the people.

The Soviet of People's Commissars has brought ruin to Russia. . . . Instead of bread and peace it has brought famine and war. The Soviet of People's Commissars has made of mighty Russia a bit of earth dripping with the blood of peaceful citizens doomed to the pangs of hunger. In the name of the people the self-styled commissars have given the most fertile land to the enemies of Russia—the Austrians and Germans. There have been wrested from us the Ukraine, the Baltic and Vistula regions, the Kuban, the Don, and the Caucasus, which fed and supplied us with bread. That bread now goes to Germany. With that bread they are feeding those who, step by step, are conquering us and with the help of the Bolsheviks are placing us in the power of the German Kaiser. With that bread they are feeding the German army, which is slaughtering our people in cities and villages of the Ukraine, on the banks of the Don, in the mountains of the Caucasus, and in the fields of Great Russia.

The Soviet of People's Commissars is a plaything in the hands of the German Ambassador, Count Mirbach.

The Soviet of People's Commissars dictates decrees in the name of the people but Kaiser Wilhelm writes those decrees. Spurning agreement with the best citizens of the country, the Soviet of People's Commissars is not only in complete accord with the German imperialists but is carrying out unhesitatingly all their orders and demands.

By its treacherous policy of executing the orders of Count Mirbach the Soviet of People's Commissars forced the rising of the Czechoslovak army, which was marching to the Western front to fight the Germans. Count Mirbach ordered the disarming of the Czechoslovak Corps, sixty thousand strong, and the Soviet of People's Commissars submissively bowed to his demand.

The Czechoslovaks, whose devotion to Russia has been proved repeatedly, had to rebel and not let themselves be disarmed. They knew that when disarmed they would be turned over to Austria, which would not stand on ceremony with them as former subjects who had taken up arms against the Austrian Emperor.

The Czechoslovaks are true republicans and serve the same sublime cause that we do. They are making war on the usurpers and will not permit the strangling of liberty. The People's Commissars, having long since betrayed the cause of the working class and knowing that the wrath of the people is terrible, now depend upon the bayonets of the Germans and the duped Letts to save their own lives and to keep in power.

The People's Commissars have brought about a terrible fratricidal war, sending detachments of Red Guards and Letts against the peasants to take their grain. The People's Commissars are arresting and shooting workers who do not agree with their policies, are manipulating the elections, and are strangling all civil liberties. . . .

The Soviet of People's Commissars convulsively seeks grain—but who will give grain to the betrayers of the fatherland? Siberia will not give them any grain, and it seems that only Siberia and part of the Don can now feed us. The Siberian Railroad is in the hands of the rebels against the Soviet Government, and we shall receive cheap grain . . . only when we ourselves have ousted the violators and betrayers of the fatherland—the Soviet of People's Commissars—and unite with the rebels.

To arms all! Down with the Soviet of People's Commissars! Only by overthrowing it shall we have bread, peace, and freedom! Long live unity and order in Russia! When we put an end to the Soviet power we shall at the same time end civil war and return once more to our former strength and power.

And then the enemies of our country will not be terrifying to us. Down with the hirelings—the People's Commissars and their tools! Long live the coming Constituent Assembly!

Long live the free mighty fatherland!

SUPPRESSION OF THE MUROM REVOLT

[Announcement of the Commission to Fight Counter-Revolution] [52]

Detachments of the Red Army have liquidated the Murom revolt. Numerous arrests were made. A levy of a million rubles was imposed upon the bourgeoisie. Ten leaders of the revolt were shot. All counter-revolutionary elements . . . fled from the city and the surrounding villages. . . . The Cheka is doing everything possible to ferret them out.

[52] *Ezhenedelnik chrezvychainykh komissii*, No. 2, 1918. p. 30.

C. The Revolt of the Socialist-Revolutionists of the Left

Whereas the groups considered in the preceding section worked for the overthrow of the Soviet régime itself, there was one party which directed its opposition not against the Soviets but against those who controlled their policies, the Bolsheviks. This was the party of the Socialist-Revolutionists of the Left, who took part in the revolution establishing the Soviet régime and later cooperated with the Bolsheviks in consolidating that régime. After a few months of collaboration, however, there developed a disagreement between the two parties on the question of peace with Germany. When in March 1918 the Bolsheviks ratified the Brest-Litovsk Treaty, the Left. S. R.'s denounced the ratification as "a betrayal of the international program of the Socialist Revolution begun in Russia" and declared that their party would not be bound by the terms of the treaty but would "fight international imperialism with all their might." [53] The Left S. R.'s thereupon resigned from the Sovnarkom, although they continued to be represented in the Central Executive Committee and other Soviet institutions. Dissension shortly arose between the two parties in connection with the food question [54] and added to the bitterness which continued on the issue of foreign policy.

In the latter part of June the Left Socialist-Revolutionists became more and more insistent in their advocacy of a rupture with Germany. On June 30 Spiridonova, a leading figure in the Left S. R. party, delivered a fiery denunciation of the government in the Peasant Section of the Central Executive Committee. She excoriated the Bolsheviks

[53] See *The Bolshevik Revolution*, pp. 533-34.
[54] See p. 463, below.

for sending food and manufactured goods to Germany and
boldly declared in conclusion that the only means of saving
the revolution was an armed uprising.[55] The next day Kamkov, another prominent member of the Left Socialist-Revolutionists, gave warning in a speech before the Moscow
Soviet that unless the Brest Treaty was repudiated and
Mirbach, German Ambassador to Russia, was expelled from
Moscow, there was bound to be trouble.[56]

On July 4 the Fifth All-Russian Congress of Soviets met
at Moscow.[57] For two days the Bolsheviks and the Left
S. R.'s aired their differences, and when the latter failed to
carry their resolution calling for a declaration of war
against Germany they decided to force that war on the
Bolsheviks. On July 6 two of their members assassinated
Count von Mirbach and immediately afterwards their
Central Committee attempted an uprising against the Bolsheviks. The uprising was quickly suppressed. The Left
S. R.'s were expelled from the Congress and several of their
members were shot.

These developments left the Bolsheviks in sole possession of political authority. Trotsky summarized the consequences of the events as follows: "The conspiracy of the
Socialist-Revolutionists of the Left deprived us of an ally
but in the end it strengthened our position. Our party
tightened its ranks, and Communist cells began to dominate
all government institutions, including the army."

[55] *Svobodnaia Zhizn*, No. 2, July 3, 1918, p. 1.
[56] *Nashe Slovo*, No. 59, July 2, 1918, p. 3.
[57] There were 1,425 delegates in attendance at the Fifth Congress of Soviets.
Of these, 868 were Bolsheviks, 470 Left S. R.'s; the rest were distributed among
the smaller parties. The statistical chart attached to the stenographic records of
the Congress shows that about two-thirds of the delegates were between the ages
of twenty and thirty, and that in aggregate the delegates had spent 1,195 years
in jail for political offenses. (*Piatyi Vserossiiskii Sezd Sovetov Rabochikh,
Krestianskikh, Soldatskikh i Kazachikh Deputatov. Stenograficheskii otchet,
Moskva 4-10 iiulia, 1918 g.*)

THE PARTING OF THE WAYS BETWEEN THE BOLSHEVIKS
AND THE SOCIALIST-REVOLUTIONISTS OF THE LEFT

[From the Proceedings of the Fifth All-Russian Congress of Soviets,
July 4, 1918]

Trotsky:[58] . . . In different army units on our front there have been certain disturbing occurrences which, . . . if not checked, . . . may seriously threaten the line of policy which you have pursued thus far and which I think you are in favor of continuing for the present. On the Kursk sector of our Ukrainian front there were alarming indications a few weeks ago that an agitation is being carried on in various units of our army to incite them . . . to attack [the Germans]. . . . There is, I believe, no one here . . . who thinks that questions of war and peace, of launching an attack and of concluding an armistice, are questions which can be left to the decision of the individual units and detachments of the Red Army.

I have a telegram from the Kursk War Commissar . . . informing me that certain units, spurred on by propaganda, . . . called for an attack, . . . that the X Regiment voted not to attack without orders from the central authorities . . . , that the Third Regiment attacked. Within the last few days, Commissar Bych was killed [by our own men] and Slovis, commander of a brigade, was wounded. . . . There are similar reports from other parts of the front. I should like to add that I sent a commission to Kursk and Lgov to investigate the matter, and that this commission was fired upon by the same band [which demanded an attack]. . . . One of the commissars reports that stories are being circulated to the effect that the Soviet Government is selling out the Ukrainians . . . , buying up all the cloth for the Germans, sending bread to Germany, etc. . . . If you were to ask me who these agitators are I could not tell you definitely. But if you were to ask me whether there might not be Socialist-Revolutionists of the Right among them, . . . or members of the parties opposed to the Brest-Litovsk Peace and in favor of resuming the war . . . , or agents of the Anglo-French bourse . . . , I would reply: "It is more than likely." . . .

Yesterday I telegraphed the following order . . . :

[58] *Ibid.*, pp. 20-23.

"Two groups are working to bring Russia into war with Germany. One group—the extreme German reactionaries . . .—not satisfied with the Brest-Litovsk Treaty, is aiming to provoke us to some hostile act that will serve as a pretext for seizing Moscow and Petrograd; the other group—the Anglo-French imperialists— is doing its best to involve Russia in the imperialist slaughter. Hired agents of our enemies are working in the Red Army to draw us into the war. I hereby order that . . . all agitators . . . be arrested and brought to Moscow for trial by the Extraordinary Tribunal. All armed agents of foreign imperialism who advocate an attack and are caught opposing the Soviet Government should . . . be shot on the spot. . . ."

[Trotsky's declaration created a great uproar in the hall. He was interrupted several times from the seats of the Socialist-Revolutionists of the Left. When quiet was restored Kamkov, a leader of the opposition, took the floor.]

Kamkov: [59] Comrades! The situation on the front adjoining the region [the Ukraine] where the heel of imperialism is crushing the hopes of the workers and peasants . . . and where workers and peasants are being shot . . . cannot be explained away so simply as by blaming it on German and French provocation. . . . [On the contrary] I am certain that it is the result of the healthy revolutionary psychology of the people, who could not swallow the bait of a breathing-spell and refuse to serve German capital and . . . Wilhelm . . . and to remain passive spectators while German imperialism is shooting down Russian workers and peasants. (*Cries: "What a shame!"*)

This is the general feeling in the region which was formerly a part of Soviet Russia. No matter how many resolutions you pass, no matter what you [Communists] say, you cannot force them [the soldiers on the Ukrainian front] to do the work of Cain . . . , to tolerate the German marauders and hangmen, to be the accomplices of those villains and plunderers who have arrived here. . . . (*Cries: "What a shame! Down with Mirbach!"*)

Chairman: Comrade Kamkov, you are called to order.

Kamkov: Comrades, I say that no matter how many telegrams you send, no matter how much Trotsky threatens . . . , you cannot

[59] *Ibid.*, pp. 24-25.

stop the march of the revolution. . . . We have most accurate
information that among the army units, especially the Ukrainian,
there is a healthy revolutionary movement. . . . You cannot compel
them to stand patiently and wait until you give orders, and you
cannot give orders until Mirbach gives them to you. (*Applause,
shouts: "Correct!"*) We declare that our party is going to support this healthy revolutionary movement . . . , to help the workers
and peasants of the Ukraine. (*Applause.*) . . . In place of this
scrap of paper [Trotsky's order], . . . which does not have an
honest revolutionary word in it . . . , I suggest that we send
greetings to these workers and soldiers who recognize their duty.
(*Applause.*)

Zinoviev:[60] . . . Comrade Trotsky expressed the hope that
after he had made the facts clear all would agree with him. It
seems, Comrade Trotsky, that you are mistaken. We have come
to a parting of the ways with the Lefts. (*Noise.*) . . . Since you
[Lefts] class as healthy psychology the crimes of those people
[on the front] who shoot your comrades, our commissars, then
. . . we say to you . . . that if this is a challenge to battle we
accept it. I raise the question whether you will pick up the gauntlet
thrown down by Comrade Trotsky. . . . The issue is clear. . . .
We stand by the workers stationed at the front who are carrying
out the decision of the Congress of Soviets. We call this healthy
revolutionary psychology but it is not what you call by that name.
Have it your way. We do not desire to exchange places with you.
Cling to those who shoot down your comrades but we cling to
the revolutionary proletariat. (*Stormy applause.*)

[After Zinoviev's remarks a recess was declared at the request
of the Socialist-Revolutionists of the Left, who went into private
conference. This conference lasted about an hour and a half.
When the Congress reassembled Mariia Spiridonova spoke as
follows:]

Spiridonova:[61] The Socialist-Revolutionists of the Left have
authorized me to make the following statement: . . . Our party,
the advance-guard of the toiling peasantry and the proletariat
(*laughter, applause*), accept your challenge. We accept it before
the International, before our oppressed Ukrainian and Finnish

[60] *Ibid.*, pp. 25-27.   [61] *Ibid.*, pp. 27-30.

brothers, before all the toilers of the world, who expect us to
go on with the fight and not to bow [to German imperialism].
Comrades Bolsheviks, we pick up the gauntlet! (*Applause.*) But
let me first of all remind you of a few historical incidents. . . .
Let us recall the days of July 16-17 [1917], when I, Lev
Davidovich [Trotsky] . . . , and other Bolshevik comrades went
to the Central Executive Committee, where we were being criticized. ·. . . There Chkheidze . . . tried to force the whole Central
Executive Committee to pass a resolution [condemning all opposition to the majority of the Soviet]. You . . . and I left the
hall because we knew that the resolution meant the death of
revolutionary socialism. . . . We refused to submit to that
resolution and we succeeded in blocking it. . . . It is now painful
. . . to realize that the Bolsheviks, with whom until now I worked
side by side, with whom I fought behind the same barricade,
and with whom I hoped to fight the glorious battle to the end,
. . . have taken over the policies of the Kerensky government.
. . . (*Laughter.*) I burn with shame that at this gathering of
Soviet representatives, of revolutionists and fighting socialists, . . .
I hear words which bring to mind the speeches of Kerensky . . .
and Avxentiev accusing Lenin of being a spy and the Bolsheviks
of being traitors in the pay of Germany. . . . All those words
and scenes . . . are now being reenacted with almost stenographic
accuracy. . . . (*Noise, applause.*)

Comrades Bolsheviks! Do you know that . . . in the occupied
regions there is not a peasant whose back is not scarred [by
German whips] . . . and that the suffering endured on one side
of the line has aroused the other? . . . It will arouse the whole
front . . . as long as there are people who possess honor and
feeling. . . . Comrades Bolsheviks! You have come out to fight
against those very slogans which according to our ideas should
be used against world capitalism, and we expect you to fight
honestly. Give us a chance to explain our position. . . . You may
carry off the victory at this meeting because you have a majority
here . . . , but you do not have a majority in the country.
(*Applause . . . and laughter.*) . . .

The majority [62] are against the Soviet Government, and even

[62] *Izvestiia*, No. 138, July 5, 1918, p. 5.

within the ranks of the toilers, even there, you lack a majority. We know this to be true because you refused to give us an equal number of seats on the committee on elections which was to examine the deputies' credentials. If [the elections] had been perfectly proper why were you afraid? . . .

First give us a chance to explain the true situation and then you may adopt whatever decision you like—you may hand us over to the Revolutionary Tribunal, condemn us to death, shoot us. Comrade Trotsky's expressions foreshadowed very clearly the outcome of the struggle between the two political parties. He urged you to condemn the activities of the Socialist-Revolutionists of the Left, who call for a struggle [against the Germans] to help our Ukrainian brothers. If those who sound such a battle-cry are to be brought before the Revolutionary Tribunal, to be shot, to be killed, then it is clear that Comrade Trotsky was trying to trick you into a resolution by which the whole party of Socialist-Revolutionists of the Left will be condemned to death. . . . If this is a challenge to battle let us fight fairly. . . . Give time for a full discussion of the subject and take no final vote until the committee on elections has verified the credentials of all delegates entitled to vote. . . .

Trotsky: [63] . . . First of all, I should like to say something in reply [to the Socialist-Revolutionists of the Left] . . . who remind us that at different times they have cooperated with us. . . . I recall that when we were . . . in prison the party of Spiridonova was a member of the firm of Kerensky. This was in June [1917] . . . , and whenever we met we used to ask when that party would have the honesty and manliness to break with the Kerensky government. In October, when we took the field against Kerensky, . . . all the Socialist-Revolutionists of the Left announced that they would not support us. . . .

Kamkov: You lie, you are a liar. (Noise.) . . .

Trotsky: . . . You know that the Socialist-Revolutionists of the Left withdrew from the [Military] Revolutionary Committee. . . . Once, when we fell in with their proposal to form a government with them, they said: "We shall enter the government only if the Mensheviks and the Socialist-Revolutionists of the Right

[63] *Piatyi Vserossiiskii Sezd Sovetov*, pp. 31-35.

are in it." There was a time when we were inclined to overlook things and forgive that party . . . because of its youth. . . . But when we are told that this party is the leader of the proletariat and the peasantry and of the whole international movement, and that we Communists are followers of Kerensky, I am bound to reply that the advance-guard of the proletariat is in Petrograd and Moscow and not in Tambov. . . . The disciplined regiments of the Red Army . . . desire to defend the Soviet Republic. They are not going to be influenced by the fact that twenty men crossed the line of demarcation and killed two or three German soldiers. . . .

[When Trotsky had finished, Lashevich went to the speaker's table to announce the resolution of the Bolshevik group. He pointed out that the resolution which he was to read had been drafted before the session started and that had the S. R.'s displayed less nervousness the debates might have been considerably shorter.]

Resolution of the Fifth Congress on War and Peace [64]

After hearing the special report of the People's Commissar of War . . . , the Fifth All-Russian Congress of Soviets . . . resolves that the power of decision in matters of war and peace belongs only to the All-Russian Congress of Soviets . . . and its organs . . . ; that no other group . . . has any authority in these matters . . . ; and that all army units must submit in these questions to the orders of the central organs of the Soviet Government and the commissars and officers appointed by them. . . .

The safety of the Soviet Republic is the supreme law. Those who oppose this law should be wiped off the face of the earth.

Karelin: [65] We [Socialist-Revolutionists of the Left] have already explained why in our opinion no vote can be taken on the questions brought up . . . by the Commissar of War. The resolution which has been kept in his [Trotsky's] pocket and only just now read raises a number of general problems and should be fully discussed. . . . Under the circumstances our party is not going to vote . . . and for the time being is leaving the hall. (*Noise, shouts.*)

[64] *Ibid.*, p. 36.   [65] *Ibid.*, p. 37.

Chairman: . . . The Socialist-Revolutionists of the Left have left the hall. The session of the All-Russian Congress continues. . . . All in favor of the . . . resolution please raise your hands. It is passed unanimously. . . . The meeting is adjourned.

POINTS OF DISPUTE BETWEEN THE BOLSHEVIKS AND THE SOCIALIST-REVOLUTIONISTS OF THE LEFT

[From the Proceedings of the Fifth All-Russian Congress of Soviets, July 5, 1918]

Sverdlov: [66] Comrades! The activity of the Central Executive Committee is so closely bound up with the work of the Soviet of People's Commissars that it is difficult to think of one without the other. The Central Executive Committee, as the supreme organ of the Soviet Republic . . . , lays down the policy . . . for the Soviet of People's Commissars to carry out. . . . I should like to report on the work of the Central Executive Committee since the last Congress. . . . In this connection I wish to remind you . . . of the terrible blow which we received at the conclusion of the last Congress . . . , when the Socialist-Revolutionists of the Left resigned from the Soviet of People's Commissars. At that time it was felt that it would take a long time to recover from the blow . . . , but by now the scar is healed and hardly noticeable in so far as concerns the functioning of the central Soviet institutions. . . .

With the All-Russian Central Executive Committee, however, it has been different. The Socialist-Revolutionists of the Left remained there and have worked with us until the very last days. . . . At first there was agreement on almost all points . . . , but lately the Socialist-Revolutionists of the Left and the Right and the Mensheviks have opposed the Bolsheviks on every important issue. We [Bolsheviks] have been bitterly attacked on all sides . . . and particularly by the Socialist-Revolutionists of the Left. . . .

Among the first questions . . . over which we fell out with the Socialist-Revolutionists of the Left was the food question. . . .

[66] *Ibid.*, pp. 44-50. Sverdlov was chairman of the Central Executive Committee.

Then came the question of organizing the village poor . . . and the Decree on Food Dictatorship. . . .[67]

We also disagreed with the Left Socialist-Revolutionists . . . on the question of excluding the Socialist-Revolutionists of the Right and the Mensheviks from local soviets. (*Applause.*) You remember that the Central Executive Committee decided on this measure at a time . . . when the Socialist-Revolutionists of the Right and the Mensheviks were organizing uprisings against us . . . in different parts of Russia . . . and . . . were working hand in hand with the Czechoslovaks. . . .

Another question on which we sharply disagreed with the Left S. R.'s is the question of organizing a supreme judicial body to fight counter-revolution. . . . We [Bolsheviks] felt that such a body was necessary . . . and that its hands could not be tied, . . . and the Central Executive Committee formed the Supreme Revolutionary Tribunal. . . . At first the Socialist-Revolutionists of the Left . . . joined it, but after the first death sentence . . . they left, refusing to assume any responsibility. (*Applause.*) . . .

. . . This brings up the question of capital punishment. . . . At a special meeting of the Presidium to discuss this matter . . . the Socialist-Revolutionists argued . . . that since the Second Congress of Soviets had abolished capital punishment no one could bring it back without special congressional action. . . . We [Bolsheviks] cannot be bound by this formality . . . because . . . we hold that between sessions of the Congress supreme power is in the hands of the Central Executive Committee. . . . We also pointed out . . . that [according to the wording of the decree] the death penalty was not abolished altogether but only so far as concerned the soldiers at the front. Our main argument, however, is that the abolition of the death penalty is for times of peace . . . and not for revolutionary times. . . . During a revolutionary period we are forced to use revolutionary methods. . . . [The shooting of Admiral Shchastny] [68] was not the first case of capital punishment in the Soviet Republic. . . . Death sentences by the dozens were being passed in every city, in Petrograd, in Moscow, and in the provinces. Both . . . Communists

[67] The decrees on the food dictatorship and the committees of the poor are given below in Chapter VIII.

[68] See p. 236, below.

and Socialist-Revolutionists of the Left . . . have been associated in this work. . . . All of you know, I am sure, that the All-Russian Extraordinary Commission to Fight Counter Revolution passed and carried out many a death sentence . . . , and we had no disagreement with the Left S. R.'s on these executions. But now the Left S. R.'s make a distinction between capital punishment with and without judicial decision. They condemn the former and approve the latter. . . . This position seems to us rather illogical. . . . Our own policy for the present is not to lessen the terror against the enemies of the Soviet Government but to intensify it. . . . We are firmly convinced that the wide circles of Russian toilers . . . will fully approve measures such as decapitating and shooting counter-revolutionary generals and other counter-revolutionists. . . .

Spiridonova:[69] Permit me, Comrades, to say something about . . . the Peasant Section of the Central Executive Committee. . . . [You recall that] at the Third Congress [of Soviets] . . . the Peasant Congress united with the Congress of Workers and Soldiers . . . and put through the greatest of agrarian reforms . . . —the socialization of land. . . . On this occasion . . . our party threw in its lot with the Bolshevik party . . . , with which it had always disagreed on the land question. . . . The union of the peasants with the workers and the soldiers led to the union of the Central Executive Committees of the two Soviets. . . . That the interests of the peasants might not be wholly overlooked it was decided to have a Peasant Section of the Central Executive Committee . . . , made up of members of the Central Executive Committee, and supplemented by . . . delegates from different gubernias in order to maintain close contact with developments in the villages. . . . Such, in substance, was the Peasant Section . . . , composed of 140 persons. . . . Its aim was to organize the peasants and draw them into the social revolution. . . . As time went on the work of the Peasant Section increased . . . ; it sent literature to the villages . . . , opened schools . . . , dispatched agitators, etc. . . .

I should like to say that from the very beginning we encountered many difficulties . . . , largely because we did not see eye to eye with the Bolsheviks. Our party was the strongest in the

[69] *Piatyi Vserossiiskii Sezd Sovetov*, pp. 50-61.

Section and I was its chairman. . . . At first we got along with the Bolsheviks fairly well; each party made concessions. But after the Brest-Litovsk Treaty . . . , when our party recalled its representatives from the Soviet of People's Commissars, the situation changed completely. . . . All the projects of our Section were blocked . . . , and I cannot tell you all the trouble we had to get money. . . . This Congress is now going to be asked to do away with the Section altogether. . . . The peasants, who are now enrolled as Communists and subject to party discipline, must vote against themselves . . . and the Peasant Section will be destroyed. . . .

Our party . . . works in the interest of the proletariat and the peasantry . . . , seeking to unite them in one family of toilers. . . . But when there were brought into play the old Social-Democratic politics . . .—the dictatorship of abstract theories, the dictatorship of individuals in love with their theories . . .—we came to a parting of the ways with the Bolsheviks. . . You Bolsheviks have betrayed the cause of the peasants. . . . You are making use of them . . . to illustrate your theories . . . and the writings of Lenin. . . . The policies which you are pursuing will kill all the good feeling which the peasant has for the Soviets. . . .

We differ radically [from the Bolsheviks] . . . on the food question . . . and on the way in which the land-socialization decree is being carried out. . . . The agrarian reform . . . will require, according to our [S. R.] calculations . . . , about a billion rubles. . . . When I approached Lenin and almost went down on my knees to ask for two hundred millions, . . . he replied in a brutal and cynical way: "They [the peasants] have grabbed the land— let them divide it by themselves." That's all the satisfaction I received. . . . As regards the food dictatorship . . . , I have evidence to prove that when the flying squadrons of the Red Army pounce on a village . . . to confiscate the surplus, it takes most from the hard-working peasant and little from the kulak. . . . Consider the committees of the poor . . . which you have set up to govern the village . . . and to establish the dictatorship of the proletariat. Dictatorship of the proletariat in an agricultural country! You are bound to fail. . . . We call for a dictatorship of the proletariat and the peasantry; . . . only that kind of dictatorship has strength. . . . The peasant question is the one on which we are fundamentally divided, and on this question we will fight you to the end with all our might. . . .

Now in regard to the death penalty. . . . Our party . . . has used terror against autocracy, against the police, . . . and we are not opposed to violent measures. . . . But we are opposed to having the courts make use of the death penalty . . . , because it smacks of the old régime. . . .

In conclusion I should like to say . . . that our party . . . will not capitulate . . . but will fight for the revolutionary cause . . . until socialism, equality, fraternity, and justice are realized. (*Applause of the Left S. R.'s.*)

[Summary of Lenin's Arguments in Defense of Bolshevik Policies] [70]

Just now the people do not desire to fight, cannot and will not fight, no matter what phrases are used to incite them. Those who demand that the Brest-Litovsk yoke be thrown off belong to the same group as do the Mensheviks, the Socialist-Revolutionists of the Right, and Kerensky. Our policy at Brest-Litovsk has been justified. During the months that have passed since then our workers and peasants made tremendous progress toward a socialist form of government, while the imperialist countries moved closer and closer to the abyss.

We have made and are making mistakes, but socialism has passed from dogma and books into the practical hands of the peasants and workers. Experience is the only teacher. Each month of such experience is worth ten or twenty years of ordinary historical development. We are not ashamed to acknowledge that we are continually changing decrees, that we are feeling our way, making it possible for the peasants and workers to solve their own economic problems and build the socialist state. We cannot as yet boast of great success, we still have tremendous opposition.

The food question is the most important and all efforts are being concentrated on its solution. It is not our country alone that is suffering the pangs of hunger; some of the most developed states of Europe are realizing for the first time the meaning of famine. Millions of people have reached the point where they say: " I would rather die in the cause of the revolution

[70] *Ibid.*, pp. 62-73.

8

than live and suffer famine." We are face to face with the most difficult period in our revolution—the time of awaiting the new crop. Yet I am shocked that just at this period there are people who say: "I am through with the Soviets." It should be clear to everyone that the only way to meet this unusual situation is by unusual measures. Socialism has ceased to be a dogma just as it has perhaps ceased to be a program. Our party has not written a new program and the old one is worthless. For the present the essence of socialism is to obtain bread. The war, Kerensky, the landholders, and the kulaks have left us in such terrible straits that we must solve every problem in a practical way and with an eye to building the new society.

Those who have watched the suffering caused by the famine are convinced that to crush the kulak extraordinary steps must be taken. Only by uniting the city workers and the village poor will it be possible to take possession of the surplus grain and divide it among the toiling population. We are not waging war on the peasants but are endeavoring to save socialism and divide the bread in Russia. We are waging merciless war on the kulak and not on the poorest peasant, not even on the middle-class peasant. We have decreed that the poor peasants be permitted to have manufactured goods at a discount of 50 per cent, and the middle-class peasants at 25 per cent, but from the kulak we take everything. Only when the Commissars of Food and Agriculture will have nationalized all manufactured goods and established fixed prices, only then shall we approach socialism and be in a position to take care of the toilers and the poorest peasants. When the peasants understand what we are trying to do, 99 per cent of them will be on our side.

We probably made a mistake in accepting your socialization of the land in our law of November 8.[71] We yielded to you on this point because otherwise you would not have entered the government. It is not true that Spiridonova humbled herself before me and asked for money which I refused.

In conclusion let me repeat that the time between the present and the new crop is our most difficult period, and that only a union of the city workers with the village poor, who do not speculate, can save the revolution.

[71] See Introduction to Chapter VIII.

[Summary of Kamkov's Attack on Bolshevik Policies] [72]

When the Bolsheviks get into a tight place they make use of their bugbears, the Mensheviks and the Socialist-Revolutionists. If one votes against the death penalty he is called a Menshevik. This is cheap demagogy designed to frighten the ignorant masses. Comrade Lenin is confident that the policy pursued will save the Russian and the international revolutions. The question is whether the peasant is satisfied and whether Bolshevik policy will not be fatal to the revolution. The representatives of the bourgeois Rada made use of German imperialism and as a result the Rada was thrown into the garbage can, and the same fate will befall the Communist government and for the same reasons. But Lenin thinks that everything is all right provided he has the committees of the village poor. If we had our way we would kick out both the committees of the poor and the food armies. They play into the hands of the counter-revolutionists and we shall oppose these counter-revolutionary measures.

In regard to the food question, we insist that only the local soviets are capable of getting the surplus from the kulaks. The food armies sent from the center are not representative of the best workers but consist of men whose ambition is to plunder the village. They get very little grain but bring about a united front of the kulaks and the hired hands and an open war between city and country. The peasants are beginning to look upon the soviets as nothing better than robber gangs. On hearing that the food armies are coming, the kulaks distribute the grain among the hired hands and arm them to fight the invaders. We know of battles where scores of workmen were killed. Of all your stupid and criminal measures the food armies and the committees of the village poor are the worst. You know nothing about the village or how to deal with the kulaks. Comrade Lenin is trying to frighten us by saying that nothing will be left of the party that leaves the Soviet. As it stands today, the Soviet is nothing but the dictatorship of Mirbach. We are not going to leave the Soviet, and you, Lenin, cannot put us out. We shall defend the cause of the peasants and workers; we shall work for real socialism and not for the make-believe socialism which now exists.

[72] *Piatyi Vserossiiskii Sezd Sovetov*, pp. 73-77.

[Summary of Zinoviev's Speech] [73]

Efforts are being made to create the impression that our Red Army soldiers are robbers. The Petrograd Soviet dispatched three thousand of its best workers to the food armies and they have sent back many cars of food. You are trying to stir up the peasants against the workers. You say that the formation of the committees of the poor means the collapse of the soviets. There are all kinds of soviets; in some of them the kulaks are in the majority, and it is our duty to replace them with the poor, who are a majority in the village. The experience of our food armies in the class struggle will teach the poor how to carry on the class war. You learned your Marx from Chernov.[74] The Russian Communist party represents true Marxism.

[At the conclusion of the debate the Bolsheviks and the Socialist-Revolutionists of the Left introduced resolutions. That of the former approved the policies of the Sovnarkom and urged mass terror against the enemies of the revolution; that of the latter condemned the Bolshevik policies and recommended the breaking of the Brest-Litovsk Treaty. The Bolshevik resolution was passed.][75]

Defeated at the Congress in their demand for a break with Germany, the S. R.'s decided to force the hand of their opponents by confronting them with an act of hostility to Germany. The decision to end the "breathing-spell" by force was made by the Central Committee of the Left S. R.'s on June 24 when it adopted a resolution to organize "a series of terroristic acts against the outstanding representatives of German imperialism."[76] At this meeting the Central Committee appointed a small group to make preparations for the terroristic acts and to concentrate S. R. forces at Moscow in view of a possible clash with the Bolsheviks.

[73] *Ibid.*, pp. 77-81.
[74] Victor Chernov was an influential leader of the Socialist-Revolutionists of the Right and Center.
[75] *Piatyi Vserossiiskii Sezd Sovetov*, pp. 98-100.
[76] *Krasnaia Kniga*, I, 129-30.

In the early afternoon of July 6 two Socialist-Revolutionists, Blumkin and Andreev, who were also members of the Extraordinary Commission to Fight Counter-Revolution, drove up to the German embassy and presented an official authorization to speak to the Ambassador. They were admitted to the embassy and received by Count Mirbach with two members of his staff. During the ensuing conversation between the Cheka members and the German diplomats, Blumkin drew a revolver and shot the Ambassador.

After the assassination of Mirbach the Left S. R.'s seized several prominent Bolsheviks, and in the evening of the 6th they occupied the central telegraph office and dispatched to the provinces several telegrams announcing a successfully accomplished revolution.

Meanwhile the Bolsheviks were taking defensive measures. They arrested the Left Socialist-Revolutionist delegates to the Fifth All-Russian Congress and locked them up in the Bolshoi Theater. At the same time they summoned several Lettish regiments and the Hungarian Internationalist Battalion under Bela Kun, and brought artillery pieces close to the insurgents' quarters.

On the 7th the Bolsheviks attacked; the S. R.'s were soon routed and fled. In another day order was reestablished, and the Fifth Congress of Soviets resumed its sessions.

ANNOUNCEMENTS OF THE GOVERNMENT ON THE
INSURRECTION OF THE SOCIALIST-
REVOLUTIONISTS OF THE LEFT

[July 6, 1918] [77]

Today, July 6, about 3:00 P. M., two scoundrels—agents of Russian and Anglo-French imperialism—entered the premises of the German Ambassador, Mirbach, after they had forged Comrade Dzerzhinsky's signature on a false document . . . , and killed

[77] *Vestnik putei soobshcheniia*, Nos. 7-8, 1918, p. 36.

Count Mirbach with a bomb. One of the scoundrels who carried out this act of provocation . . . is, according to available information, a Left S. R., a member of Dzerzhinsky's Commission [to Fight Counter-Revolution], who betrayed the Soviet Government and went over to the service of those who are trying to draw Russia into war and thereby pave the way to the rule of the landlords and capitalists. . . . On account of these S. R. scoundrels . . . Russia is now on the verge of war.

In Germany the strongest party, the military party, has long been looking for a pretext to advance toward Petrograd, Moscow, and Tsartsyn. That party now has the pretext.

In reply to the first steps taken by the Soviet Government in Moscow to capture the assassin and his accomplice, the Left S. R.'s have started an insurrection against the Soviet Government. . . . The Soviet Government seized as hostages all Left S. R. members of the Fifth Congress of Soviets who happened to be in the Bolshoi Theater. Every measure was immediately taken to suppress and liquidate the rebellion by military force. . . .

[July 7, 1918] [78]

Yesterday the All-Russian Congress of Soviets approved by an overwhelming majority the foreign and domestic policies of the Soviet of People's Commissars. The so-called Socialist-Revolutionists of the Left, who during the last few weeks adopted completely the position of the Socialist-Revolutionists of the Right, have decided to break up the All-Russian Congress. They have decided to involve the Soviet Republic in war against the will of the overwhelming majority of workers and peasants. With this end in view, they killed the German Ambassador yesterday at 3:00 P. M. . . . and attempted to carry out a plan of insurrection. Comrade Dzerzhinsky, a Bolshevik, chairman of the Commission to Fight Counter-Revolution, was treacherously taken prisoner . . . , and Comrade Latsis and Comrade Smidovich, chairman of the Moscow Soviet of Workers' and Peasants' Deputies, were likewise treacherously seized. A small force of Left Socialist-Revolutionists entered the telegraph building . . . , and before they were driven out of the building the Central Committee of the

[78] *Izvestiia*, No. 141, July 8, 1918, p. 1.

Socialist-Revolutionists sent out a number of false and burlesque telegrams. Wholly in the spirit of the lawless Black Hundred, White Guards, and Anglo-Japanese imperialists, the Central Committee of the Socialist-Revolutionists of the Left talk about the concentration of prisoners of war by the Bolsheviks in Moscow, etc.

The Soviet of People's Commissars could not, of course, permit a handful of intelligentsia to interfere by means of bombs and puerile plots with the will of the working class and peasants in the question of peace and war. The Soviet Government, in the name of the All-Russian Congress, took all measures to suppress the pitiful, senseless, and shameful revolt. The Socialist-Revolutionists of the Left . . . are now in a theater held by the Soviet Government. Soviet troops have surrounded the district in which the rebels fortified themselves against the Soviet power. There is no doubt that in the course of the next few hours the revolt of the Socialist-Revolutionists of the Left, the agents of the Russian bourgeoisie and of Anglo-French imperialism, will be suppressed. What future consequences the senseless and dishonest adventure of the Socialist-Revolutionists of the Left will have on the international position of the Soviet Republic it is impossible now to say. If the German party of extreme imperialism has its way and war returns to our exhausted and bleeding country, then the blame for it falls entirely on the treacherous and deceitful Socialist-Revolutionists of the Left.

In this critical hour let all workers and peasants clearly and firmly appraise the situation and wholeheartedly rally around the All-Russian Congress of Soviets of Workers' and Peasants' Deputies.

THE SOVIET OF PEOPLE'S COMMISSARS

APPEALS OF THE SOCIALIST-REVOLUTIONISTS OF THE LEFT

[July 7, 1918] [79]

To All Workers and Red Army Soldiers:

Count Mirbach, torturer of the Russian toilers, friend and favorite of [Kaiser] Wilhelm, has been killed by the avenging

[79] *Krasnaia Kniga,* I, 148-50.

hand of a revolutionist in accordance with the resolution of the Central Committee of the Socialist-Revolutionists of the Left.

On the very day and hour when the death sentence of the toilers was being sealed forever, when your land, treasure, forests, and other riches were being delivered to the German landlords and capitalists, when the noose was tightening around the neck of the proletariat and the toiling peasants—[on that very day] Mirbach, the hangman, was killed!

German spies and traitors, of whom there are a great number in Moscow, . . . demand the death of the Socialist-Revolutionists of the Left.

The ruling group of Bolsheviks, fearing undesirable consequences for themselves, continue to obey the orders of German hangmen.

All to the defense of the Revolution!

All to the battle against international imperialists and plunderers! . . .

Forward, all workers and Red Army soldiers, to the defense of the toilers against all hangmen, spies, and treacherous imperialists! . . .

Hail the World Socialist Revolution!

· THE CENTRAL COMMITTEE OF THE SOCIALIST-
REVOLUTIONISTS OF THE LEFT

Comrades Railroad Workers: [80]

In accordance with the resolution of the Central Committee of the Party of Socialist-Revolutionists of the Left, the German Ambassador, Mirbach, torturer of the Russian people, and his associates, have been killed. A large part of the Soviet troops are with us and on the side of the revolution.

The Socialist-Revolutionists of the Left continue along the lines of the November Socialist Revolution, fighting for the freedom and independence of the Soviets of Peasants' and Workers' Deputies from the chains of international imperialism.

The leaders of the Bolshevik party, having fallen under the influence of German capitalists, continue policies which are crimes against the Russian workers.

[80] Piontkovsky, *G. V. R.*, p. 172.

Under orders from Lenin and Trotsky military detachments have been moved to Moscow for the purpose of shooting all Socialist-Revolutionists of the Left. We have been informed that German prisoners of war throughout the Moscow district are being armed against us. It is possible that an attempt has been made to bring detachments of Germans from Orsha and other places to fight against us. Be on your guard!

Comrade Mariia Spiridonova has been arrested and with her the whole group of the Socialist-Revolutionists of the Left who are members of the [Fifth] Congress.

We do not want to shed the blood of our brothers.

We call upon our comrades the Bolsheviks again to come with us on the path of the socialist revolution. The Central Committee of the Socialist-Revolutionists of the Left appeals to you, Comrades railroad workers, to prevent the transportation of the military detachments called out by the Soviet of People's Commissars. Remember that tens of millions of Ukrainian peasants, slaughtered without mercy by the Black Hundred bandits from Berlin and Vienna, listen with fear and trembling to what is happening in Great Russia.

Because of them, because of their sufferings, Mirbach was killed.

The revolution has reached its most decisive and critical moment. Stand by us, Comrades railroad workers!

Long live the power of the Soviets, the power of the workers and peasants! Deadly, merciless war against international imperialists!

THE CENTRAL COMMITTEE OF THE SOCIALIST-
REVOLUTIONISTS OF THE LEFT

THE ASSASSINATION OF COUNT MIRBACH

[Testimony of L. G. Müller, Military Attaché of the German Embassy at Moscow, July 7, 1918] [81]

About 3:00 P. M. . . . a counselor of the Embassy entered [my office] with the statement that two members of the All-Russian Commission to Fight Counter-Revolution had come, that Dr. Riezler, Privy-Counselor, intended to receive them, and that I was

---

[81] *Krasnaia Kniga*, I, 196-97.

to be present during the audience. When I met Dr. Riezler he held in his hands a certificate signed . . . by Dzerzhinsky and stating that Blumkin, a member of the Commission, and Andreev, a member of the Court Tribunal, were authorized to negotiate with the Ambassador on strictly private business.

Dr. Riezler and I entered the reception room. . . . Blumkin then announced that he had received strict orders from Dzerzhinsky to talk with the Count himself.

Dr. Riezler answered that as the First Counselor of the Embassy he was authorized to represent the Count in [all] negotiations, including matters of a confidential nature. Blumkin replied that he was obliged to conform to the orders he had received. . . . After that, Dr. Riezler left the reception room and soon came back accompanied by the Ambassador. Blumkin then took out a large number of documents from his brief case and explained that he had to speak with the Ambassador on business concerning a certain Count Robert Mirbach whom [the Ambassador] did not know personally but who belonged to a distant Hungarian branch of his family. . . . It transpired that the said Robert Mirbach was mixed up in some espionage affair. The conversation concerning this business lasted about five minutes. . . . When Dr. Riezler proposed to Count Mirbach that the discussions be brought to an end and that a written reply be given through Commissar Karakhan, the second visitor, who hitherto had just been listening and sitting on the side, said that we would probably be interested to learn what measures the Tribunal would take in the case of Count Robert Mirbach. To this question, when it was repeated by Blumkin, Count Mirbach replied in the affirmative.

I now feel that the question was a signal for action.

With the words, "I shall show you that presently," Blumkin, who stood behind the big heavy table, put his hand into the brief case, drew a revolver, and fired across the table, first at the Count, then at me and Dr. Riezler. We were so shocked that we remained sitting in our deep chairs. We were not armed.

Count Mirbach jumped up and ran into the parlor, where the second visitor took him as his target. . . . The first visitor continued to shoot . . . and also ran into the parlor. A moment later a bomb explosion followed. . . . Probably in part through atmospheric pressure and in part through instinct, Dr. Riezler and I fell to the floor. A few seconds later we ran into the parlor, where we found Count Mirbach on the floor with blood flowing from a wound in the head. . . . Meanwhile the plotters succeeded in jumping out of the window and escaping in an automobile.

TESTIMONY OF SPIRIDONOVA [82]

[July 10, 1918]

I am a member of the Central Committee of the Socialist-Revolutionists of the Left. We passed a resolution to assassinate the German Ambassador, Count Mirbach, as a step toward the realization of our plan to break up the Brest Peace Treaty. The Central Committee of the party appointed a small group with dictatorial powers. This group undertook the carrying out of the plan under conditions of strict conspiracy. Other members of the Central Committee had no relation to this group. I organized the assassination of Mirbach from beginning to end. When I learned that the assassination had taken place, I left for the Congress of Soviets to explain what had happened and to accept the responsibility before the toilers and the International. The assassination of the agent of German imperialism, who built a nest of counter-revolution at the very center of the Russian Socialist Federated Soviet Republic, is only one of the acts by which our party intends to fight against all imperialism. . . .

I repudiate with indignation the current accusation that the Central Committee of the party was willingly or unwillingly in alliance with the English, French, or any other bourgeoisie. The program of our party and its ways are clear and direct. We renounce all agreements and coalitions with any imperialist group whatsoever and advocate the class struggle of the toilers against their class enemies—landlords and capitalists; we stand for the Revolution, the International, and the triumph of socialism, and fight against war and exploitation by the world bourgeoisie.

In all its decisions the Central Committee of the party never mentioned the overthrow of the "Bolshevik" Government. What happened was merely a result of the excitement with which the Russian Government rushed to the defense of the assassinated

[82] *Ibid.*, pp. 200-01.

agents of German imperialism, and of an attempt at self-defense
on the part of the Central Committee of the party which carried
out the assassination.

. . . Blumkin acted under my instructions. . . . I participated
in all the plans for the assassination. . . .

STORY OF THE INSURRECTION

[From an Account of Sablin] [83]

I have been a member of the Socialist-Revolutionists of the Left
ever since that party was organized. . . .

During the first session of the [Fifth] Congress of Soviets I
discovered that a bureau with extraordinary powers had been
formed by the Central Committee of the Socialist-Revolutionists
of the Left. During the intermission [of the Fifth Congress],
after Trotsky made his declaration, Kamkov told me that there
was a possibility that the Central Committee of the Left Socialist-
Revolutionists and the S. R. members of the Congress would be
arrested after their sharp differences with the Bolsheviks had come
to light at the evening session. . . . I was asked to keep in touch
with Popov's detachment, which consisted of Socialist-Revolutionists of the Left. . . .

I came to Popov's detachment at 2:00 P. M. [July 6] and found
there Kamkov, Cherepanov, Karelin, and Proshian—all members
of the Central Committee. Here I was informed that Mirbach
would soon be assassinated. . . . I left for half an hour. . . . When
I came back I was told that Mirbach had been killed and that
the assassins were here [at the quarters of Popov's detachment].
Upon entering the room at the end [of the building] I saw
Blumkin and Andreev. . . . Blumkin was wounded. . . . He told
me that he had left the documents containing his name at Count
Mirbach's office. It was clear that someone would soon come
searching for Blumkin. . . . I reported to the Central Committee,
which decided to wait. Soon Dzerzhinsky arrived and demanded
that Popov surrender Blumkin. Popov declared that he did not
know his whereabouts. Dzerzhinsky then proceeded to make a
search. Popov reported this to the Central Committee, which
decided to tell Dzerzhinsky that the assassination had been carried

[83] *Ibid.*, pp. 201-04.

out by order of the Central Committee. Kamkov and Karelin went into the adjacent room where Dzerzhinsky was and told him that. . . . [Shortly afterward] Kamkov entered the room of the Central Committee and said that Dzerzhinsky had threatened to arrest Karelin and Kamkov. The Central Committee then decided, as a measure of self-defense, to detain Dzerzhinsky. . . . After that Spiridonova went to the Congress to read the declaration of the Central Committee of the Left Socialist-Revolutionists.

Our secret agents soon reported that the sailors who had accompanied Mariia Alexandrovna [Spiridonova] in an automobile were under arrest, that the entrance to the Bolshoi Theater was closed, and that Spiridonova and the entire group [of Socialist-Revolutionist delegates to the Congress] were under arrest. . . . It was clear that aggressive acts directed against us were under way. We then detained . . . Comrades Smidovich . . . and Latsis, and two other commissars. . . .

The Central Committee drafted a telegram . . . , and Comrade Proshian with fifteen soldiers entered the telegraph office . . . and sent the telegram [to the provinces.] . . . The Central Committee followed a purely defensive course. . . . According to Popov there were about eight hundred men in his detachment. According to my own estimate there were no more than six hundred. . . .

In the morning of the seventh firing began. . . . By ten o'clock the firing reached its height. . . . Popov's detachment suffered about two or three dead and twenty wounded. At this moment Popov arrived at the session of the Central Committee and announced that it was necessary to retreat at once. It was decided to retreat. . . .

LIQUIDATION OF THE REVOLT [84]

The [S. R.] delegates to the [Fifth] Congress who were placed under arrest at the Bolshoi Theater were divided into four groups. Eighty members, who recanted, . . . were set free. Two hundred and fifty members, who remained undecided, are kept in the Malyi Theater. Ninety-five members, who remained firm, are kept in the Alexandrovsk Military School. Finally a group of twenty-five is detained in the Kremlin.[85]

[84] *Novaia Zhizn*, No. 138, July 14, 1918, p. 3.
[85] *Izvestiia*, No. 147, July 14, 1918 p. 4, gives a list of the Left S. R.'s who

THE POETS OF REVOLUTION

[A Characterization of the S. R.'s by P. Surmin] [86]

Those who frequented socialist meetings in 1905 or in our own days could not fail to observe the great psychological difference between two types of Russian socialism. The Socialist-Revolutionist and the Social-Democrat, . . . while aiming at the same end, were never brothers in spirit. When making a speech the Marxian was ordinarily dry and business-like. For his citations he would go to the *Capital* and the doctrine of scientific socialism. One could feel in him the peculiar assurance of a man who knows for certain that his ideals are not figments of the mind but will inevitably be realized. There were many figures, facts, and citations in his speech, but little pathos and less feeling.

The Socialist-Revolutionists more often proved fiery speakers. The first sentence addressed to an audience would fire the listeners' minds, like a spark which kindles a flame. They never took their stand on the class principle or viewed the people as a uniform collection of equal entities united by identical interests and identical views. . . .

The S. R.'s believed not so much in the collectivity as in the creative powers of individuality. In place of objective necessity and economic. determinism they glorified the revolutionary will to socialism.

The Marxists, prosaic, dry, and business-like, are the bookkeepers and clerks of the revolution; the S. R.'s its prophets, heroes, and poets. . . .

Accustomed to play with death and to risk their lives . . . , the S. R.'s cultivated in themselves the will to individual exploits and the capacity for self-sacrifice.

The S. R.'s were men of the people·not only in theory but in their mode of living. They took as their apostles, not Marx and Engels, but Lavrov and Mikhailovsky—viz., intellectual leaders nurtured on Russian soil. But their "populism" was not merely

were shot by order of the Cheka. The list contains the following names: V. Alexandrovich, A. Zharov, M. Zasorin, M. Filanov, F. Kabanov, M. Kostiuk. I. Kozin, I. Burkin, A. Yashmanov, C. Kulakov, A. Loprikhin, V. Nemtzev, and S. Pinegin.

[86] *Zaria Rossii*, No. 60, July 6, 1918, pp. 1-2.

of a theoretical nature. Hidden in their souls there lived myster-
iously the Russian national idea. . . .

It is true that the Soviet Government was supported not only
by the Bolsheviks but also by the Left S. R.'s. The latter were
frequently spoken of as being "almost" Bolsheviks. But they
are not.

There existed a sharp difference between the traders of the
revolution and its poets. Read the *Izvestiia* . . . and other Bolshevik journals and you will note that they have failed to attract
a single creative literary man. Even Gorky . . . abandoned them.
Around the Left S. R.'s, on the other hand, a whole literary
school has been formed. The poets of revolutionary action have
attracted the poets of the word, and the connection is not
accidental; it is a spiritual kinship.

It was among the S. R.'s that there grew the conception of
Russia as the socialist messiah. It was the S. R.'s who created
the new Slavophile myth.

In their papers and journals one finds such names as A. Belyi,
A. Blok, Kliuev, Esenin, and other poets. The Bolsheviks apparently proved aesthetically unattractive to them, for who could
really be inspired by "universal accounting and control?" . . .[87]

Like all poets the Left S. R.'s are effective in words . . . but
very seldom possess political wisdom. The Don Quixotes of the
revolution, they are attractive in the pages of a novel, but utterly
ridiculous in politics. That is why the Bolsheviks hold them in
such contempt. . . .

The revolt of the Left S. R.'s in Moscow had repercus-
sions in other places. There was an uprising in Petrograd on
July 6, led by the Petrograd Committee of the Left S. R.'s;
this, however, was very easily put down, and the troops
supporting the Committee were disarmed.

Of a more threatening character was the revolt of Muravev, the Soviet commander in chief on the Volga front.

[87] The reference here is to Lenin's famous dictum elaborated in his "theses" of
April 4, 1918, and embodied in the resolution of the Central Executive Committee of April 29. Both are quoted in *The Bolshevik Revolution*, pp. 553-60,
565-66.

Muravev, who was in contact with the Central Committee of the Left S. R.'s, arrived at Simbirsk on July 10 with a force of a thousand men. He broke up the local soviet, seized the telegraph office, and issued orders declaring an armistice on the Czechoslovak front and war against Germany. He then went to the session of the Gubernia Executive Committee with the intention of winning over the Communists to his side. In this he failed. The session turned into a fight in which Muravev was killed, and his whole enterprise came to an end.[88] Even before the failure of Muravev became known the Sovnarkom declared him an enemy of the people and in his place appointed Mekhonoshin and Blagonranov to take charge of military operations against the Czechoslovaks.

THE SOVIET COMMANDER IN CHIEF DECLARED AN ENEMY OF THE PEOPLE

[Announcement of the Sovnarkom, July 12, 1918] [89]

The former commander in chief [of the forces] opposing the Czechoslovaks, the Socialist-Revolutionist of the Left, Muravev, has been bought by Anglo-French imperialists.

Muravev deserted the staff of the Revolutionary War Council at Simbirsk and issued an order to all troops to turn against the Germans, who, according to him, had captured Orsha and were marching against us. Muravev's order had for its traitorous purpose the opening of Petrograd and Moscow and all of Soviet Russia to the attacks of the Czechoslovaks and White Guards. The treachery of Muravev has been opportunely disclosed by the Revolutionary War Council, and the troops acting against the Czechoslovaks remained loyal to the Soviet Government.

We hereby declare to all troops, to the Soviets, and to all citizens of the Soviet Republic:

1. Nowhere are the Germans attacking us; all is quiet on the German front.

---

[88] *Bolsheviki v borbe za Oktiabr*, pp. 162-63.
[89] *Izvestiia*, No. 145, July 12, 1918, p. 1.

2. Every summons to attack the Germans is provocation and must be punished by shooting the offender on the spot.

3. The former commander in chief on the Czechoslovak front, the Socialist-Revolutionist of the Left, Muravev, is a traitor and an enemy of the people. It is the duty of every loyal citizen to shoot him at sight.

4. Until further notice all orders to troops fighting against the Czechoslovaks will be signed by Mekhonoshin and Blagonravov.

VL. ULIANOV (LENIN)
President of the Soviet of
People's Commissars

L. TROTSKY
People's Commissar of War

The Fifth All-Russian Congress of Soviets resumed its sessions on July 9. It passed a resolution calling for the expulsion of the Left Socialist-Revolutionists from the Soviets, approved the report of the Commissar of Food on Soviet food policies, accepted Trotsky's recommendations for the organization of the Red Army, and adopted a Soviet constitution.[90]

---

[90] The constitution and the debates preceding its adoption are given in Chapter IX.

CHAPTER V

THE CHEKA AND THE RED ARMY

Theoretical and practical considerations alike led the Bolsheviks to concentrate upon the creation of institutions of force for the defense of the revolution. As Marxists the Bolsheviks were wedded to the idea that government is class rule, an organized system of violence by means of which one class imposes its will upon all other classes. It followed from this conception that after the proletarian revolution "the 'special repressive force' of the bourgeoisie for the suppression of the proletariat . . . must be replaced by a 'special repressive force' of the proletariat for the suppression of the bourgeoisie (the dictatorship of the proletariat)." [1] The Bolsheviks were the more inclined to apply this theory because their seizure of power was attended and followed by threatening opposition to their rule from both within and without. The two chief institutions established for the defense of the proletarian dictatorship were the Cheka, which ferreted out and punished anti-Bolsheviks within Russia, and the Red Army, which fought organized opposition on both the internal and external fronts.

A. Early Activities of the Cheka

Terror as an instrument of government was approved by the Bolsheviks immediately after their assumption of power on November 7, 1917. When on the next day the Second Congress of Soviets decreed the abolition of capital punishment, Lenin condemned that step as based upon pacifist illusion. "How can you accomplish a revolution," he argued,

[1] Lenin, *Sochineniia*, XXI, 380.

"without shooting?"[2] On December 14, 1917, at the session of the Central Executive Committee, Trotsky warned the opponents of the dictatorship that "in not more than a month's time terror will assume very violent forms, after the example of the great French Revolution. The guillotine and not merely the jail will be ready for our enemies."[3] A few days later (December 20) there was established the Extraordinary Commission to Fight Counter-Revolution and Sabotage, known as the Cheka, which rapidly spread its net throughout the country and under the able leadership of Felix Dzerzhinsky proved a highly effective agency of political terror.

A POLICY OF TERROR

[Interview with Dzerzhinsky] [4]

. . . We stand for organized terror—this should be frankly admitted. Terror is an absolute necessity during times of revolution. Our aim is to fight against the enemies of the Soviet Government and of the new order of life. Among such enemies are our political adversaries, as well as bandits, speculators, and other criminals who undermine the foundations of the Soviet Government. To these we show no mercy. We terrorize the enemies of the Soviet Government in order to stop crime at its inception. . . .

We judge quickly. In most cases only a day passes between the apprehension of the criminal and his sentence. But this does not mean that our sentences are groundless. . . . When confronted with evidence criminals in almost every case confess; and what argument can have greater weight than a criminal's own confession? . . .

EXECUTIONS AT MOSCOW [5]

During the night of July 11-12, ten army officers, members of the organization, "Save the Country and the Revolution," were

[2] L. Trotsky, *Lenin*, p. 133.
[3] *Delo Naroda*, No. 223, December 16, 1917, p. 4.
[4] *Svoboda Rossii*, No. 43, June 9, 1918, p. 3.
[5] *Novaia Zhizn*, No. 138, July 14, 1918, p. 3.

shot in accordance with the decision of the Extraordinary Commission to Fight Counter-Revolution. . . .

EXECUTIONS AT YAROSLAV [6]

A special commission of inquiry has been formed to investigate the revolt at Yaroslav.

By means of careful investigations . . . the commission has separated from the mass of prisoners a group of 350 men, mostly *former officers, counter-revolutionists, and White Guards.*

The investigation has shown that this group consisted of active participants in and organizers of the revolt. They headed the conspiracy and had connections with the Czechoslovaks.

In accordance with the decision of the commission the entire band, numbering 350 individuals, was shot.

THE CHEKA OF NIZHNY-NOVGOROD

[Report of the Chairman of that Institution to the All-Russian Cheka] [7]

Nizhny-Novgorod with its famous fair . . . is reckoned among the most important of the commercial centers. . . . Its population consists largely of petty bourgeois and merchants, all of them terror-stricken and cowardly. But recently, in connection with the capture of Kazan [by the Whites], these petty-bourgeois elements began to raise their heads. They went so far as to issue proclamations to the population which urged the overthrow of Soviet rule. The Cheka succeeded in putting an end to all attempts at insurrection. . . . Seven hundred officers and gendarmes were arrested. . . . The arrests . . . still continue. . . .

The Extraordinary Commission succeeded in breaking up a White Guard organization . . . by arresting almost its entire membership and shooting a part of it. . . .

---

[6] *Pravda*, No. 155, July 26, 1918, p. 3.
[7] *Ezhenedelnik chrezvychainykh komissii*, No. 1, 1918, pp. 21-22.

ACTIVITIES OF THE URAL REGIONAL CHEKA [8]

. . . The Ural Regional Cheka was organized in Ekaterinburg a month before its removal [from the city].[9] It had to conduct a merciless fight against the White Guard elements, who, because of the Czechoslovak movement, had begun to hope for an early liberation from the "Bolshevik yoke." The Cheka achieved substantial results in its activities and succeeded in cleansing the city of all enemies of the revolution. Then the Czechoslovaks came and the Cheka was forced to transfer itself to Viatka, where it is continuing its work. . . . It placed under arrest the most important organizers of the Right parties and the former tsarist officials. [Four hundred and forty-one arrests were made.] In addition, the Cheka at different times shot thirty-five persons . . . involved in counter-revolutionary plots. . . .

THE CHEKA OF THE VILLAGE OF BOGORODSK

[Report of the Local Commission] [10]

Bogorodsk is one of the large centers of the tanning industry . . . , with a population of thirty thousand.

The . . . Extraordinary Commission has existed since May 1 . . . and has charge of six adjacent volosts. On May 29 the Soviet and the Cheka were raided . . . , their building was destroyed, and all valuables were removed. . . . With the aid of a detachment from Nizhny-Novgorod the authority of the Soviet and the Cheka was reestablished. . . . Ten persons were shot . . . and a levy of one million rubles was imposed on the bourgeoisie and the capitalists.

In all . . . , five hundred searches and forty arrests were made. . . . We confiscated two hundred thousand rubles' worth of gold and silver articles and one million rubles' worth of sheep wool. . . . The factory owners and the bourgeoisie are in flight. The Commission decided to confiscate the property of those who fled and to sell it to workers and peasants. . . .

[8] *Ibid.*, pp. 18-19.
[9] When Ekaterinburg was captured by the Czechoslovaks on July 25, 1918.
[10] *Ezhenedelnik chrezvychainykh komissii*, No. 4, 1918, pp. 29-30.

THE EXECUTION OF THE IMPERIAL FAMILY

[From an Account by Pierre Gilliard] [11]

. . . On July 16, about 7:00 P. M., Yurovsky called in Pavel Medvedev, who enjoyed his absolute confidence . . . , and ordered him to get twelve revolvers. . . . When the order had been complied with, Yurovsky told Medvedev that the Imperial Family was to be executed . . . and that he was later to give out this news to the Russian guard. . . .

Shortly after midnight, Yurovsky entered the rooms occupied by members of the Imperial Family and woke them up . . . with orders to make ready to follow him. He told them that a riot had broken out in town and that it was necessary to remove them and [meanwhile] have them wait in the cellar. Everyone was soon ready. . . . The procession was headed by Yurovsky and Nikulin, who were followed by the Tsar, carrying Alexei Nikolaevich; behind them were the Empress, the Grand Duchesses, Dr. Botkin, Anna Demidova, Kharitonov, and Trup.[12] The prisoners stopped at the place indicated by Yurovsky. They were under the impression that carriages had been sent for to convey them to a new place. Meanwhile they asked for chairs. Three chairs were brought in. The Tsarevich, who had a sore leg and could not stand up, sat down in the middle of the room; the Tsar sat on his left, and Dr. Botkin remained standing on his right. The Empress sat by the wall to the right of the door through which they had just passed, not far from the window. Behind her stood one of her daughters. . . . On the same side stood Anna Demidova, holding two pillows. The other three Grand Duchesses were leaning against the wall, and on their right were Kharitonov and old Trup.

They waited for a few minutes; suddenly Yurovsky, accompanied by seven Austrians and Germans and two of his friends,

[11] Pierre Gilliard, *Tragicheskaia sudba rossiiskoi imperatorskoi semi*, pp. 12-13. Pierre Gilliard was the tutor of the Tsarevich and lived with the Romanovs at Tobolsk. When the Tsar and his family were moved to Ekaterinburg, Gilliard, though not allowed to live with the Romanovs, took up residence in the vicinity of Ekaterinburg. After the execution of the Romanovs Gilliard took part in the investigation of the circumstances of the execution and the account here quoted is based on the findings of that inquiry.

[12] Kharitonov and Trup were employed as servants by the Romanovs.

Ermakov and Vaganov, Cheka executioners, came in. Medvedev was also with them. Yurovsky approached the Tsar and said: "Your friends wanted to rescue you but have failed, and we are obliged to execute you." Immediately he raised his revolver and fired point-blank at the Tsar, who fell dead. This was a signal to the others. Every assassin had selected his victim. Yurovsky had kept for himself the Tsar and the Tsarevich. Death came to the majority of the prisoners almost instantaneously. A slight groan was heard from Alexei Nikolaevich and Yurovsky fired another shot at him. Anastasia Nikolaevna was only wounded and cried out when the assassin approached her. She fell under the blows of the bayonet. Anna Demidova for a time saved herself by hiding behind the pillows; in the end she too fell a victim of the assassins. . . .

When everything was over, the commissars took from the victims their valuables and carried the bodies in sheets to a truck which was waiting at the gate.

[Announcement of the Presidium of the Ural Regional Soviet] [18]

In view of the fact that the Czechoslovak bands are threatening the Red Ural capital, Ekaterinburg, . . . and that the crowned executioners [the Tsar and his family] might escape the People's Court (there was recently disclosed a White Guard plot which aimed at the spiriting away of the entire Romanov family), the Presidium of the Regional Soviet, in accordance with the people's will, has decided that the former Tsar, Nicholas Romanov, guilty before the people of innumerable bloody crimes, is to be shot.

The decision of the Presidium of the Regional Soviet was carried out during the night of July 16-17. The Tsar's family was transferred from Ekaterinburg to a safer place.

PRESIDIUM OF THE URAL REGIONAL SOVIET OF WORKERS', PEASANTS', AND RED ARMY DEPUTIES

[18] Gilliard, *op. cit.*, p. 13.

[Resolution of the All-Russian Central Executive Committee,
July 18, 1918] [14]

The Central Executive Committee of Soviets of Workers',
Peasants', Red Army, and Cossacks' Deputies, acting through
its chairman, approves the acts of the Presidium of the Ural
Soviet.

SVERDLOV
Chairman of the Central
Executive Committee

LIQUIDATION OF AN ANTI-BOLSHEVIK ORGANIZATION IN THE ARMY [15]

In the middle of August the local Cheka arrested a group of
officers who were on their way to Archangel. After repeated
questioning and attempts to determine the aim of their "journey,"
the officers finally confessed that they belonged to a counter-
revolutionary organization. . . . The Cheka . . . succeeded in
fully discovering the secrets of the organization and in taking
into custody all its leaders . . . , who included the following: [A
list of thirty names is given.] . . . As enemies of the Worker-
Peasant Government they were all shot. . . .

THE LAW OF CIVIL WAR

[From a Statement by Latsis] [16]

. . . This is the law of civil war: *Kill all wounded of the enemy
camp.* . . . It is necessary not only to exterminate the active
force of the enemy but to show that anyone raising the sword
against the existing régime will perish by the sword. This is the
whole meaning of civil war—something which the bourgeoisie
understand very well but which we are very slow in realizing. . . .

In civil war there is no place for judicial procedure. The
struggle is one of life and death. If you do not kill you will be
killed. Therefore kill that you may not be killed. . . .

[14] *Ibid.* About the same time the Tsar's brother, Grand Duke Mikhail
Romanov, was shot by the Perm Cheka, and another group of the Romanov
family were shot and thrown into an abandoned mine pit at Alapaevsk near
Perm.

[15] *Izvestiia*, No. 210, September 27, 1918, p. 3.

[16] *Ibid.*, No. 181, August 23, 1918, p. 2. Latsis (Sudrabs) was a prominent
member of the Cheka. For some time he was in charge of the secret section of
that institution.

THE PURPOSE OF THE CHEKA

[From a Statement by Fomin, Member of the All-Russian Cheka] [17]

By this time it is clear to everyone that our planet has become divided into two contradictory and hostile . . . camps: On one side is the revolutionary proletariat, . . . led by the Bolsheviks; on the other is the entire counter-revolution, including the German Junkers, the American millionaires, the party of Scheidemann, and the Russian Mensheviks and Socialist-Revolutionists. . . .

This being so, the proletariat must solve a number of problems . . . without a moment's delay. . . . The first of these problems is the creation of a strong army capable of crushing·with one blow the "Allied" counter-revolution; the second is the strengthening of the fighting organization of the proletariat, the Cheka, by means of which the dictatorship of the proletariat may be established quickly, firmly, and systematically. . . . Our party must give this question its most serious consideration. . . .

The proletariat of Western Europe . . . will do well to avoid the errors which we committed in November [1917] by being lenient to our enemies. . . . This they will be able to do if the . . . armed forces of the Russian proletariat . . . are well organized and able to lend their experience and authority to the proletariat of the West. . . .

IN A CHEKA PRISON

[From the Memoirs of A. Peshekhonov] [17a]

. . . I began to inquire about other prisoners. The more I did so, the greater became my wonder. If one had gone into a street and assembled about a hundred persons at random, there would have been just such a medley and one could have detained them in a prison with just as much justification. Even the percentage of real counter-revolutionists and speculators would probably have been the same. . . .

---

[17] *Ezhenedelnik chrezvychainykh komissii,* No. 3, 1918, pp. 1-2.

[17a] A. Peshekhonov, " Pered krasnym terrorom," in *Na Chuzhoi Storone,* II (1923), 204-07. Peshekhonov, Minister of Agriculture in the Provisional Government, begins his narrative with his arrest in August 1918 by the Cheka. No formal charges were placed against him but several weeks passed before he was released. After leaving Russia he recorded his experiences with the Cheka.

It sometimes happened, however, that the cause of the arrest would become clear during [chance] conversation. I recall how one of the prisoners began to speculate aloud as to the reasons for his arrest. He had come from Vladimir as a deputy of some trade union, stopped at a hotel, and sent in his passport for registration. Before he had time to go out or to see anyone he was suddenly arrested. "Why?"

"What is your name?" asked someone from another bunk.

"Smirnov.". . . (I do not recall the real name at present, but, as far as I can remember, it was one of the most common in Russia.)

"The name, then, was the cause of your arrest," said a man coming toward us. "Let me introduce myself. My name too is Smirnov, and I am from Kaluga. At the Taganka prison there were seven of us Smirnovs, and at the Butyrki prison, it is said, there are many more. . . .

"At the Taganka prison they managed somehow to find out that a certain Smirnov, a Bolshevik from Kazan, had disappeared with a large sum of money. Moscow was notified and orders were issued to the militia . . . to arrest all Smirnovs who came to Moscow and to send them to the Cheka. They are trying to catch the Smirnov from Kazan. . . ."

"But I have never been to Kazan. . . ."

"Neither have I. I am not even a Bolshevik, nor do I intend to become one. Just the same, here I am. Now we'll stay here together."

It was just as hard to find the reason for the arrest of an American who appeared once in our cell. He was interested commercially in Russian forests and had come to Russia to familiarize himself with its forestry. Not knowing a word of Russian, he engaged as interpreter and guide an experienced Russian forester with some knowledge of English, and they travelled together in the North. On their way back they were arrested somewhere near Vologda, and were conveyed under armed guard to Moscow. There was no reason at all for this arrest, unless it was the fact that they had been conversing in English while travelling. "But is this a crime?" wondered the American. However, he was much more absorbed in another feeling, curiosity. He studied everything about him with keen interest and never tired of questioning his companion about every prisoner. He wanted particularly to shake hands with me and asked his companion to introduce us.

When known, the reasons for arrests amazed one with their pettiness. Thus, one old man in our midst had been arrested because during a general search they found in his possession a photograph of a man in a court uniform. It was the picture of a relative of his, who had his photograph taken when he was appointed Gentleman of the Chamber. The photograph dated from the seventies. But the commissar in charge of the search would not listen to any explanations and saw fit to send both the picture and the "counter-revolutionist" possessing it to the All-Russian Cheka. . . .

That the Bolsheviks used provocation freely cannot be doubted. Among the prisoners were many who had been caught with this bait.

One man, for example, was arrested for trying to buy a gun. The story of this intended purchase was a whole epic; a number of secret agents participated in it and several secret meetings were held before the gun was finally purchased. No sooner did the purchaser lay out his money for the gun than he was arrested by the person selling it; the man, it appeared, had bought the gun from a Cheka agent.

Numerous people were arrested for the purchase of various articles from agents of the Cheka. Not all of them were professional speculators. There were some who never dreamed of engaging in speculation but merely yielded to temptation. . . . Thus, a school teacher went one day to the Kursk depot in the hope of getting some sugar. He intended to buy about five pounds, but then he met a soldier who offered him a whole pud [forty pounds]. The price was right; if one were to offer this sugar to friends they would gladly take it. The teacher counted his money and there was just enough. They set out. The soldier led the way further and further; finally they came to a yard where the teacher was arrested. As for the sugar, he did not even see it. . . .

The Cheka was not the only terroristic institution acting in behalf of the dictatorship. There was also the Supreme Revolutionary Tribunal, established on May 29, 1918,[18]

[18] *S. U. R.*, No. 41, 1918, pp. 500-01.

which also contributed its quota of death sentences. The first death sentence by that Tribunal was pronounced on June 21, 1918, in connection with the trial of Admiral Shchastnyi of the Baltic Fleet on a charge of counter-revolutionary activity. The trial lasted two days, and the sentence, after stating the findings of the court, ended thus: "The Tribunal resolves that in view of his guilt he [Shchastnyi] is to be shot within twenty-four hours." The sentence raised an important legal question in that the death penalty had been formally abolished by the Bolsheviks on November 8, 1917. The defense naturally protested against the sentence and appealed to Krylenko, Chief Prosecutor. On June 23 Krylenko published the following ironical explanation in the *Izvestiia* (No. 128): "The sentence does not say that the accused is condemned to death; what it says is that 'the Tribunal resolves that in view of his guilt [the accused] is to be shot.' "

B. THE RED TERROR

In the evening of August 30, 1918, while Lenin was leaving the Mikhelson Shops after addressing a workers' meeting, an attempt on his life took place. The person who tried to assassinate the Bolshevik leader was a woman named Fania Kaplan-Roid, a former member of an anarchist organization and later a Socialist-Revolutionist of the Right. After firing several shots at Lenin and wounding him she attempted to escape; however, she was immediately arrested and was executed a few days later. On the same day that Lenin narrowly escaped death, Uritsky, chairman of the Petrograd Cheka, was assassinated in Petrograd. These acts of individual terrorism led immediately to the inauguration of systematic "Red Terror" by the government. On September 2, at the order of Zinoviev, head of the Northern Commune, five hundred hostages were shot in Petrograd. A few days later the Sovnarkom legalized the Red Terror by ordering the "shooting of all persons associated with White Guard organizations, plots, and conspiracies." Arrests and executions spread rapidly throughout the country and continued on a wholesale scale for several weeks.

THE ASSASSINATION OF URITSKY [19]

Comrade Uritsky was assassinated between 11:00 and 12:00 A. M. on August 30. The assassin, a student by the name of Keniegisser, entered the office of the Commissar as a petitioner. . . . [20]

ATTEMPT ON THE LIFE OF LENIN

[Announcement of the Central Executive Committee, August 30, 1918] [21]

To All Soviets of Workers', Peasants', and Red Army Deputies! All, All, All!

A few hours ago a brutal attempt was made to assassinate Comrade Lenin. The rôle of Comrade Lenin, his importance for the proletarian movement of Russia and of the world in general, is known to vast circles of workers in every country.

A true leader of the working class, he never lost intimate contact with the class whose interests and needs he has championed for many years. On Friday Comrade Lenin . . . appeared at a meeting of the workers of the Mikhelson Shops. Upon leaving the meeting he was wounded. Several persons have been arrested and their identity is being established.

We have no doubt that the clues will lead to the Socialist-Revolutionists of the Right, hirelings of the British and French.

We call upon all comrades to remain calm and to redouble their efforts in the fight against counter-revolutionary elements. The working class will meet every attack on its leaders with

[19] *Izvestiia*, No. 187, August 31, 1918, p. 4.

[20] According to the account given in *Golos minuvshego no chuzhoi storone*, I (1926), 155, Uritsky was assassinated in front of the Petrograd Cheka building while leaving his automobile.

[21] *Izvestiia*, No. 187, August 31, 1918, p. 1.

greater consolidation of its forces and merciless mass terror against the enemies of the revolution.

Comrades! Remember that the safeguarding of the lives of your leaders is in your own hands. Close your ranks to deliver a mortal blow to the bourgeoisie! Victory over the bourgeoisie is the best guarantee of the preservation of the gains of the November Revolution, the best guarantee of the safety of the leaders of the working class. . . .

YA. SVERDLOV
Chairman of the Central
Executive Committee

A WARNING FROM THE ALL-RUSSIAN CHEKA

[Proclamation of August 31, 1918] [22]

Comrades Workers and Citizens!

The counter-revolution is raising its head. The enraged bourgeoisie, aided by capitalist flunkeys, is trying to snatch from our ranks the leaders who fight for the worker-peasant cause. The criminal hand of a member of the Socialist-Revolutionist party, instigated by the English and French, has dared to fire on the leader of the working class. The bullet was directed not only against Comrade Lenin but also against the working class as a whole. . . .

At this crucial moment it is your duty to tighten your ranks and crush the counter-revolutionary beast with a mighty effort. . . .

The criminal adventure of Socialist-Revolutionists, White Guards, and other pseudo-socialists forces us to reply to the criminal designs of the enemies of the working class with mass terror. The avenging hand of the working class is engaged in breaking the chains of slavery, and woe to him who stands in the way of the working class and dares to place obstacles before the socialist revolution.

Let the enemies of the working class remember that anyone caught in possession of arms without having the required permission . . . will immediately be shot, that anyone daring to agitate against the Soviet Government will immediately be arrested

[22] *Vestnik putei soobshcheniia,* Nos. 11-12, 1918, pp. 2-3.

and placed in a concentration camp. Representatives of the bourgeoisie must begin to feel the heavy hand of the working class.

All agents of plundering capital, all marauders and speculators,
will be sent to compulsory public works and suffer confiscation
of property; persons involved in counter-revolutionary plots will
be destroyed and crushed by the heavy hammer of the revolutionary proletariat. . . .

PETERS

Acting Chairman

RED TERROR LEGALIZED

[Resolution of the Sovnarkom, September 5, 1918] [23]

The Soviet of People's Commissars, having heard the report
of the chairman of the Extraordinary Commission to Fight
Counter-Revolution, Speculation, and Crime, finds that under
present circumstances it is necessary to safeguard the rear by
means of terror. In order to strengthen the work of the . . .
Commission . . . its forces must be increased by reliable party
comrades. The Soviet Republic must be safeguarded from its
class enemies by isolating them in concentration camps, by shooting all persons associated with White Guard organizations, plots,
and conspiracies, and by publishing the names of all those shot
and the reasons for the shooting.

D. KURSKY

People's Commissar of Justice

THE TAKING OF HOSTAGES

[Circular of the Commissar of the Interior, September 5, 1918] [24]

The assassinations of Volodarsky and Uritsky; the attempt on
Lenin's life . . . ; the shooting of tens of thousands of our
comrades in Finland, in the Ukraine, and on the Don . . . ; the
steady disclosure of plots in the rear of our armies; the open
confession by the Socialist-Revolutionists of the Right and other
counter-revolutionary scoundrels of their participation in these
plots . . . ; and the unusually mild measures of repression and the

[23] *S. U. R.*, No. 65, 1918, p. 789.
[24] *Ezhenedelnik chrezvychainykh komissii*, No. 1, 1918, p. 11; also *Vestnik Narodnago Komissariata Vnutrennikh Del*, Nos. 21-22, 1918, p. 1.

small amount of shooting of White Guards and bourgeois by local soviets—all go to show that the talk of mass terror against the Socialist-Revolutionists, the White Guards, and the bourgeoisie has no basis in fact.

It is time to put an end to this state of affairs. . . . Local soviets should arrest all Socialist-Revolutionists at once. A considerable number of hostages should be taken from the bourgeoisie and [former army] officers. The least opposition, the least movement among the White Guards, should be met with wholesale executions. Local gubernia executive committees should take the initiative and set the example.

Chekas and militia departments should make special efforts to locate and arrest all those living under assumed names and to shoot without formality everyone mixed up in White Guard activities.

These measures must be carried out at once. Local organs which show hesitation should immediately be reported . . . to the Commissar of the Interior.

The rear of our army must be cleared of all White Guards and other dirty plotters against the government of the working class and poorer peasantry. Show no hesitation or indecision whatever in carrying out mass terror. . . .

Petrovsky
People's Commissar of the Interior

RED TERROR AT NIZHNY-NOVGOROD

[Announcement of the Local Cheka, September 1, 1918] [25]

The criminal attempt on the life of our intellectual leader, Comrade Lenin, the murder of Comrade Uritsky and . . . of Comrade Volodarsky . . . , have exhausted the patience of the revolutionary proletariat. The workers and the village poor demand that the most severe measures be taken against the bourgeoisie. . . . The conditions of the life-and-death struggle which is now taking place require that we discard all sentiment and carry on the dictatorship of the proletariat with a firm hand.

In view of this fact the Gubernia Cheka of Nizhny-Novgorod has shot forty-one persons of the enemy camp.

[25] *Izvestiia*, No. 189, September 3, 1918, p. 4.

To every murder of a Communist or attempt at such murder we shall reply by shooting bourgeois hostages. The blood of our killed and wounded comrades cries out for revenge. Long live the Revolution! Long live the Dictatorship of the Proletariat! Long live Comrade Lenin!

[A list of forty-one persons shot follows.]

EXECUTIONS AT PETROGRAD [26]

The Petrograd Extraordinary Commission to Fight Counter-Revolution has shot over five hundred hostages.[27] The names of those shot, as well as of candidates for future shooting in case of another attempt on the lives of Soviet leaders, will be published in the newspapers.[28]

EXECUTION OF FORMER TSARIST OFFICIALS [29]

On September 5 twenty-nine counter-revolutionists were executed. Among them were the following tsarist officials: former Minister of the Interior Khvostov; his assistant, Beletsky; former Minister of Justice Shcheglovitov; Archbishop Vostorgov; [former] Chief of the Moscow Secret Police Ganko; and others.

These executions, Comrade Krylenko explained to our correspondent, came about as a result of the Red Terror proclaimed after the attempt on . . . the life of Lenin and the murder of Uritsky.

The executions took place in accordance with the decision of the Collegium of the All-Russian Cheka.[30]

---

[26] *Ibid.*

[27] "Five hundred and twelve counter-revolutionists and White Guards have been shot [at Petrograd]. Among them were ten Socialist-Revolutionists of the Right involved in the organization of an armed insurrection against the Soviet Government." (*Ibid.*, No. 193, September 7, 1918, p. 3.)

[28] The first list of "candidates" for shooting was published at Petrograd in the *Severnaia Kommuna* of September 6. The list is reproduced in part in *Izvestiia*, No. 193, September 7, 1918, p. 3.

[29] *Ibid.*

[30] The *Ezhenedelnik chrezvychainykh komissii*, No. 6, 1918, pp. 27-28, gives a list of ninety persons shot by the Moscow Cheka. The time of the executions is not indicated. The Moscow Cheka was an institution distinct from the All-Russian Cheka, which was known as the Ve-Cheka (*Vserossiiskaia Chrezvychainaia Komissia*).

9

THE TERROR AND THE WORKERS [31]

On September 6 a meeting of the Post-Telegraph Union took place. The subject discussed was "White and Red Terror."

Comrade Liubovich, chairman of the Post-Telegraph Union, said that in addition to [using] mass terror as a means of exterminating the bourgeois class it was necessary to deprive the bourgeoisie of all economic advantages.

Comrade Efretov, member of the Central Committee of the Post-Telegraph Union, declared that the bourgeoisie, which is exterminating the working class not only in Russia but also in other countries, must itself suffer extermination by mass terror. "We must talk to the bourgeoisie in their own language. For every ten lives of Red Army soldiers the bourgeoisie must pay with a hundred lives of hostages." The speaker concluded his speech by urging merciless terrorization of the bourgeoisie until the idea of communism was fully established. . . . In conclusion the following resolution was unanimously adopted:

"Having considered the question of the recent individual terroristic acts against the leaders of the working class, the meeting has come to the conclusion that the working class must at present be merciless in its fight against the bourgeoisie. . . . It is necessary, therefore, to adopt at once merciless mass Red Terror against the bourgeoisie, which can be conquered only by means of mass terror. . . . For every drop of blood shed by our leaders in their fight for the ideals of socialism, the proletariat will drown the bourgeoisie in their own blood. . . ."

RED TERROR IN THE PROVINCES

Penza. . . . Wholesale arrests are taking place in Penza and in the uezd. In the city the following persons were shot: Count Musin-Pushkin, Grachev and Meshkov (army officers), and Kudriavtsev (a gendarme). Similar news is coming from other uezds. Everywhere the kulaks are being penalized and their property is given to the poor. . . . The kulaks are terror-stricken. Revolutionary order reigns in the region.

TURLO
Chairman of the Gubernia Soviet [32]

[31] *Rabotnik pochty, telegrafa i telefona*, Nos. 7-8, 1918, p. 27.
[32] *Izvestiia*, No. 195, September 10, 1918, p. 3.

Ostashkov, September 10. In connection with the Red Terror, the local Soviet of Workers' Deputies has imposed on the local bourgeoisie a levy of 469,000 rubles.[33]

The All-Russian Cheka is in receipt of a number of telegrams about the execution of counter-revolutionists and other elements hostile to the Soviet Government.

1. By order of the Astrakhan Cheka nine Socialist-Revolutionists of the Right were shot.

2. By order of the Vitebsk Cheka . . . [eight persons] were shot. . . .

3. By order of the Grodno Cheka . . . [one person] was shot.

4. [The Nevelsk Cheka shot two.]

5. By order of the Voronezh Cheka [four persons] were shot.

Petrozavodsk. . . . On September 13 the following counter-revolutionists were shot by order of the Gubernia Cheka: Lebedev, . . . Bazarnyi, . . . Yarsha, . . . and Groshnikov.[34]

The leaders of a counter-revolutionary revolt [five names follow] which occurred in the village of Yuzh were shot by the Cheka of Vladimir Gubernia.

Four kulaks of the village of Vorony were shot by the Uezd Cheka. . . .

The Perm Gubernia Cheka, in reply to the assassination of Uritsky and the attempt on the life of Lenin, decided to shoot the following persons belonging to the counter-revolutionary camp: [A list of thirty-six people follows.]

By order of the Viatka . . . Cheka seventy counter-revolutionists were placed under arrest in the city of Orel (Viatka Gubernia). Army officers and Socialist-Revolutionists of the Right predominate among the arrested. Twenty-three were shot. . . .[35]

Penza, September 25. We liquidated a White Guard plot which aimed at . . . the freeing of hostages kept in jail. For the murder . . . of one comrade, Egorov, a Petrograd worker, the Whites paid with 152 lives. Severer measures will be taken against the Whites in the future.

TURLO

Chairman of the Gubernia Soviet [36]

[33] *Ibid.*, No. 200, September 15, 1918, p. 4.
[34] *Ibid.*, No. 202, September 18, 1918, p. 4.
[35] *Ibid.*, No. 206, September 23, 1918, p. 2.
[36] *Ibid.*, No. 211, September 29, 1918, p. 3.

The expeditionary detachment sent to quell the revolt in Kurmysh shot the following kulaks: [A list of sixty-three names follows.][37]

[Novorzhev.] In reply to the attempt on Comrade Lenin's life, the Extraordinary Commission shot eight outstanding counter-revolutionists. All the local rich were taken as hostages. . . . The Cheka is now busy fighting counter-revolutionists and kulaks in the villages. . . .[38]

[Ivanovo-Voznesenk.] The Cheka . . . took 184 hostages from the local . . . bourgeoisie and also a number of leaders of the socialist-traitors. A number of active counter-revolutionists were shot. . . . The Kineshma Cheka constructed a concentration camp for a thousand people. . . .[39]

[Kursk.] The Gubernia Cheka of Kursk, at a special session . . . , adopted a resolution calling for merciless Red Terror and the shooting of prominent representatives of the monarchical régime—landlords, members of the bourgeoisie, and Socialist-Revolutionists of the Right. . . . In all, nine persons were executed. . . .[40]

[Yaroslav.] By order of the Yaroslav Extraordinary Commission the following participants in the White Guard insurrection were shot: [A list of thirty-eight names follows.][41]

THE CHEKA OF THE CITY OF TORZHOK GIVES A WARNING [42]

To All Citizens of Torzhok!

The flunkeys of capitalism have raised their hands against the leaders of the Russian proletariat. The President of the Sovnarkom, V. Lenin, was wounded at Moscow, and Comrade Uritsky was assassinated at Petrograd. The proletariat will not permit its leaders to die by the dirty and murderous hands of the hirelings of counter-revolutionists. . . . For every head and life of our leaders, hundreds of heads of the bourgeoisie and their helpers will fall. . . . The Extraordinary Commission of Torzhok hereby

[37] *Ibid.*, p. 6.
[38] *Ezhenedelnik chrezvychainykh komissii*, No. 2, 1918, p. 30.
[39] *Ibid.*, No. 3, 1918, p. 26.
[40] *Ibid.*, pp. 29-30.
[41] *Ibid.*, No. 6, 1918, pp. 29-30.
[42] *Ibid.*, No. 1, 1918, p. 24. Torzhok is in Tver Gubernia.

announces that a number of representatives of the bourgeoisie and of their hirelings, the Socialist-Revolutionists of the Right and the Mensheviks, have been arrested and will be kept in prison as hostages. . . . Any counter-revolutionary attempt directed against the Soviets, or any attempt on the life of a leader of the working class, will cause the immediate execution of the hostages. [A list of twenty names follows.]

M. KLIUEV

Chairman of the Cheka

SPECIAL BULLETIN OF THE CHEKA OF THE CITY OF MORSHANSK [43]

Comrades!

Those who fight for a better future must be merciless to their enemies. Those aiming at the defense of the poor must harden their hearts and become cruel. A revolution is not a toy and you cannot trifle with it. They strike us on one cheek, so we will return a hundred-fold and hit them all over the face. . . . You know that a few days ago an attempt was made on the life of Comrade Lenin and that Comrade Uritsky was assassinated by . . . the bourgeoisie. They are trying to strike us on the head, . . . so now we are resorting to Red Terror as a vaccine to inoculate the bourgeoisie. . . . This inoculation is taking place all over Russia, particularly in the city of Morshansk, where . . . the following gentlemen were shot: [A list of names follows.]

RESOLUTION OF THE CHEKA OF THE WESTERN REGION [44]

[September 13, 1918]

Having learned the sad news that the bandits of international imperialism, through their hirelings, have made a daring attempt on the life of Lenin, the brave leader of the international proletariat, . . . we hereby resolve to wipe the brutal murderers off the face of the earth. We also wish to emphasize that the White Terror directed against the brave leaders of revolutionary communism is forcing the workers to rally round the Soviet Government and to resist all attacks of the international plunderers. . . .

[43] *Ibid.*, p. 24. Morshansk is in Tambov Gubernia.
[44] *Ibid.*, No. 5, 1918, pp. 29-30.

We members of the Cheka . . . declare that we shall take the most energetic measures to exterminate the hired murderers immediately so that they may not continue in this world. Shame on the betrayers and compromisers, the Mensheviks and the Socialist-Revolutionists, who help the bourgeoisie to do their reactionary work!

Down with the murderers!

Death to the betrayers of the Revolutionary International!

Long live the Red Terror! . . .

Long live the Dictatorship of the International Proletariat! . . .

A DAY'S WORK OF THE CHEKA OF THE WESTERN REGION [45]

[September 17, 1918]

The session took place in the presence of seven members of the Extraordinary Commission and two members of the Central Collegium of the Russian Communist Party.

The following were arraigned:

1. Antonevich, S., former [army] officer, an active participant in a counter-revolutionary plot to overthrow Soviet rule. . . . *Decision:* He is to be shot.

2. Gepner, Vladimir, former chief of police of Smolensk. *Decision:* He is to be shot.

3. Korshonboim, former assistant inspector of Smolensk Prison. He flogged political prisoners while holding the position of prison inspector. *Decision:* He is to be turned over to the People's Court and his case is transferred to the Department of Justice.

4. Revknev, I., arrested for serving in the Polish Corps. *Decision:* He is to be released from arrest in view of the fact that he was only a private in the Polish Corps.

5. Sorokin, V., former general and head of the secret police. . . . *Decision:* He is to be shot.

6. Mikhailov, M., a criminal, . . . charged with participation in murders and robberies. *Decision:* He is to be shot.

7. Romanov, Zakhar, former police guard, . . . notorious for cruelty to peasants. . . . *Decision:* He is to be shot.

[45] *Ibid.*, pp. 24-26.

8. Kondratiuk, G., charged with drunkenness and murder. *Decision:* He is to be transferred to the People's Court.

9. Brazhko, charged with drunkenness and murder. *Decision:* Three months in jail.

10. Toptunov, Leiba, charged with giving a bribe. *Decision:* He is to be released from arrest and to receive his money back.

11. Goncharov, E., Piroga, A., Kozlov, and Egorov, members of the militia, charged with violation of official duties. *Decision:* They are to be released.

12. Dorman, M., former general, involved in the organization of a counter-revolutionary plot against the Soviet Government. . . . *Decision:* He is to be shot.

13. Dorman, Vladimir, son of General Dorman. . . . *Decision:* Being only fifteen years old, he is to be released.

14. Vitkevich, Maria, proprietress of Smolensk, charged with insulting the Soviet Government. *Decision:* She is to be fined ten thousand rubles and freed from arrest upon payment of the fine.

15. Shustov, Evdokim, a store employee, arrested for having a false permit to carry arms. *Decision:* Because he belongs to the proletarian class Shustov is to be released from arrest.

16. Gladyshev, V., former police official of Smolensk. *Decision:* He is to be shot.

17. Filippov, I., Ventov, F., criminals. *Decision:* They are to be shot.

18. Lukstin, A., arrested for delivering 57,000 rubles to a White Guard organization. *Decision:* He is to be shot.

19. Blokh, I., Dembrovsky, I., Turchinsky, V., and Chernogubov, N., all charged with theft. *Decision:* Since they are minors their case is to be transferred to the Department of Justice.

20. Gordzialovsky, a pomeshchik, arrested for operating a gambling establishment. *Decision:* He is to be fined. The amount of the fine is to depend on the property status of the accused.

21. Petrov, former police officer. . . . *Decision:* He is to be released as a useful worker . . . of the department fighting espionage.

22. Katz, M., former ensign, participated actively in the Dorman plot. . . .[46] *Decision:* He is to be shot.

[46] General Dorman's organization was engaged in recruiting army officers and sending them to Kiev to join the ranks of the Southern (White) Army.

23. Belyi, Stepan, a physician, arrested in connection with the Dorman plot. *Decision:* Belyi is to be released because . . . he is a railway physician.

24. Fenraevsky, V., former officer, participated in the Dorman plot. . . . *Decision:* He is to be shot.

25. Sedlenek, Ekaterina, arrested with her husband and charged with participation in the Dorman plot. *Decision:* She is to be released since she did not participate actively in the plot.

26. Zakharov, A., former [army] officer, active participant in the Dorman plot. *Decision:* He is to be shot.

27. Diuna, F., member of the militia, served on the staff of the Dorman counter-revolutionary organization. . . . *Decision:* He is to be shot.

28. Liadkovsky, G., charged with active participation in the Dorman counter-revolutionary plot. . . . *Decision:* He is to be shot.

29. Mikhailov, P., teacher, arrested in connection with the Dorman plot. *Decision:* In view of the fact that Mikhailov was not an active participant in the plot, and that during the tsarist régime he published a number of articles against reaction and anti-Semitism, he is to be released.

30. Uriadov, B., active participant in the Dorman plot. . . . *Decision:* He is to be shot.

31. Schwartz, N., banker, arrested in connection with the Dorman plot. *Decision:* In the absence of proof that he participated in the plot he is to be released.

32. Reutt and Engelgardt, large landowners of Smolensk Gubernia, participated in the Dorman plot. . . . *Decision:* They are to be shot.

33. Yatsevich, arrested in connection with the Dorman plot. *Decision:* He is to be released.

34. Zhdanovich, S. O., lawyer, member of the Cadet party, participated in the Dorman plot. . . . *Decision:* He is to be shot.

35. Voznenko, Vladimir, and Voznenko, Vadim, charged with participation in the Dorman plot. *Decision:* They are to be shot.

36. Tantsov, B., physician, monarchist. . . . *Decision:* He is to be shot.

37. Zaichko, M., Oguretsky, B., Krutikov, S., and Selianinov, P., former army officers, active White Guards. *Decision:* They are to be shot.

38. Maliavkin, Morozov, Karsky, and Butsko, charged with speculation. *Decision:* To release them and confiscate the goods.

39. Liberman, Meer and Tsira, husband and wife, large speculators. *Decision:* To fine them 200,000 rubles; to set them free upon payment of 100,000, the rest to be paid within a month.

40. Chernovich, Ore-Leizar, large speculator. *Decision:* A fine of 50,000 rubles.

41. Troitsky, F., deacon, took part in the Belsk revolt against the Soviet Government. *Decision:* He is to be shot.

42. Chulkov, a priest, took part in the Belsk revolt. *Decision:* He is to be shot.

43. Diakonov, Alexander, and his son, Pavel, participated in the Belsk revolt. *Decision:* They are to be shot.

44. Baikov, A., charged with participation in the Belsk revolt. *Decision:* He is to be shot.

45. Mochonnikov, S., member of the counter-revolutionary staff which led the Belsk revolt. *Decision:* He is to be shot.

46. Efremov, E., agitated against the Soviet authorities in the village of Khalm. . . . *Decision:* He is to be shot.

47. Veling . . . , army officer, participant in the Belsk revolt. . . . *Decision:* He is to be shot.

48. Veling, Valentine, participated in the Belsk revolt. . . . *Decision:* One year of hard labor.

49. Chairman of the Nikolsk Volost . . . , a kulak, carried on propaganda among peasants in behalf of the revolt. . . . *Decision:* Confiscate his property and expel him from the Western Region.

50. Voronin. . . . The revolutionary staff met at his house. *Decision:* Confiscate all his property and expel him from the Western Region.

51. Shumin, A., Petrov, S., Petrov, A., Grigoriev, N., Ilin, A., Izmailov, O., Romanov, I., Denisov, A., Denisova, Maria, Timofeev, N., Vasiliev, P., . . . shall be released.

52. Dzunkovsky, V., Lieutenant General, former Vice-Minister of the Interior. . . . *Decision:* Imprison him. . . .

53. Baikovich . . . , charged with smuggling money abroad. *Decision:* Confirm the decision of the Section in Charge of Speculation.

54. Solomonik, M., charged with falsification of documents. *Decision:* He is to be released.

CHAIRMAN OF THE EXTRAORDINARY COMMISSION
OF THE WESTERN REGION

THE RED TERROR AT KAZAN

[From a Report of Yu. Yanel, Member of the All-Russian Cheka, September 1918] [47]

. . . According to the information supplied by Comrade Latsis, the situation here is as follows: A field court martial is at work. Uezd Chekas have been organized [in ten localities]. Punitive expeditions have been sent into every uezd. In Kurmyshsk Uezd forty people have been shot. In Kazan proper only seven or eight people have been shot by the Tribunal. This is explained by the fact that the entire bourgeoisie, including the petty bourgeoisie, the priests, and the monks, fled from the city. Half of the city houses are deserted. The property of the fugitives is being confiscated for the benefit of the city poor. . . .

ACTIVITIES OF THE PETROGRAD CHEKA

[From the Minutes of the Conference of the Cheka of the Northern Region Held at Petrograd on October 15, 1918] [48]

Comrade Boky reported on the activities of the Petrograd Cheka. . . . During the period between March and October the Commission considered 5,423 cases. . . . In all, 6,229 arrests were made. During the period of Red Terror 800 people were shot. . . .

Comrade Moroz reported on the activities of the All-Russian Cheka for the same period. . . . In all, 2,559 cases involving counter-revolution were registered with the Commission. Over 3,000 arrests were made. It was with great concern that the Commission undertook the task of carrying on mass terror. . . .

The spread of Red Terror, in particular the shooting of five hundred hostages at Petrograd in one day, evoked a

[47] *Ezhenedelnik chrezvychainykh komissii,* No. 4, 1918, p. 25.
[48] *Ibid.,* No. 6, 1918, pp. 19-20.

number of strong expressions of disapproval not merely from Russian groups but also from foreign representatives. On September 4 DeWitt C. Poole, American Consul General at Moscow, sent a note to Chicherin in which he called the Commissar's attention to the "mad career into which the Bolshevik government has now plunged" and urged that "the barbarous oppression" of the Russian people be stopped at once.[49] On the following day representatives of the Diplomatic Corps at Petrograd, including the German Consul General, expressed "their profound indignation at the reign of terror instituted in the cities of Petrograd, Moscow, etc.," and asserted that this terror was calling forth "the indignation of the civilized world." [50] A few days later Alan Wardwell, Chief of the American Red Cross Mission to Russia, added his protest in a letter to Chicherin which spoke of the recent executions as "unwarranted slaughter." [51]

Chicherin replied to the joint note of the Diplomatic Corps that the allegations made in the note had not been sustained by concrete cases, and that in any event "no outward protests and representations will deter the hand which is to punish those who raise arms against the workmen and the poorest peasants in Russia, who wish to starve them, and who wish to drive them into new wars in the interests of capital." He concluded by denouncing the interference of the "capitalistic powers" in favor of "the Russian bourgeoisie," declaring that if the representatives of these powers exceeded the legal limits to which they were entitled for the protection of the interests of their citizens, the Soviet Government would consider it an attempt to support the Russian counter-revolution.[52] In reply to the chief

[49] *U. S. Foreign Relations, 1918, Russia,* I, 683.
[50] *Ibid.,* p. 698.   [51] *Ibid.,* p. 686.   [52] *Ibid.,* pp. 707-08.

of the American Red Cross Mission, Chicherin asserted that only the guilty had been executed, that the executions were unavoidable in the class war waged by the Russian workers, and that to protest against them was to be blind to "the beauties of the heroism of the working class, trampled under the feet of everybody who were above them until now, and now rising in fury and passionate devotion and enthusiasm to recreate the whole world and the whole life of mankind." [53]

On September 20 the American Secretary of State despatched to all American diplomatic missions a circular telegram summarizing the reports of Red Terror and directing the diplomatic representatives to inquire whether the governments to which they were accredited would be disposed to take immediate action "to impress upon the perpetrators of these crimes the aversion with which civilization regards their present wanton acts." [54] However, no further diplomatic *démarches* were taken against the Soviet Government.

Meanwhile certain anti-Bolshevik groups in Russia which had the means of publicly expressing their opinion voiced their protest against the Red Terror.

THE ANARCHISTS AGAINST THE TERROR [55]

[Editorial of an Anarchist Newspaper]

. . . Red terror is a double-edged sword and too often its use brings the most unexpected results. It not only produces emotions of horror and fear in those against whom it is directed but creates a state of desperation and a thirst for revenge as well. Blood for blood has become the slogan of the day and is bound to lead to an endless mutual slaughter.

Our rulers have undertaken to destroy the bourgeois order but actually they are engaged in the killing of individual represen-

---

[53] *Ibid.*, p. 715.   [54] *Ibid.*, p. 688.
[55] *Volnyi golos truda*, No. 4, September 16, 1918.

tatives of that order. Not the murder of a bourgeois but making it impossible for him to be a parasite . . . is what socialism requires. Instead, we witness indiscriminate shooting of everyone who is in any way related to the bourgeois class. And not only those who actively participate in the counter-revolutionary ranks are being shot, but also those who stand aside from the struggle and would be glad to part with their property and become workers. . . . The indiscriminate taking of hostages as prospective victims is a disgrace which would not have embarrassed Tamerlane but cannot be tolerated in our time.

The bourgeois are being driven from their homes and deprived of food rations. But these are ridiculous measures as they compel the bourgeoisie to flee into regions under the control of counter-revolutionists. . . . The forcing of the bourgeoisie to do such filthy work as cleaning the toilets of soldiers' barracks is nothing but malice and can only damage the cause of socialism. . . . The rejoicing of the Communists at the sight of a bourgeois cleaning those toilets tends only to demoralize the ignorant masses. Instead of fighting the bourgeoisie as a class the governing party is perpetrating a medieval inquisition; for the measures are dictated not by considerations of social necessity but solely by fear, which blinds the party and drives it to a policy of useless cruelty, while the desire to retain power at any cost leads it to connive at the bloodthirsty acts of the unenlightened masses. . . .

PROTEST OF UKRAINIAN WORKERS

[Resolution of the All-Ukrainian Trade-Union Council] [56]

The news of the ever increasing brutal and frenzied terror in Russia is arousing profound anxiety in the ranks of the organized proletariat of the Ukraine. This anxiety is the more deeply felt because the cruel and inhuman deeds are being perpetrated in the name of the Russian proletariat, to which the Ukrainian proletariat is bound by most intimate and solid ties.

Blood is being shed all over Russia; thousands of victims, including loyal defenders of the working class, are perishing; prisons are full of hostages living under the constant threat of execution.

[56] *Posledniia Novosti*, No. 5,213, September 28, 1918 (Evening Edition), p. 2.

In this unprecedented . . . situation we deem it our duty to declare that the working class has always been opposed to any terror, no matter by whom practiced. The working class has always fought against such means of settling differences with political opponents. . . . The shooting of hostages and the murder of thousands of people in reprisal for the murder of one man . . . contradict in principle the methods of proletarian struggle. . . .

Bolshevik terror is dealing a heavy blow to the cause of democracy. Reactionaries are everywhere raising their heads. . . . Red Terror is used as a justification for White Terror.

When a government pretending to act in defense of workers makes use of the same methods of political struggle as those employed by reactionaries in their fight . . . against the insurgent masses, then the proletariat must raise its voice and declare openly: "The responsibility for terror falls on those who use it." The working class never has had and never will have anything in common with these methods of struggle. We appeal to the organized proletariat to support our protest.

To the bloody war waged on the battlefields at the will of the imperialists there has been added a war which is allegedly conducted for the happiness of the proletariat.

Enough of blood! Down with terror! Down with all the dark deeds perpetrated in the name of the proletariat! . . .

PATRIARCH TIKHON DENOUNCES THE BOLSHEVIKS

[Message to the Soviet of People's Commissars, October 26, 1918] [57]

". . . All they that take the sword shall perish with the sword." (Matthew 26:52.)

We address this prophecy of the Saviour to you who now direct the fate of our country, to you who call yourselves People's Commissars. You are making preparations to celebrate the anniversary of the October Revolution, which gave you power, but the rivers of blood which you have been shedding cry to heaven and compel us to speak to you these bitter words of truth. . . . You promised the people peace "without annexation and indemnity," but you have given Russia a humiliating peace the

[57] *Bulletin*, No. 1, December 18, 1918, p. 1. Published by the Crimean Government in French.

conditions of which you dare not even publish. . . . In payment of the contribution imposed, you are secretly transporting to Germany the gold which has been accumulated by others and not yourselves. In disrupting the army you have robbed it of its spirit, which had performed heroic deeds. You have tempted the soldiers . . . to abandon the defense of the country and have eradicated from their hearts the belief that "greater love hath no man than this, that a man lay down his life for his friends." (John 15:13.) . . . You refuse to defend the country against foreign enemies and at the same time you do not cease mobilizing armies. Against whom are you leading these armies? You have divided the people and have incited them to fratricide. . . . There seems to be no end to the civil war, since what you are aiming at is the triumph of world revolution and you are prepared to sacrifice Russian workers and peasants to that end. . . .

Nobody feels himself secure; everyone lives in the expectation of search, arrest, etc. Many innocent persons suffer in prison, awaiting execution without trial. You have been shooting not only those who fought against you but innocent hostages as well. . . . You have condemned to death bishops and clergymen . . . on the ground of the indefinite accusation that they were opposing the revolution. At the same time, you have refused the last consolation to the faithful.

Is not all this the utmost . . . cruelty on the part of those who pretend to be benefactors of humanity and to have suffered from the cruelties of the old régime?

Your cruelty is not sated by these rivers of blood; you instigate the people to pillage under the names of levies, requisitions, and nationalizations. You teach the people to plunder the land, manor houses, industrial establishments, factories, live stock, money, valuables, and even furniture!

At first it was the rich who were plundered, because they were "bourgeois"; then the well-to-do peasants were robbed. You have multiplied the number of paupers in complete forgetfulness of the fact that by ruining a large number of citizens you also ruin the country.

You have tempted the ignorant with the possibility of easy gain, but no matter under what attractive name you cover up your crimes, murder, plunder, and violence will always remain heavy sins crying to Heaven for revenge.

You have promised freedom.

Freedom is a great blessing when it safeguards happiness, when it torments no one and does not become violence. But this is not the kind of freedom which you have given the people; you stimulate the lowest passions of the dregs of the population, you let murder and plunder go unpunished. You supress civil liberty, which is the supreme dignity of man.

Do you call it liberty when no one dares to buy provisions, to rent an apartment, to travel from city to city without a special permit?

Do you call it freedom when whole families and sometimes all the inhabitants of a house are evicted with their belongings? Is it for the sake of liberty that citizens are artificially divided into classes some of which become the prey of famine and plunder? Is it liberty when nobody dares to give sincere expression to his opinion for fear of being accused of counter-revolution? Where are freedom of speech, freedom of the press, and freedom of religion?

The most courageous of the clergy have paid with martyrdom for their devotion; the voice of public opinion is stifled; the press is forced to keep silent; only Bolshevik papers are allowed to speak freely.

You are especially cruel to the clergy. You write lies and blasphemies about the Christian Church and the clergy. You ridicule the priests and send them to hard labor. You squander the riches of the Church, accumulated by generations of the faithful. . . . You have destroyed a large number of monasteries and churches without any cause. You prevent people from entering the Kremlin in Moscow. . . . You throw all holy images out of the schools and prohibit religious instruction of children. . . . Time does not permit me to describe all the calamities from which our country is suffering. . . .

I do not mention the disruption of our country, which was once great and powerful; the ruin of transportation; the want of provisions; the famine and cold which are menacing city and village alike. . . . This horrible period of your régime will remain long in the memory of the people. . . . As the Prophet said: "Their feet run to evil, and they make haste to shed innocent blood: their thoughts *are* thoughts of iniquity; wasting and destruction *are* in their paths." (Isaiah 59:7.)

We know well that our accusations will only awaken your wrath and that you will find in them only a reason for accusing us of rebellion against the authorities. But your wrath is additional proof of the justice of our accusations. It is not given to us to pass judgment on civil authorities. We are ready to bless any authority which God allows to be in power, provided it serves God, fights evil, and protects the good. (Romans 13:3-4.)

Stop using your power for the persecution of your neighbors and the extermination of the innocent. Celebrate the anniversary of your rule by freeing prisoners, by stopping the flow of blood, and by putting an end to violence and ruin.

Cease to destroy, begin to bring order and law, give to the people rest and peace. . . .

TIKHON

The Patriarch of Moscow and of All Russia

A DEFENSE OF THE CHEKA BY LENIN

[Speech at the Celebration of the First Anniversary of the November Revolution] [58]

In honoring the anniversary of our revolution I should like to say a few words about the Cheka.

It is not surprising that both friends and foes attack this organization. In undertaking to govern the country we assumed a difficult task. Naturally we made many mistakes, and, of course, the mistakes of the Cheka stand out more prominently than others. The accusing intelligentsia makes the most of them and does not look beyond the surface. What astonishes me is that so few are able to estimate the work of the Cheka broadly. The tendency is to pick out a mistake here and there and weep about it. . . . We, on the other hand, insist that one can learn only by making mistakes . . . , by self-criticism. What is important is not so much the personnel of the Cheka as the character of its work. The Cheka must act firmly, quickly, and loyally. When I place its achievements beside its mistakes the latter sink into insignificance. . . .

[58] *Pravda*, No. 290, December 18, 1927, p. 3.

Marx has said that between capitalism and communism lies the revolutionary dictatorship of the proletariat. The more the proletariat presses on the bourgeoisie the more will the latter resist. We know what happened to the French proletariat in 1848. Those who reproach us for severity forget the elements of Marxism. We have not forgotten the uprising of the cadets in November and we should not forget the plots for other uprisings. We have a double task to perform—to govern and to break the opposition of the bourgeoisie. The White Guards of Finland, despite their democracy . . . , did not hesitate to shoot workers. For us the important consideration is that the Cheka has made the dictatorship of the proletariat a living reality. Regarded from this point of view its work is priceless. There is only one way to free the masses and that is to crush the exploiters. This is the task of the Cheka, and for this it deserves the gratitude of the proletariat. . . .

C. Attempts to Subordinate the Cheka

During the first months of its existence the powers of the Cheka were not strictly defined, with the result that it extended its jurisdiction into spheres claimed by other organs of the Soviet state. Among the first attempts to restrict the activities of the Cheka was that of the Conference of Commissars of Justice, held in July 1918. However, their resolution calling for some check on the activities of the Cheka was without any effect.[59] The controversy over the Cheka's jurisdiction was resumed at the All-Russian Congress of Representatives of Gubernia Sovdeps early in August, and a resolution was adopted opposing the independence of the Cheka. A similar resolution was adopted by the Congress of Representatives of Revolutionary Tribunals in the early part of November.[60] But the Cheka successfully defended its claim to be "absolutely independent"

---

[59] Excerpts from the minutes of the conference are quoted in *The Bolshevik Revolution*, pp. 580-81.

[60] *Izvestiia*, No. 215, November 10, 1918, p. 3.

and free from every limitation upon its power "to carry out searches, arrests, and executions."

ADVOCACY OF SOVIET CONTROL OF THE CHEKA

[Resolution of the All-Russian Congress of Representatives of Gubernia Sovdeps, August 1, 1918] [61]

In view of the fact that the fundamental aim of local government is to establish administrative unity . . . [and] that the past practice of the Commission to Fight Counter-Revolution, which led a separate and independent existence, has resulted in constant friction and opposition among the different parts of the local administrative machinery . . . , the First All-Russian Congress of Representatives of Gubernia Sovdeps . . . considers it absolutely essential to include . . . the Gubernia and Uezd Commissions to Fight Counter-Revolution in the administrative departments of the corresponding local soviets.

OPPOSITION TO SUBORDINATION OF THE CHEKA

[Statement by Shklovsky, Member of the All-Russian Cheka] [62]

Of late the Commissariat of the Interior has developed a tendency to subordinate the Cheka to its own authority.[63] . . . The main reason for this tendency appears to have been the large number of complaints . . . from the provinces . . . of alleged outrages and unlawful acts committed by the Cheka. The Commissariat of the Interior . . . is naturally anxious to mitigate the severity of the "unlawful acts" directed against a certain portion of the population. . . .

However, the representatives of the proletariat need not pay much attention to these complaints. . . . The experience of the Cheka plainly indicates the harmfulness of subordinating to any authority an agency discharging such important tasks as the Cheka has assumed.

In the first place, it should be clear to any one that in so far as

[61] *Vestnik Narodnago Komissariata Vnutrennikh Del,* No. 20, 1918, pp. 11-12.
[62] *Ezhenedelnik chrezvychainykh komissii,* No. 3, 1918, p. 4.
[63] A reference to the resolution of the representatives of gubernia sovdeps, who were under the Commissariat of the Interior.

the proletariat is forced to adopt a policy of repression in the class struggle against its class enemies, to that extent it is compelled to create the necessary machinery by the aid of which this policy of repression can be carried out relentlessly and systematically. In the second place, . . . the carrying out of a system of repression . . . necessitates swiftness of action and suddenness of attack, which can be attained only if there is a single directing center. . . . The same consideration applies to the "legal limitations" which certain tender-minded Bolsheviks would impose upon the Cheka . . . , thus making it dependent upon the dead letter of the law. If someone should object that there are revolutionary laws [which the Cheka must observe], our reply must be that the methods of the Cheka are those very revolutionary laws, for no one can prove that the Cheka is striking at anyone but the enemies of the proletariat. . . . Thus we see that all allegations of "lawlessness" and "outrage" collapse when regarded from the point of view of the dictatorship of the proletariat. . . .

RELATION BETWEEN EXTRAORDINARY COMMISSIONS AND OTHER SOVIET INSTITUTIONS

[Order of the All-Russian Cheka, September 26, 1918] [64]

Of late much friction has occurred between the Extraordinary Commissions and the administrative departments [of the Interior]. Taking their stand on the resolution of the Congress [of Representatives of Gubernia Sovdeps], the administrative departments are trying to subordinate the Extraordinary Commissions.

We wish to make it clear that the resolution in question is a mere proposal. It was approved neither by the Sovnarkom nor by the Central Executive Committee. The All-Russian Cheka therefore makes the following ruling:

The All-Russian Extraordinary Commission is *subordinate* to the Soviet of People's Commissars only. The Commissariats of Justice and Interior have the right of control. In its activity the All-Russian Cheka is absolutely independent and has the power to carry out searches, arrests, and executions. . . .

PETERS
Acting Chairman

[64] M. Latsis, *Chrezvychainye komissii po borbe s kontr-revoliutsiei*, p. 57.

THE NATURE OF THE CHEKA

[From a Statement by Latsis] [65]

. . . The Cheka is not an investigating commission, a court, or a tribunal.

It is a fighting organ on the internal front of the civil war and makes use . . . of investigating commissions, courts, and military force.

It does not judge, it strikes.

It does not pardon, it destroys all who are caught . . . on the other side of the barricade. . . .

It is a fighting organ . . . of the Communist party, paving the way to the kingdom of communism. . . .

It is not a guillotine which cuts off heads by order of the court. The Cheka either kills those caught in the act on the spot or it isolates in concentration camps, or hands over to tribunals the cases that need to be investigated. . . . The Cheka first determines the harmfulness, . . . the degree of harmfulness, of a person to the Soviet Government,[66] and then decides whether to kill or isolate him in order to render him incapable of doing harm. . . . In time of civil war, when it is a case of life or death, the proletariat must have such an organ. . . .

In its activities the Cheka has endeavored to produce such an impression on the people that the mere mention of its name will quell the desire to sabotage and plot . . . against the revolution.

REQUIREMENTS FOR MEMBERSHIP IN THE CHEKA

. . . The Cheka performs a very important function. In its hands are the lives of the citizens of the Soviet Republic. It protects the Soviet Government and the Communist party, which directs that government.

---

[65] *Ibid.*, pp. 8-23.

[66] In an article published in *Krasnyi Terror* No. 1, November 1918, p. 1, Latsis gives the following advice for the determination of a person's harmfulness to the Soviet Government: "Do not ask for incriminating evidence to prove that the prisoner opposed the Soviet either by arms or by word. Your first duty is to ask him what class he belongs to, what were his origin, education, and occupation. These questions should decide the fate of the prisoner. This is the meaning and essence of Red Terror. . . ." (Quoted from *Pravda*, No. 281, December 25, 1918, p. 1.)

Only those belonging to government parties can be members of the Cheka. . . .

A party that ceases to be a government party, that ceases to share governmental responsibility and cooperates with the hostile opposition on the other side of the barricade, cannot be allowed to work in the organization which is fighting against counter-revolution.

Parties not belonging to the government cannot work in the Cheka. Life has taught us that lesson. When the Socialist-Revolutionists of the Left were with us in the government they were also in the Cheka. When they left the government they still remained in the Cheka . . . and used that institution . . . against the Communists. . . . On July 6, 1918, the uprising of the Left S. R.'s started in the Cheka, where one of their members, Alexandrovich, held a high office. . . .

Members of the Cheka must be Communists. This is the primary condition for effective work. . . .

The second condition is . . . that members of the Cheka must *be men of high quality* . . . , above suspicion . . . , of strong character . . . , and of good reputation. . . . The third condition . . . is that *after a certain period men in active Cheka service should be transferred to work in other fields.* No matter how honest a man is . . . , the work of the Cheka with its unlimited power, its peculiar conditions . . . , is bound to have an effect upon him . . . , upon his nervous system. . . . He must be given a rest and a change. . . .

We must not think that our Chekas, which, including all office clerks, number about thirty-one thousand people, are alone capable of handling this great task. Counter-revolutionary work goes on everywhere . . . and we must have eyes, ears, and mailed fists everywhere. . . .

Every worker and peasant must help. . . . But there are those who hold themselves aloof, who think it humiliating and degrading to take part in this work . . . , who see no difference between the Cheka and the Okhrana [67] of the old régime.

Those who see no difference understand nothing. They have slept through the March and November Revolutions and expect

---

[67] Tsarist secret police.

others to do all the dirty work necessary for the construction of the new communist order so that they can step in with unpolluted hands and clean, starched collars.

We must bring to an end once and for all these insulting attacks on the Cheka. . . .

WHO ARE COUNTER-REVOLUTIONISTS?

. . . The bourgeoisie stands in the way of the proletariat. . . . There are two hostile camps—the proletariat and the bourgeoisie. . . . In the counter-revolutionary camp . . . is also the petty bourgeoisie . . . , from which the more active counter-revolutionary elements are drafted. Cadets, officers of the old régime, teachers, students of all kinds—all these come from the petty bourgeoisie and it is these who are fighting in the White Guard ranks. . . . Mensheviks and Socialist-Revolutionists are in favor . . . of stopping the civil war . . . , of overthrowing the Bolsheviks. . . . They are, therefore, counter-revolutionary parties. . . .

In addition to the above-mentioned groups there are others. Some are counter-revolutionists because of ignorance, others because of lack of understanding. Such are the peasant masses and some workers. . . .

REPRESSIVE MEASURES USED BY THE CHEKA

Since the Cheka is not a judicial body its acts are of an administrative character. . . . Its extreme measure is shooting. . . . The second measure [in grades of severity] is isolation in concentration camps. . . . The third measure is confiscation of property. . . .

We are forced to adopt these measures in order to save hundreds of thousands of our comrades from the hands of the White Guards. . . . We do not lust for blood; we desire peace. . . . As soon as victory is ours . . . we will give up the right to shoot. . . .

SPHERE OF ACTIVITY OF THE CHEKA

The counter-revolutionists are active in all spheres of life. . . . Consequently there is no sphere of life in which the Cheka does not operate. . . . It looks into military matters, food supply, education . . . , etc.

THE ALL-RUSSIAN CHEKA AND LOCAL CHEKAS

[Decree of the Central Executive Committee, November 2, 1918] [68]

1. The All-Russian Extraordinary Commission . . . integrates the activities of the local Extraordinary Commissions and has as its direct aim the struggle against counter-revolution, crime, and profiteering in every part of the Russian Socialist Federated Soviet Republic.

2. The All-Russian Extraordinary Commission is an organ of the Sovnarkom and works in close contact with the People's Commissariats of the Interior and Justice.

3. Members of the All-Russian Extraordinary Commission are appointed by the Sovnarkom.

4. The chairman of the All-Russian Extraordinary Commission is a member of the Collegium of the People's Commissariat of the Interior.

5. The People's Commissariats of the Interior and of Justice have representatives in the All-Russian Extraordinary Commission.

6. The budget of the All-Russian Extraordinary Commission must be approved by the Sovnarkom.

7. The All-Russian Extraordinary Commission and the local Extraordinary Commissions have the right to maintain special military units. The size of such units is to be determined by the local soviet executive committees, with the concurrence of the All-Russian Extraordinary Commission. The money for the maintenance of these units is appropriated in the usual way by the local executive committees.

All military units, both of the All-Russian Extraordinary Commission and of the local Extraordinary Commissions, are under the control of the Revolutionary War Council of the Republic.

8. The local Extraordinary Commissions have jurisdiction over all cases of counter-revolution, profiteering, and crime. . . .

YA. SVERDLOV
Chairman of the Central Executive Committee

[68] *S. U. R.*, No. 80, 1918, p. 998.

INSTRUCTIONS OF THE CHIEF OF THE ALL-RUSSIAN CHEKA [69]

[December 17, 1918]

Dear Comrades:

There are three questions on which members of the Cheka need instruction in order to avoid possible error. These questions concern hostages, specialists, and arrests in general.

Who is a hostage?

He is a prisoner, a member of a group or organization which is fighting against us. But to be a hostage that prisoner must have in the eyes of our enemy a certain value which will serve as a guarantee that the counter-revolutionists will refrain for the sake of that person from killing any of our comrades. . . .

Whom do they value?

They value high state officials, landlords, captains of industry, prominent politicians, eminent scholars, relatives of those who occupy high positions in their governments, etc.

From these groups hostages should be taken. . . .

The second question concerns specialists. Most of our specialists come from the bourgeois classes, frequently from the nobility. While normally we keep members of these classes as hostages, sending them to concentration camps or public works, it would be unreasonable to adopt the same measures in regard to specialists. We have but few specialists of our own and are therefore compelled to hire bourgeois brains. . . .

In the third place, the Cheka very often resorts to arrests which cannot be justified. There is no need to arrest people on hearsay, on mere suspicion, or for petty crimes. . . . In view of the above considerations the All-Russian Cheka orders you to adopt in the future the following principles:

1. Make out a list of (a) the entire bourgeois population from which hostages can be taken, namely, former landowners, merchants, factory owners, industrialists, bankers, large real-estate owners, officers of the old army, important officials of the tsarist and Kerensky régimes, and relatives of persons fighting against us; (b) important members of anti-Soviet parties who in case of our retreat are likely to remain on the other side of the front.

---

[69] Latsis, op. cit., pp. 54-55.

2. Send in these lists to the All-Russian Cheka. . . .

3. Hostages may be taken only by permission of or order of the All-Russian Cheka.

4. Technical experts may be placed under arrest only after their participation in White Guard organizations has been established beyond doubt. . . .

DZERZHINSKY

Chairman of the Cheka

D. THE RED ARMY

The old Russian army melted away during the confusion and demoralization attending the early months of the Soviet régime. Prodded by the rising opposition to their rule, the Bolsheviks undertook on January 28, 1918, the formation of a new army, called the Worker-Peasant Red Army. The theory underlying this endeavor was expressed in part by Trotsky when he said that "there can be no change of social relationships without a bloody war," [70] and in part by the Central Executive Committee when it declared that "the Russian Soviet Republic must have a mighty army under the protection of which the reorganization of society on a communistic basis can take place." [71]

The small forces which the Bolsheviks employed during the early stages of the civil war consisted mostly of volunteer detachments and had a thoroughly democratic organization. The army was ruled by soldiers' committees, officers being elected by the soldiers themselves. In the summer of 1918 the Bolsheviks abolished this system and began to organize their army on principles of strict military authority and discipline. They decreed compulsory military service, abolished soldiers' committees, and invited officers of the old army to take charge of military operations. To prevent disloyalty on the part of the old officers, trusted Communists

---

[70] *Kak vooruzhalas revoliutsiia*, I, 47.   [71] *S. U. R.*, No. 33, 1918, p. 419.

were attached to every responsible commander to watch over his activities. Another means of insuring the loyalty of the tsarist officers was the threat to punish their families in case the officers deserted the Red Army and went over to the anti-Bolshevik camp. During 1918 the Bolsheviks succeeded in attracting over twenty-two thousand officers to service in the Red Army.[72] The administration of the army, which numbered during this period about half a million, was in the hands of the Revolutionary War Council, of which Trotsky as Commissar of War was chairman.

EMPLOYMENT OF FORMER GENERALS

[From Trotsky's Speech, April 21, 1918] [73]

. . . In order to train the Red Army we are employing . . . some of the better qualified and more honest of the old generals. I hear these questions: "What? . . . Is this not a dangerous step?" There is danger in everything. We must have teachers who know something about the science of war. We talk to these generals with complete frankness. We tell them: "There is a new master in the land—the working class. He needs instructors to teach the toilers . . . how to fight the bourgeoisie." . . . If these generals serve us honestly we shall give them our full support; if they attempt counter-revolution we shall find a way of dealing with them. They know that we have eyes everywhere. . . .

CONSCRIPTION

[Decree of the Central Executive Committee, May 29, 1918] [74]

The All-Russian Central Executive Committee of Soviets finds that present conditions in the country necessitate our changing from voluntary enlistment in the army to a general conscription of workers and peasants. . . .

[72] Zaitsov, *1918 god. Ocherki po istorii russkoi grazhdanskoi voiny*, p. 182.
[73] *Kak vooruzhalas revoliutsiia*, I, 63-64.
[74] *S. U. R.*, No. 41, 1918, p. 499. On June 12 the order of conscription was extended to the following gubernias: Simbirsk, Saratov, Ufa, Orenburg, Ekaterinburg, Tobolsk, Tomsk, Altaisky region, Turgaisk, Akmolinsk, Semipalatinsk, and the Siberian and Orenburg Cossack territories. (*Ibid.*, No. 43, 1918, p. 526.)

It is necessary to proceed without delay to a compulsory mobilization of one of several categories of recruits. . . .

. . . The People's Commissariat of War is hereby ordered . . . to prepare, within a week, plans for conscription in Moscow, Petrograd, and the Don and Kuban regions. . . .

YA. SVERDLOV

Chairman of the Central Executive Committee

THE CLASS BASIS OF THE RED ARMY

[Excerpts from Trotsky's Speech at the Fourth Trade-Union Conference, Moscow, June 29, 1918] [75]

The principal theme of my talk is the organization . . . of the armed forces of the Russian Republic. This question confronts us now . . . as one of the life and death of the country . . . [and] the working class . . . ; and when it is a question of the life and death of the working class this class must be ready to defend its freedom and to make every possible sacrifice. . . . It is up to you—trade unions and factory-shop committees—to create an army. . . . You must bring together the human material . . . to repel the attack on the revolution. . . .

Our army is a class army and will include primarily workers and poorer peasants. Why should it be a class army? . . . Because we need an army . . . to fight against all internal and external enemies. . . . We do not arm the bourgeoisie, for we want to wipe them off the face of the earth. During the entire course of history arms have been withheld from the lower classes . . . and have been placed at the service of the exploiters and the bourgeoisie. But the time has now arrived when armed force is used for the complete extermination of the exploiting classes. (*Applause.*) Universal military training will be based on this principle. We shall make it our aim to give military training and arms to the proletariat. . . . The Germans succeeded in creating among their soldiers the Kaiser cult. But we should strive to create the spirit and the readiness to fight for the freedom of the working class. . . . Every young worker, instead of drinking home-

---

[75] *Protokoly 4-oi conferentsii fabrichno-zavodskikh komitetov i professionalnykh soiuzov g Moskvy*, pp. 68-80.

brew on Sundays, should learn how to shoot. . . . The worker
must realize that in learning to shoot . . . he is accomplishing the
most important task of his own class. . . . You are worker-pro-
ducers and citizen-soldiers at one and the same time—a fact which
should be realized by every party man and every honest revolutionary worker. . . . To be sure, the less intelligent worker does
not see why he is called upon to take up arms and go to the front
while the bourgeois is left free. What we need, on the one hand,
is to make clear the class character of our army as a weapon in
the struggle for the supremacy of the working class and the poor
peasants, and, on the other, to take the bourgeoisie in our clutches.
This is something which we have not yet succeeded in doing. You
may have seen the report which was sent to the Soviet of People's
Commissars and was approved by it in principle. This report says
that along with compulsory conscription of workers and peasants
. . . there are necessary a compulsory conscription of bourgeois
youth of the same ages and formation of these into rear detachments . . . to clean the barracks and camps. For centuries the
workers and peasants have been cleaning and washing up the dirt
of the ruling classes. . . . Now these [classes] are raising their
heads once more and wish to place us in the same position. We
shall level them with the earth (*applause*) and tell them that unless they are willing to share our burdens in the pursuit of common ends they will be forced to clean up the dirt which we are
leaving behind. (*Applause.*) At the same time, Comrades, the
Sovnarkom decided to increase the levies on the bourgeoisie and
to place them in such housing and food conditions that they will
lose the desire to remain bourgeois. (*Applause.*) All this work,
Comrades, is not within the capacity of the Commissariat of War.
Workers' organizations, trade unions, [and] factory-shop committees should take part in the task. . . . Help us to make an
accounting of the bourgeoisie! Let every bourgeois house be
marked as one in which seven or eight families live . . . as parasites,
and we shall post yellow tickets on the gates of those houses!
(*Applause.*)

These and similar measures are necessitated by the fight of the
working class for socialism, for a genuine socialist economy, and
are in the interests of military affairs; for the worker will fight
loyally only when he knows that the bourgeoisie is being shown no

mercy, that the bourgeoisie is in our clutches in the true sense of the word. . . .

THE RED ARMY AND THE BOURGEOISIE

[Trotsky's Report to the Sovnarkom, June 1918] [76]

The international position of the Soviet Republic requires the creation of a powerful army. Such an army can be formed only on the basis of compulsory military service. One need not doubt that the All-Russian Congress of Soviets of Workers' and Peasants' Deputies will decide to make it compulsory for citizens of the Soviet Republic to defend their socialist fatherland. . . .

However, the institution of universal military service is now facing an obstacle in the as yet unbroken resistance of the . . . exploiting classes. . . . Having been removed from power, the bourgeoisie has demonstrated that it not only refuses to defend the country against foreign aggressors but, on the contrary, is prepared at any moment to betray the Soviet Republic to external enemies in order to strangle with their aid the Russian workers and peasants.

Not until the revolutionary dictatorship has finally broken down the criminal will of the bourgeoisie will it be possible to admit . . . the exploiting classes into the ranks of the army. The burden and honor of defending the Soviet Republic must therefore rest on the proletariat and [that part of] the peasantry which does not exploit the labor of others.

The extremely successful mobilization . . . in Moscow has shown that the proletariat is conscious of its revolutionary duty. There can be no doubt that the mobilization will prove a complete success everywhere.

However, it is absolutely impossible to endure any longer a situation in which the bourgeoisie is exempt from every effort and sacrifice needed for the defense of the Soviet Republic. The revolutionary consciousness of the toiling masses will not tolerate the shameful privileges which the bourgeoisie has temporarily gained for itself by means of crime and treason. . . .

. . . I propose that the Soviet of People's Commissars approve the following measures:

[76] *Vestnik putei soobshcheniia*, No. 5, 1918, pp. 9-10.

1. The . . . bourgeoisie of military age shall be mobilized and organized into reserve regiments to do the menial work of the army (cleaning barracks, camps, streets, digging trenches, etc.).
. . .

2. There shall be exacted from every private enterprise a payment to be applied to the maintenance fund for the families of the Red Army soldiers. . . .

3. Every bourgeois family, any member of which fails to enter the reserve regiments, shall be fined from three thousand to one hundred thousand rubles, and the head of the family shall be kept under arrest until the fine is paid. . . .

4. Pending the introduction of universal labor duty . . . , it is indispensable to bring about a complete registration . . . of all parasitical elements, i. e., all who do not discharge any socially necessary function in the Soviet Republic. These elements, perverted by their past mode of life, are the chief source of discontent, speculation, sabotage, perversion, disloyalty, and treachery. The sacred task of defending the Soviet Republic, surrounded by enemies, demands from the toilers strict surveillance over the parasitical classes. These [classes] should be placed in such conditions of life (food supply, living quarters, etc.) as will make them actually feel the clutches of the iron dictatorship of the workers and peasants. . . .

L. Trotsky

People's Commissar of War and the Navy

Approved by Ulianov (Lenin)

President of the Sovnarkom

RESOLUTION OF THE FIFTH ALL-RUSSIAN CONGRESS [77]

[July 10, 1918]

1. The Russian Soviet Republic is like a fortress surrounded on all sides by the forces of imperialism. Within the . . . fortress counter-revolution is raising its head, receiving temporary support from the Czechoslovaks in the pay of the Anglo-French bourgeoisie. The Soviet Republic must have a strong revolutionary

---

[77] *Piatyi Vserossiiskii Sezd Sovetov Rabochikh, Krestianskikh, Soldatskikh i Kazachikh Deputatov*, pp. 180-82.

army capable of crushing the counter-revolution of the bourgeoisie and landlords and of beating off the attack of the plundering imperialists. . . .

4. The Soviet Government has always considered . . . that it is the duty of every honest and able-bodied citizen between the ages of eighteen and forty to answer a call to come to the defense of the Soviet Republic against its external and internal foes. . . .

12. The bourgeoisie cannot be armed until it has been thoroughly expropriated . . . and has given up the idea of regaining its former domination. To do so would be equivalent to arming an enemy who might at any moment betray the Soviet Republic into the hands of foreign imperialists. The Congress approves the decree of the Soviet of People's Commissars ordering the formation of the bourgeois of military age into reserve regiments to do the menial work in the army. Only those of the bourgeoisie who have actually demonstrated their loyalty to the working classes may be transferred from the reserve to the active army. . . .

TSARIST OFFICERS AND THE RED ARMY

[Trotsky's Statement July 23, 1918] [78]

We hear it said again and again that former officers do not join the army because they do not wish to take part in civil war. They wish to be "out of politics." Were they "out of politics" when they served in the tsarist army . . . ? Was there ever a time when the army was out of politics? . . . The officers did carry on a civil war against the workers and peasants. It was not called civil war then, but this fact did not save those who were shot down. . . .

Someone will say . . . that the officers wish to remain "neutral" in the internal war but are ready to protect the country from foreign foes. . . . Let us examine this statement. Is the struggle against Krasnov a civil war or a foreign war? He is trying to cut off the Don and the Kuban from Russia, to deprive us of bread and oil. To do this he . . . is making use of German arms and is calling on the Germans for help.

How about the Czechoslovaks? Are they internal or external

---

[78] *Kak vooruzhalas revoliutsiia*, I, 143-45, 159.

foes? . . . How about the Anglo-French landing at Murmansk?
. . . Krasnov [works] with the help of the Germans . . . and
Alexeev . . . works with French money. . . . In their wake
there is no end of these . . . opponents of "civil war." At first
some of them willingly joined the Red Army but later they deserted to the Czechoslovak or the Anglo-French forces. . . .

A small group of officers . . . have caught the spirit of the
revolution and the new age. . . . They are doing everything they
can to increase the military power of the Soviet Republic. . . .
They should be respected and supported. . . .

Should the situation change . . . we may be obliged to go back
. . . to a policy of Red Terror and to kill all who attempt to help
the enemies of the proletariat. But to do this in anticipation . . .
would be merely to weaken ourselves. To refuse the service of
military specialists because individual officers play the traitor is
about as reasonable as to drive out all the railway engineers . . .
because there are a few *saboteurs* among them.

CALL TO NON-COMMISSIONED OFFICERS

[Trotsky's Announcement, August 3, 1918] [79]

Non-commissioned officers! The country is calling you. The
Soviet Government is forming an army to safeguard the freedom
and independence of the toiling classes . . . against the attacks of
external and internal enemies. The worker-peasant army is in
need of . . . an honest commanding personnel . . . and the
Soviet Government calls you to the *posts of commanding officers.*
You are the children of the toiling people; the worker-peasant
army is *your* army. . . . Every non-commissioned officer serving
in the Red Army . . . is hereby raised to the status of squad
commander.

The Soviet Government gives you the opportunity to complete
your military education . . . , to rise to the very height of military art.

Non-commissioned officers! Your hour has struck. Soviet Russia summons you. Forward . . . to the glorious fight for the
freedom and happiness of Soviet Russia!

Forward to a life of glory and honor!

[79] *Ibid.*, p. 174.

10

FAMILIES OF DESERTERS PUNISHED

[Trotsky's Order, September 10, 1918] [80]

Although the desertion of traitorous officers to the camp of the enemy is becoming less frequent, yet it still goes on. This monstrous crime must be ended at all costs. The deserters betray the Russian workers and peasants to the Anglo-French and Japanese-American robbers and executioners. Let them know that they are at the same time betraying members of their own families: fathers, mothers, sisters, brothers, wives, and children.

The staffs of the armies of the Republic, as well as the regional commissars, are ordered to report by telegraph to Aralov of the Revolutionary War Council the names of all deserting officers with all necessary information about their families. Aralov, in cooperation with the proper institutions, will take the measures necessary to arrest the families of the deserters and traitors.

APPEAL OF THE CENTRAL EXECUTIVE COMMITTEE TO THE RED ARMY [81]

[September 16, 1918]

To All Military Revolutionary Councils, All Armies, All Soldiers of the Red Army, All, All!

The All-Russian Central Executive Committee resolved at its session of September 16 to greet the worker-peasant Red Army which is fighting bravely on all fronts against the imperialist hirelings—the White Guards, Czechoslovaks, and other bands opposing the Soviet Government.

The enemies of the social revolution wish to return the banks, factories, and industrial enterprises to the capitalists, and the land to the pomeshchiks. The working people, who have paid with their blood for the transfer of the land, the banks, and the factories to the hands of the toilers, have selected you as their vanguard. . . .

Comrades! In fighting heroically you give your life for the triumph of socialism. You have liberated Kazan and Simbirsk. Many cities and villages are still in the hands of the plunderers

[80] *Ibid.*, p. 151.

[81] *Piatyi sozyv Vserossiiskogo Tsentralnogo Ispolnitelnogo Komiteta*, p. 145.

and robbers. You must destroy their power everywhere. Let your courage and will to victory constantly grow. . . . Forward from victory to victory!

THE CENTRAL EXECUTIVE COMMITTEE

REVOLUTIONARY WAR COUNCIL
[Decree of the Central Executive Committee, October 30, 1918] [82]

1. The Revolutionary War Council of the Russian Socialist Federated Soviet Republic is the country's supreme organ of military authority. All forces and resources of the people that are needed for the defense of the borders of the Soviet Republic are at the disposal of the Revolutionary War Council. . . .

2. The Revolutionary War Council is to include the Collegium of the People's Commissariat of War. . . .

3. All military institutions are subordinate to the Revolutionary War Council.

4. The chairman of the Revolutionary War Council of the Republic is the People's Commissar of War and the Navy. . . .

5. The Supreme Commander in Chief is entirely independent in all questions of a strategic-operative character. His orders must be countersigned by a member of the Revolutionary War Council.
. . .

YA. SVERDLOV
Chairman of the Central Executive Committee

THE COUNCIL OF DEFENSE
[Decree of the Central Executive Committee, November 30, 1918] [83]

The Soviet Republic is facing a growing danger of invasion by the united hordes of world imperialism. After entering the world slaughter with the false slogans of democracy and the brotherhood of nations, the victorious Allied plunderers are now trampling under foot the weak nations and states. The German working class, which hitherto has been the victim of the . . . Hohenzollern monarchy, is now being mercilessly strangled by Wilson, Lloyd

[82] *Ibid.*, pp. 226-27. The Revolutionary War Council came into existence on June 13, 1918, by order of the Sovnarkom of that date. (Maksakov i Turunov, *Khronika grazhdanskoi voiny v Sibiri*, p. 188.)
[83] *S. U. R.*, Nos. 91-92, 1918, pp. 1143-44.

George, and their helpers. . . . France, though among the victorious Powers, is in reality occupied by Anglo-American and colonial troops who were given the task of suppressing the revolutionary French proletariat.

Under these conditions of universal brigandage, plunder, and violence, only one country stands out as the genuine abode of the independence of the working class, as the protector of the weak and exploited peoples, and as the fortress of the social revolution. That country is Soviet Russia. The wrath and hatred of the bourgeoisie of the whole world are directed against that country.

To the north and the south, the east and the west, the Anglo-American and Anglo-Japanese plunders . . . are forming hostile fronts against Soviet Russia. They are arming the White Guards, Cossack generals, . . . city and village kulaks. . . .

By decree of the Central Executive Committee of September 2 of this year the Soviet Republic has been declared in a state of siege. . . .

In order to enforce [that decree] . . . the All-Russian Central Executive Committee of Soviets has resolved to establish a Council of Workers' and Peasants' Defense under the presidency of Comrade Lenin . . . , with Comrades Trotsky, . . . Nevsky, . . . Briukhanov, . . . Krasin, . . . and . . . Stalin as members.

The Council of Defense is to have full power in matters pertaining to the mobilization of the forces and resources of the country in the interests of defense. The decisions of the Council of Defense shall be absolutely binding upon every department and institution, both central and local, and upon every citizen.

Direct supervision over the army and navy . . . remains in the hands of the Revolutionary War Council of the Republic. In order to bring about a greater centralization in the activities of that institution, a bureau is appointed with the [following] membership: Chairman, Comrade Trotsky; Supreme Commander, Comrade Vatsetis; and Comrade Aralov.

YA. SVERDLOV
Chairman of the Central Executive Committee

V. ULIANOV (LENIN)
President of the Sovnarkom

CHAPTER VI

THE EASTERN FRONT

The success of the Czechoslovaks in resisting the Soviet Government, together with the shortly ensuing decision of the Allies to intervene in Russia, gave great encouragement and support to the growing anti-Bolshevik movement in Eastern Russia and Siberia. Immediately after the seizure by the Czechoslovaks of strategic points in the Volga region and Siberia, various anti-Bolshevik groups organized a number of governments [1] in these territories and at the same time formed armies to attack the Bolsheviks in Central Russia. The most important of these governments were the Samara Government, headed by Socialist-Revolutionists of the Right, and the Siberian Government, dominated at first by moderate socialists and later by conservatives.

[1] The following is a list of the governments which existed in Russia in the summer of 1918:
I. In the Volga region, Siberia, and Northern Russia: (1) the Samara Committee of Members of the Constituent Assembly; (2) the Kama Committee of Members of the Constituent Assembly; (3) the Bashkir Autonomous Government; (4) the Ural Cossack Voisko Government; (5) the Ural Regional Government (capital at Ekaterinburg); (6) the Provisional Government of Western Siberia; (7) the Siberian Cossack Government; (8) the Transbaikal Voisko Government; (9) General Horvath's Government; (10) the Provisional Government of Autonomous Siberia (Derber's group); (11) the Autonomous Government of the Yakut Region; (12) the National Administration of Turko-Tartars of the Interior of Russia; (13) the Provisional Administration of the North (capital at Archangel).
II. In the region under German occupation: (1) the Ukrainian Government; (2) the Crimean Government; (3) the White Russian Government; (4) the Latvian Government; (5) the Lithuanian Government; (6) the Esthonian Government.
III. In the regions not occupied by foreign armies: (1) the Soviet Government (R. S. F. S. R.); (2) the Kuban Voisko Government; (3) the Don Voisko Government; (4) the Autonomous Government of Turkestan; (5) the Regional Government of the Northern Caucasus; (6) the Political Administration of the Volunteer Army.
IV. In the former Russian Empire but by 1918 with the status of independent governments: (1) Finland, (2) Poland, (3) Georgia, (4) Armenia, and (5) Azerbaijan.

277

The landing by the Allies of a force at Archangel early in August lent further encouragement to the anti-Bolshevik forces and also gave direction to their efforts. They now began to base their operations on the hope of effecting a juncture between their armies and those of the Allies and thus of creating a united front against the Bolsheviks. The Allies likewise looked forward to military collaboration with the anti-Bolshevik governments, expecting thereby to establish an Eastern front against the Germans as well as the Bolsheviks. With this purpose in view the Allies not only supported these governments but encouraged the movement for consolidating them. On September 23, after conferences between the various groups at Ufa, this movement culminated in the establishment of the Ufa Directorate, an all-Russian government, composed of representatives of all the leading shades of political opinion.

However, the great divergence of viewpoints among its members doomed the all-Russian government to a very short existence. It was overthrown on November 18 by conservatives and was superseded by the dictatorship of Admiral Kolchak. By this time the military position of the anti-Bolshevik forces, incapable of sufficient cooperation from the outset, had been greatly weakened. They had not only failed to effect a juncture with the Allied armies but had been compelled by the growingly effective attacks of the Red Army to give up an extensive territory.

A. THE VOLGA UPRISINGS AND THE SAMARA GOVERNMENT

Moving eastward, the Penza section of the Czechoslovak Corps captured the city of Samara on June 8. A local group of Socialist-Revolutionists, headed by former members of the Constituent Assembly, proclaimed a new government in the name of that Assembly. This government, known as the Committee of Members of the Constituent Assembly (abbreviated as Komuch), immediately organized a council to take charge of the various departments of government. It then issued a statement of its aims, proclaimed its readiness to resume war against Germany, and appealed for Allied aid in organizing resistance to the Germans and the Bolsheviks.

SEIZURE OF SAMARA BY THE CZECHOSLOVAKS

[The American Vice-Consul at Samara to the American Consul General at Moscow, June 12, 1918] [2]

. . . In the morning of the 7th, the Czechs placed about ten shots in the city, in the vicinity of the cannon which were speaking to them. I saw them strike, and everyone went in the square (Khlebnaia Ploshad). . . . As these shells struck almost directly in front of this office, I moved the records, cash, etc., with Miss Elsing to another part of town.

The situation in the city was becoming unendurable; a jail delivery was effected in which about 550 criminals became free. No one knows the exact number, for all the records were destroyed and all those in any way connected with the prison killed. People were not allowed to gather on the street to talk, and I have heard from several sources of the murder of two men who had made slighting remarks regarding the Red Army. The population was very frightened, and prepared for serious excesses. Meanwhile, the Commissars were loading supplies of all kinds upon boats and making their get-away. The State Bank was quite cleaned out; no bank has been able to open since. . . .

Late in the afternoon of the 7th, the Bolsheviks began their cannonade again, and the Czechs replied, setting on fire a large flour mill on the bank of the Samarka, which burned for two days, destroying 18,500 puds of flour. The fire later spread to an adjoining oil tank, and destroyed 22,000 puds of naphtha. There

[2] The original report is in the possession of Professor DeWitt C. Poole, of Princeton University, sometime American Consul General at Moscow.

was little sleep in the city that night, and at the hour of two-thirty on the morning of the 8th the Czechs began their attack upon the city, which ended in its capture just five hours later. All of the Czechs crossed the river bridge, beginning with fifty grenadiers with hand grenades, who came first. . . . The battle was very severe . . . during the entire time. All kinds of pieces were used from five-inch guns to revolvers. Soon the Red Army was on the run. . . . At eight in the morning it was safe to go on the street.

In a moment it was evident that the Czechs had no hostile feeling against the inhabitants, and . . . [they] were received like conquering heroes. The Czechs were familiar with the plan of the city, for within two hours they had their guards in every place where the Bolsheviks had been, and were busy cleaning them up. There were various corners set aside to which guns when found were brought, and the piles mounted rapidly. Large numbers of the Bolsheviks were captured, and marched around the city on their way to the prison. The Czechs went about their task of restoring order with intelligence; within three hours men were removing the broken wires, and repairing the telephone lines, and within twelve hours, the streets were clear. Their courtesy and good nature were infectious. Soon the streets were thronged with people who celebrated a holiday. There was an enthusiastic burst of national spirit, the Russian flag appeared all over the business district, and before the day was over dozens of former officers were on the streets in their old uniforms, and some of the prominent women of the city went about with Czech soldiers, who held out their hats, and the women solicited contributions for food for the men. Every hat I saw was running over with rubles, peasants and workmen with merchants alike eagerly giving liberally, a clever way to rouse enthusiasm.

The Czechs at once issued a proclamation to the people of the city, . . . and soon the delegates to the Constitutional Assembly with commendable promptness took over the government of the city, and issued several statements, more particularly arranging to call meetings of the different classes of society, and advising in regard to the formation of a new army. . . .

After one day the Czechs turned over the guarding of the streets to the new army, and are careful not to interfere in matters of civil government. The city is quiet, and there is no longer martial law. . . .

The Czechs summarily executed about fifty Austrian prisoners whom they captured fighting against them, including two Czechs. They are for the most part releasing the Bolsheviks after disarming them. . . . Three Commissars were killed in the fight, and the others fled or have been arrested, and are held. Every place which the Bolsheviks occupied has been searched and cleaned out. . . .

THE SAMARA COUP D'ÉTAT

[From an Account by Klimushkin, Member of the Samara Government] [3]

. . . The Samara coup d'état was not a spontaneous and accidental affair. It had its history, . . . which begins with our arrival at Samara after the dissolution of the Constituent Assembly. . . . Our chief purpose at that time was to bring about conditions favorable to the overthrow of Bolshevik rule, since we understood that this rule was bound either to result in a monarchical restoration or to lead to Germany's enslavement of Russia. . . . From this it followed that along with the struggle against Bolshevism there would have to be a fight against Germanism.

. . . At first our work was very difficult. The army was demoralized and so too the working class. The workers refused to see that the ruin of industry and the bribes by which the Bolsheviks were attracting them were bound to lead ultimately to the ruin of the workers and to famine. Our aim was to open the eyes of the army and the working class. A series of talks to the soldiers produced a good impression; . . . the garrison demanded the reelection of the Soviet—a demand which caused a clash between the soldiers loyal to the Bolsheviks and those loyal to our movement. Even then it was possible to start a civil war, but we were afraid that without the support of the workers and the rest of the population it would end in disaster. We could not rely solely upon the soldiers. Therefore the Socialist-Revolutionists and the members of the Constituent Assembly decided to organize all available forces. . . . Fortunatov undertook the formation of an army, Brushvit collected necessary resources, and I assumed the duties of political leadership.

[3] Piontkovsky, *G. V. R.*, pp. 213-15.

We started intense propaganda. But we soon realized that the workers were difficult to organize. They had fallen into a marked degree of demoralization and were split into a number of camps fighting among themselves. We turned to the soldiers, especially the officers, but they constituted a small force and very few believed in the possibility of overthrowing the Bolsheviks. . . . A general to whom I appealed for aid told me that he considered the Bolshevik government well established and thought any attempt to overthrow it an adventurer's risk.

As the cities gave us little encouragement we gradually turned our attention to the villages. We believed that the peasantry still retained enough vital force to be aroused. The Balakovsky insurrection, during which the peasants took five hundred [Magyar] prisoners and a number of machine guns, confirmed us in our belief. We sent our friends to the villages to organize the peasants. The work, though steadily progressing, was very slow, and it was clear that without some external stimulus no hope could be entertained for a coup d'état in the near future. . . . At this time we heard of the Czech insurrection. Brushvit went to the Czechs . . . , while we began . . . to organize a government. . . . It was decided that the members of the Constituent Assembly would take over the government. . . . We also entered into negotiations with the Social-Democrats and the Cadets . . . , but neither party was willing to support us. The Social-Democrats argued that Bolshevism would liquidate itself, while the Cadets maintained that unless the Czechs remained at Samara our whole enterprise would be a leap in the dark. . . . It was in this way that the whole burden of the coup fell upon the shoulders of the Socialist-Revolutionists, . . . and I must say that during the first days we had to face insurmountable difficulties. In spite of the universal jubilation we were actually supported only by a few . . . citizens. The workers failed to give any help, and when we went to the City Duma [to proclaim the government], guarded, I am sorry to say, not by our own soldiers but by the Czechoslovaks, everybody thought that we were madmen. . . .

PROCLAMATION OF THE COMMITTEE OF MEMBERS OF THE CONSTITUENT ASSEMBLY

[Order No. 1, June 8, 1918] [4]

In the name of the Constituent Assembly we hereby declare the Bolshevik government in the city of Samara and in Samara Gubernia deposed. All commissars are dismissed from their posts. All organs of local self-government abolished by the Soviet Government are reinstated to full powers. City dumas and zemstvo councils are urged to resume their duties at once.

Pending the formation of governmental institutions by an all-Russian government, the authority, both civil and military, in the city and in the gubernia, passes to a committee composed of members of the Constituent Assembly, elected from Samara Gubernia. . . .

The formation of an army and the command of all military forces are entrusted to a military staff consisting of Colonel Galkin, Chief of Staff, Bogoliubov . . . , and Fortunatov. . . .

All restrictions of freedom and repressive measures introduced by the Bolsheviks are declared void. Freedom of speech, press, and assembly is reestablished. . . .

United, free, and independent Russia! All power to the Constituent Assembly! These are the slogans and aims of the new revolutionary government.

POLICIES OF THE KOMUCH

[Declaration of July 24, 1918] [5]

The Soviet Government is now deposed and Bolshevism has suffered defeat in the entire territory under control of the Committee of Members of the All-Russian Constituent Assembly. There are, however, a considerable number who hope for the return of the Soviets. These individuals, cooperating with the criminal element, are engaged in inciting the workers and peasants against the new government. . . . They tell them that the workers will again be in the power of the capitalists and that the peasants will lose the land and be subjected to the landlords.

[4] G. Lelevich, *V dni Samarskoi uchredilki,* pp. 9-10.
[5] Piontkovsky, *G. V. R.,* pp. 219-20.

The Committee, considering such agitation to be clearly provocative, declares that there is no basis whatever for it, and to end such evil inventions makes the following statement:

1. *The land has irrevocably become the property of the people and the Committee will not sanction any attempt to return it to the landlords. All transactions in land . . . are forbidden. . . .*

2. *All existing laws and decrees concerning the protection of labor shall remain in force pending their legislative revision.*

3. The Department of Labor, now acting in place of the Commissariat of Labor, is charged with the strict duty of maintaining a strong surveillance over the enforcement of these laws and decrees, while the judicial power is under orders immediately to investigate and dispose of all cases of violation of labor laws.

4. Workers and peasants are urged to defend their interests only by legal means, in order to avoid anarchy and chaos.

5. Whenever not justified by the conditions of production or resorted to by industrialists as a means of conflict with workers or the government, discharge of workers and suspension of industrial activity are forbidden under threat of strict accountability.

6. Industries may close only with the permission of the organs in charge of economic life. . . .

8. Stipulated legal rights of trade unions remain in full force until the legal provisions are revised. . . .

9. Collective agreements must remain in force until their abolition by mutual agreement or by revision of the laws affecting these agreements.

At the same time bearing in mind the interests of the industrial and economic life of the country, which has been brought to complete ruin by the Bolsheviks, and desiring to express a willingness to cooperate with the best representatives of the commercial and industrial classes, who honestly strive for the regeneration of our country and are imbued with the desire to cooperate in the restoration of normal economic life, the Committee of Members of the Constituent Assembly considers it a duty to make the following statement:

1. Industrialists have the right to demand from workers intensive work of good quality during all working hours established by law and agreement, and to discharge within the limits of the law those not complying with this demand.

2. Industrialists have the right to discharge superfluous workers provided all laws and ordinances existing for this purpose are observed.

VOLSKY

Chairman of the Committee

N. SHMELEV, I. NESTEROV, P. BELOZEROV, I. BRUSHVIT,
P. KLIMUSHKIN, I. ABRAMOV

Members of the Committee

THE KOMUCH INVITES ALLIED INTERVENTION

[Memorandum to the Allies, August 3, 1918] [6]

I have the honor to bring the following [facts] to the attention of the Allied Powers:

After six months of nightmare rule exercised by wilful usurpers of power, the so-called "Soviet of People's Commissars," the Russian people have gathered sufficient strength to take up arms against the tyrants. The territory over which the power of the "Soviet of People's Commissars" still exercises control grows narrower day by day.

The legal power of the All-Russian Constituent Assembly, elected by general popular vote, is being restored in the parts of the country which have been freed from the usurpers; and pending the opening of the Assembly this power is vested in the Committee of Members of the Constituent Assembly.

Having assumed the reins of government in the territories which have been liberated from Bolshevism, the Committee of Members of the Constituent Assembly considers it to be its duty to address the following declaration to the representatives of the Allied Powers:

The Committee . . . has the following principal aims:

To strengthen the power of the Constituent Assembly.

To restore the political unity of Russia.

To create a national army for the struggle against the foreign enemy.

The Committee of Members of the Constituent Assembly, which has been placed at the head of the nation under political,

[6] *Ibid.*, pp. 237-38.

economic, and social conditions of unparalleled difficulty, recognizes all the complications involved in these tasks and pledges its entire strength to saving the fatherland, which is now faced with dire destruction.

The Committee will act with all possible energy and resolution to realize its aims, taking every measure which the moment may necessitate and summoning to this work of reconstruction all classes and nationalities in Russia.

In the sphere of foreign policy, the Committee . . . will remain loyal to the Allies and renounces all thought of a separate peace. Therefore it does not recognize the Brest-Litovsk Peace Treaty.

The Committee is mustering a new army to fight the foreign enemy, which has invaded Russian territory and knows no limits in its imperialistic ambitions. Harboring no warlike designs in relation to other peoples or territories, the Committee cannot consent to the forcible seizure of any part of Russia and holds itself strictly bound to defend and save Russia from the enemy, in order to reunite the torn and weakened sections in one powerful state, the future form of which will be determined by the fully empowered All-Russian Constituent Assembly.

Likewise, the Committee is opposed to the suppression of the nationalities which stand at the side of Russia and her Allies in defense of their independence, and considers it a moral obligation to help these unfortunate peoples with all its strength in the realization of their aims.

The Committee is confident that Russia's renewal of military operations against the Central Powers will prove of great help to the Allies in the struggle on the Western front. However, these military operations will bring the desired results only under conditions which inspire tremendous effort. With this consideration in view the Committee will welcome Allied support in the form both of immediate armed participation of the Allies on our front and of sending war supplies. . . .

The Committee looks upon Allied aid as the expression of a sincere desire to cooperate in the struggle against the foreign foe and takes it for granted that this aid cannot carry with it any territorial or other demands. Summoning the valiant Allied troops to the borders of Russia can have but one purpose—the struggle against the foreign enemy. . . .

V. VOLSKY
Chairman of the Committee of Members
of the Constituent Assembly

M. VEDENIAPIN
Director of the Department
of Foreign Affairs

The armed forces of the Samara Government consisted in part of a few Czech battalions—those which had remained in Samara after the bulk of the Czechoslovak force proceeded east to clear the railway to Cheliabinsk—and in part of Russian officers' detachments and volunteers from various cities along the Volga who had joined the army during the period of enthusiasm following the overthrow of the Soviet régime. Throughout June and July the Czechs and the volunteer detachments, known as the People's Army, assumed the offensive and wrested from Bolshevik control a large territory in the region of the Middle Volga.

EARLY SUCCESSES OF THE KOMUCH[7]

At first [the troops on] the Samara front gained one success after another. Enthusiasm compensated for lack of knowledge and experience. . . .

The first unit of the . . . People's Army, together with a company of Czechoslovaks, took Stavropol . . . [and] Syzran. . . . Simbirsk, extremely important strategically, . . . was captured by a small detachment of 283 men after a difficult and risky march. . . . Ufa was surrendered to the Komuch . . . by F. E. Makhin, a colonel of the General Staff, who held a commanding post in the Soviet army with the approval of the Central Committee of the Socialist-Revolutionists.

The territory freed from the Bolsheviks grew in size from day

[7] M. Vishniak, *Vserossiiskoe Uchreditelnoe Sobranie*, p. 158.

to day. Success infused hopes in those who were fighting the Bolsheviks on other fronts and created confusion, alarm, and sometimes panic in the Soviet camp. . . .

The high point of our successes was the capture of Kazan by the People's Army and the Czechoslovaks on August 7.

"It seemed to us," wrote later the well-known Latsis, who had been engaged in Kazan as chairman of the Cheka to Fight Counter-Revolution on the Czech Front, "that Kazan should not have been surrendered, that the surrender of Kazan was opening all approaches to Moscow, that our army defeated at Kazan would roll farther to Nizhny-Novgorod, and that in this way the enemy would surround us in a closed circle from the east and the north."

THE PEOPLE'S ARMY

[From an Account by Popov, Quartermaster General of the People's Army] [8]

June and the first half of July . . . were a period of remarkable exploits by small detachments under Colonel V. O. Kappel, operating in conjunction with the river fleet against large Bolshevik forces. . . . The Red forces were wholly unable to hold out against these small detachments. . . . The Soviet Government had already sounded an alarm. From all sides forces were sent to the Volga. . . . At the head of our armed forces was placed the " Staff of the People's Army," consisting of three members. . . . This was a disguised Soviet system. . . .

This "Staff of Three" would never have been able to begin operations had it not been for a group of young officers of the General Staff who came to Colonel Galkin on June 9 and offered their services. [Galkin] himself was unprepared for the work and had no trained personnel at his disposal. . . . This "Staff of Three" was in control for a fairly long time. Colonel Galkin ran everything. Bogoliubov and V. I. Lebedev, who substituted for him, were concerned with political matters. . . . The third member, Fortunatov, hardly interfered at all with the work of army organization but for the most part participated in operations as a rank-and-file fighter with rifle in hand. During the Samara period . . . he was twice wounded. . . .

It was with great difficulty that we succeeded in having a set

---

[8] P. P. Petrov, *Ot Volgi do Tikhogo Okeana v riadakh belykh*, pp. 19-43.

of fundamental rules worked out in the ultra-democratic spirit of the year 1917. . . .

The Committee of the Constituent Assembly was reluctant to agree to mobilization, since it knew that this would not be approved by the people.

About the same time the Soviet Government was abandoning the volunteer system. The Volga insurrection gave the final stimulus to the reorganization of the Red Army . . . on a basis of strict discipline. . . . [In consequence, the Komuch finally agreed to a mobilization.]

The mobilized men turned out in good numbers, in some respects exceeding our expectations, but they had the spirit of the year 1917.

The mobilized officers worked reluctantly, sometimes protesting against being drawn into civil war. . . .

The material resources were pitifully small. In some units there was no equipment for training the men. . . .

As a result of the territorial system of recruiting employed, the mobilized men could not separate themselves from the interests of their village and at the first sign of a weakening of authority tried to return home.

The population was anti-Bolshevik in some localities only. . . . The situation at the front prevented us from working undisturbedly on the formation of units. . . . It was necessary to fight and to prepare at one and the same time. . . .

The middle of July was very favorable for the Samara Government and it attempted to extend its influence eastward. In the middle of July the first attempt to come to an agreement with the Siberian Government was made. . . . As is known, this ended in failure, for the Siberian and the Samara Governments were entirely different in nature. . . .

[Simbirsk was taken by Colonel Kappel on July 21] . . . but it failed to come up to expectations in respect to furnishing reinforcements to the People's Army. Fewer volunteers came from officers, the intelligentsia, and the bourgeoisie than was the case in Samara. . . .

Kazan, according to the statements of those coming from there, had a considerable military organization and could hold on with its own forces. Several Frenchmen who had come to Samara via Simbirsk stated positively that Allied forces were soon to appear. . . . And so it was very natural that the victors of Simbirsk burned with impatience not only to make secure the position . . . near the mouth of the Kama River but also to strike a blow at Kazan. Nobody doubted that this blow would be successful and preparations were made to reinforce the [Volga] River fleet. . . . In a few days two barges were provided with heavy guns and river transport for troops was secured.

The forces available at Simbirsk for the advance toward Kazan were small but of excellent spirit. . . .

At Samara [the authorities] did not believe . . . that Kazan . . . would be able to hold on with its own troops; they thought that a blow in a vulnerable spot would make the Soviet Government use all its forces to recapture Kazan so that large reinforcements would be required to retain that city. . . . Furthermore, the situation near Samara demanded close attention in view of the Nikolaevsk group of the enemy, which was steadily growing stronger and was pressing from Nikolaevsk toward Ivashchenko. . . . To liquidate that group of Red forces . . . it was necessary to strike . . . at Saratov. . . .

Saratov was of vast importance to us, not only because it was the center from which the Bolsheviks dealt us blows . . . but also because the Ural Cossacks were fighting the Bolsheviks in the direction of Saratov. . . . The troops of the Ural Cossacks were not numerous but had been hardened by long fighting. An attack on Saratov would have given the Ural Cossacks a chance to advance to the Volga and join forces . . . with Samara. Besides, the population along the Volga was more hostile to the Bolsheviks than was that in other places. . . .

On August 7 Kazan was taken. . . .

Kazan supplied us with many artillery units . . .—two battalions of officers—but it was impossible to leave the defense of the city to these forces. . . . Soon calls for reinforcements began to come from Kazan. . . .

In the middle of August . . . success was beginning to shift to the side of the Reds. Kazan was on the defensive. . . . There was no hope of having new Czech units sent to us from the Urals, and those Czech detachments which were operating at Kazan began to weaken. . . .

ON THE EVE OF THE MARCH ON KAZAN

[From Lebedev's Diary] [9]

Simbirsk, July 26

A French aviator arrived. . . . He had made his way through Kazan. He came from Lavergne with the news that the Allies were already approaching Vologda. I am sending him by aeroplane to Ček. . . .[10]

Today there arrived a delegation . . . from the Sormovo workers. Fifteen thousand workers are said to be impatiently awaiting us. The Bolsheviks at Nizhny[-Novgorod] are in panic. All their forces have been moved away to crush the peasant insurrections to the north.

Delegates . . . have come from Kazan, where everything is ready for the insurrection. The Bolsheviks are behaving like devils there. . . . They are shooting hostages. The delegates implore us to come to their aid, saying that the people of Kazan will revolt in any event. Having secured Ček's consent, I sent them back today with an affirmative reply which gave the approximate date of our entry into Kazan. . . . We must push on and on as long as the Bolsheviks are in a state of panic. . . . Moving south at present is impossible. It would mean exposing our flank to Kazan, at present the center of Bolshevik forces, the center of their supplies, and the headquarters of their commander in chief. . . . We cannot at present expect help from the rear. . . . The Siberian Government continues its terrible game. General Dumbadze . . . of the Siberian army has sent telegrams to all the units of the People's Army inviting our officers to enter the Siberian army and offering them high salaries. . . . Once more the Black Hundred are helping the Bolsheviks. . . .

Night of July 26-27

Stepanov [11] and I have become friends. What an appealing person he is! . . . An ardent democrat, a man with a strong love for Russia, and an immense will-power. I told him of my cherished dream: to march on Kazan, Nizhny-Novgorod, Moscow.

[9] *Volia Rossii*, VIII-IX (1928), 127-33. Lebedev was a member of the staff of the People's Army.
[10] A Czech officer in command of the Samara sector of the Volga front.
[11] A Russian officer in command of a Czechoslovak unit.

. . . We experienced wonderful moments. . . . We shook hands and concluded an alliance, [agreeing] to march on Moscow and do all in our power to make this dream a reality. We also decided to advance to Kazan. This morning we informed Ĉeĉek . . . that we would march on Kazan. . . . He gave a conditional consent. . . .

THE CAPTURE OF KAZAN
[Communication of the Bolshevik Commander, August 9, 1918] [12]

Kazan was captured by the Czechoslovaks around midnight, August 6-7. During the 7th the fight continued in the suburbs. The Czechoslovaks are following up their successes in two directions: to the northeast, and in the direction of Sviazhsk along the left bank of the Volga. . . . The fighting in Kazan demonstrated the complete incapacity of the workers' detachments. . . . Local party comrades in high posts displayed great energy and diligence in helping to defend the city, but their efforts were wasted in the chaos of unpreparedness. The soldiers proved utterly lacking in discipline. The whole burden of the defense fell upon the Fifth Regiment of Lettish Sharpshooters. The Fourth Regiment of Lettish Sharpshooters reestablished its former military reputation. As regards Russian units, they proved incapable of fighting in mass because of lack of preparation and discipline. . . .

VATSETIS
Commander of the Eastern Front

SEIZURE OF THE GOLD RESERVE AT KAZAN
[Communication to the Samara Government] [13]

I beg to report that at this moment the shipment of the gold reserve belonging to Russia has been completed. We have sent to Samara from Kazan the following:

1. The entire gold reserve, amounting to six hundred and fifty million rubles at par value. . . .
2. One hundred million rubles in paper money.
3. A large quantity of other valuables.
3. Platinum stocks. . . .

LEBEDEV
Assistant Chief of the
War Department

[12] *Volia Rossii*, VIII-IX (1928), 161.
[13] *Ibid.*, p. 165.

The Volga front was not limited to the region directly under the control of the Samara Government but extended on the southeast to the territory of the Orenburg and Ural Cossacks, who had reestablished their voisko governments after successful uprisings against the Bolsheviks; and on the northeast to the country along the Kama River (a tributary of the Volga) and to the Ural mining region.

Soon after the November Revolution the Orenburg Cossacks, led by their ataman, Dutov, attempted to check the spread of Bolshevism in their territory but failed. Their capital, Orenburg, fell into Bolshevik hands on January 31, and Dutov, together with his followers, fled to the Turgai steppes.

However, in the spring of 1918 the Orenburg Cossacks rebelled against the Bolsheviks. Early in the summer the Cossacks succeeded in expelling the Soviets from the region and in establishing contact with Samara. About the same time the Ural Cossacks broke up the Bolshevik Soviet and formed the Ural Voisko Government, in which Socialist-Revolutionists predominated.

But these governments, surrounded by superior Bolshevik forces and fully absorbed in the defense of their own territory, were in no position to offer assistance to the Samara Government. Though the Cossacks succeeded in maintaining themselves for a much longer period than did the Samara Government, yet their opposition to the Soviets remained strictly local and had little influence on the fortunes of the Volga front as a whole.

THE REVOLT OF THE ORENBURG COSSACKS
[From an Account by I. Akulinin] [14]

Having occupied the city of Orenburg and established themselves on the territory of the Orenburg Cossacks, the Bolsheviks

[14] I. Akulinin, "Orenburgskoe Kazache voisko v vorbe s bolshevikami," in *Kazachi Dumy,* Nos. 21-25, 1924, pp. 6-8.

showed at ónce what kind of "comrades" they were to the Cossacks. Everywhere, in the cities and in the stanitsas, they began bloody dealings with the people, accompanied by plunder and robbery. Several stanitsas were burned to the ground, millions of puds of grain carted away or destroyed, thousands of heads of cattle and horses driven off . . . , and all stanitsas . . . forced to pay huge levies in money. Believing that all Cossacks . . . were enemies of the Soviets, the Bolsheviks did not stand on ceremony with any of them. Many officers, rank-and-file Cossacks, and even Cossack women were shot; many more were thrown into prison.

Such dealings on the part of the Bolsheviks . . . sobered the Cossacks. Their Bolshevik sympathies evaporated and they took up arms [against the Bolsheviks].

The first to rebel were the so-called "Lineinyia" stanitsas, situated along the Ilek River. The signal for the revolt was given by the stanitsa Izobilnaia, the inhabitants of which wiped out the punitive detachment of Commissar Zwilling by a surprise attack.

Soon the Lineinyia stanitsas were joined . . . by Cossacks of the lower stanitsas, situated along the Ural River below Orenburg.

By the month of May practically all of the First District was in revolt and Cossack detachments surrounded Orenburg. . . .

At that time the fighting was carried on exclusively by rank-and-file Cossacks, who invited [former] officers to act as commanders. The struggle was led by the Congress of United Stanitsas, consisting of representatives of the insurgent Cossack villages, and the general direction of operations was entrusted to Major Karlikov. . . .

A delegation was sent to Ataman Dutov and the Orenburg Cossack Government at the city of Turgai, with the request that they come back and assume leadership of the military operations. [Dutov returned to Orenburg early in July.]

. . . The Ataman was greeted by the Congress of United Stanitsas, by representatives of the [Samara] Committee of Members of the Constituent Assembly, and by other city organizations.

From this time on, the struggle against the Bolsheviks was

again led by Ataman Dutov and the Orenburg Cossack Government.

The revolt of the northern and central stanitsas . . . was assisted by the Czechoslovaks and Siberian detachments, which helped the Orenburg Cossacks to expel the Bolsheviks from the Second, Third, and Fourth Districts. . . .

On the assumption that Allied troops would soon be forthcoming from Archangel and the Far East to reinforce them, the Czechoslovaks decided to seize Ekaterinburg. Thereby they hoped to gain control of the railway running from that city to Perm, Viatka, Kotlas, and Vologda, and also to facilitate contact with the Allied troops which were expected to land at Archangel. Two separate armies, one from Omsk, the other from Cheliabinsk, were sent for that purpose. Ekaterinburg was taken on July 25. At first there was established a moderate socialist government, called the Committee of the People's Authority.[15] However, under the pressure of bourgeois circles which were supported by representatives of France, negotiations were started with the non-socialist groups that resulted in the formation of a new government, named the Regional Government of the Urals. It consisted of two Cadets, two persons without party affiliation, one Socialist-Populist, one Socialist-Revolutionist, and one Menshevik.[16]

On August 20 the Government stated its political credo.

THE ALLIES AND THE VOLGA FRONT
[From an Account by V. I. Lebedev] [17]

. . . The Allies (through their representatives) promised to send a landing force to Archangel and Siberia via Vladivostok. . . . All our calculations rested on this. Briefly, our plan was as

---

[15] *Komitet narodnoi vlasti.*
[16] A. Taniaev, *Kolchakovshchina na Urale,* pp. 13-20; L. A. Krol, *Za tri goda. Vospominaniia, vpechatleniia, vstrechi,* pp. 71-96.
[17] *Volia Rossii,* VIII-IX (1928), 63-64.

follows: insurrection in the Volga region, capture of **Kazan,**
Simbirsk, Samara, Saratov; mobilization beyond this line; landing of an Allied force at Archangel; and the movement [of this
force] toward Vologda to join with the Volga front. Another
force, landing at Vladivostok, was to advance rapidly to the
Volga, where we were to hold the front until their arrival.

Under such conditions, not only anti-Bolsheviks but even those
sympathizing with the Soviets would have had to choose between
an alliance with Germany against all the Russian democratic
parties and an alliance with us against Imperial Germany, which
had seized half of European Russia.

The Volga region was chosen because it seemed to be the most
suitable. It was sufficiently far removed from the center of Bolshevik forces . . . and had large quantities of ammunition evacuated from the front. . . . Finally, it was beyond the Volga that
the democratic Ural Cossacks and the peasants of two neighboring uezds were fighting against the Bolsheviks with a fair
degree of success. . . .

THE REGIONAL GOVERNMENT OF THE URALS

[Proclamation of August 20, 1918] [18]

Our prostrate land is beginning to revive. Step by step the
brave Allies and their vanguard, our Czechoslovak brothers, in
union with the restored Russian army, the liberty-loving Cossacks,
and self-sacrificing officers, are clearing Russia of her conquerors
—the Germans and their accomplices, the Bolsheviks. The time
has come for Russia to rise in her might and . . . stand side by
side with the Allies, faithfully bearing her full share of responsibility in delivering the world from German militarism and
rapacity.

Great difficulties stand in the way of regenerating Russia,
especially the Urals, where life is completely disorganized. Industrial plants are entirely disrupted; stores of raw material and
fuel are small; food is insufficient; currency as well as gold and
other valuables in the Treasury and banks has been stolen by the
Bolsheviks to the value of hundreds of millions. Terrible ruin,
requiring incredible effort for rehabilitation! The task, however,

[18] Piontkovsky, *G. V. R.,* pp. 248-51.

would be beyond the strength of any government sending officials from the center, no matter who they might be. It is only the Regional Government which with great effort can carry out this task by forming a staff of local public workers and drawing into constructive enterprise all the vital forces of the region. Therefore, believing that not an hour could be lost in the task of restoring a united, mighty, and free Russia, the representatives of the political parties—People's Freedom [Cadets], Socialist-Populists, Socialist-Revolutionists, and Social-Democrats (Mensheviks)—set to work, immediately after Ekaterinburg, the capital of the Urals, had been freed [from the Bolsheviks], to formulate a program capable of uniting on one working platform all these parties. . . . As a result of the labor of this interparty commission, a Provisional Regional Government of the Urals has been established . . . to function until the convocation of the regional duma. Remembering that Russia must be united and not divided, that the final organization of Russia rests with the Constituent Assembly, and that a central government capable of uniting all regions of Russia must be created at once, the Government will endeavor to carry out the following program:

1. The Government will firmly protect all the liberties gained by the people, but without permitting any abuse detrimental to the order which our suffering country needs.

2. The Government recognizes the inalienable equal rights of nationalities and their right to cultural self-determination, as well as equality of rights for individuals of all faiths and freedom of conscience. The Government does not consider the Bolshevik decree separating church and state as having the force of law; the relation between church and state must be left to the decision of the All-Russian Constituent Assembly.

3. The Government will take all measures to develop the productive power and the industries of the Urals, protecting the rights of private property, attracting foreign capital, and removing all impediments to private initiative, cooperatives, stock companies, etc. Believing that the interest of the state and the development of industry are higher than the interests of single groups and classes, the Government will in all cases act in defense of the interests of the state as a whole.

4. The Government will take steps to return industrial plants

to their former owners but reserves the right, in individual cases, to declare industries national property. . . . State control over production and limitation of profits will be introduced in industry.

5. The eight-hour working day shall be maintained in industry, on condition that an established minimum of work is done. Wages shall be left to mutual agreement between employers and workers, but the Government reserves the right to interfere in behalf of the interest of labor should wages fall below the living-wage minimum, threaten the health of workers, or cause a lowering of the productivity of labor. Workers' insurance will be introduced in the same form which exists in civilized countries where there is greater protection of the interests of labor.

6. Private banks will be reestablished and their activities, without violation of business secrets, shall be open to government inspection. . . .

9. Believing that the question of food supplies can be solved best when left to the initiative of cooperatives and private trade, the Government will confine its rôle to that of mere regulation.

10. In regard to education, the Government will take all measures necessary for the speedy introduction of general and compulsory instruction. Leaving to schools complete autonomy in internal matters, the Government reserves to itself the framing and carrying out of a definite general plan of education. The study of religion in schools will not be compulsory for pupils.

11. Pending the solution of the land question by the All-Russian Constituent Assembly, the Government will leave agricultural land in the hands of its actual users and will take measures to protect national interests and to enable the All-Russian Constituent Assembly to carry out its will.

12. In the interest of reestablishing municipal and zemstvo self-government, the Government will at once frame laws providing for elections on the basis of universal, direct, equal, and secret suffrage rights, without regard to sex.

13. Recognizing that all energy must now be directed toward building a strong army and that no sacrifices in freeing our country from the foreign enemy are too great to be made, the Government will unswervingly carry out all measures concerned with military problems, not permitting anyone to shirk unavoidable burdens.

14. The Government considers all orders and decrees of the Soviet Government illegal and therefore void, but it will not permit any chaotic breaking up of existing relationships. It is now engaged in working out rules for the orderly restoration of rights and relationships which have been changed by the above-mentioned decrees and ordinances. . . .

The Government is confident that its program will make possible the immediate calling of the All-Russian Constituent Assembly, which is the only sovereign of Russia and which, deciding all questions, will also decide the question of the future destinies of the Regional Government of the Urals. . . .

N. Ivanov
President of the Council and Chief
Director of Commerce and Industry

L. Krol
Vice-President of the Council and
Chief Director of Finance

A. Gutt
Chief Director of Mines

N. Glasson
Chief Director of Justice

N. Aseikin
Chief Director of the Interior

A. Pribylev
Chief Director of Agriculture

P. Murashev
Chief Director of Labor

With the capture of Ekaterinburg and Kazan the driving force of the Czechoslovaks and the People's Army came to a stop. No reinforcements were coming from either Archangel or Siberia; and while the occupation of the Ural industrial region stimulated a number of anti-Bolshevik uprisings among the industrial workers [19] and peasants in Viatka Gubernia, yet these failed to influence the military situation on the Volga front materially.

Meanwhile the Bolsheviks were straining every effort to organize the Red Army and make it ready for action against the Czechoslovaks. The Supplementary Treaty of August 27, in which Germany promised not to engage in hostile activities against the Soviet Government,[20] enabled the Bolsheviks to concentrate large forces on the Volga front; and Trotsky was commissioned to take personal charge of operations on this front. As the following material shows, the Bolshevik generalissimo threatened and cajoled the Red Army soldiers in pronouncements designed to inspire them with fighting spirit. His efforts were successful. Kazan fell on September 10 and Simbirsk was taken on the following day. The forces of the Komuch took to full retreat and shortly Samara had to be abandoned.

REMEMBER YAROSLAV!

[Trotsky's Warning, August 1918] [21]

The revolt of the bourgeois officers in Yaroslav was crushed unmercifully. . . . Hundreds of them were killed and thrown in the Volga. More than 350 White Guards were shot after the revolt had been put down. . . .

Remember Yaroslav, you counter-revolutionary bandits of Kazan, Simbirsk, and Samara!

The ignorant and deceived soldiers and Czechoslovaks may hope for forgiveness if they repent in time and lay down their arms. But you, bourgeois conspirators, foreign agents, provocateurs, officers, and White Guards, will be exterminated. . . . *Remember Yaroslav! . . .*

---

[19] The most serious uprisings in this region were those of the Izhevsk and Votkinsk workers. An account of these revolts is given by A. Gutman-Gan, "Dva vozstaniia," in *Beloe Delo*, III, 151-55; and in Chamberlin, *op. cit.*, II, 16-17.

[20] See above, p. 129.

[21] Trotsky, *Kak vooruzhalas revoliutsiia*, I, 245.

DEATH FOR DESERTERS

[Trotsky's Announcement, August 14, 1918] [22]

. . . I hereby give warning that if any part of the army retreats of its own will the first to be shot will be the commissar and the second, the commander. The soldiers who show courage will be rewarded and promoted to positions of command. Cowards and traitors will not escape the bullets. . . .

[Trotsky's Announcement, August 30, 1918] [23]

. . . The Soviet Government has passed from warning to action. . . . Twenty deserters were shot yesterday. . . . The first to go were the commissars and commanders who left their posts; next came the cowardly liars who played sick; and finally the Red Army soldiers who deserted. . . .

Death to the coward! Death to the traitor-deserter!

WHAT THE TAKING OF KAZAN MEANS

[Trotsky's Announcement, August 24, 1918] [24]

Soldiers of the Fifth Army, Sailors of the Volga Fleet!

We have joyful news. The Second Soviet Army has drawn close to Kazan from the northeast. The Czecho-White Guards engaged us . . . but were driven back with losses . . . , and our heroic Second Army is within twelve versts of Kazan.

It is now your turn, soldiers of the Fifth Army. Move up to meet the Second Army and between you crush the Kazan counter-revolution.

SOLDIERS OF THE FIFTH ARMY, SAILORS OF THE VOLGA FLEET!

The taking of Kazan means the liberation of the Kazan workers and peasants.

The taking of Kazan is the beginning of the death agony for the bourgeois scoundrels on the Volga, in the Urals and Siberia. . . .

The taking of Kazan means rest and reward for the brave defenders of the revolution. . . .

[22] *Ibid.*, p. 235.   [23] *Ibid.*, p. 243.   [24] *Ibid.*, p. 239.

Attention! The decisive moment for the final blow is here. At the first order from your commander, Comrade Slavin, advance as one man and give the enemy a death-blow.

Commanders! Commissars! Soldiers! Sailors! Attention!

TO ALL THOSE FIGHTING AGAINST THE RED ARMY

[Trotsky's Appeal, August 26, 1918] [25]

What are you fighting for? To restore riches and power to landowners, capitalists, and army officers; to return dividends to French and Japanese bankers?

And you, Czechoslovak soldiers, workers and peasants! You are deceived. You are cannon fodder. You are shedding your blood for the rich. The White Guards are doomed. Kazan is surrounded on all sides. Our forces—land, sea, and air—greatly exceed yours. Your leaders, having seized the people's gold, are hastening to leave Kazan. They realize that they are doomed.

Czechoslovak soldiers, peasants, and workers! Do you wish to die with them?

I declare that the Soviet Government is making war only upon the rich, the usurpers, and the imperialists. To the workers we extend a fraternal hand. Everyone who comes to our camp will be pardoned and given a fraternal welcome. Many of your men have already come and have not suffered. They are now . . . at liberty. In the name of the Soviet of People's Commissars I give you a last warning: Join the Soviet forces!

DO NOT JOIN THE ENEMY!

[Trotsky's Warning, August 27, 1918] [26]

Our enemies—landowners, capitalists, officers, and their hirelings, the Czechoslovaks—are trying to mobilize the working people of Kazan Gubernia to fight against the workers and peasants.

So that no one may later plead ignorance of the revolutionary laws . . . of the Soviet Government, I hereby give notice:

1. Everyone who joins the Czechoslovak White Guards and enters the ranks of the enemies of the people commits a grave crime against the state.

[25] Ibid., p. 240.   [26] Ibid., p. 241.

2. All workers and peasants who have been forced to enter the enemy's army should come over at once to the Soviet camp, and . . . they will be forgiven.

3. Those peasants and workers who have sold themselves to the White Guards and remain in their armies voluntarily will be shot, along with the officers and the darling sons of the bourgeoisie and capitalists. All their property will be turned over to wounded and crippled soldiers of the Red Army and to the families of its deceased soldiers. . . .

VICTORY

[Trotsky's Announcement, September 10, 1918] [27]

September 10 is a red-letter day in the history of the Socialist Revolution. On this day Kazan was torn . . . from the White Guards and Czechoslovaks. It is a turning-point. The advance of the enemy has at last been stopped; his spirit is broken. After Kazan we shall recapture Ekaterinburg, Simbirsk, Samara, and the other cities on the Volga, in the Urals, and in Siberia. . . .

Soldiers and sailors of the Fifth Army! You have taken Kazan. It will be counted to your credit. Those parts of the army or those individuals who have especially distinguished themselves will be especially rewarded. . . . For the present I wish to declare, in the hearing of the country and the international proletariat, that *the Fifth Army Has Fully Done Its Duty.*

In the name of the Soviet of People's Commissars I say: "Comrades, I thank you."

WHAT WE ARE FIGHTING FOR

[From Trotsky's Speech at Kazan, September 11, 1918] [28]

. . . We value science, culture, art, and would like to make them accessible to the people. . . . But if our class enemies should again attempt to show that all these are for them only, we would say: "Perish science, art; perish the theater!" We comrades appreciate the sun which lights the world, but if the rich . . . should try to monopolize it, we would say: "May the sun cease to shine and may eternal darkness reign!"

[27] *Ibid.,* p. 249.   [28] *Ibid.,* p. 251.

Why did we fight under the walls of Kazan? Why are we fighting on the Volga and in the Urals? We are fighting to settle the question whether the homes, the palaces, the cities, the sun, and heaven are to belong to the workers and peasants or to the bourgeoisie and the landlords. . . .

B. ALLIED INTERVENTION AT ARCHANGEL

When the attempt to reestablish the Eastern front against Germany came to involve an attack on the Bolsheviks, Archangel appeared more strategic than Murmansk as a base for Allied operations. Accordingly, the British decided to transfer the bulk of their forces from Murmansk to Archangel. For the sake of appearances it was considered desirable that the landing of the British should take place at the invitation of the Russians of that city. On the day when the British fleet was expected to arrive at Archangel (August 2), local anti-Bolsheviks, prompted by Allied agents, deposed the Archangel Soviet and invited the British to land. They established a government calling itself the "Supreme Administration of the North" and consisting of moderate socialists who accepted the program of the Union for the Regeneration of Russia.[29] On August 2 the new government issued the following proclamation:

ESTABLISHMENT OF THE SUPREME ADMINISTRATION
OF THE NORTH

[Proclamation, August 2, 1918] [30]

To the Citizens of Archangel and Archangel Gubernia!

Bolshevik rule has come to an end! Hated by the entire population on account of its treachery at Brest-Litovsk, civil war, general famine, and its trampling on the rights and liberties of the country, . . . the so-called "Soviet Government," consisting of

[29] See pp. 182-85, above.
[30] *Sobranie uzakanenii i rasporiazhenii Verkhovnago Upravleniia i Vremennago Pravitelstva Severnoi Oblasti,* No. 1, 1918, pp. 6-7.

criminals and traitors, found itself abandoned by the people at a critical moment and was compelled to flee.

We representatives of the people, elected by universal suffrage, consider it our duty, at this period of transition when there is no legal central government in Russia, to assume the prerogatives of sovereignty in the country of the North.

We hereby inform the inhabitants that henceforth the sovereign state authority in the territory of the North will be in the hands of the Supreme Administration of the Northern Region. This government is composed of members of the Constituent Assembly and of representatives of the zemstvos and cities of the region.

Being a provisional body, the Supreme Administration will resign all its prerogatives immediately upon the formation in Russia of a central democratic government and as soon as there is a possibility of freely communicating with that government. The aims of the Provisional Administration are:

1. To cooperate with other regions in reconstructing a central all-Russian government and to organize the local administration of the Northern region.

2. To defend the North and the rest of the country against territorial violation by Germany, Finland, and other enemy states.

3. To reunite with Russia the regions which have been taken from her, provided the inhabitants of the regions concerned agree to such union.

4. To reestablish all . . . liberties and institutions of true popular government, namely, the Constituent Assembly, zemstvos, and municipal dumas.

5. To establish a stable legal order that will guarantee to every citizen the opportunity of full economic, social, and spiritual development.

6. To guarantee effectively the rights of toilers to the land.

7. To protect the interests of labor in accordance with the economic and political interests of the North and of Russia as a whole.

8. To fight the famine.

The Supreme Administration will soon make public more detailed instructions implied in the foregoing program. The Government seeks the support of all classes of the population which cherish the aims therein mentioned. In particular it counts upon

11

Russia's allies—England, America, and France—to aid in the defense of the North and of Russia, and it hopes to receive their assistance in combating the famine and in relieving the financial situation.

The Supreme Administration is firmly convinced of the identity of the interests of Russia and those of her allies in the struggle against the common enemy. It is certain, moreover, that the coming of the Allied troops was not for the purpose of intervening in the internal affairs of the country or of opposing the will of the people. Therefore the Administration greets the Allied forces coming to the North to fight the common enemy and urges the people to give them a friendly reception and all possible assistance. . . .

Members of the Supreme Administration of the North:

N. V. CHAIKOVSKY, Member of the Constituent Assembly, Viatka Gubernia

A. A. IVANOV, Member of the Constituent Assembly, Archangel Gubernia

C. C. MASLOV, Member of the Constituent Assembly, Vologodsky Gubernia

A. I. GUKOVSKY, Member of the Constituent Assembly, Novgorod Gubernia

G. A. MARTIUSHIN, Member of the Constituent Assembly, Kazan, Gubernia

YA. T. DEDUSENKO, Member of the Constituent Assembly, Samara Gubernia

M. A. LIKHACH, Member of the Constituent Assembly, Northern Front

P. YU. ZUBOV, Vice-Mayor, Vologda.

N. D. STARTSEV, Vice-Chairman, Archangel City Duma.[81]

---

[81] The personnel of the Archangel Government was as follows: President, N. V. Chaikovsky; Vice-President, C. C. Maslov; Secretary, P. Yu. Zubov. Department heads: Foreign Affairs, N. V. Chaikovsky; War, C. C. Maslov; Justice, A. I. Gukovsky; Interior, Post and Telegraph, P. Yu. Zubov; Supplies, Trade and Industry, Ya. T. Dedusenko; Finance, G. A. Martiushin; Agriculture, C. C. Maslov; Labor and Education, M. A. Likhach. (*Ibid.*, p. 8.)

ABOLITION OF SOVIET INSTITUTIONS IN THE NORTH
[Decree of the Supreme Administration of the North, August 2, 1918] [32]

. . . All organs of the Soviet Government in the region of the North . . . are hereby abolished. Members . . . of executive committees of soviets of workers', soldiers', and peasants' deputies and all commissars are to be placed under arrest . . . and so held until the investigating commissions have established the degree of their guilt in the crimes committed by the Soviet Government, such as murder, plunder, betrayal of the country, inciting civil war between classes and peoples of Russia, stealing and destroying state, public, and private property . . . , and other infractions of the fundamental laws of human society, honor, and morality. . . .

[A number of other decrees issued on August 2 reestablished zemstvo and municipal self-government and appointed gubernia and uezd commissars to take the place of the deposed authorities. (*Ibid.*, pp. 10-12.)]

THE GOVERNMENT AND LABOR
[Decree of August 13, 1918] [33]

1. . . . All existing decrees concerning the protection of labor and the relations between workers and employers are to remain in force pending their annulment by regular procedure.

2. A special committee of representatives of labor and employers . . . is hereby established to examine the existing ordinances on labor protection in order to bring them into conformity with the true interests of labor.

3. The decree on the so-called "workers' control," which was responsible for the disruption of Russian industry and brought incalculable evil to the working class, is now annulled. The Departments of Industry, Labor, and Agriculture are instructed to undertake immediately the formulation and enactment of the principles of state regulation of economic life in the [Northern] region.

N. V. CHAIKOVSKY
President of the Supreme Administration

A. GUKOVSKY
Head of the Department of Justice

[32] *Ibid.*, p. 9.   [33] *Ibid.*, p. 19.

The socialist government, though moderate in its program, was not to the liking of General Poole, the British commander of the Allied expeditionary force. On August 8, shortly after his landing, General Poole appointed Donop, a French colonel, as military governor of Archangel. The Supreme Administration of the North protested against the military governorship as an encroachment upon the government's authority, but the protest was disregarded.

This and similar measures taken by the British and French military authorities against the local government considerably weakened its prestige and strengthened the opposition groups of the Right. With the tacit approval of General Poole, the latter decided to depose the government and to establish a military dictatorship.

During the night of September 5 a group of officers entered the building occupied by the government, arrested five of its members, and conveyed them by steamer to the Solovetsky Islands. Those placed in custody were N. Chaikovsky, P. Zubov, S. Maslov, M. Likhach, and A. Gukovsky. The arrests were made by order of Captain Chaplin, commander of the Russian troops of the Northern region, who on the following day issued a declaration explaining the reasons for the coup d'état and an order proclaiming a military dictatorship for the region.

ATTEMPT TO OVERTHROW THE SUPREME ADMINISTRATION OF THE NORTH

[Chaplin's Order, September 6, 1918] [84]

1. The Supreme Administration of the Northern Region is deposed.

2. N. A. Startsev, Government Commissar of the Gubernia, is appointed Chief of the Civil Division of the Northern Region. . . .

[84] *Vozrozhdenie Severa*, No. 21, September 12, 1918, p. 2.

3. Until martial law is revoked, all civil authorities except the courts shall be subordinate to military authorities.

4. The Chief of the Civil Division . . . , N. A. Startsev, is hereby instructed to reorganize at once all departments of the former Supreme Administration of the North in such manner as to conform with the requirements of the moment and the demands of necessity.

5. Individual departments of the Civil Administration of the Northern Region are ordered to continue their present work.

6. Until martial law is revoked, all meetings, assemblies, and parades are absolutely forbidden.

7. Colonel Durov of the General Staff is appointed Chief of the Military Administration of the Northern Region. . . .

CHAPLIN
Captain of the Second Rank

[Chaplin's Proclamation, September 6, 1918] [35]

To the Citizens of Archangel! To the Citizens of the Northern Region!

Citizens! The country has reached the limit of its suffering. Our fatherland, torn by the struggle for power which is going on among all parties, has sunk to a state of unprecedented degradation and poverty. Russia is ruled by traitors who, having taken advantage of internal strife, delivered the country to the Germans to be plundered and humiliated. Only a strong and well-organized military force can give us freedom from German oppression and hope of a brighter future for Russia. The Supreme Administration of the Northern Region proved incapable of handling the task which it had assumed. Not elected by anyone and unknown to everyone in the Northern region, it undertook the reconstruction of the country while retaining the old party system. Its efforts failed and it has resigned its authority.

While warmly welcoming our allies and highly valuing the aid which they are now giving us in our fight for the existence of our country, we should all remember that shame and disgrace are ahead of us if the whole burden of the struggle falls on the shoulders of the Allies. We must build the welfare of our country

[35] *Ibid.*

with our own Russian hands and buy our resurrection with our own blood.

We are a people with a great historic past but today we are a sick people. We have become weak and spiritually impoverished.

We allow our country to be ruined by party struggles.

But the dawn is approaching.

From the Volga to the Baikal Mountains a mighty wave of reconstruction is rising. Russia's political organism is already growing to maturity there and a Russian People's Army is in the process of formation.

We too should exert our energies. Let us put aside party strife in the name of one great purpose: "Everything for the salvation of the country."

From the north let us go to meet Russia's faithful sons coming from the east. The hour will arrive . . . when, as in the past, the free Russian people will elect in Moscow . . . the government which best suits it.

Long live a free, great, and undivided Russia!

CHAPLIN
Captain of the Second Rank and Commander of the
Armed Forces of the Northern Region

N. A. STARTSEV
Chief of the Civil Division of the Northern Region

The military coup aroused widespread opposition in Archangel. Cooperative societies and zemstvo and city authorities protested to the Allied ambassadors against the overthrow of the government. A general strike was called by the workers, and armed peasants arrived from outlying districts to demand the restoration of the deposed authorities.

Meanwhile Ambassador Francis, who with other Allied representatives had established headquarters at Archangel, called a meeting of the Diplomatic Corps to consider the crisis brought about by the kidnapping of the members of the Supreme Administration of the North. The meeting decided to bring them back but to insist on such reorganization of the government as would give representatives of the middle class a voice in the administration of the region.

On September 8 the abducted ministers were returned to Archangel and on the 9th they were reinstated in power. Attempts to reconstruct the government in accordance with the wishes of the Allied representatives were at first unsuccessful, and the government crisis lasted over a month. The bourgeois groups refused to cooperate with the socialists and for a time Chaikovsky considered resigning from the government.

Upon learning that an all-Russian government had been formed at Ufa, the Supreme Administration of the North resigned and a governor-general was appointed for Archangel.[36] Since no contacts could be established with the Ufa Government the Allies insisted that the Archangel Government be reorganized on the lines suggested. Early in October an agreement was reached with the bourgeois groups, and a Provisional Government of the North was announced on October 7.

REORGANIZATION OF THE ARCHANGEL GOVERNMENT

[Chaikovsky's Announcement, October 7, 1918] [37]

I. On September 28, 1918, the members of the Supreme Administration of the North turned over the supreme power to Nicolai Vasilevich Chaikovsky and Alexandre Isaevich Gukovsky, members of the Supreme Administration of the North and of the Constituent Assembly. On September 29 Alexander Isaevich Gukovsky also surrendered his authority as member of the Supreme Administration of the North.

[36] S. P. Melgunov, *N. V. Chaikovsky v gody grazhdanskoi voiny*, p. 87.
[37] *Vestnik Verkhovnaro Upravleniia Severnoi Oblasti*, No. 45, October 9, 1918, p. 2.

II. The task, assigned to me by the Supreme Administration, of forming a government of the Northern region which meets the requirements of the present moment, has been accomplished. I have formed a Provisional Government composed of the following:

N. V. Chaikovsky: President of the Provisional Government and Chief of the Departments of Foreign Affairs and Agriculture.

Colonel B. A. Durov: Governor-General and Commander of the Russian Troops of the Northern Region and Chief of the Departments of War, Interior, Communication, Post and Telegraph.

Prince I. A. Kurakin: Acting Chief of the Department of Finance.

N. V. Mefodiev: Chief of the Departments of Commerce, Industry, and Food Supply.

S. N. Gorodetsky: Chief of the Department of Justice.

P. Yu. Zubov: Chief of the Department of People's Education and Secretary to the Provisional Government of the Northern Region.

The Provisional Government comes into existence under unique circumstances, at a time when war is being waged against Bolsheviks and Germans, when the general aims and interests of the Allies must take precedence over local affairs. The Allied cause is the cause of Russia, the cause of saving her from the horrors of bloody terror and from the parcelling of her national territory into many separate and weak fragments which . . . at any moment might become the prey of greedy plunderers. The Northern region is thus facing a task of colossal magnitude—to serve as a starting-point for the liberation and salvation of Russia from the oppression of her internal and external assailants. In the face of such a task everything else must be placed in the background.

That is the reason why the program of the new government gives primary place to the reestablishment of the Russian army and its advance at any cost. That is why we find it necessary to subordinate our local and class interests and to consider chiefly how to make possible and effective our collaboration with the Allies—with their troops and envoys. . . .

The Allies, the Russian officers and soldiers, the commercial and industrial circles, and the entire democracy should unite and work energetically to fulfill their sacred duty to the country, . . .

taking advantage of the presence in our territory of armed forces of the Allies, whose aim is to reestablish our own national fighting power. . . .

It is only because of these exceptional circumstances that I have ventured to assume single-handed the duties of the All-Russian Supreme Authority. . . . It is true that during the past few days it became known that a directorate of five persons had been elected at Ufa to head the All-Russian Government. My name appears among their number. I would be happy indeed if this information should prove correct. But to organize the regional government on the basis of this report would be premature; it is necessary to have direct communication with this central authority.

Under present conditions, both the Provisional Government and I find it necessary to direct all our efforts not only upon the above-mentioned principal task but also upon the preservation for the people of the benefits which have as yet remained intact amid the general state of disintegration. It [the Government] will continue the work which the Supreme Administration has already organized in order to reestablish law and order in place of Bolshevik chaos: the regulation of the exchange of goods with foreign countries, the organization of the distribution of foodstuffs in the region, the restoration of the system of money circulation, etc. With these economic problems in view the Provisional Government has already established a Financial-Economic Council, a Committee of Supply, and other organs of consultation to enable the Government to keep in close contact with organized groups of public opinion and to call on their cooperation.

N. V. CHAIKOVSKY
President of the Supreme Administration
of the Northern Region

The Allied forces at Archangel were insufficient to undertake a successful offensive against the Bolsheviks. Even after the American force of about four thousand landed at Archangel early in September, little progress could be made toward establishing contact with the anti-Bolshevik forces on the Volga front. The Allies advanced along the Dvina

River as far southeast as Shenkursk but there they were
brought to a halt. Meanwhile the People's Army on the
Volga front suffered a defeat and the center of anti-Bolshevik activities shifted to Siberia and the Russian Far East.

C. The Far East

The vanguard of the Czechoslovak army reached Vladivostok about the middle of May and for a time established
friendly relations with the local Soviet authorities. However, toward the end of June disagreements arose, and when
the Czechoslovaks decided to return to Central and Western
Siberia they overthrew the Vladivostok Soviet; thereupon
the Allied consuls proclaimed the city to be under the protection of the Allies. Immediately a number of rival governments sprang up and sought the recognition and support of
the Allied representatives, who were somewhat bewildered
by the multiplicity of claimants of "supreme authority."
There was the Socialist-Revolutionist government, headed
by Derber, which was elected by the Siberian Regional
Duma in January 1918. Opposed to the socialist government was the government led by General Horvath, manager
of the Chinese Eastern Railway, who received his support
from the propertied elements. Still another claimant to
authority was the regional zemstvo government, at the
head of which was Medvedev. Finally there were various
Cossack chiefs who refused to recognize any authority
and used high-handed methods unwelcome to both the
local population and the Allies.

CONDITIONS IN THE FAR EAST

[From a Report of General Stepanov to General Alexeev] [38]

Around the middle of May the situation [in the Far East] was
as follows: Irkutsk and the Transbaikal region were dominated

---

[38] Denikin, *Ocherki russkoi smuty*, III, 105-06.

by the Bolsheviks, who had occupied Blagoveshchensk, Khabarovsk, and Vladivostok. Part of the Czechoslovak troops (about fifteen thousand) managed by this time to reach Vladivostok. . . . In Manchuria, or rather within the zone of the Chinese Eastern Railway, I found complete chaos. . . . Russian police had been replaced by Chinese but the administration of the Railway remained in Russian hands, General Horvath being Chief Administrator.

[Large numbers of former army officers gathered at important railway centers and organized themselves into military groups.] Semenov, an esaul [39] of Transbaikal Cossacks, began his career by flogging a number of Manchurian railway officials for their alleged sympathies with Bolshevism. He then proclaimed himself ataman. [40] The Japanese and the French immediately supplied him with money, with which he proceeded to hire thugs capable of anything except keeping order in their own midst. Minor successes against scattered Bolshevik bands created for Semenov a semblance of glory. At Japanese instigation Semenov began to assert his independence, refusing to recognize any superior. . . .

Something very similar, but on a smaller scale, took place at Pogranichnaia, where the self-styled "ataman" of Ussury, Esaul Kalmykov, was operating. . . . This "ataman" is also under the protection of the Japanese, who supply him with money. . . .

Toward the end of January [1918] there arose the idea of organizing within the zone of the Chinese Railway a government consisting of Russian public leaders. . . . Major General Horvath was elected by the majority as head of the government. . . . [Russian] diplomats in China doubted that the undertaking would succeed and proposed . . . to General Horvath that he attempt to organize an armed force . . . as a preliminary step [to the assumption of power]. However, by virtue of his office as manager of the Chinese Railway, General Horvath was far removed from active military life; and, being slow and indecisive, . . . he aroused the fear that he might not be able to organize the requisite military force. Kolchak was therefore invited to undertake the task. . . . It was decided that General Horvath would select po-

---

[39] A captain in the Cossack army.
[40] A Cossack chief, usually with the rank of general.

litical leaders and that at the same time Admiral Kolchak would form an army. . . .

Kolchak accepted the offer and arrived at Harbin toward the end of April. Here he at once encountered the hostility of the Japanese, who soon recognized in him a strong and determined leader, honestly devoted to Russian interests. Some of our higher officials and the self-styled "atamans" went along with the Japanese. . . .

Everybody in Harbin was hostile to the Admiral; Semenov even refused to receive Kolchak when called upon by him at the station of Manchuria. The idea of establishing a single military organization was obnoxious to all. The Japanese feared and the higher officials suspected it; to the lower ranks it seemed a restriction of freedom, and to the masses it was counter-revolutionary. . . .

OVERTHROW OF THE VLADIVOSTOK SOVIET [41]
[June 29, 1918]

Yesterday, June 29, . . . the rule of the Bolsheviks in this city came to an end. In the morning an ultimatum was presented to the Soviet to disarm the Red Guards and Red Army. The Soviet refused to do this, whereupon the Czechoslovak forces took matters into their own hands. The Soviet premises were occupied by a strong force of Czechoslovaks. . . . The Soviet was dissolved and so far there has been no bloodshed. Simultaneously with the operations of the Czechoslovaks, British and Japanese naval forces occupied the railway station, the powder magazines, and all the public buildings of the city. At 1:00 P. M. a body of Chinese marines was landed. . . . Arrests of prominent Bolsheviks . . . were made. . . . After considerable resistance the Revolutionary Staff surrendered at 6:00 P. M.

THE CZECHS MOVE WEST TO HELP THEIR BRETHREN
[Announcement of the Czechoslovak's, July 2, 1918] [42]

The main forces of the Czechoslovaks will now resume the task of liberating their brothers whose journey through Siberia is being obstructed by Germans and Magyars.

[41] *Dalekaia Okraina*, No. 3,578, June 30, 1918, p. 4.
[42] *Golos Primoria*, No. 242, July 6, 1918, p. 2.

We are leaving in the vicinity of Vladivostok a detachment to protect our rear. This detachment has been ordered not to interfere in the domestic affairs of the city or its environs; and it is intended to forestall any armed riots which might endanger the lives of the citizens.

We are not responsible for the overthrow of the local Soviet Government. The Soviet surrendered voluntarily,. seeking protection from lynching. We therefore declare that as long as the Czechoslovaks are on Russian soil, and until there is established legal order sufficient to give full protection to everyone, we shall guard the members of the former Soviet against any unlawful violence.

At the same time we are bound to state that we cannot release these individuals and give them freedom of movement. We have lost all faith in their sincerity. After they had assured us that there were no armed Germans and Magyars in Vladivostok, we were attacked upon reaching the citadel . . . and suffered useless bloodshed among our brothers. The same thing happened in Nikolsk-Ussuriisk, where two thousand armed Germans and Magyars attempted to interfere with our movements.

GENERAL DIETRICHS

ESTABLISHMENT OF AN ALLIED PROTECTORATE OVER VLADIVOSTOK

[Proclamation by the Commanders of the Allied and Associated Powers at Vladivostok, July 6, 1918] [48]

In view of the dangers which threaten Vladivostok and the Allied forces here assembled from the open and secret activities of Austro-German war prisoners, spies and emissaries, the city and its vicinity are hereby taken under the temporary protection of the Allied powers and all necessary measures will be taken for its defense against dangers both external and internal.

All orders heretofore issued by the Czechoslovak authorities continue in force.

The authority of the Zemstvo and municipality will be recognized in local affairs but the local military forces and police will be supplemented by such Allied force as may be found necessary

[48] *U. S. Foreign Relations, 1918, Russia,* II, 271.

in emergency to prevent danger from Austro-German agencies and influence which are known to be at work in the city.

This action is taken in a spirit of sympathetic friendship for the Russian people without reference to any political faction or party and in the hope that the period of tranquillity which will result may permit the reconciling of all factions and their cooperation in a harmonious and patriotic effort for the establishment of a stable and permanent government and for throwing off the yoke of tyrannical dictation which the Austro-German powers are endeavoring to fasten permanently upon the Russian people.

All good citizens are enjoined to cooperate in the maintenance of law and order.

AUSTIN M. KNIGHT
Admiral, United States Navy
Commander in Chief, United States Asiatic Fleet

HIROGARU KATO
Rear Admiral, Japanese Navy,
Commanding Special Division Imperial Japanese Navy

PAYNE
Captain, Royal Navy,
Senior British Naval Officer

PARIS
Colonel, French Army, Chief of the French Military Mission to the Czecho-Slovak Army

H. LIU
Captain, Chinese Navy,
Commanding R. C. S. "Hai Yung"

BADUIRA
Captain, Czecho-Slovak Army, Town Mayor

DECLARATION OF THE PROVISIONAL GOVERNMENT OF
AUTONOMOUS SIBERIA "

[Vladivostok, July 8, 1918]

The Provisional Government of Autonomous Siberia hereby
makes known to all friendly Powers, both allied and neutral, that
on June 29, 1918, it assumed the rights and duties of the central
government of Siberia.

Raising its banner at this tragic moment when Russia has no
organized government, . . . the Provisional Government aims to
reestablish national political life in Siberia and to lay a foundation for the reconstruction and unification of Russia as a great
federated democratic republic. . . .

The first practical task of the Provisional Government . . . is
to convoke the Siberian Regional Duma, which . . . will determine, in full agreement with the All-Russian Constituent Assembly, the final form of the political organization of Siberia. . . .
The Provisional Government considers it as its duty to reestablish the normal functioning of state and public institutions which
was interrupted by the Soviet authorities, . . . as well as to safeguard all civil rights and property interests of private individuals.
. . .

The Provisional Government of Autonomous Siberia has the
right to assume the functions of the central government of Si-
beria because it received plenipotentiary powers from the Siberian
Regional Duma on January 28, 1918. . . . Western and Central
Siberia have already recognized the Provisional Government of
Autonomous Siberia. . . . It is also recognized by the Maritime
Province and . . . by the political organizations at Vladivostok.
The Government is sure, therefore, that in proportion as the
country is cleared of anti-social elements it will be unanimously
accepted by the rest of the population.

The Provisional Government expects the armed forces which
have been operating in the zone of the Chinese Eastern Railway
. . . to discontinue independent activities inasmuch as there is
now a legally constituted government. . . .

In accordance with the declaration of the Special Siberian Con-

" *Vestnik Vremennago Pravitelstva Avtonomnoi Sibiri,* No. 3, July 11, 1918,
pp. 1-2.

gress of December 25, [1917], reasserted by the Siberian Regional Duma on January 28 . . . , Siberia is an autonomous region of the Russian Federated Republic. In view of this fact the Provisional Government solemnly declares its intention of safeguarding Russian interests . . . and of accepting all international agreements made by Russia . . . before November 7, 1917. It follows from this that the Provisional Government . . . rejects all agreements made by the Soviet of People's Commissars, especially the Peace Treaty of Brest-Litovsk. . . .

[The rest of the declaration consists of a statement of the steps which the government planned to take in combating the German and Austrian war prisoners, of words of welcome to the Czechoslovaks, and, in conclusion, of an appeal for Allied recognition.]

P. DERBER
Minister-President

A. KRAKOVETSKY	S. KUDRIAVTSEV
A. TRUTNEV	N. ZHERNAKOV
V. TIBER-PETROV	A. NOVOSELOV
I. TARASOV	V. MORAVSKY
A. PETROV	G. NEOMETULLOV

Members of the Council of Ministers

PROCLAMATION OF A GOVERNMENT BY HORVATH

[Announcement of July 9, 1918] [45]

The government of the People's Commissars . . . has ruined the economic life of the people, deprived the country of its power of defense, and . . . treacherously betrayed our loyal allies.

Having tempted the people with fantastic promises of a speedy reorganization . . . of Russia's social life on socialist principles, the Soviet of People's Commissars . . . has thrown the country into the abyss of anarchy. All civil liberties are trampled under foot. The cultural and creative life of the country has died. Famine, lynching, plunder, and murder are going on.

German troops, notwithstanding the peace which was signed by the commissars, continue their advance into Russian territory . . . , and Magyar and German prisoners of war . . . , in cooperation

[45] Dalekaia Okraina, No. 3,587, July 11, 1918, p. 3.

with the Bolsheviks, shed Russian blood all over the country, thus preparing for its seizure by Germany.

This cannot be tolerated any longer! It is necessary to establish order at once, to organize civil life, and to restore Russia's fighting power.

The attempts of different groups to form a government have failed in consequence of their narrow party aims. A number of Russians who place the welfare of their country above everything else have appealed to me, . . . as the sole remaining representative of the Provisional Government, to do something to save the country from disaster and to assume the prerogatives of supreme state authority.

With deep faith in the bright future of the great Russian people and in obedience to a sense of duty to the country, . . . I have resolved to take charge of governmental authority until . . . order is reestablished in the country and a freely elected Constituent Assembly decides the form of government of the Russian state.

In declaring myself Provisional Ruler, and in endeavoring to establish a form of government which will guarantee the people tranquillity, law, and order . . . , I am forming a business cabinet . . . consisting of men with practical experience . . . who have the confidence of public and political circles. . . . The cabinet will be guided in its actions by the following principles:

1. The annulment of all decrees issued by the Bolsheviks.

2. The reestablishment of courts, administrative institutions, and city and zemstvo self-government.

3. The equality of all citizens before the law and the safeguarding of civil liberties.

4. Universal suffrage.

5. The reestablishment in full of all agreements concluded with the Allies and neutral Powers. . . .

6. The reestablishment of the army on principles of strict discipline.

7. The reestablishment of property rights.

8. The solution of the land question by the Constituent Assembly.

9. The reestablishment of industry and transport, including the annulment of the socialization and nationalization . . . of enterprises, and the satisfaction of the needs of workers.

10. The raising of the level of popular education.

11. The recognition of the right of Siberia and other regions to autonomy on condition that the unity of Russia is maintained.

. . .

LIEUTENANT GENERAL HORVATH
Provisional Ruler

For a time the Provisional Government of Autonomous Siberia found favor among the Allied consuls. But the opposition of local Russian groups prevented that government from forming an effective administrative machinery and gaining extensive control. Civil government was in the hands of zemstvo and municipal authorities, while military control rested with the Czechoslovaks. But despite its weakness Derber's government clung desperately to its legal authority and bent every effort to prevent Horvath's rival government from being recognized.

NOTE OF THE SIBERIAN GOVERNMENT TO THE
ALLIED POWERS [46]

[July 25, 1918]

With reference to its declaration of July 8 . . . and its note of July 15,[47] the Provisional Government of Autonomous Siberia wishes to make the following statement to the Allied Governments:

The Provisional Government . . . realizes that in consequence of Soviet rule . . . and especially the Brest-Litovsk Treaty the Allied Powers . . . were placed under the necessity of . . . safeguarding their interests and insisting that Russia fulfill her obligations as an ally. . . .

The Provisional Government of Autonomous Siberia has firmly declared its intention of assuming all obligations arising from the agreements made between Russia and the Allies during the war, as well as all other agreements existing before November 7, 1917.

[46] Maksakov i Turunov, *Khronika grazhdanskoi voiny v Sibiri*, pp. 215-16.
[47] The note is quoted in *U. S. Foreign Relations, 1918 Russia*, II, 296-97.

On July 15 the Government communicated a note urging consideration of the question as to what could be done to reestablish . . . the anti-German front and to combat German influence in Siberia. The Provisional Government of Autonomous Siberia believes that the Allied Powers now have an opportunity to carry out their strategic plans against Germany, first in Siberia and then in Russia, . . . provided that Russia's sovereignty is respected and the principles of international law are not violated.

The Provisional Government of Autonomous Siberia also wishes to warn . . . the Allied Powers that any agreement with private individuals or organizations declaring themselves to be the supreme authorities . . . of Siberia [48] will be condemned by the entire population . . . as an act hostile to the people. . . . The sole sovereign authority in Siberia . . . is the Provisional Government of Autonomous Siberia.

A. I. LAVROV

President of the Council of Ministers

P. YA. DERBER

Minister of Foreign Affairs

A WARNING TO HORVATH

[Derber's Note of July 28, 1918] [49]

To General Horvath:

The Government of Autonomous Siberia is informed that you have declared yourself dictator, assuming the title of Provisional Ruler. The Provisional Government calls your attention to the fact that the only lawful and recognized authority in Sibera is the Provisional Siberian Regional Duma, together with the Provisional Government of Autonomous Siberia elected by the Duma. . . . The Provisional Government of Autonomous Siberia calls upon you to divest yourself immediately of the power you have illegally assumed. Should you refuse to do so and attempt to accomplish your criminal plans by force you will be held entirely responsible for the possible serious consequences.

DERBER

Minister-President

[48] The reference is to General Horvath.
[49] Maksakov i Turunov, *op. cit.*, p. 215.

Early in August Allied troops began to arrive at Vladivostok. The first to land were the Japanese and the British; these were followed by the Americans and the French. Later in the same month communication with Western Siberia was reestablished, and in September a delegation of the Provisional Government of Western Siberia arrived at Vladivostok to bring an end to the confusion which existed in the Russian Far East. After lengthy negotiations the Derber government resigned, and Horvath was appointed government commissar of the region. Those arrangements, however, were of little effect since in October Japan had landed at Vladivostok a large force, which undertook a systematic occupation of the Russian Far East.

D. WESTERN SIBERIA

In Western Siberia the development of events was at first similar to that in other regions where the military success of the Czechoslovaks made possible the overthrow of the Soviets by local anti-Bolshevik forces. After the capture of Tomsk on May 30 a provisional government known as the Western-Siberian Commissariat was established. On June 7 Omsk fell and the Commissariat moved to that city.

CAPTURE OF OMSK [50]

. . . On June 7 it was decided to surrender Omsk. . . . The plan was to retreat by railway . . . , but the treacherous behavior of the railway workers who wrecked the road . . . prevented the carrying out of the plan. Under the rifle and machine-gun fire of White Guards . . . the comrades ran headlong for the boats . . . going to Tobolsk.

Due to our commander's inexperience . . . the retreat was effected in a disorderly fashion. . . . Everything was abandoned

[50] V. Karmashev, *Poslednie dni sovetskoi vlasti v Zapadnoi Sibiri 1918 goda,* p. 9.

to the Czechs: arms, ammunition, a large number of Soviet employees and Communists. Only money was evacuated.

Tomsk was surrendered a few days earlier . . . in still more disorderly manner. The Czechs had not yet arrived there . . . when an unexpected revolt of White Guards . . . caused the city to be abandoned without fighting. . . .

THE SOVNARKOM DECLARES WAR ON THE SIBERIAN PROVISIONAL GOVERNMENT [51]

[June 10, 1918]

To All Toilers!

The enemies of the working class are making a last desperate attempt to regain the power, the land, and the wealth of the country. The workers and the peasants hate their age-old oppressors. The . . . exploiters are, therefore, looking to outside help, to the aid of foreign imperialists of one camp or another. While on Russian territory the Czechoslovak Corps considered itself in the service of France, and during all this time was receiving money from that country. At the head of the Corps were counter-revolutionary officers and agents of Russian, Czechoslovak, and Allied extraction. Russian counter-revolutionists and Allied conspirators decided to use the Czechoslovaks for the purpose of overthrowing the Soviet Government. The hirelings of the Russian and Allied bourgeoisie pushed the deluded Czechoslovaks on to the road of insurrection. The Czechoslovaks . . . seized Penza and reestablished there the power of the bourgeoisie. From all sides workers and peasants rushed to the aid of the Soviet Government. The Czechoslovaks, under pressure of our troops, moved on and captured Samara. Other detachments of Czechoslovaks stationed along the railroad seized Novonikolaevsk and Omsk. The Siberian bourgeoisie and the Kornilovist officers expelled from the army as enemies of the people immediately set up in Novonikolaevsk and Omsk a "Provisional Siberian Government" of their own.

Two counter-revolutionary adventurers addressed . . . to the Soviet of People's Commissars the following note:

"Moscow, to the Soviet of People's Commissars, from Omsk.

Bolshevik power in Siberia has been abolished and the Siberian

---

[51] *Svoboda Rossii,* No. 44, June 11, 1918, p. 1.

Provisional Government, elected by the Siberian Regional Duma, . . . has assumed the task of governing Siberia. As its first task the Siberian Government intends to reestablish the organs of self-government which were elected on the basis of universal, equal, direct, and secret suffrage. It also intends to call as soon as possible the Constituent Assembly, which will settle finally the question of the political régime of Siberia and of its relation to European Russia. The Siberian Provisional Government has no intention of separating Siberia from Russia; [the Government] is deeply concerned over and regretful for the sad plight in which Russia finds itself. We are authorized . . . to announce that we are ready to undertake as soon as possible the uninterrupted shipment of supplies to the starving gubernias of Russia and to enter into negotiations concerning the conditions under which supplies can be sent to Velikorossiia. . . . However, the sending of supplies into starving Russia will be rendered impossible if the Soviet of People's Commissars makes an attempt to invade the Transural region for the purpose of restoring the deposed Sovdeps. These attempts will be met with armed force and the shipment of supplies will be stopped. We bring the above to your attention and announce it to the people in order that they may know that the responsibility for the death of people from hunger lies on the Soviet Government.

Ivanov

Corps Commander

Liakhovich

Plenipotentiary of the Siberian
Provisional Government"

We quote verbatim the proposal of the counter-revolutionary conspirators who have enthroned themselves for a few days in Omsk and are trying to play at government.

If these gentlemen had sufficient power behind them they would not address us with their pitiful false promises and threats. Colonel Ivanov, the Siberian Kornilovist, wishes to defend the Constituent Assembly against the workers' and peasants' Soviets! The Kornilovist colonel is, of course, supported by the Cadets, the Right S. R.'s, and the Mensheviks. Their armed forces consist of the deluded Czechoslovaks, who are supported by the money of the Anglo-French bourse. The hideous plot against the working people is as clear as day. The principal aim of the plotters is to cut off the Siberian Railroad, interfere with the shipment of Siberian grain, and subdue the Soviet Republic by famine. The Siberian Kornilovist impudently demands to be let alone by the Soviet Government. In return he promises bread. What will really happen, however, is that after we allow the Siberian bourgeoisie to strangle the Siberian workers and the toiling peasants, the Siberian counter-revolutionists will at once move to this side of the Urals to aid the Russian counter-revolutionists in establishing throughout the country the power of the landlords, capitalists, and Kornilov-officers. Under guise of the Constituent Assembly there is going on a fight to establish the autocratic rule of rich over poor, of idlers over toilers.

Dutov, the Ural bandit, Colonel Ivanov, the Czechoslovaks, fugitive Russian officers, agents of Anglo-French imperialism, former landlords, and Siberian kulaks have united in a holy alliance against workers and peasants. Should this alliance triumph, the blood of the people will flow like water and the power of the monarchy and the bourgeoisie will be restored in Russia.

Naturally, the Soviet of People's Commissars will not negotiate with counter-revolutionary adventurers who are merely trying to gain time to enable them to thrust a knife in the back of the toiling people.

Loyal troops . . . have been sent against the rebels. The capture of a number of railway centers on the Siberian Railroad by the counter-revolutionists will undoubtedly affect the food supply of our famine-stricken country. But the Russian, French, and Czechoslovak imperialists will fail in their attempt to subdue the revolution by hunger. The Southeast is coming to the rescue of the starving North. People's Commissar Stalin, who is now in Tsaritzyn in charge of food collection, . . . has informed us by telegraph of the enormous supplies of bread which he hopes to ship to the North during the next few weeks. People's Commissar Shliapnikov is also going to the Southeast and is accompanied by a number of food and transport specialists. Workers' food armies from Petrograd and Moscow will assist them. No matter how difficult the condition of the country, Soviet Russia cannot be starved to death.

Meanwhile, the Siberian Railroad will be cleared of rebels. In order to achieve this in as short a time as possible, as well as to sweep the treacherous bourgeoisie off the face of the earth . . . , the Soviet of People's Commissars finds it necessary to take special measures:

1. [Local mobilization is decreed.]
2. [Artillery and engineering troops in Moscow are mobilized.]
3. All soviets . . . are charged with the duty of keeping close watch over the local bourgeoisie and of inflicting severe punishment on insurgents.
4. Former [army] officers who help honestly and conscientiously in the formation of the Red Army should enjoy, of course, full inviolability and the protection of Soviet authorities. But officers engaged in plots, who are traitors and accomplices of Skoropadsky, Krasnov, and the Siberian colonel, Ivanov, should be exterminated without mercy.

Workers, peasants, Red Army soldiers, and all honest citizens! The power in the country belongs to you. Your age-old enemies and oppressors are trying to snatch that power from you. Capitalists of the whole world hate you because you have overthrown the power of the Russian capitalists and have given a revolutionary example to the workers of the world. They want to subdue you by famine. . . . But this shall not be. The liberation of the working class cannot be accomplished in a day. It is a hard struggle and we shall continue the fight until we gain complete and final victory.

Down with traitors and oppressors! Death to the enemies of the people!

Long live the power of the workers and the poorer peasants!

V. Ulianov (Lenin)
President of the Soviet of People's Commissars

L. Trotsky
People's Commissar of War and the Navy

The Western-Siberian Commissariat was controlled by Socialist-Revolutionists of fairly radical tendencies and like the Samara Komuch was inclined to tolerate existing revolutionary organizations. However, it soon aroused strong opposition among conservative groups, and toward the end of June the Commissariat was replaced by a new government. Although consisting of nominal socialists this government at once took a determined stand in suppressing every form of revolutionary radicalism. It annulled all Soviet decrees, ordered the suppression of workers' soviets and peasants' land committees, and undertook the restoration of private property in all its forms.

ESTABLISHMENT OF THE PROVISIONAL GOVERNMENT OF WESTERN SIBERIA

[Announcement of the Chairman of the Siberian Regional Duma, June 30, 1918] [52]

With the downfall of the Soviet Government in Western Siberia supreme authority in this region has been assumed by the Western-Siberian Commissariat appointed for that purpose by the Siberian Provisional Government.

A number of members of the Siberian Provisional Government elected by the Siberian Regional Duma have assembled at Omsk and are assuming supreme authority in Siberia. The personnel of the government is as follows: President of the Council of Ministers and Minister of Foreign Affairs, P. V. Vologodsky; Members of the Council of Ministers, V. M. Krutovsky (Interior), I. A. Mikhailov (Finance), G. B. Patushinsky (Justice), M. B. Shatilov (Nationalities).

I. YAKUSHEV
Chairman of the Siberian Regional Duma

DECLARATION OF SIBERIAN INDEPENDENCE [53]

[July 4, 1918]

Having assumed supreme authority in the region liberated from the Bolshevik usurpers, the Siberian Provisional Government . . . now proposes to lead Siberia out of the indefinite position in which it finds itself as a result of the breaking up of the Siberian Regional Duma by the Bolsheviks and their continuing ascendency in European Russia.

[52] *Sobranie uzakonenii i rasporiazhenii Vremennago Sibirskago Pravitelstva*, No. 1, 1918, pp. 1-2.
[53] *Ibid.*, No. 2, 1918, pp. 1-3.

The Siberian Provisional Government clearly realizes that any delay in defining the political status of Siberia is apt to lead to consequences highly detrimental to our international position. The Government would be considerably hampered in assuming legally the difficult task of moulding the future of the country were it not for the authoritative statement of the Siberian Regional Duma . . . of January 27, 1918, . . . in which it quite definitely claimed for Siberia the broadest political prerogatives. The Siberian Provisional Government therefore feels justified in its decision to settle the political question . . . without waiting for a new convocation of the Regional Duma.

. . . Considering the fact that Russia sovereignty as such no longer exists, since a considerable part of Russian territory is in the de facto possession of the Central Powers, while another part is occupied by the Bolshevik usurpers, the Siberian Provisional Government solemnly declares that henceforth it and the Siberian Regional Duma will be responsible for the future of Siberia. It also proclaims its complete freedom to enter independently into relations with foreign powers. . . .

At the same time the Siberian Provisional Government considers it a sacred duty to summon an All-Siberian Constituent Assembly. . . . It likewise wishes to declare . . . that the severance of Siberia from the territories comprising the former Russian Empire is only temporary and that every effort will be made to reestablish Russian sovereignty. . . . The future relations between Siberia and European Russia will be defined by the All-Siberian and the All-Russian Constituent Assemblies. . . .

P. VOLOGODSKY
Chairman of the Council of Ministers and
Minister of Foreign Affairs

V. KRUTOVSKY
Minister of the Interior

GRIGORII PATUSHINSKY
Minister of Justice

IVAN MIKHAILOV
Minister of Finance

MIKHAIL SHATILOV
Minister of Nationalities

POLICIES OF THE SIBERIAN PROVISIONAL GOVERNMENT

[Annulment of Soviet Decrees, July 4, 1918] [54]

In view of the fact that Soviet rule rested . . . on criminal violation of the people's will, the Siberian Provisional Government . . . resolves:

1. All decrees issued by the so-called Soviet of People's Commissars and local Soviets of Workers', Soldiers,' and Peasants' Deputies are illegal and are hereby declared null and void. . . .

P. VOLOGODSKY
Chairman of the Council of Ministers,
Minister of Foreign Affairs . . .

[Abolition of Soviet Institutions, July 6, 1918] [55]

. . . 1. All Soviets of Workers', Peasants', Soldiers', and Cossacks' Deputies are hereby abolished. . . .

3. No obstacle will be placed in the way of organizing trade unions which do not pursue a political end. . . .

P. VOLOGODSKY
Chairman of the Council of Ministers . . .

[Restoration of Estates to Former Landowners, July 6, 1918] [56]

In conformity with the resolution . . . annulling all decrees of the Sovnarkom . . . the Council of Ministers resolves:

1. Pending the solution of the land problem by the All-Russian Constituent Assembly, all estates . . . are restored to their former owners. . . .

P. VOLOGODSKY
Chairman of the Council of Ministers . . .

Of the many governments which came into existence as a result of the success of the Czechoslovaks in Siberia, only the Samara and the Omsk Governments proved to be important factors in the anti-Bolshevik movements. But these

[54] *Ibid.*, p. 4.　　　[55] *Ibid.*, p. 5.　　　[56] *Ibid.*, pp. 15-16.

governments were radically opposed in their political and socio-economic viewpoints. The opposition shortly developed into open rivalry and antagonism in the form of customs warfare and refusal of military cooperation. Representatives of the Czechoslovak National Council and of the Allied diplomatic missions, who were anxious to bring about some kind of understanding between the rivals, succeeded after considerable effort in arranging a conference between members of the Omsk and Samara Governments. This conference, which was also attended by members of the Czechoslovak National Council, of the French Mission, and of the Union for the Regeneration of Russia, took place at Cheliabinsk on July 15-16.

The first day of the Conference only served to emphasize the deep-lying difference between the standpoints of the representatives of Samara and Omsk. The Samara Government maintained that it represented the nucleus of the all-Russian government which was to be established as soon as a sufficient number of members of the Constituent Assembly were available. When this government was formed, all regional governments, including the Siberian, were to surrender their authority. The Siberian delegates refused to acknowledge the claim made in behalf of the Constituent Assembly and, without making any counter-proposal, were ready to leave the conference. The situation was saved by the representatives of the Union for the Regeneration of Russia, who proposed that the question of forming an all-Russian government be considered at a special conference of representatives of all regional governments and political organizations. The proposal was accepted and August 6 was set as the date for a second conference to meet at Cheliabinsk.[57]

[57] Argunov, *Mezhdu dvumia bolshevizmami*, pp. 12-14; Krol, *Za tri goda*, pp. 63-66; *Krasnyi Arkhiv*, LXI (1933), 62.

RIVALRY BETWEEN THE SAMARA AND OMSK GOVERNMENTS

[From the Memoirs of General Boldyrev] [58]

. . . This antagonism [between the Samara and Omsk Governments] had already brought appreciable consequences: it had engendered a customs war, ruinous for the population. Siberia gave the Urals no grain, the Urals gave Siberia no iron. Moreover, the antagonism penetrated the ranks of the two armies. . . . To the detriment of Samara, its army officers soon showed a tendency to flock to Siberia, where the ideals [of the government] seemed to them more like their own and where material conditions were better. Here shoulder straps and addressing by the old titles were reestablished—things which it had cost so much bloodshed to abolish. Siberia also had the energetic War Minister and Commander of the Army, General Grishin-Almazov, who was very popular among the military. The situation was rendered especially serious by the Omsk Government's unwillingness to send its troops to fortify the Volga front. When I arrived at Samara, Colonel Kappel, one of the most outstanding leaders of the People's Army, presented me with a virtual ultimatum—that for the sake of an army exhausted by uninterrupted marches and fighting, a general political unification was immediately imperative. Representatives of the Czechoslovaks declared the same thing.

The selfishness of the Omsk Government was justified to a certain degree by the necessity of completing the training and preparation of the newly formed Siberian army. But of course the true motive lay much deeper. Because of the political tendencies by which the Siberian Government was now dominated every failure of Samara, even the decline of the fighting capacity of the "Constituent" army, was, to be sure, an advantage to Omsk, especially in view of the negotiations which were at that time going on at Vladivostok between the Allied representatives and Vologodsky. The fact that this gave the Red Army full opportunity to beat its enemies severally was apparently not considered.

Meanwhile the position of the People's Army on the Volga, which previously had been excellent, began to grow considerably worse. The Bolsheviks managed to rally after their defeats on

[58] V. Boldyrev, *Direktoriia, Kolchak, Interventy,* pp. 30-32.

that front. The People's Army not only proved unable to consolidate its gains and thereby assure for itself the possibility of further advance into Russia, but also commenced to show clear signs of deterioration, caused, on the one hand, by the shortcomings of its organization, and, on the other, by excessive fatigue in the absence of fresh reinforcements. . . .

The People's Army hardly numbered more than ten thousand fighters, who definitely bent under the onslaught of the Red armies brought to the Volga from other fronts, with better technical equipment and a vast supply of ammunition. . . . The Allies had thus far limited themselves to giving advice.

THE FIRST ATTEMPT TO FORM AN ALL-RUSSIAN GOVERNMENT

[From the Minutes of the First Cheliabinsk Conference, July 15, 1918] [59]

The Committee of Members of the Constituent Assembly was represented at this historic session of July 15, 1918, by I. M. Brushvit . . . , M. A. Vedeniapin, . . . [and] H. A. Galkin; the Siberian Government, by Grishin-Almazov, . . . I. Mikhailov, . . . and Golovachev. I. M. Brushvit was elected chairman of the meeting.

. . . Speaking for the Siberian Government, I. Mikhailov declared that his only purpose in coming was to establish a definite coordination of practical activities with the Samara Government and not at all to discuss the question of the possibility of forming an all-Russian government.

I. M. Brushvit proposed that . . . the meeting consider first the project of the Committee of Members of the Constituent Assembly on the question of forming a central government.

The project is as follows:

1. The Constituent Assembly will be the sovereign of the country. . . .

2. Pending the meeting of the Constituent Assembly the supreme authority is to be embodied in the Committee of Members of the Constituent Assembly, composed of all legally elected members, exclusive of Bolsheviks and Socialist-Revolutionists of the Left. . . .

[59] Piontkovsky, *G. V. R.*, pp. 277-78.

3. Fundamental laws (a constitution) and general questions lying within the jurisdiction of the Constituent Assembly are to be left unconsidered by the Committee of Members of the Constituent Assembly and are to await solution until the meeting of the Constituent Assembly.

4. The Committee has the following immediate tasks: (a) the consolidation of the power of the Constituent Assembly . . . ; (b) the restoration of Russia's political unity . . . ; (c) the formation of a people's army for the defense of Russia's independence . . . ; (d) the reestablishment of democratic organs of self-government; (e) the rehabilitation of the disrupted national economy and of transportation, and the regulation of the food supply; (f) the reestablishment of friendly relations with the Allied Powers with a view to the formation of a united front against the German coalition. . . .

. . . Among its basic aims the Committee also includes a merciless struggle against Bolshevism. . . .

5. To realize the above ends, the Committee of Members of the Constituent Assembly proposes the establishment on a coalition basis of a central all-Russian government . . . in which all classes and nationalities will participate.

6. Legislative power and the general control of governmental activities are to belong to the Committee of Members of the Constituent Assembly.

7. Military affairs, finances, and foreign affairs are within the exclusive jurisdiction of the central all-Russian government.

8. All other activities of government . . . require the sanction of the Committee of Members of the Constituent Assembly. . . .

The second Cheliabinsk conference did not meet until August 20. In a memorandum circulated among the members of the conference the Czechoslovak National Council urged the necessity of united effort on the part of the Russians. But the delegates assembled at this conference were not numerous enough to make an agreement representative of the wishes of all anti-Bolshevik groups, and it was decided to hold another conference at Ufa on September 7.

THE CZECHOSLOVAKS URGE THE FORMATION OF A CENTRAL
GOVERNMENT

[Memorandum Presented to the Second Cheliabinsk Conference,
August 20, 1918] [60]

The Czechoslovak National Council (Russian Branch) sends
its fraternal greetings to the representatives of the Russian groups
and governments assembled . . . for the purpose of forming an
all-Russian government.

The Czechoslovak National Council entertains the hope that the
Conference will accomplish its aim and form a central government capable of rising to this great historic occasion of reestablishing a united and free Russian federated republic. . . .

Three months have passed since the Czechoslovak army rose
against the Bolshevik usurpers. At first we had to defend our
own freedom, but very soon we decided to . . . come to the
rescue of the Russian people. . . . We hoped that the Russians
themselves would make an effort to reestablish their military and
political organization. . . . Unfortunately, the work of reconstruction is progressing very slowly. . . . The attempts to form
a volunteer army in Siberia and within the territory of the Samara Committee have proved unsatisfactory. Thus far the partial mobilization undertaken by the Samara Committee among the
Cossacks and Bashkirs has had little influence on conditions at the
front. All this is happening at a time when the Czechoslovak . . .
forces are gradually diminishing, while those of the Bolsheviks
are steadily increasing through reinforcements from German and
Magyar prisoners of war and German and Austrian officers.

Three months of constant fighting have brought the Czechoslovaks to physical exhaustion . . . , and they naturally ask themselves the question: What will happen in the future? . . . Why
is it that after three months so little has been done by the Russians
to form organizations of their own?

Instead of a national government being established, we witness
strife among the different parts of Russia. . . . The political situation imperatively calls for the formation of a central government. . . . The various regional governments . . . , as well as
the most important political parties, appear to be unanimous in

[60] Maksakov i Turunov, *op. cit.*, pp. 230-31.

their demand for a reconstructed and unified Russia; they agree in rejecting the Brest-Litovsk Treaty and recognize the necessity of resuming war against the Central Empires in cooperation with the Allies.

An all-Russian central government would symbolize the unification of Russia. . . . Only such a government could count on the material and moral support of the Allies. . . .

Bogdan Pavlu
Josef Pateidl

While these attempts were being made to reconcile the conservative and radical elements in the anti-Bolshevik camp, the more reactionary members of the Siberian Government, headed by Ivan Mikhailov and supported by army officers, were gaining the upper hand. They decided to get rid of the Siberian Regional Duma, which had a majority of Socialist-Revolutionists and was known to be in sympathy with the Samara Government.

A pretext for the dissolution of the Duma was found when it became known that Yakushev, the president of that body, and Krutovsky and Shatilov, two S. R. members of the Siberian Government, intended to make one of their sympathizers, Novoselov, an additional member of that government. To avert this the commander of the Omsk garrison, Colonel Volkov, arrested the four "conspirators" and forced the S. R. members of the government to resign. They as well as the President of the Duma were soon released, but Novoselov was killed while being conveyed to jail. The remaining members of the Siberian Government decreed the dissolution of the Siberian Regional Duma and accepted the resignations of the S. R. members of the government. The Duma refused to dissolve. Instead it issued a decree dismissing the Administrative Council of the Siberian Government together with Mikhailov and Gratsia-

12

nov, the two members of the government most objectionable to the Duma. It also appealed for aid to the Czechoslovaks, who were known to be in sympathy with the Socialist-Revolutionists. The Czechs arrested Gratsianov, but Mikhailov went into hiding and eluded arrest.[61]

In the meantime various political groups which had assembled at Ufa for the purpose of organizing an all-Russian government made much progress toward that end. On September 23 an all-Russian government was formed and the first task which it had to face was the untangling of the chaotic conditions at Omsk.

PROROGATION OF THE SIBERIAN REGIONAL DUMA

[Decree of the Administrative Council, September 21, 1918] [62]

By virtue of Article 3 of the resolution of the Council of Ministers of September 7, 1918, . . . the Administrative Council of the Siberian Provisional Government resolves:

1. The activity of the Siberian Regional Duma . . . is to cease.

2. The Siberian Provisional Government will issue a special decree setting a date for the resumption of the activity of the Siberian Regional Duma.

3. This resolution goes into effect [upon receipt] by telegraph.

I. Mikhailov
Acting Chairman of the Administrative
Council and Minister of Finance

A. Morozov
Acting Head of the Ministry of Justice

---

[61] S. Melgunov, *Tragediia Admirala Kolchaka; iz istorii grazhdanskoi voiny na Volge, Urale i v Sibiri,*. I, 160-62.

[62] *Sobranie uzakonenii i rasporiazhenii Vremennago Sibirskago Pravitelstva,* No. 13, 1918, pp. 11-12.

THE SIBERIAN REGIONAL DUMA DISMISSES THE ADMINISTRATIVE COUNCIL

[Resolution of September 22, 1918] [63]

The Siberian Regional Duma resolves that:

1. . . . The Administrative Council [of the Siberian Government] was established illegally and is to be dissolved.

2. The resolution of the Administrative Council of September 21, 1918, ordering the prorogation of the Duma, is in violation of law.

3. I. Mikhailov, Minister of Finance, and A. Gratsianov, Assistant Minister of the Interior, are dismissed from office and turned over to the court on the charge of attempting a coup d'état.

. . .

5. In case it is unable to continue functioning, the . . . Duma will transfer its powers to a committee of the Duma. . . .

E. The Ufa Directorate

The Ufa Directorate came into existence as a result of an agreement between various political groups which met at Ufa from September 8 to September 23. The number of delegates assembled is variously estimated between 147 and 170. Twenty-three shades of political opinion were represented; the strongest group was the Committee of Members of the Constituent Assembly (73 members), belonging to the Socialist-Revolutionist party. Numerical superiority, however, was not a decisive factor since each party, however small, had the right of veto. There were only five general sessions of the conference. During the first four each faction presented its views on the character of the proposed central government; at the fifth and concluding session the conference accepted the constitution drawn up by a special committee and approved the government members whom the committee proposed.[64]

[63] Maisky, *Demokraticheskaia kontr-revoliutsiia*, pp. 251-52.

[64] M. Vishniak, "Grazhdanskaia voina," in *Sovremennyia Zapiski*, XLV (1931), p. 317; "Ufimskoe gosudarstvennoe soveshchanie," in *Russkii istoricheskii arkhiv. Sbornik pervyi*, p. 61.

THE UFA STATE CONFERENCE
[Opening Session, September 8, 1918] [65]

N. D. Avxentiev: . . . We have all gathered here for one purpose—to create at last, out of all the scattered fragments . . . of our land, one mighty, free, independent Russian state. . . . We are face to face with a serious responsibility for the blood . . . which will again be required of our people to repel the enemy trampling under foot the Russian people, its liberty and state. We have gathered here to find a solution to fundamental questions, to discover a way out of the tragic situation in which our country finds itself, and to create a strong government inspired with the ideal of Russia's freedom and independence. To attain this end we shall have to find at all costs a common language and common thoughts . . . , make superhuman efforts, and take a solemn . . . oath not to leave this place . . . without establishing a unified Russian state headed by a Russian government.

In the cause of Russian liberation, which we are about to undertake, we feel ourselves united at the outset by the same ideal and the same hope. More than this, we feel that we are not alone. At this time of difficult trials, when treason has built its nest at the very heart of Russia . . . , our valiant allies, who for three years have fought shoulder to shoulder with us in defense of European freedom, have been able to distinguish between usurpation and the genuine will of the people. They have not abandoned us but now as before are hastening to our aid. You are probably familiar with the declaration of the Allied Governments in which they stated that their help to us, directed against those who have schemed to enslave the world, is a help that pursues no selfish interests.

Chairman N. D. Avxentiev then introduced a motion to send . . . greetings to the valiant and loyal Allies and a fraternal welcome to the brave Czechoslovak troops. . . .

Volsky [66] [representative of the Committee of Members of the Constituent Assembly]:

. . . There is only one way in which the people can be welded

---

[65] "Ufimskoe gosudarstvennoe soveshchanie," in *Russkii istoricheskii arkhiv*, pp. 65-66.

[66] *Ibid.*, p. 68.

. . . into a political force: it is the way of popular sovereignty. There is no other way, and those who would attempt to organize our Russian state by some means other than popular sovereignty will . . . inevitably bring matters to this: there will be no state of Russia; [instead] there will be enslavement of Russia; the disruption of Russia will continue, with no hope of organizing the Allied front [against the Germans] of which many patriotic Russians are now dreaming. . . . We are confident that this State Conference, which is imbued with a genuine desire to reconstruct the Russian state, will not forget even for a second that there is no state without the people. . . . If the State Conference accepts this as the common point of view . . . , then the ways and means . . . of forming a provisional government, to rule until the All-Russian Constituent Assembly meets, will be found. . . .

N. N. Karpov [representative of the Siberian Regional Duma]:

The Siberian Regional Duma . . . has authorized us to greet this high assembly and to express our profound conviction that the members of the Constituent Assembly and the representatives of Russian political thought will be able to overcome all differences, individual and local, and to reach an agreement . . . on the basis of retention of the gains of the February Revolution. The Russian provisional government which is to be created should be responsible to the Constituent Assembly in its present membership. (*Applause.*)

The Siberian Regional Duma, which is opposed to any separation, thinks of Siberia as an integral part of a great and united Russia. . . . The Siberian Regional Duma considers that its most important object is to reconstruct a great democratic federated republic and to free Russia from the shameful yoke of Bolshevism and German imperialism. Russia can be regenerated only as a united whole. The different regional governments are powerless to accomplish this general task. Furthermore, they are even powerless to achieve their own welfare. The sad experience of the Ukraine, the Caucasus, and Finland is the best proof of this fact. Russia will be saved when all the energies of her people are gathered together. . . .

[Session of September 10, 1918] [67]

The chairman [Avxentiev] reported on the steps which the Presidium had taken to hasten the arrival of the representatives of the Siberian Provisional Government. . . . the chairman of the State Conference had another direct-wire conversation with I. A. Mikhailov, Minister of Finance of the Siberian Government. This conversation made it clear that the delegation of the Siberian Provisional Government did not plan to leave before September 9. . . . Mikhailov mentioned the name of one member of the delegation, Professor Sapozhnikov, Chief of the Ministry of Public Education.

In the name of the Presidium, the chairman introduced a motion to elect a council of elders to undertake a preliminary exchange of opinion between the representatives of the delegations on questions which were to come up at the plenary session, especially on the question of forming an all-Russian government. . . . The motion was passed. . . .

[Session of September 12, 1918] [68]

Pavlu [chairman of the National Council of the Czechoslovak troops] :

Gentlemen of the High State Conference! In the name of the Czechoslovak National Council and the Czechoslovak troops who are fighting for our freedom and yours, I greet you, members of the State Conference. . . . You have gathered at a critical hour in Russia's period of turmoil for the purpose of establishing a people's government . . . capable of directing Russia's ship of state. . . . We Czechoslovaks extend to you our heartfelt wishes for success in the momentous task ahead and trust that at this State Conference you will be able to form an all-Russian government which can actually depend on all strata of the Russian people. We trust that you . . . will find a common language which will unite you all in the common desire to serve your country. . . . We entertain this hope especially in view . . . of the gravity of the moment, which follows upon two warnings that have been given us. The first was the collapse of the front north of Ufa, a break

[67] *Ibid.*, pp. 77-78.   [68] *Ibid.*, p. 84.

which thus far has not been liquidated; the second was the fall of Kazan. Gentlemen, we must all unite so that we shall not need to fear a third warning. (*Applause.*)

PARTY DECLARATIONS

[Declaration of the Russian Social-Democrats (Edinstvo)] [69]

Fomin: . . . The February [March 1917] Revolution, having overthrown tsarism and the remnants of medievalism, opened to Russia a clear and wide road for economic, political, and social development. Essentially bourgeois, this revolution would have found its completion in the establishment of a social order of the capitalist type . . . , taking the form of a free democratic state. . . . In October of last year the attack of the anarcho-syndicalists interrupted the work of creating a democratic order, . . . and not until now have the different parts of Russia which succeeded in freeing themselves from the yoke of Bolshevism had another opportunity to undertake the task of reconstruction in the spirit of the February Revolution. . . .

In view of the fact that all classes and groups of Russia are vitally interested in the development of the economic life of the country; that this development can follow a normal course only in a free and independent state; that there can be no question of having a free and independent country as long as Germany and her allies occupy extensive territories [of Russia]; that such freedom and independence . . . can be attained only by the united effort of all of Russia's social forces . . .—we find that what the country needs most is the consolidation of all the social classes and groups which are not in any way concerned with the restoration of the "old order." We consider this conclusion especially true since the two years of revolution have clearly demonstrated that no single class . . . or group is capable with its own resources of leading Russia out of its present critical position and of creating a stable order. The urgent demand of the present is the unity of all active forces of the country. . . . We believe, therefore, that in solving the problem of forming a government it is important to make certain . . . that the government is organized on the principle of a coalition of all progressive forces of the

[69] *Ibid.,* pp. 88-90.

country. . . . If it be true that every government must be strong and decisive, then our future government, in view of the extraordinarily difficult conditions under which it will have to work, will need a high degree of such qualities. Furthermore, inasmuch as it will be operating under war-time conditions, the government will have to be given power to make decisions and to execute them immediately and independently.

We believe that supreme authority should belong to a collegium of three or five. . . . A business cabinet should be attached [to the collegium]. The future government should be guided in its conduct by the following principles: First, to prosecute the war against Germany in cooperation with the Allies . . . until victory is won . . . over German imperialism; second, to fight for an independent, united, and undivided Russia; third, to stimulate the development of the material [and] productive forces of the country; and fourth, to consolidate the gains of the February Revolution.

As soon as the conditions of social life permit the people to engage normally in elections, the government should make preparations for elections to a new Constituent Assembly. . . .

Taking into consideration, however, the correlation of the political points of view represented at this Conference, we deem it possible to form, in addition to the future coalition government, a representative political organ endowed with the right of interpellation in cases where the supreme power is obviously deviating from the path laid down for it by the State Conference. . . . Without any hindrance to the work of the government . . . such a representative organ could serve as a link between government and people. . . .

[Declaration of the Socialist-Populists] [70]

Chembulov: Exhausted by the long war, . . . humiliated by the foreign enemy, great and undivided Russia has still preserved in itself the aspiration for freedom and independence, for unity, . . . law, peace, and order. National spirit cannot be crushed by accidental misfortunes; a free people cannot be deprived of its natural rights. A people born in freedom is called upon to enact

[70] *Ibid.,* pp. 91-94.

its own will, is the sole source of all government, the only creator of political institutions and laws. . . . A freely elected Constituent Assembly would have been the only legitimate organ of supreme state authority. . . . But fate was against it. . . . By the onslaught of usurpers and tyrants the will of the people was strangled and suppressed. . . . Great [therefore] is the merit of the Committee of Members of the Constituent Assembly, which took the initiative in reestablishing our disrupted state; great are the accomplishments of the regional governments, which undertook the introduction of order and government in the border provinces and the regions which have freed themselves from the Bolsheviks; but greater still is their merit in so far as they direct all their strivings toward the formation of a united all-Russian government, because the Russian state is one and undivided. As it is impossible to have [now] a lawful Constituent Assembly . . . which would reflect the will of the people adequately, the assembly of all the [new] governments . . . , supplemented by representatives of all political parties and by democratic self-government, can at present be recognized as the organ most fully expressing the aspirations of the people. Under present conditions the State Conference should be acknowledged as the sole organ of state authority in our fatherland. . . . The Socialist-Populist party does not believe . . . in a government which is responsible only in theory to some organ planned for the future. . . .

In view of the above considerations, the Socialist-Populist party recommends:

1. Pending resumption of the work of the Constituent Assembly or . . . the calling of a second Constituent Assembly . . . , sovereign state authority is to be exercised provisionally by a collegium of five or seven persons . . . , bearing the name "All-Russian Provisional Government."

2. The All-Russian Provisional Government is to have administrative and legislative powers provided these do not infringe upon the rights of the All-Rusian Constituent Assembly and upon the laws which it adopted.[71]

3. The Provisional Government is to appoint a business minis-

[71] The Constituent Assembly passed only one law, abolishing private property in land. See *The Bolshevik Revolution,* pp. 377-78.

try to take charge of affairs of administration. The ministry will be responsible solely to the government.

4. The All-Russian Provisional Government will be fully responsible to the Constituent Assembly.

5. The Provisional Government is to exercise authority and issue laws under the supreme control of the State Conference, which is to be supplemented by representatives of zemstvos and cities as they free themselves from Bolshevik and enemy power. . . .

6. During their tenure of office, members of the Provisional Government are to give up party membership.

7. The State Conference shall have the power to annul legislative acts of the Provisional Government if in its opinion such acts threaten the integrity and safety of the state and the established democratic order.

8. The State Conference is to meet regularly once every three months, at the call of its Presidium. . . .

9. The State Conference and the Provisional Government have the duty of calling the Constituent Assembly as soon as possible and of transfering to it . . . sovereign authority.

[Declaration of the Ural Regional Government] [72]

Koshcheev: The Ural Regional Government considers it a duty to bring to the attention of the State Conference the following views and considerations on the subject of organizing a central all-Russian government:

Our country is beginning the work of regeneration under difficult conditions. . . . Separate territories are forming autonomous . . . governments. This process, inevitable under existing objective conditions, not only leads to the development of regional life . . . but also contributes to the emergence of all the creative forces of the country.

At the same time, in view of the absence of an all-Russian central authority capable of directing regional reconstruction, the process involves the danger of an excessive development of . . . centrifugal tendencies and the neglect of the interests of Russia as a whole.

[72] "Ufimskoe gosudarstvennoe soveshchanie," in *Russkii istoricheskii arkhiv*, pp. 94-97.

One of the chief defects of the administration of old Russia consisted in the fact that . . . the authorities attempted to govern the whole of Russia from the center. . . . It was assumed that a central apparatus was sufficient to meet all the manifold needs of the various parts and borderlands of Russia. This method of administration, which lasted for several centuries, proved its absolute inadequacy. . . . At this critical moment local initiative must be emphasized especially. But until a central government capable of directing regional reconstruction with authority and foresight is organized . . . there is danger of the development of separatist tendencies. Unfortunately, certain practices of a number . . . of local and regional governments give ample warning . . . and [force us] to conclude that our view is correct. . . . The Ural Regional Government . . . therefore thinks it necessary for the present State Conference to organize an all-Russian government . . . —one capable of solving the problem of the country's regeneration and of directing regional reconstruction into permanent channels.

The vastness and complexity of the task which the central government faces demand that all forces of the country which share the platform of non-recognition of the Brest Peace make a coordinated effort to form, together with the Allies, an all-national front to fight for the indepenednce of Russia [and] to reorganize the country on the foundations of popular sovereignty and democracy. . . .

The central government should be organized on a coalition basis . . . by reaching an understanding as regards certain candidates who are known to the country for their steadfastness, political honesty, and ability to carry out the program upon which the State Conference decides. . . . Within the limits of this program . . . the central government must possess absolute power. . . . To ensure that the central government does not deviate from the program formulated by the State Conference a state controlling organ should be formed. . . . The central all-Russian government thus established should be provisional in character. It should be its duty as soon as proper conditions arrive . . . to call a new Constituent Assembly and surrender its powers. . . .

[Declaration of the Moslems] [73]

Bukeikhanov: Citizens! I have been sent here by the Moslem members of the Constituent Assembly, by the governments of the autonomous regions of Turkestan, Bashkurdistan, Alash-Orda, and by the National Administration of Turko-Tartars of the Interior of Russia and Siberia.

Until the February [March] Revolution, Russia was an autocracy. The February Revolution promised to give us a government by the people . . . and to realize the age-old ideals of the Russian intelligentsia. The non-Russian peoples of old autocratic Russia joined the democratic part of Russia, republican Russia, in the hope that the All-Russian Constituent Assembly would establish popular government . . . , but our hopes, like the hopes of all Russian democrats, were defeated. Power was seized by demagogues who wished to establish a dictatorship of the proletariat . . . [but actually] introduced a reign of anarchy, disruption, and the absence of all government. It was under such conditions that regional governments began to appear. These governments were absolutely necessary; without them it would have been impossible to govern the region liberated from the Bolsheviks. There are those who ascribe the organization of regional governments to separatism, but they are wrong. The organizations in the name of which I now speak do not adhere to the separatist point of view. They consider themselves to be parts of an undivided Russia and believe that the autonomous regions could have played no rôle in the concert of Powers had they formed independent states. We are at one with a democratic federated Russian republic . . . and shall go hand in hand with the Russian people to create a great and happy Russia.

. . . We are of the opinion that authority in Russia should belong to the Constituent Assembly in its present membership. . . . Until that Constituent Assembly meets, the Congress of Members of the Constituent Assembly now on hand, together with a collegium elected by this Conference, should be sovereign. The collegium should be established by agreement and not by pressure on the part of a majority. . . . The collegium should form a . . . cabinet of ministers responsible to the Congress of [Members of] the Constituent Assembly. . . .

[73] *Ibid.*, pp. 98-9.

[Declaration of the Party of the People's Freedom] [74]

Krol: Members of the State Conference! The Central Committee of the Party of the People's Freedom, in discussing the question of the nature of the government which should now be established in Russia, took as its point of departure the tasks which the government will have to face. The first task . . . is the reestablishment of a great, united, and undivided Russia. . . . This can be accomplished only . . . [if we reenter the war on the side of the Allies]; but to do this we must have a strong army. . . . To form an army is not very easy . . . , and the government will be forced to make great demands on every class of the population. . . . The army will have to be fed . . . and clothed . . . , but the productivity of the country has fallen enormously. . . . To wage war there must be order in the country. . . . Unfortunately our people . . . confuse liberty with license, and the government will have to conduct affairs in such a way that liberty does not interfere with order. I have no doubt that this will require a strong government. . . . The Committee of the Party of the People's Freedom therefore believes that the best form of government is a one-man government. To the great misfortune of Russia, our revolution has produced giants of destruction, anarchy, and disorder . . . but has failed to produce a man whom the country as a whole . . . could trust with [unlimited] power. . . . It is therefore necessary to become reconciled to a less perfect form of government—a directorate. But in our view this directorate . . . cannot be responsible to anyone. . . . In opposition to the proposal that we have a government responsible to some other organ, I advocate a government which stands outside any control. . . . I know beforehand that many of you will be shocked by our proposal, but I trust that the wisdom of this high assembly will rise to the importance of the task before us.

[Volsky, representing the Committee of Members of the Constituent Assembly, delivered a long speech emphasizing the importance of the Constituent Assembly as the symbol of popular government and the banner around which to rally in the struggle against the Bolsheviks. The fact that the Assembly was broken up by the Bolsheviks did not invalidate, he said, its claim to

[74] *Ibid.,* pp. 99-102.

represent the will of the people. He repudiated the charge that the S. R.'s, who had a majority in the Assembly, were aiming at party dictatorship. On the contrary, he asserted that they were willing to cooperate with other parties provided the Constituent Assembly in its existing membership was taken as the basis of the new government.[75] The concrete proposals of the Socialist-Revolutionists were embodied in the following program:]

[Program of the Right Socialist-Revolutionists] [76]

1. Pending the resumption of the work of the All-Russian Constituent Assembly, which is to take place at the nearest possible date, to be determined by the Congress of Members of the Constituent Assembly, there should be established an all-Russian government in the form of a collegium of from five to seven persons. The membership of this body will be determined by the State Conference, and its platform should include the safeguarding of the unity and independence of Russia, the principles of popular sovereignty, and the social and political gains of the February [March] Revolution. The Congress of Members of the All-Russian Constituent Assembly . . . shall then proclaim the [elected] body as the All-Russian Provisional Government. The All-Russian Provisional Government shall have the right of provisional administration and legislation within limits which do not infringe upon the rights of the All-Russian Constituent Assembly and the laws which it has already adopted. For administrative tasks the All-Russian Provisional Government will appoint a business cabinet of ministers.

[Declaration of the Siberian Provisional Government] [77]

1. The All-Russian Government should be organized as a directorate of not more than five persons, selected by the State Conference. . . .

2. The directorate is to form a business cabinet of ministers, responsible to the directorate.

3. The directorate is responsible only to the future plenipotentiary organ elected by a regular expression of the will of the people.

[75] *Ibid.*, pp. 105-13.   [76] *Ibid.*, pp. 115-16.   [77] *Ibid.*, p. 122.

4. The directorate should be animated by a united will, directed first of all toward the restoration of a great Russia and the resumption of war against Germany and Austria in cooperation with the Allies and the Czechoslovaks.

5. The directorate is to take charge of affairs which concern the state as a whole, leaving such matters as relate to local government and economic life to . . . the autonomous regional governments.

THE STATE CONFERENCE WELCOMES THE LANDING OF ALLIED TROOPS

[Resolution of September 12, 1918] [78]

The State Conference . . . assembled to form an all-Russian government welcomes the friendly troops of the Allied Powers, which by mutual understanding have entered Russian territory . . . to fight against Germany. . . . The aid of these troops, which are sent to us in fulfillment of the solemn declarations of the governments of Great Britain, the United States, France, and Japan, . . . for the purpose of helping to free Russia from the yoke of our common enemy and of reestablishing the Eastern front, comes at a time when the front of internal struggle is being transformed into an external front of war against Germany, which has made a formal agreement with Russia's betrayers.

The Ufa State Conference faced a difficult task in attempting to reconcile the different points of view presented by the various groups. Since the reaching of an agreement at the general sessions was obviously impossible, it was proposed during one of the early sessions to form a council of elders which would seek a compromise between the divergent programs. This council held fourteen meetings. As was to be expected, its members split into two camps—one advocating military dictatorship and the other upholding the principle of popular rule. After a good deal of bickering,

---

[78] *Ibid.*, pp. 104-05. A similar message of greeting was sent by the Samara Government. Subbotovsky, *Soiuzniki, russkie reaktsionery i interventy*, p. 314.

there was finally reached a compromise by which the Constituent Assembly of January 1918 was recognized as the source of authority, but without any limitation of the government before the next meeting of that assembly. This compromise was embodied in a constitution of the Directorate.

CONSTITUTION OF THE UFA DIRECTORATE

[Resolution of the State Conference, September 23, 1918] [79]

The State Conference composed of the Congress of Members of the Constituent Assembly; the plenipotentiary representatives of the Committee of Members of the All-Russian Constituent Assembly; the Siberian Provisional Government; the Regional Government of the Urals; the Cossack Voiskos of Orenburg, the Urals, Siberia, Irkutsk, Semirechie, Yenisei, and Astrakhan; the Governments of the Bashkirs, Alash[-Orda], and Turkestan; the National Adminstration of the Turko-Tartars of the Interior of Russia and of Siberia; the Esthonian Provisional Government; representatives of the Congress of Cities and Zemstvos of Siberia, the Urals, and the Volga Region; representatives of political parties and organizations—the Socialist-Revolutionists, the Russian Social-Democratic Labor Party, the Socialist-Populists, the Party of the People's Freedom [Cadets], the All-Russian Social-Democratic Organization ("Edinstvo"), and the Union for the Regeneration of Russia—in a unanimous desire to save the country, to reestablish its unity, and to assure its independence, resolves:

Supreme authority over all the territories of the Russian state is to be entrusted to an All-Russian Provisional Government composed of the following five persons: Nikolai Dmitrievich Avxentiev, Nikolai Ivanovich Astrov, Lieutenant General Vasily Georgievich Boldyrev, Petr Vasilievich Vologodsky, and Nikolai Vasilievich Chaikovsky.

The All-Russian Provisional Government will be guided in its conduct by the principles established under the present constitutional act.

[79] "Ufimskoe gosudarstvennoe soveshchanie," in *Russkii istoricheskii arkhiv*, pp. 247-51.

General Principles

1. Until the convocation of the All-Russian Constituent Assembly, the All-Russian Provisional Government will be the sole trustee of sovereign authority over all territories of the Russian state.

2. All functions of sovereignty which in view of existing conditions have been exercised provisionally by the different regional governments will be turned over to the All-Russian Provisional Government when claimed by it.

3. The determination of the jurisdiction of regional governments, within the limits of local autonomy and on the basis of the governmental program set forth below, will be left to the discretion of the All-Russian Provisional Government.

The Duties of the Government in Relation to the All-Russian Constituent Assembly

The All-Russian Provisional Government takes upon itself the following tasks:

1. To assist in every way the Congress of Members of the Constituent Assembly, which is functioning as a legislative organ, in its efforts to insure the arrival of the members of the Constituent Assembly and to make all necessary preparations for the quickest resumption of the work of the Constituent Assembly in its original membership.

2. To be guided in all its conduct by the indisputable sovereign rights of the Constituent Assembly, and to exercise unrelaxing vigilance that nothing be permitted in the activities of the various bodies subordinate to the Provisional Government which might tend to diminish the rights of the Constituent Assembly or to postpone the resumption of its activity.

3. To render an account of all its activities to the Constituent Assembly as soon as the Assembly resumes its functioning, and to consider itself thenceforth entirely under orders of the Constituent Assembly—the sole sovereign of the country.

Note: Attached hereto is a resolution of the Congress of Members of the All-Russian Constituent Assembly of September 13, 1918.[80]

[80] The *A. R. R.*, XII, 190, gives September 16 as the date of the resolution. This resolution calls for the Constituent Assembly to open on January 1, 1919,

PROGRAM OF THE PROVISIONAL GOVERNMENT

In its endeavor to reestablish the national unity and independence of Russia, the All-Russian Provisional Government undertakes the following urgent tasks:

1. To fight for the liberation of Russia from the Soviet Government.

2. To reunite the regions of Russia which have been annexed, separated, and partitioned.

3. To repudiate the Brest Treaty and all other international agreements made after the revolution of March, 1917, by any power save the Russian Provisional Government, whether in the name of Russia or of any of her provinces; and to reinstate all agreements entered into with the Entente Powers.

4. To continue war against the German coalition.

In the domain of internal policy the Provisional Government will pursue the following program:

I. MILITARY POLICY

1. The formation of a united and powerful Russian army, placed outside the influence of party politics and subordinated through its supréme command to the All-Russian Provisional Government.

2. The complete non-interference of military authorities in civil government, except in the zone of military operations or in regions which have been declared by the Government under martial law. . . .

3. The establishment of strict military discipline based on the principles of law and respect for personality.

4. The exclusion from the army of all political organizations. . . .

II. CIVIL GOVERNMENT

1. In anticipation of the final establishment of the state on federal principles by the fully empowered Constituent Assembly, the organization of liberated Russia is to proceed on the basis of broad local autonomy for the various provinces, with recognition of geographical, economic, and ethnic differences.

if 250 members are present, or on February 1, 1919, if 170 members are present. (Boldyrev, *op. cit.*, p. 513.)

2. National minorities which do not occupy separate territories are to be granted the right to national-cultural self-determination.

3. Democratic city and zemstvo governments are to be re-established in regions liberated from the Soviets. . . .

4. All civil liberties are to be restored.

5. Effective measures are to be taken to ensure public safety and order.

III. ECONOMIC POLICY

1. To fight against economic disorganization.

2. To develop the productive forces of the country with the help of private Russian and foreign capital, and to stimulate private initiative and enterprise.

3. To introduce government regulation of industry and commerce.

4. To increase the productivity of labor and reduce the unproductive use of national revenues.

5. To promote labor legislation which is based upon principles of true protection of workers and regulates conditions of employment and dismissal.

6. To recognize complete freedom of association.

7. In its food policy, the Government stands for abolition of the bread monopoly and the fixing of prices, and for retention of control over the distribution of products of which there is a shortage. Government food purchases will be made with the help of private and cooperative trade agencies.

8. In its financial policy, the Government will fight the depreciation of paper money, endeavor to stabilize the fiscal structure, and increase direct income taxes and indirect taxes.

9. In its land policy, the All-Russian Provisional Government will refrain from introducing such changes in the existing system of land tenure as would interfere with the subsequent and final solution of the land question by the Constituent Assembly. The land will, therefore, be left for the time being in the hands of its de facto holders. . . .

IV. THE ORDER OF SUCCESSION IN THE GOVERNMENT

1. In its exercise of supreme authority on the above principles, the All-Russian Provisional Government acts as a collective body.

Its members cannot be recalled prior to the meeting of the Constituent Assembly and are responsible only to that body.

2. Should any vacancy occur in the membership of the Provisional Government the following have been elected as substitutes: A. A. Argunov, V. A. Vinogradov, General M. V. Alexeev, V. V. Sapozhnikov, and V. M. Zenzinov.

3. . . . Succession in the membership of the All-Russian Provisional Government shall take place in the . . . [following] manner: A. A. Argunov shall take the place of N. D. Avxentiev; V. A. Vinogradov, of N. I. Astrov; M. V. Alexeev, of V. G. Boldyrev; V. V. Sapozhnikov, of P. V. Vologodsky; and V. M. Zenzinov, of N. V. Chaikovsky.

4. Since the exercise of its authority must immediately be assumed by the All-Russian Provisional Government . . . in its full membership, the substitutes should enter the Government at once, [remaining there] until the arrival of the absentee members.[81]

5. At the time of assuming their duties members of the All-Russian Provisional Government will take a solemn oath, the text of which is hereto attached.

THE SOLEMN OATH

We, members of the All-Russian Provisional Government, elected by the State Conference at the city of Ufa, solemnly swear to be loyal to the Russian people and state and to discharge our duties in full accord with the constitutional act adopted by the State Conference on September 23, 1918, in establishing the supreme authority.

[Signatures follow.]

The Directorate had at first decided to make Ekaterinburg the seat of government, but the delegates from Omsk pressed for a reconsideration in favor of their city. The Minister of Finance of the Siberian Government, Ivan Mikhailov, was particularly concerned to have the Directorate located at Omsk, hoping thus to insure the removal

[81] Astrov, Alexeev, and Chaikovsky were elected *in absentia*. Astrov declined membership (see below, pp. 366-68), Alexeev died on October 8, and Chaikovsky was then at the head of the Archangel Government.

to that city of the gold reserve which had been seized at Kazan and which the Directorate had inherited from the Samara Government.[82] The Directorate finally decided in favor of Omsk as the capital, and the new government moved to that city in the early part of October.[83]

From the very outset the Directorate found itself in an atmosphere of intrigue and hostility coming from both the Right and the Left. The radical Socialist-Revolutionists, headed by Chernov, charged the Directorate with having surrendered to the Siberian reactionaries, while the conservative Omsk leaders could not reconcile themselves to the presence of socialists in the Directorate.

A matter of particular difficulty was the formation of a cabinet of ministers, and negotiations on this question with the Siberian Government lasted for several weeks. Finally an agreement was reached, and a Council of Ministers was announced on November 4. But the days of the Directorate were numbered. On November 18 conservatives overthrew it and put in power a dictator, Admiral Kolchak.

THE FIRST DAYS OF THE DIRECTORATE

[General Boldyrev's Account] [84]

The first steps of the Directorate were exceedingly difficult. It possessed neither an administrative machinery nor a reliable armed force. It found shelter in the . . . Grand Siberian Hotel in a city [Ufa] saturated with hostility and intrigue. We [members of the Directorate] were undoubtedly animated by a common desire to work for the good of the people . . . ; in reality, however, we were merely representatives and champions of different groups . . . with divergent and hostile political and social ideals—a fact which made it difficult to form a definite and solid majority. . . . Under normal conditions, in a country with a constitutional form of government in which the adminis-

---

[82] *Krasnyi Arkhiv*, LXI (1933), 66 ff.   [84] Boldyrev, *op. cit.*, pp. 54-55.
[83] Boldyrev, *op. cit.*, p. 52.

trative machinery . . . is not disturbed by frictions at the apex, this situation would not necessarily be considered as menacing. But in Russia, consumed as it was by revolutionary conflagration, . . . the situation of the Directorate was very difficult indeed.

The most vulnerable spot of the Directorate was its detachment from the masses. A child of the intelligentsia, it was absorbed too much in high-sounding principles . . . and abstract slogans such as "the good of the country," "the people"; it had no contact with actual life. It remained cut off from the real life of the peasant, the worker, and even the petty artisan; cut off from those problems . . . which on the other side of the civil-war front were solved so radically. . . .

The groups which established the Directorate continued their . . . quarrels . . . and intrigues, bringing about conditions under which any ambitious minister . . . had the opportunity to play politics for himself. . . .

ORGANIZING THE MINISTRY OF THE DIRECTORATE

[Excerpts from General Boldyrev's Diary] [85]

Omsk, October 23

. . . Had a visit from Mikhailov. He cautiously questioned me concerning himself and Rogovsky.

Knox called. He urged that we hurry in concluding an agreement with the Siberian Government. . . .

According to General Stepanov, who visited me after Knox, it was decided . . . to support a Russian general whom the Allies can trust. This general will be given both financial and military assistance. Stepanov hinted at the identity of that general. This was the first temptation. I met it calmly.

Stepanov reported many interesting things about the Japanese. [It appears] that the atamans of the Far East spread anarchy in that region at the direct instigation of the Japanese.

Knox cautiously inquired about my attitude toward Savinkov's candidacy for the post of Minister of Foreign Affairs. I gave an unfavorable reply. . . .

Knox paid no official call on Avxentiev and views him skeptically as a type akin to Kerensky. He [Knox] avoids having direct

---

[85] *Ibid.*, pp. 82-88.

relations with the Directorate as a body. I expressed my views with great emphasis to let him understand that the leadership of the [anti-Bolshevik] movement in Siberia belongs not to any of the generals but to the Government—the Directorate. But Knox obstinately follows his own line. He admits no point of contact between a general and a socialist. . . .

October 24

. . . Rozanov and Kolchak called. The latter is noticeably being subjected to treatments in the "Siberian" spirit. . . .

The session of the Government became very stormy when the question of the prorogation of the Duma came up. . . . Vologodsky threatened at first with ultimata. . . . Our side met the ultimata with firmness and Vologodsky gave in. . . .

October 25

In the morning Kolchak was again very eager to find out who was going to be Minister of Finance, of the Interior, and of Supplies. I argued for some time to show that Mikhailov, in the capacity of Minister of the Interior, would not be likely to contribute the necessary tranquilizing influence. . . .

At four o'clock Knox came with Rodzianko. . . . Drinking his tea, he threatened to gather a gang and overthrow us if we did not come to terms with the Siberians.

"I am getting to be a Siberian myself," he concluded his joke.
. . .

October 27

Rozanov and Kolchak came to make the customary morning report. We discussed the general situation. Both of them appear to be definitely in favor . . . of reducing the Directorate to one person. . . . I soon suceeded in bringing them back to reality and in showing that the resignation of the Directorate's left wing at the present time would lead to grave consequences and cause complications with the Czechs—a fact which, in view of the growth of Bolshevism in the country and at the front, would spell ruin to the attempt to regenerate Russia.

The Government met at one o'clock. . . . The depressed atmosphere was aggravated by Vologodsky's declaration that under the pressure of local "public opinion" he considered Mikhailov's candidacy for the post of Minister of the Interior as irrevocable. Avxentiev declared that he would resign from the Government. He was supported by Zenzinov. . . . Vinogradov also expressed himself to the effect that it would be impossible for him to remain in the Government.

Vologodsky was confused; he declared that evidently the thing for him to do was to renounce his purpose of forming a Council of Ministers.

Avxentiev, with characteristic effervescence, declared that he had decided to become a soldier, to join the army, which does not meddle in politics.

The All-Russian Provisional Government was thus coming to an inglorious end. . . .

After the session, Vinogradov told me that in case all the other four members resigned from the Directorate he would advise me to take over power in my capacity of Supreme Commander in Chief.

October 28

This day also has failed to yield any results. Again a split over Mikhailov's candidacy. Avxentiev is under great nervous tension. So is Vologodsky. Mikhailov is ready to withdraw on condition that the Czechs sign a statement that they had exerted pressure on him and on the Administrative Council. Avxentiev feels that this is calculated to impress upon the public mind the idea that the Czechs are interfering in our internal affairs in behalf of himself and Zenzinov. . . . The idea of a dictatorship is gaining ground. . . . I hear hints from many sides. This time the idea will most probably be connected with Kolchak.

October 29

The French and American Consuls called to feel the ground. . . . Our delay in selecting candidates [for the Cabinet] has acted most unfavorably on the financial situation. Deposits are being withdrawn from the banks.

In the evening I again had a call from Kolchak, Zhardetsky, Lopukhin. . . . They are playing a desperate game, hinting at the dissolution of the Directorate and at the retention of the Supreme Command alone. This they consider to be the only acceptable solution of the Ufa State Conference. The names of Avxentiev and Zenzinov are hateful to them. They suspect them of being in communication with the Central Committee [of the S. R.'s].

"Do you know that Chernov is negotiating a peace with the Bolsheviks?" stated the enraged Zhardetsky. I remarked that many more rumors had been reaching me . . . but that rumors proved nothing.

The excitement subsided. They began to assure me that I had their entire support. It was becoming tedious. I remarked curtly that their interference in state affairs surprised me and that they were entering upon a path reminiscent of the sad memory of the Petrograd Soviet. They were offended. . . .

A new complication. Vologodsky declared that Rogovsky is entirely unacceptable for the post of Chief of State Police. Avxentiev leaped to his feet. Kruglikov delivered himself of a philippic. Even Vinogradov, ready to accept the candidacy of Mikhailov, was puzzled. . . . [The meeting adjourned.]

I was asked to talk things over with Kolchak, who was responsible for this new complication.

October 30

. . . Vinogradov called and declared with emotion that the military circles and the "Muses"—Zhardetsky & Co.—had designated Kolchak for the post of dictator.

THE SOCIALIST-REVOLUTIONISTS AND THE UFA DIRECTORATE

[From an Account by Sviatitsky] [86]

. . . Notwithstanding the fact that the Central Committee [of the S. R.'s] . . . approved the Ufa Agreement officially, there was no unanimity on that question among its members. . . . When Chernov and Rakitnikov arrived at Samara and learned of the nature of the proposed agreement . . . and the composition of the Directorate, they sounded an alarm. V. M. Chernov urged by telegraph . . . "not to ruin the party and the democracy" by sanctioning the [Ufa] agreement. . . . But Chernov's plea had no success. Of the seven Central Committee members present at

---

[86] N. Saviatitsky, K istorii Vserossiiskogo Uchreditelnogo Sobraniia, pp. 59-60. N. Sviatitsky was a member of the Constituent Assembly and prominent in S. R. circles.

Ufa, three were against the agreement and four in favor. The agreement was thus approved by a majority of one. . . .

When the State Conference came to a close, all members of the Central Committee (except V. M. Zenzinov) departed for Samara to call a plenary session [of the Central Committee] and to consider the extremely delicate situation in which the party found itself. . . . Two points of view at once asserted themselves: that of M. Hendelman, approving the Ufa Agreement . . . , and that of V. Chernov, sharply denouncing it. Chernov's point of view prevailed, and on October 24 the Central Committee . . . passed a lengthy . . . "declaration" which was destined to play an important political rôle. . . .

THE SOCIALIST-REVOLUTIONISTS REPUDIATE THE UFA AGREEMENT

[Circular Letter, October 24, 1918] [87]

In the struggle which is now going on between Soviet Russia and the Russia of the Constituent Assembly, between ochlocracy and democracy, the latter is dangerously threatened by counter-revolutionary elements who have allied themselves [with democracy] for the purpose of ruining it.

The Socialist-Revolutionist party, which has assumed the whole burden of the defense of the Constituent Assembly, must therefore make . . . certain that it will not be submerged in the counter-revolutionary tide as it was a year ago in the tide of Bolshevik anarchy. One of the most important guarantees against this danger would be the establishment in that part of Russia which has been freed from Bolshevism of a central state authority to keep the banner of popular rule unblemished by compromise with its open or disguised enemies, give energetic support to the organizations of the toiling democracy, and just as energetically suppress every attempt to rally counter-revolutionary forces for the purpose of organizing conspiracies. At the same time, the existence of such an authority would greatly enhance not only the popularity of the Constituent Assembly among the toiling masses of Soviet Russia but also the likelihood of its cause being victorious.

[87] *Sovremennyia Zapiski*, XLV (1931), 348-52. The circular is sometimes referred to as the "Chernov Manifesto."

However, the task of organizing a government at the Ufa State Conference was not accomplished satisfactorily . . . because of the highly unfavorable international situation, . . . the stubborn resistance on the part of the reactionary imperialist group which has made its nest in the Siberian Government and is supported by the upper strata of Cossacks, and the menace of plots which threatened civil war at a time when the military front of the Constituent Assembly, weakened by secret and open defeatists, was suffering setbacks.

Furthermore, the results of the [Ufa] State Conference were influenced by the general weakness of the Socialist-Revolutionist group, which suffered from lack of unity and discipline, was terrorized by military defeats and the menacing attitude of conservative elements, and consequently was unable to secure for the Socialist-Revolutionist party the place in the government to which its moral and political prestige among the masses entitled it.

The party's principal victory at the Ufa Conference—the de jure recognition of the Constituent Assembly in its present membership—is in danger of becoming a purely nominal victory, as a result of the fact that in their most recent declaration the leading Cossack elements and the Cadets of the Siberian orientation appear to ignore completely all the political obligations which they undertook at Ufa.

The concessions which the party was forced to make in connection with the membership [of the Directorate], the irresponsibility of the Directorate, and the setting of the date for the meeting of the Constituent Assembly . . . have already resulted in a number of political mistakes. . . . These are the choice of residence [for the Directorate], the territorial separation between the Government and the Congress of Members of the Constituent Assembly, the transfer of the most important state functions to the . . . ministries of the Siberian Government, the ratification of the temporary prorogation of the Siberian Regional Duma, the prolonged impunity of the instigators and leaders of the Omsk counter-revolutionary plot, the reinstatement of shoulder straps and old-time [army] discipline, the attempt to do away with the activities in the army which aimed at propaganda and education, and a number of appointments which handed the army over to reactionary generals and atamans.

The weakness of the Provisional Government was shown particularly by the passivity with which it met such acts as the abolition by the Siberian Government of the land law passed by the Constituent Assembly, Dutov's militarization of labor, the rough treatment which the Congress of Trade Unions and other labor organization and peasant movements received in Siberia, and the many outrageous infringements upon freedom of speech and person from which private individuals, as well as organizations of socialist parties, suffer more and more frequently.

In spite of these blunders and evidences of weakness and indecision the Socialist-Revolutionist party, in accordance with the obligations which it assumed at Ufa, continues by every means to support the central government in its fight against commissar autocracy and is equally prepared to uphold that government in every possible way in its fight against the adventurous groups of reactionaries into whose hands local authority has in some places fallen. . . . The S. R. party is also prepared to give the Provisional Government all possible assistance in defending democratic freedom and Russian independence and in establishing normal relations with the Allies on conditions which will guarantee the country against curtailment of its sovereignty in consequence of the occupation of its territories by foreign troops. At the same time, the party believes that the country has a right to be fully informed of every measure taken toward this end by the Provisional Government, whose irresponsible status must not in any case be allowed to bring back all the defects of old-time secret diplomacy.

Whether or not the Provisional Government in its present composition has the power and will to act in the direction here indicated, the . . . tactics of the S. R. party should be to rally its forces . . . around the Constituent Assembly and the Congress of Members of the Constituent Assembly, which is a preliminary to the former. . . .

In anticipation of possible political crises resulting from counter-revolutionary schemes, all party forces must be mobilized immediately, given military training, and armed, in order to be able to withstand at any moment the attacks of counter-revolutionists who organize civil war in the rear of the anti-Bolshevik front. . . .

A natural supplement to these activities of the Central Committee should be work in Soviet Russia aiming to attract to the party standard all those elements of the masses who have succeeded in recovering from Bolshevik intoxication—work showing that only the Constituent Assembly with its leading S. R. group can safeguard the people against a change from Bolshevik tyranny to that of counter-revolution.

The party should be thoroughly cleansed of all alien elements who bring disintegration into its ranks and destroy the consistency of its socialist doctrines and the unity of its tactics. . . . Only on condition of thus straightening its line of policy can the work of the S. R. party rise to the tragic historical moment through which Russia and the world are now passing . . . , and become more and more the party of the people, drawing from this indissoluble bond with the people its strength for the solution of the political problems which are questions of life and death for the Russian people.

CENTRAL COMMITTEE
OF THE SOCIALIST-REVOLUTIONIST PARTY

AGREEMENT BETWEEN GENERAL BOLDYREV AND GENERAL KNOX
[October 24, 1918] [88]

I shall do all in my power to assist the Russian Government in organizing a Russian army, on the following clearly understood conditions:

1. The new Russian army must be a real army, under complete control of its officers. It is to have no committees nor commissars. Neither officers nor private soldiers are to mix in politics.

2. There is to be only one Russian army. The Russian Government is to request the Allied representatives to agree that military assistance will be given to the Russian Government only, and not to various Russian military chiefs such as Semenov or Kalmykov. The troops of General Horvath are to be disbanded.

3. All appointments and promotions of officers are to be made by the Supreme Commander in Chief.

4. The German and Austrian war prisoners are at present allowed to do anything they please. Every small officers' "battal-

[88] Boldyrev, *op. cit.*, p. 524.

ion" keeps a hundred Germans as cooks, servants, and grooms; and every company of new recruits has three German cooks to prepare Russian shchi [cabbage soup] for Russians. Were this situation known in England it would provoke a storm of indignation. All war prisoners of non-Slavic origin should be interned and kept under guard in prison camps. It would be still better if these camps were situated in Transbaikalia or the Far East, where American or Japanese troops could guard them.

5. Measures must be taken at once to compel the workers in the [railway] shops to work in the most energetic and conscientious manner. Otherwise the number of freight trains will decrease next spring to four pairs daily; and assistance from the Allies, as well as military operations, will become impossble. The shops must be made to work.

A large number of railway cars in the rear are occupied by officers and their families, refugees, and troops. General Horvath's troops, for example, occupy several hundred cars. . . . All these cars must be immediately released, and, if there is not enough housing space for the refugees, barracks must be built.

6. It is very disappointing to the Allies, who are trying to help Russia to regain her strength, that the Russian leaders have failed for so long a time to come to an agreement about the membership of the Provisional Government. We have the right to demand that all personal and party interests be set aside and that a strong government be formed which will place no obstacles in the way of organizing an army to save Russia.

GENERAL BOLDYREV
Supreme Commander in Chief

MAJOR GENERAL A. V. KNOX

ASTROV DECLINES MEMBERSHIP IN THE DIRECTORATE

[Letter, November 26, 1918] [89]

I learn from the newspapers that I have been honored with election to the Directorate which was formed by the State Conference at Ufa. Not until now have I been able to acquaint my-

[89] "Ufimskoe gosudarstvennoe soveshchanie," in *Russkii istoricheskii arkhiv*, pp. 274-75.

self with stenographic reports of that conference and to learn how the Directorate was formed. On this occasion I wish to state the following:

In Moscow, last April, there was formed with my direct participation a political organization named *Soiuz Vozrozhdeniia* [Union for the Regeneration of Russia], which aimed to establish as extensive a political front as possible and to effect unity in our relations with the Allies. The Union consisted of individuals of different political tendencies who had agreed on a simple and clear platform: to continue the struggle against Germany, to fight the Soviet Government, and to reestablish a united and independent Russia.

In accordance with the program of the Union, the government to be established for this transition period was intended to take the form of a directorate of three. This government was to lead the country to the Constituent Assembly, which would determine the final form of Russia's political organization. Among the candidates to the Provisional Government my name was mentioned. It is only natural to suppose that the people who agreed on that platform should also have agreed as to which Constituent Assembly they meant: a new one or the old one of 1917. I state emphatically that what was taken as the basis of the Union's program was a new Constituent Assembly, to be elected by the country after it had been freed from the enemy and after its parts, now torn asunder, had been united.

The members of the Union departed to the Volga to assist there in the formation of an Eastern front and to carry out the ideas of the Union. Evidently the necessity of forming an Eastern front has since passed; [but] the program of the Union was accepted at the Ufa Conference as the foundation for an all-Russian government. The Directorate as elected consists mostly of individuals who had been nominated at Moscow. However, one essential change was admitted into the Moscow program and the Moscow agreement. This change consists in the attempt to call to life the old Constituent Assembly.

I shall not enter on a discussion of the question whether that Assembly was good or bad. I shall say only that it simply does not exist and that to build on this [Assembly] an all-Russian government is the greatest delusion. The members of the Ufa Conference knew that as originally formed the Constituent Assembly no longer existed, and they therefore identified the Assembly with a gathering of any 250 members, if they should meet next January, or of any 170 members, if they should meet in February.

Since I myself advocate the recognition of the Constituent Assembly as the supreme plenipotentiary organ, having as its final aim the determination of the form of Russia's political order, I repudiate the more resolutely any thought of possible participation in a government which makes itself dependent on the old, defunct Constituent Assembly.

This settles the question of my participation in the Provisional Government formed by the Ufa Conference. . . . Not wishing to become divorced from actuality, I cannot help recognizing that the whole political situation has now radically changed and no longer justifies our considering as an all-Russian government the political body created at Ufa. Under present conditions, it is but one among many political bodies formed on the long and difficult path of reuniting Russia. . . .

PROCLAMATION OF THE ALL-RUSSIAN PROVISIONAL GOVERNMENT [90]

[November 4, 1918]

To All Regional Governments and All Citizens of the Russian State!

Having assumed sovereign state authority, with the unanimous consent of all members of the State Conference, at the city of Ufa on September 23, 1918, the All-Russian Provisional Government at once undertook the performance of the important tasks of state with which it had been charged. First of all, it undertook the reestablishment of the fighting capacity of the country, so indispensable during a time of struggle for the restoration of Russia to greatness and unity.

The inflexible resolution of the Government to make every sacrifice for the realization of this great task suffered defeat because of the absence of a unified and harmonious system of administration and the presence in the different regions of Russia

[90] *Vestnik Vremennago Vserossiiskago Pravitelstva*, No. 1, November 6, 1918, p. 1.

of separate governments. . . . Reaffirming its inflexible determination to acknowledge and to put at the disposal of the different parts of the Russian state the right to extensive autonomy which was granted in the declaration issued on September 24, 1918, at the city of Ufa, the All-Russian Provisional Government, conscious of its responsibility to the peoples of Russia and of a historical moment which calls for the creation of a unified and strong state, has found it necessary to enact the following:

1. All regional governments and regional representative bodies, without exception, shall cease their existence upon the formation in the near future of central administrative organs of the All-Russian Government.

2. The reestablishment of regional administrations, resulting from the recognition by the All-Russian Government of the rights of certain regions of Russia to autonomous administration, must presuppose as preliminary an exact and clear delimitation by the supreme state authority of the jurisdiction of regional administrations over questions of purely regional import.

3. While assuming in full the prerogatives of administration previously exercised by local governments, the All-Russian Government leaves in force the legislative acts of the regional governments; the amendment and repeal of these legislative acts shall take place in the order of general legislative procedure.

4. In order to facilitate the speediest possible organization of an all-Russian administrative organ, the ministries and central administrative organs of the Siberian Provisional Government shall continue to act, as invested with the authority pertaining to all-Russian administrative organs, until in the course of general legislative procedure the [above] institutions and their personnel are altered.[91]

5. While unifying the entire Russian army under a single su-

[91] The Council of Ministers which was announced on November 4 consisted of the following: P. V. Vologodsky, Chairman of the Council of Ministers; V. A. Vinogradov, Vice-Chairman; A. V. Kolchak, Minister of War and Navy; Yu. V. Kliuchnikov, Assistant Minister of Foreign Affairs; A. N. Gattenberg, Chief of the Ministry of the Interior; I. I. Serebrennikov, Minister of Supplies; I. A. Mikhailov, Minister of Finance; N. S. Zefirov, Minister of Food; S. S. Starynkevich, Minister of Justice; L. A. Ustrugov, Minister of Ways and Communications; V. V. Sapozhnikov, Minister of Education; L. I. Shumilovsky, Minister of Labor; N. I. Petrov, Minister of Agriculture; N. N. Shchukin, Assistant Minister of Trade and Industry. (*Ibid.*)

13

preme command, the All-Russian Government hereby grants to certain parts of the Russian army regional designations and distinctive regional colors, provided that the national tri-color flag is displayed at the same time.

In taking these measures the All-Russian Provisional Government profoundly believes that every part and nationality of the great Russian state, realizing the mortal danger which is threatening the country from the German-Magyar hordes and their henchmen, the Bolsheviks, will unite in a single mighty whole, under the resolute guidance of the all-Russian supreme authority, to lead our tormented fatherland out of the abyss of disintegration to the predestined path of regeneration of the all-Russian state.

The All-Russian Provisional Government

NIKOLAI AVXENTIEV

VASILII BOLDYREV

PETR VOLOGODSKY

VLADIMIR VINOGRADOV

VLADIMIR ZENZINOV

THE OVERTHROW OF THE DIRECTORATE

[Resolution of the Council of Ministers, November 18, 1918] [92]

I.

In view of the extraordinary events which have terminated the activity of the All-Russian Provisional Government, the Council of Ministers, with the consent of the remaining members of the All-Russian Provisional Government, has resolved to take over the government.

II.

In view of the critical situation in which the state finds itself and of the necessity of concentrating supreme authority in one individual, the Council of Ministers has resolved to resign tempo-

[92] Maksakov i Turunov, *Khronika grazhdanskoi voiny v Sibiri,* pp. 264-65.

rarily the exercise of supreme governmental authority to Admiral Alexander Vasilevich Kolchak, conferring upon him the title of Supreme Ruler.

PETR VOLOGODSKY
Chairman of the Council of Ministers

Yu. Kliuchnikov	G. Krasnov
L. Ustrugov	N. Petrov
N. Zefirov	I. Serebrennikov
A. Kolchak	A. Gattenberger
G. Guins	N. Shchukin
C. Starynkevich	I. Mikhailov
L. Shumilovsky	

Members of the Council

[Direct-Wire Conversation Between Boldyrev and Kolchak, November 19, 1918] [93]

[Boldyrev:] General Boldyrev, Supreme Commander in Chief, is at the apparatus.

[Kolchak:] Admiral Kolchak is at the apparatus. . . .

[Boldyrev:] Greetings, Admiral. I called you to the apparatus to learn what has happened in Omsk during my absence and also to learn of the orders, of which I have heard indirectly, concerning the Russian Supreme Commander in Chief.

[Kolchak:] It is impossible to relate everything over the wire. The Omsk events occurred unexpectedly during [the session of] the Council of Ministers. When the question of the future of the Directorate became clear and Vologodsky and Vinogradov recognized the impossibility of its further existence, the Council of Ministers . . . assumed sovereign power and then proceeded to discuss the question whether it was possible under present conditions for the Ministers to exercise power as a body. It was decided that such a collective exercise of authority was at present impossible. There was then raised the question of vesting two or three individuals with supreme power. This was also recognized as unacceptable. The question then reduced itself to a uni-personal sovereign power, and two individuals were proposed. I suggested

---

[93] Boldyrev, *op. cit.*, pp. 111-12.

you, arguing that it would be simpler to bring about a uni-personal sovereign power by transferring civil authority to the Supreme Commander in Chief of the army. . . . This was debated in my absence. I left the session chamber after giving my opinion. The Council of Ministers resolved that I should assume supreme authority; they stressed the fact that the situation was critical and that my refusal was unacceptable. I shouldered this heavy cross as a necessity and as a duty to the country. That is all.

Boldyrev: Thus no measures whatsoever were taken either by yourself as War Minister, or by the Commander of the Siberian Army, or by the Council of Ministers, to restore the rights of those who had suffered and to liquidate the criminal acts against the members of the All-Russian Government. . . . I have already witnessed, both here and at the front, the ruinous effects of the coup d'état which at one stroke has undone everything accomplished with such enormous effort during the past month. I cannot possibly adopt so placid an attitude toward the government which, imperfect though it may have been, had as its foundation the fact that it was popularly elected. I have not received from you an answer on the question of the Supreme Command and must inform you that . . . in this respect too a fatal blow has been dealt to the ideal of popular sovereignty in so far as it found its visible expression in the esteem which through my person was accorded both by the Russian troops and the Allies to the title of Supreme Commander in Chief. I shall not be mistaken if I say that your orders as Supreme Commander in Chief will not be obeyed. I have not permitted myself during the past two days to utter a single word, either spoken or written, and have refrained from addressing the troops, expecting that Omsk would realize the utter madness of what has happened and would consider the situation more seriously, so that the front might be saved and order preserved in the country. As soldier and citizen, I must tell you honestly and frankly that I am not at all in sympathy with what has happened and what is now going on, and consider absolutely necessary the reestablishment of the Directorate, the immediate release and restoration to their rights of Avxentiev and others, and the surrender by you of your powers. I have considered myself in honor bound to express my profound conviction and hope that you will have the courage to listen with even temper. I cannot admit the thought that in a state based to any extent on legality such methods as were used in relation to members of the government will be allowed, or that government representatives will assume such a placid attitude toward what has happened and merely state it as an accomplished fact. I beg to have this opinion brought to the knowledge of the Council of Ministers. I have finished.

Kolchak: I fail to understand the expression of your feelings as to my attitude toward the Government. . . . I am relating as briefly as possible the facts and beg you to speak of them and not of your attitude toward them. The Directorate was leading the country to civil war . . . and because of Avxentiev and Zenzinov was destroying everything accomplished before their advent to the posts of supreme authority. The fact of their arrest was, of course, a criminal act, and the culprits have been brought by me before a military court martial; [94] but the Directorate, which has aroused the opposition of all social groups, especially the military, cannot continue to exist. . . .

[94] The kidnappers of the Left members of the Directorate were led by three Cossack officers: Volkov, Katanaev, and Krasilnikov. On November 19 Kolchak signed two orders relating to these officers—one appointing a special court to investigate their crime, the other promoting, "for excellent military service," Volkov to the rank of major general and the other two to the rank of colonel. The two orders are given in Subbotovsky, *op. cit.,* pp. 64-65.

CHAPTER VII

TOWARD THE COMMUNIST ECONOMIC ORDER

Foreign intervention and civil war by no means diverted all the energies of the Bolsheviks from their principal aim, the reorganization of the economic life of Russia on communist principles. A number of measures aiming at such a reorganization were taken in the early months of the Soviet régime when the Bolsheviks placed industry under workers' control, nationalized the banks, foreign trade, transport, and a number of industrial establishments, and annulled domestic and foreign state loans. But these and similar measures [1] were designed primarily to deprive the propertied classes of their influence in the economic life of the country and to paralyze their opposition to the proletarian dictatorship. It was not until eight months after their seizure of power that the Bolsheviks undertook a systematic reconstruction of the national economy in accordance with communist principles. The reconstruction was not completed in the period covered by this chapter, and certain features of the system which finally emerged as a result of communist experimentation did not appear until 1919 and 1920. But the basic elements of the communist economic order—the socialization of the means of production and distribution, the establishment of rigid control over raw materials and products of industry and agriculture, the abolition of money and markets, and the conscription of labor—were introduced during the summer and fall of 1918. [2]

[1] Materials relating to early Soviet economic policies are given in *The Bolshevik Revolution*, Chaps. VI, X, and XI.

[2] A controversy has arisen in connection with the interpretation of the economic policy which the Bolsheviks pursued during the period of 1918-1920. It is maintained by a number of Russian writers that the economic measures of

374

The materials of this chapter relate to the application of communist principles to industry, labor, distribution, and finance. Because it raised special problems the agrarian application of these principles is treated in a separate chapter.

A. INDUSTRY AND LABOR

In the spring of 1918, when economic disorganization was increasing at a rapid tempo throughout the country, Lenin took the view that there could be no improvement in the situation unless the Communists changed their tactics in the economic sphere. At a meeting of party leaders on April 4 he argued that the task of the revolutionary "expropriation of the expropriators" had been successfully accomplished and that the time had arrived for a consolidation of

this period resulted not so much from the original program of communism as from the exigencies of civil war. Hence these writers use the name "War Communism" to characterize the economic system which prevailed in Russia from 1918 to the end of 1920. This point of view was developed by L. Kamenev at the Ninth All-Russian Congress of Soviets in 1921 (see the stenographic report of the Congress, Moscow, 1922, p. 50) and by Trotsky (in *Sochineniia*, XII, 308-09, 311, 346-48). On the other hand, many prominent Communists hold that Soviet economic policies of 1918-1920 aimed at communism pure and simple, and they refer to the system, not as War Communism, but as Integral Communism. (Cf. N. Bukharin, *Ekonomika perekhodnogo perioda*, pp. 6, 102, 111, 135; and L. Kritsman, *Geroicheskii period russkoi revoliutsii*, p. 75.) Lenin's characterizations of the economics of that period vary with different pronouncements. Commemorating the fourth anniversary of the revolution he wrote:
"Lifted up on a wave of exaltation, and having behind us the general political and, later, the military enthusiasm of the people, we intended on the basis of this enthusiasm to carry out . . . similarly exalted economic tasks. We expected— or perhaps it would be more correct to say that we assumed without sufficient calculations—that by the direct fiat of the proletarian state we would be able to establish state production and state distribution of products on a communistic basis in a country of small peasants. Life has exposed our error. There was need of a series of transition stages . . . to communism. . . . Thus spoke life itself to us. Thus spoke the facts revealed by the progress of the revolution." (*Sochineniia*, XXVII, 29.) Similar views were expressed by Lenin in speeches delivered at the Moscow Gubernia Conference of the Communist Party in October 1921 (*ibid.*, pp. 55-72) and at the Eleventh Congress of the Russian Communist Party on March 27, 1922 (*ibid.*, pp. 228-31). On the other hand, at the preceeding congress in March 1921, Lenin declared that the economic measures of the foregoing years were due to the necessities of war and not to economic needs (*ibid.*, XXVI, 241).

the gains already made. "We conquered," he said, "by methods of suppression, but we shall also be able to conquer by methods of administration." He therefore recommended the abandonment of what he termed the "Red Guard" attack on capitalism and the establishment of a *modus vivendi* with those capitalists who were willing to cooperate with the Soviet Government.

Lenin's proposals aroused strong opposition in the left-wing Communists, who argued that a moderate economic policy was bound to suppress the "creative forces" of the revolution and to result in the complete defeat of the proletariat. They therefore advocated the continuation of the policy of expropriation until it had effected "the complete ruination of the bourgeoisie" and the thoroughgoing socialization of the national economy.[3]

The disagreement between the Right and Left Communists on the question of what economic policy would best serve the interests of the proletarian dictatorship lasted through most of the spring. Meanwhile the industrial workers continued the seizure of factories and shops, the ejection of the old administrations, and the operation of the enterprises without any regard to the interest of the state as a whole. Toward the summer of 1918 conditions reached such a state that government intervention in industry was considered by both Right and Left Communists as the only means of averting an economic collapse. In the middle of May the conference of representatives of nationalized industries passed a resolution favoring a general nationalization of industry. A similar resolution was adopted on June 3 by the first All-Russian Congress of Councils of National Economy. These were followed on June 28 by the Sovnar-

[3] Lenin's economic proposals and the program of the Left Communists are quoted in *The Bolshevik Revolution*, pp. 553-65.

kom's decree declaring the great majority of larger enterprises the property of the socialist state.

CONDITIONS ON THE RAILROADS [4]

At the second session of the conference of [representatives of] nationalized machine-shops the delegate of the Central Transport Committee delivered a report . . . dealing with conditions on the railroads. . . .

According to the speaker, self-government of the railroads has assumed abnormal forms and has finally turned into trade-union syndicalism. Railroad workers pursue only their personal interests, in complete disregard of the interests of the country. . . . Some of the railroads ignore the Soviet Government and the Commissariat of Ways and Communications, and their sole concern is to get money from the government. . . . The collegia in charge of the different railway branches do their work in a clumsy way, interfering with the establishment of order. The speaker thought that the collegia should be removed. They may be entrusted with nominal control, but all administrative orders should come from one person and no one should have the right to interfere with his orders.

The collegia are packed with unworthy people who feel no responsibility whatever for anything that may happen.

By way of illustrating the activities of the collegia, the speaker related how an inspector of one of the roads . . . discovered that the bolts were loose. He reported the fact to the road collegium, and the railway watchman was reprimanded. Thereupon the collegium of railway watchmen . . . warned the inspector that he would be discharged if he continued to complain.

The speaker then touched upon the financial difficulties of the railways. Every railway station appropriates the money which it collects. On the Vladikavkaz Railroad passengers are forced to buy tickets at every station; the same is true of freight, the reason being that each station is trying to get its share of receipts. . . .

Among the causes of the railway crisis are the shortage of locomotives, the superfluity of governing organs, and food difficulties.

[4] *Svoboda Rossii*, No. 25, May 5, 1918, p. 4.

Half of the blame for the disruption of the railroads must be put upon objective conditions, the other half upon the conduct of the railway employees. They have insisted on the abolition of piece-work wages, with the result that the number of workers is constantly growing while the number of disabled locomotives is not diminishing. . . . The increase in personnel has affected not only the workers of the railroad shops but the porters and locomotive crews as well. Despite the curtailment in train movement this [condition] still prevails.

The speaker then touched upon the subject of railroad leadership. . . . As a rule, experienced orators and demagogues are elected to office; experienced administrators are voted down. . . . Railway expenditures have increased ten times in relation to the pre-war period. . . . Expenditure estimates of the Commissariat of Ways and Communication have reached the sum of nine and a half billion rubles for 1918. One and a half billion rubles are for material and fuel; eight billions for personnel. The income of the railroads is not quite three billion rubles. . . .

CONDITIONS IN THE TEXTILE INDUSTRY

[Report of the Union of Textile Workers of the Volga Region
to the Presidium of the Textile Section of the Supreme
Council of National Economy] [5]

All factories present the same picture: There is no money, no food, and the workers are condemned to starvation. There are no raw materials, no necessary machine parts, . . . no oil, no fuel, etc. But the most appalling fact—and this is bound to deal a death-blow to the factories—is the superfluity of workers coming from the ranks of the peasants. This superfluity is as high as 25 per cent, and [the peasants] use force [to be hired] to work. The soldiers are especially notorious for using force. The peasants stream to the factories in large crowds. Those who have never . . . worked in factories are also coming, and no amount of persuasion can help [keep them away]. . . .

What is it, then, that attracts the peasants to the factory? (1) Wages which are starvation pay for [regular] workers because of

[5] *Ibid.*, No. 28, May 18, 1918, p. 1. The report was the outcome of an investigation of a number of factories in the Volga region.

the criminally high cost of living, but which are very high for the peasant, who has everything, including food supplies. . . . (2) The peasar ᵥ is also drawn to the factory by this: As soon as he comes to the factory he demands cloth for himself and his family at [the reduced] prices which the worker is paying. . . . The factories are thus being plundered.

Without enlarging on our report . . . , we declare that stringent measures should be taken at once against these plunderers. The situation is such that it requires a state law to eject peasant proprietors from the factories.

CALL FOR NATIONALIZATION OF INDUSTRY

[Resolution of the Conference of Representatives of Nationalized Industries, May 17, 1918] [6]

The utter exhaustion of Russia's productive forces makes the question of a planned and organized utilization of its remaining resources one of life and death.

In industry this can be achieved by consolidating in one technical unit the different factories engaged in the same industry. In the transport industries such a consolidation is especially imperative in view of the shortage of metal and fuel. . . . The importance of a technical consolidation of factories of the transport group in one enterprise, which has been acknowledged at the present conference by technical and scientific experts,[7] is especially urgent at this time because of the protracted state of uncertainty and the disrupted condition [of the country]. . . .

As a preliminary, a single centralized administration must be formed to serve as a point of departure for the necessary technical and economic reorganization of factories on up-to-date principles and for the preparation of a general technical program of work.

In view of the above considerations, the Conference is in favor of the immediate nationalization of factories and the establishment of a unified administration. It also declares that the present indefinite situation can no longer be tolerated.

[6] *Izvestiia*, No. 98, May 18, 1918, p. 5.

[7] The engineers who participated in this conference opposed nationalization on the ground that Russia was not prepared for it. Hence they refrained from voting for the resolution, although they declared that they would continue to work in the nationalized industries. *Ibid.*

PLAN FOR THE ADMINISTRATION OF NATIONALIZED
ENTERPRISES

[Account of the Conference of Representatives of Nationalized Industries,
May 18, 1918] [8]

. . . Yu. Larin read a letter received from Lenin . . . in
which the President of the Soviets greeted the Conference. . . .
Lenin thought that the Conference should adopt the following
[program] : (1) the organization of a provisional committee to
do the preliminary work required in connection with the nationalization of factories; (2) the application . . . to all factories of
the rules of internal organization worked out at the Briansk Factory . . . to provide for strict discipline; (3) the selection by
the workers of representatives to take part in the administration
of nationalized factories. The more able workers with long experience should be sent to assist badly organized factories where
more experienced and practical workers are lacking. In conclusion, Lenin expressed the hope that . . . it might be possible in
the near future to bring about the complete nationalization of factories as painlessly as possible. . . .

Yu. Larin also reported on the project for the control of nationalized enterprises. The project has in view the establishment of a
central committee for the administration of these enterprises . . .
and the appointment of itinerant control groups of three persons
to inspect the activities of the factories. Enterprises which are
sufficiently supplied (i. e., which have fuel, raw material, and a
food supply), but do not fulfill the assigned program of work will
be declared in the danger zone of production, and a control commission consisting of representatives of the particular factory and
of the central [authorities] will be sent there. After the commission has reported its findings, the factory will be closed, or the
employees and workers discharged, or there will be taken other
special measures such as establishment of collective responsibility,
penalization of workers, etc.

Every two months all factories will be required to send to the
central committee detailed information concerning their receipts,
expenditures, and production. . . .

After that the rules for factory regulation were announced.

[8] *Svoboda Rossii,* No. 28, May 19, 1918, p. 3.

These rules were recently formulated at the Briansk Factory. According to the rules, every factory is placed in charge of an administrative body consisting of [representatives] elected by the workers and of appointees of the Council of National Economy. The administration appoints the director and the technical personnel. Strict labor discipline is the basis of the project. . . . Workers are not to interfere with technical measures. Infractions of labor discipline are punished by various fines. . . .

LABOR INSPECTION
[Decree of the Sovnarkom, May 18, 1918] [9]

1. Labor inspection has the purpose of protecting the lives, health, and work of all persons engaged in any form of economic activity, and is carried out . . . not only in their place of work but outside it as well.

2. Labor inspection is under the control of the People's Commissariat of Labor and its local organs (the Bureaus of Labor Protection).

3. Inspectors and inspectresses . . . are selected by trade-union councils and city or regional insurance departments.

4. In the absence of the organizations referred to in the preceding article, the local commissar of labor is to call a conference consisting of equal numbers of representatives of insurance and labor organizations for the selection of inspectors and inspectresses. . . .

9. Inspectors and inspectresses have the right to bring before the court and to fine within specified limits violators of the decrees, regulations, and other acts of the Soviet Government in regard to the safety . . . of the workers.

10. In the performance of their duty inspectors and inspectresses have the right to enter all (without exception) places of work, places of rest, and living quarters of workers and their families. . . .

V. ULIANOV (LENIN)
President of the Sovnarkom

A. SHLIAPNIKOV
People's Commissar of Labor

[9] *S. U. R.*, No. 36, 1918, p. 449.

REGULATION OF WAGES

[Instructions of the All-Russian Central Council of Trade Unions, May, 1918] [10]

1. Every trade union engaged in production and intending to establish by legislation a definite wage-scale for workers and office employees in its trade must submit three copies of that scale to the trade-union councils and the Commissariat of Labor for ratification.

Note: Wage agreements cannot be ratified by separate enterprises without the consent of the unions.

2. Wage agreements of workers and office employees in state and public institutions where no trade unions exist are considered in the course of general procedure . . . by the [trade] union councils and the Commissariat of Labor.

3. Wage agreements which concern workers and office employees of a given locality are submitted to the local trade-union councils and the [local] commissar of labor; regional [wage agreements are submitted] to regional [unions]; while those on an all-Russian scale require the consideration and approval of the All-Russian Central Council of Trade Unions and the People's Commissar of Labor.

4. Wage agreements not signed by the [trade] union councils concerned have no validity.

5. Wage agreements not signed by the Commissar of Labor have no validity.

Note: Paragraphs 4 and 5 apply also to wage agreements between trade unions and employers.

6. In case of disagreement between local unions and the Commissar of Labor on questions relating to the ratification of wage agreements, the dispute . . . goes for consideration to the All-Russian Central Council of Trade Unions and the People's Commissariat of Labor.

7. To become a law every wage agreement must contain:

(a) An estimate of the degree of (1) the labor skill, complexity, and precision of the work, . . . the skill in reading blueprints, drawings, or models, the ability to use precise measuring instruments; (2) the worker's self-guidance and the importance

[10] *Professionalnyi Vestnik*, Nos. 7-8, May 25, 1918, p. 22.

of the work; (3) the training and experience [of the worker];
(4) the difficulty of working conditions as well as the danger involved in production. . . .

(b) A division of the workers of a particular trade into groups
(wage categories) on the basis of the above qualifications. . . .

(c) A guarantee that every worker will produce a certain
amount of work, or a precise statement of the production standard for every . . . wage category. . . .

8. All rates of an approved wage agreement are fixed rates
and cannot be increased or diminished without a reconsideration
of the wage agreement.

9. Wage agreements become law from the time they are signed
by the Commissar of Labor.

10. [Wage agreements have no retroactive force.]

Presidium of the All-Russian Council of Trade Unions

CONGRESS OF COMMISSARS OF LABOR
[May 19, 1918] [11]

At the plenary session of the Congress on Sunday [May 19],
A. G. Shliapnikov, People's Commissar of Labor, gave a report
on the activity of the Commissariat of Labor. The Bolsheviks
[he said] aimed to satisfy all the . . . demands of the working
class. They had introduced the eight-hour working day . . .
[and] workers' control. . . . As regards measures against unemployment, we now have 160 employment bureaus, as against
ten or fifteen which existed before. There are about five hundred
thousand unemployed, mainly in the regions of Petrograd and
Moscow. The situation in the Petrograd region is especially critical, as there are no means of getting coal and raw materials for
the factories. . . . The unemployed are being helped with the
thirty million [rubles] appropriated in accordance with the decree on social insurance.

The decline in productivity of labor is explained by the fact
that the best [labor] force was taken by the war, as well as by
the existence of a food crisis. The workers' organizations should
take a hand in matters of food supply.

[11] *Svoboda Rossii*, No. 30, May 21, 1918, p. 3.

The Commissar of Labor is now facing the problem of creating discipline in production. In this [endeavor] there were many failures because of the transitional character of the time. The speaker declared that it was important to fight against the syndicalist tendencies of the workers who look upon whole branches of industry as belonging to the trade, forgetful of the fact that it is the state which owns the industries.

The realization of all our aims, said the Commissar, is dependent upon the activity of the international proletariat. At present the imperialist ring is drawing closer. Only the insurrection of the Western-European proletariat can help us to accomplish our purposes fully.

[Schwartz, a Menshevik, criticized the speaker.] . . . The Bolsheviks prided themselves on the decree of the eight-hour working-day. Already they repudiate that decree. Lenin himself declared that it would be necessary to do away with the eight-hour day. The Bolsheviks promised to give work to everybody but the number of the unemployed is growing. Instead of demobilizing industry . . . they have closed a number of enterprises. A vast scheme of public works was formulated by specialists . . . but the plans have been buried because the Soviet Government is surrounded by a crowd of careerists. (*Noise in the hall.*)

[The speaker was not allowed to continue, and the meeting closed with the adoption of a Bolshevik resolution.]

THE TASK OF THE WORKING CLASS

[Lenin's Speech at the Congress of Commissars of Labor, May 22, 1918] [12]

Comrades! First of all, permit me to welcome the Congress of Commissars of Labor in the name of the Soviet of People's Commissars. At yesterday's meeting of the Soviet of People's Commissars, Comrade Shliapnikov reported that your Congress has accepted the resolution of the trade unions in regard to labor discipline and production standards. In my opinion, Comrades, you have made a very important move, which not only concerns the productivity of labor and the conditions of production but . . . also affects vital principles relating to the present situation in gen-

[12] *Sochineniia*, XXIII, 32-34.

eral. You are in constant and close touch with the large masses of workers and are aware that our revolution is going through one of the most important and critical periods of its development. It is well known to you that our enemies, the Western imperialists, are waiting for a favorable chance to send their armies against us. In addition to these external enemies we now have dangerous internal foes—disruption, chaos, and disorganization, made worse by the bourgeoisie in general but especially by the petty bourgeoisie with their various hirelings and flunkies. You know, Comrades, that from the terrible war into which we were led by the tsarist régime and the compromisers, headed by Kerensky, we inherited nothing but disorganization and extreme devastation. We are now in a most critical situation, when famine and unemployment are knocking at the doors of an ever increasing number of workers, when hundreds and thousands of people are feeling the pangs of hunger. The lack of bread at a time when it can be had makes the situation even worse. We know that a proper distribution depends on orderly transportation. Shortage of fuel, resulting from the fact that a region rich in fuel has been taken away from us, and the breakdown of the railways, threatened by a complete stoppage, are the factors which create difficulties for the revolution and fill with joy the hearts of the Kornilovists of various colors. They are scheming daily, and possibly hourly, to take advantage of the difficulties besetting the Soviet Republic and the proletarian government and to put a Kornilov into power. They are still quarreling as to the nationality of this Kornilov but [agree] that he must help the bourgeoisie, no matter whether that Kornilov wears a crown on his head or sits in a presidential chair. By this time the workers fully realize all this and they will not be surprised at it after what the Russian Revolution had to go through since the fall of Kerensky. But the strength of . . . the workers' revolution consists in the ability to keep an open eye and face the facts as they are. We maintain that the war is threatening by its dimensions and the unprecedented suffering to submerge European culture. The only way to salvation is to transfer authority to the hands of the workers for the purpose of organizing an iron rule. After 1905, because of the development of the Russian Revolution and the peculiar historical situation, our Russian proletariat found itself for a certain time far ahead of the other international armies of the proletariat. Just now, we are passing through a period when revolution is ripening in all Western-European countries, when the armies of German workers are beginning to realize the helplessness of their position. We know that there in the West the toilers are being opposed not by the rotten régime of the Romanovs nor by the empty braggarts [moderate socialists], but by the organized bourgeoisie equipped with the most up-to-date technique and culture. That is why it was so easy for us to start the revolution but so difficult to carry it on, and why in the West it is so difficult to start the revolution although it will be easy to carry it on. Our difficulty arises from the fact that everything has to be done by the efforts of the Russian proletariat alone, which must hold its posts until the time when our ally, the international proletariat, becomes strong. We feel as time goes on that there is no other way out. It is our lot to bear the brunt of the burden because, in addition to the fact that we have no outside help, we are facing a ruined transport and a food shortage. This situation should be made clear to everyone. I trust that the Congress of Commissars of Labor, which, more than anyone else, is in direct contact with the workers, . . . will not only serve as a stepping-stone to the immediate improvement of the system of labor which we must place at the foundation of socialism but will also undertake to clarify the minds of the workers as to the significance of the present situation. The working class is engaged in carrying out a very difficult but noble task, on the performance of which depends the fate of socialism in Russia and perhaps in other countries as well. That is why the resolution on labor discipline is so important. Now that power is held firmly by the workers, the future depends entirely on proletarian discipline and proletarian organization. It is a question of discipline and of the dictatorship of the proletariat, a question of establishing an iron rule. A government which meets with the warmest sympathy and the most active support of the poor, such a government must have an iron hand, because unheard-of calamities are ahead of us. . . .

Of considerable importance in the development of Bolshevik economic policy during the early summer of 1918 was the First All-Russian Congress of Councils of National

Economy, which met at Moscow from May 25 to June 4. The discussions at this congress showed that the indecision and hesitancy characteristic of Soviet economic policy during April and May had largely been superseded by a determination to continue the policy of "expropriating the expropriators" which had been initiated during the early months of the revolution. There was still a disagreement between the Right and Left Communists with respect to the tempo that expropriation should take, but both groups approved of nationalization as a policy making for the complete elimination of the bourgeoisie from economic power and the transference of that power to the proletariat.

RUSSIA'S ECONOMIC CONDITION AND BOLSHEVIK ECONOMIC POLICY

[From Radek's Speech at the First All-Russian Congress of Councils of National Economy] [13]

. . . I am not going to give you . . . all the statistical data [relating to the Treaty of Brest-Litovsk]; these are familiar to you from the newspapers. Nor am I going to remind you of the extent of Russia's losses resulting from the surrender of Poland, Lithuania, the Baltic region, the Ukraine, and, for the time being at least, of the Donetz Basin.

You know very well what this means. It means a loss of 40 per cent of our industrial proletariat and a similar decline in the productivity of our industries. It means the loss of important sources of raw materials such as the Donetz Basin, which formerly supplied us with iron and coal. You fully understand what a decline of 90 per cent in beet-sugar production . . . and the surrender of regions from which surplus grain was received . . . [will mean to the country]. Russia's territorial losses are very great, and her losses in productive capacity colossal. . . . In the case of raw materials, especially pig iron and steel, the loss is as high as 70 per cent. This means a shortage of the industrial products

[13] *Trudy I Vserossiiskago Sezda Sovetov Narodnago Khoziaistva. Steno-grafìcheskii otchet*, p. 15.

upon which . . . the economic organism of every nation rests and without which a socialist form of economy is impossible of realization.

Nor . . . is the Brest Treaty merely a precisely worded document which once and for all defines [political] relationships. . . . [The situation] created by the Treaty threatens us with additional . . . and very serious economic losses. . . . In the Caucasus . . . it menaces our oil supplies . . . , and in the East it has served as a pretext for some of our former allies to seize . . . Russian territory which plays a very important part in Russia's economic recovery. . . .

[Miliutin's Report to the First All-Russian Congress of Councils of National Economy, May 28, 1918] [14]

Comrades! To form a clear idea of the economic policy which we intend to introduce in the near future we must study . . . the present economic condition of the country. The present economic situation cannot be studied apart from the historical period of the last few years. When people say and show that the present situation in Russia is difficult they forget the economic position of the country before the November Revolution, they forget the legacy which was left on our hands. It is necessary to remember that before the November Revolution, i. e., as early as 1915-1916 and during the whole of 1917, both individual economists and public congresses considered the economic situation exceedingly difficult; they actually believed that this situation was rapidly leading the country to an economic collapse. The inevitability of a highly serious economic crisis was apparent to everyone. . . . What is more, even people who were not in our camp, i. e., those who stood at the helm and were therefore inclined to view the situation in a more optimistic light, believed that the condition of the country . . . was desperate. I could cite a number of opinions to this effect. . . . After six months of activity, we must state that if we had not seized power conditions would have been terrible. As it is, the situation has been saved by the fact that we undertook the work [of reconstruction].

To be sure, the situation is not satisfactory in every respect . . . ,

[14] *Ibid.*, pp. 47-52.

but this is due solely to the fact that our machinery of government is not adequately organized. Let me give you an account . . . of the resources in our possession. . . .

The harvest of 1917 yielded 3,503 million puds of grain. . . . The Ukraine can give us approximately 516 million puds. The Ukraine had surpluses of grain with which it supplied Russia. It is quite true that under no circumstances are we in a position to obtain these surpluses now, but, apart from the Ukraine, other regions of Soviet Russia also had grain surpluses. These surpluses in Soviet Russia were considerable during the years of 1917-1918: there were 261 million puds of grain in the Northern Caucasus, 52 million puds of grain in Siberia. Moreover, old supplies of grain, amounting to 132 million puds, were left from previous years in Samara, Ufa, and Tomsk gubernias. Thus we see that we are actually in possession of grain surpluses. If we take the list of orders of grain for the next six months (i. e., until the new harvest), and compare them with all our grain resources, even supposing that half of the grain had already been consumed . . . we may still say that we shall have sufficient supplies until the next harvest. Though we know of a number of cities and gubernias which at present are actually starving, for example, Petrograd and Moscow, we believe that this is due mainly to lack of organization and not to the fact that we have no surpluses of grain. . . . Soviet Russia has bread until the next harvest, but the organization of our food supply must be improved. I shall now pass to the fuel question.

At first glance our fuel situation seems exceedingly bad. But a more detailed analysis will lead us to draw somewhat different conclusions. At the preceding . . . session, Comrade Lomov said that with the loss of the South and the Donetz region we were actually deprived of 90 per cent of our fuel. . . . I may say that those who make such statements are very seriously mistaken; they overlook the fact that the South was also an important *consumer of fuel.* . . . The loss which we suffer from the separation of the Ukraine amounts, as far as fuel is concerned, to about 300-350 million puds of coal. Soviet Russia can obtain her own coal from Moscow, the Urals, and Western Siberia. . . . In our negotiations with the Ukraine we must insist that it deliver to us a minimum of 300 million puds of coal. . . .

Our oil production is about 600 million puds. At present . . . we need about 150 million puds of oil for the railways, 400-450 million puds for export. The Caucasus is using 150 million puds. . . . Thus far we have shipped 14 million puds out of the 18 millions stored in Astrakhan. We have yet to ship from the Caucasus the enormous quantity of 400 million puds of oil.

Soviet Russian railroads use about a million cubic sazhens [15] of firewood annually. Because of the shortage of coal it will be necessary to provide about two million cubic sazhens. If we include the needs of industry five million cubic sazhens will be required.

Thus we can see that as far as fuel is concerned our position is not absolutely hopeless. . . .

Now about our metallurgy.

Here too we are given a hopeless picture when we are told that 70 per cent of our metal is lost to us with the separation of the South. . . . Once more a most serious error is made. There is left out of account not only the consumption of the Ukraine, as was the case in regard to fuel, but also the changed character of production. Before the November Revolution more than 50 per cent of our metal was used for non-productive purposes (i. e., for war-time needs) ; . . . thus when we are told that the total production of steel and iron is 265 million puds a year, of which 160 millions are supplied annually by the South, and that only 100 million puds are produced within Soviet Russia, and further that with the loss of the South only 35 per cent is left to us, it is apparently altogether forgotten that the South itself consumed about 35 per cent of our iron and steel, and that of the remaining supplies left for Central Russia more than 50 per cent, or even 60 per cent, was used by the Ministry of War. Only 30 to 35 per cent was used for the country's productive needs. . . . My conclusion is that we shall be able to satisfy our requirements in iron and steel. The same conclusions must be drawn in regard to cast iron. . . .

Such is the present situation. These data force me to the belief that people who say that the system which we have adopted does not work and that the rule of the proletariat has been established too soon are making a colossal mistake.

If we could turn back the wheel of history and return to past

[15] A cubic sazhen is 2.68 cords.

conditions economic ruin would be inevitable; even with the resources of the South our existence would have been impossible.
The capitalist system, the imperialist war, the unproductive use
of fuel, cast iron, steel, etc., would have brought about the economic collapse and complete distintegration of the country. These
data convince me that the productive and consumptive needs of
the country can be satisfied only by a system which uses all the
resources of the land for such needs. Only the socialist system
can save the country from ruin. . . . The road which we have
chosen is not an artificial one but a road to which we were brought
by objective economic conditions. In this respect the introduction
of socialism in Russia is not a utopia, not an abstraction, but a
necessity dictated by the iron conditions of life, their logic, and
the correlations of forces which have come into existence in the
country. . . .

*Hence this is my first conclusion: The basis on which our eco-
nomic policy must be built is the rule of the proletariat. Considering fully the objective economic situation of the country,
the proletariat must carry on the policy of consolidating further
the socialist order, which alone can lead the country on the path
of healthy economic life.*

I believe that after the war a return in capitalist countries to
the old economic structure will be impossible. . . . We cannot
predict now how soon the socialist revolution will take place in
the West. . . . It is not easy to destroy the powerful capitalist
system of Western Europe, but the very fact that the end of the
war is not in sight signifies that the destructive tendencies of
Western capitalism have penetrated deeply . . . and that the
overthrow of this system is inevitable. . . . The existing situation in Russia demands that temporarily and until the socialist
revolution takes place on a world scale there be a certain shifting
of our industrial centers . . . farther east, to the Urals and
Western Siberia. . . . Thus, if we summarize our economic situation and the prospects of our economic development, we may
say that in spite of great difficulties we have reason to look ahead
with courage, provided we have a definite system of government.
. . .

[In the remainder of his speech Miliutin outlined a program of
economic reconstruction which, in accordance with prevailing cus-

tom, was summed up in a number of "theses." These "theses," quoted below, pp. 396-97, were adopted by the Congress in the form of a resolution.]

[Obolensky's Report to the First All-Russian Congress of Councils of National Economy, May 28, 1918] [16]

Comrades! I do not entirely agree with Comrade Miliutin's opinion of the economic condition of the country. . . . I find that Comrade Miliutin is painting the condition in very optimistic colors. . . . He believes that everything will turn out well provided we adopt a definite plan of demobilization and economic organization. The separation of the Ukraine he views under the aspect of historical necessity . . . , *sub specie aeternitatis*. Of course, it is possible to maintain that if a man has one leg amputated it is *inevitable* that he walk on one leg. But I do not believe that it is possible to walk on one leg. On one leg a man must jump and jump very badly. I do not, therefore, share Miliutin's point of view. . . . I see the present economic condition of the country in an altogether different light. . . . Our material productive forces have reached a stage where the economic system is beginning to wither away. . . . The workers are exhausted from constant starvation. . . . The loss of the Ukraine has divided our economic system into two separate . . . regions. . . .

It is impossible for me to enter into a detailed polemic against Comrade Miliutin, who so optimistically sweeps aside these alarming phenomena. . . . I should like, however, to pause to consider what was said concerning our bread supply. Comrade Miliutin . . . counted the Northern Caucasus among our sources of supply. Hardly any optimist will maintain that we shall succeed in keeping the Northern Caucasus. If we omit the Northern Caucasus . . . we shall have a shortage of five million puds. . . . The bread available has to be shipped from one place to another, and a third of our locomotives are disabled. . . . If we look at the question in this way we see that we have a catastrophic shortage of food. . . . [Obolensky then proceeded to other questions of fuel, metal, etc., to show that Miliutin's calculations were not sound.]

[16] *Trudy I Vserossiiskago Sezda Sovetov Narodnago Khoziaistva*, pp. 56-64.

. . . To reestablish normal productivity it is not enough to proceed along socialist principles. Our industrial machine is so shattered that . . . nothing short of energetic intervention can salvage it. I do not mean that this has to be a foreign capitalist intervention. . . . The only method of reestablishing the productive forces of our country and of the world as a whole is to stop the World War . . . , to overthrow the power of finance-capital in all countries and then, with the energetic international intervention of the world proletariat, to heal the wounds inflicted by the war. . . . But what are we to do . . . before this international intervention makes it possible for us to heal the wounds in our economic body? . . . It is clear that we must transfer the center of our activities to the regions which have remained intact . . . —the Urals, the Kuznetsk Basin, etc. . . . We must refrain from hasty investments and bold schemes which promise much for the future but can yield nothing at present.

All the electrification projects which can yield results only in four years, provided we can get turbines . . . , should be severely criticized. . . . Preference should be given to those industries . . . which are capable of drawing food and money out of the village. . . . An account should be made of all the basic means of production and a state monopoly declared on them. . . . This brings me to a number of radical socialist proposals. We need absolute public control over all means of production, not only over raw materials but also over machinery which uses raw materials. . . . This implies complete nationalization of industry, which should be carried into effect as soon as possible and on a wide and well-planned basis. . . .

When I put the problem in this way, I shall be told that really Comrade Miliutin and I do not differ. I advocate nationalization and he proposed nationalization. But I should like to insist that there is a difference. . . .

Comrade Miliutin's report of today grew out of a long argument on economic policy carried on among responsible workers of the Supreme Council of National Economy. The argument evolved in the following stages. In the first stage, those holding the ideas which Comrade Miliutin was developing maintained that "socialism should be built under the leadership of trust organizers," and what they advocated was something different from nationalization. Their socialism, modeled after Morgan-Rockefeller, was to take the form of the ownership of half of the shares of the nationalized enterprises by the state and of half by finance-capitalists. . . . The capitalists were to assume the management of industry, which, in its internal structure, was to have the form of a trust. . . . Other officials of the Soviet Government drastically attacked these ideas, which soon disappeared from discussion.

What is important to notice, however, is that during these arguments and negotiations between the organizers of the trusts and the builders of socialism the process of nationalization slowed down appreciably. . . . Then came the second stage, under the following slogan: "If we should attempt to continue the previous tempo of expropriating capital we would suffer quite certain defeat. Our work of organizing proletarian accounting and control . . . is lagging behind the work of expropriating the expropriators. . . . We shall assume only the task of accounting and control, while the capitalists will manage the industries which have not been nationalized. This we shall call *state capitalism."* [17] During this period nationalization was at a standstill. . . . Now we are entering the third stage . . . , which I would call the *resumption* of nationalization. . . . [He then criticized Miliutin's plan of nationalization as being too cautious and slow.] I am quite ready to accept Comrade Miliutin's formula on condition that we state clearly that what we need is a rapid and energetic nationalization of the basic branches of industry and provided that this nationalization is a transition to socialism. . . .

[Lozovsky's Speech at the First All-Russian Congress of Soviets of National Economy, May 28, 1918] [18]

The two reports which we have just heard gave us a general picture of the economic condition of Russia, although the speakers differed in their estimates of this condition and in their conclusions. On the one hand, we have an optimist, Comrade Miliutin, who wished to prove by figures that the situation is not as bad as many people are inclined to think. I must say that the figures

[17] The reference here is to Lenin's theses of April 4, 1918, cited in *The Bolshevik Revolution*, pp. 553-60.
[18] *Trudy I Vserossiiskago Sezda Sovetov Narodnago Khoziaistva*, pp. 76-78.

presented by Comrade Miliutin revealed a lack of careful investigation. . . .

Comrade Obolensky has given us a more realistic picture of the situation, and while Comrade Miliutin drew pessimistic conclusions from his optimistic estimate, Comrade Obolensky, on the other hand, while drawing a pessimistic picture of the situation . . . , wound up by advocating . . . the immediate socialization and general nationalization of industry. . . . What are the suggestions of both of these speakers? Comrade Miliutin. recommends the nationalization of the basic branches of industry, and, having behind him the experience of six months of exceedingly unsuccessful partial nationalization, tells us quite reasonably . . . that nationalization must be carried out carefully, gradually, and without hurry. Comrade Obolensky, on the other hand, . . . advocated a policy of universal mass nationalization. . . . Comrade Obolensky . . . did not mention the name of the author who wrote about state capitalism and said that we have expropriated and nationalized so many enterprises that we do not know what to do with them. He ought to have said that these were the words of Comrade Lenin, who has given us in his articles . . . a number of very practical considerations showing that sudden and universal nationalization will not strengthen our economic organism but, on the contrary, will weaken the results already achieved. That is why . . . I agree with Comrade Miliutin's conclusion rather than with that of Comrade Obolensky. . . . Comrade Obolensky, as head of the [Supreme] Council of National Economy, has applied broadly this principle of sudden and universal nationalization. I should like to ask Comrade Obolensky what the results of his activity were? Perhaps he can teach us something from his own experience. . . . Comrade Obolensky has apparently forgotten the experience with Vikzhedor, . . . Kavomar [the Kama-Volga-Mariinsk water system], etc., . . . when the administration of the enterprises was transferred to trade unions on the assumption that we must go full speed through socialization to socialism. But those were abstract dreams which are being shattered by hard realities. . . . The fact that the principle of centralization is now being applied . . . is good reason why we should reexamine our views on the transfer of the administration to factory-shop committees and trade unions. Therein, perhaps, lies the fundamental error of your policy. . . .

RESOLUTION OF THE FIRST ALL-RUSSIAN CONGRESS OF
COUNCILS OF NATIONAL ECONOMY [19]

[June 3, 1918]

1. Our economic policy, the basic aim of which is to over-throw the bourgeois and landowning classes and to transfer power to the proletariat, is at present directed toward the establishment of a socialist order in Russia and the struggle against the aggression of international imperialism. All our measures in transition to socialism are influenced by the bitter fight which we must wage against the bourgeoisie inside and outside of Russia.

2. The conditions of Russia's economic development are determined, on the one hand, by the change in its boundaries in consequence of the Brest-Litovsk Treaty, and, on the other hand, by the change in its mode of production.

3. The most important consequence of the Brest-Litovsk Treaty is the separation [from Russia] of the Ukraine and Poland, a separation which changes in a vital way the industrial development of the rest of Russia. This separation has deprived Russian industry of a considerable part of its fuel supply (70 per cent of its coal)—a circumstance which makes it necessary to shift the main centers of industry to the coal mines of the Urals and Siberia and to hasten the development of the productive forces in those regions.

4. The change of production [from a war to a peace-time basis] is certain to improve the economic situation in spite of the utter financial exhaustion, the disorganization of transport, the decrease in the productivity of labor, etc. . . . The closing of factories and shops and the increase of unemployment are due chiefly to the transition from war to peace-time production and from a capitalist to a socialist economy. As the new order becomes more firmly established . . . [it] is bound to result in an increase of production.

5. The present economic situation after seven months of Soviet rule necessitates a continuation of the policy. . . . which liquidated the landowning class in the village and removed the bourgeoisie from control of the economic life of the country.

[19] *Narodnoe Khoziaistvo,* No. 4, 1918, p. 16.

6. As far as the organization of production is concerned, nationalization must be completed by passing from a [sporadic] nationalization of separate enterprises . . . to a systematic nationalization of whole branches of industry, and first to the nationalization of the metal, engineering, chemical, oil, and textile industries. The policy of nationalization must be divested of its haphazard character and come either from the Supreme Council of National Economy alone or from the Soviet of People's Commissars with the approval of the former.

7. The development of the productive forces of the country necessitates the establishment of production standards for individual workers and plants; the correlation of wage scales with production standards; strict labor discipline, enforced by the workers themselves; the introduction of compulsory labor . . . ; the mobilization of technical . . . specialists; [and] an organized redistribution of labor in accordance with shifting of the regions and centers of industry.

8. As far as the organization of exchange and distribution [of commodities] is concerned, the whole apparatus of trade must be centralized in the hands of the state and the cooperative societies by gradually eliminating all private trade. The [government] monopoly in goods of general consumption makes it necessary to adopt the system of exchange in kind . . . and of fixed prices. . . .

9. The village should be amply supplied with agricultural machinery, manufactured goods, and fertilizers. The work of amelioration should be undertaken on a large scale, and a regular exchange of goods between city and village should be established.

10. In the domain of finance the nationalization of banks must be completed . . . , a system of current accounts . . . for the entire population established . . . , and a comprehensive system of bookkeeping introduced for all nationalized enterprises.

NATIONALIZATION OF LARGE-SCALE INDUSTRY
[Decree of the Sovnarkom, June 28, 1918] [20]

For the purpose of combating decisively the economic disorganization and the breakdown of the food supply, and of establishing more firmly the dictatorship of the working class and the village poor, the Soviet of People's Commissars has resolved:

[20] S. U. R., No. 47, 1918, pp. 566-70.

I. To declare all of the following industrial and commercial enterprises which are located in the Soviet Republic, with all their capital and property, whatever they may consist of, the property of the Russian Socialist Federated Soviet Republic.

[At this point there is given a long list of the most important mines, mills, factories, etc.]

II. The administration of the nationalized industries shall be organized . . . by the different departments of the Supreme Council of National Ecomony. . . . All previous decrees issued on the subject of nationalization remain in force. . . .

III. Until the Supreme Council of National Economy issues special rulings for each enterprise, the enterprises which have been declared the property of the R. S. F. S. R. by this decree shall be considered as leased rent-free to their former owners; the boards of directors and the former owners shall continue to finance the enterprises . . . and also to receive the income from them. . . .

IV. Beginning with the promulgation of this decree, the members of the administration, the directors, and other responsible officers of the nationalized industries will be held responsible to the Soviet Republic both for the intactness and upkeep of the business and for its proper functioning. Those who leave their posts without the permission of the . . . Supreme Council of National Econmy, or are found guilty of negligence in the management of the business, are liable both civilly and criminally to the Republic.

V. The entire personnel of every enterprise—technicians, workers, members of the board of directors, and foremen—shall be considered employees of the Russian Socialist Federated Soviet Republic; their wages shall be fixed in accordance with the scales existing at the time of nationalization and shall be paid out of the funds of the respective enterprises. Those who leave their posts . . . are liable to the Revoluntary Tribunal and to the full penalty of the law.

VI. All private capital belonging to members of the boards of directors, stockholders, and owners of the nationalized enterprises will be attached pending the determination of the relation of such capital to the turnover capital and resources of the enterprises in question.

VII. All boards of directors of the nationalized enterprises must prepare at once a financial statement of their respective businesses as of July 1, 1918.

VIII. The Supreme Council of National Economy is authorized to formulate at once and send to all nationalized plants detailed instructions on the organization of management and the problems of labor organization connected with the carrying out of the present decree.

IX. Enterprises belonging to consumers' cooperative societies . . . are not to be nationalized.

X. The present decree becomes effective on the day it is signed.

V. ULIANOV (LENIN)
President of the Soviet of
People's Commissars

TSIURUPA, NOGIN, RYKOV
People's Commissars

THE SIGNIFICANCE OF NATIONALIZATION

[From an Article by V. Molotov] [21]

The "expropriation of the expropriators" about which Marx wrote is in reality occurring less simply and gradually than those who call themselves . . . followers of Marx thought it would occur. The entire development of the socialist revolution, which is taking place in Russia for the first time, has assumed forms and a general aspect far removed from those which the majority of socialists pictured to themselves. The economic revolution in particular has brought forth much that was new and unexpected from the point of view of previously held ideas.

"The hour of capitalist property has struck. The expropriators are expropriated." In these dramatically brief and forceful words Marx characterizes the principal moment of the socialist revolution. More than nine months have elapsed since the beginning of the socialist revolution in Russia, and yet the "hour" has not yet struck for all the property of the capitalists. Furthermore, it is difficult to predict how long it will take to expropriate the expro-

[21] *Novyi Put,* No. 3, August 1, 1918, pp. 3-5. The *Novyi Put* was the official organ of the Council of National Economy of the Northern Region.

priators and to transfer completely all means of production to the
hands of the socialist society.

This process started in the very first days after the November
Revolution. . . . But it followed neither a definite system nor an
approximate plan; . . . it affected in the majority of cases separate, large enterprises, and was of punitive character . . . with
respect to failures to accept workers' control, opposition to the
new Soviet Government, sabotage, etc.

It is also necessary to bear in mind that orders for the nationalization of industry came not only from the central government
but also from local authorities, even workers' organizations. All
this cannot, of course, be termed "nationalization" in a legal sense;
but, de facto, in all such cases the owners were deprived of their
possessions and new administrations were appointed to take complete charge of their properties. The central government found
out about these [nationalizations] only after some time and quite
often accidentally; even now many of these are still unknown. . . .
Thus it is difficult to give a rough estimate of the extent to which
industry was nationalized. . . .[22]

Gradually the principle of nationalizing whole branches of industry in which the state had a special interest came to the fore.
In this way there were nationalized water transport, the sugar
industry, oil. . . .

Finally, . . . on June 28, there was published the decree nationalizing the great majority of larger enterprises. . . . According
to the information of the Society of Factory and Shop Owners
(see *Torgovo-Promyshlennaia Gazeta,* July 8 of this year) this
decree affects 1100 joint-stock companies with a capital of over
three billion rubles (according to estimates of 1914-1915 and
partly of 1916), excluding the previously nationalized enterprises
and private railroads.

The distribution according to separate branches is as follows:

---

[22] The computations of T. Weinberg, an official of the Supreme Council of
National Economy, show that up to June 1, 1918, 513 industrial enterprises were
confiscated, nationalized, or sequestrated. Of these, only 100 were confiscated
by the central authorities, and the rest by local soviets. *Narodnoe Khoziaistvo,*
No. 4, 1918, pp. 45-46. See also V. P. Miliutin's report, quoted in *The Bolshevik
Revolution,* p. 613.

Branches of Industry	Number of Enterprises	Capital (in millions)
Metal	215	1,100
Textile	311	779
Mineral fuel	99	253
Mines	57	205
Electricity	40	135
Cement	40	82
Wood-carving	69	66
Rubber	5	54
Flour mills (steam)	48	65

The importance of the decree will be found in its legal implications. It puts an end to all transfers of property rights and especially to the artificial transfer of enterprises to privileged foreigners. . . .

So far the decree is primarily of legal significance. But essentially . . . it is the most important . . . step in the direction of "expropriating the expropriators" . . . , and Russian industry can be considered as having passed into the hands of the state. . . .

STRIKERS DECLARED ENEMIES OF LABOR

[Resolution of the Joint Conference of Factory-Shop Committees and Trade Unions, July 1, 1918] [23]

The decree of the Soviet of People's Commissars of June 28 transferred all large-scale factories and shops, all organized productive forces of the country, to the disposal and management of the R. S. F. S. R.

From now on, the organized forces of the working class—the trade unions—must shoulder a new, large, and important task. Under the guidance of the Supreme Council of National Economy they must establish new organs to administer industry in conformity with the principles formulated by the All-Russian Congress of Councils of National Economy. The general introduction of labor discipline, supervised by the new administrations, will enable the workers to raise the productive forces of the country and by their concentrated efforts to end economic disorganization.

[23] *Professionalnyi Vestnik*, Nos. 11-12, 1918, p. 15. This resolution was adopted in connection with the strike movement among railway workers. See pp. — above.

14

Under these conditions any stoppage of work, any strike, amounts to a betrayal of the proletarian cause. Those instigating a strike do the work of the enemies of the proletarian revolution, assist capital in its fight to regain power, and inevitably help to increase starvation and disorganization.

The joint session of representatives of Factory-Shop Committees of Moscow, Trade Unions, and the Moscow Soviet of Workers' and Red Army Deputies hereby proclaims that all those who under existing circumstances interrupt the work of enterprises are enemies of the labor movement and are to be handed over to the court of the international proletariat.

The time has arrived when the working class has a right to expect from workers in every enterprise and every trade the ability to subordinate, in the name of the common proletarian cause, their group interests to the interests of the working class as a whole. At the same time, the joint session declares in the name of the working class and its central organizations that the interests of [separate] groups of workers, including those of railwaymen, will be protected in every possible way.

The counter-revolution will not stop short of any violence or provocation in order to bring about a paralysis of the railways. . . . In this case, as in all others, the counter-revolution uses the Mensheviks and Right Socialist-Revolutionists.

The working class and the railway workers should put an end to every provocation aiming to bring about strikes on the railways or in other branches of industry.

Hail the Soviet Government!

Hail the International Proletarian Revolution!

SOCIAL INSURANCE

[Decree of the Sovnarkom, August 7, 1918] [24]

1. After it has been nationalized and sequestrated every enterprise is to continue payment of the amounts which it owes for social insurance.

2. In preparing estimates for the operation of the individual nationalized enterprises the Supreme Council of National Econ-

---

[24] *Biulleten otdela sotsialnago strakhovaniia i okhrany truda*, Nos. 2-3, 1918, pp. 38-39.

omy, as well as the regional and provincial councils, shall include in the estimates [the following]:

(a) The amount due to the hospital insurance fund . . . at the rate of 10 per cent of the total wage paid to workers and office employees of the enterprises; (b) the amount due to the unemployment insurance fund at the rate of 4 per cent of the total wage paid to regular workers and employees and 6 per cent of that to seasonal [workers]; (c) the amount due to ,the accident insurance fund at the rate . . . determined by local insurance companies. . . .

3. Since employees and workers in government institutions and enterprises are covered by [the law of] compulsory insurance . . . , all government institutions and enterprises shall include in their estimates of expenditure items a, b, and c of Article 2 of this decree. . . .

Note: The formation of special insurance funds for individual trade-union groups of workers is forbidden.

4. Private enterprises and individual employers must pay all amounts due to the [general] insurance funds. . . .

8. Interest-bearing securities owned by workers, insurance funds, and such insurance partnerships as are reorganized on the basis of complete [workers'] self-rule are not subject to annulment in accordance with the decree of January 21, 1918, provided these securities were bought prior to the promulgation of this decree.

V. Ulianov (Lenin)
President of the Sovnarkom

A. Rykov
Chairman of the Supreme Council
of National Economy

P. Stuchka
People's Commissar of Justice

From the Communist standpoint one of the most glaring defects of capitalist economy is the existence of a number of uncoordinated and competitive units of production and distribution giving rise to economic chaos and wastefulness.

To overcome that defect Communists advocated the establishment of a logically planned and balanced system of production and distribution. With this in view the Bolsheviks created during the early months of the revolution a Supreme Council of National Economy, which was given the broad function of framing "general standards and plans for the regulation of the economic life of the country," together with the correspondingly broad power "to confiscate, requisition, sequestrate, and consolidate various branches of industry, commerce, and other enterprises in the fields of production, distribution, and state finance." [25]

During the first eight months of its existence the Supreme Council of National Economy exercised very little influence on the economic development of the country and was concerned mainly with problems of its own organization. The original division of the Council into departments in charge of a number of related branches of the national economy was gradually replaced by committees (called glavki) which had a more restricted scope and controlled single branches of production.

After large-scale industry had been nationalized by the decree of June 28, the Supreme Council of National Economy was concerned chiefly with organizing the administration of the nationalized industries. Although the decree of August 8, quoted below, still defined the functions of the Council in broad terms, in practice its activity became considerably narrower and was mainly in the sphere of industrial production and distribution.

[25] See *The Bolshevik Revolution*, p. 314.

THE FUNCTIONS OF THE SUPREME COUNCIL OF NATIONAL ECONOMY

[Decree of the Sovnarkom, August 8, 1918] [26]

1. The Supreme Council of National Economy is the economic section of the Central Executive Committee and is responsible to it as well as to the Soviet of People's Commissars.

2. The Supreme Council of National Economy is to regulate and organize all production and distribution and to manage every enterprise of the Republic.

Note: All decrees and ordinances which the People's Commissariats of Food and Agriculture issued in regard to the distribution of supplies remain in force.

3. All drafts of the state budget must be presented for preliminary consideration to the Supreme Council of National Economy, and after this body has given its decision shall be brought before the Soviet of People's Commissars.

4. The financing of all branches of the national economy shall be undertaken by the Supreme Council of National Economy in cooperation with the Commissariats of Finance and of State Control.

5. To direct—within the limits of the general economic policy of the Sovnarkom and the All-Russian Central Executive Committee—the activities of the Supreme Council of National Economy as well as the regional and local councils of national economy, there is established a plenum of the Supreme Council of National Economy, with the following membership:

a) The All-Russian Central Executive Committee—10.

b) The All-Russian Council of Trade Unions—30.

c) The Regional Councils of National Economy—20.

d) The All-Russian Council of Workers' Cooperatives—2.

e) The People's Commissariat of Food—2.

f) The People's Commissariat of Ways and Communication—1.

g) The People's Commissariat of Labor—1.

h) The People's Commissariat of Agriculture—1.

i) The People's Commissariat of Finance—1.

[26] *Narodnoe Khoziaistvo,* No. 11, 1918, pp. 63-64.

j) The People's Commissariat of Commerce—1.

k) The People's Commissariat of the Interior—1.

Note: The people's commissariats not mentioned above have the right to send their representatives to the meetings of the Plenum of the Supreme Council of National Economy in a consulting capacity only.

6. Members of the Plenum are appointed for six months.

Note: The different commissariats shall be represented by the commissars themselves or by their assistants.

7. The Plenum is to meet not less than once a month.

8. The executive business of the Supreme Council of National Economy shall be entrusted to a Presidium of nine members, of which eight shall be elected by the Plenum and approved by the Soviet of People's Commissars, while the chairman shall be elected by the All-Russian Central Executive Committee and vested with all the rights of a people's commissar.

V. Ulianov (Lenin)
President of the Soviet of
People's Commissars

A. Rykov
Chairman of the Supreme Council
of National Economy ·

TRANSACTIONS BETWEEN NATIONALIZED ENTERPRISES AND SOVIET INSTITUTIONS

[Decree of the Supreme Council of National Economy, August 30, 1918] [27]

In order to simplify and regulate the accounts of nationalized enterprises and Soviet institutions, the Supreme Council of National Economy has resolved:

1. Every nationalized or sequestrated enterprise, including those nationalized by the decree of June 28, 1918 (*S. U. R.* No. 47, 559), must deposit all receipts on their current accounts in the People's Bank, leaving only enough cash for current needs.

2. All nationalized enterprises must consign the products of their industry to the appropriate centers and glavki . . . , re-

[27] *S. U. R.,* No. 63, 1918, p. 770.

ceiving in return . . . all necessary equipment and raw materials. These transactions of consigning and receiving products shall be carried on by means of book entries and without the use of money. If, in case of necessity, products are not consigned or received through the distributing centers, the transactions must be carried on by means of checks on the People's Banks.

3. In like manner, all payments to and from consumers and Soviet organizations and institutions shall be made by book entries.

Until special orders for each industry have been issued by the Supreme Council of National Economy, the industries declared the property of the Russian Republic by the decree of June 28, 1918, are recognized as being in free lease to their former owners. The directors and former owners must finance them as before; thus obligations of every kind accrued by them for the future operation of the enterprises, as well as agreements arising out of commercial transactions, settlement of bills, merchandise loans, etc., must be recognized by these enterprises and be paid from the returns on the property.

A. RYKOV
Chairman of the Supreme Council
of National Economy

THE UNEMPLOYED FORBIDDEN TO REFUSE WORK

[Decree of the Commissar of Labor, September 3, 1918] [28]

1. Provided the conditions of work do not deviate from the scales established by the appropriate trade unions, the unemployed who are registered in employment bureaus have no right to refuse. work in their special occupation.

2. In case of a shortage of manual laborers, employment bureaus have the right, upon the consent of the local trade unions, to put to work the unemployed of some other labor category with the rating of manual laborers. . . .

3. The unemployed have no right to refuse temporary work. If the temporary work is for a period of less than two weeks,

[28] *Ibid.,* No. 64, 1918, p. 783. In the Labor Code of October 31, 1918, this regulation was made applicable to everyone subject to labor duty. See pp. 418-19, below.

the unemployed does not lose his turn on the waiting-list of the employment bureau.

4. Work connected with the harvesting and delivery of food supplies is compulsory for all unemployed regardless of the trade category and must be carried out in accordance with Articles 2 and 5 of this decree.

5. The unemployed have no right to refuse to leave town for work, no matter where it is offered, provided the terms of the work are in accordance with Article 1 of this decree. For such out-of-town work single men are called upon first and married men next.

6. Persons violating Articles 1, 2, 3, and 5 . . . are refused assistance (in money and in kind) for three months . . . and lose their places on the waiting-list. They are to register again as if applying for the first time. Persons violating Article 4 and Articles 1, 2, 3, and 5 a second time lose the right to register again with the employment bureau and are reported to the local civil authorities. . . .

V. NOGIN

Acting People's Commissar of Labor

GOVERNMENT REGULATION OF LABOR AND WAGES

[Resolution of the Central Committee of the all-Russian Union of Metal Workers, October 3, 1918] [29]

Taking into consideration the fact that the decree of June 28 concerning nationalization transferred all large-scale metal industry to the Government of Workers and Peasants, the Central Committee is of the opinion that this transfer marks the beginning of a new wage-scale policy, consisting in a complete break with [the system of] agreements with private capitalists and the inauguration, by the aid of the Soviet Government, of a workers' trade-union policy.

Inasmuch as the dictatorship of the proletariat is a dictatorship of the political and economic organizations of the proletariat, and since in this period only the organized workers are in a position to determine the conditions of work and wages, the Central Committee finds it necessary to organize an all-Russian council for the regulation of labor in the metal industry, consisting of repre-

[29] *Metallist*, No. 7, 1918, p. 6.

sentatives of the Union of Metal Workers and the Supreme Council of National Economy.

LABOR BOOKS FOR NON-WORKERS
[Decree of October 5, 1918] [20]

In order to carry into effect the fundamental principle of the Constitution of the R. S. F. S. R. with respect to universal labor, the Soviet of People's Commissars decrees:

1. To introduce labor books in place of identification cards, passports, etc., for the following classes of citizens:

   a) Persons living on unearned incomes from property or interest on capital.

   b) Persons deriving profits from hired labor.

   c) Directors of stock companies, partnerships, etc. . . .

   d) Merchants, brokers, middlemen.

   e) Persons belonging to the so-called liberal professions, if they do not perform a socially useful function.

   f) Others having no definite occupation, i. e., former officers, graduates of military academies, former attorneys, etc.

2. Local soviets . . . will be in charge of the distribution of labor books. . . .

3. At stated intervals, . . . no less than once a month, notations should be entered in the labor books . . . by duly authorized organs of local soviets to the effect that the holders of such books have performed their share of assigned public work. . . .

4. A labor book is valid only if it bears the monthly notations referred to in Article 3. . . .

5. Non-workers are allowed to travel . . . and to receive food cards . . . only when in possession of labor books. . . .

9. Persons listed in Article 1 who fail to exchange their identification papers for labor books or give false information about themselves . . . are liable to fine up to ten thousand rubles or to imprisonment up to six months.

G. Petrovsky
People's Commissar of the Interior

V. Nogin
Acting People's Commissar of Labor

[20] *S. U. R.*, No. 73, 1918, pp. 893-94.

The plan for the administration of the metallurgical trust, quoted below, was fairly typical of plans adopted in other branches of industry. While accepting complete subordination to the Supreme Council of National Economy in administrative matters, the trade unions insisted on having a majority of their representatives (two-thirds) on the administrative boards. But the Council of National Economy was willing to give the trade unions only a third of the seats in the central administrations. Disagreement on this question was the cause of numerous conflicts between the Supreme Council of National Economy and the trade-union workers, who, as in the case of the tanners' union cited below, wished to build the administration "on the principle of the dictatorship of the proletariat" and demanded an absolute majority in the management of the tanning industry.

ADMINISTRATION OF NATIONALIZED METALLURGICAL
WORKS

[Resolution of the Conference of Metal Workers, October 18, 1918] [31]

CENTRAL ADMINISTRATION

1. At the head of the State Combine of Metallurgical Works [32] is the Central Administration. . . .

2. The Central Administration shall consist of fifteen members, one-third of whom are appointed by the Supreme Council of National Economy . . . and two-thirds of whom are elected by a conference of trade-union workers and employees of the combine, in conformity with the regulations of the All-Russian Union of Metal Workers. The elections must be ratified by the Presidium of the Supreme Council of National Economy.

3. The term of office of the Central Administration is one year. However, the Supreme Council of National Economy shall have

[31] *Metallist,* No. 7, 1918, pp. 15-17.

[32] The combine in question was among the first to organize into one trust all large locomotive and car shops in Russia, and included such works as the Sormovo-Kolomna, Vyksunsky, Kulebaksky, Briansk, Phoenix, Tverskoi, Russko-Baltiisky, Mytishchensky. The combine was known by the name of "Gomza."

the right on particularly important occasions to alter the membership of the Administration, on its own initiative or at the suggestion of the All-Russian Union of Metal Workers.

Note: The Supreme Council of National Economy reserves the right to retain the appointed members of the Central Administration for future terms.

4. The Central Administration shall be directly subordinate to the Metallurgical Section of the Supreme Council of National Economy. It shall be guided in all its acts, measures, and decisions by the existing decrees and laws of the Soviet Republic as well as by the decisions, principles, and ordinances of the Supreme Council of National Economy, and shall be responsible for its conduct of business to the Supreme Council of National Economy

5. The Central Administration is in charge of the enterprise as a whole and is the supreme organ, acting within the limits of the estimates and plans of the Central Government Administration, in matters relating to general administrative, technical, economic, and financial phases of the enterprise. . .

6. The sphere of jurisdiction of the Central Administration comprises the following duties :

(1) To examine the estimates of the Central Administration and those submitted by the separate shop administrations, and to work out a general annual estimate of the enterprise for presentation to the Supreme Council of National Economy.

(2) To frame both a general plan of production and a plan for additional plant construction.

(3) To frame a plan for supplying the enterprise . . . with raw materials, fuel, and [food] products.

(4) To keep accounts of manufactured products, take orders, distribute the manufactured products in accordance with the directions given by the central government, and sell in the market the products which were not included in the plans of distribution. . . .

(8) To increase the productivity of labor and see that the workers, employees, and higher personnel . . . carry out their duties.

(9) To organize [departments of] labor statistics in all branches of production. . . .

(10) To appoint responsible managers of technical, administrative, and commercial sections. . . .

(13) To improve the material and cultural life of workers and office employees. . . .

(14) To furnish the Supreme Council of National Economy with regular reports on the technical and general activities of the enterprise.

7. The Central Administration is to guide, consolidate, and harmonize the activities of the administrations of the different shops, and has the right to veto any decision made by them. . . .

8. The Central Administration has the right to call periodically congresses of representatives of [local] shop administrations. . . .

10. The Central Administration is to select from its membership a Presidium consisting of one chairman and two vice-chairmen. The Presidium sees that the orders of the Central Administration are carried out and represents the Central Administration in its official dealings with the Supreme Council of National Economy and other state institutions. . . .

11. The Presidium calls the meetings of the Central Administration whenever necessary, but not less than once a week. . . .

12. All resolutions of the Central Administration require a majority for passage. . . .

LOCAL ADMINISTRATION

1. A local shop administration is formed in every shop which enters the combine. The number of members, ranging from three to six, is to be determined in every case by the Central Administration in concurrence with the All-Russian Union of Metal Workers. At least one-third of the local administration must be elected by the workers' and employees' trade unions of a shop; and at least one-third must consist of technical and commercial shop-heads appointed by the Central Administration. The membership of the [local] shop administration must be confirmed by the Supreme Council of National Economy.

2. The term of office of a shop administration is one year.

Note: The Central Administration has the right to secure . . . a tenure of office for subsequent terms for its appointed specialists in the shop administrations.

3. The local shop administration is in charge of all business

in the producing unit . . . and is guided by the estimates, plans, and instructions of the Central Administration. The local administration is fully responsible to the Central Administration and must carry out all its orders.

4. In addition to current business the following .duties appertain to [local] shop administrations. . . .

[The ten duties which are set forth follow very closely the points under Article 6 of the instructions relating to the duties of the Central Administration.]

ABOLITION OF WORKERS' CONTROL IN NATIONALIZED MACHINE SHOPS

[Resolution of the Conference of Metal Workers, October 18, 1918] [83]

Having considered the question of the place which the organs of workers' control should occupy in nationalized enterprises, particularly in the State Combine of Metallurgical Works, the Conference hereby resolves:

1. The organization of the administrative bodies of these enterprises guarantees that the representatives of the trade unions of the proletariat and the regulative organs of the state will have a decisive influence in the management of the amalgamated shops; the need for the previously existing special organs of workers' control is thereby removed.

2. In view of this fact workers' control shall cease functioning and its organs shall be dissolved as soon as the administrative organs of the amalgamated shops have been fully established.

CONFLICT BETWEEN THE COMMISSAR OF RAILWAYS AND VIKZHEDOR

[Commissar of Railways to the Sovnarkom] [84]

Kobozev, People's Commissar of Railways, has sent the President of the Sovnarkom and the Chairman of the Central Executive Committee a telegram calling attention to certain misunderstandings which have arisen between the Commissar of Railways and Vikzhedor:

[83] *Metallist,* No. 7, 1918, p. 18.
[84] *Svoboda Rossii,* No. 34, May 25, 1918, p. 2.

" . . . A situation has arisen which might further complicate the already critical condition of the transportation system. According to the statute of Vikzhedor, supreme authority in matters pertaining to railway administration is vested in that institution. On the other hand, according to the laws relating to the administration of the Republic, that authority is delegated by the Central Executive Committee to the Sovnarkom. Having been confirmed in the post of Commissar of Railways by the Central Executive Committee, and bearing full responsibility for the administration of transport before the Sovnarkom and the Central Executive Committee, I am now face to face with all the difficulties which follow from the peculiar interpretation of the division of power contained in the statute of Vikzhedor. . . . Adhering strictly to the Sovnarkom's decree of March 25,[35] I consider it my right to appoint chiefs of divisions . . ., responsible to me. . . . This is likely to provoke undesirable conflicts between myself and Vikzhedor. . . . I therefore urgently request that it be made clear whether this dual system of administration . . . can continue to exist. . . . "

ORGANIZING THE TANNING INDUSTRY

[From the Proceedings of the All-Russian Conference of Tanners, November 13, 1918] [36]

The report of the All-Russian Council of Tanners indicated that the Council had connections with fifty-nine local unions. . . . The main attention of the Council centered on the organization and regulation of the tanning industry. . . . "We made," said the speaker, "many errors, but the comrades who will pass judgment on our actions must not overlook the serious condition of the country in general as well as the fact that the local unions give us no financial support."

The next speaker reported on the activities of the Central Tanning Committee. All tanning goods have been monopolized and are accounted for by the central and regional committees. . . . Production is gradually being organized but the committee is not

[35] This decree ordered the suspension of workers' control over the railroads. See *The Bolshevik Revolution*, pp. 655-56.
[36] *Professionalnyi Vestnik*, Nos. 17-18, 1918, pp. 21-22.

in a position to manufacture more than a limited number of shoes. For every thousand people there will be only 129 pairs of shoes. . . .

The Central Tanning Committee will be the sole provider of shoes; orders for the population will be received from the Commissariat of Supplies, and for the army from the Military-Economic Division of the Red Army. . . .

The productivity of large factories is about 90 per cent of the total production. . . . Local authorities have nationalized about fifty enterprises; about twenty [enterprises] are subject to nationalization in accordance with the decree of June 28. . . .

The Conference proceeded to consider the . . . question of the reorganization of the regulative centers, a question which was decided in the following way:

"All administrative organs of the tanning industry shall be built on the principle of the dictatorship of the proletariat, by giving the workers as represented by their . . . trade unions an absolute majority. By the decree of June 28, 1918, concerning nationalization of industry, representatives of property-owning elements have lost all legal right to manage industry. As regards the representatives of small home industry, it is not advisable to allow their participation in the organs of administration as they are not capable of contributing anything creative and constructive. . . ."

The Conference decided to insist before the Supreme Council of National Economy that two-thirds of the membership of the Central Administration consist of workers of the tanning industry, elected by the All-Russian Conference and responsible to the All-Russian Council of Tanners; and that one-third of the membership go to the Presidium of the Supreme Council of National Economy. . . .

On the question of workers' control the Conference resolved: "To transfer control from the trade unions to the regulative organs of the tanning industry. A control-accounting section shall be established in connection with the Central Committee of the Tanning Industry and placed under the direction of a collegium of three, representing the All-Russian Council of Tanners, the Division of Statistics, and the Technical Division. Similar control sections shall be established in connection with regional committees of tanners. . . ."

CONTROVERSY BETWEEN THE TANNERS' TRADE UNION AND THE SUPREME COUNCIL OF NATIONAL ECONOMY

[Meeting of the Presidium of the All-Russian Trade-Union Council, December 3, 1918] [87]

. . . The representative of the Union of Tanners reported to the meeting on the conflict which took place between the Trade Union of Tanners and the Supreme Council of National Economy.

The Tanners' Section of the Supreme Council of National Economy presented a plan for the organization of a committee in charge of the tanning industry . . . and recommended its administrative representatives. Ratification or non-ratification depends entirely on the Supreme Council of National Economy. In view of the fact that such a procedure reduces the Union to a secondary position, it presented the ultimatum that the Union be allowed two-thirds of the membership of the administration and that those members be elected by the Union.

Comrade Libin pointed out that . . . the Union insisted on its right of recall . . . while the Supreme Council of National Economy proposed that one-third of the members of the administration represent the Union, one-third the scientific-technical personnel, and one-third the Supreme Council of National Economy. In other words, the Council is trying to create an arrangement by virtue of which the Union of Tanners actually ceases to take part in [the regulation of] production.

Comrade Labkovsky insisted that the resolution of the Tanners' Union remain in force. In so far as it reduces the masses [to a secondary position] the Supreme Council of National Economy is becoming a bureaucratic institution. . . .

Comrade Schmidt called attention to the fact that the Supreme Council of National Economy adopted a similar decision with regard to metal workers, textile workers, and others. The trade unions displayed an ambition to dominate the centers which regulate production, thereby manifesting syndicalist tendencies. At first the metal workers also refused to accept the government policy of the Supreme Council of National Economy, but later they sent their representatives. . . . The resolution of the Su-

[87] *Professionalnyi Vestnik*, No. 1, 1919, pp. 34-35.

preme Council of National Economy is correct. The administration of Glavkozha should be responsible to the Supreme Council of National Economy and not to the [trade] unions. . . .

[Resolution of the Trade Union Council:] . . . The question of organizing a section of the Supreme Council of National Economy should be postponed until a plenary session of the All-Russian Council of Trade Unions and of the Supreme Council of National Economy takes place. As regards the resolution of the Congress of Tanners, the Presidium is of the opinion that the resolution . . . is binding only in so far as it does not conflict with the general policy of the proletariat.

RELATIONS BETWEEN TRADE UNIONS AND THE UNION OF STATE EMPLOYEES

[Tomsky's Argument at the Plenary Session of the All-Russian Council of Trade Unions, October 18, 1918] [88]

1. During the first stages of the workers' revolution . . . the liberal professions came out in decisive opposition to the proletariat. With the consolidation of the Soviet power these liberal professions . . . are ready for compromise. . . .

2. The proletariat alone is the active creator of new economic relationships. A whole group of complicated economic problems forces the proletariat, while retaining its hegemony in politics and economics, . . . to lean (sometimes through compromise) on petty-bourgeois circles. . . .

3. The system of individual bargaining with intellectuals and technical specialists failed to produce expected results, and the government . . . is obliged again and again to appeal to collectives . . . and organizations of the middle and petty intelligentsia to take part in state and economic construction under the control and supervision of the proletariat.

4. On the other hand, . . . the intelligentsia . . . aims to substitute collective bargaining . . . for individual compromise, . . . for which purpose it is organizing into unions and is endeavoring as a socio-economic group to find its place in the economic life of the country. . . .

5. Granting the right of association to all toiling elements of

[88] *Ibid.*, Nos. 17-18, 1918, pp. 14-15.

the country, the proletariat . . . cannot withhold such rights from employees . . . at a time when a *rapprochement* with the latter is necessitated by the economic tasks of the working class. . . . [However,] the intensity of the class struggle . . . makes it imperative to place these in-between elements within such limits as will safeguard the proletarian unions against becoming contaminated by the petty-bourgeois ideology characteristic of these groups. . . .

6. . . . [The unions of state employees] may be allowed to enter the family of proletarian unions, provided they are not given an active vote and they agree to accept as binding all resolutions of the leading trade-union organs. . . .

[Lozovsky and Riazanov objected to Tomsky's argument on the ground that it would create a division between sheep and goats, but Tomsky's theses were approved by a majority vote of the Council. (*Ibid.*, p. 19.)]

UNIVERSAL LABOR DUTY
[Decree of the Sovnarkom, October 31, 1918] [39]

1. All citizens of the R. S. F. S. R., with the exception of those specified in Articles 2 and 3, are subject to compulsory labor.

2. The following are exempt from compulsory labor: (*a*) persons under sixteen years of age; (*b*) persons over fifty years of age; (*c*) persons who are incapacitated as a result of injury or illness.

3. The following are temporarily exempted from compulsory labor: (*a*) persons who as a result of illness or injury are temporarily incapacitated, for a period necessary to their recovery; (*b*) pregnant women, for a period of eight weeks before and eight weeks after confinement.

4. Students in all institutions of learning perform compulsory labor at school.

5. Permanent or temporary incapacity must be established by medical examination. . . .

Note 2: Persons subject to compulsory labor and not engaged

[39] *S. U. R.*, Nos. 87-88, 1918, pp. 1099-1100.

in socially useful work may be summoned by local soviets of deputies for public work on conditions determined by the sections of labor in agreement with local trade-union councils.

6. Work takes the form of: (a) organized collaboration; (b) individual services; (c) performance of special services.

7. Conditions of labor in state (Soviet) institutions are regulated by wage-scales approved by the . . . People's Commissariat of Labor.

8. Conditions of labor in all other establishments . . . are regulated by wage-scales established by trade unions in concurrence with the directors or owners of the establishments . . . and with the approval of the People's Commissariat of Labor. . . .

COMMERCIAL AND INDUSTRIAL EMPLOYEES AND THE SOVIET GOVERNMENT

[Proceedings of the All-Russian Conference of Trade Unions of Employees, November 12-15, 1918] [40]

Comrade Tartakovsky: The German Revolution, the intensification of Entente imperialism, and the approaching world revolution—these are the three factors which must force anyone to revise his tactics. A year ago, when in isolated Russia there occurred a revolution which has been justly described as a soldiers' revolution, and when . . . there was inaugurated an economic policy which could be characterized as "home-brewed" socialism, we adopted a certain policy [hostility to the Bolsheviks]. But now, when the great majority of the Russian proletariat follow the Soviet Government, when Russia is no longer isolated, when, on the one hand, the flames of world revolution are spreading, and, on the other, Entente imperialism is trying to strangle the revolution, our attitude toward the Soviet Government should be of a different character.

The speaker then proposed a resolution declaring that, in view of the fact that the Russian and the world revolutions were in great danger from international imperialism, the task of the trade unions was to support actively the policies of the Soviet Government, designed to combat international imperialism and assist the organization of the economic life of the country.

[40] *Professionalnyi Vestnik,* Nos. 17-18, 1918, p. 23.

The second speaker was Comrade Tomsky. . . . The Soviet Government [he said] has been in existence for over a year, and if it had not been a government expressing the will and the hopes of the workers and poorer peasants it would not have lasted so long. We saw this in the example of all the provisional governments. . . . The workers' movement of Western Europe could not and cannot teach us how to build life on socialist principles. The Russian proletariat has achieved greater results in this respect and has facilitated considerably the struggle of the Western proletariat. The Soviet Government has been able to create an army powerful in spirit and equipment.

It is time to give up bookish determinism. There are certain movements which even now cannot become reconciled to the fact that things are not being done in the way described in "clever books." Life has proved the correctness of the Bolshevik prognosis. The bet on world revolution has been justified, and consequently there can be no question for any section of the proletariat as to whom it should follow.

Unconditional support of the Soviet Government is the course for the trade unions because their interests and those of the Soviet Government coincide. . . .

Comrade Aronson . . . pointed out that the German Revolution was no reason why one should give up his views as to the tasks of the working class. The fact that the Soviet Government has lasted a year does not prove its stability. The revolution in Western Europe does not follow the Bolshevik path, and the Soviet Government is therefore doomed.

Comrade Holtzman, supporting in a general way the position of Aronson, said that it was necessary to attract wider circles of the democracy to the business of government. He proposed "to straighten out the line of the Russian Revolution to parallel the front of the German Revolution." . . .

[When the resolution of the Presidium favoring support of the government was put to a vote the Conference divided into two equal parts—one favoring, the other opposing, support.]

Notwithstanding the general tendency of Soviet economic policy toward centralization of management in one institution, no complete unification of control was achieved during the summer and fall of 1918. Alongside the Supreme Council of National Economy there continued to exist the Commissariats of Agriculture, Finance, Trade, Industry, and Ways and Communications, discharging functions similar to those of the Supreme Council of National Economy.

Larin, a thoroughgoing advocate of centralization, urged subordination of the economic commissariats to the Supreme Council of National Economy; but at no time during the entire period of so-called War Communism was the duplication of the functions of the S. C. N. E. by the economic commissariats eliminated.

PROPOSED INCREASE OF THE POWER OF THE SUPREME COUNCIL OF NATIONAL ECONOMY

[Larin's Speech at the Second All-Russian Congress of Councils of National Economy, December 20, 1918] [41]

. . . I should like to call your attention to the external conditions which have affected the national economy of Russia during the past year and are likely to continue. [Russia] is in complete economic isolation . . . , and the existing international situation holds out no promise that relations with foreign markets will soon be reestablished. . . . Even if the Soviets triumph in Germany and the French and English proletariat join the German Revolution, these countries will be as exhausted as we. In order to maintain its power in relation to the outside world an isolated economy . . . must have all its resources . . . concentrated in one agency. . . . During the first year of our work it was impossible to accomplish this. . . . We must create a single economic center, embodied in the Supreme Council of National Economy. . . . When this institution was first conceived . . . it was thought of as . . . the one economic center . . . , as the principal fighting organ of proletarian dictatorship. In reality, however, we have not succeeded in creating a single economic center. What we have instead is an unsystematic division of commissariats which either

[41] *Trudy II Vserossiiskogo Sezda Sovetov Narodnogo Khoziaistva. Stenograficheskii otchet*, pp. 18-20.

pursue independent policies or have no policies at all. . . . It is high time that the Supreme Council of National Economy assume control of the different economic commissariats. . . . Just as in time of war, so now, it is fatal to have forty general staffs each of which is conducting operations on its own risk and responsibility. . . .

During the past year we were able to tolerate this situation because plenty of goods had been left us by the bourgeoisie. We inherited large quantities of metal, cotton, wool, etc., . . . which enabled us to exist this year in spite of the unsystematic character of our work and the absence of any plan. . . . To be sure, we shall continue to exist . . . even if we have to put down more insurrections . . . , but if we are to become a force on which the proletariat of Germany, France, and other countries can rely . . . we must establish a unified economic administration, must subordinate all commissariats to the Supreme Council of National Economy. . . .

PROGRESS OF NATIONALIZATION

[From Rykov's Report to the Second All-Russian Congress of Councils of National Economy, December 21, 1918] [42]

. . . Since the First Congress [of Councils of National Economy] [43] the . . . nationalization of factories, shops, and other enterprises has been very rapid. . . . We have nationalized 1,125 businesses (exclusive of trade establishments), . . . divided as follows: Metal works . . . [343]; fuel, 28; fibrous substances, 83; chemical, 88; paper works, 116; mineral, 113; food, 138; animal products, 55; printing, 52; miscellaneous, 47.

During the past six months nationalization has usually been accompanied by the consolidation of the various branches of industry into . . . separate trusts with central administrations for every large enterprise. . . . Our aim is to raise the productivity of labor, to improve the supply of raw materials . . . for the [nationalized] enterprises, and to introduce production standards. . . .

[42] *Izvestiia*, No. 281, December 22, 1918, p. 2.
[43] May 25-June 4, 1918.

ORGANIZATION OF CREDIT [44]

. . . Recently the People's Commissar of Finance presented to . . . the Soviet of People's Commissars a number of theses on the function of the People's Bank . . . during the transition period.

According to his project, the People's Bank of the R. S. F. S. R. is to be the sole credit . . . institution of the Republic. It is to finance . . . all nationalized enterprises, the operations of the Commissar of Food . . . , foreign trade, railway construction, agriculture . . . , and is to supply credit to enterprises not yet nationalized and to cooperative societies. . . .

The Sovnarkom discussed mainly the theses concerning the financing of nationalized enterprises. . . . The People's Bank is to establish a special account for nationalized industry. The money in this account is to be appropriated . . . by the Soviet of People's Commissars and distributed by the Supreme Council of National Economy among the different centers and glavki, which allocate it to the different enterprises. . . .

The People's Bank is to enter in its books all manufactured products of nationalized enterprises. . . . The theses of the People's Commissar of Finance were accepted as a basis for the reorganization of the People's Bank.

Further attacks on the institution of private property came with the promulgation in the spring and summer of 1918 of the decrees abolishing the right of inheritance and of owning real estate.

ABOLITION OF INHERITANCE

[Decree of the Central Executive Committee, April 27, 1918] [45]

I

Inheritance by law or testament is hereby abolished. After the death of the owner, his property (personal and real) becomes the property of the Russian Socialist Federated Soviet Republic.

Note: All questions relating to the transfer and use of agri-

[44] *Izvestiia*, No. 288, December 31, 1918, p. 2.
[45] *S. U. R.*, No. 34, 1918, pp. 7-9.

cultural lands are determined in accordance with the Fundamental Law of Land Socialization.

II

Pending the promulgation of a decree relating to general social insurance, the needy, i. e., those lacking the necessary living minimum, the disabled relatives (direct and indirect), full-brothers, half-brothers, full-sisters and half-sisters, and the spouse of a decedent receive maintenance from his estate.

Note 1: No distinction is to be made between relationship in wedlock and out of wedlock.

Note 2: Relatives by adoption and their descendants . . . are of the same status as relatives by birth.

III

In case the property left is not sufficient to provide for the maintenance of the spouse and other surviving relatives listed in the preceding article, the neediest are to be provided for first.

IV

The amount of the maintenance due from the property of the deceased to the spouse and the other surviving relatives is determined by an agreement among the persons who have the right to receive maintenance and the institutions in charge of social welfare attached to the gubernia soviets or, in Moscow and Petrograd, the institutions of social welfare attached to the city soviets. . . . In case of dispute the matter is taken to the local court. Cases of this kind are under the jurisdiction of the Soviets of Workers' and Peasants' Deputies and of the local court of the place where the decedent last resided.

V

All the property of the decedent, except that which is listed in Article IX of this decree, is taken over by the soviet of the place where the person resided before his death or where the property in question is located. The soviet turns over this property to the local institutions in charge of the various properties belonging to the Russian Republic.

VI ·

The local soviet publishes notice of the death of the property owner and summons the persons who enjoy the right to receive maintenance from this property to appear within one year from the date of publication of the notice.

VII

Persons who fail to assert their claims within one year from the date of the above-mentioned notice lose the right to receive maintenance from the property of the decedent.

VIII

The expense of administering the property is a first lien on the property of the decedent. Relatives and the spouse of the decedent receive maintenance from his property in preference to any creditor's claim. Creditors of the deceased, if their claims are recognized, are provided for out of the property which remains after the above-mentioned deductions. If the property is not sufficient to cover all the claims of the creditors the general rules of preference are to be followed.

IX

If the property of the decedent does not exceed ten thousand rubles and consists principally of house and garden, furniture, and implements of a worker's establishment, in city or village, it becomes subject to the direct control and disposal of the surviving spouse and relatives mentioned in Article II of this decree. The manner of control and disposal of the property shall be determined by mutual agreement between the spouse and the relatives; and in the event of a dispute between them by the local court.

X

This decree is retroactive in all cases of inheritance arising prior to the promulgation of this decree, provided that the heirs have not yet established their rights of possession, or, if such rights have been established, that they have not yet come into possession of the property.

XI

All disputed cases of inheritance, cases concerning probation of wills and the ratification of the rights of inheritance, etc., which are now before the courts are hereby dismissed, and the properties in dispute are handed over immediately to local soviets or to the institutions named in Article V of this decree.

Note: A special ruling will be issued concerning the inheritance cases enumerated in Article IX of the present decree if these cases arose prior to the promulgation of this decree.

XII

The People's Commissariat of Justice, in concurrence with the People's Commissariats of Social Welfare and Labor, will issue detailed instructions concerning the enforcement of this decree. The present decree becomes effective on the day of its signing and is to be promulgated by telegraph.

YA. SVERDLOV
Chairman of the All-Russian Central
Executive Committee

ABOLITION OF THE OWNERSHIP OF REAL ESTATE

[Decree of the Central Executive Committee, August 20, 1918] [40]

1. The right to own a tract of land . . . within a city is abolished without exception.

2. The right to own buildings located in cities with a population of ten thousand or over and having . . . a value . . . in excess of the amount fixed by local authorities is abolished.

Note 1: This law applies also to buildings on leased land.

Note 2: The local authorities of any city have the right to fix rentals on tracts of land remaining in the use of private individuals or organizations. . . .

Note 3: If, as provided in this Article, a building in a given estate remains the private property of an individual, all land attached to it which exceeds the norm fixed by local authorities is transferred to the general land fund.

Note 4: The local authorities have the right to lower by special

[40] *Ibid.,* No. 62, 1918, pp. 744-46.

decree the original valuation . . . of real estate remaining in private ownership. . . .

4. This decree does not apply to buildings which form an essential part of industrial plants. . . .

5. All city buildings and plots on which property rights have been abolished in accordance with this decree shall be turned over to the local authorities.

6. The right to erect new buildings in cities with a population of ten thousand or over belongs exclusively to the local authorities. In cities with a smaller population this right may be given . . . to private individuals. . . .

9. All mortgages of ten thousand rubles or over on confiscated lands and buildings are annulled. Mortgages of less than ten thousand rubles become state loans subject to regulations of the decree annulling state loans. (*S. U. R.* No. 27, Chap. 353.)

10. Former owners of real estate must pay rentals on the same terms as other tenants. . . .

11. In case of inability to work and the absence of other means of subsistence, former owners of real estate are entitled to receive from the local authorities a sum of not more than ten thousand rubles.

12. The local authorities are entitled to use . . . one-third of the net profit from real estate for local needs. . . . One-tenth of the profits is to go to the general building fund of the state . . . for the construction of new cities; . . . the rest of the net profit . . . will go to the local city building fund to be used for buildings, construction, repairs, street improvements, etc. . . .

YA. SVERDLOV
Chairman of the Central Executive Committee

B. DISTRIBUTION

Whereas all production was placed in charge of the Supreme Council of National Economy or the Commissariat of Agriculture, the distribution of commodities was entrusted exclusively to the Commissariat of Food. The decree of May 27 [47] charged that commissariat with the duties of "provisioning the population with articles of prime necessity, of organizing on a national scale the distribution of these articles, and of paving the way for the nationalization of trade in articles of prime necessity." These duties were subsequently (November 21) enlarged to include charge of all products of "personal and household use." To obtain his ration of food and other commodities every citizen had to become a member of a cooperative store, which apportioned goods in accordance with the class-qualifications of its members.

The class principle of food distribution was first introduced in Moscow and Petrograd during August. It established four categories of consumers: (1) those engaged in hard physical labor, (2) those in light physical labor, (3) those in intellectual work, and (4) the "non-toiling" elements.[48] According to the Russian publicist Izgoev, citizens of the fourth category were allowed one-eighth of a pound (Russian) of bread every two days, and Zinoviev, the head of the Petrograd Commune, explained that the reason for establishing the fourth category of citizens was "to insure that the bourgeoisie do not forget the smell of bread." [49]

DISRUPTION OF PRIVATE TRADE [50]

Tambov. Because of frequent requisitions and levies, private trade is in a hazardous state throughout the gubernia. In the cashier's office of almost every store in Tambov there is a Soviet agent collecting all receipts to cover the levies which the owners of the stores have failed to meet. . . . A number of merchants have been put in jail. Similar conditions prevail in [other] cities. . . . Fear of requisition is forcing merchants to close their stores.

[47] See below, pp. 466-67.
[48] Lenin, op. cit., XXIII, 543.
[49] A. Izgoev, "Piat let v sovetskoi Rossii," in A. R. R., X, 28.
[50] Svoboda Rossii, No. 33, May 29, 1918, p. 4.

. . . Cooperative stores continue to function in the villages but are in no position to meet the demands of the population.

COOPERATIVE SOCIETIES AND THE SUPREME COUNCIL OF NATIONAL ECONOMY

[Resolution of the First All-Russian Congress of Councils of National Economy, June 4, 1918] [51]

1. The work of cooperative organizations . . . should be co-ordinated . . . with the activities of Soviet institutions . . . , above all with the councils of national economy, and should be directed toward the aim of socialist construction. . . .

3. The work of coordinating the activities of cooperative organizations with those of Soviet institutions should not be restricted to the consumers' cooperatives alone, but should include also other forms of cooperative activity, such as credit and agriculture.

4. In undertaking the reorganization of cooperative organizations the Soviets should follow a consistent plan; measures which might hamper or paralyze the activity of cooperative organizations should be avoided.

5. Cooperative bureaus should be established in conjunction with the councils of national economy in order to consolidate all measures in connection with the cooperative movement. . . . Representatives of cooperatives must participate in the work of state supply organs.

6. . . . Control over cooperative organizations is vested in local councils of national economy, oblast councils of national economy, and the Supreme Council of National Economy, but not in employees of cooperatives.

A COMMUNIST VIEW OF THE FUNCTION OF COOPERATIVES [52]

In a capitalist society the principal aim of cooperatives is to free the consumer from the tyranny of the middleman, to secure trading profits for the union of consumers, and to provide consumers with high-quality merchandise. . . . Cooperatives adapted

[51] *Trudy I Vserossiiskago Sezda Sovetov Narodnago Khoziaistva,* pp. 484-85.
[52] Bukharin i Preobrazhensky, *Azbuka kommunizma,* pp. 258-61.

themselves to capitalism and came to play a definite part in the
capitalist system of distribution. . . .

Considering the class to which their members respectively belong, distributive cooperatives may be divided into workers' cooperatives, peasants' cooperatives, and the cooperatives of the
comparatively well-to-do city-dwellers, petty bourgeoisie, and
state officials. The workers' cooperatives were always on the extreme left of the cooperative movement but on the extreme right
of the proletarian movement. In peasants' cooperatives the well-
to-do peasants were in control, while in the city cooperatives the
predominant place was occupied by the petty-bourgeois intelligentsia, which looked upon itself as the spokesman of the movement as a whole, believing that the cooperatives had a great mission to fulfill in the destruction of capitalism by loaves of cooperative bread and bushels of cooperative potatoes.

The true nature of the cooperative movement was disclosed by
the November Revolution in Russia. Except for some of the
workers' cooperatives, the movement as a whole, especially its intellectuals and kulak leaders, assumed a definitely hostile attitude
toward the socialist revolution. The Siberian cooperatives . . .
sided openly with the White Guard counter-revolution and advocated the crushing of the Soviet Republic with the assistance of
international imperialism. . . .

. . . In the Soviet system the cooperative is destined either to
die out gradually with the rest of the capitalist system of distribution or else to enter the system of socialist distribution and rise
to the importance of a state distribution agency. The older leaders of the cooperatives—the Mensheviks, the Socialist-Revolutionists—would like to insure for the cooperatives independence
of the proletarian state, which means to insure for them the freedom to die out. The Soviet Government, on the other hand, having at heart the real interests of the great masses of the workers
and caring in particular for the interests of the workers' cooperatives, pursues another path. . . . The Soviet Government has
continually endeavored to fuse the cooperative apparatus of distribution with the whole system of its own distributive organs.
. . . In this connection the practical aims of the Soviet Government and of the Communist party have been as follows:

The normal cooperative of the bourgeois type is a voluntary

union of citizens having a definite interest in the organization. Such a cooperative serves the interests of its members only. . . . We, on the other hand, consider it necessary that the entire population be organized in cooperatives, that every member of the community belong to a cooperative. Only then will distribution through cooperatives signify distribution to the whole population. . . . After enrolling the entire population in the cooperatives, it is necessary that the leading part. in these organizations be given to the proletarian strata of the population . . . by securing the election of a communist and proletarian majority in the administrative bodies, and above all by transforming the proletarian—not the bourgeois—cooperatives into city consumers' communes. For the same reason, it is imperative that there be an intimate association between the cooperatives and the trade unions, that is to say, between the respective organs of distribution and production. . . . In time the function of the state will be reduced to that of a central accountant's office, and then the living union of productive and distributive organizations will become of great importance.

Finally, it is essential that the Communists participate as a compact group in the construction of this system of cooperative distribution and that they secure the dominant rôle in the work.

In the villages it is important that the kulaks be excluded from management of the cooperatives, that the privileges of the wealthy be withdrawn, and that the entire apparatus of village cooperatives be controlled by the poor and the class-conscious middle peasants. . . .

FOREIGN TRADE POLICY

[Resolution of the Supreme Council of National Economy, June 4, 1918] [53]

. . . 3. The war and the revolution have greatly changed the position of Russia in the international market. Whereas before the war [Russia's] protectionist tariff policy on the one hand aimed to prevent an influx of industrial products, and on the other hand sought to increase the export of grain and raw material, in the near future the substance of our foreign economic policy

[53] *Rezoliutsii Pervago Vserossiiskago Sezda Sovetov Narodnago Khoziaistva,* pp. 20-21.

will be just the opposite. It will endeavor to increase the import
of machinery needed for the reconstruction of the national economy, and to decrease the export of raw materials and food
products.

4. Our immediate aim in the domain of foreign commodity
exchange is to secure machinery for the most important branches
of the raw-material and manufacturing industries, as well as for
agriculture; . . . to reduce as far as possible the import of commodities of mass consumption ([e. g.] ready-made footwear);
and to stop completely the import of articles of luxury and personal use. As a temporary exception, the import of foodstuffs
(sugar, fish, grain) should be permitted.

5. The fundamental principle of our export is the exchange of
commodities. . . . Payment for imported machinery may be
made in the form of definite concessions in territories heretofore
not touched by Russian productive forces, on condition, however,
that the government have a share in the products and that the
social and industrial legislation [of the country] be binding on
the holders of concessions.

6. The altered conditions of the internal life of the country
necessitate a change in the organization of foreign trade. Since
the import of commodities necessitates export, it is essential to an
economical utilization of our internal resources to regulate deliberately the import as well as the export of commodities. The
existing methods of this regulation, such as the tariff policy and
the license and embargo systems, do not sufficiently satisfy this
need. The license system leaves initiative in the exchange of commodities to private commercial capital, which is guided not by the
needs of the country but by motives of a speculative character.
It is necessary to regulate foreign trade from the standpoint of
the interests of the national economy as a whole, and in accordance with a general plan of production and distribution. . . .

10. In the interest of a proper distribution of the existing resources in accordance with the general plan of our internal economic policy, it is necessary to concentrate all foreign orders . . .
in the hands of the Council for Foreign Trade. . . .

BUREAU IN CHARGE OF COOPERATIVES [54]

1. A bureau in charge of cooperatives is [hereby] established in connection with the Supreme Council of National Economy. It will consist of two representatives of the S. C. N. E., one of the Commissariat of Food, one of Finance, three of the cooperatives, and one of the Bureau. . . .

2. The Bureau of Cooperatives will take charge of all matters relating to the cooperative movement, issuing decrees and ordinances . . . and seeing that they are properly executed. . . .

WAGES IN KIND

[Plan Presented to the Conference of Metal Workers, October 19, 1918] [55]

At the evening session Comrade Larin reported on the payment of wages in kind. . . . He made reference to the extension of Soviet activities in the sphere of [rural] economy. About four hundred estates, with a total of a million and a half desiatins, were taken over by the government. Eight hundred more estates are to be taken over. All Soviet estates combined will yield between forty and fifty million puds of grain. . . . It is desirable to attach some of the estates to factories . . .—[a measure] which will help not only to prevent food crises but also to make possible the payment of wages in kind. . . .

[THESES]

1. Wages in kind must include living quarters, the principal manufactured and food products, and certain cultural needs.

2. To introduce wages in kind, it is necessary to organize every producing group of state factories into a separate unit of supply. Every such group should be included . . . in the state plan of commodity distribution framed by a central organ of supply such as the Commissariat of Food or the "Tsentrotextil." . . .

3. To make certain that workers obtain supplies through the portion of their wage which is paid in kind, it is necessary to bring about a union of industry and agriculture by attaching to factories certain agricultural tracts of the large capitalistically

[54] *Narodnoe Khoziaistvo*, No. 3, 1918, p. 45.
[55] *Metallist*, No. 7, 1918, pp. 18-19.

15

used farms. The administration of these farms will consist of representatives of the factories to which the farms are attached, representatives of farm workers, and specialists. The Commissariat of Agriculture will supervise the agronomic side of the enterprise and lend all possible assistance.

The products of these farms will be used for the distribution of wages in kind to factory workers within the limits laid down by the general state plan of supply. . . . What is left over will go to the Commissariat of Food.

On their part the factory workers, in case of necessity during rush periods, will send from their midst the required number of workers to help on the farm.

4. Under the system of wages in kind, the repair and maintenance of workers' living quarters, as well as the construction and supply of necessary furniture, will devolve upon the state. . . .

7. The price of goods distributed as wages in kind will be calculated at fixed prices and the sum deducted from the [total] wages. In the future, no matter what the fluctuation of prices may be, the quantity of the products supplied in kind shall not diminish and the amount deducted not increase.

8. The quantity of goods required by a woman and a child . . . will be calculated separately. . . .

9. To make it absolutely certain that the guaranteed goods will be supplied, a [special] reserve of goods to be used as wages will be established. Every branch of economy is to set aside the part of production which is required for wages in kind. The transportation of goods . . . which are used for wages in kind will take precedence over all other shipments, in the same way as do shipments for the active army.

10. The fixing of norms for the distribution of goods under the system of wages in kind will be undertaken by a commission attached to the Supreme Council of National Economy and consisting of representatives of the S. C. N. E., the All-Russian Council of Trade Unions, the All-Russian Unions of Metal Workers, Textile Workers, Railway Workers, Employees of Trade and Industry, and the Commissariats of Trade and Food. On the basis of the decisions of that commission the Supreme Council of National Economy will set aside a certain quantity of products which will go to the fund of wages in kind. The Com-

missariat of Food will then distribute [that fund] among the workers and employees.

11. Wages in kind will be introduced first for workers and employees of Moscow, Petrograd, and other cities with a population of more than twenty thousand, and also for other large and medium-size enterprises situated outside cities. . . .

12. The Central Committee of the All-Russian Union of Metal Workers and the Central Administration of the State Combine of Metallurgical Works are charged with the immediate undertaking of all necessary practical steps to introduce wages in kind at the factories of which they have charge.

ABOLITION OF PRIVATE TRADE

[Decree of the Sovnarkom, November 21, 1918] [56]

1. In order to eliminate all private trade and supply the population systematically with all necessary products from the state and cooperative stores, the Commissariat of Food . . . is commissioned to provide the population with articles of personal and household use.

2. These articles, manufactured in nationalized factories . . . as well as in plants controlled by the Supreme Council of National Economy, shall be turned over to the Commissariat of Food . . . to be disposed of in accordance with definite utilization projects. (See Article 7.) The remainder of the goods required shall be furnished by the Commissariat of Food.

3. A chain of state and cooperative wholesale and retail . . . stores shall be established to maintain the supply and proper distribution of goods. The wholesale warehouses and retail stores of the cooperatives shall remain in the hands of the cooperatives and under the control of the Commissariat of Food. (Article 15.)

4. From the date when this decree becomes effective no central or local state institution, except the Commissariat of Food and its local organs, shall have the right to regulate trade in goods affected by this decree, or to issue prohibitions or permits concerning the import or export of such goods. Permits issued by the Commissariat of Food and its organs for the purchase of these

[56] *S. U. R.*, No. 83, 1918, pp. 1045-49.

goods from some other province and for transit shipments within the Soviet Republic shall be final, and no additional permits shall be required to carry out the above orders.

Note: The Supreme Council of National Economy . . . reserves the right to ship, and to issue permits for shipments of, such goods affected by the present decree as are intended for manufacturing purposes (supplies for factories, shops, etc.).

5. The requisition and confiscation of wholesale warehouses and the nationalization of companies which own these warehouses can be undertaken only by the People's Commissariat of Food and organs duly authorized by it. The requisition, confiscation, and "municipalization" of retail stores and companies can be undertaken only by the local organs of the People's Commissariat of Food and with the approval of the local executive committee.

All articles of personal and household use requisitioned . . . by any institution other than the Supreme Council of National Economy and its organs shall be turned over to the People's Commissariat of Food.

The above articles, as well as those confiscated in the future by any organization (including the railroads, the court, and the Cheka), must be turned over to the central or local organs of the People's Commissariat of Food not later than two weeks after the date of their requisition or confiscation.

Note: The requisition and confiscation of wholesale warehouses and the nationalization of trading companies handling goods other than articles of personal and household use can be undertaken only by the Supreme Council of National Economy in concurrence with the various people's commissariats.

6. The Central Distribution Bureau of the People's Commissariat of Food shall take charge of supplying the population with goods of industrial and kustar manufacture, including both goods under state monopoly and those in free circulation. The Collegium of the Central Distribution Bureau shall include two representatives of the Supreme Council of National Economy and one representative of the People's Commissariat of Commerce and Industry.

7. Utilization projects (referred to in Article 2) include: (1) the determination of the quantity of goods required for export, for reserve, for industrial use, and for distribution among

the population; (2) the fixing of factory, wholesale, and retail prices of commodities; (3) the determination of ways and means for the distribution of goods among the population. . . . Items 1 and 3 of this article shall be entrusted to a special commission of the Supreme Council of National Economy, the membership of which shall consist of three representatives of the S. C. N. E. and three representatives of the People's Commissariat of Commerce and Industry. Item 2 shall be entrusted to the Central Committee of the S. C. N. E. All utilization projects . . . must be approved by the Presidium of the S. C. N. E. in concurrence with the People's Commissariat of Food. . . .

10. The list of commodities under state monopoly must be drawn up by the Presidium of the S. C. N. E. in concurrence with the People's Commissariat of Food.

Every factory, shop, and mining enterprise must turn over to the Central Distribution Bureau . . . all commodities required for distribution among the population in accordance with the utilization projects of the S. C. N. E.

11. All wholesale warehouses of factories . . . remain under the supervision and management of the . . . Supreme Council of National Economy . . . , with the exception of that part of the commodities [of such warehouses] which, in accordance with the plans of the S. C. N. E., is intended for distribution among the population. These commodities shall be turned over . . . to the Central Distribution Bureau of the Commissariat of Food. . . .

12. The Central Distribution Bureau and its authorized agencies are expected to make payment within two weeks to . . . either the factories or the S. C. N. E. for commodities received. . . . Goods distributed by cooperatives shall be paid for directly . . . by the cooperatives.

13. All existing internal revenue taxes are abolished. Extra charges for the benefit of the state may be added to the prices at which the Commissariat of Food purchases goods from the S. C. N. E. The necessity for and the amount of the extra charge shall be determined in each case by the Presidium of the S. C. N. E. with the participation of representatives from the People's Commissariats of Finance and of Food. In cases of dispute representatives of the Soviet of People's Commissars shall be consulted. Whenever such extra charges are due to the state, the People's Com-

missariat of Food must make corresponding payment to the State Treasury within two weeks of the transfer of the goods from the factories to the Central Distribution Bureau.

Note: Prior to the announcement of new scales for the extra charges, such charges shall be computed in accordance with existing internal revenue taxes.

14. Each gubernia branch of the Commissariat of Food must establish by January 1, 1919, a . . . chain of retail stores to handle the monopoly goods. . . . In order to obtain goods . . . , every citizen must register at one of the stores included in this chain.

15. The local soviets of deputies, together with food departments, shall be guided by the following rules for the municipalization of retail trade:

a) All retail stores and those wholesale stores which carry local trade shall be municipalized.

Note: In cases of doubt, the Central Distribution Bureau shall have the right to decide whether or not a particular wholesale store is carrying on trade of more than local character; [if its trade is more than local] it may be taken over by the Central Distribution Bureau.

b) Stores handling goods on which there is a state monopoly shall be municipalized first.

c) Stores handling non-monopoly goods shall be municipalized only when facilities have been established . . . for the distribution of non-monopoly goods . . . through Soviet and cooperative stores.

d) . . . Stores municipalized according to the above rules must not remain closed for more than seven days. On the eighth day they must resume their operation in charge of an agent of the food department. . . .

e) Cooperative stores and warehouses cannot be nationalized. Those already nationalized or municipalized . . . shall be restored to their former status and receive back their goods with an accounting for goods already disposed of. Henceforth all lawful activities of the cooperatives must not be interfered with in any way.

Note: Care should be taken to prevent any meddling on the part of kulaks and counter-revolutionists in the activities of the reinstated cooperatives. For this purpose strict and systematic supervision by the committees of the poor and local soviets shall be instituted.

16. The administration of the All-Russian Central Union of Consumers' Societies (Tsentrosoiuz) and of each of the regional and gubernia consumers' cooperative societies must include one representative of the People's Commissariat of Food. . . .

The Collegium of the Central Distribution Bureau has the right to annul such decisions of the Tsentrosoiuz and the regional cooperative societies on the distribution of products as appear to contravene or hamper the plans of the Central Distribution Bureau. . . .

18. Persons violating this decree are liable to arrest and confiscation of their property. . . . Employees are liable to arrest and forced labor for a term of not less than one year.

V. Ulianov (Lenin)
President of the Soviet of People's Commissars

KULAKS EXCLUDED FROM COOPERATIVES

[Decree of the Supreme Council of National Economy, November 30, 1918] [57]

In order to eliminate kulaks and counter-revolutionary elements from the cooperative organizations, the following persons shall be deprived of the right to elect and be elected officials of cooperatives:

1. Those hiring labor with the purpose of gain.

Note: Temporary hiring of help does not disqualify for election.

2. Those living on unearned incomes, such as interest on capital, incomes from business or real estate.

3. Those engaged in trade at present or during the past three years, as well as those occupied as middlemen at any time during the past three years.

Note: The three-year period may be shortened to one year in the cases of those who have proved themselves useful cooperative workers.

4. Monks and nuns.

[57] Piontkovsky, *G. V. R.,* pp. 72-73.

5. Ministers of religion, except those who have proved themselves useful workers in the cooperative movement.

6. Agents of the former police, gendarmes, and secret-service
agents.

A. Rykov

Chairman of the Supreme Council
of National Economy

PLAN FOR DISTRIBUTION OF GOODS

[Resolution of the Second Congress of Councils of National Economy,
December 27, 1918] [58]

1. The limited quantity of products and mass-consumption
goods requires an effective organization of distribution, which
until now has been inadequate.

2. A regular exchange of goods between city and village
should be established, and the village supplied with articles of
necessity. . . .

5. Cooperative organizations should be enlisted in the work
of requisitioning and distributing goods.

6. It should be made compulsory for the entire population to
become members of cooperatives.

7. As a measure of transition to the system of wages in kind,
workers in industry, in agricultural communes, and on Soviet
farms should be supplied with goods . . . in place of money (or
of part of their money wage).

C. Finance

Soviet financial policies were determined by two disparate
aims—to pave the way to the communist economic' order
and to meet the immediate problems of a transitional order
which still retained certain features of the capitalist system. In the pursuit of the first aim the Bolsheviks nationalized all private banks, merging them with the State (Peo-

---

[58] *Trudy II Vserossiiskogo Sezda Sovetov Narodnogo Khoziaistva,* pp.
392-93.

ple's) Bank, the function of which was to assist the People's Commissariat of Finance in issuing paper money and in distributing it among the various state institutions and nationalized enterprises. The People's Bank thus became the cashier and accountant for the national economy as a whole. A more radical measure in behalf of communism was the decree of August 30, 1918, which introduced a system of moneyless movements of raw materials and manufactured products between nationalized enterprises.[59] This was a step toward the communist ideal of a moneyless and exchangeless economy. Still another policy dictated by this ideal was that of greatly increasing the issuance of paper money with a view to depreciating it and thus rendering it ultimately worthless as a medium of exchange. Finally, the Communists introduced to some extent the system of wages in kind, that is, the payment of workers not in money but in goods.

At the same time, since a moneyless economy was introduced only in part it was necessary to meet the enormous monetary expenditures arising from the expansion of governmental functions. The Soviet Government sought to derive the required revenue by resort to the printing press and to various forms of extraordinary taxes. However, these measures raised many difficulties, the discussion of which is the principal theme of the documents that follow.

TAXING THE BOURGEOISIE
[Editorial in *Izvestiia*] [60]

. . . Reports are coming from the provinces to the effect that there is no end to the levies which are being laid on the bourgeoisie.

---

[59] See pp. 406-07, above.
[60] *Izvestiia*, No. 106, May 28, 1918, p. 7.

Levies, taxes, and requisitions are being resorted to by local soviets, and in most cases without any system or definite plan. The Commissariat of Finance is endeavoring to evolve some system . . . of taxing the bourgeoisie.

The local authorities use the levies exclusively for the needs of local institutions. . . . The state has no objection to the taxing of the bourgeoisie, but it desires to modify somewhat the methods of imposing the levies. . . . Local soviets must realize that over and above the local interests are the interests of the state, which is entitled to a certain portion of the levy. A too frequent taxation of the same people is likely to cause the failure of the state's efforts to impose and collect its own taxes.

The Commissariat of Finance intends to fix the amount of these levies by setting legal limits to them. . . .

THE STATE BUDGET

[Gukovsky's Speech at the First All-Russian Congress of Councils of National Economy, May 31, 1918] [61]

Comrades! I have been invited by the Presidium of the Supreme Council of National Economy to address you on our state budget. But in view of the fact that Comrade Sokolnikov spoke to you yesterday on our financial plans, I shall have to extend the limits of my report and discuss not only the budget but also our general financial situation. I do not know in whose name Comrade Sokolnikov spoke—whether he gave his private opinion or that of some organization. . . . As the representative of the Commissariat of Finance of the Russian Federated Republic, I view our financial plans differently. . . . While Comrade Sokolnikov looks to foreign loans as a way out of our critical financial condition, I, on the other hand, think that we shall hardly succeed in negotiating a loan, for the simple reason that we repudiated our old loans . . . and until we settle those loans cannot expect a kopek from abroad.

Comrade Sokolnikov thinks that gold can no longer serve as security for our money. He thinks that gold can be exported only as a commodity in exchange for other commodities. . . . I [on the other hand] think that as long as there is circulation of money

[61] *Trudy I Vserossiiskago Sezda Sovetov Narodnago Khoziaistva*, pp. 129-42.

—and we are likely to have it for some time—gold should be used as the security of the circulating currency. . . . At present it is impossible to say that our paper money has a gold backing, because for a billion and a half rubles' worth of gold there have been issued thirty-seven billion rubles' worth of paper money, excluding the different money surrogates. The security is insignificant . . . but the paper money is being accepted for the reason that it is . . . the only standard of value and the sole medium of exchange. However, we cannot exist exclusively on the printing-press. Paper money has thus far been accepted by the workers . . . because by means of it they were able to exist in the cities and the villages. As soon as confidence in these money tokens is lost we shall receive neither supplies nor labor. . . .

I come now . . . to our budget. Comrade Sokolnikov pointed out yesterday that after my report to the Central Executive Committee on April 16,[62] there was an impression that our budget would reach a figure between eighty and a hundred billion [rubles]. . . . My report was not quoted accurately in the newspapers. . . . Today I have more precise information, based on estimates submitted by the various departments and checked by a committee for the reduction of the budget. According to the figures submitted, . . . the sum of twenty-four billion rubles is demanded from us for the first six months of 1918. This sum has been reduced by the committee . . . to fourteen billions, but the final figure . . . will be somewhat higher. . . . In reality the estimates presented do not cover all our expenditures. There were omitted the expenditures for the upkeep of the All-Russian Central Executive Committee and the institutions of the Supreme Council of National Economy. These institutions will require large amounts, from one to two billion rubles. . . . The upkeep of the railways has also been omitted, and the amount required is from nine to ten billion rubles semi-annually. These are the principal items not included [in the budget]. After including them our budget will [still] be less than what I originally supposed. . . . We shall allow between twenty-five and thirty billion [rubles] for the first six months . . . ; thus our budget for the year will amount to from fifty to sixty billion [rubles]. . . . I must say

[62] The report, which was actually made on April 15, is quoted in part in *The Bolshevik Revolution*, pp. 604-06.

further that the estimates do not include the expenses of local
Soviet organs . . . and a large number of expenditures of which
it is difficult to give an estimate. . . . For example, we annulled
[state] loans but in the act of annulment assumed the obligation
. . . to pay the holders of small securities as well as socially useful institutions holding securities. . . . We shall also have to pay
the Germans . . . , in accordance with the Brest Treaty. . . .
There is another important item which has been omitted [from
the budget]. You may know that there exists a law according to
which the Commissariat of Labor is to receive 10 per cent of the
wages of all workers. The decree was issued at a time when there
were not very many nationalized enterprises, and the payment of
this 10 per cent was imposed not upon the workers but upon the
employers and was to go to hospital funds, accident insurance
. . . , and the unemployed. The Commissariat of Labor is now
insisting that similar payments be made for employees and workers in nationalized enterprises. This will amount to over a billion
[rubles]. . . .

Where can we obtain the means to cover these expenditures?
. . .

On a number of occasions I have stressed the fact that with the
contraction of the rôle of private capital [in our economy] . . .
we are under the necessity of finding other sources of income.
The rôle of direct taxation is bound to become less important.
The more the state concentrates in its own hands industry, trade,
transportation, and other branches of industrial activity which
were yielding profit to private capital, . . . the fewer are the objects of taxation. . . . Undoubtedly we still have a large field of
taxation in the taxing of the independent workers, who are not
employed in nationalized enterprises. . . . [But the average income of city dwellers is hardly above the minimum wage; as for
the peasants, they constitute a difficult problem.] From an economic standpoint the peasant population gained more from the
revolution than did any other class. . . . It received the land . . . ,
the forests, and other things. . . . Yet it will prove very difficult
to get anything from the peasant. According to the law of land
socialization, land cannot be taxed. We can tax [only] property
and income. A number of commissions are now working on this
question. But it is very difficult and complicated . . . to deter-

mine how much a peasant's income exceeds his minimum standard of living. . . . We may have to adopt some external [arbi-
trary] criterion of taxation. . . . I do not know how much this
taxation will yield . . . , perhaps three hundred million [rubles].
It will be hard on peasants, but our finances will not thereby
improve. . . .

We might be able to meet [the deficit] by increasing indirect
taxes. This is the surest method of taxing the large masses—the
peasantry. To be sure, by taxing consumption goods we raise the
cost of living not only for the peasant but for the worker as well
. . . , [but] we have no way of collecting taxes from the peasant
other than by exchanging goods for his products and taxing those
goods for the benefit of the state. . . . We have already increased
a number of [indirect] taxes . . . , which are expected to bring
in 841 million [rubles] for six months. . . . Thus, by scratching
here and there, we expect to collect five billion [rubles] to cover
the twenty-five or twenty billions which we must spend. . . .

I have forgotten to mention one important item of revenue—
levies. I consider these levies altogether an evil. . . . The money
collected is being spent without any system, and improper measures are being taken in collecting these levies. . . . In the city of
Kaluga there was published the following announcement: "Those
who do not subscribe to *Kaluzhskaia Pravda* will be guilty of
sabotage and failure to comply with the ordinances of the Commissariat. The penalty is three thousand rubles." . . . I cannot
accept this kind of financial policy. . . .

DEBATES ON THE BUDGET

[From the Proceedings of the First All-Russian Congress of Councils of
National Economy, May 31, 1918] [63]

Lozovsky: The two reports—the one by Sokolnikov, the other
by Gukovsky—produced a very sad impression on me. I say a
"sad" impression because, in the first place, here are two official
representatives whose accounts differ by no less than thirty billion
rubles. Comrade Sokolnikov maintains that our annual budget
is from twenty-five to thirty billion rubles, while Comrade Gukovsky says that our semi-annual expenditure is from twenty-five to

---

[63] *Trudy I Vserossiiskago Sezda Sovetov Narodnago Khoziaistva,* pp. 143-47.

thirty billions. The divergence is not slight, even though the
figures are so stupendous that no one seems to be frightened by
sums like twenty-five or thirty billions. However, the crux of
the matter is not so much in the figures as in the difficulty of
knowing where the money is being spent. When we lived under
the bourgeois order it was customary . . . to make estimates.
These estimates were made out by the different departments and
passed on to those who in one way or another had to watch over
the number of rubles spent. . . . Not only here, in the Councils
of National Economy, but even in the [Central] Executive Committee, which is considered . . . the supreme organ of the [Soviets
of] Workers', Peasants', and Soldiers' Deputies, even there we
are given no estimates, no budget plans. We are told that such
and such a commissariat, let us say the Commissariat of Agriculture, wants seven hundred million rubles. . . . But how is this
money going to be spent . . . ? Neither the representatives of
the Councils of National Economy, nor Sokolnikov, nor Gukovsky
know anything about it. . . . There is a new commissariat, called
the Commissariat of Social Welfare, which, according to Comrade
Gukovsky, cares for no one in particular, but which requires ninety-
one million rubles for running expenses. . . . How many officials
are there in this Commissariat of Welfare which requires ninety-
one million [rubles] to minister to its own welfare? This we do
not know. It is true that, as Comrade Gukovsky has told us . . . ,
there are some comrades who think that estimates are bourgeois
prejudices. But I am infected with bourgeois prejudices to the
extent of wishing to know how many billions we need—twenty-
five or fifty. . . .

The two speakers agree that our situation is desperate and both
of them hope that we shall somehow pull through. . . . Let us
see then how they conceive of our financial-economic policy.

Yesterday Sokolnikov made the discovery . . . that the bour-
geois-capitalist order, which all of us thought was 99 per cent
dead and only needed the finishing blow, is pretty much alive.
Sokolnikov said that the Russian bourgeoisie is still in existence,
that it can be taxed, and that much can be gotten out of it. . . .
The question then arises why it is that until now the finance
department has failed to accomplish anything in this direction.
Comrade Sokolnikov was in charge of that department and it

was under his auspices that the very theatrical nationalization of banks was carried out. . . . Obviously, there must be definite reasons which prevented the taxation of the very bourgeoisie that should have been taxed. What happened during the past six months? . . . This is what happened.

It seemed at first that during these six months socialist policies were being applied, that socialism was being directly introduced. . . . Sokolnikov's speech, after six months of experimentation, was a confession not only that we have failed to arrive at socialism but that we have not even reached its beginnings, that what took place cannot even be called a real nationalization. . . . Yesterday a comrade quoted from a resolution of workers of the water transport which read as follows: "Fight by all means and measures for wages. Do not stop short of nationalization." (*Laughter.*) . . . Those who spoke thus about nationalization were considering the question from the point of view of their own interests . . . , of their wages. . . . To our great misfortune, too many nationalizations were undertaken in this manner . . . , and [the state] lost many millions. . . . The amount of paper money is constantly increasing, and we have reached a stage where the printing of one paper ruble costs one ruble and seventeen kopeks. . . . However, the printing of paper money did not improve our financial situation. . . . We had no definite financial or economic plan to begin with . . . , no comprehension of the resources at our disposal. . . . We listened yesterday to Comrade Obolensky's amusing story: how Comrade Lenin introduced a proposal to confiscate immediately all joint-stock companies; how Comrade Obolensky, believing that Comrade Lenin was too much to the left, ignored the project; and how after several months Comrade Obolensky proposes the very same thing. . . . What we need first of all is to reduce our expenses. . . . We must require the commissariats, the Sovnarkom, and the Central Executive Committee to count every kopek. . . . We must give up fantastic experiments of sporadic nationalization. . . . These are some of the things which are necessary . . . in order to reduce our budget. . . .

Smirnov: [64] Comrades! It is easy to tear our policies to pieces. . . . Had we followed Comrade Lozovsky's advice, i. e., not to

[64] *Ibid.*, pp. 147-49.

spend a kopek before a detailed estimate was made, we would not
be in power now. . . . The same is true of the policy of nationalization. If we had studied the details of every nationalization
. . . , selecting only [those enterprises] which were profitable,
we would not have nationalized anything and the bourgeoisie
would not have been overthrown. . . .

I come now to Comrade Gukovsky's report. . . . Our problem
is not at all a problem of reducing the money in circulation. We
need not fear the decreasing value of the ruble. . . . When
socialism triumphs completely the ruble will not be worth anything and we shall have moneyless exchange. . . . Comrade
Gukovsky was critical in regard to levies. I, on the other hand,
believe that levies are quite proper . . . but that they should be
kept within certain limits. . . . Local authorities should impose
levies on condition that a certain part is deposited in the Soviet
Treasury. (*Riazanov: "A share in the plunder!"*) Yes, a share
in the plunder of the bourgeoisie. . . . These levies should yield
large amounts. . . . We must adopt the system of monopolies
and trade regulation. Only under these conditions can we direct
profits from nationalized trade . . . into proper channels. In
proportion as industry becomes organized on socialist principles
the village must be taxed more and more. . . . Goods which the
peasants buy in the city should be sold at prices above normal.
. . . The introduction of the card system . . . and the nationalization of trade . . . will enable us to adopt a clear-cut policy
toward the village. . . .

Riazanov:[65] . . . Comrade Smirnov has been advocating the
very things which I consider to be the fundamental vice of the
whole economic and financial policy of the Soviet Government.
This [vice] is the granting of legislative power to local sovdeps.
. . . The enjoyment of this power by separate sovdeps is a death
sentence to any attempt to maintain a consistent financial policy.
. . . The method by which the Soviet Government took its first
money [from the State Bank] is perhaps the best testimony to
its incompetence in financial matters. . . . Future historians will
reconstruct the famous conference of regimental delegates in
which Comrade Trotsky urged that each regiment send its representatives to the State Bank to obtain . . . ten million [rubles].

[65] *Ibid.,* pp. 149-52.

. . . *Izvestiia* and other papers carried an account of the march of the Guard . . . Regiments with music to the State Bank. . . . And yet all that was necessary was to ask any official . . . to sign an order [for the money]. . . . Here is a government which has fallen into the hands of drum-beating financiers . . . , and we have witnessed one error after another. As early as December [1917] I advocated control over workers. I am an old opponent of factory-shop committees, and when the nationalized banks became a reservoir for these committees I sounded a warning. I should like to ask our financiers to secure information from the nationalized State Bank as to how the administration of the Treugolnik [66] managed, through the factory-shop committee, to pump out all its deposits [from the State Bank]. We could then see (unfortunately, we have no accounts, no data) how many millions of rubles the capitalists pumped out of the nationalized bank . . . through factory-shop committees. . . .

Comrade Gukovsky's speech . . . shows not only that we have retained all the defects of the old bureaucratic régime and kept superfluous commissariats, but that we have managed to add . . . a number of new ones. . . . Water transport was taken away from the Commissariat of Ways and Communications . . . and placed under the Supreme Council of National Economy. . . . It then became necessary to create an interdepartmental commission to coordinate the activities of water transport and railroads. . . .

Serkov: [67] Comrades! I shall not pause much on the reports. Upon me, as a man of the village, they produced a sad impression. The speakers contradicted each other . . . , while the things that matter most remained unconsidered. . . . As a representative of the village I should like to say a few words on the food question, the most critical of our problems. Comrade Rykov said that we have one billion arshins of fabrics. . . . [In the villages] we have bread but are going naked, while here the people are starving. Instead of sending thirty thousand Red Guards our government should send, I suggest, manufactured goods in exchange for bread. As a man of the village I know that you will not succeed in getting bread by bayonets. . . . You will not succeed in ex-

[66] A large rubber factory.
[67] *Trudy I Vserossiiskago Sezda Sovetov Narodnago Khoziaistva*, pp. 156-57.

propriating the peasant's toil. . . . (*Noise.*) . . . The peasant works twenty-hours a day, and the bread which you intend to seize from him by means of bayonets he gained by hard work. [The speaker was not allowed to continue.]

EXTRAORDINARY REVOLUTIONARY TAX ON THE BOURGEOISIE

[Decree of the Sovnarkom, October 30, 1918] [68]

. . . The All-Russian Central Executive Committee has . . . resolved to levy on the propertied classes in cities and villages a lump-sum tax of ten billion rubles, to be imposed on the following basis:

1. The extraordinary lump-sum tax is levied upon persons belonging to the propertied classes of the cities and villages.

2. Persons whose sole source of income is a wage . . . of not more than fifteen hundred rubles a month . . . are exempt from the extraordinary . . . tax.

3. All nationalized and municipalized enterprises as well as consumers' cooperatives and agricultural communes are exempt from the extraordinary tax.

4. The extraordinary . . . tax is to be distributed among the different gubernias of the Republic in accordance with the instructions laid down in the Appendix to this decree.

Note: The People's Commissariat of Finance, in concurrence with the People's Commissariat of the Interior, has the right to change the gubernia allotment of the extraordinary tax at the recommendation of the corresponding gubernia executive committee of soviet deputies.

5. The amount of the extraordinary . . . tax assessed on a gubernia on the basis of the preceding paragraph (4) is distributed by the gubernia executive committee of soviet deputies among the uezds and cities which participate in the gubernia congresses of soviets. (Constitution of the R. S. F. S. R., Article 53 b.) The amount of the tax which has been fixed by the gubernia executive committee is distributed by the uezd executive committee . . . among the volosts, and by the volost soviets among the villages and hamlets. (Constitution, Article 57 b.)

[68] *S. U. R.,* No. 80, 1918, pp. 996-98.

6. Committees of the poor and village, volost, and city soviets of deputies are to prepare lists of persons liable for the payment of the tax, and to distribute the amount of the tax which has been assessed on the village or city among the taxpayers in accordance with the property and income of each person. The distribution is to be made in such a way that the city and village poor shall be completely exempt from the extraordinary tax, that the middle classes shall be taxed lightly, and that the whole burden of the tax shall fall on the rich part of the city population and on the rich peasants.

7. The extraordinary tax does not replace any of the previous taxes.

8. Personal and property liability is established for the non-payment of the tax.

9. The extraordinary tax is to form a part of the general resources of the state and is entered in the estimates of the revenue department of the People's Commissariat of Finance.

10. The present decree becomes effective at once. Assessments must be completed by December 1 and the tax collected not later than December 15 of this year.

11. The People's Commissariat of Finance is instructed to send local soviets general regulations for the execution of the present decree and to see that the time limits indicated in paragraph 10 are strictly observed.

YA. SVERDLOV
Chairman of the Central
Executive Committee

V. ULIANOV (LENIN)
President of the Sovnarkom

EXTRAORDINARY REVOLUTIONARY TAX TO BE IMPOSED BY
LOCAL SOVIETS
[Decree of the Sovnarkom, October 31, 1918] [69]

1. Uezd, city, and gubernia soviets of deputies have the right to impose extraordinary revolutionary taxes, to be paid in a lump sum, on members of the bourgeois class.

Note: Extraordinary revolutionary taxes are preferably to be collected in ready cash.

[69] *Ibid.,* No. 81, 1918, pp. 1001-1002.

2. Collection of the local extraordinary tax is in addition to other current taxes . . . , local and state, and in addition to the state extraordinary revolutionary tax.[70]

3. Nationalized and municipalized industries, as well as consumers' cooperatives and agricultural communes . . . , are exempt from extraordinary taxes. . . .

V. ULIANOV (LENIN)
President of the Soviet of
People's Commissars

TAXES IN KIND

[Decree of the Central Executive Committee, October 30, 1918] [71]

The principle of the equal distribution of land in accordance with the "consumption-labor standard" [72] set forth in Article 12 of the Law of Land Socialization . . . is as yet far from being a reality. . . . As in the past, there are everywhere rich peasants who own more and better land and whose crops are far in excess of what they can consume. At the same time the state, after four years of costly warfare, finds itself in great need of agricultural products—a fact which makes it necessary to impose a tax in kind on the well-to-do peasants.

Under such conditions, a continuation of the system of taxation by which all peasants were assessed for an equal sum of money would amount to the perpetuation of conditions under which the wealthy are given an opportunity to exploit the poor. In view of this fact, and in an effort to achieve complete emancipation of the poor from the burden of taxation by transferring this burden to the economically well-to-do classes . . . , the All-Russian Central Executive Committee has decreed the levying of a tax in kind upon all peasants who have an excess of agricultural products. . . .

YA. SVERDLOV
Chairman of the Central
Executive Committee

V. ULIANOV (LENIN)
President of the Sovnarkom

[70] See the decree of October 30, 1918, quoted above.
[71] S. U. R., No. 82, 1918, p. 1024.   [72] See footnote on p. 458, below.

KRESTINSKY ON THE EXTRAORDINARY TAX [73]

. . . It is not always possible to count upon such measures [extraordinary taxes] as a way out of budgetary difficulties, for their application leads to the extinction of the very objects of taxation. Yet, in the present period of transition to a new economic order, this extinction does not represent any danger for the economic development of the country. After all, everything that is economically valuable and productive (viz., factories, shops, mines) becomes the object of state development and the source of state revenue; whereas this kind of tax affects mainly the unproductive savings of the propertied class. We can go even farther in this direction. If we can introduce compulsory current accounts and a new extraordinary tax like the last we shall extract a few more billions from the profiteering bourgeoisie. After that, Soviet Russia will have to defray its expenditures by developing nationalized industries and improving agriculture.

The calculations of Krestinsky in connection with the extraordinary tax proved to be highly overoptimistic. A year later, when the results of the tax became known, the Commissar of Finance had to admit that only one billion, two hundred thousand rubles had been collected through the extraordinary tax.[74] Industry and agriculture showed no signs of improvement, while state expenditures grew by leaps and bounds. Under the circumstances, the printing press had to be called into assistance to increase state income. Reviewing the situation which existed during 1918, the official organ of the Commissariat of Finance wrote as follows:

"It was clear to everyone that during the transition period the Soviet Government could not help but base its budget on paper money, i. e., finance the administrative and economic machinery through the issue of paper money. Under such conditions, with the possibility of unlimited issue, the old

[73] *Rospis obshchegosudarstvennykh dokhodov i raskhodov. Iul-Dekabr, 1918* (N. Krestinsky, ed.), p. 59.   Krestinsky was People's Commissar of Finance.
[74] *Izvestiia Narodnago Komissariata Finansov*, No. 10, 1919, p. 3.

demands upon the budget for strict calculation, economy in spending, and correspondence between proposed expenditure and expected revenue became unnecessary." [75]

BUDGET FOR JULY-DECEMBER 1918

Estimated Receipts	In Millions	
Fixed Sources of Revenue	2,726.9	
Revolutionary Tax	10,000.0	
	12,726.9	
Expenditures	29,103.0	
Deficit		16,376.1 [76]
Collections		
Fixed Revenues	1,252.3 [77]	
Revolutionary Tax	1,200.0	
	2,452.3 [78]	
Expenditures	29,103.0	
Deficit		26,650.7

ISSUE OF BANK NOTES

[Decree of the Sovnarkom, October 26, 1918] [79]

For the purpose of balancing the accounts of the People's Bank, the Soviet of People's Commissars hereby authorizes the Bank to issue additional bank notes to the amount of 35.5 billion rubles.[80]

KRESTINSKY ON PAPER MONEY [81]

The new issue of paper money may be dangerous and even

[75] *Ibid.,* Nos. 10-11, 1920, p. 20.

[76] *Rospis obshchegosudarstvennykh dokhodov i raskhodov. Iul-Dekabr 1918,* p. 56.

[77] G. Dementiev, "Gosudarstvenye dokhody respubliki," in *Izvestiia Narodnago Komissariata Finansov,* No. 10, 1919, p. 15.

[78] N. Krestinsky, "Itogi," in *Izvestiia Narodnago Komissariata Finansov,* No. 10, 1919, p. 3.

[79] *Obzor finansovogo zakonodatelstva,* pp. 33-34.

[80] The amount of money in circulation for the period of May-December 1918 is estimated by S. S. Katzenellenbaum to have been as follows: May 1, 37.8 billion rubles; June 1, 40.3; July 1, 43.3; August 1, 45.3; September 1, 48.2; October 1, 51.3; November 1, 53.8; December 1, 56.8. *Russian Currency and Banking, 1914-1924,* p. 57.

[81] *Rospis obshchegesudarstvennykh dokhodov i raskhodov. Iul-Dekabr 1918,* pp. 58-59.

catastrophic if the complete depreciation of our ruble should occur before we have had time to complete our economic reconstruction. However, this is not likely to happen. The toiling masses of Russia and the international proletariat have faith in the prospective economic reconstruction of Russia upon a new socialist basis. Our bourgeois neighbors in Europe appreciate this country's economic power, as is proved by the rise in the rate of exchange of the ruble on the European markets. Finally, the world revolution is fast approaching and we need not fear an economic failure.

MONEYLESS ECONOMY [82]

Communist society will know nothing of money. Every worker will produce goods for the general welfare. He will not receive any certificate to the effect that he has delivered a product to society; in other words, he will receive no money. Likewise, he will pay no money to society when he receives from the common store what he requires. . . .

Socialism, however, is communism in the process of construction . . . , and in the proportion that the work of construction is successfully carried on the need for money will disappear. In due time the state will probably be compelled to put an end to the expiring monetary circulation. This is particularly necessary to bring about the complete disappearance of the bourgeois classes, which with hoarded money continue to consume products created by the worker in a society which has proclaimed: "He who does not work shall not eat."

Thus at the very outset of the socialist revolution money begins to lose its significance. . . . By degrees a system of moneyless accounting will be introduced. . . . The gradual disappearance of money will likewise be promoted by the extensive issue of paper money on the part of the state. . . .

But the heaviest blow to the monetary system will be delivered by the introduction of budget books and the payment of workers in kind. In the work-book will be entered what the holder has produced, and this will represent how much the state owes him. The worker will receive from the consumer's store products corresponding to the entries in his book.

[82] Bukharin i Preobrazhensky, *op. cit.*, pp. 284-86.

CHAPTER VIII

THE BOLSHEVIKS AND THE PEASANTS

In their attempt to introduce a communist economic order the Bolsheviks found no problem more perplexing than that presented by agriculture. While realizing that the social revolution which they were initiating could not succeed without the support or at least the acquiescence of the peasantry, the Bolsheviks also had to acknowledge that the agrarian solution to which they were committed by their Marxian doctrines was contrary to the desires of the peasants, who constituted the great bulk of the Russian people. As Marxists the Bolsheviks looked upon agriculture as an organic part of the national economy, a part which was to be included in a unified scheme of socialized production and distribution by introducing large-scale methods of farming, by transforming the peasants into proletarians, and by establishing rigid control over agricultural production. But the peasant was mainly interested in receiving an additional allotment of land and was least of all willing to give up individual forms of farming or to relinquish the right of disposing of his products as he saw fit.

In their desire to win over the peasants to the new régime, the Bolsheviks for a considerable time compromised with their Marxist doctrines and fell in with some of the wishes of the peasants. The land decree announced by Lenin at the Second Congress of Soviets on November 8, 1917, adopted in entirety the agrarian program of the Socialist-Revolutionists in that it not only declared the land state property but also affirmed the principle of its equal distribution. This principle was popular among the peasants and Lenin declared [1] that the Bolsheviks' adoption of the land program of their political opponents was but an expression of the ultra-democratic character of the new government. The interparty negotiations which followed the establishment of the Soviet régime resulted in an agreement between the Bolsheviks and the Left Socialist-Revolutionists by which the latter were placed in control of the Commissariat of Agriculture and given a free hand to carry out the agrarian reform in accordance with their own principles of land socialization.[2]

The carrying out of the agrarian reform soon disclosed fundamental divergencies between theory and practice. In the first place, the land decree was not administered uniformly. The country was broken up into thousands of small units in which the local soviets or the land committees began to execute the reform in accordance with their own conceptions. Knipovich, an agricultural expert of the Commissariat of Agriculture, gives the following account of the prevailing practices in connection with the land reform:

"The transformation of Russia into an all-embracing commune with frequent redistribution of land on the basis of equality, contemplated in the program of the Socialist-Revolutionists, could not be realized. In practice the land was simply appropriated by the local peasants, who made no attempt to migrate from localities where land was scarce to those where it was in greater abundance. Equal distribution of land inside a village took place everywhere, but equalization between volosts was less frequent. Still less frequent were the cases of equal distribution between uezds and gubernias." [3]

---

[1] See Lenin's speech at the Second Congress of Soviets, in *The Bolshevik Revolution*, p. 132.

[2] These were embodied in the law of land socialization of February 19, 1918. See *ibid.*, pp. 673-78.

[3] B. Knipovich, "Napravlenie i itogi agrarnoi politiki 1917-20gg.," in *O zemle*, I, 24-25.

In the second place, the bulk of the peasantry interpreted the socialization law as affecting landlord and state lands only, so that in the majority of cases peasant lands remained untouched by the reform. In the law-abiding regions where an attempt was made to cut off surplus lands from individual farms having more than the "consumption-labor standard" [4] allowed, the wealthy peasants, in order to save their land, cattle, and implements, would break up their farms, dividing them among the members of their households. This practice reduced considerably the size both of the average peasant family and of the average farm.[5] Moreover, the peasants showed no disposition to adopt the large-scale collective farming which the Bolsheviks urged upon them.

But the most disquieting element in the situation was the stubborn refusal of the peasants to acquiesce in Soviet food policies, which from May 9 on required the surrender of all food surpluses to the government. Peasant opposition to these policies led to an open war between the government and the peasants and resulted eventually in a break between the Bolsheviks and the Socialist-Revolutionists of the Left.[6] After that break the Bolsheviks abandoned the land policy of the Socialist-Revolutionists and reverted to a strictly Marxian program of collective farms and large-scale methods of agriculture.

A. THE BREAD WAR

During the early period of the revolution the Bolsheviks hoped to obtain necessary foodstuffs by an exchange in

[4] The "consumption-labor standard," as defined in the law of land socialization, was an area of land large enough to enable a farmer to provide an adequate living for himself and his family without hired labor. See *The Bolshevik Revolution*, p. 676.

[5] Yu. Larin i L. Kritsman, *Ocherk khoziaistvennoi zhizni i organizatsiia narodnago khoziastva v sovetskoi Rossii*, pp. 10-11.

[6] See pp. 197 ff., above.

kind between city and village. A few months of such exchange only served to intensify the food crisis. The requisite supplies of food were not forthcoming, partly because after the separation of the grain-producing regions, viz., the Ukraine, the Don, the Northern Caucasus, and Siberia, not much surplus grain was left in Central Russia, and partly because of other circumstances. The chaotic demobilization of the army had ruined transport; there was no efficient machinery of distribution; and the countryside was invaded by speculators who offered the peasant much higher prices than the government, in its adherence to a policy of fixed prices, was willing to give.

Toward the spring of 1918 the grain-consuming regions [7] of Russia were reduced to a condition of starvation. Seeing that the revolution was in serious danger, the Bolsheviks decided to change their food policy. Through Sverdlov, its chairman, the Central Executive Committee declared on May 20 that the class struggle had to be carried into the village, where the peasants were to be divided into two hostile camps. For this purpose armed detachments of city workers were sent to the villages to requisition grain surpluses. At the same time special committees of poor peasants were created and given full power to redistribute the land, requisition horses, and help the city workers to extract the grain forcibly from the well-to-do peasants.

THE FOOD SITUATION IN NORTHERN RUSSIA

[From the Proceedings of the Food Congress of the Northern Region, April 30, 1918] [8]

The Congress of Food Organizations of the Northern Regions held its opening session. V. G. Groman was elected chairman.

---

[7] The name given by Russian agricultural economists to regions which do not raise their own food supplies.

[8] *Svoboda Rossii*, No. 17, May 1, 1918, p. 4.

Reports by local delegates drew a gloomy picture of famine and bloody fights for food which are taking place among the people.

In Petrograd Gubernia there have been cases in which armed detachments [guarding] food trains . . . were disarmed by peasants and bread was plundered. Butter and meat are rationed in Petrograd Gubernia in the quantity of one pound [Russian] to a person per month. Eggs are allowed only to children and the sick.

In Vologodsky Gubernia . . . it is expected that about nine hundred thousand will be starving in June and July. Two and a half million food rations will be required every month during the winter and spring of 1919. In certain places the peasants refuse to sow, hoping to save the seeds for food.

In Pskov Gubernia the German advance and the evacuation completely disrupted the organization of food supply. Over three hundred railway cars have been plundered during the past year. Unauthorized requisitions and searches are going on in every volost. There has been no sugar since November.

In Novgorod Gubernia there are no seeds and no means of acquiring them.

In Archangel Gubernia a shipment of bread en route to France was seized. A bread reserve was thus formed. The daily ration in Archangel is three-quarters of a pound.

The situation is especially bad in the parts of Vitebsk Gubernia under [German] occupation. No bread rations have been issued in Vitebsk for the past six days. . . .

The critical food conditions were not confined to the North. Parts of Central Russia and especially the large cities were experiencing a similar shortage of food. The Bolsheviks undertook to solve the crisis by forcing the peasants to surrender all grain surpluses.

FOOD DICTATORSHIP

[Decree of the Central Executive Committee, May 9, 1918] [9]

. . . Having considered the general situation and the fact that Russia can overcome the food crisis only by taking the strictest

[9] S. U. R., No. 35, 1918, pp. 437-38.

account of and effecting an equal distribution of grain reserves, the All-Russian Central Executive Committee of Soviets has resolved:

1. To reaffirm its stand in favor of the grain monopoly and fixed prices, as well as to recognize the necessity of continuing a merciless fight against the bread speculators and bagmen [10] and of compelling every possessor of surplus grain to declare within a week from the promulgation of this resolution in the volost that he is ready to hand over all in excess of what he needs, according to the established living standard, for sowing and consumption until the new crop. The order of these declarations shall be determined by the Commissariat of Food through the local food departments.

2. To call on all the toilers and propertyless peasants to unite at once and begin a merciless fight against the kulaks.

3. To denounce as enemies of the people all those who have surplus grain but do not bring it to the delivery stations, as well as those who use their grain for illicit distilling. These shall be handed over to the Revolutionary Court to be sentenced to prison for a term of not less than ten years, and shall be expelled forever from their communes and suffer confiscation of their property. Those guilty of illicit distilling shall be sentenced, in addition, to compulsory public work.

4. To confiscate without compensation any surplus grain which has not been reported in accordance with Article 1. One half of the value of the confiscated grain, determined on the basis of fixed prices and after it has actually reached the delivery station, shall go to the person who gave the information about the concealed surplus; the other half shall go to the village community. Information about concealed surpluses shall be given to the local food organizations.

Taking also into consideration the fact that the fight against the food crisis required the adoption of quick and decisive measures, that the most effective way of carrying out these measures requires the centralization into a single institution of all ordinances relating to food, and that the People's Commissariat of Food is such an institution, the All-Russian Central Executive Committee of

[10] People carrying bags with food which had been bought from peasants with the view of selling it at high prices.

Soviets has resolved to confer on the People's Commissariat of Food the powers named below. . . .

1. To issue binding orders in relation to food which are usually beyond the powers of the People's Commissariat of Food.

2. To repeal such orders of the local food organs and other organizations and institutions as are in conflict with the plans and acts of the People's Commissariat of Food.

3. To demand from all governmental institutions and organizations immediate and unconditional obedience to all food orders issued by the People's Commissariat of Food.

4. To use armed force in cases of resistance to the requisition of grain and other food products.

5. To dissolve or reorganize local food departments if they oppose the orders of the People's Commissariat of Food.

6. To dismiss, remove, arrest, and turn over to the Revolutionary Tribunal the officials and employees of governmental and public institutions who interfere with the execution of the orders of the People's Commissariat of Food.

7. To delegate these powers, except the power of arrest (Article 6), to local agents and institutions approved by the Soviet of People's Commissars.

8. To consult with the Commissariat of Communication and the Supreme Council of National Economy on all matters in which their several departments are involved. . . .

9. The orders and decrees of the People's Commissariat of Food issued by virtue of the authority herein conferred are subject to the scrutiny of the Collegium of the People's Commissariat of Food, which has the right, without interfering with the execution of the orders, to lodge complaints with the Soviet of People's Commissars.

The present decree becomes effective on the day of its signing and is to be promulgated by telegraph.

YA. SVERDLOV
Chairman of the Central
Executive Committee

V. ULIANOV (LENIN)
President of the Sovnarkom

OPPOSITION TO THE FOOD DICTATORSHIP

[From Karelin's Speech in the Central Executive Committee, May 9, 1918] [11]

. . . We Socialist-Revolutionists of the Left find that the decree . . . contains very risky orders. . . . Who are the kulaks . . . against whom the decree is directed? . . . It is necessary to define this category with greater precision. . . . The decree is characterized by a bureaucratic approach . . . and all bureaucracy is dangerous. . . . The decree is based on the idea . . . of dictatorship . . . and our party is opposed to dictatorship. . . . The dictatorship in the village will produce nothing but fighting in the village. . . .

[From Dan's Speech in the Central Executive Committee, May 9, 1918] [12]

. . . The policy . . . of [food] dictatorship is calculated to cause an armed conflict with the peasantry. . . . Since they incite the city population against the village such methods of settling the food problem will result in arousing the peasants against . . . the revolution. As far as the collection of grain is concerned the results will be negative, and the intensification of civil war is not likely to induce the peasants to increase the area under cultivation. . . .

FAMINE IN PETROGRAD

[Appeal of the Sovnarkom, May 10, 1918] [13]

Petrograd is experiencing an unprecedented catastrophe. There is no bread. The population is receiving what was left of potato flour and hardtack. The Red capital is on the brink of ruin from starvation. The counter-revolutionists are raising their heads, inciting the dissatisfied, starving masses against the Soviet Government. Our class enemies, the imperialists of all countries, are aiming to crush the Socialist Republic. . . . The situation can be saved only if the Soviet organizations do their utmost . . . to send food trains at once. We demand in the name of the Soviet Socialist Republic that Petrograd be given help at once. . . .

[11] *Protokoly zasedanii Vserossiiskogo Tsentralnogo Ispolnitelnogo Komiteta 4-go sozyva,* pp. 255-56.
[12] *Ibid.,* p. 257.
[13] *Svoboda Rossii,* No. 22, May 11, 1918, p. 3.

Failure to help is a crime against the Soviet Socialist Republic, against the world socialist revolution.

LENIN

President of the Sovnarkom

TSIURUPA

People's Commissar of Food

THE BOLSHEVIKS DECLARE WAR ON THE KULAKS

[From a Speech by Sverdlov in the Central Executive Committee, May 20, 1918][14]

. . . The kulak elements among the peasants are growing stronger every day and will soon prove a formidable source of trouble. We have succeeded thus far in destroying the bourgeoisie in the cities, but the same cannot be said of the villages. . . . We must direct our most concentrated attention upon the problem of splitting the village by creating two diametrically opposed and hostile camps. . . . This we can accomplish by fanning the flames of civil war in the village . . . , by arming the village poor against the village bourgeoisie. . . .

[Resolution of the Central Executive Committee, May, 20, 1918] [15]

The All-Russian Central Executive Committee, having discussed the question of the tasks of the soviets in the village, considers it imperative to point out the urgent necessity of uniting the toiling peasantry against the village bourgeoisie. Local soviets must undertake immediately the task of explaining to the poor that their interests are opposed to those of the kulaks, and of arming the poor with the purpose of establishing their dictatorship in the village.

HOW TO FIGHT THE FAMINE

[From Lenin's Speech at the Congress of the Commissars of Labor, May 22, 1918] [16]

. . . The mass of workers still live under the impression of the past and believe that we shall somehow muddle through. These

---

[14] *Protokoly . . . Tsentralnogo Ispolnitelnogo Komiteta 4-go sozyva*, p. 294.
[15] *Ibid.*, p. 310.   [16] *Sochineniia*, XXIII, 34-35.

illusions, however, are daily being crushed. It becomes more and more evident that the World War threatens whole countries with hunger and extinction unless the working class organizes to prevent ruin. Alongside the class-conscious elements of the working class, which are endeavoring to build a new cooperative discipline, there are millions of small owners and petty-bourgeois elements who are guided by no other ideals than their own narrow interests. We cannot fight the approaching famine and catastrophe in any other way than by the rule of class consciousness. Short of this we are helpless. On account of the enormous size of Russia . . . bread is plentiful in one corner and lacking in another. We must not deceive ourselves into believing that we can avoid a defensive war which [our enemies] may impose upon us. We must not deceive ourselves into believing that the towns and large industrial centers can be fed without organized transportation. We must keep track of every pud of bread [and see to it] that not one is lost. But we know that at present this is not being done. . . . Small speculators demoralize the village poor by telling them that the shortage can be overcome by [permitting] private trade. . . .

Russia can have enough bread for all . . . , enough fuel for industry, if all available supplies are accurately distributed among all citizens so that no one receives an extra pound of bread and not a single pound of fuel remains unused. Only in this way can the country be saved from famine. This communistic lesson of dividing up, of keeping track of everything in order to provide people with bread and industry with fuel, is a lesson learned not from books but from bitter experience. The mass of workers may not realize at once that we are face to face with a catastrophe. The workers must· organize a crusade against disruption, against the concealment of grain. It is necessary to organize a crusade, to spread throughout the country the idea of labor discipline, . . . in order that the masses may understand that there is no other way out. The strength of class-conscious workers during the course of our revolution lay in their ability to face bitter and dangerous reality . . . and to estimate accurately their own strength. We can rely only upon the class-conscious workers; the rest of the masses—the bourgeoisie and small owners—are against us. They do not believe in the new order . . . , as is evidenced by their acts in the Ukraine and Finland. . . . We know that the . . .

16

class-conscious workers in Russia are not numerous . . . , [but] the time is not far off when the masses will realize the uselessness of half-measures. . . . We live at a time when whole countries are being destroyed and millions of people are condemned to ruin and military slavery. History has called upon us to end this condition, brought about not by the evil will of certain individuals but by the collapse . . . of the whole capitalist system.

Comrades, Commissars of Labor! Make use of . . . every opportunity to explain the present situation to the workers in order that they may know that we are doomed to complete extermination unless we defend ourselves . . . , unless the poor organize a crusade and conquer the chaos and disruption. . . . [17]

THE COMMISSARIAT OF FOOD

[Decree of the Central Executive Committee, May 27, 1918] [18]

1. Recognizing the necessity of centralizing in one institution the entire provisioning of the population with articles of prime necessity and foodstuffs, of organizing on a national scale the distribution of these articles, and of paving the way for the nationalization of trade in articles of prime necessity, the All-Russian Central Executive Committee of Soviets of Workers', Soldiers', Peasants', and Cossacks' Deputies has resolved to charge the People's Commissariat of Food with the execution of the above-mentioned tasks.

2. Central organs regulating the production and distribution of certain articles of prime necessity shall make their policy of distribution conform to all regulations issued by the People's Commissariat of Food. Agencies which have a purely distributive function are placed within the jurisdiction of the People's Commissariat of Food.

Note: General plans of distributing articles of prime necessity,

---

[17] Commenting on Lenin's speech, *Svoboda Rossii,* No. 34, May 25, 1918, p. 1, says: "The President of the Sovnarkom speaks very eloquently. There is only one thing he fails to tell his "advance-guard"—where bread supplies are to be found. It is a well-established fact that Great Russia has no bread. As for the supplies in the Ukraine and elsewhere, the Soviet Government's arms are too short to reach them. As regards the "crusades" for bread—those have been declared long ago . . . by the "speculators."

[18] *S. U. R.,* No. 38, 1918, pp. 471-75.

the production of which is regulated by the Supreme Council of National Economy, are ratified by the People's Commissariat of Food in concurrence with the Chairman of the Supreme Council of the National Economy. . . .

3. Prices of articles of prime necessity are established by the Supreme Council of National Economy in conjunction with the People's Commissariat of Food.

4. Distribution of goods to the population shall be carried out by local food organs and cooperative organizations in accordance with the decree on cooperative organizations of April 11, 1918 (*S. U. R.*, No. 32, Chapter 418).

Note: Private trade in articles of prime necessity is allowed only under the control of regional and gubernia food organs and in accordance with the general instructions of the People's Commissariat of Food. . . .

5. A Council of Supply attached to the People's Commissariat of Food is hereby established for the purpose of drafting plans for the distribution of articles of prime necessity, the obtaining of agricultural products, the exchange of goods, and the coordination of activities of organizations in charge of food supply. This Council is vested with advisory powers and shall consist of representatives of the People's Commissariat of Food, the Supreme Council of National Economy, the People's Commissariats of Trade and Industry, Ways and Communication, Agriculture, and War and the Navy, local and central food committees, and the Central Union of Cooperative Societies. The Council shall act in accordance with special rulings issued by the Commissariat of Food. . . .

[The rest of the decree provides for the organization of local food organs, the formation of workers' detachments for the collection of grain, the enforcement of the grain monopoly, and the distribution of articles of prime necessity among the rural population.]

Ya. Sverdlov
Chairman of the Central
Executive Committee

V. Ulianov (Lenin)
President of the Sovnarkom

THE FIGHT FOR BREAD

[From Lenin's Speech in the Central Executive Committee, June 4, 1918] [19]

. . . We are engaged in building up a dictatorship, a régime of violence against the exploiters; whoever does not grasp this simple truth we cast away from us . . . so as not to waste words with him. . . . We are facing a new historical task. We need . . . agitators from the workers . . . to preach the Soviet idea . . . , to arouse the poor against the rich . . . , to lead in the food war against the kulaks.

The fight against the kulaks is taking the form of uniting the poor against them. . . . In order to obtain bread we must be ready to make common cause with the poor, . . . and this we have already done. We are adopting a policy of violence against the kulaks, the criminals who torture tens of millions of the population with hunger. . . . To the village poor we are offering all kinds of rewards. . . . We are ready to help them if they will help us . . . to get food from the kulaks. We shall use every means to . . . accomplish this end.

[From a Speech by Trotsky, June 9, 1918] [20]

Comrades! I come before you in a very trying . . . period of the history of our . . . Soviet Republic. Of all the difficulties which confront us . . . , the most pressing . . . is that of food. . . . How to live tomorrow is the concern that is uppermost in the minds of all. . . . Instead of the situation becoming better it is daily growing worse. It is bad in Petrograd, it is bad in Moscow, but it is still worse elsewhere in Russia. . . . Here is a telegram . . . : "Give us bread or we perish." . . . Here is another . . . : "The death-rate is terrible . . . , hunger-typhus is raging." . . . I could go on and on citing similar telegrams but it is unnecessary. . . . Famine is not a new thing in Russia. . . . In the time of Alexander III and Nicholas II the Americans sent shiploads of grain to Russia. . . .

Are we perishing from hunger now because there is no food in the country or because we do not know how to get hold of it and

[19] *Sochineniia,* XXIII, 58-61.
[20] *Kak vooruzhalas revoliutsiia,* I, 74-86.

. . . distribute it properly? . . . There is food in abundance, but it must be said to our shame that the workers and the village poor have not yet learned state management, have not yet learned to seize the food reserves and distribute them to the toilers and famine-stricken masses. . . . There is enough grain to last not only until the new crop but even until 1919. . . .

The question is how to get hold . . . of the millions of bushels of grain . . . in the hands of the village bourgeoisie, the kulaks, and the speculators. . . . The bourgeoisie says . . . : "Remove the grain monopoly, do away with price-fixing, declare free trade in grain." . . . If that were done, they say, . . . "our wives, mothers, and sisters would have no difficulty in providing our dinners and suppers." This is not true. Such a solution would be ruinous. . . .

If the Soviet Government were to remove the grain monopoly, . . . all the speculators . . . would make a rush . . . for the bread reserves, and prices would soar to . . . a hundred or more rubles for a pud of grain. . . . That is not all. To transport the grain . . . the spectators would compete for freight-cars with all the accompanying evils of graft and crookedness. . . . By the time a pud of grain reached Moscow it would cost about two hundred or more rubles . . . , quite out of reach of the poor workman . . . , who would suffer more than he does now. . . .

[To raise the price of bread is equally unsound.] The people who would benefit by this . . . are the kulaks. . . . They would hold on to the grain . . . until it went up still higher. . . . Just now the kulak is not in need of paper money. As a matter of fact he has so much of it on hand that he no longer counts it but weighs it by the pound, seals it up in bottles, and buries it in the ground.

[The kulak has still another motive.] He thinks that . . . if he can starve the city for a while longer there will be hunger uprisings . . . which will lead to the overthrow of the Soviet Government and the restoration of the bourgeoisie. . . .

The bourgeoisie is tricky. . . . It is mobilizing against us all its forces . . . —the village bourgeoisie, the newspapers, and the propagandists, who shout: "Don't let the grain go to the cities. Hold it. . . . Starve Petrograd and Moscow into submission; break the spirit of the workingman . . . and bring back the rich to lord it over the poor."

The kulaks are the advance-guard of the counter-revolution.
. . . They are the worst enemies of the city and of the village
poor. They hide food in barns . . . while people in the city are
dying of hunger and typhus. . . . The Central Executive Committee . . . was more than right when it announced that the
Soviet Government would not tolerate such a condition. . . . We
are against private property in general and private property in
grain in particular. . . . As Communists we recognize only one
sacred right—the right of the toiler, his wife, and his child to
live. . . .

The question may be asked: "If the lives of our wives and
children. . . are so dear to us why not pay two hundred or four
hundred rubles for a pud of flour . . . ?"

In order to provide for the increase in the cost of living . . .
it would be necessary to raise wages. . . . In the end we would
get nowhere. It would be like trying to quench thirst by drinking
salt water. . . .

There is still another question . . . : "Why take the grain
. . . by force when we can get it . . . in exchange for manufactured goods?" Unfortunately . . . the kulak does not need
our goods. . . . Five puds of grain will supply him with all the
nails and calico that he can possibly use. This still leaves him
hundreds and thousands of puds of grain on hand. . . . The
people who really need the calico and nails are the village poor, but
they have no grain to exchange. . . . We therefore propose to
take grain from the kulaks through the committees of the poor
. . . without exchanging it [for manufactured articles]. . . .
We did not hesitate to wrest the land from the landowner, the
factories . . . from the capitalist, . . . the crown from the
stupid head of the Tsar. Why, then, should we hesitate to take
the grain from the kulak . . . ?

With this in mind the Central Executive Committee has made
the following announcement: "Peasants! The cities are ready to
part with . . . cloth, leather, machines [etc.], but not to give
them to the kulak. They will give these things to the village poor,
who in turn must take the grain from the kulak. If the kulaks
should refuse to give it up voluntarily, it must be taken by force
. . . and divided up in a brotherly manner among the hungry in
the city and the village." If we cannot do this we have failed. . . .

. . . The bourgeoisie, Socialist-Revolutionists, and Mensheviks are trying to frighten us by saying: "You are starting a civil war—the city against the village." . . . That is not true. It is not a war of the city against the village but a . . . struggle of the city and the village poor on the one side against the rich and the kulaks on the other. . . .

In order to carry out this policy . . . the Soviet Government issued a decree on May 13.[21] This decree . . . makes it compulsory for everyone to declare how much grain he has, how much he needs for his family, stock, and seed, and what surplus he has. This surplus he must surrender to the Soviet food organizations at fixed prices. Whoever fails to do so will be regarded as a criminal, and it will be the duty of every person . . . to denounce him to the Soviet authorities. . . . They will take his grain from him without . . . paying for it and will turn him over to the iron hand of the court to be treated as a murderer and sentenced to ten years of compulsory labor. . . . This is a good law . . . and we have already had echoes of it from different parts of the country. . . . Here is a telegram from Elts: "Agents have been ordered into every volost to keep an eye on the volost soviets. Committees of the poor . . . are being organized in every village and are making an inventory of the surplus grain." . . . Here is another from Voronezh: "Special detachments of workmen have been called out to requisition grain . . . from the kulaks." . . . It is clear that to enforce the decree of May 13 we must have committees of the poor everywhere. . . .

We have still another problem. . . . Ufa telegraphs us to send food detachments from the famine area. This . . . is necessary and important . . . because only those from the famine belt know what the pangs of hunger are like. . . . When these detachments reach their destination they should address themselves to the poor of the village and say: "We, hungry workmen, have come to you, village poor, to make you this friendly proposition. We have cloth, metal, nails, and similar things which we want to exchange for bread. . . . Have you any bread to exchange?"

"No. . . . We have barely enough to last until the next crop."

"How about your neighbors?"

"They have more than enough."

[21] The decree on "Food Dictatorship," quoted above, pp. 460-62.

"Let's go to their places and find out how much they have. . . . Have they horses and carts?"

"Yes, they have both."

"We shall load the grain on the carts. Half we shall leave for the poor of this region . . . and the other half we shall send to Petrograd and Moscow."

These Moscow and Petrograd detachments should include a few women, wives, and mothers, who know better than anyone else what suffering means. . . . When these women . . . face the kulaks they will tell them what they think of them. . . . The kulaks will not dare to oppose this combination of village poor and city workers. . . . After all, the kulaks are outnumbered . . . twenty to one by the toilers who are suffering from hunger. . . . Of course, if the kulaks put up a fight, if they make use . . . of rifles and machine guns, we shall have to fight them mercilessly. But it will not come to that. . . . What we need in the fight for bread is determination and courage. . . . Comrade Zinoviev reported today that four thousand Petrograd workmen, fully armed, have just started for the bread front. They have not only good rifles but also persuasive tongues . . . and will make excellent agitators among the village poor. . . . On June 8 the Soviet of People's Commissars discussed the question of forming, along with the volost and village soviets, committees of the poor. These people know as well as do the workers what it means to be hungry and undernourished. With these committees it will be possible to carry out the Soviet policies in the village. . . .

COMMITTEES OF THE VILLAGE POOR

[Decree of the Central Executive Committee, June 11, 1918] [22]

1. Volost and village committees of the poor, organized by local Soviets of Workers' and Peasants' Deputies with the participation of the [local] food departments and under the general control of the People's Commissariat of Food and the All-Russian Central Executive Committee, shall be established everywhere. . . .

2. Both native and newly arrived inhabitants of the village may elect and be elected to volost and village committees of the poor, with the exception of notorious kulaks . . . who possess

[22] *S. U. R.*, No. 43, 1918, pp. 522-24.

grain surpluses and other food products, and owners of commercial and industrial enterprises using hired labor, etc.

Note: Peasants employing labor on farms which do not exceed the consumption standard may elect and be elected to the committees of the poor.

3. The volost and village committees of the poor discharge the following duties:

a) Distribution of food, goods of prime necessity, and farming implements.

b) Assistance to local food departments in requisitioning surplus grain from kulaks and the rich. . . .

7. The distribution of grain, goods of prime necessity, and farming implements must accord with the standards set up by the gubernia food departments and conform to the general plans of the People's Commissariat of Food. . . .

8. For the time being and until the People's Commissar of Food makes special rulings, the basis of grain distribution shall be as follows:

a) Grain is distributed among the village poor in accordance with the established standards and free of charge, at the expense of the state. The distribution is made out of the grain surpluses which have been fully requisitioned from the kulaks and the rich in accordance with the decision of the gubernia and uezd soviets . . . and have been delivered to the state grain storehouses. . . .

10. Volost committees of the poor are to take charge of the more complicated agricultural machinery and to organize communal cultivation of the fields and harvesting for the village poor; no charge will be made for the use of such machinery in places where the volost and village committees of the poor give energetic support to the food departments in requisitioning the surplus from the kulaks and the rich.

11. The Soviet of People's Commissars will place at the disposal of the People's Commissariat of Food such money as may be needed from time to time to execute this decree.

YA. SVERDLOV

Chairman of the Central
Executive Committee

V. ULIANOV (LENIN)
President of the Sovnarkom

CIVIL WAR IN THE VILLAGES

[*Pravda's* Account, July 2, 1918] [23]

All parties, from the Cadets to the Left S. R.'s, are opposing the organization of committees of the village poor, the crusade of the class-conscious city proletarians fighting against the kulaks and the rich, the gospel of the class struggle among the peasants.

All these parties blame the Soviet Government and our party for artificially fanning civil war in the village, maintaining that our food detachments will do only harm to the countryside.

Nevertheless, the local news which we receive from the villages indicates that the decree of the Central Executive Committee relating to the committees of the village poor was not invented by our party, which, it is presumed, desires to instigate . . . useless bloodshed.

All news points to the fact that fighting of the poor against the rich, of the village proletarians against the kulaks, is of common occurrence, and that the decree in question is the appropriate and timely expression of an urgent need.

The class struggle which is taking place between the poor and the kulaks . . . often assumes the form of armed clashes. We find in the provincial newspapers . . . interesting accounts of the . . . revolutionary struggle conducted by the village poor against their own kulaks.

The volost soviets and the committees of the poor appear to be eyesores to . . . the village bourgeoisie, which . . . is engaged in organizing counter-revolutionary offensives against the Soviet Government. . . .

Conditions in Nizhegorodsky Gubernia give many such examples. One is the village of Shargoli, of Pavlovsk Uezd, where the kulaks had organized themselves, murdered three Bolsheviks, and "knocked down the Soviet." But then comrades from Bogoroditskoe and Pavlovsk came to the rescue and "knocked down the kulaks."

Take, for example, Kozievskaia Volost of Vasilevsky Uezd. The poor, numbering about two hundred men, had elected an Executive Committee. The kulaks gathered a crowd of about a thousand people and attacked the Soviet. . . . But the poor did not

[23] Piontkovsky, *G. V. R.*, pp. 183-85.

give up their positions; a small group of men armed with . . . rifles succeeded in dispersing the angry mob.

It is clear that the poor are forced to defend their organizations with arms. The kulaks are practical men and do not fight the soviets with empty hands. They act with arms, and naturally the fight against them turns into bloody clashes. The armed detachments of city workers which come to the villages render all possible assistance to the poor in their struggle against their enemies and those of the city proletariat.

Very often the poor succeeded in defeating their enemies without any outside help. Thus in the village of Migalikhi, in Nizhegorodsky Gubernia, a small but well-organized group of former soldiers who had recently returned from the front . . . succeeded in warding off an attack on the Volost Soviet led by the kulaks and supported by the ignorant masses, who blindly followed these kulaks because they promised an earthly paradise if the free sale of grain were introduced.

The Migalikhi bourgeoisie, like our Mensheviks and Right S. R.'s, play on the ignorance and darkness of the masses. . . .

The class struggle in the village is in progress. No effort of the parties, from the Cadets to the Left S. R.'s, can stop the cleavage which began long ago in the village. The decree of the Central Executive Committee gave definite meaning and organization to this struggle, and the Soviet Government, being a government of workers and peasants, is helping the village poor against the kulaks and the rich. . . .

FOOD-REQUISITION CORDONS

[Decree of the Sovnarkom, August 4, 1918] [24]

In order to establish strict order and regularity in the work of requisition cordons, all such cordons, without exception, must carry out undeviatingly the following instructions:

1. When undertaking the search of the baggage and freight of passengers en route all cordons must present credentials of an authorized organ which warrant the search and requisition of freight. . . .

2. The right of search applies not only to passenger but also

[24] *S. U. R.*, No. 57, 1918, pp. 690-91.

to service coaches and engines, with the exception of coaches of the State Bank and mail coaches, which are not subject to search.

3. All freight and hand luggage of passengers are subject to search.

4. The work of the cordons must as far as possible avoid interference with regular railroad and steamship transportation; in cases of extreme necessity and in the interest of a thorough search, trains and steamers may be delayed one hour but no more.

5. Food products may be transported in quantities limited to the amount necessary for one passenger, i. e., not more than twenty pounds [Russian] per consumer in all. This may not include flour or grain in any quantity whatsoever; it may include butter up to two pounds and meat products up to five. . . . Whatever exceeds this norm will be requisitioned. . . .

7. All requisitioned goods must be consigned by the chief of the cordon, on his personal responsibility, to the food department of the institutions in the name of which the cordon has been acting. . . .

V. ULIANOV (LENIN)
President of the Soviet People's Commissars

· FOOD-REQUISITION DETACHMENTS

[Decree of the Sovnarkom, August 6, 1918] [25]

1. The more important workers' trade unions (including those of railway workers), associations of factory and shop committees, and Uezd and City Soviets of Workers' and Peasants' Deputies are authorized to organize food detachments among the workers and poorest peasants, and to send them to the food-producing gubernias to obtain grain by either purchase at fixed prices or requisition from the kulaks.

2. At the head of each detachment shall be a group of responsible leaders chosen by the organization which has formed the detachment. This group shall include representatives from organs of the central and gubernia Soviet Government. All these leaders are responsible to the Soviet Government for the acts of the detachment.

3. The collection of grain by these detachments . . . is al-

[25] *Ibid.*, p. 690.

lowed only upon presentation of certificates from organizations which have sent the detachments and is to be conducted according to the instructions and under the control of the district food organs of the grain-producing gubernias. . . .

4. One-half of the collected grain is to be sent to the gubernia which fitted out the detachment and is to be used to fill directly the needs of the organization which procured this grain in the manner described below (Article 5); the other half is to remain at the place of collection to be turned over to the People's Commissariat of Food for distribution among all the famine-stricken workers and the poorest peasants of the Republic.

5. When the grain brought in by the detachment has reached its destination the organizations which have sent the detachment shall distribute the grain under the supervision of local supply organs and in accordance with established norms; the share received shall then be subtracted from the ration to which the party is entitled.

6. In case of attempts on the part of detachments to depart from or violate the above ordinance (e. g., buying grain above the fixed price, evasion of control of food organs, etc.) all the grain collected by them shall be taken away by the food organs and turned over to the state at established prices; the chiefs of such detachments and those of their members found to have violated the law shall be turned over to the nearest Extraordinary Commission to Fight Counter-Revolution, Sabotage, and Speculation, for the purpose of bringing them before the Revolutionary Tribunal.

7. Detachments which go out to collect grain are under obligation to help the local population in harvesting crops.

V. Ulianov (Lenin)
President of the Soviet of People's Commissars

ORGANIZATION OF FOOD-REQUISITION DETACHMENTS

[Ordinance of the Commissariat of Food, August 20, 1918] [26]

1. Every food detachment is to consist of not less than seventy-five men and two or three machine guns.

[26] *Sistematicheskii sbornik dekretov i rasporiazhenii pravitelstva po prodovolstvennomu delu,* I, 106-07.

2. At the head of every detachment is a commander, appointed by the chief commissar in charge of the organization of food armies, and a political commissar, appointed by the Commissariat of Food. . . .

The commander is in charge of the purely military and economic activities. The duties of the political commissar are: (a) to organize local committees of the poor; (b) to see to it that the detachment fulfills its duty and is imbued with revolutionary zeal and discipline. . . .

3. Uezd and gubernia military commanders are in charge of all food detachments operating in a given uezd or gubernia. . . .

4. General plans for grain requisition in a given uezd are framed by the chief of the requisition department, appointed by the gubernia food commissar. Plans for grain requisition in a gubernia are framed by the chief of the requisition department appointed by the gubernia. . . .

5. Food detachments are under the orders only of their immediate commanders. . . .

7. The detachments . . . should be distributed in a way that will make it easy for two or three detachments to unite in a short time. There should be continuous cavalry communication between different detachments. . . .

A. Tsiurupa

People's Commissar of Food

INSTRUCTIONS FOR REQUISITIONING GRAIN

[Ordinance of the Commissariat of Food, August 20, 1918] [27]

1. Upon arriving at a village with his food detachment the political commissar shall call a meeting of the village poor and explain not only the meaning of the decree on organizing the poorer classes of the village but also the rôle which the Russian counter-revolution and the kulaks are playing. He shall then . . . organize a committee to collect grain from the kulaks and distribute it . . . among the needy peasants. . . .

2. The committee of the poor and the political commissar of the detachment shall then issue an order to the population to sur-

[27] Ibid., pp. 107-08.

render all firearms. A part of the firearms is turned over to the newly elected committee in order to form an armed guard in connection with it; the rest must be sent by the commander of the detachment to the military commander of the gubernia. All machine guns and hand grenades must be confiscated. . . .

3. Having done this the food agents, assisted by the detachment and the members of the committee of the poor, shall proceed to make an inventory of all grain stores on hand . . . as well as to uncover those that have been hidden, with the exception of the grain which . . . the peasants need for their families, for seed, and for their cattle.

4. After the entire grain surplus of a given village has been ascertained, part of that surplus shall be distributed among the local poor . . . and the rest shipped to the nearest government storage depot. . . .

7. Grain voluntarily surrendered in due time is to be paid for at a fixed price. . . . The grain of those failing to comply with the law . . . shall be requisitioned at 25 per cent less than the fixed price. Hidden grain is subject to confiscation. . . .

11. Those who violate the law of grain monopoly by selling grain to bagmen or wasting it for home-brew shall be arrested and given up to the gubernia Cheka.

12. The food-requisition detachment shall not leave a village until all grain surpluses have been delivered. . . .

A. Tsiurupa
People's Commissar of Food

THE FOOD ARMY ADMINISTRATION [28]

[Fall of 1918]

The main purpose of the Food Army Administration is to assist . . . the Commissariat of Food in carrying out its program . . . of extracting grain surpluses from the peasants. At the head of the Food Army Administration shall be placed a committee of three, one member of which must be a military specialist. . . . A fourth member shall be appointed to keep the Food Army Administration in contact with the Commissariat of Food. . . .

The Food Army Administration is divided into three sections:

[28] *Ibid.,* p. 54.

(1) Food Army General Staff; (2) Division of Supplies; (3) Political Section. . . .

THE FOOD ARMY

[Report of the Commissariat of Food for 1918-1919] [29]

Since the promulgation of the decree on food monopoly, the Soviet Government has been endeavoring to create a machinery of coercion by the aid of which it could carry out the policies of the Commissariat of Food. In order to centralize all armed forces (food armies) required for that purpose, the Commissariat of Food appointed on May 20, 1918, a military commissar to take charge of all food detachments. Later that office developed into the Food Army Administration.

The idea of a food army was talked about everywhere but required a considerable period of time to take clear and definite form. At first there was no unified plan of action either at the center or in the provinces. Instead, under the pressure of necessity, separate food armies came into existence, sometimes at the suggestion of the central government, at other times through the initiative of the gubernia food committees. . . .

The Food Army Administration introduced a number of measures for the purpose of coordinating the various detachments. . . .

Apart from the question of the quantity of grain which the state managed to extract with the aid of the Food Army, one cannot fail to notice the almost unanimous testimony of all gubernia food committees to the effect that without the help of the Food Army they could not have collected whatever supplies they did succeed in assembling. The reports show that the people would not surrender their grain voluntarily and that only the presence of a Food Army rendered it possible to make an inventory of the grain surpluses and compel their surrender. . . .

During the food campaign [30] of 1918 the Food Army numbered from twenty thousand to forty-five thousand men. . . . It resembled the Red Army in its organization and was subject to all decrees affecting the army.

The methods employed by the Food Armies in requisitioning grain from the peasants are graphically described in a

[29] *Vtoroi god borby s golodom*, pp. 5-6.   [30] *Ibid.*, Introduction, p. vii.

report to the Commissariat of Food by L. Kaganovich, one of the leading requisitioning officers.[31]

The author tells how he arrived with a food-requisition detachment five thousand strong in the gubernia where he was "to collect the harvest," divided his army by regions, and formed "operative staffs." Within forty-eight hours the eleven million puds of grain for which the gubernia was assessed were apportioned to the individual villages at rates varying from five to thirty-five puds per desiatin. The detachment then proceeded to collect the grain by force, ignoring the principle of "exchange of goods." At times it was necessary to search the same farm ten times in order to find the hidden supplies. Refractory mobs of peasants were dispersed by sharpshooters and bombs; large villages were occupied at daybreak; and house-to-house searches were conducted. These measures produced the "necessary moral effect." The peasants were "brought to reason" and the grain tax was delivered in full.

ACTIVITIES OF THE COMMITTEES OF THE POOR [32]

. . . In the spring of 1918, when the political power of the proletariat was finally set up and established in the towns, there were formed everywhere . . . committees of the poor, composed exclusively of peasants who owned little or no land. They had practically complete power in their hands and were all armed. In the course of a few months these committees carried out a redistribution of land in the villages, requisitioned horses from the peasants who had more than the necessary minimum, and gave them to farmers who were just establishing themselves. . . . At the same time they helped factory workers in forcibly extracting grain surpluses from the . . . kulaks. The village and volost soviets established by the constitution were reduced to a secondary rôle

---

[31] The report is quoted in an unpublished manuscript in the Hoover War Library, Stanford University, entitled "Russian Agriculture and the Revolution."

[32] Larin i Kritsman, op. cit., pp. 13-14.

for a period of more than six months.[88] The committees of the poor practically controlled the agrarian revolution in the village, but their activities led in all parts of Soviet Russia to armed uprisings of the peasants—the very peasants who had welcomed the proletarian revolution when it abolished the political and economic yoke of the landlords but who rose against the revolution when in the course of its progress it brought about an economic leveling among the peasants themselves. However, all these uprisings were suppressed. . . .

B. AGRICULTURE

The Bolsheviks advocated radical innovations not only in the means of obtaining food but also in the methods of its production. In general their agrarian policy during the summer and fall of 1918 aimed at the replacement of the millions of small peasant holdings by large-scale collective farming, better adapted to the communist program of bringing agriculture into a governmentally controlled and integrated scheme of national economy. Specifically, the Communists proposed to pool the holdings of individual peasants, to organize peasants without land into large agricultural communes, and to have the state itself operate farms on specially selected lands.

Although aggressive in their food policy, the Bolsheviks were reluctant to coerce the peasants in bringing about collective farming. They believed that the peasants could be won over to the new ideas of agriculture by persuasion and encouragement. Accordingly, the huge machinery of Soviet propaganda was set in motion to spread the ideas of agrarian socialism throughout the land by broadsides, party instructions, and newspaper articles. In addition, both financial and agronomic aid was offered to the peasants

[88] The committees of the poor were formally abolished by decree of the Central Executive Committee, December 2, 1918. This decree also ordered a reelection of local soviets. *S. U. R.*, No. 86, 1918, pp. 1092-97.

as an inducement to form agricultural collectives and communal farms.

AGRARIAN TENDENCIES IN THE VILLAGE
[Letter from Syzransky Uezd] [34]

The village is experiencing a reaction from the stormy events which followed the November Revolution. One sees there evidences of a tacit dissatisfaction with existing conditions. Although much has come to the surface during this time, what stands out as the most prominent characteristic of the peasantry is not at all a tendency toward communism but the acquisitiveness and the economic egoism of the proprietor. Years of privation have made the peasant indifferent to the interests of others, and a sense of the obligation to make a sacrifice for the common good has failed to appear. . . . The peasant psychology is far removed from socialism. The seizure of somebody else's property is not socialism. . . .

The agrarian question is being solved in a simple way. The landlord's land is becoming the property of the peasant community. Each village takes the land which belonged to its former lord, and no other village can get an inch of that land. This is irrespective of the fact that the land in question may be in excess of the needs of the particular village and that the neighboring [village] population may have insufficient land. Such a viewpoint has taken deep root and . . . the attempt at equal distribution is encountering serious opposition. [The peasants argue that] it is better to leave the superfluous land with the landlord than to give it to peasants of another village. They say that they can always earn something from the landlord while he is using his land and that when necessity arises they can take the land away from him. The idea of land nationalization is entirely foreign and unintelligible to our agriculturists. Nationalization is bound to eventuate in a change of proprietorship. The place of the landlord will be taken by the village community or the [individual] peasant. . . .

[34] *Svoboda Rossii*, No. 26, May 18, 1918, p. 6.

Kostroma. In numerous uezds there is a movement on foot among the peasants to reestablish the authority of the old volost and village starshinas [elders]. . . . In most cases the former authorities are reinstated in the offices thus reestablished. The land committees remain intact but their members are reelected. In place of those who call themselves socialists there are elected old peasants with experience. . . .

The peasants do not even think of socializing the land. They simply add the allotments to their possessions as private property. The congress of land committees of Kostroma Gubernia was forced recently to sanction that procedure, but with the reservation that socialization was postponed for one year until statistical and other data were available.

Yaroslav. The peasants have dismissed the volost soviets in almost the whole uezd of Moloka and have reestablished the old volost authorities. . . .

THE COMMUNAL FARM MOVEMENT

[Newspaper Report] [36]

Forty agricultural communes have been formed in twelve uezds of the Ural Oblast. The Oblast Commissariat of Agriculture is supplying the communes with agricultural machinery. In certain villages labor duty has been introduced for the kulaks. Consumption goods are being distributed on communistic principles in the majority of communes.

OPPOSITION TO COMMUNAL FARMS [37]

The Soviet of Terekhovsky Volost has resolved to give the experimental farms back to the landlords in order to prevent their falling into the hands of labor artels.

"To hell with these 'labor' artels!" was the motion of the chairman of the Volost Soviet.

[35] *Ibid.*, No. 33, May 24, 1918, p. 4.
[36] *Novaia Zhizn*, No. 129, July 4, 1918, p. 4.
[37] *Nashe Slovo*, No. 61, July 4, 1918, p. 4.

The motion of the chairman was accepted unanimously by the Soviet.

APPROPRIATION FOR COMMUNAL FARMS

[Decree of the Sovnarkom, July 3, 1918] [38]

To help organize agriculture on socialist principles the Soviet of People's Commissars has resolved:

To appropriate . . . ten million rubles for the use of the People's Commissariat of Agriculture in organizing agricultural communes and subsidizing already existing communes.

V. Ulianov (Lenin)
President of the Sovnarkom

S. Sereda
People's Commissar of Agriculture

COMMUNAL AND SOVIET FARMS

[Resolution of the Moscow Congress of Soviets, July 27, 1918] [39]

The Moscow Congress of Soviets of Workers' and Peasants' Deputies, having considered . . . the question of the present status of land reform at the session of July 27, 1918 . . . , has adopted the following resolution:

The present land policy of the proletariat and the poor peasantry should be directed toward the organization of agricultural communes and Soviet farms.

Division among the agricultural population of the land, cattle, and agricultural implements formerly belonging to privately owned estates . . . is profitable only to the rich peasants. Such citizens as had no land or agricultural implements will not profit by this division. All they will obtain is a semblance of right to the land, for they are not in a position to cultivate it and will soon find themselves enslaved by kulaks. . . .

The only salvation of the poor is to organize communes . . . for the collective cultivation of land and to establish large and properly cultivated farms. . . . Land departments must supply

[38] *Syn Otechestva*, No. 4, July 6, 1918, p. 1.
[39] *Izvestiia*, No. 164, August 3, 1918, p. 4.

such communes with all necessities: seed, cattle, implements, money, etc.

Another very urgent need is the organization of communistic Soviet farms which will pave the way . . . to a socialist economy in agriculture and help to combat the food shortage. All vacant and uncultivated lands should at once be taken over by the soviets for this purpose. . . .

[Decree of the Commissariat of Agriculture, August 3, 1918] [40]

The ultimate purpose of the communal farms is to reorganize agriculture on a socialist basis. To achieve this end the communes must engage in a merciless fight against capital and resist by force of arms every counter-revolutionary attempt of the landlords, capitalists, and kulaks. Acting in full agreement with the organs of the Soviet Government, . . . [the communes] shall guard firmly the rights and interests of the proletariat and the village poor.

The communes shall endeavor:

1. To develop large-scale socialized agriculture by amalgamating communes. . . .

2. To institute a proper exchange of products between city and village.

3. To assist in the wide dissemination of political and agricultural information.

4. To raise the productivity of labor by introducing strict labor discipline and applying scientific methods of agriculture. . . .

5. To unite agriculture and industry in a single planned economy.

Those wishing to enter a commune must waive all claims to private property and surrender their estate (both real and movable) . . . to the commune. Each member of the commune is to perform the work for which he is best fitted, giving all his energies and abilities to serving the commune. Whoever does not work is not entitled to the goods of life. To each according to his needs, from each according to his capacities.

The commune must endeavor to build common living quarters for its members and to take care of their physical and spiritual

[40] *Instruktsii i polozheniia o kommunakh,* pp. 14-18.

development. . . . The charter of a commune shall contain . . . the following provisions:

I. GENERAL PRINCIPLES

1. The commune is a voluntary union of laborers aiming to live according to the principle of equality and devoted to large-scale . . . collective agriculture.
2. The commune is a potent instrument for the overthrow of every form of exploitation and for the organization of a socialist agriculture employing scientific and technological improvements.
3. The commune is a potent instrument of socialist education of the laboring classes . . . and a means of promoting the fraternal union of the proletariat and the poor peasants and of furthering the struggle between labor and capital.
4. The fundamental principle of the commune is: To each according to his needs, from each according to his capacities.
5. Everything in the commune belongs to everyone. Hiring of labor is prohibited.
6. The commune supports the Soviet form of government.

II. HOLDINGS OF THE COMMUNE

a. Land granted to the commune for use.
b. All real and movable property, including the money belonging to its members. . . .
c. Grants and loans from the Soviet Government.
d. All products of the labor of the commune.

III. ORGANIZATION OF THE COMMUNE

1. The commune consists of citizens of the working class . . . who accept the constitution of the commune.
2. Membership in a commune is open to all able-bodied persons of both sexes, with their families, who have reached the age of eighteen, no restriction being made on account of religion, nationality, or citizenship. . . .
3. New members may be accepted by the general assembly.
4. Members may be expelled by the general assembly.
5. Members of the commune are free to leave at any time.

6. All members are equal in their rights; each has a right to the products of common labor.

7. Every member is under obligation to work to the extent of his powers and capacities, to observe the . . . rules of the commune, and to assist in every way the successful development of the commune and the fraternal union of its members.

8. The internal regulations of the commune are established and modified by the general assembly of members.

9. Communes have no right to hire labor, and members of a commune cannot hire themselves out.

10. The executive organ of a commune is the soviet elected by the general assembly. . . .

IV. Distribution and Use of Communal Goods

Strict account must be kept of all products of communal economy. After provision for the needs of the commune, all remaining products on which there is a state monopoly must be turned over to Soviet food organizations. The remaining products on which there is no state monopoly may be exchanged for products and manufactured goods of which the commune may be in need.

V. Control Over Communal Activities

The land department of the uezd is charged with controlling the activities of the commune. . . .

VI. Liquidation of Communes

1. A commune may be liquidated by the Soviet organs of government. . . .

2. A commune may end its existence . . . by the resolution of the general assembly of members. In this case all communal property passes to the uezd land department. . . .

S. Sereda
People's Commissar of Agriculture

BUREAU OF COMMUNAL FARMS

[Decree of the Commissariat of Agriculture, August 17, 1918] [41]

I. Aim and Purpose

In order to place the organization of agricultural communes on a broad and planned basis, there should be formed at once a Bureau of Communes to operate in connection with the uezd and gubernia land departments.

II. Functions of the Bureau of Communes

The principal aims of the Bureau of Communes are:

1. To assist in every way the economic and cultural activities of the communes.

2. To consolidate the communes into a single planned socialist economy.

3. To train instructors who believe firmly in communal land cultivation and have had organizing experience. (It is desirable that they possess agronomic knowledge also.)

4. To prepare plans of communal farms in cooperation with the gubernia agronomic organization and to see that these plans are carried out.

The duties of the Bureau are as follows:

1. To register all communes which already exist as well as those to be formed. . . .

2. To examine and ratify estimates presented by the communes.

3. To see that all ordinances of the Soviet Government . . . relating to communes are strictly and accurately adhered to.

4. [To supply the government with information concerning existing communes.]

5. [To exercise control over communal activities.] . . .

N. Petrovsky
Acting People's Commissar of Agriculture

[41] *Ibid.,* pp. 21-22.

DELIVERY OF LIVE STOCK

[Ordinance of the People's Commissar of Food, August 24, 1918] [42]

In accordance with the decree of the Central Executive Committee of May 27, 1918,[43] and in modification and supplementation of existing rules on the obtaining . . . of . . . cattle, meat, and meat products, the following rules for the delivery of live stock . . . are hereby established:

1. If there is a shortage of deliveries, gubernia food committees (gubprodkoms) of regions where the delivery of live stock is compulsory are to proceed with the requisition of live stock and meat products at prices 15 per cent less than fixed prices.

2. Gubernia food committees have the right to prohibit the exportation from gubernias of live stock, meat, and lard, as well as meat products, with the exception of live stock exported for fattening, herds in transit, and breeding cattle.

3. In order to preserve the state's supply of horned cattle deliveries of sheep and pigs may be substituted for cattle. . . .

4. The exportation of large horned cattle abroad is hereby prohibited.

5. In supplying the population . . . with meat, the gubprodkoms shall at no time exceed the norms established by the People's Commissar of Food, viz., two pounds of meat weekly for workers and one pound weekly for the remainder of the population.
. . .

A. TSIURUPA
People's Commissar of Food

AID TO COLLECTIVE FARMING

[Decree of the Sovnarkom, November 2, 1918] [44]

In order to improve and develop agriculture and to facilitate the speediest reconstruction of agriculture on socialist principles, the Soviet of People's Commissars has resolved:

[42] *Sistematicheskii sbornik dekretov i rasporiazhenii pravitelstva po prodovolstvennomu delu*, I, 265.

[43] On the organization of the Commissariat of Food. See above, pp. 466-67.

[44] *S. U. R.*, No. 81, 1918, p. 1014.

1. To form a special fund of one billion rubles to subsidize measures for the improvement of agriculture.

2. Grants and subsidies out of this fund are advanced to: (*a*) agricultural communes and . . . associations; (*b*) village societies . . . , on condition that they change from individual to collective tilling . . . of land. . . .

V. ULIANOV (LENIN)
President of the Sovnarkom

S. SEREDA
People's Commissar of Agriculture

TOWARD SOCIALIST AGRICULTURE

[Resolution of the Second Congress of Councils of National Economy, December 27, 1918] [45]

The development of farming and the raising of the productivity of agriculture necessitate the following:

1. The intensive development of collective and communal land tilling and as a means to this end the consolidation of small peasant farms. . . .

2. The supplying of agricultural communes . . . with all necessary machinery and seeds.

3. The organization of large Soviet state farms under the auspices of the People's Commissariat of Agriculture or the Supreme Council of National Economy. . . .

4. The placing of the administration of agriculture and industry in the hands of one supreme organ—a policy demanding . . . consolidation of the People's Commissariat of Agriculture and the Supreme Council of National Economy. . . .

The principal legislative act of this period was entitled: "Regulations Concerning the Socialist Organization of the Land and Measures for Facilitating the Introduction of the Socialist System of Agriculture." This law was not formally issued until February 14, 1919. However, it had been in actual operation in a much earlier period in spite of the

[45] *Trudy II Vserossiiskogo Sezda Sovetov Narodnogo Khoziaistva*, pp. 391-92.

fact that it was in direct opposition to the Socialist-Revolutionist Law of Land Socialization.

SOCIALIST PRINCIPLES OF AGRICULTURE

[Resolution of the Central Executive Committee, February 14, 1919] [46]

CHAPTER I

GENERAL PRINCIPLES

Article 1. All land within the boundaries of the R. S. F. S. R., regardless of who is using it, shall be considered a single state fund.

Article 2. This single state fund is under the direct control and supervision of the various people's commissariats and the local authorities subordinate to these commissariats.

Article 3. In order to abolish completely every form of exploitation of man by man; to organize agriculture on socialist principles with the application of all the conquests of science and technology; to educate the toiling masses in the spirit of socialism; and to unite the proletariat and the village poor in their fight against capital—it is imperative to pass from individual to cooperative forms of agriculture. Large Soviet farms, communes, collective farming, and other forms of cooperative agriculture are the best means to attain this end. All forms of individual agriculture are therefore to be regarded as transitory and as having outlived their time.

Article 4. The main object of the organization of agriculture is the creation of a unified economy of production capable of supplying the Soviet Republic with a maximum of economic goods at a minimum expenditure of the people's labor.

Article 5. To attain this object the land departments are charged with the following duties in connection with the regulation of agriculture: (a) The separation of lands used for agriculture from those used for other purposes; (b) the exclusion from the agricultural land fund of lands which are not to be distributed for individual cultivation; (c) the elimination of scattered strip holdings, holdings far removed from any village,

[46] S. U. R., No. 4, 1919, pp. 50-61.

etc.; (*d*) the distribution of the land among the toiling population for the purpose of developing agriculture; (*e*) the distribution of land used for other purposes; (*f*) the investigation of
means of enlarging the agriculutral land fund; (*g*) the taking of
a census of the land and the agricultural population.

Article 6. Gubernia land departments have the right to take
under control and supervision any piece of land, regardless of who
is using it, for such purposes as: (*a*) the protection of natural
resources of the land; (*b*) the taking of measures for the increase
of the productivity of land by artificial irrigation . . . , etc.;
(*c*) the building of roads other than railroads; (*d*) the building
of experimental stations, experimental fields, as well as sanitary,
medical, charitable, educational, and other social institutions.

CHAPTER II

DISTRIBUTION OF LAND

Article 7. Land reform is to embrace the entire land fund.

Article 8. This land fund is to be used, in the first place, for
the needs of Soviet farms and communes; in the second place,
for labor artels, partnerships, and collective farming; and, in
the third place, for individual farmers desiring land as a means of
subsistence.

Article 9. The following [lands] cannot be distributed for individual use: (*a*) lands under the jurisdiction of Soviet and
social cultural-educational institutions (agricultural schools, experimental farms, etc.); (*b*) lands which formerly were used
capitalistically [and] on which Soviet farms have already been
established or are about to be established; (*c*) lands which formerly were used capitalistically [and] are now retained by the
land departments for the purpose of organizing cooperative
farms; (*d*) lands reserved for special purposes, viz., cities, . . .
health-resorts, . . . factories, ways of communication, etc.; (*e*)
lands, in general, which up to the passage of the present decree
have not yet been distributed for individual cultivation. . . .

Article 10. All other lands may unquestionably be distributed
for individual cultivation within the limits of the standards established in every region.

[Articles 11-28 give rules for the drafting of local, regional, and state plans of land organization and for taking an agricultural and population census.]

CHAPTER V

Soviet Farms

Article 29. Soviet farms are organized for the following purposes: (a) to raise as much as possible the level of agricultural production and to increase the area under cultivation; (b) to create conditions for a complete transition to the communist system of agriculture; (c) to set up and develop a network of centers of scientific agriculture.

[Articles 30-31 enumerate the kinds of land on which Soviet farms are to be formed. Among the lands listed are tracts formerly owned by landlords or the state, and those considered important because of the character of the crops raised.]

Article 32. Soviet farms of national importance are under the direct control of the People's Commissariat of Agriculture. . . .

Article 36. For the organization and management of Soviet farms there shall be formed gubernia, regional, and local departments . . . , subordinate to the Section of Soviet Farms of the Department of Socialized Agriculture of the People's Commissariat of Agriculture. . . .

Article 38. ' Direct management of every farm is in the hands of either a manager or a collegium, appointed by the regional or gubernia departments or by the People's Commissariat of Agriculture. There shall be formed on each farm a workers' control committee which shall function until a gubernia control committee is organized or until management by workers, which has already been established in the best organized branches of industry, is introduced on Soviet farms.

Article 39. The means for the organization and upkeep of Soviet farms shall be supplied by the People's Commissariat of Agriculture. All profits from such farms are turned over to the Treasury. . . .

Article 41. The scales, forms, and conditions of compensation for workers on Soviet farms shall be established by the gubernia departments in concurrence with the gubernia department of labor. . . .

Article 43. Rationed products which go to the laborers and

their families are to be calculated at fixed prices established by the Commissariat of Food; prices for non-rationed products are to be set by the gubernia department in concurrence with the gubernia food committee.

Article 44. All rationed products remaining after the needs of the farm in connection with production have been taken care of are to be surrendered by the gubernia departments to the People's Commissariat of Food. . . . Non-rationed products are to be turned over to the appropriate Soviet organizations. . . .

CHAPTER VI
INTERNAL MANAGEMENT OF SOVIET FARMS

Article 47. The manager, . . . the collegium, and the workers' committee are subordinate to the regional and gubernia departments and carry out strictly all its ordinances and instructions.

Article 48. The workers' control committee is to consist of from three to five members elected by the permanent laborers and employees of the farm. . . .

Article 50. The duties of the workers' committee are as follows: (*a*) to examine the estimates and accounts of the farm and report their conclusions to the regional and gubernia departments; (*b*) to see that the estimates and accounts of the farm are made on time; (*c*) to supervise the conditions of life and work . . . of laborers and employees; (*d*) to supervise food rations. . . .

Article 51. Members of the workers' committee are responsible to the People's Commissariat of Agriculture for the proper discharge of their duties, particularly for the safety of [farm] property and for labor discipline. . . .

Article 53. The workers' committee must not interfere with the orders of the manager of the farm or the collegium. Any disagreement . . . is to be settled by the appropriate regional or gubernia department. . . .

Article 55. The duties of the farm managers are those of administrative and technical management. . . .

CHAPTER VII
AGRICULTURAL COMMUNES

Article 60. Agricultural communes . . . are voluntary associations of toilers . . . aiming at the organization of agriculture on communist principles in the domains of both production and distribution. . . .

Article 61. In view of the fact that . . . the purpose of the Soviet Government is the organization of agriculture on the principles of socialization of the means of production, cooperative work, and management on a national scale, the People's Commissariat of Agriculture is to render every form of assistance and support to agricultural communes and to the same extent as to other forms of cooperative farming. . . .

Article 64. Agricultural implements of estates formerly owned by private individuals, monasteries, and churches, and assigned to communes, will be given to the communes provided that these implements are not needed on the neighboring Soviet farms. . . .

Article 66. Agricultural communes . . . are under the control of the People's Commissariat of Agriculture. . . .

Article 67. Agricultural communes . . . are under obligation to adopt the agricultural plans approved for the region by the People's Commissariat of Agriculture or the gubernia land department. . . .

Article 69. All surplus products . . . subject to rationing must be turned over, in conformity with general regulations, to Soviet agencies . . . for distribution on a national scale. Surplus products not rationed must also be turned over to state or public organizations in accordance with special regulations formulated by the People's Commissariat of Food. Part of the value of the surplus products surrendered by the commune to [Soviet] organs of supply . . . is intended to cover the subsidies received by the commune from the state and to defray state and local expenses.

Article 70. Profits received from a communal farm shall be used exclusively for the improvement and the development of that farm. . . .

Article 72. Exploitation of labor with a view to profit (hiring of labor) is forbidden in a commune. . . .

Article 74. During the plowing, sowing, [and] harvesting . . . seasons the commune has a right to invite in workers . . . who are not its members. . . .

Article 79. Agricultural communes located in the same . . . region shall unite in a regional union of communes.

Article 80. The uezd land department has the right to consolidate communes in one, two, or more communes if the lands on which the communes are established are contiguous or adjacent. . . .

Article 81. Communes are to be managed by elected councils, consisting of from three to five members . . . approved by the uezd land department.

Article 82. To coordinate the economic plans of the communes with those of the Soviet farms of a given region, the gubernia department may send a representative of the administration of the Soviet farms to the administrative councils of the neighboring communes. Such a representative will act in an advisory capacity only. . . .

[Articles 83-93 define the relations of the communes with the higher Soviet authorities and formulate rules for the dissolution of communes.]

CHAPTER VIII

COLLECTIVE FARMING

Article 94. Collective farming is a cooperative application of labor on the part of a [village] community, or different groups of a community, in which the means of production and machinery employed in plowing, sowing, harvesting, etc., are used in common.

Article 95. Collective farming may be organized either on the whole area of land of a given community or on a part of that land. . . .

Article 96. The decision for a transition to collective farming requires a majority of the members present at the meeting.

Article 97. In case the majority of members of the community is opposed to collective farming, the minority wishing to adopt that system should be assigned . . . a single parcel of land equivalent to the standard land allotment. . . .

Note 1: Farms established on the basis of this article form an artel or partnership for the collective cultivation of the land. . . .

Note 2: Resolutions of village communities relating to the redistribution of land do not apply to lands assigned for collective farming. . . .

[Articles 98-134 set forth in detail the internal workings of collective farms.]

17

CHAPTER IX

ENCOURAGEMENT AND AID TO SOCIALIZED AGRICULTURE

Article 135. The People's Commissariat of Agriculture and its organs are charged with the duty of giving every assistance to agricultural communes, associations, and societies which have adopted socialized farming . . . , by supplying them with seed, machinery, and cattle, as well as by giving them every kind of agronomic and cultural-technical aid. . . .

Article 137. In the granting of subsidies from the billion [ruble] fund decreed on November 2, 1918 . . . , and in the distribution of machinery, cattle, etc., preference shall be given to those associations which have achieved the highest measure of socialization of agriculture and have the best organized farms.

Article 138. The People's Commissariat of Agriculture may award prizes to workers . . . , Soviet farms, communes, and partnerships . . . for the most efficient organization of the farm and for success in production.

YA. SVERDLOV
Chairman of the Central
Executive Committee

SEREDA
People's Commissar of
Agriculture

THE FUTURE OF COMMUNIST AGRICULTURE [47]

A developed network of Soviet farms under the general direction of a single plan of national economy, working for the benefit of the community as a whole . . . , engaged not only in the production of raw materials but also in the processing of agricultural products . . . —such is the spectacle which is now witnessed in its initial stages and which in a few years is bound to reach enormous dimensions.

Soviet farms will improve the technique of production. Electricity, already becoming the chief motive power in industry, will be applied on the largest scale in the country districts and in agriculture.

[47] Miliutin, *Sotsialism i selskoe khoziaistvo*, pp. 90-91.

Soviet farms will organize a network of mills and factories for the manufacture of canned goods, leather products, agricultural implements, woodenware, textiles, etc.—enterprises all of which must be developed to the fullest extent.

Soviet farms will be the promoting agencies of scientific agronomy; they will maintain establishments for cattle and horse breeding and will conduct experiments for the improvement of every branch of agriculture.

Lastly, Soviet farms will be centers of socialist culture, education, and art; in short, places for the development of a new human nature.

CHAPTER IX

THE CONSTITUTION

From the point of view of the development of Communist ideology, an event of considerable importance in the first year of the Soviet Republic was the adoption of a constitution by the Fifth Congress of Soviets on July 10, 1918. More than any other single document this constitution reflects the principles and aspirations, political, social, and economic, which, while not entirely carried out in practice, formed the credo of Communists in the early years of the Republic.

The first formal expression of this credo was the Declaration of the Rights of Toiling and Exploited People, generally attributed to Lenin, Bukharin, and Stalin, which was adopted by the Third Congress of Soviets on January 23, 1918. The declaration, however, comprised for the most part broad abstract generalizations and did not state the specific forms of Soviet political organization and procedure. To fill this gap the Third Congress instructed the Central Executive Committee on January 28 to draft a constitution. On April 1, 1918, the Central Executive Committee delegated the task to a special committee consisting of five of its own representatives and of representatives of each of the following commissariats: Interior, Justice, Nationalities, National Economy, and War. On April 4 seven other members were added: four Bolsheviks, two Socialist-Revolutionists of the Left, and one Maximalist. As finally formed, the committee had the following membership: Ya. Sverdlov, chairman; M. P. Pokrovsky, vice-chairman; V. Avanesov, secretary; A. Berdnikov, D. Bogolepov, N. Bukharin, G. Gurvich, M. Latsis, D. Mage-

rovsky, M. Reisner, E. Skliansky, A. Smirnov, I. Stalin,
Yu. Steklov, and A. Shreider. On July 3 the draft of the
constitution was approved by Lenin and on July 10 it was
ratified by the Fifth Congress of Soviets as the fundamental
law of the Russian Socialist Federated Soviet Republic
(R. S. F. S. R.). The constitution remained in force until
July 1923, when it was replaced by a new constitution of
the Union of Socialist Soviet Republics (U. S. S. R.).[1]

DEBATE ON THE CONSTITUTION

[Steklov's Speech at the Fifth All-Russian Congress of Soviets, July 10, 1918] [2]

Comrades! The constitution which is submitted for the approval of the Fifth Congress of Soviets consists of two parts.
The first, the Declaration of the Rights of Toiling and Exploited
People, has already been approved by the Third Congress of
Soviets. Since then the Soviet Republic has lived through a
stormy period, brief from the point of view of time but rich in
social and political experience. This experience . . . has been
embodied in . . . the constitution submitted for your consideration. . . .

Our constitution . . . is not the first in the history of mankind. In the course of its struggle . . . mankind has seen many
constitutions, in fact too many, and it is no wonder that among
the toilers there is a certain skepticism, I might say hostility, toward constitutions. . . . They were all bourgeois constitutions,
and although, due to pressure from below, certain concessions
were made to the toiling masses . . . , yet their object . . . was
to give privileges to the propertied and ruling classes and keep the
toilers in subjection and slavery. . . . Even the Jacobin constitution of 1793 . . . erred in this respect.

Our constitution is the first in the world which tries to give
expression in constitutional form to the hopes of the workers,

[1] The principal work on the history of the Soviet Constitution is G. C.
Gurvich's *Istoriia sovetskoi konstitutsii*; see also W. R. Batsel, *Soviet Rule
in Russia*, pp. 51-75. A critical analysis of the constitution is given in *Pravo
sovetskoi Rossii*, I, 34-45.
[2] *Piatyi Vserossiiskii Sezd Sovetov*, pp. 183-91.

the peasants, and the oppressed, and to abolish political and economic inequality once and for all. That is why one may rightly say that our constitution has been evolved by the toilers themselves in the course of struggle . . . , by the Russian proletariat and revolutionary peasantry in the heat of battle for the rights of the people. . . . This bill of rights sets an example . . . to other nations which have not yet reached, but are surely approaching, our stage.

. . . The Declaration of Rights has made it clear that the great aim of Soviet Russia is to destroy the bourgeois régime and the exploitation of man by man, and to create in their stead a form of government under which all the wealth produced by the workers and peasants shall belong to all the people, united in one fraternal labor collectivity. . . . When this socialist state finally comes into being . . . we shall have true communism and the application of the principle: . . . "To each according to his needs and from each according to his capacities." We shall then be able to realize the political implication of our communist ideal—the elimination of every form of force, coercion, and oppression, in other words, government.

. . . The constitution before you is not a finished product . . . but is intended merely . . . for the period of transition . . . from capitalism to socialism. . . . In this transition period . . . we are occupied politically in fighting the bourgeoisie and its agents. Thus in the interest of that end it is necessary to remove the machinery of government from them and to turn it over . . . to the toiling masses, who will utilize it to attain their freedom and to suppress the bourgeoisie. . . . In this transition period it is necessary to establish a dictatorship of the proletariat, a powerful centralized government, which, however, will also permit freedom of activity and development to local soviets, toiling peasants, and proletarians. . . . We must build a mighty machine capable of beating off attacks on Soviet Russia . . . from within and from without, and of laying the foundations of a new social- ist order. This, Comrades, explains why we have in our constitution what is known as democratic centralism.

While bourgeois constitutions, sustained by doctrinaire ideas of the propertied classes . . . , make an artificial distribution of executive, legislative, and judicial powers, we, in our constitution, have attempted as far as possible to concentrate all these functions in such central authorities as the All-Russian Congress of Soviets and the Central Executive Committee elected by the Congress, with the Soviet of People's Commissars subordinate to them. . . .

Both in the constitution and in the Declaration of Rights, . . . you know, we approved a federation. . . . In this we did not contradict ourselves. Remember that at the present moment, on account of accidental and transitory causes, certain territories have separated from Russia. . . . If those territories . . . had the possibility of self-determination . . . they would undoubtedly be with us. . . . While our constitution now applies only to Great Russia . . . , it also has a world significance. As the workers and peasants of other countries . . . follow in our footsteps, overthrow the bourgeoisie, and gain control of the government, the Russian Soviet Republic will be surrounded by sister and daughter republics which, by uniting, will lay the foundation first for the federation of Europe and then for the federation of the world. . . .

Another basic characteristic of our constitution . . . which differentiates it from other democratic constitutions . . . is the electoral law. You know, of course, that this law has been bitterly attacked by the bourgeois press. . . . I should like to point out that the bourgeoisie has for centuries denied the vote to peasants and workers, and even today universal suffrage is by no means practiced everywhere. Even if it were, it is nothing more than an empty shell, for the capitalist régime makes it impossible for the working class to free itself from oppression and . . . improve its lot. . . . We have need of this law in the transition period of the dictatorship of the proletariat . . . , and our limitation of the right to vote is not a reactionary measure, is not against the interest of the people. On the contrary, it aims at progress, revolution, the freedom of the toilers . . . , and the abolition of all oppression and exploitation.

Just as you have denied to the bourgeoisie the honor to bear arms in the defense of the country, so also you will approve the law . . . vesting all the power of government in the toilers and in them only, . . . taking it from those who live directly or indirectly on the toil of others. . . .

These, Comrades, are some of the fundamental principles of

our constitution . . . —principles which are embodied in every soviet throughout Russia, from the lowest . . . to the highest, the All-Russian Congress of Soviets. . . .

I have already said that this constitution . . . is merely for the transition period . . . ; it can be changed at any time. . . . In this respect also it differs from other constitutions . . . , which are spoken of as "eternal" and as based on the eternal laws of nature, economics, and society. . . . Our constitution . . . is one more weapon . . . in the hands of the proletariat. . . . It is not a finished product . . . ; it lacks polish . . . ; it deals with realities. . . .

This constitution . . . has a historical importance not only for the Russian proletariat . . . but for the whole world and all oppressed peoples. For the first time . . . the ideas of the International are brought to the foreground. All bourgeois constitutions . . . were concerned with the interests of one particular state and . . . nation. . . . But we have formulated our constitution . . . for every nation where there is a proletarian class. . . .

The Jacobin constitution of 1793 was the most democratic constitution until today. It was the first to raise its hand against "sacred" bourgeois property; it proclaimed universal suffrage . . . and recognized some of the rights of the toilers. . . . This constitution was never put into effect; the bourgeoisie . . . killed it. Nevertheless, it remained as a flag around which all democratic classes rallied, and when the working classes came forth with revolutionary protests against the shameful domination of the bourgeoisie they shouted for "bread and the constitution of '93." If our constitution were to meet a similar fate . . . the workers of the world would still regard it as their own. . . . But I am convinced, Comrades, that it will live and grow strong. . . . It is living . . . and has lived long before it was put on paper. . . .

There are several historical documents . . . that mark the painful road followed by the working class in its fight for freedom. Among these one may count the "Manifesto of Equals" by Gracchus Babeuf . . . , the "Communist Manifesto" of Marx and Engels, and the "Inaugural Address" of the First International, written by Marx in 1864. I am profoundly convinced that our constitution, even with all its legal and grammatical mistakes, will have the same world importance. . . .

[Poliansky's Speech, July 10, 1918] [8]

Poliansky: . . . I should like to call your attention to several points in the constitution to which the Maximalists are going to offer amendments. . . . One of these has to do with representation . . . in the Congress of Soviets. . . . It is quite right that this body should be made up of toilers and toilers only . . . , but it is not right that there should be inequality among the toilers, as is provided in the chapter [of the constitution] according to which a representative is sent by one group for every 25,000 votes and by another group for every 125,000 inhabitants. . . .

Another point which needs correction is the method of indirect representation of . . . the masses. The gubernia congress sends delegates to the All-Russian Congress, but there is no reason to suppose that this will give us the most direct representation of the masses. It would be much better to have delegates from the uezd. . . . I should propose representation . . . of the city and uezd soviets. . . .

A third point . . . concerns the membership of the Central Executive Committee. It should, of course, represent the masses . . . but it should also include men of experience and action, men who are engaged in the constructive work of developing the Soviet state. . . . It should have . . . representatives from regional executive committees . . . , trade unions, and other organizations—cooperative, cultural, etc. . . .

A [fourth] point relates to the distribution of the executive power among . . . the various commissars. . . . We think it would be better to have collective responsibility than individual responsibility. . . . We should suggest that there be a collegium at the head of each commissariat, . . . if necessary a small collegium within the larger collegium. . . .

In conclusion I should like to recommend that we discard our archaic terminology, which we have inherited from the past. . . . I refer to our division of the toilers into workers, peasants, soldiers, sailors, etc. Labor should be represented . . . as one and undivided. . . . We suggest that in the future we speak of the "Congress of Labor Soviets," "Soviets of Labor Deputies," . . . and "Labor Soviets." . . . We should also discard the word

[8] *Ibid.,* pp. 191-95.

state. . . . The old idea of the domination of a majority by a minority clings to that word. . . . A word better for our purpose is commune . . . , "All-Russian Labor Commune." . . .

Steklov: . . . In reply to Comrade Poliansky I should like to say . . . that in the cities the adult population is larger . . . , and that is why representation in the cities is on the basis of the number of voters. The 125,000 inhabitants in the country have a smaller proportion of voters than the same number of inhabitants in the city. . . . As it stands, the city is not favored as against the country. . . . Petrograd with its two million inhabitants has never had more than twenty or twenty-five delegates in the congress. . . .

In regard to [the indirect system of] elections, it is necessary to say that the uezds themselves have developed this system. The representatives of the uezd congresses meet in the gubernia congresses . . . , and the chances are that the men chosen in the gubernia congress will represent the uezd more ably than in the direct way. . . . The uezds themselves are in a better position to take care of this question. If the arrangement proves unsatisfactory they will change it. . . .

. . . As regards the suggestion that we include in the Central Executive Committee men of experience . . . , it must be said that this has been tried and the result . . . was a coat of many colors. . . . In view of the fact that the congress is composed of toilers . . . , including trade unions and other organizations, it follows that the Central Executive Committee is made up of these same toilers. . . . It is to be assumed that those selected will be men of experience, regardless of whether they come from trade unions . . . or from other organizations. . . .

. . . At one time all of us favored a collegial system . . . , but experience has caused us to change our minds. . . . At the head of each commissariat is the commissar . . . , who reports his decision to the collegium [of the commissariat]. If any member disagrees with the decision he may bring the matter before the Soviet of People's Commissars or the Central Executive Committee, but he cannot stop the carrying out of the decision of the commissar. For this reason, the collegium of a commissariat (five or six people) is not so authoritative a body as the Sovnarkom or the Central Executive Committee . . . , which has the final word. The constitution preserves the collegium but gives final authority to the higher body. . . . In these trying times there must be prompt decisions and prompt action, and for this reason the responsibility has been placed in the individual commissars. . . .

In order not to prolong the discussion I move that the constitution be approved as a whole and that its final draft and publication be left to the new Central Executive Committee. . . .

Chairman: . . . All in favor raise your hands. . . . The constitution is unanimously approved. (*Applause.*)

CONSTITUTION (FUNDAMENTAL LAW) OF THE RUSSIAN SOCIALIST FEDERATED SOVIET REPUBLIC

[Adopted by the Fifth All-Russian Congress of Soviets, July 10, 1918]

The Declaration of the Rights of Toiling and Exploited People, approved by the Third All-Russian Congress of Soviets in January 1918, together with the Constitution of the Soviet Republic, adopted by the Fifth All-Russian Congress, constitute the Fundamental Law of the Russian Socialist Federated Soviet Republic.

This Fundamental Law becomes effective upon its publication in final form in the *Izvestiia* of the All-Russian Central Executive Committee of Soviets.[5] It shall be republished by all organs of the Soviet Government and shall be displayed prominently in all Soviet institutions.

The Fifth All-Russian Congress of Soviets charges the People's Commissariat of Education with the introduction of the study, exposition, and interpretation of the basic principles of this Constitution into all schools and other educational institutions of the Russian Republic.

PART I

DECLARATION OF THE RIGHTS OF TOILING AND EXPLOITED PEOPLE

CHAPTER ONE

1. Russia is proclaimed a Republic of Soviets of Workers',

[4] *S. U. R.*, No. 51, 1918, 599-609.
[5] It was published on July 19, 1918.

Soldiers', and Peasants' Deputies. All central and local authority is vested in these Soviets.

2. The Russian Soviet Republic is established on the basis of a free union of free nations and is a federation of National Soviet Republics.

CHAPTER TWO

3. With the fundamental aim of abolishing all exploitation of man by man, of eliminating completely the division of society into classes, of ruthlessly crushing exploiters, of establishing the socialist organization of society, and of bringing about the triumph of socialism in all countries, the Third All-Russian Congress of Soviets of Workers', Soldiers', and Peasants' Deputies further decrees:

a) In order to introduce the socialization of land, private ownership of land is abolished and all land is hereby declared the property of the people and is turned over to the toilers without compensation and with equal rights to its use.

b) All nationally important forests, subsoil resources, and waters, as well as all live stock and farm appurtenances, model farms, and agricultural enterprises, are declared national property.

c) As a first step toward the complete transfer of factories, shops, mines, railroads, and other means of production and transportation to the Soviet Republic of Workers and Peasants, and in order to insure the supremacy of the toiling masses over the exploiters, the Congress ratifies the Soviet laws establishing Workers' Control and the Supreme Council of National Economy.

d) The Third All-Russian Congress of Soviets considers the Soviet law repudiating the debts contracted by the governments of the Tsar, the landlords, and the bourgeoisie to be a first blow to international banking and finance-capital, and expresses its confidence that the Soviet Government will firmly follow this course until the international labor revolt against the yoke of capital is completely victorious.

e) The transfer of all banks to the ownership of the Workers' and Peasants' Government is ratified as one of the prerequisites for the emancipation of the toiling masses from the yoke of capital.

f) In order to exterminate the parasitic classes of society and to organize the economic life of the country, universal labor duty is introduced.

g) In order to give the toiling masses absolute power and to render the restoration of the power of the exploiters impossible, [the Congress] decrees the arming of the toilers, the establishment of a socialist Red Army of workers and peasants, and the complete disarming of the propertied classes.

CHAPTER THREE

4. Expressing its firm determination to rescue mankind from the claws of capitalism and imperialism, which during this most criminal of all wars have drenched the world with blood, the Third All-Russian Congress of Soviets approves wholeheartedly the policy of the Soviet Government in repudiating secret treaties, in organizing the most extensive fraternization among the workers and peasants in the ranks of the belligerent armies, and in its efforts to bring about, by revolutionary means, at all costs, a democratic peace of toilers on the principles of no annexation, no indemnity, and the free self-determination of nations.

5. With the same purpose in view the Third All-Russian Congress of Soviets demands a complete break with the barbarous policy of bourgeois civilization which enriches the exploiters in a few chosen nations at the expense of hundreds of millions of the toiling people in Asia, in colonies in general, and in the small countries.

6. The Third All-Russian Congress of Soviets welcomes the policy of the Soviet of People's Commissars in granting complete independence to Finland, in beginning the withdrawal of troops from Persia, and in giving the right of self-determination to Armenia.

CHAPTER FOUR

7. The Third All-Russian Congress of Soviets of Workers', Soldiers', and Peasants' Deputies believes that at the present moment of decisive struggle of the proletariat against the exploiters there is no place for the exploiters in any organ of government. The government must belong wholly and exclusively to the toiling masses and their fully empowered representatives—the Soviets of Workers', Soldiers', and Peasants' Deputies.

8. At the same time, desiring to bring about a really free and voluntary, and consequently a more complete and lasting union of the toiling classes of all nations in Russia, the Third Congress of Soviets confines itself to the formulation of the fundamental principles of the federation of the Soviet Republics of Russia, leaving the workers and peasants of each nation free to decide independently at their own plenipotentiary Soviet congresses whether they desire, and if so, on what conditions, to take part in the federal government and other federal Soviet institutions.

Part II

General Principles of the Constitution of the R. S. F. S. R.

CHAPTER FIVE

9. The fundamental aim of the Constitution of the Russian Socialist Federated Soviet Republic, designed for the present transition period, is to establish a dictatorship of the city and village proletariat and the poorest peasantry in the form of a powerful All-Russian Soviet Government which has the purpose of crushing completely the bourgeoisie, of ending the exploitation of man by man, and of establishing socialism, under which there will be no division into classes and no state authority.

10. The Russian Republic is a free socialist society of all Russian toilers. Authority within the boundaries of the Russian Socialist Federated Soviet Republic is vested entirely in all the working people of the country, organized in city and village soviets.

11. Soviets of regions which have distinctive customs and national characteristics may unite in autonomous regional unions, at the head of which, as well as at the head of all other regional unions which may be formed, stand the regional congresses of soviets and their executive organs. These autonomous regional unions enter the Russian Socialist Federated Soviet Republic on a federal basis.

12. Sovereign power in the Russian Socialist Federated Soviet Republic is vested in the All-Russian Congress of Soviets and, in the interim between congresses, in the All-Russian Central Executive Committee.

13. To secure for the toilers real freedom of conscience, the church is separated from the state, and the schools from the church, and freedom of religious and anti-religious propaganda is recognized as the right of every citizen.

14. To secure for the toilers real freedom of expression of opinion, the Russian Socialist Federated Soviet Republic does away with the dependence of the press on capital, turns over to the working class and the poorer peasants all technical and material resources necessary for the publication of newspapers, pamphlets, books, and other printed matter, and guarantees their free circulation throughout the country.

15. To secure for the toilers real freedom of assembly, the Russian Socialist Federated Soviet Republic, recognizing the right of the citizens of the Soviet Republic freely to organize assemblies, meetings, processions, etc., places at the disposal of the workers and the poorer peasants all premises suitable for public gathering, together with their furniture, lighting, and heating.

16. To insure for the toilers real freedom of association, the Russian Socialist Federated Soviet Republic, having destroyed the economic and political power of the propertied classes and having thereby removed all obstacles which hitherto, in bourgeois society, have prevented the workers and peasants from enjoying freedom of organization and action, is now offering to the workers and poorer peasants every assistance, material and otherwise, in uniting and organizing.

17. To secure for the toilers and poorer peasants real access to knowledge, the Russian Socialist Federated Soviet Republic undertakes to provide for the workers and poorer peasants a complete, well-rounded, and free education.

18. The Russian Socialist Federated Soviet Republic regards work as the duty of every citizen of the Republic and proclaims the slogan: "He who does not work shall not eat."

19. To safeguard in every possible way the conquests of the great Worker-Peasant Revolution, the Russian Socialist Federated Soviet Republic considers it the duty of every citizen of the Republic to defend his socialist fatherland and establishes universal military service. The honor of bearing arms in defense of the Revolution is granted only to the toilers; the non-toiling elements shall have other military duties to perform.

20. Acting on the principle of the solidarity of the toilers of all nations, the Russian Socialist Federated Soviet Republic grants all political rights enjoyed by Russian citizens to foreigners resident within the territory of the Russian Republic provided they belong to the working class or to the peasantry not using hired labor. Local soviets are authorized to confer the rights of Russian citizenship upon such foreigners without any formalities or difficulties.

21. The Russian Socialist Federated Soviet Republic offers asylum to all foreigners persecuted for political and religious offenses.

22. The Russian Socialist Federated Soviet Republic, recognizing the equality of all citizens, regardless of race or nationality, declares it contrary to the fundamental laws of the Republic to institute or tolerate any privileges or advantages based upon such grounds, or to repress national minorities, or to limit their rights in any way.

23. To safeguard the interests of the working class as a whole, the Russian Socialist Federated Soviet Republic deprives individuals and groups of rights which they may use to the detriment of the Socialist Revolution.

PART III

THE STRUCTURE OF THE SOVIET GOVERNMENT

A. Organization of the Central Government

CHAPTER SIX

The All-Russian Congress of Soviets of Workers', Peasants', Cossacks', and Red Army Deputies

24. The All-Russian Congress of Soviets is the supreme authority in the Russian Socialist Federated Soviet Republic.

25. The All-Russian Congress of Soviets consists of representatives of city soviets on the basis of one deputy for every 25,000 electors, and of representatives of gubernia congresses of soviets on the basis of one deputy for every 125,000 inhabitants.

Note 1: In case the gubernia congress of soviets does not precede the All-Russian Congress of Soviets, delegates to the latter are sent directly by uezd congresses of soviets.

Note 2: In case a regional congress of soviets immediately precedes the All-Russian Congress of Soviets, delegates to the latter may be sent by the regional congress of soviets.

26. The All-Russian Congress of Soviets is called at least twice a year by the All-Russian Central Executive Committee.

27. An Extraordinary All-Russian Congress is called by the All-Russian Central Executive Committee, either on its own initiative or at the demand of local soviets representing at least one-third of the total population of the Republic.

28. The All-Russian Congress of Soviets elects an All-Russian Central Executive Committee of not more than 200 members.

29. The All-Russian Central Executive Committee is responsible in all matters to the All-Russian Congress of Soviets.

30. In the interim between congresses the All-Russian Central Executive Committee is the supreme authority of the Republic.

CHAPTER SEVEN

The All-Russian Central Executive Committee

31. The All-Russian Central Executive Committee is the supreme legislative, executive, and regulative organ of the Russian Socialist Federated Soviet Republic.

32. The All-Russian Central Executive Committee directs in a general way the activities of the Workers' and Peasants' Government and of Soviet organs throughout the country. It unifies and coordinates legislative and administrative functions and supervises the enforcement of the Soviet Constitution, the decrees of the All-Russian Congresses of Soviets, and those of the central Soviet organs.

33. The All-Russian Central Executive Committee examines and ratifies drafts of decrees and other proposals submitted by the Soviet of People's Commissars or by separate departments, and also issues its own decrees and ordinances.

34. The All-Russian Central Executive Committee calls the All-Russian Congress of Soviets, to which it gives an account of its activities, together with a statement on general policy and specific questions.

35. The All-Russian Central Executive Committee establishes a Soviet of People's Commissars for the general direction of the

affairs of the Russian Socialist Federated Soviet Republic, and various departments (People's Commissariats) for the direction of the different branches of administration.

36. Members of the All-Russian Central Executive Committee work in the departments (People's Commissariats) or perform other duties laid upon them by the All-Russian Central Executive Committee.

CHAPTER EIGHT

The Soviet of People's Commissars

37. The Soviet of People's Commissars has the general direction of the affairs of the Russian Socialist Federated Soviet Republic.

38. In the execution of this task the Soviet of People's Commissars issues decrees, ordinances, and instructions, and undertakes such other measures as are necessary for the prompt and proper conduct of state affairs.

39. The Soviet of People's Commissars immediately reports to the All-Russian Central Executive Committee all its enactments and decisions.

40. The All-Russian Central Executive Committee has the right to repeal or suspend any enactment or decision of the Soviet of People's Commissars.

41. All enactments and decisions of the Soviet of People's Commissars which are of great political importance are submitted to the All-Russian Central Executive Committee for consideration and approval.

Note: Emergency measures may be enacted on the sole authority of the Soviet of People's Commissars.

42. Members of the Soviet of People's Commissars are in charge of the various People's Commissariats.

43. There are seventeen [eighteen] [6] People's Commissariats: Foreign Affairs, Army, Navy, Interior, Justice, Labor, Social Welfare, Education, Posts and Telegraph, Nationalities, Finance, Transportation, Agriculture, Commerce and Industry, Food, State Control, Supreme Council of National Economy, and Health.

[6] Error in the text.

44. Attached to each People's Commissar and under his chairmanship is a Collegium, the members of which are appointed by the Soviet of People's Commissars.

45. The People's Commissar has the authority himself to decide all questions under the jurisdiction of his commissariat but must report his decisions to the Collegium. In case the Collegium disagrees with any of the decisions of the People's Commissar it may, without suspending the execution of the decision, appeal to the Soviet of People's Commissars or the Presidium of the All-Russian Central Executive Committee. The same right of appeal belongs to every member of the Collegium.

46. The Soviet of People's Commissars is responsible in all matters to the All-Russian Congress of Soviets and the All-Russian Central Executive Committee.

47. The People's Commissars and the Collegia of the People's Commissariats are responsible in all matters to the Soviet of People's Commissars and the All-Russian Central Executive Committee.

48. The title of People's Commissar belongs exclusively to the members of the Soviet of People's Commissars, who have charge of the affairs of the Russian Socialist Federated Soviet Republic, and cannot be used by any other representative of the central or local government.

CHAPTER NINE

The Jurisdiction of the All-Russian Congress of Soviets and the All-Russian Central Executive Committee

49. The All-Russian Congress of Soviets and the All-Russian Central Executive Committee of Soviets have jurisdiction over all matters relating to the life of the state as a whole, namely:

a) The ratification, amendment, and supplementation of the Constitution of the Russian Socialist Federated Soviet Republic.

b) The general direction of foreign and domestic policies of the Russian Socialist Federated Soviet Republic.

c) The establishment and alteration of boundaries, as well as the alienation of parts of the territory of the Russian Socialist Federated Soviet Republic or of the rights belonging to it.

d) The establishment of the boundaries and jurisdiction of the Regional Soviet Unions composing the Russian Socialist Federated Soviet Republic, and the settlement of disputes between them.

e) The admission into the Russian Socialist Federated Soviet Republic of new members of the Soviet Republic and the recognition of the withdrawal of different parts from the Russian Federation.

f) The setting up of the general administrative divisions of the territory of the Russian Socialist Federated Soviet Republic and the ratification of Regional Unions.

g) The establishment and alteration of the system of weights, measures, and currency within the territory of the Russian Socialist Federated Soviet Republic.

h) Relations with foreign powers, declaration of war, and conclusion of peace.

i) The negotiation of loans, tariff and trade treaties, and financial agreements.

j) The establishment of principles and of a general plan for the whole national economy and its different branches in the territory of the Russian Socialist Federated Soviet Republic.

k) The approval of the budget of the Russian Socialist Federated Soviet Republic.

l) The levying of state taxes and the imposition of public duties.

m) The establishment of principles for the organization of the armed forces of the Russian Socialist Federated Soviet Republic.

n) General state legislation, judicial organization and procedure, civil and criminal legislation, etc.

o) The appointment and dismissal both of individual members of the Soviet of People's Commissars and of the Soviet of People's Commissars as a whole, as well as the confirmation of the appointment of the President of the Soviet of People's Commissars.

p) The issuance of general regulations concerning the acquisition or loss of the rights of Russian citizenship and the rights of foreigners within the territory of the Republic.

q) The right of granting complete or partial amnesty.

50. In addition to the above matters the All-Russian Congress of Soviets and the All-Russian Central Executive Committee may decide any other question which they deem within their jurisdiction.

51. Within the exclusive jurisdiction of the All-Russian Congress of Soviets come the following:

a) The establishment, supplementation, and amendment of the fundamental principles of the Soviet Constitution.

b) The ratification of peace treaties.

52. Decisions on questions enumerated in Sections *c* and *h* of Article 49 may be made by the All-Russian Central Executive Committee only in case it is impossible to convoke the All-Russian Congress of Soviets.

B. Organization of Local Soviet Government

CHAPTER TEN

Congresses of Soviets

53. Congresses of soviets are formed as follows:

a) Oblast [7] congresses consist of representatives of city soviets in the proportion of one deputy for every 5,000 electors, and of uezd congresses of soviets in the proportion of one deputy for every 25,000 inhabitants, and are not to consist of more than 500 deputies for the entire oblast. Oblast congresses may also be composed of representatives of gubernia congresses of soviets, elected on the same basis, if the latter congress immediately precedes the oblast congress of soviets.

b) Gubernia congresses consist of representatives of city soviets in the proportion of one deputy for every 2,000 electors, and of [representatives of] volost congresses of soviets in the proportion of one deputy for every 10,000 inhabitants, and are not to consist of more than 300 deputies for the whole gubernia. In case the uezd congress of soviets immediately precedes the gubernia congress, elections are held on the same basis, not by the volost but by the uezd congress of soviets.

c) Uezd congresses consist of representatives of village soviets in the proportion of one deputy for every 1,000 inhabitants, but of not more than 300 deputies for the entire uezd.

d) Volost congresses consist of representatives of all the vil-

[7] Oblast, gubernia, uezd, volost, and selo are the territorial divisions of Russia, descending in size in the order here given. An oblast comprises several gubernias, a gubernia several uezds, and so on.

lage soviets of the volost in the proportion of one deputy for every 10 members of the soviet.

Note 1 : In the uezd congresses of soviets representation is given to the soviets of cities the population of which does not exceed 10,000 inhabitants. Village soviets of localities numbering less than 1,000 inhabitants combine in electing representatives to the uezd congress of soviets.

Note 2 : Village soviets numbering less than 10 members send one representative to the volost congress of soviets.

54. Congresses of soviets are convoked by the executive organs of the Soviet Government of the district (the executive committees) upon their own initiative, or upon the request of local soviets comprising not less than one-third of the entire population of the given district, but in either case not less than twice a year in the oblast, once every three months in the gubernia and the uezd, and once every month in the volost.

55. Each congress of soviets (oblast, gubernia, uezd, volost) elects its own executive organ (the executive committee), the membership of which shall not exceed: (*a*) in the oblast and gubernia, 25; (*b*) in the uezd, 20; (*c*) in the volost, 10. The executive committee is responsible in all matters to the congress of soviets which elected it.

56. Within the limits of its jurisdiction the congress of soviets (oblast, gubernia, uezd, and volost) is the supreme authority throughout the given territory; in the interim between the congresses this authority is vested in the executive committee.

CHAPTER ELEVEN

Soviets of Deputies

57. Soviets of deputies are formed as follows :

a) In cities, one deputy for every 1,000 inhabitants but not less than 50 nor more than 1,000 members.

b) In rural districts (villages, hamlets, stanitsas, towns, cities with less than 10,000 inhabitants, auls [mountain settlements], farms, etc.), one deputy for every 100 inhabitants, but not less than 3 and not more than 50 members. The term of office of the deputies is three months.

Note: In rural districts where it is considered possible, questions of administration shall be directly decided by the general assembly of electors of such districts.

58. For the transaction of current affairs the soviet of deputies elects from its members an executive body (executive committee), numbering not more than 5 in villages, and in cities at the ratio of one for every 50 members, but not less than 3 and not more than 15 (in Petersburg and Moscow not more than 40). The executive committee is responsible in all matters to the soviet which elected it.

59. The soviet of deputies is convoked by the executive committee upon its own initiative or upon the demand of not less than half of the members of the soviet, at least once a week in cities and twice a week in villages.

60. Within the limits of its jurisdiction the soviet is the supreme authority in the district, except in cases provided for by Article 57*n*, when that authority is the general assembly of electors.

CHAPTER TWELVE

Jurisdiction of Local Organs of the Soviet Government

61. The oblast, gubernia, uezd, and volost organs of the Soviet Government, as well as the soviets of deputies, have the following functions:

a) The enforcement of all orders of the higher organs of the Soviet Government.

b) The adoption of appropriate measures for the cultural and economic development of their districts.

c) The settlement of all questions which have a purely local character (for the given territory).

d) The coordination of all soviet activities in a given territory.

62. The congresses of soviets and their executive committees have the right to exercise control over the acts of the local soviets (i. e., the oblast congress exercises control over all soviets of the oblast, the gubernia over all soviets of the gubernia, except city soviets which are not included in the uezd congresses of soviets, etc.). The oblast and gubernia congresses of soviets and their executive committees have in addition the right to repeal decisions

of the soviets in their areas, provided they notify the central Soviet Government in the most important cases.

63. To enable the organs of the Soviet Government to perform the duties laid upon them, corresponding departments in charge of executives are formed in connection with every soviet (city and village) and every executive committee (oblast, gubernia, uezd, and volost).

Part IV

Active and Passive Electoral Rights

CHAPTER THIRTEEN

64. The right to elect and be elected to the soviets belongs, irrespective of religion, nationality, domicile, etc., to all the following citizens of the Russian Socialist Federated Soviet Republic, of both sexes, who have reached the age of eighteen at the time of the election:

a) All those gaining their livelihood by productive and socially useful work, and also persons engaged in domestic pursuits which enable the former to undertake productive work, e. g.: workers and employees of all kinds and categories engaged in industry, commerce, agriculture, etc., peasants and Cossack farmers who do not use hired labor for the sake of profit.

b) Soldiers of the Soviet army and navy.

c) Citizens coming under the categories specified in Sections *a* and *b* of the present Article who have in any way lost their capacity for work.

Note 1: Local soviets may, with the approval of the central government, lower the age limit established by the present Article.

Note 2: Of the persons who have not adopted Russian citizenship those mentioned in Article 20 (Part II, Chapter Five) also enjoy active and passive electoral rights.

65. The following persons cannot vote or be elected even though they come under one of the above-mentioned categories:

a) Persons employing hired labor for the sake of profit.

b) Persons living on unearned incomes—interest on capital, revenue from businesses, income from property, etc.

c) Merchants and industrial and commercial agents.

d) Monks and clergymen of all religious denominations.

e) Employees and agents of the former police, of the special gendarme corps and secret service, as well as members of the former reigning dynasty of Russia.

f) Persons legally recognized as mental defectives or imbeciles, together with those under guardianship.

g) Persons convicted of mercenary or infamous crimes and sentenced for a term set by law or judicial decision.

CHAPTER FOURTEEN

Electoral Procedure

66. Elections take place according to established custom, on days fixed by local soviets.

67. Elections take place in the presence of an electoral commission and a representative of the local soviet.

68. In cases where the presence of the representative of the soviet is technically impossible his place is taken by the chairman of the electoral commission, and, in his absence, by the chairman of the electoral assembly.

69. A report of the proceedings and results of the election is drawn up and signed by the members of the electoral commission and the representative of the soviet.

70. The exact order of the electoral procedure, as well as the participation of trade unions and other workers' organizations in elections, is determined by the local soviets in conformity with instructions issued by the All-Russian Central Executive Committee.

CHAPTER FIFTEEN

Verification and Annulment of Elections and Recall of Deputies

71. All records of elections are sent to the appropriate soviet.

72. The soviet appoints a credentials committee to examine the elections.

73. The credentials committee reports to the soviet the results of its examination.

74. The soviet decides disputed elections.

75. In case of the non-confirmation of any candidate the soviet calls a new election.

76. In case the election as a whole was carried out contrary to law the question of annulling the election is decided by the next superior soviet organ.

77. The final court of appeal in matters of soviet elections is the All-Russian Central Executive Committee.

78. Electors who have sent a deputy to the soviet have the right to recall him at any time and to hold new elections in accordance with the general statute.

Part V

Budgetary Law

CHAPTER SIXTEEN

79. The financial policy of the Russian Socialist Federated Soviet Republic during the present transition period of the dictatorship of toilers has as its fundamental aim the expropriation of the bourgeoisie and the creation of the conditions for the general equality of citizens of the Republic in the fields of production and distribution. With this in view it aims to place at the disposal of the organs of the Soviet Government, without hesitating to encroach upon rights of private property, all resources needed to meet the local and general state requirements of the Soviet Republic.

80. The state revenues and expenditures of the Russian Socialist Federated Soviet Republic are combined in the general state budget.

81. The All-Russian Congress of Soviets, or the All-Russian Central Executive Committee, determines what revenues and receipts shall be credited to the general state budget and what revenues and receipts shall go to the local soviets; it also fixes the limits of taxation.

82. Soviets levy taxes and imposts exclusively for the needs of local economy. General state needs are met by grants from the State Treasury.

83. No expenditure may be made from the funds of the State Treasury unless it is included in the state budget or has been specially authorized by the central government.

84. To meet general state requirements necessary credits from

the State Treasury are placed at the disposal of local soviets by the appropriate People's Commissariats.

85. All credits granted to the soviets by the State Treasury, as well as credits appropriated through estimates of local needs, must be expended in accordance with their direct assignment as set forth in the estimates (paragraphs and clauses), and cannot be diverted to any other purpose without the special authorization of the All-Russian Central Executive Committee and the Soviet of People's Commissars.

86. Local soviets draw up semi-annual and annual estimates of revenues and expenditures. The estimates of village, volost, and city soviets participating in uezd congresses of soviets, as well as the estimates of uezd organs of the Soviet Government, are approved by the respective gubernia and oblast congresses or by their executive committees; the estimates of the city, gubernia, and oblast organs of the Soviet Government are approved by the All-Russian Central Executive Committee and the Soviet of People's Commissars.

87. In cases of expenditures not provided for in the estimates, as well as in cases of insufficiency of the budgetary appropriations, the soviets apply to the appropriate People's Commissariats for supplementary credits.

88. In case the local funds are inadequate to meet local needs, the subsidies and loans needed to cover urgent expenditures are granted from the State Treasury to the local soviets by the All-Russian Central Executive Committee and the Soviet of People's Commissars.

Part VI

Emblem and Flag of the Russian Socialist Federated Soviet Republic

CHAPTER SEVENTEEN

89. The emblem of the Russian Socialist Federated Soviet Republic consists of a golden sickle and hammer, with handles crossed and pointing downward, placed upon a red background in sunrays, and surrounded by a garland of wheat ears with the inscription:

(a) Russian Socialist Federated Soviet Republic

(b) Proletarians of All Countries, Unite

90. The commercial, naval, and military flag of the Russian
Socialist Federated Soviet Republic is of red (scarlet) material,
in the upper left corner of which, near the staff, are the letters in
gold "R. S. F. S. R." or the inscription "Russian Socialist Federated Soviet Republic."

YA. SVERDLOV

Chairman of the Fifth All-Russian Congress of
Soviets and the All-Russian Central Executive
Committee

T. I. TEODOROVICH
F. A. ROZIN
A. P. ROZENGOLTS
A. KH. MITROFANOV
K. G. MAKSIMOV

Members of the Presidium of the All-Russian
Central Executive Committee

CHAPTER X

EDUCATION

The Communists aimed not merely at the political and economic reorganization of society but also at the transformation of the entire cultural life of Russia, particularly its educational institutions. Education was conceived as the means for bringing young and old to the habits, ideas, and feelings harmonious both with communist politico-economic institutions and with communist ideals of human nature. It followed that the existing system of education, regarded as steeped in bourgeois prejudice, would have to be replaced by a system informed throughout by the communist spirit and ideology.

During 1918 the Communists made considerable progress in breaking up existing educational institutions. At the same time some of their leaders devoted themselves to the development of programs for a new school system. Particular importance was attached to the grandiose project of a "unified labor school" which would furnish a well-balanced and harmonious education to every child. In the sphere of higher education the Bolsheviks abolished all requirements for admission to universities and eliminated distinctions in the rank of university teachers. In order to "liberate science from the yoke of capitalism" they established the Socialist Academy of Social Sciences.

However, lack of material resources, together with the opposition of a great majority of the teachers to the Communist dictatorship, prevented the state from making much headway with its educational programs and projects.

EDUCATION IN THE PROVINCES

[From the Reports of Local Instructors] [1]

The masses in the provinces are besieging the central authorities with requests for help in cultural problems, libraries, schools, etc. Educational institutions grow up spontaneously in the provinces. For example, an instructor of Vasilsurky Uezd, Nizhegorodsky Gubernia, writes that "there are numerous educational circles in the villages about which the Department [of Education] does not have the slightest information. These circles, in the absence of guidance, often end in failure." Adult education courses and proletarian universities organized by the Department of People's Education have capacity audiences. Peasants come from the uezd to attend [the lectures]. An instructor in Simbirsk Gubernia reports that in [educational] activity the uezd is far ahead of the gubernia center. The people are anxious to educate their children and anticipate the Department [of Education] in establishing schools. . . . The peasants are especially fond of the name "labor school."

However, there are tendencies of a different nature. Writers of letters cite cases of popular opposition to the Department [of Education], caused chiefly by the exclusion of the teaching of religion from the schools. . . . Cases are known of the reinstallation of icons in schools. . . . Cultural workers and teachers are greatly needed for the new labor school. An instructor in Nizhegorodsky Gubernia writes [thus] about the teaching staff: "There are many high school girls . . . , and the peasants are greatly dissatisfied with them. Their main fault is that they are not familiar with their jobs in a practical way, and, being tenderfeet, they cannot assimilate with the local population. . . ."

The records of teachers' conferences . . . indicate that the teaching profession, irrespective of political coloring, is much interested in school reform and is accepting it in a spirit of great sympathy. . . . The masses are forcing the teacher to work for the toilers' school . . . , the school which the people need. . . . Unions of Teachers-Internationalists are being formed and the influence of the All-Russian Teachers' Union is on the decline.

[1] *Narodnoe Prosveshchenie*, Nos. 23-25, 1918, p. 14.

. . . The teaching profession is now coming over to the support of the Soviet Government. The teachers' congress of Yukhanovsky Uezd (Smolensk Gubernia) which took place at the end of October elected Lenin and Lunacharsky as its honorary presidents, and passed a resolution hailing "the Sovnarkom and the great apostles of the social revolution—Comrades Lenin, Trotsky, and Lunacharsky." The resolution further declared: "We are ready to sacrifice our lives for the ideals of the world revolution. We curse all those who have dared or dare to raise their dirty hands against the government of Soviets. Our slogan is: Red Terror against the enemies of the toiling people and the Soviets!"

. . .

The fact that a part of the intelligentsia sides with the working class and the toiling peasantry does not insure a sufficient number of [educational] workers. In the same Yukhanovsky Uezd the Department of People's Education decreed that the intelligentsia be forced into cultural-educational service.

All the reports of the instructors complain about the lack of money. The delay in distributing the funds which were appropriated for education—a failure for which the central authorities are to be blamed—is interfering with the development of the schools.

CONFERENCE OF RUSSIAN TEACHERS [2]

[May 13, 1918]

The conference of the Joint Council of the All-Russian Teachers' Union and representatives of regional and gubernia organizations came to a close yesterday. The conference, after hearing reports from the provinces on the relations between teachers and government authorities, came to the conclusion that in certain cases teachers may take part in the work of Soviets of Workers' Deputies, educational councils, and cultural-educational committees because such participation may bring some positive results in the way of protecting the professional interests of the teachers and preventing the total disruption of the schools. However, the Joint Council finds no basis for a general and lasting cooperation with the Soviet Government, the acts of which are guided neither

[2] *Svoboda Rossii,* No. 24, May 14, 1918, p. 4.

by creative ideas based on principles nor by a popular-democratic conception of questions relating to school affairs. . . . Therefore, as in former days, the teaching profession is faced with the necessity of developing an intense and independent professional and cultural activity to serve as a basis for the regeneration of the country and at the same time as a means for closer contact between the teachers and the people. [The conference] also passed the following resolution:

"The reports of the delegates have made it clear that in numerous places the decree on the councils of people's education is being obscured, and that administration is being vested not in collegial organs [as the decree provides] but in individuals, that is, the uezd commissars of people's education, who take complete charge of school life and the teachers. The Joint Council considers this [practice] as brutal arrogance and a return to the worst period of arbitrary rule over schools. [The Joint Council] expresses the hope that the teachers and the people will come to the defense of their right to manage the schools and will defend successfully the principles of collegial management of people's education and the autonomy of school administration. . . ."

INVESTIGATION OF POLITICAL SYMPATHIES OF TEACHERS [3]

Kazan. The Commissariat of Education is demanding that every teacher send in a report containing a statement of his political sympathies and his views relating to school reform. Three schools made collective reports, but the Commissariat was not satisfied and insisted that each teacher present a separate statement.

COEDUCATION

[Decree of the Commissariat of Education, May, 31, 1918] [4]

1. Coeducation is introduced in all schools. . . .
2. From the date of publication of this decree all vacancies in schools are to be filled by students of both sexes on an equal footing. . . .

A. V. LUNACHARSKY
People's Commissar of Education

[3] *Ibid.*, No. 30, May 21, 1918, p. 3.   [4] *S. U. R.*, No. 38, 1918, p. 475.

THE STATE DEPARTMENT OF EDUCATION
[Decree of the Sovnarkom, June 26, 1918] [5]

1. The general control of education in the R. S. F. S. R. is entrusted to a State Commission of Education under the chairmanship of the People's Commissar of Education.

2. The State Commission consists of the following members: (a) By APPOINTMENT: Members of the Collegium of the Commissariat of Education, all department heads of the Commissariat, the director of the Commissariat, and the secretary of the State Commission; (b) By ELECTION: Three representatives of the All-Russian Central Executive Committee, three of the teachers' unions which accept the platform of the Soviet Government, two of the Central Bureau of Trade Unions, one of the Central Bureau of Workers' Cooperatives, and one of the Educational Committee of the Central Council of Railwaymen; (c) REPRESENTATIVES OF COMMISSARIATS: One of the People's Commissariat of Nationalities and one of the Supreme Council of National Economy.

Note 1: The delegate of the People's Commissariat of Nationalities has the right to invite to the sessions of the State Commission, in advisory capacity, a representative of the nationality the educational institutions of which are under discussion at the session.

Note 2: Each newly organized region may send a representative to the State Commission of Education. He shall have the right to vote.

Note 3: The State Commission has also the right to increase its membership by adding representatives of other organizations —educational, professional, student, etc.—provided that these organizations are of national scope and accept the platform of the Soviet Government.

3. The administration of the People's Commissariat of Education is entrusted to a Collegium composed of the People's Commissar, his assistant, and five other members.

4. The People's Commissar is elected by the All-Russian Central Executive Committee of Soviets. . . . His assistant and the

[5] *Ibid.*, No. 46, 1918, pp. 557-60.

18

other members of the Collegium are elected by the Soviet of People's Commissars, at the recommendation of the People's Commissar of Education. . . .

6. In addition to the activities specified in other articles of this decree, the following duties shall come within the scope of the State Commission: the formulation of a general plan of education for the R. S. F. S. R.; the development of fundamental principles of education and school organization; the coordination of all cultural activities in the provinces; the preparation of a state budget and the distribution of the funds appropriated for federal educational needs; also any other matters of fundamental significance submitted by the Collegium to the Commission. . . .

[Articles 7-30 provide for the establishment of local councils of education and the calling of the all-Russian congresses of education.]

V. ULIANOV (LENIN)
President of the Soviet of
People's Commissars

M. POKROVSKY
Acting People's Commissar
of Education

THE SOCIALIST ACADEMY OF SOCIAL SCIENCES

[Decree of the Central Executive Committee, June 25, 1918] [6]

1. The Socialist Academy of Social Sciences is a free association of persons aiming at the study and teaching of the social sciences and related subjects from the point of view of scientific socialism and communism.

2. The membership of the Socialist Academy of Social Sciences consists of students who attend the different departments and sections with the status of associate members, of persons permanently connected with the different departments as candidates, and, finally, of those elected as active members, viz., professors, lecturers, and assistants.

3. The Socialist Academy of Social Sciences is divided into

[6] *Narodnoe Prosveshchenie,* Nos. 4-5, 1918, pp. 15-21.

two main sections: (1) Academic Research; (2) Scientific Education. . . .

4. In pursuance of the above-stated aims the Socialist Academy of Social Sciences may announce contests, award prizes, publish books and manuals . . . , and invite to associate membership any Russian citizen or foreigner. . . .

5. The Socialist Academy of Social Sciences is attached to the All-Russian Central Executive Committee and is to send reports of its activity to that institution.

6. All expenditures of the Socialist Academy of Social Sciences shall be included in the estimates of the People's Commissariat of Education.

SECTION OF ACADEMIC RESEARCH

7. The Section of Academic Research of the Socialist Academy of Social Sciences has the following aims: Scientific study of questions relating to socialism and communism, scientific investigation in the field of the social sciences, philosophy, and the natural sciences in so far as they touch upon the social sciences, and training of scientific specialists in the field of the social sciences.

[Articles 8-19 define the duties of the different categories of members.]

SECTION OF SCIENTIFIC EDUCATION

20. The Scientific-Educational Section of the Socialist Academy of Social Sciences is a free higher institution which aims to teach the social sciences to anyone who wishes to learn, and to spread the teachings of scientific socialism and communism among the masses. . . .

[Articles 21-65 define the duties of the Scientific-Educational Section and deal with the administration of the Academy. An additional article charges the All-Russian Central Executive Committee with the election of the first active members of the Academy.]

YA. SVERDLOV
Chairman of the Central
Executive Committee

PRINCIPLES OF THE NEW SCHOOL

[From Lepenshinsky's Report to the First All-Russian Congress of Teachers-Internationalists, June 3, 1918] [7]

. . . Our conception of a school completely bars religious services and teachings from it. A people's school must be compulsory and accessible to all; . . . tuition, books, etc., must be free. Lastly, we conceive of the new school as a unified labor school. It must he homogeneous in the sense of having a uniform structure with a definite minimum of instruction, a uniform set of problems grouped around two large centers of gravitation—the harmonious development of the individual and the realization of his social capacities. The different grades of the school must have an organic connection between them which leads the pupil gradually from one grade to the other.

The principles of the labor school may be summarized as follows:

1. An early combination of productive labor with academic instruction is a potent factor in the reconstruction of modern society.

2. The technique of present-day production requires an all-around development of the individual. He must be equipped technically for the various types of industrial work. It follows, therefore, that a general school education must be of a polytechnical nature. Specialization and professional training should remain outside the scope of general education and be left to the higher schools. . . .

3. Manual labor should form an integral part of school life. All school children should participate in productive labor and . . . be made to understand the usefulness of such labor, aiming at the direct creation of useful objects of consumption (chiefly to meet the needs of the particular school) or the performance of such tasks as tend toward indirect creation of material goods, for example, maintaining cleanliness . . . in school.

4. The school should become a productive commune, i. e., a producing and consuming collective based on principles designed to further the social development of the children. Those principles are as follows:

[7] *Sbornik vserossiiskogo soiuza uchitelei internatsionalistov*, No. 1, 1918, pp. 32-33.

(*a*) School autonomy and collective self-determination in the process of mental and physical work.

(*b*) Self-help of children in the satisfaction of their needs.

(*c*) The group study principle (scientific groups, reading circles, collective work, etc.).

5. The labor school must offer the widest possible opportunity for the unimpeded development of the creative faculties of the child. For this purpose the child must be reared in surroundings favorable to his mental and physical growth and conducive to the harmonious development of his individuality. The essential prerequisites for such a free development are:

(*a*) Spontaneous activity of the child in the various fields of school life; independence and initiative in work; and a spirit of self-reliance in matters of every-day routine. . . .

(*b*) The application of the method of eurythmics to education as a stimulant to the development of the creative energies of the child.

(*c*) Encouragement of artistic activity as an essential element in the child's aesthetic development and a factor tending to dominate the passive emotional phases of his spiritual life. . . .

ZEALOTS OF POPULAR EDUCATION

[Announcement of the Moscow Soviet] [8]

The Presidium of the Moscow Soviet of Workers' Deputies has imposed on all house committees the duty of subscribing to the *Izvestiia* of the All-Russian Central Executive Committee, the official Soviet newspaper.

[Announcement of the *Severnaia Kommuna*] [9]

On July 20 of this year there was promulgated under No. 27 the following compulsory ordinance:

"Every house committee of the city of Petrograd and all cities which comprise the Union of Communes of the Northern Region

[8] *Novaia Zhizn,* No. 138, July 14, 1918, p. 3.
[9] *Severnaia Kommuna,* No. 150, November 10, 1918, p. 1.

is under obligation to subscribe to one copy of the paper *Severnaia Kommuna,* the official organ of Soviets of the Northern Region. . . .

G. ZINOVIEV
President of the Union of Communes
of the Northern Region

N. KUZMIN
Commissar of the Press"

However, until now the majority of houses, occupied mostly by the bourgeoisie, have failed to comply with the above compulsory ordinance, and the workers living in these houses are not in a position to secure the *Severnaia Kommuna* from their house committees.

The editors of *Severnaia Kommuna* hereby give notice . . . that special emissaries have been appointed to ascertain whether the compulsory ordinance No. 27 is being complied with. House committees which fail to produce a receipt of subscription to the *Severnaia Kommuna* will be held strictly accountable for violation of a compulsory ordinance.

Subscriptions are received at the main office and the branches of the *Severnaia Kommuna* daily except Sundays and holidays, between 10:00 A. M. and 4:00 P. M.

ADMISSION TO HIGHER INSTITUTIONS OF LEARNING
[Decree of the Sovnarkom, August 2, 1918] [10]

1. Any person, regardless of citizenship or sex, who is sixteen years of age may be admitted to any of the higher institutions of learning without presenting a diploma or certificate of graduation from a secondary or any other school.

2. To require that the candidate present any credentials other than an identification card is forbidden.

3. All higher institutions of learning in the Republic . . . are accessible to all, regardless of sex, in conformity with the decree on coeducation. Violators of this provision are subject to criminal prosecution by the Revolutionary Tribunal.

[10] *S. U. R.,* No. 57, 1918, p. 689.

4. Admissions of first-year students (for 1918-1919) already made on the basis of either school certificates or competitive examinations are hereby declared void. New entrance conditions . . . will be published not later than September 1 of this year.

5. Tuition fees in higher educational institutions of the R. S. F. S. R. are henceforth abolished. Tuition fees already paid for for the first half of the academic year 1918-1919 shall be refunded accordingly.

V. ULIANOV (LENIN)
President of the Soviet of
People's Commissars

M. POKROVSKY
Acting People's Commissar
of Education

SCIENCE AND THE WORKING CLASS

[Resolution of the First All-Russian Conference of Proletarian Educational Organizations, September 15-19, 1918] [11]

The First All-Russian Conference of Proletarian Cultural-Educational Organizations looks upon science as an instrument for the organization of socialized labor. Until now science has been used by the ruling classes as an instrument for domination. In the hands of the working class science must become a weapon in the social struggle. . . . We therefore advocate the socialization of science [as follows] :

1. All scientific data should be systematically reexamined from a collectivist-workers' point of view.

2. The systematic exposition [of science] should be coordinated with the . . . requirements of proletarian work . . . and revolutionary struggle.

3. This reorganized scientific knowledge should be widely disseminated. . . .

---

[11] *Rabotnik pochty telegrafa i telefona*, Nos. 9-10, 1918, p. 15.

ABOLITION OF ACADEMIC TITLES AND RANKS
[Decree of October 1, 1918] [12]

1. All titles of learning . . . , together with the rights and privileges associated with them, are hereby abolished. Any person having the reputation of a scholar . . . or a teacher may compete for the position of professor.

2. All ranks . . . such as professor . . . , instructor, etc., are abolished. Any person who has carried on independent instruction in an institution of higher learning is called a professor.
. . .

5. Professors . . . of higher institutions of learning . . . who have taught at any institution for ten years . . . , or whose teaching career at various institutions will amount by October 1, 1918, to fifteen years . . . , shall be retired from their positions . . . , with the right to compete for the same position in accordance with the rules of the all-Russian competition. . . .

M. POKROVSKY
Acting Commissar of
Education

REGULATIONS CONCERNING THE UNIFIED LABOR SCHOOL
[Decree of October 16, 1918] [13]

I. GENERAL REGULATIONS

1. All schools of the Russian Socialist Federated Soviet Republic . . . except institutions of higher learning shall be known under the name of "The Unified Labor School." . . .

2. The Unified Labor School has two divisions: the first for children from eight to thirteen (a five-year course), and the second for children from thirteen to seventeen (a four-year course).
. . .

3. Instruction in schools of the first and second divisions is free.

4. Attendance at schools . . . is compulsory for children of school age. . . .

[12] *S. U. R.*, No. 72, 1918, pp. 888-89.   [13] *Ibid.*, No. 74, 1918, pp. 915-20.

5. Schools of the first and second divisions are coeducational.
. . .

6. The teaching of religion or the holding of religious cere-
monies on the premises of the school is forbidden.

7. Different ranks among instructors in schools are abolished.
All school workers referred to in Article 8 are paid according to
the first category of the scale for remuneration of teachers decreed by the Soviet of People's Commissars. . . .

8. All school workers, viz., teachers, physicians, instructors in
physical labor, are selected in accordance with the rules of February 27, 1918, of the People's Commissariat of Education. . . .

II. Principles of School Organization

12. Productive labor shall be the core of school life. . . .
There should be a vital connection between labor and education,
which is capable of throwing the light of knowledge upon every
aspect of life. . . .

Note 1: To be an effective pedagogical method work must be
creatively joyful, free from compulsion, and at the same time
systematic and socially organized. In this respect the school assumes the character of an educational commune, organically connected . . . with the rest of life.

Note 2: The old discipline, with its iron-bound system hinder-
ing free development of the child, can have no place in the new
labor school. The very processes of labor will educate the child
in a new internal discipline, which is the necessary condition for
every form of rationally conducted collective work. . . .

13. Education in the labor school is of a general and poly-
technic nature . . . , with special emphasis on physical and
aesthetic development. . . .

III. Organization of School Work

14. The school year is divided into three periods: (*a*) regular
instruction from September 1 to June 1; (*b*) open-air school from
June 1 to July 1 . . . ; (*c*) vacation period. . . .

17. Home lessons are abolished. . . .

18. The punishment of school children is prohibited.

19. All examinations . . . are abolished.

20. Division into classes must be replaced by division of students into groups in accordance with the degree of their preparation to do certain work. . . .

21. Free hot lunches shall be served in all schools. . . .

IV. SCHOOL ADMINISTRATION

26. The school collective consists of all pupils and all school workers.

27. The responsible organ of school self-government is a school soviet consisting of (*a*) all school workers, (*b*) representatives of the toiling population of the school district . . . , (*c*) representatives of higher-grade pupils of the ages of twelve and on . . . , and (*d*) one representative of the Department of People's Education.

YA. SVERDLOV
Chairman of the Central Executive
Committee

M. POKROVSKY
Acting People's Commissar of
Education

THE TASK OF COMMUNIST STUDENT YOUTH [14]

It is necessary to indicate in a general way the ends and organizational aims which the Communist Student Youth should set for itself in the endeavor to achieve a new organization of the school. . . . *One aim is to bring about a complete reorganization of the school, based on new socialist principles.* Only new men can accomplish this task. The old pedagogues have become ossified in their petty-bourgeois ideology to such an extent . . . that they are absolutely unfitted for the task. It follows that we students must unite our ranks in a final effort to destroy the old, rotten school and to build in its place a new, magnificently beautiful edifice of the Unified Labor Socialist School.

The task of the present, in so far as it concerns the school, is to bring about a November Revolution, i. e., to introduce into

[14] *Narodnoe Prosveshchenie,* No. 21, 1918, pp. 7-8.

school management the dictatorship of the student proletariat [and] to draw a sharp dividing-line between our supporters and our enemies. . . .

The time in which we live is among the most turbulent periods of history. In this epoch of the great world revolution any person capable in some degree of using his intellect must define in one way or another his attitude toward this great event; he must join either the ranks of the followers of the revolution or of its enemies. Indifference is unthinkable, because all the threads of individual and social life have become woven in one knot.

The elements which until now have considered themselves outside politics are unsuited for the rôle of active workers. By separating the best proletarian communist youth we shall bring about a revolution in every sphere of school life. We shall destroy the [old] school and rebuild it in the spirit of communism. The sooner we bring about the pedagogic revolution in the minds and the feelings of youth, the more secure will prove the conquests of the other revolutions (political and social).

It is important to educate student youth in such a way that it will prove a loyal inheritor of the work already done, understand . . . the meaning of the class struggle which is now going on, and help the proletariat to bridge the gap between capitalism and socialism.

In order to achieve this aim, student youth . . . should immediately organize a communist nucleus in every school of the Russian Federated Republic. . . . This communist nucleus will serve as the active fermenting element of the school and will be endowed with the widest powers in its reorganization. . . . It should send its representatives into every organ of school administration . . . , and no aspect of school life may remain outside its attention.

The first aim [of the nucleus] is to establish a political center . . . where students may undertake the study of various political questions connected with current world events. The study should aim to develop the class consciousness of every student and to prepare politically mature communist fighters. The Union of Communist Student Youth is to stand for the defense of all the Soviet Government's undertakings and to strive for their realization in school life. . . .

A central bureau of student organizations . . . will be established in connection with the Commissariat of Education to lead the youth movement throughout the country. The Central Bureau of the Union of Communist Youth will take charge of all propaganda and educational work . . . , will send party workers and instructors to the schools . . . , and will offer systematic courses to train experienced communist organizers. . . . The bureau will work in cooperation with the Union of Internationalist Teachers, the Party, and the People's Commissariat of Education. . . .

SCHOOLS OF NATIONAL MINORITIES

[Decree of the Commissariat of Education, October 31, 1918] [15]

1. All nationalities inhabiting the R. S. F. S. R. have the right to use their native language in instruction in both grades of the Unified Labor School and in the higher institutions of learning.

2. Schools of national minorities can be opened wherever there is found a sufficient number of students of one nationality. The required minimum number of students is twenty-five for each age group.

3. In order to bring about . . . a greater class solidarity of the toilers of various nationalities, the language of the majority of the population of a given area must be taught in the schools of national minorities. . . .

5. The administration of the schools of national minorities is centralized in the People's Commissariat of Education and in the Oblast and Gubernia Departments of People's Education. . . .

POKROVSKY
Acting Commissar of Education

WORKS OF SCIENCE AND ART DECLARED STATE PROPERTY

[Decree of the Sovnarkom, November 26, 1918] [16]

1. Every published or unpublished scientific, literary, musical, or artistic work, regardless of who possesses it, may upon the decision of the People's Commissariat of Education be declared the property of the R. S. F. S. R. . . .

[15] S. U. R., No. 80, 1918, p. 990.   [16] Ibid., No. 86, 1918, pp. 1091-92.

2. A work of art which becomes state property may be reproduced and distributed only by the People's Commissariat of Education or by some other Soviet institution acting with the approval of the People's Commissariat of Education.

Note: Productions of drama, music, etc., which are declared to be state property can be performed in public only with the permission of the People's Commissariat of Education and on such conditions as it may prescribe. . . .

3. Works not declared state property cannot be reproduced and distributed without the consent of the author if he is living, and no one may publish or republish his works within six months after his death. . . .

7. After the author's death all remunerations due him become state property. The needy and disabled relatives of the deceased have the right to receive assistance . . . in accordance with the general rules provided in the decree on the abolition of inheritance. . . .

10. The right of translation . . . into Russian . . . and from Russian may be declared . . . the monopoly of the Republic. . . .

V. ULIANOV (LENIN)
President of the Soviet of People's
Commissars

THE DEPARTMENT OF SOVIET PROPAGANDA

[Decree of the Central Executive Committee, December 5, 1918] [17]

1. A Department of Soviet Propaganda . . . shall be formed in connection with the People's Commissariat of Foreign Affairs and shall be under the direction and control of the Collegium of that Commissariat.

2. The budgetary funds of the Department of Soviet Propaganda . . . are appropriated directly by the Central Executive Committee. . . .

3. The Chief of the Department of Soviet Propaganda . . . is appointed by the Central Executive Committee in concurrence with the Collegium of the People's Commissariat of Foreign Affairs. . . .

[17] *Ibid.*, No. 90, 1918, p. 1141.

5. The Department of Soviet Propaganda . . . is to organize foreign bureaus of the Russian Telegraphic Agency. These bureaus are subordinate to the Department of Soviet Propaganda.
. . .

6. Radiograms and telegrams sent abroad for publication by the bureaus of the Russian Telegraphic Agency (Rosta) shall be written by the Department of Soviet Propaganda. . . .

7. All information received from abroad through the Rosta bureaus is to be released for publication in the Russian press by the Department of Soviet Propaganda. . . .

YA. SVERDLOV
Chairman of the Central Executive
Committee

MOBILIZATION OF LITERATES FOR PROPAGANDA

[Decree of the Sovnarkom, December 10, 1918] [18]

In order that the population may have the widest possible information concerning the nature of the Soviet régime and the activities and policies of the Worker-Peasant Government, the following steps shall be taken:

1. The People's Commissariat of Education, working in cooperation with other institutions having charge of propaganda and agitation, shall undertake at once the preparation of a collection of popular articles dealing with the above-described themes and suitable for the widest dissemination, especially for reading to illiterate citizens of the Soviet Republic.

The People's Commissariat of Education is to formulate instructions defining more clearly the character and theme of such collections.

2. Regional and city Soviet institutions, as well as soviets and committees of the poor in the villages, assisted by local organizations and nuclei of the Russian Communist party, are to undertake at once [the following]:

a. To register the entire literate population, separating those who are able to read aloud clearly and intelligently.

[18] *Narodnoe Prosveshchenie*, Nos. 23-25, 1918, p. 22.

b. To mobilize as readers all literate citizens except those whose full time is taken up by Soviet work.

c. Mobilized citizens of both sexes between the ages of sixteen and fifty shall be divided into groups directed by local teachers . . . and under control of local party organizations.

d. Each group is to take charge of a certain part of the city or village and is under obligation, in the first place, to read to the illiterate population all the ordinances of the Government, and, in the second, to help in the general political education of the people by reading to them [Government] decrees and Communist newspapers. . . .

5. Citizens who are subject to mobilization under Article 2 (Sections *a* and *b*) have no right to refuse to discharge the duties of readers. . . . All such work is gratis.

V. Ulianov (Lenin)
President of the Sovnarkom

M. Pokrovsky
Acting Commissar of Education

ABOLITION OF LAW FACULTIES

[Decree of the Commissariat of Education] [19]

In view of the totally antiquated character of the teaching curricula of the law faculties of Russian universities and other institutions of higher learning of the same grade, as well as of the utter incapacity of these curricula to satisfy the requirements of scientific methodology and the need of Soviet institutions for highly qualified [legal] workers, it is hereby decreed:

1. All law faculties are abolished. . . .

2. All credits intended for the maintenance of these faculties . . . shall be stopped on January 15, 1919.

3. Separate chairs of the above-named faculties, viz., the chairs of political economy, statistics, finance, laws, and international law, shall be transferred temporarily, pending the establishment of faculties of social sciences, to the historical division of the historico-philological faculties; the chair of constitutional

---

[19] *Ibid.,* pp. 22-23.

law shall be changed to the chair of Soviet legislation. This subject shall be introduced into the regular curriculum of all faculties. All other chairs shall be abolished and their incumbents excluded from the teaching staff beginning with January 15, 1919. . . .

4. The Socialist Academy of the Social Sciences shall have ready by January 15, 1919, a curriculum for the faculties of social sciences.

DISSOLUTION OF THE ALL-RUSSIAN TEACHERS' UNION

[Decree of the Central Executive Committee, December 23, 1918] [20]

The All-Russian Central Executive Committee has learned the following:

(1) The All-Russian Teachers' Union, immediately after the November Revolution, cooperated with . . . the counter-revolutionary Committee to Save the Country and the Revolution. (2) The All-Russian Teachers' Union supported the activity of the Committee by spreading literature directed against the Soviet Government. (3) [The Union] incited the teachers to sabotage and strike and [advocated] insubordination and opposition to the ordinances of the Soviet Government. (4) [The Union] offered opposition to the decree concerning reelection of teachers. (5) [The Union] strove in every possible way to undermine the confidence of the teachers in the activities of the People's Commissariat of Education in relation to school reform. (6) It adopted a reactionary attitude toward the effort to free the schools from the yoke of religious superstition and chauvinism, insisting on teaching religion in the schools and on national principles in education in opposition to the ideas of internationalism. . . . (8) The All-Russian Teachers' Union took part through its provincial organizations . . . in the counter-revolution of the Czechoslovaks and White Guard insurrections.

In view of the above considerations the All-Russian Central Executive Committee decrees the dissolution of the All-Russian Teachers' Union, including its central and local organizations. Its press organs, *Izvestiia Vserossiiskago Uchitelskago Soiuza, Petrogradskii Uchitel, Uchitel* (published by the Moscow Region-

[20] *Ibid.*, p. 22.

al Bureau of the All-Russian Teachers' Union), and other central and local organs of the All-Russian Teachers' Union, shall be suppressed. All properties and funds of the Teachers' Union shall be used to satisfy the professional and cultural needs of the teachers under the control of the Collegium of the People's Commissariat of Education.

Members of the All-Russian Teachers' Union will not be subject to persecution or discrimination on account of membership in the Union.

YA. SVERDLOV
Chairman of the Central
Executive Committee

CHAPTER XI

SIDELIGHTS OF THE RUSSIAN SCENE

An upheaval which extended far beyond the politico-economic sphere, the Bolshevik Revolution evoked in the great mass of the Russian people changes of attitude and behavior which are revealed only incompletely by the documents portraying governmental policy and action. These changes in the people's ideas, ways, and mores are often shown more clearly by news items and personal reminiscences which, while incidental from the viewpoint of the ordinary categories of political and economic history, center upon the aspects of the revolution most prominent for those pursuing humble walks of life in places far removed from the main centers of political activity. It is from this point of view that the materials given below may be presented as sidelights of the Russian scene. They give glimpses into the states of mind engendered by the revolution in the worker, peasant, soldier, and bourgeois—reactions as varied as fanatical enthusiasm, dark pessimism, and utter bewilderment. They reveal at the same time many of the characteristics of the turbulent scene which stimulated such sharp reactions. The spread of new ideas to the villages; the bewilderment of the new local authorities and their expedients for retaining power; the degradation and penalization of the bourgeoisie; the struggle against famine; the various innovations in social valuations and customs—these and other themes of the materials give evidence of a social revolution no less dramatic than the politico-economic changes introduced by governmental fiat.

546

A DAY IN THE VILLAGE [1]

Colorless, lazy, tedious Riazan has not changed much since the days of Gogol. The raven continues as of old to clamor from the church steeples. All is quiet in the city except for a dance here and there.

In the uezds it is frightful. The sleepy Russian village has been aroused by Bolshevism and threatens to destroy everything in sight. In the robbing and killing of landlords Riazan Gubernia is notorious. . . . Conditions are worst in the localities where the deserters and the hidden stills are most numerous. . . .

Father Alexander and I took a walk through the village.

"Take note," said the Father, "of the people's blindness . . . and the use that is being made of it. . . . At the time of the elections [Constituent Assembly] the women came to me to ask how to vote and while doing so kept looking around to see if anyone was listening. Soldiers went from hut to hut telling the occupants that if they did not vote the Bolshevik ticket their cows, grain, and huts would be taken from them."

While talking we arrived at the schoolhouse. . . . A meeting had been called to hear a lecture on how good the Bolsheviks are and what they would give to the people and . . . why other parties are bad. A soldier was reading from a paper. It was not quite clear who sent him here, whether the Riazan Soviet or an emissary of the People's Commissars. . . .

During the reading there appeared the commissar himself, in soldier's uniform. He walked with a certain assurance, stepped up to the speaker's desk, took off his cap, knocked on the table, and began to talk:

"Comrades! I should like first of all to call your attention to the importance of the period we are living in. It is a time of the freedom of the people, the triumph of the proletariat, and the solution of important problems. . . ."

He spoke rather quickly but not altogether ungrammatically. His speech sounded like an article in *Pravda*, but it was quite evident that he had not assimilated what he had read. He likened Kerensky to a dog whose tail had been cut off but [said that] "it should have been the head." When he talked about the bourgeoi-

[1] *Nash Vek*, No. 21, 1918, p. 4.

sie he became so excited that it seemed as if his eyes would pop out. . . .

I looked at the auditors. They sat there quietly, drinking in everything, believing everything. . . . The village believes him who shouts, beats his breast, and foams at the mouth. The last and loudest speaker has the best chance of carrying his audience with him. But I must return to the speaker of the day.

"Comrades" said the orator, "the time has come when every true peasant and proletarian can say and say loudly: 'Enough! Take the land from the landlords! It is time for them to go down on their knees before the suffering people! Go through their bags and pocketbooks!' Do you agree with me, Comrades?"

"We agree!" shouted back the younger men, but the women nudged each other and tried to keep from giggling.

The first speaker was followed by the teacher of the school. He did not know the arts of eloquence, he did not jump up and down, did not fume, and could not get the attention of the audience. . . . His arguments, too, were childish. "The Bolsheviks," he said, "will soon disappear, for how can it be otherwise?" He failed completely.

Father Alexander came next. He had no more than opened his mouth when someone began to make remarks about him.

I left the room and went outside. Three peasants with long beards stood talking, and I approached them.

"How can you listen to such rot, lies, and foolishness?" I remarked.

"Who are you?" asked one.

"One of those city fellows," said another.

"Of course, he does not like to let go of his property," added a third.

The meeting ended and we went home. I spent a miserable night. My room was cold, the baby cried, and the wind howled. . . .

When I awoke in the morning and looked out I noticed a streak of light against the grey sky. Later I learned that it was the flames from one of the manor houses which had been set on fire. . . .

On my way to the station I passed a number of peasant carts, loaded down with furniture, pictures, and a piano. The piano was without its top and rested on its side. A peasant woman was steadying it with one hand and striking the keys with the other. . . .

The train was more than crowded. Every bit of space, including the aisle and the toilet, was occupied. The air was so thick that one almost choked. . . . But even under these conditions a young soldier made a speech. He explained the origin of the bourgeoisie:

"Once upon a time there lived Adam and Eve. They had many children. The children settled in villages and cities. In the cities there grew up 'individuals.' These 'individuals' are people of strong will. They united with the priests, that is to say, with all kinds of clergy, and through this combination the bourgeoisie came into existence. What a bourgeoisie! It has been crushing us and it is about time that we got rid of it. . . . Tolstoy said the same thing. . . ."

I broke in with the question, "What did Tolstoy say?"

He gave me a wicked look of contempt . . . , spat on the floor, and turned his back on me. . . .

Russia has lost herself in the darkness. Lord of Heaven, lead Russia out of the darkness!

THE NEW LIGHT

[Narrative of a Traveller from Siberia] [2]

While I was sitting on the platform of a railway station several hundred miles from Omsk, there was close beside me a robust peasant smoking his pipe. "How far are you travelling?" I asked him.

"To Omsk, to buy *lectrical* lamps. We have in our village *lectricity* running from wires, you know."

"How long has this been going on?"

"Not so very long."

Then he told me the following story:

"In November news reached our village that the government at Omsk had changed, that it called itself the Soviet and was going to bring in *sicilism*. At a village meeting we decided to find out what it was all about. We elected Levonty, the oldest peasant, and gave him these instructions: 'Levonty, take these thirty rubles, go to Omsk, and find out everything about the Soviet—

[2] *Novaia Zhizn*, No. 117, 1918, p. 1.

what sort of people the Bolsheviks are, how strong they are, and what is meant by *sicilism.*'

"After two weeks Levonty came back and brought with him a soldier. We called a meeting, and Levonty mounted the table and made a speech.

" 'Well, it's this way,' he said. 'Everything seems to be in order, and as for the rest, the soldier can explain it to you better than I.'

"We then turned to the soldier.

" 'Who are you?' we asked him.

" 'I am a Bolshevik and a *communir*,' he said. 'I'll stay with you if you appoint me your commissar.'

"We thought for a while and said, 'Be it as you wish.'

" 'Thank you humbly, Comrades,' he said. 'Give me a little time to look around.'

"A week later a soviet was organized. By this time Levonty had learned a lot and at the meeting of the Soviet he said: 'Now that we have adopted the point of view and become Bolsheviks our duty is to destroy and reorganize.' When we pointed out that there was not much in our village to destroy, the soldier interrupted.

" 'If you are *communirs*,' he said, 'you have to requisition. Don't you have a *bourgeoisiat*?'

"We were all silent. We could not see at first what he was talking about. But the soldier insisted: 'Where is your *bourgeoisiat*?'

" 'We are sorry,' we answered, 'but we have none.'

" 'Well,' said the soldier, 'you do not seem to know your own condition. I will find the *bourgeoisiat* for you. Let me have a few men.'

"He took about sixty peasants with him and went to the neighboring village, about forty versts away. The next day they came back bringing twelve rich peasants and ten thousand rubles with them.

"The soldier said to us, 'Here is the *bourgeoisiat*.'

"When we asked the peasants if this was true they answered yes. 'Well,' we said, 'we are *communirs* and we want to requisition you.'

" 'How much do you want?' they asked.

"We went aside to hold a council.

" 'Three thousand from each of you,' was the answer.

"The *bourgeoisiat* held out at first. 'Too much,' they said, 'take two thousand.' At last they agreed. They left one of their number as a hostage and went to fetch the money. In a day they sent us forty-two thousand rubles. We thus had fifty-two thousand in all. We called a meeting of the Soviet. Levonty was chairman and said: 'We have requisitioned the money, and now what shall we do?'

"Somebody thought that we should build a school. Somebody else thought that we should buy an automobile and let everybody drive it in turn. These ideas were turned down and the soldier once more helped us out.

" 'In the cities,' he told us, 'there is *lectricity*. . . . Installing it is an easy matter. You let a wheel rotate in water and connect it with a dynamo, then you attach one end of a wire to the dynamo and an electric lamp to the other, and the lamp begins to burn. Is that clear?'

" 'Clear enough,' we said, 'let us have *lectricity*.'

"The soldier then went to Omsk to buy the machine. Levonty went with him, carrying the money. . . . When they came back they brought with them four strangers. They were the mechanics. . . .

"After the machine was uncovered we all looked at it, and it seemed very strange indeed. But we could not help realizing that it was a good machine and was worth the money. The mechanics got busy. They made a big wheel, lowered it into the water, and connected it with the machine, which began to move so quickly that sparks flew from it. We were all frightened. We then decided to put the *lectricity* in the house of our priest first. 'Levonty had found out somewhere that the church and the state were being separated. . . . So he said to the priest: 'You had better get out of the house.'

"We all went to the priest . . . , chased him out of the house, and while the mechanics were busy with the wires everybody made speeches. . . .

"One of the mechanics then gave the order: 'Blind the windows in any way you can.'

"We put on blinds. It became dark and mysterious. We were all silent.

"Suddenly a glow of light struck our eyes. The lamp was burning.

"We then decided to put a lamp in every house. . . .

"Before long the peasants of a neighboring village found out what we had done and asked us if they could use our light.

"The soldiers advised us not to allow those who weren't *communirs* to use the light, so we told the neighboring peasants: 'If you wish to use the light, declare yourselves *communirs*.'

"Of course, they declared themselves *communirs*; it's a simple thing to do that. They chased out their priest, opened a library in his house, and said they were *communirs*.

"The soldier then gave us another piece of advice: to connect a wire to the other village and charge money for the light. To this we agreed.

"Our neighbors searched out a *bourgeoisiat* of their own, requisitioned sixty thousand rubles, and built a school to teach the children and others without schooling. They hired a good teacher and connected four lamps. One of our men, pretending that he is going to school, makes sure with a timepiece in his hand that no more *lectricity* is being used than is paid for. It is a good business and we are making money.

"Everybody in the neighborhood talks about this cold fire, which brings so many conveniences. . . . But there is one thing about it we find very strange: You cannot light a cigarette with it."

DISCOVERING SOURCES OF INCOME

[A News Report from Dankov] [3]

Beginning with December of last year the uezd authorities embarked upon new . . . ways of finding sources of income. The Revolutionary Committee conducted searches . . . and took everything it could. The searches were conducted in a very polite manner and receipts were given for every article taken. Early in January new authorities, representing the Executive Committee of Peasants' Deputies, came into power. They continued the policies of their predecessors except for the fact that the receipts [given for articles taken] were written in a new way: "Expropriated and not subject to payment."

[3] *Svoboda Rossii*, No. 5, 1918, p. 3. Dankov is in Riazan Gubernia.

After a number of turbulent peasant congresses a Soviet of Soviets was finally formed. . . . With the aid of a Moscow detachment of Red Guards it succeeded in establishing its power, and it continues to rule the city to this day. . . .

The emergence of the Soviet of Soviets signified the advent of a new era in methods of discovering sources of income.

The house of the [former] city mayor, Lebedov, . . . was confiscated . . . and was occupied by members of the Soviet and Red Guards. His corn mill was also taken. . . . All the goods of M. A. Ivanov, the [former] vice-mayor and a local merchant, were confiscated. The goods brought in 150,000 rubles when sold to village organizations. One hundred and thirty members of the Union of Land Proprietors—a union which had ceased to exist a long time ago—were placed under arrest. . . . Four . . . were killed, the rest released. The Soviet collected about 200,000 rubles in ransom. . . . Those who had bank accounts . . . were forced by threat of imprisonment to make out checks to the account of the Soviet. These checks yielded about 100,000 rubles.

CIVIL-WAR JUSTICE

. . . The Soviet sent a workmen's delegation of which I was a member to the front, with several cars of presents for the soldiers. . . . I lost some time at Gomel, because for quite a distance the line was in the hands of the Ukrainians. One of the revolutionary officers took charge of the cars and promised to put a guard over them. A few days later I was informed that the cars could not go through and that the presents had better be distributed among the revolutionary soldiers on the spot. I called attention to the possibility of getting the cars through, but the officers insisted on sending them a different way. When I examined the cars I discovered that the locks were broken and half the goods gone. . . .

We managed to reach Bakhmach. . . . Along the line I noticed naked bodies and was told that they were former army officers who had been shot.

[One day] two officers were brought into our car and put in a compartment. As the door was open I could hear the questions

⁴ *Novaia Zhizn,* No. 21, 1918, p. 3.

and answers. Bashmakov, a soldier who impressed me as rather abnormal, conducted the investigation. He asked the officers why they were in this neighborhood. The replies which they gave apparently did not satisfy the examiner for he told them that they were lying and that they had come to fight against the revolutionists. The examiner had no evidence of any kind for he had burned all the papers he found on the officers. . . .

I turned to one of the soldiers in the car and asked what would become of these officers. He said that they would be sent to "Dukhonin's staff." I did not know what he meant, and on further questioning he explained that they would be taken out of the car and shot.[5]

I was so shocked that I did not know what to say. While I was looking on I noticed two men, one a sailor and the other a Red Guard, holding a conversation, and I heard enough to realize that they were bargaining over the clothes of the officers.

A little later Bashmakov gave the order to take the officers out. They were led away and I watched them through the car window until they disappeared from sight. A few minutes later I heard several shots. Not long afterwards I saw two men coming back, and as they approached I recognized the sailor and the Red Guard. In their hands were the clothes of the two officers. . . .

THE COMMISSAR OF THE CITY OF KOTELNICH
[Official Notice] [6]

Citizens!

In a few days all counter-revolutionists will be sent to Fort Petropavlovsk in Petrograd. There they will be brought before the Military Revolutionary Tribunal.

The trial will be an honest and just one. The guilty will be punished and the innocent will be brought back to Kotelnich.

I ask the citizens of Kotelnich not to become excited about the sending of the arrested [counter-revolutionists to Petrograd] and not to start different reports and rumors. I especially warn

[5] General Dukhonin, commander in chief of the Russian army, was killed by Bolshevik sailors on December 3, 1917, after Krylenko had occupied the Stavka at Mogilev. See *The Bolshevik Revolution,* pp. 267-68.
[6] *Novaia Zhizn,* No. 30, 1918, p. 4.

the women not to behave like empty-headed market-women and not to imitate Mrs. Myshkina, the physician.

This ignorant member of the species of empty-headed market-woman, who carries the title of physician by some misunderstanding and was only recently released from arrest, . . . continues her open counter-revolutionary propaganda among the citizens of Kotelnich both inside and outside the zemstvo hospital of which she is in charge.

Her hostile activities are bound to lead her to bitter tears.

I trust that upon reading my public denunciation this market-woman [Myshkina] will come to her senses . . . and stop her slanderous talk. If that does not happen I shall take the most stringent measures to segregate Mrs. Myshkina from the other citizens of Kotelnich. No protest on the part of the women's union of which Mrs. Myshkina is a member will be of any avail. No pleading in her behalf by any citizen will succeed in awakening a single spark of sympathy in my heart. I shall show no mercy!

After the arrested [counter-revolutionists] are sent away life in Kotelnich must go on as usual. All voices of protest will be stifled within prison walls. . . .

LENID ZHARBA
Commissar

STRICT ACCOUNTING AND CONTROL

[From the Official Transactions of the Skopin Soviet] [7]

Russian Federated Republic
Uezd Executive Committee of the Soviet of Soviets
of Workers' and Peasants' Deputies.

City of Skopin, Riazan Gubernia
June 5, 1918

AFFIDAVIT

This affidavit is issued by the Presidium of the Skopin Soviet of Workers' and Peasants' Deputies to the Russian traveller Valen-

[7] *Svobodnaia Zhizn*, No. 5, 1918, p. 4.

tin Lensky as authorization of his carrying from Skopin Uezd a quarter of a pound of bread.

SMIRNOV

Chairman of the Soviet

BATRAKOV

Executive Secretary

THE ZEAL FOR TEMPERANCE

[Resolution of the Kargopolsky Soviet] [8]

Commissars of temperance, both uezd and volost, are to be elected from those who completely abstain from drink. In case no teetotaler can be found, it is permissible to elect a drinking man.

COMMUNIZATION OF WOMEN [9]

From Saratov comes the news that the Anarchist Club of that city has issued a "decree" declaring all women between the ages of seventeen and thirty-two the property of the state. The rights of husbands are to be abolished; the women will receive 232 rubles a month from the state and are to be distributed among those who want them.[10]

THOUGHTS OF RETURNING SOLDIERS

[Narrative of a Traveler] [11]

. . . There are certain advantages in traveling in a small freight car. It is less crowded, easier to get in and out of; all are equal for all lie on the floor; the conversation is general, and in the dark one is more apt to say what he thinks. . . .

Our car is full of soldiers returning from the front. . . . There are also two or three Chinamen, who grin and say nothing, a few workmen, my companion and I.

Each of us carries a sack of food of one kind or another. . . .

[8] *Narodnaia Mysl,* No. 4, 1918, p. 3.
[9] *Svoboda Rossii,* No. 4, 1918, p. 4.
[10] This item is perhaps one source of the legend about Bolshevik communization of women which received much publicity in foreign countries.
[11] *Novaia Zhizn,* No. 54, 1918, p. 2.

The conversation is mainly about food, bagmen, and Red Guards who lie in wait to confiscate the food of workers and soldiers. . . . The Red Guards are as thoroughly hated as were the old police. . . .

"They are worse than the old secret police, because the old gang knew the law and these scoundrels do not. They do just as they please."

"That's because the Soviets are just as ignorant of the law and do as they please."

"Let up on the Soviets! Who isn't stealing now, who of us isn't doing as he pleases? Didn't the soldiers sell government supplies? Didn't the workmen demand unreasonable pay? We are all thieves. . . ."

There is a lull in the conversation but after a while it flares up again.

"After two years of military service," says one soldier, "I am now on my way home, a wiser and a sadder man. The Bolsheviks have ruined Russia, destroyed industry, closed the factories, killed credit, and have now handed us over to the Germans. Believe me, I am ashamed to go home. . . . We dreamed of peace but not this kind of peace. . . . The Bolsheviks claim that the soldiers were interested in their program. Nothing of the kind! The Bolsheviks knew how to touch the tender spots. The soldier who thought that freedom was worthless to a dead man was ashamed to say it out loud. The Bolsheviks said it for him and added that if the Russian soldiers stopped fighting, the Germans would do likewise. On hearing this the ignorant soldiers began to clamor for an end of hostilities. . . . What did the soldier understand about Bolshevik ideas?"

"Would you say," interrupted someone, "that we should have gone on with the struggle? Enough have been killed."

"Is it any better to be in bondage to the Germans? We have lost the Baltic coast, the Ukraine, some of the best parts of the Caucasus, and now Japan is getting ready to seize Siberia. Let them grab the whole of Russia!"

"Let them grab, let them grab everything! We fools are getting what is coming to us. What business had we to get into the war? We must rest now; we cannot go on."

Just then a new voice made itself heard. "It would have been a good thing if Kornilov had captured Petrograd. We played the fool then. We were told that he wished to restore the death penalty and to ruin the revolution. I learned lately that this was not so and that all Kornilov planned to do was to equalize the pay of the workers and the soldiers. That's fair. But we fools believed what Kerensky said. It is a good thing that the Bolsheviks got rid of him."

"What are you, a Kornilovist?" came a voice from somewhere.

"How in the devil do I know what I am? When I marched against Kornilov I thought I was a Bolshevik, but now that I am with the Bolsheviks I begin to think that I am a Kornilovist. I understand that Trotsky has invited the old generals to come back. That means that he has restored the death penalty."

"Lenin and Trotsky did that a long time ago."

"They are all sons of bitches," interrupted a soldier. "All of them—Lenin, Trotsky, Kerensky, Tsereteli—have sold themselves to imperialists and capitalists."

"For God's sake, tell me, is there an honest man left? Is there anyone we can follow?"

"Follow your own head. . . . If we only had Nicholas Nikolaevich [12] back. There was a man!"

"Are you in favor of the monarchy?"

"Monarchy or revolution, what in the devil do I swollen from hunger care? I was against Kornilov because he tried to restore Nicholas II; but Grand Duke Nicholas was a friend of the people."

"I don't agree with you!" shouted another soldier. "If he was the fine man you say, why was he dismissed? I am told that he held back thousands of letters belonging to prisoners of war. . . . Was that decent? I am glad they dismissed him."

"The only decent fellow was Kerensky, a real patriot. . . . I have always stood up for him," declared another soldier. . . .

In this manner the conversation runs on and on until we all fall asleep.

---

[12] The Tsar's uncle, one-time commander in chief of the Imperial armies.

HOW THE BOLSHEVIKS RETAINED POWER IN TAMBOV [18]

. . . The Tambov paper *Iskra* gives [the following] account of the breaking up of the local Soviet:

Early in April there were held new elections for the City Soviet of Tambov. The Social-Democrats (United) and the Socialist-Revolutionists [Right] received a majority . . . , the Bolsheviks about a third of the vote. Thus the situation was clear . . . ; the Bolsheviks were losing power [in the city]. This, however, was not to the liking of the Bolsheviks, and they decided to do everything to retain power. At the meeting of the newly elected City Soviet the Bolsheviks presented an ultimatum that they be given seven of the twelve places in the Soviet Executive Committee. The ultimatum was rejected, and the Bolsheviks left the meeting declaring that they reserved for themselves freedom of action. The meeting of the Soviet continued and elected an Executive Committee, . . . leaving vacancies for Bolshevik representatives as is provided by the Soviet system of proportional representation. . . . The Bolsheviks, however, did not wish to take part in the work of the Soviet. . . . They held a joint meeting with the [old] Gubernia Executive Committee and discovered a pretext for breaking up the City Soviet. The reason they offered was that the members of the old Soviet had not been notified about the pre-election meetings. For that reason the Gubernia Executive Committee decided that the elections were not legal . . . , that new elections should take place, and that the old Executive Committee should remain in power. . . .

On April 5, when the newly elected City Soviet was to meet again, . . . all entrances . . . to the City Duma . . . were occupied by Red Guards. No one was allowed to enter the building. Members of the Soviet were searched, their [Soviet] membership cards taken away and destroyed. A few members succeeded in penetrating into the building and opening the session. Thereupon the Bolsheviks gave orders to evict them by force. . . .

Meanwhile the Gubernia Executive Committee announced that authority in Tambov was transferred from the Soviet to the Bolshevik and Left Socialist-Revolutionist parties. . . .

[18] *Novaia Zhizn,* No. 87, 1918, p. 4.

RAISING MONEY IN HASTE

[A News Report from Kislovodsk] [14]

Quite recently a number of people received notice to appear at 11 : 00 A. M. at the Grand Hotel to hear the demands of the representatives of the Terek central authorities. Thirty-two persons came. At the appointed hour [Terek Soviet] officials appeared. [They said :] "We summoned you here to tell you that a levy of thirty million rubles has been imposed on Kislovodsk. We give you an hour and a half in which to collect that amount and hand it over to us, the commissars. You are at liberty to elect a committee from your midst . . . and distribute the sum of thirty millions [among the different watering resorts in the neighborhood]. In order that the bourgeoisie of Essentuki, Zheleznovodsk, and Piatigorsk may not escape their share of the levy, we place at your disposal the entire government apparatus—the army, the railway, rifles, [the right to make] arrests, etc."

When the summoned persons expressed their astonishment at . . . being expected to collect thirty million rubles in an hour and a half, the commissars agreed to extend the time limit to 6 : 00 P. M. and left the hotel. The guards who surrounded the hotel and refused to let anyone out were a clear indication that the commissars were not joking. Work had to be started. . . . It was soon found that to collect thirty million rubles was impossible. . . . A number of committees and sub-committees were organized. . . . [Attempts were made to bring to the hotel members of the bourgeoisie, real-estate owners, and bankers.] The bankers declared that the money on hand in all local banks, including all current accounts, was fourteen million rubles. One committee was sent to Essentuki in an automobile, accompanied by all the attributes of state power—a machine gun and Red Guards. When evening came the commissars made their appearance. They were informed that the money could not be collected. The commissars then gave a forty-eight hour extension but demanded a written guarantee that at the expiration of the forty-eight hours at least ten million rubles . . . would be paid.

At the dictation of the commissars the following note of guarantee was given: "We, the undersigned, agree to pay within

[14] *Svoboda Rossii*, No. 32, 1918, p. 6. Kislovodsk is a well-known resort in the Northern Caucasus.

forty-eight hours thirty million rubles. Of these, ten millions are
to be paid in cash. The amount is to be collected from the propertied classes of the visiting bourgeoisie and from the local population. In case the obligation which we have voluntarily assumed is
not fulfilled, stern consequences will fall not only upon those who
signed this agreement but upon all those who were assessed."

In the evening there took place a stormy session . . . which
ended in another extension of two to three days. An attempt was
made to send a telegram to Moscow . . . but Kislovodsk refused
to accept it, while the special messenger sent to Tikhoretskaia was
detained by the guards who were surrounding the city. The work
of assessing [the bourgeoisie] began, and those liable to payment
were divided into fourteen categories. The first category was
250,000 [rubles], the second 100,000, the third 75,000, and so
on. . . . The assessments were made in a purely arbitrary way
and brought forth a horde of complaints. The Grand Hotel was
surrounded by a crowd of people watching what was going on.

SOVIET AGAINST SOVIET

Samara, May 23.[15] The Commander in Chief of the Orenburg
front, acting with the approval of the Executive Committee of
the City Soviet of Deputies, on May 21 broke up the Gubernia
Executive Committee of Soviets. This case, unique in the history
of the Russian Revolution, is explained by the fact that in the
almost complete absence of workers' deputies the Peasant Section [of the Committee] consisted of kulak elements much influenced by anarchists and nationalists. During the three months
of its existence the Gubernia Executive Committee proved barren
of creative work. Of late it interfered greatly with the work of
the Extraordinary Revolutionary Staff which the Soviet of Deputies organized to fight against Dutov. Finally, the Committee
played an important rôle in the revolt of the Anarchist-Syndical-
ists and various hooligan bands who made an unsuccessful attempt to overthrow the Samara Soviet.

Yaroslav, July 4.[16] The Left Socialist-Revolutionists formed
their own Executive Committee of Soviets, in opposition to that
of the Bolsheviks. The two committees do not recognize each
other.

[15] *Ibid.,* No. 33, 1918, p. 4.   [16] *Nashe Slovo,* No. 63, 1918, p. 4.

19

MEASURES AGAINST THE BOURGEOISIE

Bologoe, September 12. By order of the Uezd Executive Committee the city bourgeoisie are being evicted from their homes, which workers are occupying.[17]

Labor duty of the bourgeoisie in the Spassky section [of Petrograd] is assuming well-organized forms. About 150 men are being sent daily to work in vegetable gardens and to clean soldiers' barracks.[18]

Balashov, October 6. The Uezd Executive Committee has resolved . . . to expel the entire bourgeoisie from . . . the uezd.

Tambov, October 3. Public works are being organized by the Gubernia Commissariat of Labor. Over five hundred individuals, mostly members of the bourgeoisie, have been forced to work.[19]

LEVIES ON THE BOURGEOISIE

[Newspaper Reports]

In Temnikov [Tombov Gubernia] the local soviet imposed on merchants and well-to-do inhabitants a levy of 10,000 to 35,000 rubles each and demanded that the amounts be paid in cash. In view of the fact that no one had the cash, the bank not paying on deposits, all had to go to jail. . . .

Tomsk. The Tomsk Sovdep presented an ultimatum to the Chamber of Commerce demanding the payment of 5,000,000 rubles. . . . The local merchants discussed the question at a meeting of the Chamber of Commerce . . . and by a large majority decided to reject the demand of the Sovdep. . . . When the meeting came to an end . . . the Chamber of Commerce building was surrounded by soldiers. The soldiers placed everyone under arrest. Those arrested were taken to jail. . . .

Orel. The question of the 6,000,000 rubles which the local soviet levied on the city of Orel has not yet been settled. Payments have reached to date the sum of 2,000,000 rubles. The . . . Gubernia Executive Committee has decided that the capitalists who fail to pay their share within forty-eight hours . . . will be arrested, sentenced to hard labor, and be subjected to confiscation of their property.

[17] *Izvestiia*, No. 200, 1918, p. 4.   [19] *Ibid.*, No. 217, 1918, p. 4.
[18] *Ibid.*, No. 203, 1918, p. 4.

Kazan. The Sovdep of the city of Spassk imposed upon well-to-do inhabitants the payment of 500,000 rubles.

The Village Soviet of Bolgary . . . exacted from the local "bourgeoisie" the payment of 30,000 rubles for the needs of the "poor inhabitants." Bolgary has a population of 3,200.

Simferopol. By order of the Military Revolutionary Committee, about 1,500,000 rubles have been transferred from the bank accounts [of private citizens] to the account of the Military Revolutionary Committee. . . . [20]

The Soviet of Verkhne-Uralsk (Orenburg Gubernia) has resolved to place on the bourgeoisie of Verkhne-Uralsk a levy of 2,365,000 rubles. Since April 5 [1918], the sum of 11,797,000 rubles has been exacted.[21]

Vyshny-Volchek, September 9. A fine of 100,000 rubles and 2,000 puds of grain was imposed upon the volost of Lugininsk for disarming Red Guards. . . . For similar reasons . . . Podubskaia Volost was fined 50,000 rubles and 1,000 puds of grain. . . . [22]

STARVATION [23]

The Moscow Regional Food Committee has received the following telegrams:

From Viksa (Nizhny-Novgorod). Workers are starving and fall at their benches from weakness. . . . We implore you to send us bread . . . , else the factory will have to close. Please understand that this is not a threat but a last cry of desperation.

KOSOLAPOV

Chairman of the Viksa Factory Workers

From Moshka (Vladimir Gubernia). We are dying of hunger. For God's sake send us bread!

MOSHKA PEASANT COMMITTEE

From Bogorodsk. The Bogorodsk industrial region . . . is starving. This is the sixth day on which the workers have received no bread. Disturbances are taking place. . . .

[20] *Svoboda Rossii*, No. 2, 1918, p. 4.   [22] *Izvestiia*, No. 196, 1918, p. 5.
[21] *Novaia Zhizn*, No. 105, 1918, p. 4.   [23] *Svoboda Rossii*, No. 35, 1918, p. 4

CHRONOLOGY

1918

April 4 Japanese force lands at Vladivostok.

5 The Sovnarkom denounces the Japanese landing.

14-30 The Don Cossacks rise against the Soviets.

27 Right of inheritance is abolished by the Central Executive Committee. Chicherin protests against Germany's advance into Central Russia and the Crimea.

28 The Don Voisko Government is reestablished.

29 The Ukrainian Rada is overthrown by the Germans.

30 General Skoropadsky is proclaimed hetman of the Ukraine. German troops occupy Sevastopol.

May 1-7 The Germans occupy parts of the Don region.

9 A food dictatorship is decreed by the Central Executive Committee.

11 The Transcaucasian Republic resumes peace negotiations with Turkey. The Krug to Save the Don meets at Novocherkassk.

14 The Central Executive Committee, the Moscow Soviet, and the representatives of trade unions and factory-shop committees meet in plenary session to discuss foreign policies. First clash of the Czechoslovaks with the Bolsheviks occurs at Cheliabinsk.

16 Revolt in the Red Army breaks out at Saratov. General Krasnov is elected ataman of the Don Cossacks.

20 The Central Executive Committee declares war on the kulaks. The Sovnarkom orders the disbanding of the Czechoslovak Corps.

22 Czechoslovak leaders in conference at Cheliabinsk decide not to surrender arms.

23 The Sovnarkom starts peace negotiations with Skoropadsky's government. Conference of factory-shop delegates at Moscow calls for a strike against the Soviet Government.

May 25-June 4
First All-Russian Congress of Councils of National Economy meets at Moscow.

May 25 Trotsky orders the Siberian soviets to shoot every armed Czechoslovak.

26 Socialist-Revolutionists of the Right invite Allied intervention in Russia. The Transcaucasian Republic is dissolved. Georgia is proclaimed an independent republic.

565

27 Distribution of commodities is taken over by the Commissariat of Food.

28 Armenia and Azerbaijan are proclaimed independent republics. Penza is captured by the Czechoslovaks.

29 The Central Executive Committee decrees conscription for the Red Army. The Supreme Revolutionary Tribunal is established by the Central Executive Committee. The Sovnarkom declares martial law in Moscow.

30 Tomsk is captured by the Whites. The Western-Siberian Commissariat is established at Tomsk. Dutov, Ataman of the Orenburg Cossacks, starts an offensive against the Bolsheviks.

June 1 A Crimean-Tartar government is formed at Sevastopol.

5 The Don is proclaimed an independent republic.

7 Omsk is occupied by the Czechoslovaks. Lenin orders. the Mumansk Soviet to oppose the Allied forces of occupation.

8 Samara is captured by the Czechoslovaks. A government of the Committee of Members of the Constituent Assembly is established at Samara.

10 The Sovnarkom decrees military measures against the Siberian Provisional Government.

11 The Central Executive Committee decrees the establishment of committees of the poor. The Czechoslovak National Council is dissolved by the Sovnarkom.

14 Right Socialist parties are expelled from the Soviets. An armistice between Soviet Russia and the Ukraine is concluded.

17 Anti-Bolshevik insurrection breaks out in Tambov.

18 Part of the Black Sea fleet is sunk by Russian sailors at Novorossiisk.

21 The Supreme Revolutionary Tribunal passes the first death sentence.

22 The Volunteer Army begins its second Kuban campaign.

24 The Socialist-Revolutionists of the Left resolve upon terroristic acts against German diplomatic representatives in Russia.

25 The Central Executive Committee decrees the establishment of a Socialist Academy of Social Sciences.

28 The Sovnarkom decrees the nationalization of large-scale industry.

29 The Vladivostok Soviet is overthrown by the Czechoslovaks.

30 The Murmansk Soviet approves cooperation with the Allied forces in Northern Russia. The Western-Siberian Commissariat is replaced by the Provisional Government of Western Siberia.

July 1 Strikers are declared enemies of labor by the Soviet Government.

2 The Allies decide to intervene in Russia.

4 Siberia is proclaimed an independent republic.

4-10 The Fifth Congress of Soviets meets at Moscow.

6 Savinkov's group starts a revolt against the Soviets at Yaroslav. The German Ambassador, Count von Mirbach, is assassinated in Moscow by Left S. R.'s. The Left S. R.'s begin a revolt in Moscow and Petrograd. Vladivostok is declared under an Allied protectorate. An agreement between Allied commanding officers and the Murmansk Soviet is signed.

7 The Bolsheviks suppress the revolt of the Left S. R.'s in Moscow.

8 The Provisional Government of Autonomous Siberia makes claim at Vladivostok to sovereign authority.

9 General Horvath proclaims himself Provisional Ruler. The Fifth Congress of Soviets expels the Left S. R.'s.

10 The Soviet commander in chief on the Volga front rebels against the Bolsheviks. The Fifth Congress of Soviets adopts a constitution for the R. S. F. S. R.

10-14 Soviet troops in the Northern Caucasus are defeated by the Volunteer Army of General Denikin.

12 Chicherin protests against Allied intervention.

14 Germany demands permission to send to Moscow a battalion of German troops.

16 The Imperial Family is executed at Ekaterinburg.

21 Simbirsk is captured by the forces of the Samara Government.

23 The Bolsheviks suppress the Yaroslav revolt.

25 Czechoslovaks capture Ekaterinburg. The Regional Government of the Urals is established at Ekaterinburg. The Allied Diplomatic Corps leaves Vologda for Archangel. The Provisional Government of Autonomous Siberia appeals for Allied recognition.

28 Helfferich, the new German ambassador, arrives at Moscow.

29 Lenin proclaims a state of war between Soviet Russia and the Allies.

30 Field Marshal von Eichhorn, commander in chief of German forces in the Ukraine, is assassinated by a Left S. R.

31 The Bolshevik Soviet of Baku is overthrown by Caspian sailors.

August 2 An Allied force is landed at Archangel. The Supreme Administration of the North is established at Archangel.

3 The Samara Government invites Allied intervention. Japanese and British troops land at Vladivostok.

4 The Sovnarkom decrees the establishment of food-requisition cordons.

5 French and British nationals are arrested in Moscow.

6 The German Ambassador leaves Moscow. The Sovnarkom authorizes workers' trade unions to send armed detachments to the villages for the requisitioning of bread.

7 The Czechoslovaks and the People's Army capture Kazan. The Russian gold reserve is transferred to Samara. Social insurance is decreed by the Sovnarkom. The Izhevsk workers revolt against the Bolsheviks.

15 The Siberian Regional Duma meets at Tomsk.

16 American troops land at Vladivostok. Ekaterinodar is captured by the Volunteer Army.

20 Right to own real estate is abolished by the Central Executive Committee.

26 Novorossiisk is captured by the Volunteer Army.

27 Supplementary treaty between Germany and Soviet Russia is concluded.

28 General Denikin establishes a civil administration for the regions occupied by the Volunteer Army.

30 Uritsky is assassinated in Petrograd and Lenin is wounded in Moscow. The Supreme Council of National Economy establishes moneyless transactions between nationalized enterprises.

31 The British Embassy at Petrograd is raided by the Cheka.

Sept. 1 Lockhart, British unofficial representative, is arrested in Moscow.

2 Five hundred and twelve persons are executed by the Petrograd Cheka. The Sovnarkom accuses British and French representatives of plotting against the Soviet Government.

3 Unemployed are forbidden to refuse work.

4 American troops land at Archangel.

5 The Sovnarkom legalizes Red Terror against the bourgeoisie. The Diplomatic Corps at Petrograd enters an official protest against the Red Terror.

6 Members of the Supreme Administration of the North are arrested by conservatives.

7 General Wrangel joins the Volunteer Army.

8-23 Anti-Bolshevik groups meet in state conference at Ufa to form an All-Russian government.

9 The Supreme Administration of the North is reinstated.

10 The Red Army recaptures Kazan.

12 The Ufa State Conference welcomes the landing of Allied troops at Vladivostok.

14 Baku is captured by the Turks.

20 The Sovnarkom repudiates the treaty between Turkey and Soviet Russia.

23 The Ufa State Conference adopts a constitution and elects an All-Russian Provisional Government.

Oct. 3 Lenin urges preparations for world revolution.

4 The Central Executive Committee pledges support of the German proletariat.

7 Samara is captured by the Red Army.

8 General Alexeev, organizer of the Volunteer Army, dies at Ekaterinodar.

16 The Unified Labor School is established by the Central Executive Committee.

26 The Sovnarkom authorizes the issue of additional bank notes to the amount of 35.5 billion rubles.

30 The Central Executive Committee decrees the formation of a Revolutionary War Council. The Sovnarkom levies on the bourgeoisie a tax of ten billion rubles. The Central Executive Committee decrees taxes in kind.

31 Universal labor duty is decreed by the Sovnarkom.

Nov. 2 The Sovnarkom appropriates a billion rubles for collective farming.

5 The Soviet Embassy is expelled from Berlin.

13 The Central Executive Committee repudiates the Brest-Litovsk Treaty.

17 The Crimean Tartar Government relinquishes authority. A Provisional Crimean Government is formed at Sevastopol.

18 The All-Russian Directorate is overthrown at Omsk. Kolchak is proclaimed Supreme Ruler.

20 A Ukrainian Soviet Government is formed by Ukrainian Bolsheviks.

21 Private trade is abolished by the Sovnarkom.

26 Allied troops arrive at Odessa. The Sovnarkom decrees the nationalization of works of science and art.

30 A Council of Defense is established by the Central Executive Committee.

Dec. 5 The Central Executive Committee establishes a Department of Soviet Propaganda.

10 The Sovnarkom decrees the mobilization of literates for propaganda.

14 Skoropadsky relinquishes authority. Forces of the Ukrainian Directory enter Kiev.

17 Latvia is proclaimed a Soviet Republic.

23 The All-Russian Teachers' Union is dissolved by the Central Executive Committee. The C. E. C. resolves to recognize Latvia, Esthonia, and Lithuania as independent Soviet Republics.

1-31 The Red Army wins victories in the Ukraine.

BIBLIOGRAPHY

The following bibliography does not purport to give all the materials relating to the subject of this work, or even all those consulted in its preparation. The list includes merely the sources cited in the foregoing pages. At the same time, it provides such annotations as are necessary to indicate the general character of the materials which are in Russian.

GOVERNMENT PUBLICATIONS

Dokumenty i materialy po vneishnei politike Zaravkazia i Gruzii (*Documents and Materials Relating to the Foreign Policies of Transcaucasia and Georgia*). Tiflis, 1918.
A publication of the Georgian Government.

Grazhdanskaia voina. Boevye deistviia na mariakh, rechnykh i ozernykh systemakh (*Civil War. Naval Operations on Seas, Rivers, and Lakes*). Egorov, I. i Shvede, E., eds., 3 vols., Leningrad, 1925-1926.
A publication of the Historical Commission of the Naval General Staff.

Instruktsii i polozheniia o kommunakh (*Instructions and Principles Relating to Communes*). Moscow, 1919.
A publication of the Commissariat of Agriculture.

Kliuchnikov, Yu, i Sabanin, A., *Mezhdunarodnaia politika noveishego vremeni v dogovorakh, notakh i deklaratsiiakh* (*Recent International Politics in Treaties, Notes, and Declarations*). 3 vols., Moscow, 1925-1928.
A publication of the Commissariat of Foreign Affairs.

Knasnaia Kniga V. Ch. K. (*The Red Book of the All-Russian Extraordinary Commission*). Makintsian, ed., 2 vols., Moscow, 1920.
A publication of the All-Russian Extraordinary Commission to Fight Counter-Revolution. The work contains data on the different plots directed against the Soviet Government and the measures taken by the Cheka to suppress those plots. It was withdrawn from circulation soon after publication and copies are difficult to obtain. The Hoover War Library has a typewritten copy of the book.

Obzor finansovogo zakonodatelstva (*A Review of Financial Legislation*). Petrograd, 1921.
A publication of the People's Commissariat of Finance.

O zemle (*Concerning the Land*). 3 vols., Moscow, 1921-1922.
A publication of the People's Commissariat of Agriculture. It contains valuable data on the results of the land reform of 1918.

Piatyi sozyv Vserossiiskogo Tsentralnogo Ispolnitelnogo Komiteta Sovetov Rabochikh, Krestianskikh, Kazachikh i Krasnoarmeiskikh Deputatov. Stenograficheskii otchet (*The Fifth Assembly of the Central*

572   BIBLIOGRAPHY

*Executive Committee of Soviets of Workers', Peasants', Cossacks',
and Red Army Deputies. Stenographic Report*). Moscow, 1919.
    A publication of the Central Executive Committee of the R. S.
F. S. R.

*Piatyi Vserossiiskii Sezd Sovetov Rabochikh, Krestianskikh, Soldatskikh
i Kazachikh Deputatov. Stenograficheskii otchet, Moskva, 4-10 iiulia,
1918g. (The Fifth All-Russian Congress of Soviets of Workers',
Soldiers', and Cossacks' Deputies. Stenographic Report, Moscow,
July 4-10, 1918*). Moscow, 1918.

*Protokoly 4-oi conferentsii fabrichno-zavodskikh komitetov i professional-
nykh soiuzov g Moskvy (Protocols of the Fourth Conference of
Factory-Shop Committees and Trade Unions of Moscow*). Moscow,
1918.

*Protokoly zasedanii Vserossiiskogo Tsentralnogo Ispolnitelnogo Komiteta
4-go sozyva. Stenograficheskii otchet (Protocols of the Sessions of
the All-Russian Central Executive Committee, the Fourth Assembly.
Stenographic Report*). Moscow, 1920.

*Rezoliutsii Pervago Vserossiiskago Sezda Sovetov Narodnago Khoziaistva
(Resolutions of the First All-Russian Congress of Councils of
National Economy*). Moscow, 1920.
    A publication of the Supreme Council of National Economy.

*Rospis obshchegosudarstvennykh dokhodov i raskhodov, Iul-Dekabr 1918
(An Estimate of State Revenues and Expenditures, July-December
1918*). N. Krestinsky, ed., Moscow, 1919.
    A publication of the People's Commissariat of Finance.

*Rossiia v mirovoi voine 1914-18gg. v tsifrakh (Russia in the World War,
1914-1918, with Figures*). Moscow, 1925.
    A publication of the Central Statistical Department.

*Sistematicheskii sbornik dekretov i rasporiazhenii pravitelstva po prodo-
volstvennomu delu (A Systematic Collection of Decrees and Ordinances of the Government Relating to Food*). Nizhny-Novgorod,
1919.
    A publication of the People's Commissariat of Food.

*Sobranie uzakonenii i rasporiazhenii Rabochego i Krestianskogo Pravi-
telstva (A Collection of the Laws and Ordinances of the Workers'
and Peasants' Government*). Moscow, 1918, 2d ed.

*Sobranie uzakanenii i rasporiazhenii Verkhovnago Upravleniia i Vremen-
nago Pravitelstva Servernoi Oblasti (A Collection of the Laws and
Ordinances of the Supreme Administration and the Provisional Government of the Northern Region*). Archangel, 1918.

*Sobranie uzakonenii i rasporiazhenii Vremennago Sibirskago Pravitelstva
(A Collection of the Laws and Ordinances of the Provisional
Siberian Government*). Omsk, 1918.

*Trudy I Vserossiiskogo Sezda Sovetov Narodnago Khoziaistva. Stenog-
raficheskii otchet (Proceedings of the First All-Russian Congress of*

Councils of National Economy. Stenographic Report). Moscow, 1918.
A publication of the Supreme Council of National Economy.
Trudy II Vserossiiskogo Sezda Sovetov Narodnogo Khoziaistva. Stenograficheskii otchet (Proceedings of the Second All-Russian Congress of Councils of National Economy. Stenographic Report). Moscow, 1919.
A publication of the Supreme Council of National Economy.
United States Department of State, *Papers Relating to the Foreign Relations of the United States, 1918, Russia.* 3 vols., 1931-32.
Vtoroi gad borby s golodom (The Second Year of the Fight against Famine). Moscow, 1919.
A report of the Commissariat of Food.

Manuscripts

Cheriachukin Papers. Hoover War Library, Stanford University.
Private papers of the ambassador of the Don Government to the Ukraine.
Crimean Government Documents. Hoover War Library, Stanford University.
Papers from the private archives of Vinaver, Minister of Foreign Affairs of the Crimean Government.
Report of the American Vice-Consul at Samara to the American Consul General at Moscow. In the collection of Professor DeWitt C. Poole, Princeton University.
Russian Agriculture and the Revolution. Hoover War Library, Stanford University.
A study by a Russian agricultural expert.

Collections of Writings and Documents

Arkhiv Russkoi Revoliutsii (Archives of the Russian Revolution). Hessen, I. V., ed., 21 vols., Berlin, 1921—.
Memoirs and other materials relating to the Russian Revolution.
Beloe Delo. Letopis beloi borby (The White Cause. A Chronicle of the White Struggle). Lampe, A. von, ed., 7 vols., Berlin, 1926-1933.
Reminiscences of civil war and revolution by White leaders.
Bunyan, James and H. H. Fisher, *The Bolshevik Revolution 1917-1918. Documents and Materials.* Stanford University, 1934.
Donskaia Letopis (The Don Chronicle). 3 vols., 1923-1925.
A collection of materials relating to the revolution in the Don region in 1917-1918. Published by the Don Historical Commission.
Golder, F. A., *Documents of Russian History 1914-1917.* New York and London, 1927.

Lenin, V. I., *Sochineniia (Works)*. 30 vols., 2d ed., Moscow, 1926-1932.

Lutz, R., *Fall of the German Empire 1914-1917*. 2 vols., Stanford University, 1932.

Maksakov, V. i Turunov, A., eds., *Khronika grazhdanskoi voiny v Sibiri 1917-1918 (A Chronicle of Civil War in Siberia in 1917-1918)*.
A collection of documents, with a detailed chronology and a bibliography of works relating to the civil war in Siberia.

Piontkovsky, S. A., ed., *Grazhdanskaia voina v Rossi 1918-1921gg. (Civil War in Russia in 1918-1921)*. Moscow, 1925.
A selection of materials which present the history of the civil war from a Bolshevik viewpoint.

Pravo sovetskoi Rossii. Sbornik statei, sostavlennyi professorami russkogo iuridicheskogo fakulteta v Prage (The Law of Soviet Russia. A Collection of Papers by Professors of the Russian Law Faculty in Prague). 2 vols., Prague, 1925.

Revoliutsiia na Ukraine po memuaram belykh (The Revolution in the Ukraine as Described in the Memoirs of the Whites). Alexeev, S. A., ed., Moscow, 1930.
Selections by a Soviet historian.

Russkii istoricheskii arkhiv (Russian Historical Archives). Prague, 1929.
Published by the Russian Historical Archives at Prague.

Russian-American Relations, March 1917–March 1920. Documents and Papers. (Cumming, C. K. and Pettit, W. W., eds.), New York, 1920.

Seymour, Charles, *Intimate Papers of Colonel House*. 4 vols., Boston and New York, 1926-1928.

Sibirskaia sovetskaia entsiklopediia (The Siberian Soviet Encyclopedia). 3 vols., Novosibirsk, 1929-1932.

Trotsky, L., *Kak vooruzhalas revoliutsiia (How the Revolution Armed Itself)*. 5 vols., Moscow, 1923-1925.
A collection of articles by Trotsky relating to the organization of the Red Army.

MEMOIRS

Antonov-Ovseenko, V. A., *Zapiski o grazhdanskoi voine (Notes on the Civil War)*. 4 vols., Moscow, 1924-1933.
An account of the civil war in Southern Russia by the Soviet commander in chief.

Argunov, A., *Mezhdu dvumia bolshevizmami (Between two Bolshevisms)*. Paris, 1919.
A criticism of the Siberian Government by a Socialist-Revolutionist member of the Ufa Directorate.

Avalov, A., *Nezavisimost Gruzii v mezhdunarodnoi politike 1918-1921gg. (The Independence of Georgia as an Issue in International Politics)*. Paris, 1924.

Beneš, Édouard, *Souvenirs de guerre et de révolution, 1914-1919.* 2 vols., Paris, 1928-1929.

Boldyrev, V., *Direktoriia, Kolchak, Interventy. Vospominaniia (The Directorate, Kolchak, and the Interventionists. Reminiscences).* Novonikolaevsk, 1925.
   The reminiscences and diary of the Supreme Commander in Chief of the Directorate's army.

Borisenko, I., *Sovetskie respubliki na severnom Kavkaze v 1918 godu (Soviet Republics in the Northern Caucasus in 1918).* 2 vols., Rostov-na-Donu, 1930.
   An account of the civil war in the Northern Caucasus by a Bolshevik.

Bosh, E. B., *God borby. Borba za vlast sovetov na Ukraine s Aprelia 1917g. do nemetskoi okkupatsii (The Year of Struggle. The Fight for Soviet Rule in the Ukraine from April 1917 to the German Occupation).* Gosizdat, 1925.
   Reminiscences of a Bolshevik who took part in the events.

Denikin, A. I., *Ocherki russkoi smuty (Sketches of the Russian Turmoil).* 5 vols., Berlin, 1924-1926.
   Memoirs of the commander in chief of the Volunteer Army, containing a number of documents.

Dunsterville, L. C., *The Adventures of the Dunsterforce.* London, 1921.

Francis, David, *Russia from the American Embassy.* New York, 1922.

Gilliard, Pierre, *Tragicheskaia sudba rossiiskoi imperatorskoi semi (The Tragic Fate of the Russian Imperial Family).* Reval, 1921.

Grenard, F., *La révolution russe.* Paris, 1933.

Hoffman, M., *Der Krieg der verzäumten Gelegenheiten.* München, 1924.

Janin, General Maurice, *Moje účast na československém boji za svobodu (My part in the Czechoslovak Struggle for Freedom).* Prague [1930].

Karmashev, V., *Poslednie dni sovetskoi vlasti v Zapadnoi Sibiri 1918 goda (The Last Days of Soviet Rule in Western Siberia).* Moscow, 1921.
   A Bolshevik account.

Kedrov, M., *Bez bolshevistskogo rukovodstva (Without Bolshevik Guidance).* Leningrad, 1930.
   Reminiscences of civil war in the Murmansk region by a Bolshevik commissar.

Khrīstiuk, P., *Zamitki i materiali do istorii Ukrainskoi revoliutsii 1917-1920rr. (Notes and Materials Relating to the History of the Ukrainian Revolution).* 3 vols., Wien, 1921.

Kratochvil, Jaroslav, *Česta Revoluče (The Road of Revolution).* Prague, 1928.
   A well-documented account of the Czechoslovaks in Russia.

Krol, L. A., *Za tri goda. Vospominaniia, vpechatleniia, vstrechi* (*Three Years. Reminiscences, Impressions, Encounters*). Vladivostok, 1922.
Memoirs of a liberal member of the Ural Regional Government, describing conditions in Siberia during 1918-1921.

Kudela, Josef, *S našim vojskem na Rusi* (*With Our Army in Russia*). 2 vols., Prague, 1923.

Latsis (Sudrabs), M. Ya., *Chrezvychainye komissii po borbe s kontr-revoliutsiei* (*Extraordinary Commission to Fight Counter-Revolution*). Moscow, 1921.

——, *Dva goda borby na vnutrennem fronte* (*Two Years of Struggle on the Internal Front*). Moscow, 1921.
Statements of the nature and activities of the Cheka by a prominent member of that institution.

Lelevich, G., *V dni Samarskoi uchredilki* (*The Days of the Samara Committee of the Constituent Assembly*). Gosizdat, 1921.
A Bolshevik account of the policies of the Samara Government.

Lockhart, R. H. Bruce, *British Agent*. New York, 1933.

Ludendorff, E. von, *Meine Kriegserinnerungen*. Berlin, 1918.

Maisky, I., *Demokraticheskaia kontr-revoliutsiia* (*The Democratic Counter-Revolution*). Gosizdat, 1923.
Reminiscences of a member of the Samara Government who later joined the Bolsheviks.

Margolin, A., *Ukraina i politika antanty* (*The Ukraine and the Policies of the Entente*). Berlin, 1922.

Masaryk, J. G., *The Making of a State*. New York, 1927.

Noulens, J., *Mon ambassade en russie sovietique*. 2 vols., Paris [1933].

Papoušek, Jaroslav, *Chekhoslovaki i Sovety: Kak proizoshlo stolknovenie chekhoslovatskikh legionov s sovetami* (*The Czechoslovaks and the Soviets: How the Clash of the Czechoslovak Legions and the Soviets Came About*). Prague, 1928.

Pasmanik, D. S., *Revoliutsionnye gody v Krymu* (*Revolutionary Years in the Crimea*). Paris, 1926.
Reminiscences of civil war and revolution in the Crimea by a conservative observer.

Petrov, P. P., *Ot Volgi do Tikhogo Okeana v riadakh belykh 1918-1922* (*From the Volga to the Arctic Ocean in the Ranks of the Whites in 1918-1922*). Riga, 1930.
Reminiscences of the chief of staff of the People's Army.

Sadoul, J., *Notes sur la révolution bolshevique, Octobre 1917–Janvier 1919*. Paris, 1919.

Savinkov, B. V., *Borba s bolshevikami* (*The Struggle against the Bolsheviks*). Warsaw, 1920.

Steidler, F. V., *Československi hnuti na Rusi* (*The Czechoslovak Movement in Russia*). Prague, 1922.

Sviatitsky, N., *K istorii Vserossiiskogo Uchreditelnogo Sobraniia, chast III, sezd chlenov Uchreditelnogo Sobraniia* (*The History of the All-Russian Constituent Assembly, Part III, Congress of Members of the Constituent Assembly*). Moscow, 1921.

> An outline of events in Eastern Russia during September–December 1918 by an S. R. member of the Constituent Assembly.

Taniaev, A., *Kolchakovshchina na Urale* (*The Kolchak Régime in the Urals*). Gosizdat, 1930.

> Reminiscences of a Bolshevik.

Vinaver, M., *Nashe pravitelstvo. Krymskiia vospominaniia 1918-1919gg.* (*Our Government. Reminiscences of Crimea in 1918-1919*). Paris, 1928.

> A memoir by the Minister of Foreign Affairs of the Crimean Government.

Vishniak, M., *Vserossiiskoe Uchreditelnoe Sobranie* (*The All-Russian Constituent Assembly*). Paris, 1932.

> Reminiscences of civil war in Eastern Russia by a Socialist-Revolutionist who was secretary of the Constituent Assembly.

Secondary Works

Batsell, W. R., *Soviet Rule in Russia.* New York, 1929.

Broide, S., *Yaroslavskii miatezh; po zapiskam generala Perkhurova* (*The Yaroslav Revolt; a Study Based on the Notes of General Perkhurov*). Moscow, 1930.

Bukharin, N., *Ekonomika perekhodnogo perioda* (*Economics of the Transitional Period*) Moscow, 1920.

> A consideration of the economic processes involved in the transition from capitalism to communism.

———— i Preobrazhensky, E., *Azbuka kommunizma* (*The A B C of Communism*). Gosizdat, 1920.

> A popular exposition of the communist program.

Chamberlin, William H., *The Russian Revolution 1917-21.* 2 vols., New York, 1935.

Delo Borisa Savinkova (*The Trial of Boris Savinkov*). Gosizdat, 1924.

Doroshenko, D., *Istoriia Ukraini 1917-1923rr.* (*A History of the Ukraine 1917-1923*). 2 vols., Uzhgorod, 1930-1932.

> The second volume of this work is an apologia for the Hetman régime.

Fischer, Louis, *The Soviets in World Affairs.* 2 vols., London, 1930.

Gurvich, G. C., *Istoriia sovetskoi konstitutsii* (*A History of the Soviet Constitution*). Gosizdat, 1923.

> This work gives some of the early drafts which influenced the final form of the Constitution of the R. S. F. S. R.

Katzenellenbaum, S., *Russian Currency and Banking 1914-1924.* London, 1925.

Klante, Margarete, *Von der Volga zum Amur. Die tschechische Legion und der russische Bürgerkrieg.* Berlin, 1931.

Kritzman, L., *Geroicheskii period russkoi revoliutsii (The Heroic Period of the Russian Revolution).* Moscow, 1924.

Larin, Yu. i Kritsman, L., *Ocherk khoziaistvennoi zhizni i organizatsiia narodnago koziaistva sovetskoi Rossii (A Sketch of the Economic Life and the Organization of the National Economy of Soviet Russia).* Gosizdat, 1920.

Levidov, M., *K istorii soiuznoi interventsii v Rosii (A Contribution to the History of Allied Intervention in Russia).* Leningrad, 1925.

Melgunov, S., *Tragediia Admirala Kolchaka; iz istorii grazhdanskoi voiny na Volge, Urale i v Sibiri (The Tragedy of Admiral Kolchak; a Study in the History of Civil War on the Volga, in the Urals, and in Siberia).* 3 vols., Belgrade, 1930-1931.

———, *N. V. Chaikovsky v gody grazhdanskoi voiny (N. V. Chaikovsky during the Years of Civil War).* Paris, 1929.

Miliutin, V., *Sotsialism i selskoe khoziaistvo (Socialism and Agriculture).* Gosizdat, 1919.

Mintz, I., *Angliiskaia interventsia i severnaia kontrrevolutsiia (English Intervention and the Northern Counter-Revolution).* Moscow, 1931.

Renner, Karl, *Das Selbstbestimmungsrecht der Nationen in besonderer Anwendung auf Oesterreich.* Leipzig, Wien, 1918.

Schuman, F. L., *American Policy toward Russia since 1917.* New York, 1928.

Subbotovsky, I., *Souizniki, russkie reaktsionery i interventy (The Allies, the Russian Reactionaries, and the Interventionists).* Leningrad, 1926.
   Contains a number of documents from the archives of the Kolchak Government.

Trotsky, Leon, *Lenin.* New York, 1925.

Vladimirova, V., *God sluzhby " sotsialistov " kapitalistam; ocherki po istorii kontrrevoliutsii v 1918 godu (A Year of Service of " Socialists " to Capitalists; Sketches of the History of Counter-Revolution in 1918).* Moscow, 1927.

Zaitsov, A., *1918 god. Ocherki po istorii russkoi grazhdanskoi voiny (The Year 1918. Sketches of the History of the Russian Civil War).* [n. p.], 1934.

Za svobodu. Obrázková kronika československeho revolučniho hnuti na Rusi 1914-1920 (In the Cause of Freedom. Illustrated Chronicle of the Czechoslovak Revolutionary Movement in Russia in 1914-1920). Prague, 1926.
   An official history of the Czechoslovaks in Russia.

MAGAZINES

Biulleten otdela sotsialnogo strakhovaniia i okhrany truda (Bulletin of the Department of Social Insurance and Labor Protection). Moscow, 1918.

A publication of the People's Commissariat of Labor.

Ezhenedelnik chresvychainykh komissii (Weekly of the Extraordinary Commissions). Moscow, 1918.

Six numbers were issued.

Golos minuvshego na chuzhoi storone (The Voice of the Past in a Foreign Land). Paris, 1926. See *Na chuzhoi storone*.

Istorik i Sovremennik (The Historian and the Contemporary Observer). Berlin, 1922-1924.

A historical and literary journal containing reminiscences of civil war and revolution in Russia. Five numbers appeared.

Izvestiia Narodnago Komissariata Finansov (News of the People's Commissariat of Finance).

An official publication.

Krasnyi Arkhiv (Red Archives).

A historical journal published by the Central Archives of the R. S. F. S. R. at Moscow since 1922. Contains documents and materials on the developments of the revolution and the civil war.

Krasnyi Terror (Red Terror).

Published by the Kazan Cheka. Only two numbers appeared in 1918.

Letopis Revoliutsii (Annals of the Revolution).

A historical journal published in Berlin in 1923. Only one number appeared.

Metallist (Metal Worker).

The official organ of the Central Committee of the Metal Workers' Trade Union.

Na chuzhoi storone (In a Foreign Land).

A historical and literary journal published irregularly in Berlin and Prague in 1923-1925. Thirteen numbers appeared. Continued in 1926 under the title *Golos minuvshego na chuzhoi storone*.

Narodnoe Khoziaistvo (People's Economy). Moscow, 1918.

Published by the Supreme Council of National Economy.

Narodnoe Prosveshchenie (People's Education). Moscow, 1918.

Official organ of the People's Commissariat of Education.

Professionalnyi Vestnik (Trade-Union Herald).

Official organ of the All-Russian Trade-Union Council.

Proletarskaia Revoliutsiia (The Proletarian Revolution).

A monthly historical journal published in Moscow since 1921 by the Central Committee of the Communist Party.

Rabotnik pochty, telegrafa i telefona (*The Post, Telegraph, and Telephone Worker*). Moscow, 1918.
> A trade-union journal.

Sbornik vserossiiskogo soiuva uchitelei internatsionalistov (*Proceedings of the All-Russian Union of Teachers-Internationalists*). Moscow, 1918.
> A publication of the People's Commissariat of Education.

Sovremennyia Zapiski (*Annales Contemporaines*).
> A literary and political journal published in Paris since 1920, at first monthly, later bi-monthly, and still later irregularly. The journal is under the influence of moderate Socialist-Revolutionists.

Vestnik Narodnago Komissariata Vnutrennikh Del (*The Herald of the People's Commissariat of the Interior*).
> An official publication.

Vestnik putei soobshcheniia (*The Herald of Ways and Communications*).
> Organ of the railway workers' trade union.

Volia Rossii (*The Will of Russia*).
> A journal of politics and culture, published by émigré Socialist-Revolutionists of the Right and Center. In 1922 it appeared weekly. At the end of 1922 it was issued fortnightly, later monthly, and still later irregularly.

NEWSPAPERS

Bulletin.
> A French daily, published by the Crimean Government in 1918.

Dalekaia Okraina (*The Distant Borderland*).
> A liberal daily, published in Vladivostok.

Delo Naroda (*The People's Cause*).
> The official organ of the Central Committee of the Socialist-Revolutionists of the Right.

Golos Primoria (*The Voice of the Maritime Province*).
> An anti-Bolshevik daily, published in Vladivostok.

Izvestiia Vserossiiskago Tsentralnago Ispolnitelnago Komiteta Sovetov Krestianskikh, Rabochikh, Soldatskikh i Kazachikh Deputatov.
> The official organ of the Soviet Government.

Narodnaia Mysl (*The People's Thought*).
> An independent Moscow daily.

Nash Vek (*Our Age*).
> The central organ of the Constitutional Democrats, published in Petrograd.

Nashe Slovo (*Our Word*).
> A liberal Moscow daily.

Novaia Zhizn (*The New Life*).
> The central organ of the Social-Democrats (Internationalists), published in Petrograd by Maxim Gorky, who in 1918 was opposed to the Bolsheviks.

Novyi Put (The New Way).
A Bolshevik daily, published in Petrograd by the Council of National Economy of the Northern Region.

Prosledniia Novosti (The Latest News).
An independent progressive daily, published in Kiev.

Pravda (The Truth).
The central organ of the Communist party, published in Moscow by the Bolshevik Central Committee.

Rannee Utro (The Early Morning).
An independent progressive daily, published in Moscow. It was suppressed on July 6, 1918.

Strana (The Country).
A liberal daily, published in Petrograd.

Svoboda Rossii (Russia's Freedom).
The spokesman of the Moscow Cadets.

Svobodnaia Mysl (Free Thought).
A progressive Moscow daily.

Severnaia Kommuna (The Northern Commune).
An official Soviet organ, published in Petrograd.

Syn Otechestva (The Son of the Fatherland).
A Moscow daily, reflecting the views of the Socialist-Revolutionists of the Right. Only four numbers appeared. The paper was suppressed on July 6, 1918.

Svobodnaia Zhizn (Free Life).
The Moscow edition of *Novaia Zhizn.* Only six numbers appeared. The paper was suppressed on July 6, 1918.

Vestnik Verkohvnavo Upravelniia Severnoi Oblasti (The Herald of the Supreme Administration of the Northern Region).
The official organ of the Archangel Government.

Vestnik Vremennago Pravitelstva Avtonomnoi Sibiri (The Herald of the Provisional Government of Autonomous Siberia).
The official organ of the Derber Government at Vladivostok.

Volnyi golos truda (The Free Voice of Labor).
An anarchist daily, published in Moscow.

Vozrozhdenie Severa (Resurrection of the North).
A moderate socialist daily, published in Archangel from August 1918 to May 1919.

Zaria Rossii (Russia's Dawn).
An independent progressive daily, published in Moscow. It was suppressed on July 6, 1918.

Zhizn Natsionalnostei (The Life of Nationalities).
The official organ of the People's Commissariat of Nationalities.

Znamia Truda (The Banner of Labor).
The organ of the Central Committee of the Socialist-Revolutionists of the Left, published in Moscow.

INDEX